The
BOOKER T. WASHINGTON
Papers

The BOOKER T. WASHINGTON *Papers*

VOLUME 4
1895-98

Louis R. Harlan
EDITOR

Stuart B. Kaufman
ASSISTANT EDITOR

Barbara S. Kraft
ASSISTANT EDITOR

Raymond W. Smock
ASSISTANT EDITOR

University of Illinois Press
URBANA · CHICAGO · LONDON

Library of Congress Cataloging in Publication Data

Washington, Booker Taliaferro, 1856?-1915.
 The Booker T. Washington papers.

 Includes bibliographies.
 CONTENTS: v. 1. The autobiographical writings —
v. 2. 1860-89. — v. 3. 1889-95. — v. 4. 1895-98.
 1. Negroes — History — Sources. 2. Washington,
Booker Taliaferro, 1856?-1915.
E185.97.W274   301.45'19'6073024   75-186345
ISBN 0-252-00529-5 (v. 4)

To the Memory of
Emmett Jay Scott

CONTENTS

CONTENTS

CONTENTS

CONTENTS

xiii

CONTENTS

CONTENTS

CONTENTS

INTRODUCTION

THE FOURTH VOLUME OF *The Booker T. Washington Papers* begins with the aftermath of the Atlanta Exposition address on September 18, 1895, which thrust Washington into public prominence as the black spokesman whom whites were willing to listen to. It ends in December 1898, when President William McKinley's visit to Tuskegee symbolized Washington's growing fame and public acceptance.

The Atlanta address was followed by a flood of comment that made clear that Washington's compromise formula struck a responsive chord in the national mood. Northern and southern whites united in their endorsement, many of them in the belief that he had conceded to white supremacy more than he had. Blacks, on the other hand, in many cases believed that he had conceded more than he should. Washington gained the support, however, of a surprising number of black spokesmen who would later be more critical.

Washington's reputation as an orator soared dramatically as a result of the publicity, and while he continued to speak to small audiences in behalf of Tuskegee Institute, he also took to the general lecture circuit. All over the country he spoke to overflow audiences of both races, using a conversational tone, conventional ideas, and humor, amusing his listeners with Negro, chicken, and mule stories that often offended other blacks. Among his oratorical triumphs were his speech on receiving an honorary master's degree at Harvard in 1896, the dedication of the Robert Gould Shaw monument in Boston in 1897, and the Peace Jubilee in Chicago in 1898, at the end of the Spanish-American War. The speech at the Peace Jubilee was an effort to go beyond the Atlanta address formula for race relations by calling on the South to bury racial and sectional prejudice in the trenches of San Juan Hill, where black and white, northerner and southerner, had harmonized in a fight for freedom. Washington warned that race hatred, unless cut out, would be a cancer in the heart of the South. A wave of southern criticism, however, forced Washington to explain away his speech and return to the Atlanta address formula.

In these years Washington made new allies among the wealthy and powerful. William H. Baldwin, Jr., became the head of the Tuskegee trustees in 1895 and Washington's closest white adviser. Baldwin began an aggressive campaign to secure contributions to Tuskegee from the multimillionaires. Among those who began or substantially increased their annual gifts to Tuskegee in these years were Andrew Carnegie, Henry H. Rogers, and John D. Rockefeller. This fresh flow of money and the growing fame of Washington and his educational philosophy brought about an enlargement of Tuskegee, including new buildings, a larger student body, and a more specialized faculty. A new addition to the faculty was George Washington Carver, who took charge of the federal agricultural experiment station on the Tuskegee campus and began his career in applied scientific agriculture.

Emmett Jay Scott, a young Texas newspaper editor, marked an important step in Washington's developing role as a black leader when he came to Tuskegee in 1897 as Washington's private secretary. Scott worked day and night to make his chief the dominant figure in the national black community, managing a larger office force to handle Washington's growing correspondence, combing the black and white press for signs of matters needing attention, answering Washington's mail with the carefully learned nuances of Washington's thought and expression.

With Scott as his surrogate, Washington was able to leave Tuskegee for long intervals, secure in the knowledge that no important detail would escape notice. In the black communities of the northern cities, Washington relied heavily on T. Thomas Fortune, the New York journalist, to inform and advise him. He began in these years, however, to seek other black allies in the North.

As late as 1898, Washington still considered Tuskegee Institute his primary concern and principal base of operations. Opposition to him was silently developing among black intellectuals, but he was not openly challenged. He had for years shunned black conventions and race organizations, and it was not until 1899 that he took part in the Afro-American Council, spoke out against lynching, albeit in characteristically conservative language, and began the first of a number of secret civil-rights activities.

Though Washington continued his close paternal watch over his institution, the years covered by this volume marked his growing involvement in all of the experiences of the black community throughout the country. His papers, therefore, represent somewhat of an odyssey of the color line, from the beating of his employee Robert W. Taylor on the train the night after the Atlanta Exposition address, through the discussion of the Plessy decision in 1896, to the controversy over the Peace Jubilee speech in 1898.

During the course of work on Volume 4, assistant editor Stuart B. Kaufman resigned to become editor of his own project, the Samuel Gompers Papers, and Barbara S. Kraft became assistant editor in his place. Other staff members whose work contributed to the quality of this volume are Janet P. Benham, Patricia A. Cooper, Barry A. Crouch, Sadie M. Harlan, John Lenihan, Virginia V. Molvar, Denise P. Moore, Judy A. Reardon, and Elaine Smith.

Others whose editorial help we are glad to acknowledge are Herbert Aptheker, Dennis A. Burton, Hal Chase, Charles Cooney, Pete Daniel, Kay L. Dove, Charles F. Downs, Casper LeRoy Jordan, Sandra K. Lindsay, Richard M. McConnell, Richard E. McEvoy, Manning Marable, Nerissa L. Milton, Alfred A. Moss, Jr., Fred Nicklason, Cynthia H. Requardt, Hannah Schoenbach, Constance B. Schulz, Richard A. Striner, Jerry Thornbery, and Thomas E. Weir, Jr.

This publication would have been impossible without the continuing support and encouragement of the University of Maryland, the National Historical Publications Commission, and the National Endowment for the Humanities.

ERRATA

VOLUME 2, p. 262, John Massey died in 1918, not 1911.

VOLUME 2, p. 351, the Afro-American Cotton Mill Company should be the Afro-Alabama Cotton Mill Company.

VOLUME 3, p. 162, Reverend Pitt Dillingham was the brother, not the father, of Mabel Wilhelmina Dillingham.

VOLUME 3, p. 243, Livingstone College is an A.M.E. Zion school, not an A.M.E. school.

VOLUME 3, illus. 7, following p. 290, should be Daniel Alexander Payne, not Daniel Augustus Payne.

CHRONOLOGY

1895 Nov. 4: Open letter to Benjamin Ryan Tillman on the South
      Carolina constitutional convention.

1896 June 24: Honorary Master of Arts degree awarded by Harvard
      University.

1897 May 31: Speech at the unveiling of the Robert Gould Shaw
      monument.

1898 Feb. 19: Open letter to the Louisiana constitutional convention.
      Oct. 16: Address at the National Peace Jubilee, Chicago.
      Dec. 16: President William McKinley visits Tuskegee.

SYMBOLS AND ABBREVIATIONS

Standard abbreviations for dates, months, and states are used by the editors only in footnotes and endnotes; textual abbreviations are reproduced as found.

DOCUMENT SYMBOLS

1. A — autograph; written in author's hand
   H — handwritten by other than signator
   P — printed
   T — typed

2. C — postcard
   D — document
   E — endorsement
   L — letter
   M — manuscript
   W — wire (telegram)

3. c — carbon
   d — draft
   f — fragment
   p — letterpress
   t — transcript or copy made at much later date

4. I — initialed by author
   r — representation; signed or initialed in author's name
   S — signed by author

Among the more common endnote abbreviations are: ALS — autograph letter, signed by author; TLpI — typed letter, letterpress copy, initialed by author.

Symbols used for repositories are the standard ones used in *Symbols of American Libraries Used in the National Union Catalog of the Library of Congress,* 10th ed. (Washington, D.C., 1969).

A-Ar	Alabama Department of Archives and History, Montgomery
ATT	Tuskegee Institute, Tuskegee, Ala.
DHU	Howard University, Washington, D.C.
DLC	Library of Congress, Washington, D.C.
DNA	National Archives, Washington, D.C.
GAGTh	Gammon Theological Seminary, Atlanta, Ga.
Ia-HA	Iowa State Department of History and Archives, Des Moines
MB	Boston Public Library, Boston, Mass.
MdBJ	Johns Hopkins University, Baltimore, Md.
MeB	Bowdoin College, Brunswick, Me.
MH	Harvard University, Cambridge, Mass.
MHi	Massachusetts Historical Society, Boston
MNS	Smith College, Northampton, Mass.
NIC	Cornell University, Ithaca, N.Y.
NN	New York Public Library, NYC
NN-Sc	Schomburg Collection, New York Public Library, NYC
NNC	Columbia University, NYC
ViHaI	Hampton Institute, Hampton, Va.

OTHER ABBREVIATIONS

BTW	Booker T. Washington
Con.	Container
RG	Record Group
Ser.	Series

Documents, 1895-98

An Article in the New York *World*

Atlanta, Sept. 18 [1895]

SOUTH'S NEW EPOCH

Its Spirit Indicated at the Opening
of Atlanta's Big Exposition

A NEGRO MOSES SPOKE FOR A RACE

And Booker T. Washington's Consummate Plea
Made Him the Hero of the Occasion

CREELMAN'S[1] STORY OF THE GREAT DAY

Hundreds of Miles Away President Cleveland
Touched the Button and Sent Good Wishes

While President Cleveland was waiting at Gray Gables to-day to send the electric spark that started the machinery of the Atlanta Exposition a negro Moses stood before a great audience of white people and delivered an oration that marks a new epoch in the history of the South and a body of negro troops marched in a procession with the citizen soldiery of Georgia and Louisiana. The whole city is thrilling to-night with a realization of the extraordinary significance of these two unprecedented events. Nothing has happened since Henry Grady's immortal speech before the New England Society in New York that indicates so profoundly the spirit of the New South, except, perhaps, the opening of the Exposition itself.

When Prof. Booker T. Washington, principal of an industrial school for colored people in Tuskegee, Ala., stood on the platform of the Auditorium, with the sun shining over the heads of his hearers into his eyes and his whole face lit up with the fire of prophecy, Clark Howell, the successor of Henry W. Grady, said to me: "That man's speech is the beginning of a moral revolution in America."

It is the first time that a negro has made a speech in the South on any important occasion before an audience composed of white men and women. It electrified the audience, and the response was as if it had come from the throat of a whirlwind.

"Dixie" Has a New Meaning Now

The hosts of soldiers gathered to-day on the battlefield of Chickamauga, not 150 miles from this place, celebrating a struggle the

3

fruits of which were exposed to the world in Atlanta, through whose streets of fluttering flags rivers of bayonets, plumes and banners billowed towards the gigantic amphitheatre where the New South demonstrated that she is no longer a mere agricultural dependency of the North, but a serious rival in every branch of industry, commerce and the arts, would have been astonished by the spectacle when Prof. Booker stepped to the front of the platform. A moment before the strains of "Dixie" from Gilmore's Band were filling the big hall; a moment later "Dixie" had a new meaning for the people of the South.

Thirty years ago Sherman burned Atlanta to the ground. It was a heap of blackened ashes when he left on his march to the ocean. But on these ashes the ruined and loyal South has built the foundation of a new career. And the amazing thing about this Exposition is that the work was undertaken in the middle of the silver excitement, when the Southern banks were actually issuing scrip to save the people from utter bankruptcy. This might not have been considered in Chicago, but in the slothful South, which has been paying its share of the $1,717,275,718 of pensions for Northern soldiers without a murmur — the beaten, broken, harassed South, with its almost hopeless problems of race, climate and politics — it seems a miracle.

CLEVELAND AND THE SOUTH

And the hand that set the machinery of this almost miraculous enterprise in motion is the same hand that raised two Southern men to the bench of the Supreme Court of the United States and restored the South to a substantial political equality with the rest of the country. There is material in this day's work here for John Sherman and his friends to think about.

Since the sun rose this morning over the green hills of Atlanta, where Sherman's breastworks still stand, the city has been in a state of breathless excitement. Trains from all parts of the country bore thousands of visitors into the streets, and the multitude of men who had been working all night on the Exposition grounds were still at their task. The heat was appalling.

By noon the procession of Georgia and Louisiana soldiers, headed by four companies of the Fifth United States Regiment, commanded by Col. Kellogg, had formed at the junction of Broad and Marietta streets. At 1.30 Gov. Atkinson, the managers of the exposition and the guests took their places in the line and the march was begun.

The route was lined with cheering crowds of whites and blacks. There were miles of bare chocolate-colored legs fringing the gutters.

STARS AND STRIPES EVERYWHERE

The Stars and Stripes were everywhere. Many of the houses were completely covered with them. It was a picture beyond words to express — waves of dark blue bodies with light blue legs, gleaming gold lace, jingling spurs, rumbling cannon wheels, clattering horses, white helmets, acres of Georgia colonels, scarlet, yellow, gray, every color under heaven, sparkling, blazing, glowing and dancing with the liltings of music.

The procession was made up as follows: Chief Marshal, W. L. Kellogg, with Col. W. G. Obear, Chief of Staff, Col. James W. Austin, Col. Usher Thomson, Col. Peter Reiley, of Savannah; Col. Eugene Hardeman, Col. Frank West, Major E. L. Higdon, of Birmingham; Capt. George S. Obear and Capt. John A. Milner, as his staff. The band of the Fifth United States Infantry and then six companies of United States regulars, of the same regiment, commanded by Major Mason Carter, came next. The band of the Washington Artillery, of New Orleans, preceding one hundred members of the famous New Orleans company, the Washington Artillery, drilling as infantrymen, followed with Lieut.-Col. John B. Richardson in command.

Then came Gov. Atkinson and the members of his staff. Following was Col. John S. Candler, of the Fifth Georgia, with Capt. George S. Lowman, Adjutant; Capt. Everett, Capt. C. C. Bardley, Capt. J. A. Childs and Lieut. W. Blalor, as his staff.

GEORGIA TROOPS IN LINE

The band of the Fifth Georgia Volunteers came next and behind marched the following companies: Atlanta Zouaves, Capt. Amos Baker commanding; Hibernian Rifles, Capt. W. D. Ellis; Atlanta Rifles, Capt. Joe Nash; Griffin Rifles, Capt. A. J. Burr; Marietta Rifles, Capt. S. F. Sanford; Barnesville Blues, Capt. J. T. Howard; Atlanta Reserves, Capt. W. C. Mass.

The Fifth Regiment machine gun platoon, Lieut. C. H. Plyer commanding and Colonel Usher Thomason, commanding the Third Regiment with Capt. Von der Lieth, Capts. Shannon and Crain as his staff were next in line. They were followed by the following companies: Clarke Rifles, under command of Capt. J. H. Beuse, Athens;

5

the Conyers Volunteers, Capt. Irwin; Hill City Cadets, from Rome, Capt. Stewart; the Atlanta Artillery, Capt. J. F. Kempton; Troop B, Governor's Horse Guards, Capt. J. S. Dosier.

Behind these came the second battalion of colored troops, commanded by Lieut.-Col. F. H. Crumbly, and the Lincoln Guards of Macon.

PROMINENT GUESTS IN CARRIAGES

Among the more prominent outside people who were in the carriages were Dr. C. W. Dabney,[2] Mr. J. M. Biddle (representing the State Department), Commander C. J. Train, Capt. H. Barry, Major Frank Strong, W. D. Ravenel, Charles E. Kemper, Prof. G. Brown Goode and Kerr Craige, of the Government Commission; Gen. E. P. Cotteraux, Col. L. C. Waller, Col. J. C. Andrews, Col. George H. Varnard, Major Maurice Generelly, Major George S. Koster and Col. Fred A. Obear, of the staff of Gov. Foster, of Louisiana.

The following foreign representatives were also in line: Consul-General d'Auglade, representing France; Louis M. Jove, Venezuela; A. Macchi, European Commissioner; Gregorio E. Gonzales, Mexico; Dr. Niederlin, Argentina; Theodore H. Mangel, Costa Rica; M. Sanda, France; Herbert Hillman, Great Britain; Prof. Trentanove, Italy; and M. Seasagaili, Italy.

Of the State Commissioners these were seen in the parade: James E. Graybill, President of the New York Commission; Messrs. Frank Weeks and J. H. Vaill, Mrs. D. Ward Northrup and Mrs. Sarah T. Kenney, Connecticut Board; Willis J. Abbott, Illinois Board; W. M. Wilson and L. P. Mead, Iowa; Mrs. Helen M. Winslow, Massachusetts; Mr. J. Vincent Heller, Arkansas; E. P. McKissick, North Carolina.

The following representative colored men, members of the commission in charge of the negro department, were in line: I. Garland Penn, Commissioner in charge; Prof. Booker T. Washington, Bishop W. J. Gaines, W. O. Emery, Arkansas; W. C. Coleman,[3] North Carolina; B. V. Clark, Tennessee; W. M. Brown, Virginia; T. B. Gibbs and M. Lewey, Florida.

WHAT THE VISITORS SAW

When the procession entered the exposition grounds the visitors saw spread out before them a great hollow space, comprising 189 acres, surrounded by three miles of white fence. On the level ground, inclosed by the slopes, was a beautiful green park, dotted with little pine trees, and a lake covered with graceful gondolas, rowboats and steam launches, and surrounding this, on the higher ground, the beautiful buildings erected by the South, her sister States and foreign nations. The Fine Arts and Women's buildings were snowy white, the rest drab and white, save the buff colored baronial castle occupied by the Administration offices and the yellow Georgia Manufacturers' Building, clusters of tall white fluted columns, capped with winged figures holding wreaths and trumpets and in the midst of them a golden eagle, a gray shingled tower with a chime of bells, the monster Phoenix wheel, revolving against the sky, and beyond it a confusion of domes, minarets and quaint architectural angles where the polyglot and sometimes demoralizing pleasures of the midway terrace were hidden along a little street.

This street swarmed with horn-blowing Dahomeyans, gorgeous pig-tailed Chinamen, sombre-eyed Mexicans, blowsy, fat Germans, American Indians, swaggering cowboys, old-time negroes in old-time costumes and South Americans in every conceivable garb.

On the terrace were beds of cotton plants in full blossom. Here and there were splotches of unpainted pine, with the carpenters still hammering at their work, and overhead a blue sky, with sunlight shining on the little lily-white clouds.

The troops curved and counter-marched across the greensward and then stacked their arms.

In the auditorium every man and woman who could get into the building was waiting for the exercises of the day to begin. The guests, officials and orators, headed by Bishop Nelson, in his picturesque robe, took their places on the platform. After a prayer by the Bishop, ex-Gov. Bullock introduced Albert Howell, who read Mr. Frank L. Stanton's[4] ode, the poet modestly declining to read his own lines.

PRESIDENT COLLIER, HISTORIAN AND PROPHET

President Collier, whose brain and energy directed the building of the exposition, followed. He rehearsed the beginnings of the undertaking, praised the unanimity, ardor and liberality of Atlanta, and expressed gratitude for the co-operation of the many States, cities and foreign nations and the various societies of all kinds, without which success would have been impossible. The support of the Federal Government was gratefully acknowledged. Speaking of the aid the exposition had received from women, he said:

"The advancement of the race and the adoption of truer ideals have enabled us to profit inestimably by that expanding force in our civilization — the genius of women. The part it plays here is large, and the use it has made of this opportunity will unquestionably conduce to the fuller recognition of woman's righteous claims and a fairer estimate of the value of her work. The way for women who must needs struggle with the world will be widened by the triumphs of feminine capacity and skill which are here arrayed."

Next President Collier thanked the colored citizens for their cooperation, saying: "They have accepted the responsibility of a department of their own, and have filled it with proofs of the progress they have made as freemen. They were employed largely in the preparation here, as they are in almost all our industries, and they will share largely in the honors and practical benefits of the exposition."

In conclusion the speaker said: "The work begun beneath the frown of adverse fortunes has reached its completion under the smile of heaven upon our common country. Elsewhere we see plenteous harvests, reviving commerce, restored confidence, industrial activity, capital busy in new enterprises, labor abundantly employed and reaping increased rewards, all sections of the country welded together in the bonds of common interest and the ardor of a broad patriotism."

Then Mrs. Joseph Thompson, who is the Mrs. Potter Palmer of Georgia and the head of the Woman's Department of the Exposition, stepped to the front of the platform, tall, slender, beautiful, her face covered with a white veil and her hands trembling with excitement as she laid her manuscript on the reading desk and addressed the audience in a voice which could not be heard ten feet away.

PROF. WASHINGTON THE NEGRO MOSES

Mrs. Thompson had scarcely taken her seat when all eyes were turned on a tall, tawny negro sitting in the front row on the platform. It was Prof. Booker T. Washington, President of the Tuskegee, Ala., Normal and Industrial Institute, who must rank from this time forth as the foremost man of his race in America. Gilmore's band played the Star Spangled Banner, and the audience cheered. The tune changed to Dixie and the audience roared with shrill hi-yi's. Again the music changed to Yankee Doodle and the clamor lessened.

8

All this time the eyes of the thousands looked straight at the negro orator. A strange thing was to happen. A black man was to speak for his people with none to interrupt him. As Prof. Washington strode forward to the edge of the stage the low, descending sun shot fiery rays through the windows into his face. A great shout greeted him. He turned his head to avoid the blinding light and moved about the platform for relief. Then he turned his powerful countenance to the sun without a blink of the eyelids and began to talk.

There was a remarkable figure, tall, bony, straight as a Sioux chief, high forehead, straight nose, heavy jaws and strong, determined mouth, with big white teeth, piercing eyes and a commanding manner. The sinews stood out on his bronzed neck, and his muscular right arm swung high in the air with a lead pencil grasped in the clenched brown fist. His big feet were planted squarely, with the heels together and the toes turned out. His voice rang out clear and true, and he paused impressively as he made each point. Within ten minutes the multitude was in an uproar of enthusiasm, handkerchiefs were waved, canes were flourished, hats were tossed in the air. The fairest women of Georgia stood up and cheered. It was as if the orator had bewitched them.

No Cause Ever Pleaded Better

And when he held his dusky hand high above his head, with the fingers stretched wide apart, and said to the white people of the South on behalf of his race: "In all things that are purely social we can be as separate as the fingers, yet one as the hand in all things essential to social progress" the great wave of sound dashed itself against the walls and the whole audience was on its feet in a delirium of applause and I thought at that moment of the night when Henry Grady stood among the curling wreaths of tobacco smoke in Delmonico's banquet hall and said "I am a Cavalier among Roundheads."

I have heard the great orators of many countries, but not even Gladstone himself could have pleaded a cause with more consummate power than did this angular negro standing in a nimbus of sunshine surrounded by the men who once fought to keep his race in bondage. The roar might swell ever so high, but the expression of his earnest face never changed.

A ragged ebony giant, squatted on the floor in one of the aisles, watched the orator with burning eyes and tremulous face until the supreme burst of applause came and then the tears ran down his face. Most of the negroes in the audience were crying, perhaps without knowing just why.

AN ELOQUENT PLEA FOR A RACE

Prof. Washington said, in part: "It is well to bear in mind that whatever other sins the South may be called upon to bear, when it comes to business pure and simple it is in the South that the negro is given a man's chance in the commercial world, and in nothing is this exposition more eloquent than in emphasizing this chance. Our greatest danger is that in the great leap from slavery to freedom we may overlook the fact that the masses of us are to live by the production of our hands, and fail to keep in mind that we shall prosper in proportion as we learn to dignify and glorify common labor and put brains and skill into the common occupations of life; shall prosper in proportion as we learn to draw the line between the superficial and the substantial, the ornamental gewgaws of life and the useful.

"No race can prosper until it learns that there is as much dignity in tilling a field as in writing a poem. It is at the bottom of life we must begin, and not at the top. Nor should we permit our grievances to overshadow our opportunities.

"There is no defense or security for any of us except in the highest intelligence and development of all. If anywhere there are efforts tending to curtail the fullest growth of the negro, let these efforts be turned into stimulating, encouraging, and making him the most useful and intelligent citizen."

At the close of the speech Gov. Bullock rushed across the platform and seized the orator's hand. Another shout greeted this demonstration, and for a few moments the two men stood facing each other, hand in hand.

Gov. Atkinson,[5] having just come from a sick bed, was unable to speak and simply bowed to the audience. He was represented by George R. Brown, who spoke for the State of Georgia, and he in turn was followed by Mayor King, of Atlanta.

JUDGE SPEER[6] ON RACE PROBLEMS

Judge Emory Speer, the formal orator of the day, followed. Speaking of the utility of the big show to Georgia and the South he said:

"Slavery diverted the army of emigration from the South. When slavery was abolished the negro problem proved to be almost as insurmountable an obstacle to emigration as slavery. There never was any danger of continued negro control of the local affairs of a Southern State. There are many millions of colored people who live and who will live among many millions of white people. Why shall any one force a race issue?"

In closing the speaker paid an eloquent tribute to the loyalty of the South.

"When was there ever before presented the spectacle we daily see where men who but a few years ago exerted their energy of mind and body to disrupt and destroy the Government, who were defeated, and not only find their effort condoned and themselves restored to all the rights of citizenship but actually for nearly a quarter of a century are entrusted with the duty of governing? If there is any parallel in the history of the world for this trustful magnanimity it has wholly escaped my attention.

"Our Government has lavished upon Southern harbors and Southern public buildings millions of the people's money. Our Southern people know and appreciate these facts, and let no military staff of other nations when it is taking into account the military power of this American Union fail to estimate the full fighting strength of the men who wore the gray and the sons of their blood."

The sensitive nature of Presidential candidates can be understood from the fact that both ex-President Harrison and Congressman Reed were invited to deliver the formal oration, and each pleaded lack of time to prepare themselves for the trying ordeal.

When Judge Speer had concluded the sun had sunk behind the hills. Bishop Nelson spread his hands out and blessed the people in the gloom of the great hall.

Electric lights began to flash, and from the windows one could see the 20,000 visitors watching the dry fountains which were to spout at the touch of President Cleveland's hand. On the left side of the stage was a little stand, a telegraph instrument and an operator. There was silence. The operator clicked the key and stopped.

Then the instrument itself began to click and this message came from Gray Gables, where Mr. Cleveland had been waiting for hours for the signal:

"Operator at Gray Gables says: President is sitting at my elbow. Ruth is playing with his watch. Esther is looking at me from her papa's back. Mrs. Cleveland just had the baby in here, but has taken her back to her nurse. Secretary Thurber sits at my left, opposite end of the table from the President."

MESSAGE TO THE PRESIDENT

Ex-Governor Bullock sent this despatch to Gray Gables:

"Cotton States and International Exposition Grounds, Atlanta, Ga., Sept. 18 — Honorable Grover Cleveland, President of the United States, Gray Gables, Mass.: The Committee on Ceremonies are instructed by the president and director-general and by the Board of Directors to express to the President their high appreciation of and thanks for the great interest the President has shown, both on this and other occasions, in behalf of the success of the Cotton States and International Exposition.

"Under the guidance of the hand of President Cleveland one of the most important commercial and industrial efforts ever attempted in our section has now started on its career for the upbuilding of our material interests by closer commercial relations with all portions of our own country and other sister republics south of us. The mingling of practical people from all sections made possible by the President's approval and aid to our efforts will render future ill will between the sections impossible.

RUFUS B. BULLOCK, Chairman."

CLEVELAND SENDS GOOD WISHES

The answer promptly came as follows:

"GRAY GABLES, Mass., Sept. 18. The President and Board of Directors Cotton States and International Exposition, Atlanta, Ga.: Fully appreciating the value and importance of the Exposition inaugurated to-day, I am especially gratified to be related to its inception and progress and to participate in its opening ceremonies. I sincerely congratulate those whose enterprise and energy have accomplished such splendid results and heartily wish the Exposition they have set on foot will be completely successful in consummating all the good results contemplated by its promoters.

GROVER CLEVELAND."

There was another pause and a click. Instantly the great fountains in the lake and on the plaza burst into action and 15,000 gallons of water a minute was tossed up in spray. The buildings and the grounds became glorious with beaded lines and festoons of light, million candle power arc lights and 200,000 candle power incandescent lights.

The chimes in the tower were jangled, whistles blew, drums throbbed, trumpets sounded and a hundred bombs were thrown into the air from mortars. The Exposition was open and the people swarmed into the buildings — black and white, Georgia Colonels and all.

UNCLE SAM THE ONLY ONE ON TIME

The only building absolutely in readiness to-day was the United States Government's structure. This is the most perfect exhibit ever prepared at Washington. It contains the cream of all that was seen at Chicago, with many new additions, and the arrangement was admirable. The Fine Arts Building is nearly ready. It is under the direction of Horace Bradley, late art superintendent of Harper's.

Machinery Hall is still in a state of confusion, and the only important exhibits in sight are the battery of eight boilers and fourteen engines with a capacity of 2,250 horse-power; the six enormous pumps, the largest of them sending a stream of 5,000 gallons a minute.

OTHER INTERESTING EXHIBITS

Then there is a chocolate-colored model jail suitable for small towns, although a first-class burglar could break out of it in half an hour; a model fire-department building, equipped with a well-trained force; a transportation building, a manufactures and liberal arts building, crowded with foreign and domestic wares; a Georgia manufactures building and an elaborate fisheries display by the United States, smaller but handsomer than the display at Chicago, and the Mexican village, with a bull ring, where there may yet be bull fights in spite of the protest that has been made; a life-saving corps experimenting on the waters of the lake; a Dahomey village, a Costa Rica building, Capt. Boyton's water chutes, a scenic railway, a Chinese village, a negro village, an Indian camp, a display of the Plant railway system inside of a huge gray pyramid structure, a Southern railway building and buildings erected by New York, Massachusetts, Pennsylvania, Georgia and other States.

13

On the whole the architecture is not impressive and scarcely instructive, but the exposition in its entirety is a marvellous revelation of the New South, which is no longer a land devoted simply to cotton, tobacco and sugar. The man whose genius inspired the enterprise has passed away, but everywhere the dead hand of Henry W. Grady moves and controls this new thing which has come to life.

James Creelman

New York *World,* Sept. 19, 1895, 3.

¹ James Creelman (1859-1915), a leading newspaper reporter, worked for the New York *World* from 1894 to 1897 and from 1900 to 1906. Born of Scotch-Canadian parents in Montreal, he was a foreign and domestic correspondent of the New York *Herald* from 1878 to 1893. He also wrote for the New York *Journal,* a British edition of *Cosmopolitan,* and *Pearson's Magazine,* and was the author of several books. He died in Berlin on assignment as a war correspondent for the New York *American.*

² Charles William Dabney (1855-1945) was at the time assistant secretary of agriculture in the Cleveland administration, and in charge of the federal government exhibits at the exposition. Born in Hampden-Sydney, Va., the son of a Presbyterian minister and professor, Dabney was educated at Hampden-Sydney College, the University of Virginia, and the University of Göttingen, where he received a Ph.D. in chemistry in 1880. A leading agricultural chemist in North Carolina and at Washington, Dabney was also an educator. He was president of the University of Tennessee and the University of Cincinnati. One of the most active members of the Conference for Education in the South and the Southern Education Board from 1898 to 1915, Dabney was in large part responsible for the emphasis these organizations put on the education of whites, to the neglect of the black schools. A highlight of his involvement with the Ogden Movement was his establishment at Knoxville of the Summer School of the South for the training of white teachers.

³ Warren C. Coleman, born a slave, was said to be the wealthiest black man in North Carolina at the turn of the century. Shortly after the Civil War he invested the profits from the sale of a small grocery store, probably founded with funds supplied by his putative white father, in land and about 100 cabins which he rented to freedmen. Hoping to be the black man's Moses, and a wealthy man as well, he organized the Coleman Manufacturing Company, a cotton mill in Concord, N.C., an ostensibly cooperative venture for which he actively sought funds from southern black workers. His campaign succeeded, but the mill did not. The causes of failure were inefficient machinery, insufficient materials, inexperienced management, untrained workers, and an employment policy that grievously exploited the very workers the enterprise was established to help, according to Holland Thompson. Other factors, undoubtedly, were marketing problems and the reluctance of white bankers to aid a black business. By an unwritten understanding in the southern Piedmont region, cotton-mill management and labor were white monopolies. Finally, in 1903, Coleman employed a white manager. When he died a year later the mill was sold to whites, who employed white operatives. (Thompson, *From the Cotton Field to the Cotton Mill,* 253-63.)

⁴ Frank Lebby Stanton (1857-1927) for nearly forty years wrote a daily column of anecdotes, essays, and poems in the Atlanta *Constitution,* many of them in dia-

lect. In 1925 he was made poet laureate of Georgia. His lengthy dedicatory ode began:

> Behold to-day the meeting of the lands
> In pride and splendor; from far foreign strands
> Great State with State clasps hands!
> Here, on this Southern soil, supreme and free,
> Meet now no hostile bands;
> But all flags wave where one of Liberty
> Shakes stars down like the sands!
> And from sky-cleaving towers
> Time strikes the thrilling hours
> Of golden promise for the years to be!

[5] William Yates Atkinson (1854-99), governor of Georgia from 1894 to 1898.
[6] Emory Speer (1848-1918) was born in Georgia and graduated from the University of Georgia in 1869. He was state solicitor general from 1873 to 1876. A champion of the mountain whites in Georgia, he served in Congress as an Independent Democrat and then as an Independent from 1879 to 1883. He was a Georgia district attorney until 1885, when he was appointed to the federal bench in Georgia. He presided over many important cases involving expansion of federal power. He was also active in the prosecution of peonage cases.

To the Editor of the New York *World*[1]

Atlanta, Ga. Sept. 19 [1895]

To the Editor of The World: My present feeling is that yesterday was the brightest, most hopeful day in the history of the negro race. It was the day for which Garrison and Douglass and Grady worked and prayed. It has been my privilege to address audiences in all parts of the North and West. It has remained for the South, and here in the heart of the South, where Sherman and Hood fought, and where lived Toombs and Brown and Stephens, and our beloved Grady, to give my words the most hearty and overwhelming reception in the history of my public speaking. I had no dream that any colored man thirty years after slavery could be received and treated in Atlanta with such distinction and honor.

As I sat on the platform, with the flower and culture and beauty of the South on either side, and in front of me black men who were slaves, and near them ex-Confederate soldiers, who only a little while ago were the masters of these slaves and on this very ground fought to keep enslaved these black men, and as I saw these Southern men and these black men and beautiful and cultured Southern women wave their hats and handkerchiefs and clap their hands and shout in approval of what I said, I seemed to have been carried away in a vision, and it was hard for me to realize as I spoke that it was not all a beautiful dream, but an actual scene, right here in the heart of the South.

I care nothing for the personal commendation. It is the race that I speak for. This is the year of jubilee of the negro. It is the beginning of an era. The heart of the South is open to-day to the negro as it has never been before. The greatest problem is now with the negro himself. Will he throw aside his vagaries and enter in and reap the harvest that is right about him. It is an equality of industrial opportunity that the negro should seek, rather than spend time over questions of social equality, which has no existence among any people.

As I have received during the last few hours the hearty handshake of hundreds of Southern men and women, and as they have spoken in my ear the "God bless you" and the "I am with you," I can see and feel that we are on the threshold of a new life. The South is the negro's home. Here he is surrounded by them that know him and by those whom he knows. Here the black man and the white man work in the same field and on the same house and at the same bench.

Let us as a race throw aside complaints and useless criticism and enter with hand and mind as we have never done before the industrial field. No one will scorn the negro that has a half million dollars to lend. As a race we must decide within the next ten years whether we are going to hold the place we now have in the industrial world or whether we are going to give it up to foreigners. To hold our place we have no time to spend in fretting and fussing over nonessentials.

The hand as well as the head of every black boy and girl in the South should be trained to useful occupation. We want to make ourselves so skillful that we will be indispensable. No one cares much for a man with empty hand, pocket and head no matter what his color is.

Beginning from to-day let the negro register an oath in heaven that from henceforth he will cast his lot materially, civilly and morally with the South; that he will cultivate the closest friendship with the Southern white man; that when he can he will vote for and with the Southern white man; that he will praise his good deeds, and that he will in a dignified and sensible manner tell the white man of his wrongs to the negro. And I am more convinced to-day than ever that if this course is followed there will be soon not only a new South but a new negro.

Though we are not yet where we want to be, yet, thank God, we are not where we used to be.

Booker T. Washington

New York *World,* Sept. 20, 1895, 2.

[1] Clark Howell, editor of the Atlanta *Constitution,* also wrote to the New York *World:* "I do not exaggerate when I say that Prof. Booker T. Washington's address yesterday was one of the most notable speeches, both as to character and the warmth of its reception, ever delivered to a Southern audience." Howell described BTW's address as "epoch-making" and a "turning point in the progress of the negro race." Howell mentioned that there was initial opposition to having a Negro speak, but the directors of the exposition decided otherwise. "There was not a line in the address," Howell proudly reported, "which would have been changed even by the most sensitive of those who thought the invitation to be imprudent." He described the address as "a platform on which the whites and blacks can stand with full justice to each race." Howell maintained that BTW's speech was "full vindication" of the New South views of Henry Grady. He believed, furthermore, that the issue of social equality was laid to rest by BTW's phrase "in all things that are purely social we can be as separate as the fingers." (New York *World,* Sept. 19, 1895, 2.)

From Mary Elizabeth Preston Stearns

[Tufts College P.O., Mass.] Sep 19th 1895

Dear and Honored Friend, Your address is glorious! Beyond all words glorious! One of the historic Speeches of the century — worthy to rank with Lincoln's "Gettysburg" in eloquence, elevation, and far-reaching influence. You have struck the keynote of *Twentieth* century civillization in America! Can the South fail to hear its sublime pathetic pleadings: its unanswerable truth?

My old eyes overflowed with tears of joy; tears of pitiful memories as I read aloud your glowing sentences from the everlasting "Rock of Ages,["] on which you were planted.

I cannot express what I feel. Such an uplifting of the spirit as makes all ordinary life and motives "flat, stale, and unprofitable." As I read, a glorious spirit seemed to hover around and above you inspiring and sustaining with angelic power your sublime faith in the cause of justice & humanity. She wore the Crown of Martyrdom and the Palm was in her hand.

If departed spirits can approach kindred ones in this earthly sphere, *than* Olivia was with you yesterday! It is my faith that she was. Another also walks visibly with you, dear friend, a "lamp and a light unto your feet."

Had Gen'l Armstrong been present, what rewards would have been his! Let us believe that such *reward* was his exceeding deserts. "The night is fleeing away." The Dawn is at hand: and this second "Washington," is its Heaven appointed Herald. I can no more.

Mary E. Stearns

How rejoiced G. L. S.[1] would have been to see this day!

ALS Con. 113 BTW Papers DLC.

[1] George Luther Stearns.

From William Still

Philadelphia, Sept. 19th 1895

My Dear Mr. Washington I have no words to express my delight with your noble speech yesterday at the opening of the "First Day of The Cotton Exposition."

I do not wonder that your speech produced such wide spread demonstrations among all classes. And even the weeping among the colored people reached my eyes, in my office, alone, as I read your speech, and of course, I attributed their emotion as well as my own simply to the cause for rejoicing it had awakened in the breasts of the people who were compelled to listen to such grand truths under such grand circumstances.

In my judgement our cause was absolutely advanced many degrees and henceforth many friendly persons identified with either race will find it much easier to battle for freedom & education than they have ever done hitherto.

But I meant in taking up my pen to write to you for quite a different purpose than for what I have done, nam[e]ly, to invite you to attend a memorial meeting to commemorate the bi[r]th of Stephen Smith, the Founder of the Home for Aged and Infirm Colored Persons; Likewise the Birth of Edward T. Parker, the Founder of the Annex a new & imposing edific[e] adjoining the old Building.

The day fixed for the memorial meeting will take place on Thursday Oct. 17th. We desire that it shall be a very grand occasion in every respect, with regard to speakers white & colored and we dont want you under any circumstances to deny us this petition.

While I cannot definitely promise you any material aid, I can nevertheless say to you I think it will pay you to accept. I think I can influence the old Pennsylvania Anti Slavery to donate you $100. at our next meeting besides give you other evidences of our appreciation & encouragement.

Of course I shall be very glad to entertain you at my house what time you may be in our city.

I will send you our last Annual Report of our home for Aged & Infirm Colored Persons in which you will find Parkers Life & labors; Likewise I will look up an old Report which will contain Stephen Smith's life, and will send that also. Yours Very Truly

W. Still

ALS   Con. 113   BTW Papers   DLC.

From Samuel Laing Williams

Chicago, Sept 19 1895

My Dear friend– Permit me to extend a hearty word of Congratulation for your great utterance of yesterday. In my humble opinion no word uttered by a colored man during the past 20 years will go farther and do more to set us right in public opinion than your eloquently apt and philosophically sound words that have become a part of yesterdays remarkable event. Sincerely Yours

S. Laing Williams

ALS   Con. 113   BTW Papers   DLC.

From John Webster Cochran[1]

N.Y. City   Sept 21st 1895

My Dear Sir & Brother, Sing ye to the Lord — Bless God, the "day of Jubilee am come." As a white man and old time abolitionist an ex Union Veteran I bless God from inside out, up and down for the great speech which He told you to make & which you did make to the assembled thousands. When I read it and of the manner of its glorious reception by a mixed Southern audience my soul from out the old shadow which lay floating on the floor of the old ideas of caste was lifted, elevated to the 7th Heaven — Glory to God — the old gulf is bridged — the ax is covered forever — not to be unburried on Election Day! No, Atlanta will live in the hearts of the peaceful world by this act, as it will live for all time made memorable by Shermans great March from Atlanta to the Sea.

Oh — could I have witnessed the scene. Today you may hear the "Havelock of the Union Army" our Gallant Gen. Howard.

Indeed we have entered upon the outer rim of the shining of the sun of the mellenial Dawn as it comes up over the Mountain tops. God bless the Management of the Atlanta Exposition for their *bravery,* and good judgement in asking you to speak as the foremost advocate of your Race of Black-Americans. I like that word *Black!*

I hope to meet you, at Atlanta. I intend to arrange for some concerts under Mrs. Thompsons[2] management if she will give us an opportunity.

I met Brother Taylor last eve who let me see a type copy of your Oration which he will publish next week.

I gave him 2 programs of Concerts given [by] my little daughters who are wonderfull musicians. He will send to you. I want them to be attached to the exposition if possible, for they would be an attraction after once *heard.* Cant something be done about it? God bless you is my prayer.

John W. Cochran

ALS   Con. 110   BTW Papers   DLC.

[1] John Webster Cochran (1844-1929), a white man born in Plattville, Wis., served in an Illinois regiment in the Civil War. He settled in New York City as a newspaperman and lawyer.

[2] Mrs. Joseph Thompson was in charge of the women's department of the Atlanta Exposition.

From Robert Wesley Taylor

Boston, Mass. Sept 23, 1895

Dear Mr. Washington— Possibly ere this reaches you you will have heard of the rather disgraceful affair that happened last Thursday night after we left Atlanta.

I will enclose you a copy of the charge sent to Mr. Baldwin which will explain the whole affair.

I was advised to take rash steps concerning the matter but because of Mr. Baldwin's connection with Tuskegee and my acquaintance with his father I shall not do it if I can avoid it, without too great a sacrifice of principle and manhood.

I saw Mr. Baldwin, Sr. to-day and let him read the charge which he endorsed and wrote his son a personal letter concerning it.

Again I take this step because I despise notoriety.

Rev. Dr. Clinton,[1] Editor "Star of Zion" got on the train at Charlotte N.C. and wanted to write up the affair but I positively objected to his using my name or referring to me in any way as to have others infer that it was I.

In Washington, D.C. I was interviewed but declined to give any one permission to use my name directly or indirectly.

Later on I shall let you know the particulars.

Such a matter is too grave to be overlooked. Your friend,

Robert W. Taylor

P.S. Your speech has created a profound impression here in Boston.

R. W. T.

ALS Con. 792 BTW Papers DLC.

[1] George Wylie Clinton (1859-1921) was a leading A.M.E. Zion clergyman, elected bishop in 1896. Born a slave in Lancaster County, S.C., he attended the University of South Carolina from 1874 until the end of Reconstruction closed the university's doors to blacks in 1877. Clinton then studied theology at Livingstone College and was ordained in 1879. A staunch supporter of BTW, he joined the Tuskegean on five statewide speaking tours in the South in behalf of black self-improvement, and frequently lectured at Tuskegee Institute. He was founder of the A.M.E. Zion *Quarterly Review* (1889), and from 1902 to 1906 he edited the denominational weekly *Star of Zion*. Though a conservative on many intraracial matters, Bishop Clinton was an active member of the Southern Sociological Congress and the Southern Interracial Commission.

Robert Wesley Taylor to William Henry Baldwin, Jr.

Boston, Mass. Sept. 23, 1895

(Confidential)

Sir: I left Atlanta, Ga. Thursday night Sept 19th en route to Framingham, Mass. about Ten O'clock on train No. 36 over the Southern Rail Road, accompanied by Prof. B. T. Washington's little daughter, Portia.

Upon entering the coach in Atlanta we found two seats facing each other — that is, one was turned backwards.

As I always prefer riding backwards I sat down in the seat as I found it and Portia occupied the one in front of mine.

Before the train made its first stop, for reasons entirely unknown to me, I was ordered by the conductor to get up so as to have the seat in which I was sitting turned over.

I told him that I preferred riding back wards but he replied in a very contemptuous and ungentlemanly way that he cared nothing for my preference, at the same time handing me the tickets which I had given him to punch, etc.

I took the tickets, folded them, put them in an envelope given to Prof. Washington for that purpose, and put them in the inside pocket of my coat.

Before I could button my coat it seems that the conductor became enraged at the idea that I did not obey him even before he spoke, plunged at me like a mad bull with the intention evidently of getting his hand in my collar.

I threw up my hands and thwarted his intention so far as my collar was concerned, but he got his left hand in my vest, from which he tore three buttons and before I could get my equilibrium, struck me in the mouth with his right hand containing the punchers, which blow cut my upper lip through.

After that blow I caught hold of the hand containing the punchers and prevented his further disfiguring my face. His malignant attempt being again frustrated he took unbounded pleasure in kicking me until passengers from different parts of the car ran around him and the disgraceful scene was closed. It is hard for me to realize that a more needless, unprovoked and cowardly assault has ever been received by a passenger at the hands of a conductor.

The result of it all is, I was humiliated, disgraced and my mouth disfigured for life.

If necessary I can refer you to my witnesses at any time.

I tender this charge to you, sir, against the conductor that had charge of the train that left Atlanta Ga. about Ten O'clock Thursday night Sept 19th over the Southern Rail Road, and who, as I understand, was acting as your representative.

I have stated the particulars of the unprovoked assault upon my person, and believing that you will take the right course of action in the matter, I will now subscribe myself, Very respectfully,

R. W. Taylor

Let me have your opinion of the above and what should really be expected of the company.

R. W. T.

ALS Con. 863 BTW Papers DLC. The postscript may have been written to BTW.

From John Wesley Gilbert[1]

Augusta, Ga., Sept. 23, 1895

My Dear Prof., Allow me to congratulate you upon the success of your excellent speech in Atlanta at the opening of the exposition. I am sorry I did not hear it, but I have read it most carefully and as thoughtfully as I can. It was the most opportune speech ever made before a Southern mixed audience, and is destined to set our race upon higher and rising ground in the estimation of these white people whom we *must make our friends* upon grounds which brook no compromise of Negro manhood on the one hand, nor breathes an incendiary spirit of race antagonism, socially speaking, on the other. Utterances like yours upon that occasion and the recent "write up" concerning you and your work in *Harper's Weekly,* justly make you a historic character in the history of the South. I hope you [have] a long life of just such usefulness as has heretofore characterized your manful efforts. I rejoice with your family, your institution, your state, your race, your country, and the world that you were

23

born to meet with the olive of peace, and the honey of sweet persuasion the critical conditions of both races in the South at this crisis of their history. Here's my hand and my heart in the advocacy of your words and work. God speed you. Would that I could identify myself with you in some way that would familiarize our acquaintance, breed a strong friendship between us, and help the race which we represent. I hope it may be my privilege to talk with you personally at some time. I propose whenever I may happen to be near you to hunt you up. I am not a man of ceremonies, flattery, or reserve, when I like a thing. Therefore, I have spoken very freely heretofore, and now concerning your work. I would have done so had my words been unfavorable instead of favorable, if the occasion demanded any utterance from me. I rejoice to offer my encouragement to men who, like yourself, deserve it.

The papers all over Georgia have had the best things to say of your great address. With best wishes,

Jno W. Gilbert

ALS   Con. 111   BTW Papers   DLC.

¹ John Wesley Gilbert was a leading minister and teacher of the Colored Methodist Episcopal Church. Born in Hepzibah, Ga., in 1865, he was educated in the public schools of Augusta, Ga., Atlanta Baptist Seminary (later the theological department of Morehouse College), Brown University, and the American School of Classical Studies, Athens, where he earned an M.A. degree in Greek. He took part in a number of archaeological excavations in Greece and elsewhere in the Mediterranean. In 1889 he became a teacher of Greek at Paine College, a C.M.E. school in Augusta, Ga. In 1895 he became a C.M.E. minister, but he continued his teaching and made two more trips abroad. On one of them he accompanied Bishop Walter Russell Lambuth of the Southern Methodist Church to the Belgian Congo, where he founded a mission.

To Francis James Grimké

Tuskegee, Ala. Sept. 24, 1895

My dear Dr. Grimke: You cannot realize how much satisfaction your kind words of congratulation bring to me.¹ I know that no utterance comes from your lips that is not sincere. The reception given my words at Atlanta has been a revelation to me. I had no idea that a Southern audience would treat a black man's utterances in the way that it did.

The heart of the whole South now seems to be turned in a different direction.

You can easily see that I had rather a difficult task. First I wanted to be very sure to state the exact truth and of not compromising the race. Then there were some things that I felt should be said to the colored people and some others to the white people; and aside from these considerations I wanted to so deport my self as not to make such an impression as would prevent a similar opportunity being offered to some other colored man in the South. The Southern Press seems to be trying to outdo the Northern press in commendation of my remarks. By this mail I send you a copy of the Springfield Republican which contains the address in full. After you have read it I should like to have your opinion on it. Mrs. Washington desires to be remembered to you and Mrs. Grimke. Yours truly,

Booker T. Washington

TLS Con. 1 BTW Papers DHU.

¹ Grimké wrote that he wished he could have been present to hear BTW's speech, and added: "It is a great satisfaction to us all to know that you had the opportunity of speaking on so important an occasion, and that you acquitted yourself so nobly. I am greatly delighted with the extracts from your address that I have seen." (Grimké to BTW, Sept. 20, 1895, Con. 111, BTW Papers, DLC.)

From Ellen Collins

New York. Sept 24/95

My dear Mr. Washington We are much gratified that so soon after the day of highest excitement you were willing to write to us. My sisters fully share my interest but Miss Mary said "He is too generous to them."

Do not be doubtful about the recognition of your good work. There is no reason as yet, why the newspapers should say flattering things — they were surprised and much impressed. You struck the right chord. It is my full belief that when we follow the Divine leading, we will find ourselves over & over again surprised & awed by the response. What does He say? "Ask of Me, and I will show thee great and mighty things which thou has not known."

The times are ripening, the consummation is drawing nearer, it may yet be a long way off to our reckoning, but you can rejoice to be allowed to be one of the forerunners. We are glad for you and with you.

Three papers have come, we thank you. This can hardly fail to set forward the school work; you may find that the darkness of the summer presaged the dawn.

May I add "Keep close to the Leader?" With sincere goodwill I am

Ellen Collins

ALS Con. 110 BTW Papers DLC.

From William Edward Burghardt Du Bois

Wilberforce, 24 Sept., '95

My Dear Mr Washington: Let me heartily congratulate you upon your phenomenal success at Atlanta — it was a word fitly spoken.[1] Sincerely Yours,

W. E. B. Du Bois

ALS Con. 113 BTW Papers DLC.

[1] Du Bois also wrote to the New York *Age* suggesting of the Atlanta address that "here might be the basis of a real settlement between whites and blacks in the South" if whites opened to blacks the doors of economic opportunity and blacks cooperated with whites politically. Du Bois later said the aims of the Atlanta Compromise were frustrated by the mass disfranchisement of blacks by the southern whites. (Du Bois, *Dusk of Dawn,* 55.)

From Edward Wilmot Blyden

New York. Sept. 24. 1895

Dear Mr. Washington, I have read with great delight your wonderful address at the opening of the Atlanta Exposition. I congratulate you on having been made by Providence the instrument of such a message to the whites and blacks of this country at the present time. Your address was an inspiration. It will go down to posterity with such documents as Washington's Farewell Address. By a singular coincidence you are the namesake, not probably by inheritance but by gift, of the "Father of his country." But your work in some respects is greater than his. He freed one race from foreign domination, leaving another chained and manacled. But your words and your work will tend to free two races from prejudices and false views of life and of their mutual relations which hamper the growth of one and entirely cripple the other.

There are several sentences in your address that ought to be printed in bold letters and set up as mottoes in various parts of your Institute; for it seems to me that they are really the maxims which have guided your life work.

They are the following:

"No race can prosper until it learns that there is as much dignity in tilling a field as in writing a poem."

"It is at the bottom of life we must begin and not the top."

"In all things that are purely social the races can be as separate as the fingers, yet one as the hand in all things essential to mutual progress." (This simile, by the way, so apt and expressive, is a common one among the aborigines of Africa.)

"There is no defense or security for any of us except in the highest intelligence and development of all."

"The opportunity to earn a dollar in a factory just now is worth infinitely more than the opportunity to spend a dollar in an opera house."

When, oh when, will our people learn the common sense of this last sentence?

I recognize as healthful and encouraging elements in the condition of the Negro in the South his desire for material and intellectual improvement, his thirst for physical comfort, his craving for justice, which your work tends to stimulate. I do not understand his hunger for social equality with the dominant race, because equality depends upon so many things. It is a matter of taste which it is not in our power to regulate.

I arrived in this country on the 20th of July last, landing at Baltimore. I was at once besieged by newspaper reporters anxious to hear

27

about Africa. General Bryce,[1] Editor of the North American Review, sent his assistant to Baltimore to meet me and request me to write an article for the September number of his Review on the African question, which I at once did. In this article I felt it my duty to refer to your work. I hope you have seen a copy of the Review.

I have received invitations from Chicago, Washington, Danville, Atlanta, New Orleans to deliver addresses. After to the best of my ability fulfilling these engagements I hope to avail myself of your invitation to visit Tuskegee.

Please present my kindest regards to Mrs. Washington whom I know only through her writings which I always peruse with great interest. Yours faithfully,

Edwd. W. Blyden

P.S. You will permit me to say that I am particularly pleased that you did not introduce the word "Afro-American," as descriptive of the race in so important and dignified a public document. That word excludes in discussing race questions, the whole of the people of the Fatherland. It excludes me. It limits all views and discussions of the race question. It is narrow and provincial and not a statesmanlike word. I am glad to see that Southern leaders of the race, as a rule, ignore that word.

EWB.

ALS Con. 110 BTW Papers DLC.

[1] Lloyd Stephens Bryce (1851-1917) was editor of the *North American Review* from 1889 to 1896.

From Benjamin Tucker Tanner

Phila. 9-25-'95

Dear friend. I am so often away from my desk, that at times what I write may seem to be inopportune, as is the present case.

I have read your magnificent oration at Atlanta with positive delight. Allow me to thank you for your noble utterances on behalf of the race; especially for the epigrammatic word:

"The opportunity to earn a dollar in a factory, is infinitely to be preferred in our present condition to the opportunity to spend a dollar in an opera."

God bless you for the word and make you more and more to increase in favor with God and man. Fraternally,

Benj. Tucker Tanner

NB. Brother Penny[1] has written me to be with him in February — it is all right I suppose.

ALS   Con. 113   BTW Papers   DLC.

[1] Edgar J. Penney.

From Burwell Town Harvey

Atlanta, Ga. 9-25-'95

Dear Prof. Washington: I was in the Exposition auditorium when you delivered your very able, and manly plea for the race. It was the best effort of your past life. I consider the speech was worth millions in many ways to our people in making friends for them. It has raised you prominently before the whole country as being the race's best champion and wisest leader. In fact, the Evening Journal here stated in bold letters that your speech was the speech of the occasion. I truly felt proud of you and cheered from the depth of my heart. Leadership along the vital lines which you so earnestly and manly advocate will carry the race up the sure road to success in all walks of life.

I was sorry that I could not get the opportunity to speak to you at the grounds, but I was compelled to leave. I am now located here in Atlanta, Ga., having been called to the pastorate of Antioch Baptist church here. My family is still in Columbus, Ga., and I don't think I will move up here entirely until after Xmas. I will have to allow the newspaper matter to rest awhile until I get a little settled. I think I could publish it and do my church service too. I trust the School is still flourishing as ever.

I hope to be able to run down sometime this winter to visit the School, kindest regards to Mrs. Washington. Let me hear from you at your convenience.

29

Tuskegee has a most creditable exhibit at the grounds. Sorry that I was not able to have my poems printed so as to exhibit them. Your Friend,

B. T. Harvey

ALS Con. III BTW Papers DLC.

From William J. Cansler[1]

Knoxville. Sep. 26 –95

Dear Sir: Allow me to congratulate you upon the success of your speech at Atlanta.

I had the pleasure of hearing your address given last spring to students and residents at Knoxville College, and say now as I have often said since, that I wish every Negro on the continent could hear the same.

I believed then, and know now, that you are our Moses destined to lead our race out of the difficulties and dangers which beset our pathway and surround us on all sides. I have often said and long believed that our peculiar position in the U.S. would only be bettered by gaining the sympathy and cultivating the friendship of the Anglo-Saxon race; your speech and reception at Atlanta has proven this. May you live long to carry on this good work just begun, and tis my earnest wish that you will be able on many more occasions to bear the olive branch of peace to our white neighbors. Upon you has fallen the mantle of the illustrious Douglas[s], to you we accord the title as leader, all intelligent and thinking colored men will follow.

Wishing you a long life, an illustrious career, I am Respectfully,

W. J. Cansler

P.S. Couldnt that expression of yours, "We can be as separate as the fingers, yet one as the hand in all things essential to mutual progress," be symbolized in the form of a button worn on lapel of coat as are worn by Grand Army men, Oddfellows, Masons &c: represented as an open hand, fingers extended and diverging? This could be sold on Exposition grounds at the Negro exhibit and would be bought and worn by thousands both white and colored. It would fittingly symbolize the new epoch in the Negroes history in the South, as well as immortalize the expression.

W. J. C.

ALS Con. 110 BTW Papers DLC.

[1] William J. Cansler was a black teacher in the Knoxville, Tenn., public schools for forty-five years. He was the eldest son of Laura Ann Cansler, who had opened the first school for blacks in Knoxville.

From Timothy Thomas Fortune

New York, Sept 26, 1895

Dear Friend: Can't you see your way to use the term Afro American when speaking of the race as a whole? We are not all black and colored and yellow, but we are all Afro American, and are never spoken of as proper noun except when the legitimate term Afro American negro, colored or yellow person is spoken of. Think it over. I want to be in Atlanta Nov 21. Can't you make it an object for me to spend a week at Tuskegee and deliver a lecture on Douglass and write one article for the Sun and one for the Chicago Sunday Times Herald? If so send along a check $125 and called it settled.

It looks as if you are our Douglass and I am glad of it. I state the case in an article that way handed in to day for the Sunday Sun.[1] I hope it will go. You are the best equipped of the lot of us to be the single figure ahead of the procession. *We must have a head*, and it ought to be in the South and every one of us should hold up his hands. Yours truly

T. Thomas Fortune

ALS Con. 116 BTW Papers DLC.

[1] Fortune must have been chagrined that, instead of publishing his article, the New York *Sun* said editorially on Sept. 28, 1899, 6: "Comparing Principal Washington's oratorical ability with that of the late eminent colored man, Frederick Douglass, we are bound to say that Mr. Douglass stands far beyond the rivalry of Mr. Washington. The oratory of Douglass was also destitute of negroism, and was modeled upon that of the white man; but it was often elevated and commanding, greatly superior to that of any other colored man known to us."

31

From Emily Howland

Sherwood N.Y. Sept. 26, 1895

Dear friend   I have read your noble and eloquent address at the opening of the Exposition once; and I mean to read it many times more. It was the true word fitly spoken. I felt when reading it as Fred'k Douglass did when Pres't Lincoln asked him how he liked that immortal inaugural spoken by Lincoln on the 4th of March 1865. Douglass replied, "it was inspired." Much that is called so bears less evidence in itself of being an inspiration. By the way that inaugural message has become a classic, and [I] have read is conned as a model of style by students at Oxford.

In reading your speech, I could not discover that any point had been left untouched, and all is so terse so brief that the listener must have wished for more.

It is perfect in form, style and fitness, and will help widely and deeply the cause for which you live.

Before the Columbian Exposition Susan B. Anthony[1] said on some occasion that that Exposition would be a great protracted Woman's Suffrage Convention, others felt like hushing her up, it proved her prophecy true, every day a woman's m.t.g. was held where some phase of woman's interests was up. And when Susan B. herself was to speak the jam was a hard one to live through. The Woman's cause and broader religious sympathy were great gainers there, the specific benefit of this Exposition will be to the colored people of the nation I think. They will hereafter hold a higher place, the world having seen collected, the best that they can do.

This is too long a letter for you to take time to read. Skip it. Thanks for the press notice & the Atlanta papers. The Inter-Ocean has published the speech & noticed it, even our local paper mentions it. Cordially

E. Howland

ALS Con. 113   BTW Papers   DLC.

[1] Susan Brownell Anthony (1820-1906), reformer and champion of women's rights, president of the National Woman Suffrage Association from 1892 to 1900.

From Ellen Collins

New York. Sept. 28/95

My dear Mr. Washington, Your letter of the 23rd was duly recd and I have written to W. J. Edwards.

You ask me to express my opinion of your Atlanta address. Already you have received, no doubt, our acknowledgment of the papers, and expression of our interest & gratification. I would have responded to your request however, more promptly, but felt it would be due to you that I should read the address again and with special care, if my comments were to be worth anything. Having lent the copy, I had to wait for its return, & that was this evening. Do not think that I mean to praise unduly when I say it seems to me your remarks were in good taste, sound sense, manly in their claims, and expressed in good English. I do not wonder that the hearers were greatly surprised. Your people have so much love for what strikes the imagination that there is a tendency to the florid in style, you have escaped that, avoided it too. But I believe your mind moves well under the control of principle and the guidance of judgment. Perhaps you might have been a little more independent; in view of the long, long, suffering of your people a little irritation would have been pardonable. I am glad you avoided it. I should be a little sorry for a part of what you promise of loyalty &c, if it were not followed by the demand for the administration of absolute justice. I believe you spoke with great effect, and shall look for a general advance in public sentiment toward a recognition of the rights of the colored people as men; not the extension of privileges.

There, that is the first time I was ever asked to criticise a "notable address"; thank you. I believe it is honestly done. I was glad of the use of the Amazon story. Sincerely

Ellen Collins

P.S. What you say about dignifying labor was a lesson for them to learn as for your people.

ALS Con. 110 BTW Papers DLC.

A News Item in the Chicago *Inter Ocean*

Atlanta, Ga., Sept. 28 [1895]

IS HE A NEW NEGRO?

"We have a new woman and a new negro in the South, and you will find them both in this Cotton States Exposition." So said a brilliant Southern woman, one of the social leaders of Atlanta, to me. She spoke only of what have been the greatest subjects of talk since the exposition opened. The new woman and the new negro are in evidence here, and they are attracting universal attention. I propose to take up both these subjects, and shall reverse the order of their consideration — not because I would put the new negro ahead of the new woman, but because the opening address of Booker T. Washington, of Tuskegee, Ala., was the sensation of that great day in Atlanta. Mr. Washington opened the eyes of the white people of the South. They heard his address in amazement. They applauded him as a new Moses of his people. They talked about it and about him. The papers wrote about both speaker and speech. Booker T. Washington is still the subject of more talk than any other man who figured in the exercises at the formal opening of the Cotton States Exposition. The Atlanta papers receive requests from all over the country for copies of Mr. Washington's address. I was in the Atlanta Journal office when a Californian came in and asked for the paper containing that address. "I understand that it was a great speech for a negro." "A great speech for a man," said the editor. "One of the greatest speeches I ever heard from any man, black or white." This is the sample of the comment. Southern men refer to this speech and the negro exhibit as evidences of an awakening of the race. It seems to me, however, that it would be more appropriate to speak of the awakening of the white race to the real merit of the earnest effort, the work accomplished, and the possibilities of the colored people.

Booker T. Washington may be a new type of a negro to most white men; but he is not a new discovery. His work is not new. He has been working on the lines laid down in his exposition address for fifteen years, and he has accomplished a great deal in that time. Five years ago The Inter Ocean told the story of Washington and his work. It has made both well known in the Northwest — so well known that Mr. Washington was invited to Chicago to take a conspicuous part in the labor congress at the World's Fair. When I first visited the Tuskegee Normal and Industrial Institute, five years ago, I began my first letter to The Inter Ocean with this paragraph:

"What are the colored people doing for themselves in the South? Many Northern people ask this question every year, and they hear different answers to the question, but these do not encourage. They hear only of what is being done for the colored people by good missionaries. I came to the Black Belt of Alabama with that impression. I had heard only of that kind of work, and of colored politicians; but I found that there was another and a more hopeful work here. In telling the story of that work, I can answer the question, 'What are the colored people doing for themselves?' Just in the suburbs of an old-time aristocratic Southern town there is a group of a dozen buildings, large and small, brick and frame, covering the highest ground in Macon County. These buildings are the most conspicuous in the landscape. They dwarf the grand old houses of the planters, which still stand as monuments to a past that was looked upon as glorious. They are the most modern in architecture that are to be found in the whole county. They are known as the Tuskegee Normal School for Colored People, and every one of them was designed by colored skill and built by colored labor. Colored men made the drawings, colored men made the working plans, colored men cut the timber and sawed the lumber, colored men made the brick, colored men laid these brick, fashioned the timbers, and colored men alone are represented in the construction of these most modern buildings in the Black Belt; but the work of colored creation does not stop there. Grouped around among these school buildings and colleges are shops, where colored boys are making wagons to sell to the white merchants of Tuskegee; harness, buggies, house, office, and church furniture, for white people to buy; boots and shoes, clothing, bed mattresses, and, in fact, carrying on, in a small way, almost every industry known in the South. These colored boys and girls are not learning to handle tools in toy shops, to waste material in becoming familiar with them. They are making their own tools in many instances, and in every school shop they are turning out goods ready for the market which the whites are glad to buy, and acknowledge that they do so because they cannot do better elsewhere."

The story of Washington and his practical work was then told in these columns and it has been told again and again, but when the man appeared on the platform at the opening of the Cotton States Exposition and delivered his address, saying what he had said many times before and giving utterance to ideas he had already worked out most successfully in a practical way, he was a revelation to the great majority of the people who heard him, and he was heralded as the new negro. But the awakening was on the part of the white men, not the negro. Booker T. Washington has been awake and working and talking for fifteen years, but the white people of the South have not heard him until he was here given an audience as the first negro to be placed on an official programme in the South to stand beside a white man and speak for his race with the same freedom. The white people heard him and awoke to the realization that there was a new negro in the South, a negro who had as much promise in him as the white man, a negro who had a plan to solve the race troubles.

When it came to the selection of the negro for this address Mr. I. Garland Penn, the chief of the negro commission, wrote to negroes in all parts of the country for suggestions as to the man. Langston and Bruce and others were named and a few named Booker T. Washington. Mr. Penn knew Washington and his work and proposed his name. He told the committee on ceremonies about the work at Tuskegee, and the selection was made. Mr. Washington was invited to deliver the address. He did it, and talk with the people who were present at the opening of the exposition and you will get the impression that there was but one speech, and but one speaker there — Booker T. Washington, the new negro.

The negro building and the negro exhibit at the fair are not new. They are the product of negro skill and industry and largely the product of just such industrial training as Booker T. Washington has been giving his pupils at Tuskegee, and advocating for negro youth all over the South. Commissioner Garland Penn, who has charge of the negro building, says that it was not because the race desired to draw the line that they demanded separate representation at the World's Fair, but because in the mass the colored people can in no wise equal the dominant race, but they do measure up very well when their past and present environments are considered. They presented their request for separate exhibit to the directors of the Cotton States Exposition and it was granted. The colored people offered to erect their own exposition building, but the exposition company would not allow them to do what was not asked of others. It paid for this building as for others. But it let the contract for the building to negroes and they employed negro workmen, so that the negro building stands as an example of negro skill and work.

This building is in the southeastern corner of the park at the main entrance from the railway terminal station. It covers 25,000 square feet. It is 276 feet long by 112 feet wide. It has a central tower and four corner pavilions, and the pediment over the main entrance is decorated with relief work, representing the past and the present conditions of the negro. The one side of the pediment represents the slave mammy, with the one room log cabin, the rake, and the basket in 1865. On the other side is the face of Frederick Douglass, a true representative of the growth and intelligence of the colored man. Near the relief of Douglass are the comfortable residence, the stone church, and symbols of the race's progress in science, art, and literature, all representative of the new negro in 1895. The well-fed mule and the plow occupy the center of the grouping, representing the negro's property and industry. There is no building at the fair which attracts more attention than this one built by negroes and for the exhibition of the products of negro labor.

The largest exhibits in the building are from schools and colleges, but there are many individual exhibits and one of them is a painting marked "30 equals 453." It was painted by a negro, Mr. Freeman,[1] of Washington, and it represents two boys at work at a blackboard. One is a white boy and the other is a colored boy. They both have the same figures before them and are subtracting 30 from 453. The colored boy has put down the result and has a look of triumph on his face. The white boy has a puzzled expression as he looks at the result and still sees the statement that "30 equals 453." But the result is the colored boy by his side, who represents thirty years of emancipation for his race, while the white boy represents 453 years of emancipation for his race. The two races stand equal before the law and in their work here at the exposition, as the two boys stand equal in their work at the blackboard. It is not a striking picture, except in the story it tells, but it is well executed and it attracts much attention from whites and blacks for the conception and the story told. In the central square under the dome of the building there is quite a large collection of pictures and several pieces of statuary. Most of the work is from the Amateur Art Club, of Washington. Mr. Freeman has portraits of Douglass, Bruce, and Langston, and several other figure pieces which are very creditable. Mr. W. C. Hill, of Washington, has several pieces of statuary that are very good, one of them called "The Stubborn Shoe," representing a little girl trying to put on her shoe with her toes stuck into the heel of the shoe and puzzling her brain how to get it on. Another represents the negro with chains broken, but not free. The same society has a large collection of crayons, photographs of colored churches and schools and hospitals in Washington and some exquisite art needlework.

In the art collection there are also three pictures by Mr. H. O. Tanner,[2] the son of Bishop Tanner, of the African M.E. Church. Mr. Tanner is a talented and finely educated young negro, and is now studying art in Paris. One of his pictures in the last Salon received honorable mention this year. There is also a marble bust of Charles Sumner, by Edmonia Lewis,[3] the colored sculptor, who has her studio now in Italy.

Two of the largest and best exhibits of industrial work are from the Tuskegee Normal and Industrial Institute and Hampton Normal and Agricultural Institute. Tuskegee is known as the child of Hampton, because Booker T. Washington had his training at Hampton, and was recommended as president of the Tuskegee Institute by General Samuel C. Armstrong, the founder of Hampton. But Tuskegee's exhibit in the negro building is almost, if not quite, equal to that from Hampton, and both show what industrial training has done for the negro.

In the Tuskegee exhibit there are large cases containing the work of the sewing, dress-making, and millinery departments, the tailor shop, the harness and shoe shops, desks, chairs, and tables from the furniture shop, a handsome carriage, a light buggy, a phaeton, and a farm wagon from the carriage shop, a steam engine built by the boys in the iron-working department, tools made in the same shops, a dairy exhibit, farm products, fruits and vegetables of every variety, and, in fact, some example of work in every department of industry known in the South, showing that the colored boys and girls who take the courses at Tuskegee are fitted for some trade before they are allowed to graduate. The work is not amateurish, but equal in finish to that put upon the market by manufacturers of these products.

In the Hampton Institute exhibit there are similar examples of students' work, some of it of a more pretentious character than that from Tuskegee. There is a handsome revolving bookcase, a richly-carved sideboard, a mantel, and a hall tree of exceptionally fine workmanship, and any of these pieces will compare favorably with any furniture exhibit to be found in the exposition. There are carriages, buggies, phaetons, and wagons from the Hampton shops, a large drill press and a half-power engine to run it. These were both made for use in the shops by the students who work there. Hampton also shows some fine ornamental iron work in banquet and large standard lamps, to show that there are artists in iron as well as artists in bronze, marble, and clay, some fine samples of book printing and binding from the printing department, and a large exhibit of various kinds of work to show how complete is the great industrial school established by General Armstrong, who had charge of the freedmen at that point at the close of the war, and started a school to teach colored youths how to earn their own living by systematic work from trained hands and developed intellects.

There are many other school exhibits from the Knoxville College, Clark University, at Atlanta; the Georgia State Industrial College, at Savannah; the State Normal College, at Montgomery, Ala.; the State Normal and Industrial School, Normal, Ala.; the Gammon Theological Seminary, at Atlanta; the Atlanta Baptist Seminary; the Central Tennessee College, at Nashville; the Fisk University, at Nashville; the Atlanta University; the Spelman Female Seminary, at Atlanta; the Schofield Normal and Industrial Institute, at Aiken, S.C., and a number of other educational and industrial institutions for negroes. The colored people of Chicago have an exhibit of various kinds of work, and there are many individual exhibits of art, mechanical, and agricultural work. There are a number of patents by colored men, some fine tile mantels from a colored manufacturer at Atlanta; a large drug exhibit from the pioneer negro druggists in the South, fancy needle work, collections of fine fruits and grains, and enough excellent work of great variety to demonstrate the capabilities and development of the negro in every department of labor. The negro building has in its exhibits more variety than any other building at the exposition, because it shows the work of the race in all departments.

There is one small corner of the negro building which represents the other extreme of the race. It is marked "Uncivilized Africa," and is an exhibit of some of the natural resources and some of the crude manufactures of the west coast of Africa. Bishop Turner, who has been for years urging the negroes to emigrate to Liberia, brought this exhibit home with him when he returned from Africa, a few weeks ago. He says that it does not represent civilized Africa, but the uncivilized natives, the heathen of that country. He has a collection of their swords, knives, and spears, which, he says, were hammered out of iron ore found there so rich that the natives use it without any knowledge of smelting; samples of the woods that grow on the west coast of the Dark Continent; palm and cocoanut oils, made by the natives; samples of leather and cloth, made by the heathen; and many other curious specimens of African products. Over this exhibit the Bishop has strung a line of delicately woven birds' nests, which are shaped like the long-handled gourd. They are the nests of the weaver bird, and they are as carefully woven as a bit of wicker work. The long arm is attached to the limb of a tree, and through it the bird passes to the large and bulb-like nest in the bottom. There is one article in the Bishop's collection which is not heathen. It is a beautiful silk quilt of the same pattern as that made by a Liberian woman and presented to Queen Victoria. She duplicated the work for Bishop Turner. It is a delicate and intricate piece of patch work, and represents the African coffee tree in bloom.

Bishop Turner has little patience with those who talk about the new negro. He strolled through the negro building with me, but saw little that was new in the workmanship that was evidenced by the exhibits.

"There is nothing new in all this fine work," said he. "The negroes always did the finest kind of work in the South. The slaves were skilled carpenters and wheelwrights and blacksmiths. They did all the work in the old days of slavery. They were not mere drudges without skill. They built the grand old mansions of the planters. They made the carriages and wagons and buggies used by their masters; they did the iron work, as well as the wood work. They made much of the furniture, and were skilled cabinet-makers. In fact, the slaves did all of the work in the South then; and there were skilled mechanics and carpenters among them — more than we now have, perhaps. In that respect, we have a very old-fashioned negro exhibit here. The men who owned slaves gave the best testimony to their skill and intelligence as workmen when they had their own carpenters, blacksmiths, wheel-wrights, and cabinet-makers among their slaves, and trusted them to build all the houses [and] manufacture most of the comforts which surrounded the Southern home. The women could do as fine sewing then as now, and they were the skilled cooks, famous for their dishes. No, this work is not the evidence of a new negro. It is the skill of the same old negro who was in slavery. The only thing new about it is the freedom of the negro to learn what trade he pleases and work out his own salvation in his own way. I am as proud of this exhibit as any one, but I have no patience with the talk about the new negro as a workman. Why, that was the reason he was kept in slavery so long. He was too valuable to be set free."

"Do you still think the negroes should emigrate to Africa?"

"Yes; several million of them. They can be spared from this country, and they can do much better in Africa. They will become the leaders and the civilizers of that continent."

The stalwart old negro Bishop strolled out of the negro building with me, and we turned our steps to the Midway. In front of the Dahomey Village there was a big-nosed white man urging the visitors to not miss seeing the wild cannibals from the west coast of Africa. The old Bishop stopped and heard the stereotyped speech, and remarked that here must be the "new negro." Then he walked up to the showman and said:

"Why do you white men pursue the negro to Africa with your lying? You have for years lied about the negro in this country, and now, when you are being found out, you are lying about the negro at home on his native heath."

The showman stopped, startled for a moment, while the crowd gathered about. Then he asked, "What do you know about it?" and began again on his speech. But the Bishop was not to be ignored.

"I know all about it, sir," he replied. "I am a negro, and I live in Africa a good part of the time. There are not, and never have been, any cannibals on the west coast of Africa. You are simply repeating some of the lies told by white men who went to Africa and had to lie about the country to magnify their own efforts and pose as heroes of great courage and endurance. The natives of the west coast of Africa may be heathens and uncivilized, but they are more peaceable and gentle than many of you civilized and enlightened white men here in America, and these wild negro cannibals you have here, cavorting around like apes and baboons, never saw Africa. They are lazy, good-for-nothing negroes from New York, or some other town, where they have been taught to jump about like monkeys and yell like hyenas, while you tell these people that they are talking in their native tongue. Stop your lying about the negro!"

The crowd shouted, the showman looked stupefied, and the Bishop walked on down the Midway, telling me that there was no new negro. He was simply the same old negro, showing his capacity as he was given opportunity by the new white man; and I am not sure that he is wrong. Booker T. Washington and Bishop Turner are not so far apart, except on the question as to where the negro is to work out his own salvation. Washington insists that by applying the industry and capacity that made the negro valuable in slavery to the new condition of freedom the negro can do the work and become independent here in America. Bishop Turner wants the negro to go to Africa and apply these new conditions in a new country. General Armstrong said to me, just before he died:

"This man Washington is worthy the name he bears. He will live to be known as the Washington of his race."

The speech of Washington has awakened the white men of the South to the realization that there has been a change. The negro building, with its exhibits of the work of negroes, offers its testimony to the truth of Booker T. Washington's teachings.

L. W. B.

Chicago *Inter Ocean,* Oct. 2, 1895, 7.

¹ Probably Daniel Freeman, a Washington, D.C., artist. He may also have been the E. D. Freeman who exhibited his work in the First Industrial Exposition by the Colored Citizens of the District of Columbia at the Union Bethel Church in September 1886.

² Henry Ossawa Tanner (1860-1937) was the leading black painter of his time. Born in Pittsburgh, the son of the A.M.E. bishop Benjamin Tucker Tanner, he grew up in Philadelphia. Inspired by the work of an obscure black painter, James Hess, he sought to learn painting by taking lessons from a local artist. He felt the instruction was too mechanical, however, and left to work on his own, sketching animals and painting outdoor scenes during a long stay in the Adirondacks for his health. In 1880 he enrolled in the Pennsylvania Academy of Fine Arts, studying for two years there under Thomas Eakins. After seven years of unsuccessful effort

to establish himself as an artist in Philadelphia, Tanner tried his hand at photography in Atlanta, but this venture was also a failure. He taught for a time at Clark University in Atlanta, but he found teaching a poor substitute for life as an artist.

In 1891 Tanner moved to Paris and studied at Julien's Art Academy, the most popular private one in Paris. The French painters Benjamin Constant and Jean Paul Laurens took an interest in Tanner and criticized his work. Soon Tanner was exhibiting in Paris salons and selling enough to support himself. In 1895 he started *Daniel in the Lion's Den,* the first painting on the religious themes that typified his later work. In the following year he did *The Raising of Lazarus,* which was hung in the Luxembourg. Rodman Wanamaker, the Philadelphia department-store executive, was so impressed with this work that he sent Tanner to Palestine for travel and work. Robert C. Ogden, a Wanamaker partner, was also a patron of Tanner and bought several of his paintings for Hampton Institute. Tanner's most faithful patron, however, was the wealthy American art enthusiast Atherton Curtis, whom he met in 1897. Tanner married an American white woman, Jessie Macauley Olssen, in 1899, and they had one son. In 1902 Curtis and his wife persuaded the Tanners to come to the United States, but in 1903 they returned to France, where Tanner's work prospered and where he was relatively free from race prejudice. As painting fashions changed in the early twentieth century to cubism, futurism, expressionism, and other styles, Tanner remained conservative, though he did begin using lighter colors and experimenting with pigments and techniques. BTW visited Tanner's Paris studio in 1899 and may also have seen him during his stay in New York in 1903. Their outlooks were radically different, however, and it is improbable that they became close friends. In later years Tanner made an annual contribution to the NAACP. (Mathews, *Henry Ossawa Tanner;* Porter, *Ten Afro-American Artists of the Nineteenth Century;* Locke, ed., *The Negro in Art.*)

[3] Edmonia Lewis was a leading black sculptor. She was born in Greenbush, N.Y., in 1845, of a black father and a Chippewa Indian mother. Both parents died when she was very young, and she grew up with the Chippewas near Niagara Falls. Her brother, Sunrise, who had attended an Indian school, helped her to attend Oberlin College from 1859 to 1863. She was accused of poisoning two white classmates, and though the charges were eventually dropped, she left college and moved to Boston.

Through the influence of William Lloyd Garrison, Edmonia Lewis studied under the sculptor Edmund Brackett. Her first two works, a medallion of the head of John Brown and a bust of Robert Gould Shaw, received much praise. She sent twenty copies of the Shaw bust to the Sailors' Fair in Boston, and using money from this and perhaps aid from philanthropists, she traveled to Rome in 1865. There she was helped by the actress Charlotte Cushman and sculptors Harriet Hosmer and Anne Whitney. She produced several Indian groups relating to Longfellow's *Hiawatha.* One of her first pieces, *Forever Free,* which she sent to Garrison for exhibition, depicted a slave man and woman rejoicing at the news of emancipation.

Edmonia Lewis's work was in the neoclassical style, and her themes usually related to her Negro and Indian background. By the 1870s her reputation in the United States and Europe had grown and she had aristocratic patrons in Italy and England. Her studio was busy, employing at one time nine helpers. She gave her bust of Longfellow to his family, and it ultimately went to the Harvard College Library. To the Centennial Exposition in Philadelphia in 1876 she sent six works, including *The Death of Cleopatra*. Contemporary critics felt almost offended by the emotional intensity and realism of her work, but she was popular in America for a period. Ex-President U. S. Grant sat for her in 1877-78. Her vogue passed, however, and she died in such obscurity, presumably in Rome, that the date is not known. Unfortunately, many of her works have been lost or destroyed.

From Thomas A. Harris

Selma Ala. Sept 29, 1895

Dear friend, I remember all of your kindness to me. I will not take time to mention them. As you know them all. I have been very anxous to hear from you. I am very thankful to be able to say to you that I am getting well. I think I will [be] able one day to walk on my leg as well as ever. It will be a little shorter than the other. I am traveling and lecturuing to the people. They take up corlection for me. I am very [sorry?] to learn that Wiley[1] has or have been notifyed to leave Tuskegee. Of couse to keep him from appearing before the grand Juory. I am a friad that that matter, between them white Caps and myself will go on untell it will affect your School. I will you would see Wiley, and find out what is being done. Please write me all you know about the matter, you need not be affrid to say anything you want to me, no one shall see your letters, I am your friend,

Thos. A. Harris

P.S. Put my letter in an envolope address the out side to Rev. C. S. Dinkins Selma Ala. I dont want it to leave Tuskegee in my name. I will get it.

H.

ALS Con. 862 BTW Papers DLC.

[1] Wiley Harris helped his father to escape to Montgomery, where BTW's friend Dr. C. N. Dorsette attended Harris's wounds. Wiley Harris then returned to Tuskegee in spite of the tense racial atmosphere. (See above, 3:558-61.)

From William Henry Baldwin, Sr.[1]

Boston, Sept 29 1895

Dear Friend Booker Washington   I *always* did believe in you, but when I read yr. *Atlanta speech* of yesterday, as I did just as soon as I saw the Transcript report — I felt that I had not, up to date, *rated you quite high enough*! ! !

It was "A No 1" — "tip-top" — "gilt-edged" — "super extra" and I thank you for it. When shall we have that Sunday Eveg at the Union in Boston?

I always plan *ahead*. Please drop me word. Always Yours Truly

Wm. H. Baldwin

If you name a date to be at the Union will yr. singers (Quartette) be with you.

ALS   Con. 113   BTW Papers   DLC.

[1] William Henry Baldwin, Sr. (1826-1909) was the father of the Tuskegee trustee William Henry Baldwin, Jr., and a longtime friend of BTW. Born in Brighton on the outskirts of Boston, the senior Baldwin became at a young age head of the woolen firm of Baldwin, Baxter and Curry in Boston. He retired in 1868 to become president of the Boston Young Men's Christian Union. This organization had been discontinued during the Civil War, but Baldwin revived and enlarged it, remaining president until two years before his death. About once a year BTW spoke without fee to the boys at the union.

From Daniel Coit Gilman

Baltimore. Sept. 30, 1895

Dear Mr. Washington, Would it be agreeable to you to be one of the Judges of Award in the Department of Education at Atlanta? If so, I shall be glad to place your name upon the list. Yours very truly

D C Gilman

a line by telegraph will be welcomed.

TLS   Con. 110   BTW Papers   DLC.

To Wilbur Patterson Thirkield

Tuskegee, Ala. Oct. 1, 1895

My dear Dr. Thirkield: I am in receipt of your kind favor and am very grateful for your encouraging words regarding my Atlanta Address. The way in which it was received and the attention which has been given it through-out the country has given me a great deal of surprise. You can readily see that I had a trying position. First I wanted to state the exact truth as I saw it and at the same time be true to the colored people and say something that would prove helpful to both races especially in their relation to each other.

When I am in Atlanta again I hope to have the privilege of seeing you in your home. Mrs. Washington desires to be remembered to you and regrets that she did not get to see you in Boston. Yours truly,

Booker T. Washington

TLS   GAGTh.

From Ben Bell, Sr.

Tison Ga   Tattnall Co   Oct the 1irst 1895

Dear sir   I saw your briliant Oration in the Atlanta Constitution which the Editor himself announced could not be surpassed for the Welfare of the Feuture Generation   I my self first read the Biography of your Life in the New York Freeman and it was my own Hearts Delight   I have been trying to be a law bideing Citizen   I did not know my age but did not refuse to pay my tax when they came Due and have been paying them yearly every since my first year but though they are some thing liken, and that was Elevating the Brains I have got a pair of willing hands but by many years of experiment did not know how to controle them for the feuture. but now by guess Work this December comeing I will be 49. fortynine years of age and you may judge by that that there is not much that I can do. but I have got 10 ten Children Seven Boys and three Girls under one roof which is only 14 by 20   My God   My God deliver me, to see some of this amount of Children in a better shape than that. I learn that you are

46

an Educator of the Head and the hand too, and I am in the same notion that I heretofore Wrote to you of sending my oldest Son which is 20 twenty years of age and is now pening these lines to you the reason that I have not made any further efforts in sending him, the rest of my Children was so small until I needed his assistance to help me to sustain them, and just as soon as I can I want him to Walk out and hold up a light for the rest of my Children to see how to walk by. I am still yet unable to send him as I need his assistance for a while yet but I expect to send him just as soon as Possible and please Write me do you still hold the same enducement as you have in the past which was to work so many Hours in the day and go to school so many Hours at night the first year was good for two years Schooling hence. for I do not want to see him with a white Jacket and an apron on Dead–heading in a Hotel because I want him to learn a trade and my Daughters part I had rather see them Burried at Sea makeing their way to Liberia than rolling the White child around the Streets and the clerk a winking at her. now please send me one of your Catalogues. yours

Ben. Bell. Sr

ALS   Con. 8   BTW Papers   ATT.   Original destroyed.

From William Henry Baldwin, Jr.

Atlanta   October 4, 1895

Dear Sir: I return you herewith Mr. Taylor's letter to you. I wrote Mr. Taylor immediately in reply to his communication, and have the matter under most serious investigation. I have had the conductor off ever since I heard of it, and I shall take proper steps to see that such a disgraceful scene will not occur again. I do not yet know the full merits in the case. On Mr. Taylor's simple statement of the fact, it is a perfect outrage. I shall not let up on this matter until I know all the facts and until justice is done. I was very much mortified to hear of the complaint.

I had meant to write you before this and to tell you how much I was impressed with your speech at the opening of the Exposition. I knew you would make just such a speech, and I told many people before that you would say just the right thing, because your work is in just the right lines, and I have heard nothing but praise for your speech and for your philosophy. I remain   Very truly yours,

W H Baldwin Jr

TLS   Con. 792   BTW Papers   DLC.

From William Richard Carter[1]

Brunswick, Ga. Oct 5/95

Dear Prin: I do most heartily approve of "Casting down your buckets where you are"; but I would like to bring up good water. I have labored hard here in the educational line but it seems to no effect. We have not been treated rightly in regards to our Public School here. The Board of Education has made the Schools a political issue and has placed such a man as Principal as will cater to its wishes. And it has reduced salaries below expenses. I received my appointment here again as Asst Prin but the salary is entirely too low for me. I have worked hard to get up an independent school (As Henry Johnson[2] will tell you) but I wanted it nonsectarian and the Baptists wanted it Baptist and the Methodists wanted it Methodist so it fell through. I am now trying to work up another school but have no encouragement whatever. I have about become discouraged and want to leave. Do you know of a school that I can get? How about the school at Aneonto or Snow Hill or anywhere else? Please let me hear from you as soon as possible.

James[3] wants to come back to school and I must find a way to keep him there. If you dont know of a school do you know of any other position that I can get?

I am getting on nicely in my ministerial studies. Have been preaching quite often here lately as my pastor is taking his vacation and I have most of his church duties to perform. Some future day I hope to be able to take a regular Theological course.

Please let me hear from [you] as soon as possible. Give Regards to Mrs. Washington also all of my dear teachers who are still there. Yours of '93

Wm. R. Carter

ALS   Con. 862   BTW Papers   DLC.

[1] William Richard Carter graduated from Tuskegee in 1893. After graduation he taught school and preached in Florida, Georgia, and Tennessee. In 1900 he became principal of the Topeka Educational and Industrial Institute in Topeka, Kan.

[2] Henry Edwin Johnson.

[3] James Garnette Carter, apparently William's brother, graduated from Tuskegee in 1897 and established his own business as a tailor.

To Hollis Burke Frissell

Tuskegee, Ala. Oct. 6 95

My dear Dr. Frissell: I meant to have written earlier in reply to your kind favor regarding my Atlanta remarks. When your letter came I had already sent the text of my speech to Miss Ludlow for the Southern Workman.

Nothing could have given me a greater surprise than the manner in which my address was received. The next day I could hardly walk the streets of Atlanta because of the large number of Southern whites who wanted to shake hands with me. Every Southern paper has had something to say editorially of my remarks and all in a favorable spirit. So far not a single colored paper that I have seen has made adverse criticism. It does seem as if there is a better state of feeling between the races than there has ever been.

Letters from South and North pour in upon me. Ever since my Atlanta speech these letters have taken my time. Reque[s]ts to write books, magazine articles, and from lecture bureau managers, and to make addresses in all parts of the country fill my mail every day, but I am determined that none of these things shall turn me aside from my work.

Dr. Curry was with us this week. Yours Sincerely

Booker T. Washington

Gr[e]atly to my surprise I have just been appointed one of the judges in the department of Liberal Arts and education. This refers to the whole exposition.

B. T. W.

ALS BTW Folder ViHaI.

From Grover Cleveland

Gray Gables, Buzzards Bay, Mass. Oct 6th., 1895

My dear Sir: I thank you for sending me a copy of your address delivered at the opening of the Atlanta Exposition.

I thank you with much enthusiasm for making the address. I have read it with intense interest and I think the Exposition would be fully justified if it did no more than furnish the opportunity for its delivery. Your words cannot fail to delight and encourage all who wish well for your race; and if our colored fellow-citizens do not from your utterances gather new hope, and form new determinations to gain every valuable advantage offered them by their citizenship, it will be strange indeed. Yours very truly,

Grover Cleveland

TLSr Copy BTW Folder ViHaI. The letter also appeared in the Indianapolis *Freeman,* Oct. 19, 1895, 5.

From Mary Caroline Moore[1]

Framingham. [Mass.] 6 Oct. 1895

My dear Mr. Washington: Your note with the enclosed check came in due season.

Payments for board are usually made at the beginning and in the middle of each term, $45. at one time, $30 at another, the larger sum first. The reverse order is, however, quite satisfactory in this case and will make not the slightest difference to us.

Portia seems happy. She is eager for every word from home, but I think she has not been seriously home-sick.

I shall be very glad to see you when you come North for I want to talk with you about what line of work you want emphasized. She has already taken two music lessons, and has wisely told her teacher that you wish her to have thorough scientific training rather than ability to play a few things. Miss Hartwell, the music teacher does excellent work. She charges fifty cents a lesson and is happy to let Portia practise on her piano. I thought you would certainly want her to take two lessons a week and have, therefore, so arranged her work.

Please give my kind regards to Mrs. Washington and tell her that I will write her again soon. Yours very truly

Mary C. Moore

ALS Con. 112 BTW Papers DLC.

[1] Mary Caroline Moore (1854-1949) was born in England and immigrated to Massachusetts with her parents in 1864. She graduated from Framingham Normal School in 1872. From 1877 to 1886 she taught in the Perkins Institute for the Blind. Returning to Framingham in 1893, she taught English until her retirement in 1916.

From Thomas A. Harris

Demopolis Ala. Oct 7. 1895

Dear friend, Yours of 30th inst come duely to hand, and contents noted. I was indeed glad to hear from you. I am still mending as I think. My leg is weak. I still have to use crutches. I think it will be some time before I can put them down. Though I hope to get alright some day again. I hope the Lord may direct all things for the best. I have been very much bothered about Wiley. I hope he will come out alright. He has done nothing to cause him to have to leave home, either have I. But the *un*-written law is much more in frorce than the written. You will do me a great favor to keep a watch after the matter concering Wiley, and advise him along that line. I received your letter second handed, at this place, and did not get your address. I would be glad to have it. I am traviling, and lecturing as I go. I charge nothing. But they give me what they mind to. I have taken up as much as $4.00 and $5.00 at a time, and less. I ofton come in contack with your name and interest. I have tried best I could to defend you and your intentions. I know I have made you many friends, out of those who do not or did not understand you, and in other words have been mislead as to you and your School. I have done it because I thought it was my duity to do so. The news papers mislead the people regards you and myself, on the night I come to the School when shot. I explain that to many. Do you think it advible for me to come back to Tuskegee? I would like to come. Every body is just as fraid of me in Tuskegee as I am of them. But for the good of my family and others, I have staided away from there, find out all you

51

can and write me. Those who shot me know that I know who they were. Old Tip Huddleson[1] shot me, and I know the others who were with him. Let me know if the grand Jury tried to get a true bill against any of them. I would have come before the grand Jury if I had been offored any protection. Talk to Brewer[2] about the matter. I will be here untel today week. If you will write me at once, I will get your letter before I leave here. You can put my letter in an envelope and put that in another envolpe back the first to me and the second to Mr. R. B. Jones, and no one will know it is coming to me. I have had some good recommendations given me in Montgomery and Selma, and I would like to be able to carrie yours too. If you feel like you would like for me to have it you may send it in your letter to me. I have been thinking of going to the Exposition in Atlanta. Do you think it would be advible for me to go there? Let me hear from you at once. I am ever your friend.

Thos. A. Harris

ALS Con. 111 BTW Papers DLC.

[1] Possibly Charles Huddleston, a white bartender in Tuskegee, twenty-five years old.

[2] Samuel Louis Brewer was born in 1864 near Tuskegee, taught for a while in Mobile, and was admitted to the bar in 1889. He was elected solicitor of the fifth judicial circuit in 1892 and 1898 and was elected judge in 1904, 1910, and 1916.

From Portia Marshall Washington

Framingham Mass. Oct. 7. 1895

My Dear Papa   I receved your letter the orther day and I was real glad to hear from you.

I was here two weeks yesterday. To day is my busy day because we dont go to school on Mon. but we do on Sat. Mamma wanted me to wash and iron my clothes but I dont see how I am to get time. We get up at six eat breakfast at seven clean up after breakfast then I practice until school time we are let out at 11-30 then come home study until lunch after lunch go to school from school to practice then go for a walk with Miss Moore come home get ready for dinner after dinner read sew etc now you have my days work.

I have a very nice teacher her name is Miss Smith.[1] she has charge of a little girl in Crocker Hall. My room is in Normal hall I have a very nice room I have yours and mamma's picture and also Davidson's I would like to have one of Bakers with pants on. The young ladies were very much pleased with your speech. Miss Moore says she would like to have some more copies and some orther circulers and things to send to Montreal Canada.

She for got to put the reciete in her letter so I put it in mine. Tell mamma I have not gotten those things yet. I got her letter to day. Love to all   Your loveing daughter

Portia

ALS   Con. 113   BTW Papers   DLC.

[1] J. Angelina Smith of Springfield, Mass., an 1888 graduate of Framingham Normal School, taught there in the practice school from 1890 to 1899.

From George V. Clark[1]

Memphis Tenn. Oct. 12th 1895

Dear Bro. & Friend: Yours to hand this morning. Am glad to give you my word of condemnation against the iniquity in the form of that saloon annex.[2]

The schools can ask to withdraw their exhibits. As many of the Chief Commissioners, who will lend their aid, might send in a petition carefully and respectfully worded asking its removal out of the building. If their be failure of the above let us, *by all means,* send out an address to the country showing our disapproval of the thing and the previous steps taken, by us, to get rid of it. A young miss, the daughter of a member of my church, was sent to your school, this week via Atlanta. She is, ere this in your midst. Take the best care of her. She is most worthy. Is of one of our best families. Her name is Ella Wallace.[3] Her father is a very successful business man. Sorry I could not drop in to see you on my way home. Fraternally yours

G. V. Clark

Let me hear from you. Am with you from tip to tip.

ALS   Con. 110   BTW Papers   DLC.

[1] George V. Clark, a graduate of Howard University, was minister of the Second

Congregational Church in Memphis until 1897, when he moved to Boston. Later for many years he was minister of the Mount Zion Congregational Church in Cleveland.

2 The Tuskegee Woman's Club, of which BTW's wife was president, complained that the restaurant in the Negro Building had a barroom attached that was "a stigma upon the entire race." The club passed three resolutions that condemned the selling of liquor in the Negro Building because "we feel it an insult to at least the womanhood of the Negro race." Since it was the only bar on the grounds, it attracted men of both races. The club women appealed to the exposition authorities to remove the bar, which "must bring to the face of every self-respecting member of the race the blush of shame, as he enters the doors darkened by the shadow of this disreputable traffic." Finally the club women resolved to petition the officials of the exposition and to make their appeal in the public press. (*Tuskegee Student,* 10 [Oct. 17, 1895], 1.) R. T. Pollard, a black minister in Montgomery and one of the Atlanta Exposition's Negro commissioners, wrote BTW that the woman's club resolutions were "fitting and timely." (Pollard to BTW, Oct. 14, 1895, Con. 120, BTW Papers, DLC.) Isaiah T. Montgomery, another Negro commissioner, also was in favor of eliminating the saloon. (Montgomery to BTW, Oct. 14, 1895, Con. 113, BTW Papers, DLC.) The matter was probably dropped on the ground that the bar was not actually in the Negro Building but in the annex. (W. H. Crogman to BTW, Oct. 19, 1895, Con. 110, BTW Papers, DLC.)

3 Maggie Ellen Wallace of Memphis was a member of the Tuskegee junior class in 1895-96.

From Rufus Brown Bullock

Minneapolis, Minn., Oct. 13, 1895

My Dear Professor: I have had it in mind to express more formally my congratulations to you and thanks for your most admirable address at the opening of our Exposition, than was convenient to do on the stage at the moment, but absence from home and other duties have intervened. I am here as a delegate from our State to the Triennial Convention of our Church and having been laid up in my room by a somewhat serious illness, I now take advantage of a comfortable moment to say that you may, without egotism, take to yourself credit for the fact that your speech will fortify everything that has been done in the right direction in the past toward bringing about proper relations between our people — relations which in my judgment should never have ceased to exist, but grew out of the unfortunate political controversy that occurred between Congress and President Johnson after the War.

The sound philosophy, the manly self assertion, and the eloquent presentation of the subject as it is today, made by you on an occasion which had no predecessor will be accepted by our people, and by the people of the United States, as the truest solution of the mistaken sentiments engendered by the political controversy to which I have alluded.

It has given to the Press of the country, without political bias, an opportunity to make known in their columns the exact sentiment of the best elements of our colored fellow-citizens, and will continue to be an educator until many mistaken notions heretofore in the minds of the people North and South, will be dissipated.

Let me renew my congratulations and thanks. Very truly yours,

Rufus B. Bullock

P.S. I find in our Sunday morning's edition of today's Minneapolis Tribune[1] a very liberal and extended editorial which I enclose.

R. B. B.

TLSr Con. 110 BTW Papers DLC.

[1] The Minneapolis *Tribune* called BTW "A Modern Moses" and recounted his rise from ignorance and poverty to a place of national leadership. The *Tribune* asserted that BTW's "masterly oration at the opening of the Atlanta Exposition has raised him into sudden prominence as the man of the hour in this country." (Minneapolis *Tribune*, Oct. 13, 1895, 6.)

From John Edward Bruce[1]

Albany [N.Y.] Oct 14 1895

My dear Mr Washington, I give you hearty thanks for your letter of Oct 9th containing a copy of your great speech. You may well feel proud of that effort. Like old wine it improves with age. I appreciate all that you say touching the embarrassments under which you labored in efforts to strike the happy mean. In the language of an Ohio politician you have did nobly!! The Negro cannot occupy relative position in the South or anywhere else until he makes himself intellectually, morally, and industrially the equal of the white man. The negro (?) of mixed blood and the white men of the north with more zeal than judgement or sagacity, have conspired by their interminable twaddle about Negro equality in the South to intensify the feeling against the black race and to retard its progress. You hold the key to the solution of the problem of the century and you can do much toward making the Bible and the spelling book the sceptres of national power and in inculcating the idea that *personal worth* is the one thing needful in the development of Negro character. Yours truly

Bruce-Grit

ALS Con. III BTW Papers DLC.

¹ John Edward Bruce (1856-1924?), a free-lance journalist in Washington, New York City, and Albany, N.Y., was one of the leading exponents of black nationalism in his day. Born a slave in Maryland, he secured an education in an integrated school in Stafford, Conn., before beginning a fifty-year career as a journalist. He wrote for scores of newspapers, founded several of his own, and wrote poetry, plays, and music. Unable to live by his writings, Bruce held minor federal posts. Though he used several pen names, he was best known as "Bruce-Grit." An exponent of black pride and solidarity, he opposed miscegenation and championed the legitimacy of violence in the struggle for equal rights. Though not consistent, he was usually in the protest camp in opposition to BTW, but he soon parted company with the integrationists of the NAACP. BTW occasionally paid Bruce through Fortune for favorable newspaper editorials, but Bruce often criticized BTW when not in his pay.

In 1912 Bruce became one of the founders of the Negro Society for Historical Research and served as its president. Arthur A. Schomburg was its secretary. Bruce was an active promoter of black history because he believed that ancient African civilization was superior to that of modern western civilization and that whites had stolen much of their vaunted culture from Africa. A believer in Pan-Africanism, the common interest and destiny of black peoples, Bruce in his last years was in the inner circle of Marcus Garvey's Universal Negro Improvement Association. (Gilbert, ed., *Selected Writings of John Edward Bruce*, 1-9; Meier, *Negro Thought*, 262-63.)

To Ednah Dow Littlehale Cheney

Tuskegee, Ala. Oct. 15, 1895

My Dear Mrs. Cheney: I received your kind letter which came through Mrs. Washington several days ago, and meant to have written you earlier.

I appreciate thoroughly anything you say because I know you always speak as you feel whether the criticism pleases or not. I do not know whether you have had opportunity to read my Atlanta address in full so I enclose a copy. In referring to the social condition I simply meant to emphasize the condition which I think obtains throughout the world, that is, I simply meant to say that each individual regulated his own social intercourse, and then again I find by experience that the southern people often refrain from giving colored people many opportunities that they would otherwise give them because of an unreasonable fear that the colored people will take advantage of opportunities given them to intrude themselves into the social society of the south. I thought it best to try to set at rest any such fear. Now of course I understand that there are a great many things in the south which southern white people class as social intercourse that is not really so. If anybody understood me as meaning that riding in the same railroad car or sitting in the same room at a railroad station is social intercourse they certainly got a wrong idea of my position. When I see you I hope to have an opportunity of talking the matter over.

Knowing how deeply you are interested in all that pertains to the interest of our race I respect most highly anything you say and I hope you will always write or speak freely. Yours truly,

Booker T. Washington

TLS   Ednah Dow Cheney Papers   MB.

From Timothy Thomas Fortune

New York, Oct 15, 1895

Dear Friend: The *People's Advocate* of Atlanta, of October 12, contains an *extraordinary* article on "The Fake of all Fakes," in which the consideration shown Afro-American patrons on the Exposition grounds to be of the most astounding character in the discriminations practiced. Please write me at once *in confidence* if Hagler tells the truth. Do we have the same consideration on the grounds and in the buildings that other patrons have?[1] Yours truly

T. Thomas Fortune

ALS   Con. 111   BTW Papers   DLC.

[1] A search of black newspapers revealed no reference to the editorial mentioned. An Atlanta *Constitution* editorial defended the exposition against "a few sensation mongers" and denied that black visitors were discriminated against or were "not wanted in some buildings." It said: "Since the exposition opened its gates thousands of respectable colored people have attended the big show, and they have been

as well treated as their white neighbors. This is a part of the programme. Our exposition is national and international in its scope, and there is no room in it for sectional or racial discrimation." (Atlanta *Constitution,* Oct. 23, 1895, 6.) Among the blacks who reported courteous treatment by whites in public places and public conveyances in Atlanta were Alice M. Bacon and Charles R. Douglass. "I entered a car with three ladies," said Douglass, "and three white typical 'Georgia Crackers' gave up their seats and invited these ladies to sit down." (Bacon, *The Negro and the Atlanta Exposition,* 24-25.)

From Robert Curtis Ogden

Philadelphia   October 17th, 1895

My dear Sir: It has been in my mind many times to congratulate you upon your speech at the opening of the Atlanta Exposition and upon the widespread and beneficent results that appear to be flowing from it. I trust that something more than merely surface impressions are being made and, although we cannot hope for a complete revolution all at once, yet I hope the principles are reaching a more popular comprehension that will give the race question a rapid impetus forward.

I also desire to ask your interest as far as possible in the exhibition of Mr. Tanner's pictures which I have had associated somewhat with the Hampton exhibition. My reason for this was twofold: first, I could not learn that the art department of the Negro Building would offer any adequate position for pictures that are so important, and second, that they would lose their distinctive race influence and character if placed in the general art exhibit. My purpose was to get the influence of Mr. Tanner's genius on the side of the race he represents and at the same time I did not want it degraded by inharmonious associations with inferior work.

A proposition was made in this city some time ago for the colored people to purchase his large picture "The Bagpipe Lesson" and present it to the Academy of Fine Arts in this city. The movement did not make much progress, resulting in the collection of only about $100. and with the advice of the local committee I have formulated a plan by which subscriptions are to be taken up for this purpose at the Atlanta Exposition. If local justification for the national appeal is necessary, it will be found in the fact that the Academy of Fine Arts gave Mr. Tanner his first opportunities for art education. Some good reproductions of the picture are in the hands of Harris Barrett,[1] and a copy will be presented to any subscribers of 25¢ and upward to the fund. The amount needed is something over $1000. If you think this a worthy matter, please give it your influence for at least the 25¢ subscriptions. I have bestowed time, thought and money upon the plan and I certainly hope it will succeed.

My friends of the Hamilton Club in Brooklyn have been very much interested in the position you have taken in consequence of your Atlanta speech. I am a member of that Club and my brother is quite important in its management. Some suggestions have been made concerning the influence of the Club in behalf of the educational work now being carried on at Hampton and Tuskegee, and, in a very crude way, the idea is being formulated to tender a reception to Dr. Frissell and yourself about the first of February next, at which the most distinguished and influential citizens of Brooklyn would be invited to meet you both as the representatives of the highest ideas in practical negro education. I mention this now with the request that you inform me if the plan meets your approval and whether you will authorize me to act for you in carrying it forward to completion, in case it seems feasible. I do not think there would be any immediate financial result for either of our institutions but I am sure the influence of such an occasion could not fail to be good and will bear fruit in the future. Please let me hear from you at your early convenience, and oblige

Yours very truly,

Robert C Ogden

TLS Con. 113 BTW Papers DLC.

[1] Harris Barrett, an 1885 graduate of Hampton Institute, was bookkeeper in the treasurer's office at Hampton. He was also secretary-treasurer of the Colored People's Building and Loan Association in the town of Hampton.

An Interview in the Atlanta *Constitution*

[Atlanta, Ga., Oct. 18, 1895]

Washington Talks of the Future

Booker T. Washington, president of the Industrial college of Tuskegee, Ala., and member of the board of awards, is sanguine over the results that will be accomplished by the exposition. He is the only negro on the jury and is also the only negro who spoke at the exposi-

59

tion on opening day. His speech, which was printed in nearly every paper in the country, will be long remembered by the people of the south as the greatest oration ever delivered by a colored man.

"Were the exposition to fail now, if such a thing were possible, its mission would have been accomplished. The colored people of the south and the colored people of the north have been greatly benefited and much good will be done. The exposition is great in all things, but greatest in the work it has done for the negro race. It has sealed old friendships anew and healed old wounds.

"The negro race the entire country over is solidly in favor of the exposition and will attend and inspect the exhibits before the gates close. I base my statements upon information that has been furnished me. There are today 300 papers published in the United States that are conducted and owned by negroes. With the exception of three of these papers they are working hard for the success of the exposition. Every one is edited by strong and influential men and will accomplish a vast amount of good. The people of my race are coming to the exposition and the negro building will be visited and inspected by many of the colored people of the United States and other countries.

"The future of the negro is brighter today than ever before and I am most sanguine over the promise that the future holds out to us who are working for the elevation of the race. I have no fear of what is to come and can assure you that as a race we are moving onward and upward."

Washington is working for the success of the negro exhibit and has done much to advertise the progress that has been made.

Atlanta *Constitution,* Oct. 18, 1895, 3.

To the Editor of the New York *Herald*

[Tuskegee, Ala., ca. Oct. 20, 1895]

COLORED MEN ADVANCE

PROFESSOR WASHINGTON TELLS OF THE DEVELOPMENT OF HIS RACE IN THE SOUTHEAST

My belief is that it is with a race as with an individual, in the long run the race is given that place in the civil fabric which it wins and deserves. Force could free the negro, but there it had to end. It could not make him industrious. It could not make him frugal. It could not make him skilled in hand. It could not make him an intelligent voter. It could not make the Southern man love and treat him as an equal.

The negro, ignorant and inexperienced as a voter and officer, immediately after the war had not only his ignorance to contend with, but the opposition of his former master. Unfortunately, the Southern white man felt for twenty years after the negro's freedom that outside parties were trying to force him into unnatural positions at too rapid a rate. The white South not only held back, but opposed the political advances of the negro. It said to Congress, "You can pass laws putting the negro on equality with the white man, but without local public sentiment these laws cannot be executed," and they were not. While this experiment of artificial forcing was being tried the negro was not only alienating himself from the Southern white man, but in the great rush for office he lost sight of the fact that his life success must be conditioned on industrial ability — his ability to create something that the white man wanted, something that would make the white man to some extent dependent on the negro.

Wise men in the North, like the sainted General S. C. Armstrong, of the Hampton Institute in Virginia, early saw the mistake that the politicians were making with the negro. They said let us stop emphasizing the political side of the negro, and give attention to making him an industrial factor in the South; let us make him so skilled in hand, so strong in head, honest in heart, that the Southern white man cannot do without him. They said it was more important that the negro be prepared for voting than that he should vote. So, during the last dozen years, led on by such institutions as the Hampton Institute in Virginia and the Tuskegee Normal and Industrial Institute in Alabama, and stimulated by gifts here and there by the John F. Slater fund under the wise administration of the Hon. J. L. M. Curry, the negro has practically dropped out of politics, and is now giving his time and strength to the acquiring of industrial skill, education, character and property in a way that he has never done since the war. Within ten miles of the Tuskegee Institute, in one community there are twenty negroes buying homes. This is brought about by the stimulus of industrial education at this institution.

Now that the leading Southern whites, led by such liberal and strong papers as The Montgomery Daily Advertiser, Atlanta Constitution and

Atlanta Journal, note the change in the method of developing the negro, they are taking hold with a strong hand and are ready to assist and encourage in making the negro a man. The recognition that the negro has received in connection with the Atlanta Exposition is an indication of the change of Southern whites. In the future they are going to be more willing to help us than they have been in the past, if the negro will only be sensible and conservative. One step has been taken, another will come.

The South does not want to wrong the negro. The wisest whites understand that even if for no better reason than that of self-preservation the whites do not want to wrong the negro. They know that the man who murders a negro will soon murder a white man. They know that the white man who will steal a negro's ballot will soon steal a white man's ballot or dollar.

What all classes want is for progress to be made by natural methods, and that the negro be given all the rights and privileges that his ability and character entitle him to, and there be no artificial forcing. On this ground, the best people in the South will join hands with the best people in the North, and we, as a race, will make more progress, I believe, in the next ten years than we have in the last twenty years.

Booker T. Washington

New York *Herald,* Oct. 20, 1895, sec. 5, p. 5.

To Robert Curtis Ogden

Tuskegee, Ala. Oct. 25, 95

My dear Mr. Ogden: I thank you for your kind words of congratulation regarding my Atlanta remarks. The reception of the speech in Atlanta and its effects upon the country have given me a great surprise.

I have spoken with Mr. Barrett about the purchase of the Tanner pictures, but as I shall not be in Atlanta very much from now on I fear there is little that I can do, but I have asked Mr. Barrett to use me in any way he thinks well.

For a week I have been associated on the Jury of Award with Dr. McAlister[1] and have learned to appreciate him very much. He and I worked much together in Atlanta. Dr. McAlister can tell you about the Hampton and Tuskegee exhibit.

I am glad to hear about the Hamilton Club matter and hope it will materialize. It will help the cause much I am sure.

Rev. Mr. Turner[2] from Hampton is here this week.

Wednesday in Atlanta I had the pleasure of receiving the President and showing him through the Hampton exhibit.[3] He expressed himself as pleased and surprised.

We are planning to hold a meeting in Phila about Nov 18 and want you to be one of the speakers. Yours Sincerely

[Booker T. Washington]

ALd Con. 112 BTW Papers DLC.

[1] James McAlister (1840-1913) was president of Drexel Institute of Art, Science and Industry in Philadelphia from 1890 until shortly before his death. Born in Scotland, he immigrated to Wisconsin at the age of ten. A graduate of Brown University, he practiced law for a time and was superintendent of schools in Milwaukee. He directed a reorganization of the Philadelphia public schools through curriculum changes and introduction of industrial training.

[2] Herbert Barclay Turner.

[3] Grover Cleveland visited the Atlanta Exposition on Oct. 23, 1895, and, at BTW's request, spent an hour shaking hands and signing autographs in the Negro Building. BTW wrote in *Up from Slavery* that Cleveland "seemed to give himself up wholly, for that hour, to the coloured people." (See above, 1:335; Atlanta *Constitution*, Oct. 24, 1895, 2.) Vice-President Adlai E. Stevenson also visited the building and met Washington, Penn, and Bishop Turner. Stevenson said: "From what I have seen of industrial progress in the colored race and the manner in which it is permitted to be displayed, I can say that it may safely be left for the southern people and the negroes to settle their own problems without outside interference." (Atlanta *Constitution*, Oct. 19, 1895, 5.)

From Laura Evangeline Mabry[1]

[Tuskegee, Ala.] Monday Oct. 28—1895

Breakfast — Minu.
Grits, Stewed Beef, Corn-bread, Coffee. Grits were scorched and not well done. Beef was not seasoned. I think it would have been much improved by the addition of salt pepper and onions. Coffee was hot and looked very well.

Dinner — Minu.
Boiled Peas with bacon. Boiled Sweet potatoes. Corn-bread. Peas were not well done, but the bacon was. The sweet potatoes were done and hot and evidently had been cleaned well.

· ·

Supper — Minu.
Baking Powder Biscuit, Syrup, Tea. Perhaps a little improvement could have been made on the biscuits by having them a little thiner, but other wise they were fairly good. The syrup was very nice. The tea was also very nice and hot.

Laura Mabry

ADS   Con. 111   BTW Papers   DLC.

¹ Laura Evangeline Mabry, of Birmingham, graduated from Tuskegee in 1895 and taught laundering there until 1901.

From Laura Evangeline Mabry

[Tuskegee, Ala.] Tuesday Oct. 29—1895

Breakfast — Menu.
Stewed Beef, Boiled sweet potatoes, Corn-bread, Coffee. The beef was badly scorched, and not well seasoned. Coffee was hot and looked nice. Bread was hot, & potatoes were nicely cooked and cleaned.

· ·

Dinner — Menu.
Boiled Peas. Boiled Sweet-potatoes. Stewed beef and Corn bread. The peas were boiled without fat. Enough hard corn was found in the peas to make them unpalatable and unattractive. The beef was not seasoned with pepper and salt, but onions added much to the taste. Potatoes and bread were nice and hot.

· ·

Supper — Menu.
Light bread, Syrup, and tea. Very nice bread and syrup. The tea was very cold.

Laura Mabry

ADS   Con. 111   BTW Papers   DLC.

From William Jenkins

Tuskegee, Ala., Oct. 30 1895

Mr. Washington: Pursuant to orders I made a tour of inspection today with the following result:

Slops are thrown too near the well in rear of Ala. Hall. Student's kitchen sewer needs cleaning. A conduit is needed to carry slops from S. kitchen to sewer. The slop pipe leading from the pantry to the garbage cart needs an exterior washing. There are too many loose brick bats lying around the laundry. Drainage pipes are very much needed about the laundry.

A new brick drain is needed in rear of annex to carry the water from the girls bath-room. The heater (for water) of the girls bath room is in a bad fix and is likely to set the annex on fire. The wood, old boxes etc. in rear of students kitchen should be cut and piled up in an orderly manner in the wood house. There are too many ruts in rear of Willow Cottage; they should be filled in with the loose brick bats which are scattered about the premesis.

The closets in every instance on the Varner property are in a most deplorable condition. The contents, instead of being hauled away, are allowed to accumulate in the rear of each. The well in rear of Varner Cottage contains a dead rabbit. This ought to be attended to at once as the veins of this well may be the same as those of other wells on the grounds.

Remains of trash pile fire should be carted off. The filthy condition about the Torbert Cottage is enough to create a pestilence.

An under-ground trough or pipe should be placed in rear of Armstrong Hall to carry away slops. Slops are now emptied upon the surface and produce a very bad odor. The bucket stand under boys water-closet needs cleaning.

Benches are needed at the urinal to enable small boys to reach the trough. Deodorizers as well as disinfectants are needed for all water-closets and damp places. There is plenty of lime. But I am under the impression that lime is a disinfectant only. The old unsightly Commencement pavilion should go. The post might be put under shelter for future use. The library shelves might be kept better if Miss Thompson were given a step ladder (and there is not a good one on the place) a cob-web brush and a hair duster. A common complaint is that our students do not dust the ledges of anything nor the window frames. This is specially true of Porter Hall Chapel.

The trash boxes in all buildings are too prominent. They should all be put in the most secluded places.

I found the Scott Cottage water closet worse, if possible, than the Varner closets.

The grounds about the Model School should be graded.

About the Varner Cottages there is a strong smell of urine.

The grounds about the Hospital which ought to be a thing of beauty are the worse kept of all.

A water-closet is very much needed at the Cropper cottage. There is entirely too much soiled paper floating about near the cottages. A Deodorizer should be used about the B. T. Washington stable yard, as the odor emenating from there on a warm day is very disagreable.

Of course, I found many things to commend. I find a most wonderful improvement since my visit of twelve months ago. Resptfly

W. Jenkins

ALS   Con. 111   BTW Papers   DLC.

From Edward Alexander Clarke[1]

Washington, D.C. October 31/95

My Dear Sir, The Bethel Lit. and Histor. Assocn extends an invitation to you to lecture before it some time this season. It has had a very brilliant opening with Dr. Blyden, Comsr of Labor Wright,[2] Prof. Schoenfeldt,[3] and others.

Your Atlanta address received one evening's discussion and received, in the main, favorable comment.

We might arrange to have a pay-lecture and divide the proceeds, if it meet your approval. We can give you the best audience to be had in this city.

You have struck a keynote that will repay elaboration. Accept my personal congratulations.

Edw. A. Clarke
Pres't.

ALS   Con. 110   BTW Papers   DLC.

¹ Edward Alexander Clarke, born in Wilberforce, Ohio, in 1861, was a graduate of Wilberforce University, from which he received both A.B. and A.M. degrees. After experience as a high school principal in Evansville, Ind., and as science professor at Lincoln Institute (now Lincoln University) in Missouri, Clarke lived in Washington, D.C., from 1893 to 1896, serving as assistant examiner in the Patent Office. He then returned to Lincoln Institute as a faculty member, ascending to the presidency in 1902. He became pastor of St. Paul A.M.E. Church in Lexington, Ky., in 1909. Three years later he became pastor of Quinn Church in Louisville.

² Carroll Davidson Wright, who became in 1895 the first U.S. Commissioner of Labor Statistics in the Department of the Interior, had previously been chief of the Massachusetts Bureau of Labor Statistics for fifteen years. In his speech before the Bethel Literary and Historical Association on Oct. 29, 1895, Wright emphasized the benefits of mechanization to the laborer. He declared the mills and factories of the day much healthier places of work than in the past. When asked by a member of the audience how blacks could gain admittance into the higher "class" of labor, Wright replied that they should make themselves useful in some particular class of work. He stressed here the advantages of manual training, which he declared superior to the apprenticeship system. (Washington *Post,* Oct. 30, 1895, 4.)

³ Hermann Schoenfeld was a Prussian-born professor of German at George Washington University.

To Henry Melville Jackson¹

[Tuskegee, Ala., October? 1895]

Dear Bishop Jackson: Please forgive the delay in answering yours of Sept 19.

You ask for suggestions from me as to topics and speakers for the proposed Atlanta meeting. First allow me to say that I believe such a meeting as has been suggested could be made to serve a good purpose. One weakness in meetings usually held for the good of our people is, that the representatives of the *masses* seldom get a chance to be heard — that is the colored people who have had more education and an opportunity to learn about "points of order" do all the talking *for* the people. It will surprise any one who has never observed it to see how much sense the ignorant masses have and how well they can express their condition as well as tell what is needed to better their condition. I should suggest by all means, get into the convention as many of the common men and women as possible and give them a chance to speak for themselves. They will not need to prepare their speeches much before hand. If they prepare they will think more about how they are going to say it than what they are going to say.

Aside from representatives from the common working men and women I would suggest that several of the strongest best teachers and ministers speak.

Among the subjects I would suggest:

1. "Do colored Parents exercise as much control over their children as during slavery.
2. "Are the educated young men and women using their education in a way to help the masses?"
3. "What effect does owning property have [on] the religious and moral life.
4. How can the lowest classes in the cities be reached and Help[ed]?
5. What is the condition and needs of the colored ministry? (1) in the cities (2) in country.
6. Is the religious life of the race, now so much a thing of the emotions as it used to be.
7. False standards of morality.
8. Mistakes in the rearing of colored girls.
9. Show vs. reality.
10. The kind of leaders needed.

If what I have outlined does not meet your views I shall be glad to help further if I can. Yours Sincerely

[Booker T. Washington]

ALd Con. 862 BTW Papers DLC.

¹ Henry Melville Jackson (1848-1900) was an Episcopal bishop at Eufaula, Ala., from 1891 until his death. Born in Virginia, he was educated at Virginia Military Institute and Virginia Theological Seminary.

To Nathan B. Young

[Tuskegee, Ala.] Nov. 1, 1895

Mr. Young: From now on I wish an especial effort made to have a more direct connection made between the class-room and industrial work, that is, I wish the one dovetailed into the other. I wish you to be very careful to see that this is done throughout the year. I do not attempt now to lay down rules by which this can be done, I only repeat the instances mentioned in one of the teachers meetings. The students in their composition work can go to the brick yard and write compositions about the manner of making brick or harnessing horses. Many of the examples in arithmetic can be gotten out of actual problems in the blacksmith shop, tin shop, or farm. The physics I think could be made to bear more on the industrial work. I wish as early as possible you would have a consultation with Mr. J. H. Washington on this subject and come to an understanding as far as possible as to the best methods of carrying out this plan.

Booker T. Washington

TLSr Copy   Con. 112   BTW Papers   DLC.

From Edward Elder Cooper[1]

Washington, D.C., Nov 2nd., 1895

Friend Washington: We wrote you recently asking for a copy of your lithograph but have not heard from you. Hope you will send one at your convenience. The small fry of the colored press, as well as a few of the so called "big guns," are worrying a little about your speech.[2] You have a champion in THE COLORED AMERICAN at all times. The more these fellows bray about your speech, the greater the speech appears. You are too philosophical we are sure, to lose any sleep over it. Let us hear from you. Yours very sincerely,

E. E. Cooper

TLS   Con. 112   BTW Papers   DLC.

[1] Edward Elder Cooper was a leading black journalist and a devoted and uncritical follower of BTW. Born near Smyrna, Tenn., he attended an old barracks school for blacks in Nashville which was later the nucleus of Fisk University. Moving to Indianapolis, he attended high school there. From 1882 to 1886 he was employed in the postal service. In 1888 he founded the Indianapolis *Freeman,* which was, under his editorship and that of his successors, one of the leading black weeklies. In 1893 he founded the Washington *Colored American,* a consistently pro-BTW paper that received occasional financial assistance from the Tuskegean.

[2] W. Calvin Chase in the Washington *Bee* on the same day said of the Atlanta speech and its reception: "He said something that was death to the Afro-American and elevating to the white people. What fool wouldn't applaud the downfall of his aspiring competitor?" (Washington *Bee,* Nov. 2, 1895, quoted in Harlan,

BTW, 225-26.) A few weeks later the Philadelphia *Christian Recorder* complained that BTW should "never allow any of his addresses to appear as if he were trying to temporize, palliate or lessen the facts as they exist." (Philadelphia *Christian Recorder,* Nov. 28, 1895, in Foner, ed., "Is Booker T. Washington's Idea Correct?," 343.) In December the *Voice of Missions,* Bishop H. M. Turner's journal in Atlanta, published an article by George N. Smith of Washington, calling BTW a "cat's paw" of the white directors of the exposition. "Money, money, money, is the sole purpose of the exposition," wrote Smith. He deeply resented BTW's "chickens from miscellaneous sources" reference, and said: "To compare Mr. Booker T. Washington with Frederick Douglass is as unseemly as comparing a pigmy to a giant — a mountain brook leaping over a boulder to a great, only Niagara." (*Ibid.,* 344-46.)

From Irvine Garland Penn[1]

Atlanta, Ga. Nov 2nd 1895

My Dear Friend: I write you a confidential letter which I am sure you will treat in the spirit written. I think you have to your credit here about "One Hundred Dollars" which you have not gotten. The Exposition is now cutting down and cutting off right and left on account of the slim attendance and the receipts. Our Department has been cut fearfully and even no appropriation made for my clerk and the clerk ordered cut off. I cannot do the work and have this thing end up in a final success unless I have some means upon which to go, and, I therefore write you as advised by General Lewis[2] asking you to sign the within order allowing me $50. They will not send more money out into the states, but I can I believe get part of it to cover my general expenses if you will simply make an order payable to me. I trust you will help me in this matter to the extent requested. This matter has been an up hill load and I have tugged to success thus far but cannot do a thing without the help which has been now cut off. Write me at your earliest. Yours Faithfully

I. Garland Penn

HLS Con. 120 BTW Papers DLC.

[1] See above, 3:517. Penn always signed his name I. Garland Penn and he was variously reported in newspapers as Irving or Irvine. New evidence — letterhead stationery and the 1900 census — indicates the proper spelling is Irvine. He died in 1930.
[2] John Randolph Lewis.

An Open Letter to Benjamin Ryan Tillman[1]

Tuskegee, Ala. [ca. Nov. 4, 1895]

[Dear Sir:] I am no politician. I never made a political speech, and do not know as I ever shall make one, so it is not on a political subject that I address you.

I was born a slave; you a freeman. I am but an humble member of an unfortunate race; you are a member of the greatest legislative body on earth, and of the great, intelligent Caucasian race. The difference between us is great, yet I do not believe you will scorn the appeal I make to you in behalf of the 650,000 of my race in your State, who are to-day suppliants at your feet, and whose destiny and progress for the next century you hold largely in your hands.

I have been told that you are brave and generous, and one too great to harm the weak and dependent; that you represent the chivalry of the South, which has claimed no higher praise than that of protectors of the defenseless. I address you because I believe that you and those associated with you in convention have been misunderstood in the following, from the pen of Mr. James Creelman, in the New York World:

"An appalling fact that may not be obvious at a first glance is that the course proposed means the end of negro education and negro progress in South Carolina. This is openly admitted by Senator Tillman and his friends."[2]

It has been said that the truest test of the civilization of a race is the desire of the race to assist the unfortunate. Judged by this standard, the Southern States as a whole have reason to feel proud of what they have done in helping in the education of the negro.

I cannot believe that on the eve of the twentieth century, when there is more enlightenment, more generosity, more progress, more self-sacrifice, more love for humanity than ever existed in any other stage of the world's history — when our memories are pregnant with the scenes that took place in Chattanooga and Missionary Ridge but a few days ago, where brave men who wore the blue and the gray clasped forgiving hands and pledged that henceforth the interests of one should be the interests of all — while the hearts of the whole South are centered upon the great city of Atlanta, where Southern people are demonstrating to the world in a most practical way that

71

it is the policy of the South to help and not hinder the negro — in the midst of all these evidences of good feeling among all races and all sections of our country, I cannot believe that you and your fellow members are engaged in constructing laws that will keep 650,000 of my weak, dependent and unfortunate race in ignorance, poverty and crime. You, honored Senator, are a student of history. Has there ever been a race that was helped by ignorance? Has there ever been a race that was harmed by Christian intelligence? It is agreed by some that the negro's schools should be practically closed because he cannot bear his proportion of the burden of taxation. Can an ignorant man produce taxable property faster than an intelligent man? Will capital and immigration be attracted to a State where three out of four are ignorant and where poverty and crime abound? Within a dozen years the white people of South Carolina have helped in the education of hundreds of colored boys and girls at Claflin University and smaller schools. Have these educated men and women hindered the State or hurt its reputation? It warms my heart as I read the messages of the Governors of Alabama, Georgia and other Southern States, and note their broad and statesman-like appeals for the education of all the people, none being so black or miserable as not to be reached by the beneficent hand of the State.

Honored sir, do not misunderstand me; I am not so selfish as to make this appeal to you in the interest of my race alone, for, thank God, a white man is as near to my heart as a black man; but I appeal to you in the interest of humanity. The negro can afford to be wronged; the white man cannot afford to wrong him. "Whatsoever a man soweth, that shall he also reap."

It is my belief that were it the purpose of your convention, as reported, to practically close negro school-houses by limiting the support of these schools to the paltry tax that the negro is able to pay out of his ignorance and poverty after but thirty years of freedom, his school-houses would not close. Let the world know it, and there would be such an inflowing of money from the pockets of the charitable from all sections of our country and other countries as would keep the light of the school-house burning on every hill and in every valley in South Carolina. I believe, Senator Tillman, you are too great and magnanimous to permit this. I believe that the people of South Carolina prefer to have a large part in the education of their own citizens; prefer to have them educated to feel grateful to South Carolina for the larger part of their education rather than to outside parties wholly. This question I leave with you. The black yeomanry of your State will be educated. Shall South Carolina do it, or shall it be left to others?

Here in my humble home, in the heart of the South, I beg to say that I know something of the great burden the Southern people are carrying, and sympathize with them, and I feel that I know the Southern people, and am convinced that the best white people in South Carolina and the South are determined to help lift up the negro.

In addressing you this simple message I am actuated by no motive save a desire that your State in attempting to escape a burden shall not add one that will be ten-fold more grievous, and that we all shall so act in the spirit of Him who when on earth went about doing good that we shall have in every part of our beloved South a contented intelligent and prosperous people. Yours respectfully,

Booker T. Washington

New York *World,* Nov. 5, 1895, 3. The letter was introduced with the following paragraph: "Tuskegee, Ala., Nov. 4 — Booker T. Washington, of this place, known as the Moses of the negro race, has sent an open letter to Senator Tillman, of South Carolina. Mr. Washington, who is a negro, was the orator of the day at the opening of the Atlanta Exposition. He is principal of the Tuskegee Normal and Industrial Institute."

[1] Benjamin Ryan ("Pitchfork Ben") Tillman (1847-1918) was governor and U.S. senator from South Carolina. A leader of the white small farmers, Tillman was a virulent and flamboyant racist. As governor from 1890 to 1894, he was largely responsible for constitutional provisions for disfranchisement of blacks in the state. He served in the U.S. Senate from 1894 until his death and often used the Senate floor to propagate his anti-Negro views.

[2] See Creelman's article, headlined "Tillman Said Nothing about Educating Negroes," New York *World,* Oct. 31, 1895, 9. On Oct. 11, 1895, Creelman had written BTW urging him to write "a ringing appeal to the nation" that at the same time would be conciliatory to South Carolina whites. (Con. 1, BTW Papers, DLC.)

To Robert Charles Bedford

Tuskegee, Ala. Nov. 5th, 1895

Mr. Bedford: Can you write this article for me on the subject mentioned in this letter? I wish especially to bring out the fact of the large proportion of colored people to the white and that it is impossible for the whites to reach the highest success unless they take the colored people along with them, and that it will pay the whites in dollars and cents to help develop the colored people along all lines especially industrially; and I also wish to show that the colored people will contribute in the support of institutions by taxation in proportion as the colored people are developed and that the moral and religious life of the colored people will not be what it should be until they get an industrial foundation on which to stand. Show the value of an educated farmer over that of an ignorant one. I think you can find matter for a good deal of this in some of my published addresses as I have covered the subject pretty thoroughly. Miss Jackson[1] I think can help in this matter.

Booker T. Washington

TLS   Con. 112   BTW Papers   DLC.

[1] Estelle M. Jackson was a clerk in the principal's office from 1893 to 1897, when BTW fired her and a co-worker, Blanche Florence Saffold, for speaking too freely about the business of the school. (See BTW to Saffold, May 27, 1897, and BTW to Jackson, May 27, 1897, below.)

From Francis James Grimké

Washington D.C. Nov 7th 1895

Dear Prof. Washington: In my last letter I told you that your speech at Atlanta was to be discussed at the Bethel Literary of this city. Anxious to know what would be said about it I went around. The meeting was largely attended and there was quite an animated discussion. The opinions expressed by nearly all the speakers were in commendation of the speech. There were a few who thought you were playing in the hands of the Southern Whites. Among those who criticised the speech was a man, whose name I have forgotten. In the course of his remarks he said that he had some information to give to the audience, that would perhaps be a surprise to them. He then went on to say that recently a colored man[1] of the town of Tuskegee was shot for entertaining some white preacher over night at his house who was lecturing in that place to the colored people that he was

74

badly wounded, and could get no attention from a single white physician in the town, whereupon in sheer desperation they took him up and brought him to the gate of your school hoping that he might receive some attention from the resident physician there; but that you positively refused to allow him to be brought in or the physician to attend him. He stated this as a positive fact, that he knew to be true.

I felt it to be my duty to apprise you of what was said. I thought that you ought to know what is being circulated.

I hope that you are all well. I saw Rev. Mr. Turner of Hampton a few evenings ago, who told me that he spent a most pleasant time with you.

Mrs Grimke joins me in kindest regards to you and Mrs. Washington. As ever your true friend

Francis J. Grimke

ALS   Con. 111   BTW Papers   DLC.

[1] Thomas A. Harris. (See above, 3:558-61, and BTW to Grimké, Nov. 27, 1895, below.)

From William J. Stevens

Anniston, Ala., Nov 8 1895

My dear Sir: You are well aware of my effort to erect & have operated a Cotton Mill[1] exclusively by colored labor, at this point the movement is meeting with favorable re[s]ponses from all over the country.

The southern people (white) especially are manifesting an interest. I little hope for at first, so much so until success seems a certainty. However, I want and kindly ask for a letter of indorsement from you bespeaking for myself & company just such words as may seem best to you.

You are in a position to greatly aid this enterprise, that will go a long ways toward obliterating racial prejudices in the different manufacturing institutions of the country.

You are no other prominent colored man can afford for this movement to fail, because it means much for good or woe, in the future

for our people. Trusting to hear from you soon I have the honor
to be, Your friend,

Wm J Stevens

HLS Con. 113 BTW Papers DLC. Written on stationery of the Afro-Alabama Cotton Mill Company, W. J. Stevens, president.

¹ The Afro-Alabama Cotton Mill Company was chartered with $100,000 au-
thorized capital. (*Acts of the General Assembly of Alabama, 1892-93,* 236-38.)
Directors at the time of incorporation were Stevens, Wiley A. Hudson, a bricklayer,
Stephen E. Moses, principal of a black school, Handy Crook, G. Washington de
Armand, William Hooper Councill, Iveron Dawson. Later the letterhead listed also
as directors Dr. Charles E. Thomas, a physician and druggist, Dr. C. N. Dorsette,
Lydden (or Lytton) Green, and James E. Bush.

From Henry Frederick MacGregor¹

Houston, Texas, Nov 11th 1895

Dear Sir: I have read your address at the Atlanta Exposition carefully
and with a great deal of interest and I believe your views approximate
mine as to the future of the colored people in this country. I believe
the Negro should "cast down his bucket" where he is and "grow up
with the country" and that he can best do this by not disclaiming any
difference between the two races, but by asserting the distinction and
being proud of it emphasizing the distinction by race effort and individual effort as a Negro. A Negro endeavoring to improve his condition and that of his race has the encouragement of the white race,
but when he throws the guantlet down and demands that the white
race shall consider him of their race and be blind to all his shortcomings growing out of slavery and his incapacity to lead the Anglo Saxon
or stand at present on equal footing socially and politically then his
troubles begin, and the hand of the white man though his friend is
against him. Socially the necessary division has been recognized generally by both races and the result is that Schools like yours have been
encouraged — and Negro churches Schools Newspapers and enterprises have been successful, while on the other hand by endeavoring
to force a condition they cannot hope to attain at present the race has
become offensive and a menace to capable government in States having
a large colored population, and as a political factor a weakness to the

76

party they are presumed to belong to. The Republican organization is weakest where the Negro is most plentiful.

The Negro exhibit at Atlanta if it had not been individualized by making it a race exhibit would have attracted but little attention and would have fallen short of the world of benefit it is going to be to your race, and to the white race as well as a stimulant to one and bringing a tolerating and encouraging spirit toward your race from the other.

The Negro politically it must be admitted is a failure from several causes but chiefly from his endeavor to force a recognition he does not get socially. It is offensive for white people to go into a primary and have the white delegates selected by Negroes and offensive to the Negroes to have the whites say what Negroes shall be elected as representing the Negro Republicans. The Negro has not been admitted into the Democratic primaries on account of its overstepping the social line. The purpose of this letter is to get a letter from you as a specially prominent and successful leader of [the] race covering your views on the advisability of extending the social division to political primaries where delegates of both races will be strictly represen[ta]tive and not forced on the other race by the one that happens to have the greatest number present. I do not think a division necessary beyond the primaries as I believe the repugna[n]ce to coming in contact with educated capable men of your race is fast dying away — but the trouble is in forced contact with a lot of ignorant or vicious Negroes in the hands of some unscrupulous politician overriding decency and right. With a social and political difference recognized I think the future of the Negro will be brightening all the time that the doors of all parties will be open to him on these terms, and he will not be led by a lot of politicians who utilize him for selfish ends and whose occupation and opportunity of trafficking will be gone — and the Negro will be able to fulfil the obligations and duties of citizenship faithfully which he has not done under the old leadership. The basis of our organization is on the back of this sheet. Your race gets 40% of the delegation in a State Convention although your numerical strength is but 23% in this state. It comes from allowing a delegate at large from each race for each County.

The enclosed clipping covers my views of the race problem. If you are the practical man your work indicates and as indicated by your address I feel that you must agree with me that where the conditions are such that the political organizations would be best advanced by seperate primaries then on demand of either race they should be thus held where no demand is made it will be unnecessary. Trusting to hear from you I am   Respectfully

H. F. MacGregor

ALS   Con. 119   BTW Papers   DLC.

1 Henry Frederick MacGregor (1855-1923), born in New Hampshire, moved to Texas after graduation from college. He was vice-president and general manager of the Houston Street Railway from 1883 to 1903 and had other business interests. He was chairman of the Republican state executive committee (1894-96), Republican nominee for Congress in 1904, and member of the Republican national committee (1912-16).

From John Wesley Edward Bowen[1]

Atlanta, Ga. Nov. 12th 1895

Dear Friend and Brother: I have delayed purposely in writing you concerning your speech delivered here in Atlanta on Sept. 18th ult. at the opening of the Fair. Some have written you with large and generous appreciation of your effort; some wrote under the momentary excitement of enthusiasm with perhaps no genuine or far reaching conception of your work and principles so happily stated in your words, while perhaps there may be a few who wrote you that they may be classed with the thoughtful and progressive.

I write not for the newspapers. I wish to say, having heard you deliver that oration, and having read it again and again, that you have done more for the Negro in that speech than has been done in a generation by a thousand political speeches. Your crusade for industrial revolution among Negroes is sound and has the approval of all the better thinking persons of the race. I believe that there are two keys to unlock the gate to future prosperity for the Colored Man viz. the Moral Key and the industrial Key. The Negro must be pure in heart and upright in life and he must also be strong in his arm, clear in his eye, accurate with his fingers, a workman that needeth not to be made ashamed and diligent in his business with a love for work not so much as an end to a means but as an end in itself. These lines represent your work and my work — either one of which is only one half of lifes duty, both together give us the perfected whole. I believe

78

in your thought and spirit and work. You can afford to be criticized even by good and clear thinking friends. You were placed in a peculiar position and you had the good sense, courage and wisdom to fill that position with astonishment to the disinterested and with gratification to your admirers and your race.

We are rapidly approaching a trying hour for the industrial development of the South. Wealth and immigration are to turn thitherward within a few years as they have not been for fifty years past. With the influx of these two factors there will come a competition for the mastery in the industrial lines that will surpass in intensity the late struggle in the civil war. Now unless the Negro can be induced and educated to *love work,* all kinds of work and to prepare along the higher mechanical lines and to excell, he will [be] driven to the wall. We must boost this sleeping Negro and breathe into his nostrils the breath of a noble purpose. Varnish it as we may, the Negro has not a ghost of [a] chance along industrial lines in the North; the competition is too great. In addition to this fact it ought to be stated that the original Northern Negro never had any chance while the immigrant Negro was unskilled and unprepared, he was merely a *freedman* in the industries as well as a freedman in civil life and freedmen are not the stuff out of which great empires are built or industries carried on or civilizations established. The freedman must be transformed into a freeman before we may hope for successful competition. This work is the Kings business and the Kings business demands haste.

You are right; stand by your guns until the walls fall or until you fall but either fall will bring victory. I mean to stand by mine for moral purity in the individual, the sanctity of the marriage relation and an elevated, consecrated and broadly educated ministry for our people. Mrs. Bowen agrees in toto with you. I pray for your success. Your Friend

J. W. E. Bowen

ALS Con. 110 BTW Papers DLC.

[1] John Wesley Edward Bowen (1855-1933) in 1895 was professor of historical theology at Gammon Theological Seminary in Atlanta. From 1906 until his death Bowen was president of Gammon. In 1904-6 Bowen helped to found and edit the influential monthly magazine *The Voice of the Negro.* Though his background and work were radically different from BTW's, he was a loyal supporter of the Tuskegean. After the Atlanta Riot in 1906 he worked with BTW in the effort to restore order and a measure of interracial goodwill.

From Horace J. Smith[1]

London [England] Nov. 15 95

My dear Sir   I was greatly pleased to get your letter — & sent your report to the Revd W Hughes[2] who was a Missionary in Africa — & has come back to Wales to establish an Ins. for teaching Africans to be self supporting while they are acting as Missionaries.

I have urged him to go to America & learn from you & at Hampton how to conduct an Industrial Training Home — which, as you will see from his enclosed letter, he proposes to do. He proposes to put himself in communication with you and I beg you to pour out to him with generous cordiality the information you possess that will aid him. He is a resolute, wise, & devoted friend of the African — & withal enthusiastic. He has refused to be bound by the cords of Sectarian bondage — and tho' a Baptist he is most wide & natural in his sympathies. It is, as you may imagine, an education for a man to go out as a Missionary, *provided* his mind is open to be taught by Mahometans & Pagans.

I send you his letter that you may learn something about this gentleman who I trust you will see when he does go to America. He & others have told me that the Medicine man by playing tricks &c was able to delude the natives. I therefore arranged for a Prestidigitateur to give the young men an exhibition of his art in that line & in ventriloquism also — & I have encouraged Mr H. to have the lads taught so that when they go back they may be able to turn the tables on the Fetish man.

I also enclose my check for $10.00 to your order to be spent, *provided you approve such* disposition of it — either

First in teaching some of your pupils feats of Prestidigitation or Ventriloquism — or

Second in purchase of books or appliances for teaching such tricks — or

Third — in premiums for the best display of such tricks.

Please understand that this is not primarily intended merely to amuse your pupils — but to *stimulate* their minds — to tempt them to nimbleness of their hands & dexterity — & to perpetuate in your School the teaching to the other scholars of these feats, so that they may not be carried away or deceived by trickery — to establish in fact a chair & *Professorship of Legerdemain.*

Perhaps you may not think the subject worth the care & attention requisite — in that case apply the money in any other way you choose.

If you have any young people who wish to go to Africa to teach I think they wd. do well to put themselves in communication with Mr Hughes. Yours truly

Horace J Smith

ALS   Con. 113   BTW Papers   DLC.

¹ Horace J. Smith (b. 1832), a wealthy Pennsylvanian who corresponded with BTW on many schemes for educating and improving mankind, made small and irregular contributions to Tuskegee. In frequent letters from Germantown, Pa., and Birmingham, England, he urged BTW to use his influence to institute a postal savings bank, to honor an early Pennsylvania opponent of slavery, and to distribute *Up from Slavery* as widely as the American Bible Society had distributed the Bible.

² William Hughes, an Englishman, was a Baptist missionary in the Congo for ten years before deciding that the work of civilizing and converting the black Africans could be more efficiently accomplished by the Africans themselves. To that end he founded in 1885 the Congo Training Institute in Colwyn Bay, Wales. He described his purposes there in detail in *Dark Africa and the Way Out: or A Scheme for Civilizing and Evangelizing the Dark Continent* (1892). He reasoned that the African climate was unsuitable for Europeans and that Africans needed to remove themselves from the unhealthy moral climate of their heathen surroundings before they could be genuinely converted. He outlined a curriculum stressing the moral value of labor and the need for the African to become trained in a trade so that he would be of practical as well as spiritual usefulness when he returned to evangelize his own people. It was perhaps because of the similarity of their programs that he wished to see the work of Tuskegee.

From Cornelius Nathaniel Dorsette

Montgomery, Ala., 11/23rd 1895

Dear Prof   I have for some time intended writing you, but keep so busy all the while trying hard to get shaped up again & make something.

Its needless for me to tell you that all Montgomery *White & Black* feel that of all that has been, or will be said of the Exposition & the race, that your address far eclipsed all. There is here from both races unstinted & out spoken praises & compliments.

Are you coming this way some time again?

Wiley Harris has been writing & talking to me about giving him credit for the $12.00 you sent for his Fathers traveling exp, and I have stated to him that I had no such authority from you & could not without, tho I would like to credit him with paying something. I made him a most reasonable [offer] of $50.00 for an excellent piece of surgery that I should have gotten cash $100.00 to 150.00 dolls for, & now his only talk is of your money & no effort to pay himself. I shall put the matter into the hands of a collector & sue on it & get Judgment & watch my chances for collection.

I have paid the Campbell matter down to 51.00 cost court & att'y fee & Int ran it up nearly $75.00.

How is school? Hastily yours

Dorsette

P.S. Do you need a fine yoke of oxen extra large 5 & 6 yrs old raised here in fine condition, I know a man 6 mls in country having such & is selling out, asks $75.00 [for] them. They work any where plow or wagon.

ALS   Con. 110   BTW Papers   DLC.

From Warren Logan

Tuskegee, Ala. 11-23 1895

Barn burned last night with contents including cows other stock saved insurance fifteen hundred in Hartford.

Warren Logan

HWSr   Con. 539   BTW Papers   DLC.

To Warren Logan

New York, Nov 24 1895

Dear Mr Logan: I am *very* sorry about the loss of the barn and especially the cows and feed. We have needed for some time a larger and better barn and now I hope we shall get it.

I leave matters regarding the barn to your judgement.

I am going to have the loss published in all the papers and I hope there will be gifts to make up the loss.

Will write more fully later. Yours truly

Booker T. Washington

ALS   Con. 9   BTW Papers   ATT.   Original destroyed.

From Robert Robinson Taylor

Tuskegee Inst. Nov. 25, 95

Dear Sir: In view of the present financial condition of the country, and the unexpected expense which is entailed on the Institution by the loss of the barn I feel willing and ready to contribute something towards bearing the expense. I shall give twenty-five dollars which you will please accept on condition that my name be not mentioned nor any allusion made to it. Yours sincerely,

R. R. Taylor

ALS   Con. 116   BTW Papers   DLC.

From Warren Logan

Tuskegee, Ala. 11/26/1895

Dear Mr. Washington: Knowing that Mr. J. H. Washington had written you in regard to the fire and being very busy myself I have not before this written you regarding the great loss which we sustained on the night of the 22nd. The fire occurred about quarter past one and in about an hour the building and contents were in ashes. The flames had gained such headway when we reached the barn that it was impossible to do anything in the way of extinguishing them. Our efforts were directed toward the saving of the stock and preventing the fire from spreading to the adjoining buildings and fences. Notwithstanding our best efforts the milch cows and bulls that were on the second floor were lost. According to the best information that I can get there were seventeen cows, five calves, and two bulls in the barn. There was quite a quantity of feed — especially corn and fodder — stored in the barn. Some of the corn was saved in a damaged condition. The dairy outfit was lost as also were the harness, Mr. Chambliss' personal effects and some clothing belonging to students. The whole loss is put at $5,000 which is reduced by the insurance which we had on the building amounting to $1,500.

Mr. Thompson[1] telegraphed to the company about the fire and tells me that the company will send an agent here in a few days to adjust the matter. The insurance will not be paid for sixty days. As yet we have no idea as to the origin of the fire. We are loth to believe that it was incendiary and yet there was at least one circumstance that tends to show that the building was set on fire. The guard reports that a short while before the fire the dogs were barking very fiercely — a thing they had never done before. We mean to make an investigation but have no idea that we will be able to discover any clew as to the origin of the fire farther than we have.

The people of the town have expressed great sympathy with us in our loss. The young men deserve special commendation for the manner in which they turned out and worked to save the property of the school. We are going ahead erecting temporary sheds for the cattle and horses. Two of the teachers have made contributions for the rebuilding of the barn.

George Stewart, a young man from Omaha, Ga. died at the school Sunday evening after a little more than a week's illness of fever. His father and sister were at the school at the time of his death and carried his remains home for interment.

The measles is gaining headway among the students. There are now eight or nine cases in the hospital and new cases are developing almost every day. We have been obliged to fit up another room for hospital use.

Mr. Carr[2] is very ill. You know he was taken down before you left for the North. The doctor has some doubt as to whether he will recover.

Mr. Torbert[3] died Saturday night and was buried on Sunday. He had been ill but a short time.

Matters in general are moving along fairly well at the school but we still feel the need of money very keenly. I trust you are well and that the meetings are proving successful. Very truly yours,

Warren Logan

TLS Con. 113 BTW Papers DLC.

¹ Charles Winston Thompson.

² William Ramsey Carr was in charge of the tailoring department at Tuskegee from 1893 to the 1895-96 school year.

³ Possibly a relative of Alice A. Torbert of Tuskegee, who graduated from Tuskegee Institute in 1885 and was a clerk in the treasurer's office.

To Francis James Grimké

New York, Nov. 27 1895

My dear Dr. Grimke: I have delayed an answer to your kind favor of Nov. 7 in the hope that I might see you in person on my way North. Although I return to Tuskegee within a few days I am not quite sure that I can see you.

I thank you sincerely for informing me about the charge made against me by some one in the Bethel Literary Association. Once before I heard this same matter mentioned from some other source. I will not take time to go into all the details as to the white minister being driven out of Tuskegee except to say that there was a traveling white minister there for a few days about whom no one in Tuskegee knew anything and while in Tuskegee he stopped in the family of a colored man who was worthless and very foolish. The white man was seen associating with the daughters of the colored man and some of the whites in Tuskegee say that there was improper association. This I do not believe. Any way this charge led to his being asked to leave Tuskegee which he did.

Now the shooting of this colored man occurred several days after the white minister had gone and occurred about another matter. It was the result of trouble between the colored man and a half dozen of the rougher element of the whites in Tuskegee that had been brewing for some time, and any one who knows the facts will state that the shooting occurred on account of a personal matter and not about the white preacher. There is never a week that I do not have two or three white persons and often ministers stopping at my house and at the homes of other teachers. At this very moment this is true.

After the man was shot his son brought him to my house for help and advice, (and you can easily understand that the people in and about Tuskegee come to me for help and advice in all their troubles). I got out of bed and went out and explained to the man and his son that personally I would do anything I could for them but I could not take the wounded man into the school and endanger the lives of students entrusted by their parents to my care to the fury of some drunken white men. Neither did I for the same reason feel that it was the right thing to take him into [my] own house. For as much as I love the colored people in that section, I can not feel that I am in duty bound to shelter them in all their personal troubles any more than you would feel called on to do the same thing in Washington. I explained my position fully to the man and his son, and they agreed with me as to the wisdom of my course. And I now state what I have not to any one before. I helped them to a place of safety and paid the money out of my own pocket for the comfort and treatment of the man while he was sick. Today I have no warmer friends than this man and his son. They have nothing but the warmest feelings of gratitude for me and are continually in one way or another expressing this feeling. I do not care to publish to the world what I do and should not mention this except for this false representation. I simply chose to help and relieve this man in my own way rather than in the way some man a thousand miles away would have had me do it.

I thank you sincerely for writing me and hope you will always feel free to speak to me about such matters.

Please remember me kindly to Mrs. Grimke. Yours Sincerely

Booker T. Washington

ALS   Con. 1   BTW Papers   DHU.

From Alice J. Kaine

[Tuskegee, Ala.] 11-30-95

Dear Mr Washington   My work begins to move. The plumbers have been in the laundry about 10 days.

Mr Thomas[1] wished to know to day how the underground drain pipe can be put in since the floor is already down. I have decided to excavate from the outside rather than ruin the new floor. I hope I may have boys for that on Monday morning.

We expect also to begin on the laundry boxes, 2d floor, Monday. They have been delayed because of the need for sheds for the animals. That could not be helped.

The halls in new part of Alabama Hall are being finished to day. On Monday we begin on the old part.

Your letter in reference to Mr J. H came to day. I do not like to speak of it. I so deeply regret the occurrence. You must never believe for a moment Mr Washington that I could or would say one disparaging word to the Slater trustees or any one else, about Tuskegee. No mistake of Mr J. H. Washingtons could lead me to that. I too fully realize the earnest work you and your wife are doing to criticize outside of your grounds anything weak that I come in contact with on the inside and too, the virtues so outnumber the faults here.

I am very sorry for Mr J. H and in spite of his temper I like him and supposed I was on the best footing with him. In his highly nervous condition I do not believe him capable of self control and his responsibility is too heavy for him.

I appreciate the support you give me, without which I could not succeed.

I gave the letter and yours to Mrs Washington to read.

It seems to me now that I shall meet with no more delays.

The slop arrangements about Ala Hall are not so good as last year — the odors are *bad*. I have talked with Mr Thomas a simple plan which he thinks a good one. I suggested it to Mr J. H. but he has some idea of his own which I fear will not work out well, if at all. Back of Willow Cottage is an unsafe slop deposit. It is simply emptied on the ground not more than four feet from the house and becomes a disease breeder. The girls who carry the slops out *will not* climb over the style into the field and I cannot blame them. I was distressed last year at the girls carrying heavy pails of slops up and down steps. I do not see how they can escape the diseases that women are heirs to, and I am sure they do not.

A gate has been suggested in place of the style and I very much wish that could be had.

No cook has been secured for the students kitchen. I wish you could find a competent woman up there.

Mr Calloway spoke to me yesterday about Miss Chapman's mother taking that place. The kitchen is kept pretty well under Mr Penny and some pieces of new furniture improve the appearance.

We will try to be in as good shape as possible for visitors and I am glad Mrs Hobson & Hopkinson[2] were so well impressed. Very Sincerely

Mrs Kaine

ALS Con. 111 BTW Papers DLC.

[1] Harry E. Thomas.

[2] Mrs. Elizabeth C. Hobson and Mrs. Charlotte Everett Hopkins were white women of Washington, D.C., who toured five southern states in late 1895 for the John F. Slater Fund. They had been designated by the fund trustees to investigate means of improving the condition of southern black women. (See Hobson and Hopkins, *A Report Concerning the Colored Women of the South.*) While they were at Tuskegee, Margaret Murray Washington gathered a group of about thirty women to meet with the two investigators.

From Leonora Love Chapman

Tuskegee, Ala., Dec. 3, 1895

Dear Mr. Washington: I am very sorry to feel obliged to worry you.

Mrs. Kaine and I have consulted as to the best method of putting down the noise. We decided that so far as the girls were concerned, it was the fault, to a great extent, of the lady teachers, who seemingly try to set no example for the girls. We further decided, that, since we had both spoken to the teachers in a body, the only way to correct it, is to take the teachers and speak to them individually. It happened that the lot fell on Mrs. Bond[1] and Miss Thompson[2] *first.* While Mrs. B. was not discourteous, she said: "It is a shame that teachers must be subjected to the same discipline as students." Mrs. Kaine complains of Mrs. B. also.

Miss Thompson said she did *not intend to try* to improve as she considered herself one of [the] quietest women on the place. She showed very great disrespect for my position, leaving personal indignity out of it entirely. I wished my talk with her to be private. As my mother and one of the students were in my sitting room, I took her to my bed room; but persons in the sitting room heard every word she said — and people in the hall, if there were any there, *could* have heard her. Mrs. Kaine complains also of Miss T., the opposition evinced toward suggestions.

I need your support in this matter. I wish the teachers to understand that the authority incumbent upon my position must be respected. I do not care as to personal feeling.

I wish you would write to Miss Thompson. You cannot censure her too sharply. I feel she has insulted my position. Very truly

Leonora L. Chapman

P.S. Mrs. Bond talks loudly in the halls *very* frequently.

L. L. C.

ALS Con. 110 BTW Papers DLC.

[1] Irene Bond was an instructor of dressmaking and sewing at Tuskegee from 1892 to 1898.
[2] Either Beulah Thompson Davis or Ida Belle Thompson McCall.

To Nathan B. Young

[Tuskegee, Ala.] Dec. 4, 1895

Mr. N. B. Young: Please send into my office by the 16th of Dec. a report showing what progress has been made in dovetailing the academic work into the industrial in the manner that I suggested to you and Mr. J. H. Washington sometime ago.[1]

Booker T. Washington

TLcSr Con. 113 BTW Papers DLC.

[1] See BTW to Young, Nov. 1, 1895, above.

From Nathan B. Young

Tuskegee, Ala., Dec 9, 1895

Dear Sir: In reply to your note of the 5th inst. asking me to file in your office by the 16th inst. a statement setting forth just how far the academic and industrial work are being dovetailed as per your previous order to myself and Mr. J. H. Washington, I beg to say that as yet no *organized* effort has been made toward this end; but I am sure that *individual* efforts are being made to make the academic work more and more practical — the end to be attained by an organized effort. Respectfully,

Nathan B. Young

ALS   Con. 113   BTW Papers   DLC.

An Account of a Speech and an Interview in Chicago

[Chicago, Ill., Dec. 11, 1895]

IN HIS RACE'S BEHALF

BOOKER T. WASHINGTON'S PLEA

NEW LEADER OF THE COLORED PEOPLE
VOICES BEFORE THE HAMILTON CLUB
THEIR PROGRESS AND TUSKEGEE'S
EDUCATIONAL METHODS

Booker T. Washington, principal and founder of the Tuskegee Normal and Industrial Institute, the colored man whose address at the opening of the Atlanta exposition made him famous and installed him as the recognized leader of his race in the United States, spoke to the members and guests of the Hamilton Club last night on "The Problems of the Colored Race in the South."

The assembly-room of the clubhouse was crowded when A. C. Barnes,[1] chairman of the political committee, introduced the speaker. He was received with a round of applause, and in the course of his address was frequently interrupted by the clapping of hands and laughter provoked by the humorous anecdotes with which he illustrated his points. A modest-appearing man, plainly dressed in brown, his earnest manner impressed his hearers with the truth of the message he brought.

Mr. Barnes, in his introductory remarks, after reviewing the conditions that have prevailed in the south since the war, said:

"But it seems like a stroke of destiny — like a providential event, that all at once, after years of sectional strife and bitterness, and after the vain appeal of that down-trodden people to the nation, that conferred upon them the right of citizenship, there should arise out of the very darkness of these conditions, out of the race itself, one who should grasp the situation with the fullness of its significance and by the genius of his common sense furnish a plan and a theory for the betterment of his race, so harmonious with existing conditions as not only to secure the unreserved indorsement of the north, but to elicit the most enthusiastic commendation of the south."

EQUAL CHANCE SOUGHT FOR ALL MEN

Professor Washington began his talk by saying that his interest in addressing the club was that he might in some humble way speed the day, now fast approaching, when there should not be a northern heart and a southern heart, a black heart and a white heart, but all should be melted by deeds of sympathy and patience and forbearance into one heart — the great American heart — whose highest aspirations should be to give to all men everywhere unrestricted opportunity for the fullest growth and prosperity.

The speaker then briefly recounted the events of his childhood and youth; how he worked in a coal mine after the war, and how he worked for his education in Hampton Institute. While at Hampton he resolved to enter the far south and give his life in providing, as best he could, the same kind of opportunities for self-help for the youth of his race as he had found for himself at Hampton. Professor Washington told of the founding and growth of the Tuskegee school. Continuing, he said:

"All, I think, agree that one of the results of education is to increase an individual's wants.

"Now, I claim that any training that increases the individual's wants, especially as that training is applied to a people whose condition is that of the masses of the negroes in the black belt of the south, any education that increases want without increasing ability to supply these increased wants is rather a mistake, and wherever it is done, whether among white or black people, you will find unhappiness, unrest, or, too often, dishonesty. As we watch from year to year the work of the young men and women who go out from our institutions, with not only trained heads but trained hands as well, we find that, so far from becoming drones in society, they are happy, strong, progressive leaders in the literary, religious and industrial world, who soon enhance many per cent the productive value of their community."

OBJECTS OF THE TUSKEGEE PLAN

"While friends in the north and elsewhere have given money to buy material which we could not produce and to pay our teachers very largely, still almost wholly by the labor of the students we have built up a property at Tuskegee that is now valued at $225,000.

"The object that Tuskegee Institute keeps constantly in front of it is to educate men and women who shall go out and become leaders of the masses of the colored people in the black belt. That is the greatest need of the black man to-day, strong, unselfish leaders, well grounded in industry and education, religion and common sense ideas of life. If you wish to help the south help educate the kind of leaders I have mentioned.

"The greatest injury that slavery did my people was to deprive them of that executive power, that sense of self-dependence which are the glory and the distinction of the Anglo-Saxon race. For 250 years we were taught to depend on some one else for food, clothing, shelter and for every move in life, and you cannot expect what was 250 years getting into a race to be gotten out in twenty-five or thirty years, unless we at best put into their midst Christian leaders.

"I am not ashamed to confess to you that I have the greatest sympathy for the south in working out the problem which God in His providence has laid at the door of the black man and the white man. I believe I have grown to the point where I can love a white man as much as a black man. I have grown to the point where I can love a southern white man as much as a northern white man. To me 'a man is a man for a' that.'"

ILL WILL'S FATAL REACTION

"As a race I believe that we strengthen ourselves at every point by extending this sympathy, for no race can cherish ill will and hatred toward another race without its losing in all of those elements that tend to create and perpetuate a strong and healthy manhood. I propose that no man shall drag me down by making me hate him.

"South Carolina nor any other state can make a law to harm the black man which does not harm the white man in a great measure. Men may make laws to hinder and fetter the ballot, but men cannot make laws that will bind or retard the growth of manhood.

"We went into slavery a piece of property; we came out American citizens. We went into slavery pagans; we came out Christians. We went into slavery without a language; we came out speaking the proud Anglo-Saxon tongue. We went into slavery with the slave chains clanking about our wrists; we came out with the American ballot in our hands.

"Progress, progress is the law of nature; under God it shall be our eternal guiding star."

At the close of Professor Washington's address Mr. Barnes announced that contributions to aid the Tuskegee school would be received and forwarded by the Hamilton Club.

MAN OF EFFECTIVE ADDRESS

Professor Washington arrived in Chicago yesterday morning from the east. He was met at the Union station by Albert C. Barnes, chairman of the committee on political action of the Hamilton Club, whose guest he is while in the city, and escorted to the Leland Hotel. He is young, his manners are easy and his voice pleasant and especially convincing when talking on the subject of his life's work — the education and uplifting of his race.

When asked concerning his famous address at the opening of the Atlanta exposition, and of the exposition itself, Mr. Washington replied that the benefits resulting from the exposition were to be seen on every hand — in the organization of other expositions, where his race would be recognized, in the improved conditions of travel and in the increased consideration, not to say respect, shown to negroes in public places generally. Professor Washington said the fact that he himself was placed on the jury of awards at Atlanta was a remarkable and significant recognition of his race by the people of the south.

CHANGING ATTITUDE TOWARD THE NEGRO

"I do not wish to be understood as saying there has been a revolution in this respect," said he, "but there are marked changes in the feeling toward my people, especially among the better classes in the south. Perhaps the most important result has been the message of the Governor of Georgia to the legislature on lynching. He not only recommended measures strong and wise to suppress this crime, but spoke out in the strongest terms in condemnation of it.

"I think the exhibit of the colored people at Atlanta is having a great influence on the common class of whites, who have never felt so kindly toward us as the better classes have. It is pleasant to note their surprise at what they see."

Since the delivery of his Atlanta speech Professor Washington has received letters from all over the country asking him to deliver lectures before various bodies. These offers have been almost invariably declined. He says he is willing to talk about his work when opportunity offers, but will not allow himself to be switched off on other lines.

In connection with the work at the Tuskegee Institute Professor Washington said he found the negro conferences held at the school were of great benefit not only to the negroes, but to the whites. These conferences are attended by farmers and planters living within a radius of 200 miles. They are instructed in modern methods of agriculture, exchange views and experiences and are aided in many ways at these meetings.

"Let a white man see a negro living in a first-class house," said Professor Washington, "and he has respect for him. That is why I push the industrial features of the school to the front. They show something tangible, and it is the tangible that appeals most forcibly to the average mind."

UPWARD RISE FROM SLAVERY

Booker T. Washington was born in slavery in Virginia about the year 1857 — he does not know the exact date. His mother was a slave on the plantation of a Mr. Burroughs, and his father was a white man, a neighboring planter. The name Washington he assumed himself. He was educated at the Hampton Institute, in Virginia, and at the age of 24 founded the Tuskegee Normal and Industrial Institute in the "black belt" of Alabama.

Beginning in 1881 with a borrowed capital of $200 and a few pupils, the school has grown to large proportions. It has now 800 pupils, half of whom are girls, and an equal number is turned away every year through lack of accommodations. The institute has 1,400 acres of land, on which are thirty-seven buildings, all but three of which were built by student labor. It costs $70,000 a year to maintain the school, $3,000 of which is given by the state and the remainder is contributed by philanthropists. The students receive fundamental instruction in mathematics and literature, but industrial education is the main feature of the course, and agriculture is the chief branch. Twenty-seven trades or industries are taught, including brickmaking, masonry, plastering, carpentry, carriage and wagon making, harness-making, millinery, dressmaking and cooking. The seventy teachers are all colored.

Professor Washington, while not an active politician, is a republican. At the close of the interview he was asked what he thought of the action of the national committee in sending the republican convention to St. Louis.

"I think it was an excellent plan to have the convention held in the south. It will have great influence in keeping Kentucky in line, and may bring Missouri into the republican ranks."

Professor Washington leaves for the south to-day.

Chicago *Times-Herald,* Dec. 12, 1895, 5.

[1] Albert C. Barnes (1853-1931), a leading Chicago lawyer, later a judge. A close friend of Dr. Daniel Hale Williams, who was one of the few black members of the Hamilton Club, Barnes aided Williams in raising funds among wealthy whites to build Provident Hospital.

From Francis James Grimké

Washington D.C. Dec 12th 1895

Dear Prof. Washington: I was very glad to receive your letter, and to have your statement in response to the matter referred to in my last letter. It will give me the opportunity surely of setting the matter in its true light before some of the friends here. It fills me with indignation when I think of how the facts were exaggerated and distorted by the speaker on the night when it was narrated before the Bethel Literary. I cannot understand what possible satisfaction people can find in stating a thing so as to make an entirely erroneous impression, especially when the impression is detrimental to another.

Prof Clarke of the Bethel Literary tells me that you are to read a paper before the Literary next month some time. If you are not otherwise engaged we shall be glad to have you stop with us. Hoping that you are well and with kindest regards for yourself and Mrs Washington   I am as ever   Your sincere friend

Francis J. Grimke

ALS   Con. 111   BTW Papers   DLC.

From Daniel Cranford Smith[1]

Hampton, Va., Dec 20th 1895

Dear Sir, Your telegram of even date received, reading "Wish to secure you to look through our acc'ts. Can you come, Answer" I wired in reply "Can come, when Hampton no longer requires me. Probably shortly after Jany 1st.["]

I will make my report to Hampton's board at a meeting to be held shortly after Jany 1st. I cannot make a definite engagement before then, but will doubtless be disengaged at once after the meeting.

It is with great pleasure that I anticipate being able to utilize at Tuskeegee the special experience I have had at Hampton. Trusting that it may be to our mutual advantage, I am   Yours respectfully,

Daniel C. Smith

ALS   Con. 113   BTW Papers   DLC.

[1] Daniel Cranford Smith (1866-1945) was born in Brooklyn, and graduated from Princeton in 1886. He was a certified public accountant who systematized the accounting procedures at Tuskegee from 1896 until 1912, when he was dismissed. Smith insisted on having the books the way he ordered, and a strained relationship developed between him and BTW. It was Smith whom BTW said he was seeking on Mar. 19, 1911, when he was attacked by Henry A. Ulrich in the celebrated "New York Affair." (See Gatewood, "Booker T. Washington and the Ulrich Affair," 286-302.) Smith's denial that he had ever telegraphed BTW to meet him there may have been partially responsible for the termination of his auditing arrangement with Tuskegee. On the other hand, Smith's services were less needed in 1912 than in 1896. In addition to his auditing work at Hampton and Tuskegee and other black institutions, Smith was an accountant for the American Cotton Company. In 1919 he became co-founder of the Oakley Chemical Company, of which he was vice-president at the time of his death.

From Thomas A. Harris

Okolona Miss. Dec 22, 1895

Dear friend, Your favor of Oct 11th in reply to me; come to hand. Contents carefully noted. I am always glad to hear from you. I am as well as I could expect. I walk with my stick; and without my crutches. I would like to come home and sell out and get my fumily away from Tuskegee. I know I can never do well there. If those who mob[b]ed me could understand that I was not going to try to prosicute them, They would not; I think interfear me. I think I have some white friends in Tuskegee. If you will see Mr. G. W. Campbell, Drakeford & Co. S. Q. Hale, Pery Magruder,[1] old man Story, and any others you may think best to see, And talk the matter of my case over with them, giving them to understand that I will not bother them, They will give you to understand that, that will be alright. I dont think any of the better class of the white people have got anything aganst me. But all of them had rather I would not practice law in Tuskegee. You see what you can do and let me hear from you. As I have been unable to do anything since I was shot, I am in great need of some money. If you could help me as much as $8.00 or $10.00 I would be very thankful. You may write me as before, (under cover) c/o, of Mr. P. McIntosh, a colored merchant. If I am not here he will send it to me. He has a larger dry good store than Drakeford & Co. in Tuskegee. I hope to hear from you soon. I will be here until Jan the 1st. I am your friend,

Thos. A. Harris

ALS   Con. 111   BTW Papers   DLC.

[1] Perry Magruder was reported in the 1880 census as a white eighteen-year-old who lived with his parents in Tuskegee and was a clerk in a store.

From Robert Curtis Ogden

Philadelphia. December 31, 1895

My dear Prof. Washington, If I may be allowed a suggestion concerning the dinner at the Hamilton Club[1] in Brooklyn on the evening of

January 11th, it would be that you could score a good point by some allusion to Alexander Hamilton's feeling toward the institution of slavery. I am not prepared to quote any authorities on that subject but I think it will be found that he was intense on the point.

It is quite possible that Mr. Chauncey Depew[2] and Professor Woodrow Wilson[3] of Princeton may both be on the Hamilton program for that evening. These engagements, however, are not at all certain.

What arrangements have you for Sunday, January 12th, and if you have none, would you like a good engagement in Brooklyn for that day or evening? Yours very truly,

Robert C Ogden

TLS Con. 113 BTW Papers DLC.

[1] The Hamilton Club, founded in 1882, was an outgrowth of the Hamilton Literary Society established in 1830. It was a literary and social club that maintained its own library and gallery and promoted libraries and the arts. BTW's address on Jan. 11, 1896, the 139th anniversary of Alexander Hamilton's birth, contained no ideas or expressions he had not frequently used before. He delivered it so effectively, however, that there were "cheers," "roars of laughter," and the waving handkerchiefs of the Chautauqua salute. He was interrupted by outbursts of "Good" and "Bravo." (Brooklyn *Daily Eagle*, Jan. 12, 1896, 1, 7.)

[2] Chauncey Mitchell Depew (1834-1928) of New York was a prominent lawyer, politician, and railroad executive. He served in the U.S. Senate from 1899 to 1911. Newspaper reports indicate that Depew was not on the Hamilton Club program on Jan. 11.

[3] Woodrow Wilson (1856-1924), then professor of jurisprudence and political economy at Princeton, later president of the United States (1913-21). He was one of the speakers with BTW on Jan. 11, and therefore he presumably sat with the black man at the head table for dinner. The southern-born Wilson was a segregationist, however, both as president of Princeton from 1902 to 1910 and as president of the United States.

From William Edward Burghardt Du Bois

Wilberforce University, Ohio. 3 January 1896

Special

My Dear Mr Washington: Professor Hart[1] of Harvard on writing me recently asked me to communicate with you — I do not know that he had anything definite in mind, but I nevertheless follow his suggestion. This is my second year at Wilberforce, and although the field here is a good one, yet I am not wholly satisfied and am continually on the lookout for another position. There is a little too much church politics in the management and too little real interest and devotion to the work of real education. Then again I have no chance to teach my spec[i]alty of History and Sociology at all. I have had the good fortune to have a monograph of mine accepted at Harvard and it will be published in the spring as the first of a series of historical studies. It is on the suppression of the slave trade.

I am thinking somewhat of trying to organize a summer School of Sociology here next summer — it is a delightful and cheap place to spend the summer and I might be able to do some good.

If you hear of any opening which you think I am fitted to fill, kindly let me know. I trust you[r] work is prospering as it deserves to. My best regards to yourself and Mrs. Washington. Sincerely Yours,

W. E. B Du Bois

ALS   Con. 116   BTW Papers   DLC.

[1] Albert Bushnell Hart (1854-1943), a well-known American historian, was a member of the Harvard faculty from 1883 to 1926. He directed Du Bois's doctoral dissertation. Hart maintained a friendship with both BTW and Du Bois, and later, when Du Bois became one of BTW's outspoken critics, Hart failed to comprehend their differences and believed that both men were really working for the same goals. Hart included excerpts from BTW's essay on "The Future of the American Negro" (1899) in Vol. IV of his *American History Told by Contemporaries* (1901). In the introduction to that essay Hart wrote that because of BTW's grasp of the race problem he was "a valuable factor in the future of American progress."

From Hugh Shepard Darby Mallory[1]

Selma, Ala., Jany 13 1896

Dear Sir: You are interested in the welfare of your race and have, to a large extent, the confidence of the white people of the country, North and South.

I have for some time been impressed with the belief that much good might be accomplished in the advancement of the colored race and to society generally by the employment of colored labor in our cotton mills in the south. You are aware that there is great activity in the

99

development of this industry in the Cotton States and that mills are not only being erected at various points with Southern capital but that Northern mills are in some instances being moved south. Here in Selma we have a large colored population, equaling the white population or nearly so in the corporate limits and if the suburbs are included then very considerably exceeding the white population. This colored population is constantly growing from immigration from the surrounding country. Very many of these people have no constant employment and I fear the result will be the permanent growth of a large idle class with the natural sequence of poverty and vice. It has occurred to me that no better outlet for Northern philanthropy can be found than the establishment of cotton mills in the South to be managed, at least for the present by expert white superintendents and white room bosses; the other labor to be exclusively colored. I know of no better point for such an experiment than Selma, which is in the midst of a large colored population with super abundant colored labor. We have here one large mill worked by white labor and another mill about to be erected, to be worked by the same character of labor. I would like to see established here a mill to be operated by colored labor, for the several reasons, indicated in this letter. In this matter I have no personal interest aside from the interest I have in the good of my country. Will you aid me in this matter? Yours truly,

H. S. D. Mallory

TLS Con. 1 BTW Papers DLC.

[1] Hugh Shepard Darby Mallory (1848-1920), an activist in Baptist church work and a trustee for several schools in Alabama, was a Selma lawyer and former mayor of Selma (1885-87). In 1910 he was an unsuccessful candidate for governor as a leader of the Braxton Bragg Comer faction of Alabama Democrats. Mallory, for example, supported railroad regulation but opposed wage and hour regulation in what one historian calls "business progressivism." (Hackney, *From Populism to Progressivism in Alabama,* 167.)

An Interview in the St. Paul *Dispatch*

[St. Paul, Minn., Jan. 14, 1896]

A COLORED LEADER

BOOKER T. WASHINGTON, WHO
MADE A SENSATION AT THE
ATLANTA EXPOSITION

INTERVIEWED BY DISPATCH

HE GIVES A FREE LECTURE THIS EVEN-
ING AT THE PEOPLE'S CHURCH — HIS
GREAT WORK AMONG HIS PEOPLE IN
THE SOUTH — AN INTERESTING TALK

Booker T. Washington arrived in St. Paul this morning direct from Brooklyn, N.Y., and took up his headquarters at the Metropolitan hotel.

A slight, graceful figure of a young man, light of color, but of distinctively African type, stood in the doorway of the parlor to receive a member of the Dispatch staff. "How did you come by your name Mr. Washington?" was the first question asked.

"Well, you know we colored people in the old days had no names but those our masters chose to give us; scarcely ever a last name; Booker is an old Virginia name, and I was given that by my master; my mother added Telfiero, but that was not her name only her fancy, and I was never called anything but Booker."

"When did the Washington come?" He smiled and said:

"That came the first day I went to school; I heard all the white children giving two names, and I said, 'what name can I say?' So before the teacher came to me I had made up my mind to call myself 'Washington,' and by that name I have since been known."

"Are you in the hands of a 'lecture bureau' Mr. Washington?"

"No, indeed," with greatest fervor, "I am a free man, to go and come and say what I like. I have been offered high prices a night to speak. I have letters every day nearly, asking me to lecture for money, but I could not do that, and do the good I want to do for the 'cause' to which I have given myself. The public would never believe I was telling the absolute truth if I were in the hands of some one; and talking for money. I should feel like a machine grinding out what I had to say at so much an hour."

"How are you received by the South in general?"

"There is no sectional South for me; all is my country; and I believe in the grand human brotherhood of all; sections in natives and races have no interest for me. I wish only to think and speak on broad, liberal lines."

"What is the outlook for the colored man in the country?"

"Our greatest danger is, that in the great leap from slavery to freedom, we may overlook the fact that the masses of us are to live by the productions of our hands, and fail to keep in mind that we shall prosper in proportion as we learn to dignify and glorify common labor and put brains and skill into the common occupations of life; shall prosper in proportion as we learn to draw the line between the superficial and the substantial, the ornamental gewgaws of life and the useful. No race can prosper till it learns that there is as much dignity in tilling a field as in writing a poem. It is at the bottom of life we must begin, and not at the top. Nor should we permit our grievances to overshadow our opportunities.

"There is no defense or security for any of us except in the highest intelligence and development of all. If anywhere there are efforts tending to curtail the fullest growth of the negro, let these efforts be turned into stimulating, encouraging and making him the most useful and intelligent citizen. Effort or means so invested, will pay a thousand per cent interest. These efforts will be twice blessed — 'blessing him that gives and him that takes.'

"There is no escape through law of man or God from the inevitable.

> The laws of changeless justice bind,
> Oppresser with oppressed;
> And close as sin and suffering joined,
> We march to fate abreast."

Mr. Washington delivers a free lecture this evening at the People's church, Bishop Gilbert presiding.

St. Paul *Dispatch,* Jan. 14, 1896, clipping, Con. 1029, BTW Papers, DLC.

Viola Knapp Ruffner[1]
to Margaret James Murray Washington

Baltimore   Jan 21st/96

Dear Mrs Washington   Your two letters in. I send the "widows mite" & hope it will be fruitful. Tell your pupils Be sure you are right, then go ahead, with the motto upward & onward. I have lost the use of one eye, & am rapidly losing the other. Hope you will never be thus afflicted. Tell Booker I have been looking for his letter, telling of the places & speeches & receipts of his trip, & when he reached home. Shall continue to look. Cannot write more. May you all be blessed. Your friend

V. Ruffner

ALS   Con. 116   BTW Papers   DLC.

[1] Viola Knapp Ruffner (1815-1904) was the second wife of General Lewis Ruffner, who owned the mines in Malden, W.Va., where BTW worked as a child. Born in Arlington, Vt., Viola Knapp attended an academy in Bennington. After graduation, she taught at the academy for two years and then at schools in North Carolina and New Jersey. At the latter school she headed the English department until she founded her own school, which she later gave up on account of poor health. While recuperating at home, Viola Knapp learned that the widowed General Ruffner was seeking a governess for his children, and she applied for the position, expecting to remain only until she was well enough to resume her profession. Her marriage to the general so disappointed several of his older children that they never entered his home again. Shy and sensitive but strong-willed, Mrs. Ruffner quickly gained a reputation for strictness partly because of the rapid turnover of her servants.
  "I had heard so much about Mrs. Ruffner's severity that I was almost afraid to see her, and trembled when I went into her presence," BTW recalled years later. (See above, 1:237.) He was so anxious to leave the dirt and dark of the mines, however, that he urged his mother to apply in his name for the job of Mrs. Ruffner's houseboy. Thus, just at the beginning of his impressionable adolescent years, BTW entered an upper-class white household whose mistress was the prototypical New England Yankee schoolmarm, devoted to the Puritan precepts of thrift, work, truth, and cleanliness. Though the youth left Mrs. Ruffner's employ occasionally during the years he worked for her, he always returned; and a strong and lasting bond of affection and respect grew between them. Mrs. Ruffner wrote years later: "He never needed correction or the word 'Hurry!' or 'Come!' for he was always ready for his book. There was nothing peculiar in his habits except that he was always in his place and never known to do anything out of the way, which I think has been his course all thru life." (Willets, "Slave Boy and Leader of His Race," 3.) BTW's passion for education and self-improvement probably appealed to the lonely woman, whose son Ernest and daughter Stella were away at school. She allowed her servant to attend school, gave him books and

urged him to accumulate his own "library," and employed him to peddle the produce she grew in her back yard. BTW became as punctilious in his habits as his mistress, and all his life he continued to practice the virtues she had taught him. "She was a stern, almost tyrannical woman," a neighbor remembered, "but she was good to Booker." (Charleston [W.Va.] *Daily Mail,* June 18, 1939, 8.)

After General Ruffner's death in 1883, Viola Ruffner lived with her son at his various army posts until her death. Both mother and son continued their interest in BTW, who paid them occasional visits during his speaking tours.

From Amanda Ferguson Johnston

[Malden, W.Va.] Jany 22/1896

Malden W Va Jany 24 Via Grand Rapids Mich

Uncle wash[1] is barely alive

Mrs Amanda Washington

HWSr Con. 539 BTW Papers DLC. Received at Ann Arbor, Mich.

[1] Washington Ferguson, BTW's stepfather.

From Amanda Ferguson Johnston

Malden W Va Jan 23 1896

Your message received we think furgeson is dying.

Amanda Johnson

HWSr Con. 539 BTW Papers DLC.

From James Nathan Calloway

Washington D.C. Jan 23 1896

Dear Mr Washington I got Mr. Harrison[1] of Opelika to take in a bill before the House today. I shall go for Senate tomorrow. Every thing looks very favorable now. I expect it will be good to have you come before the House committee when this bill come up for discussion. The Gov.² & Supt³ gave me good letters. I shall use all means in my power to make it a success here. I will write often now. Yours

J. N. Calloway

ALS Con. 112 BTW Papers DLC.

¹ George Paul Harrison (1841-1922), a Democrat who served in Congress from 1894 to 1897. An Auburn lawyer and former Alabama state senator (1876-84), he was counsel for the Western Railway of Alabama and the Central of Georgia Railroad.
² William Calvin Oates.
³ John Orman Turner.

A Bill before Congress

[Washington, D.C.] January 23, 1896

To grant land to the State of Alabama for the use of the Tuskegee Normal and Industrial Institute.

Be it enacted by the Senate and House of Representatives of the United States of America in Congress assembled, That the governor of the State of Alabama be, and he is hereby, authorized to select out of the unoccupied and uninhabited lands of the United States within the said State, twenty-five thousand acres of land, and shall certify the same to the Secretary of the Interior, who shall forthwith, upon receipt of said certificate, issue to the State of Alabama patents for said lands: *Provided,* That the proceeds of said lands, when sold or leased, shall forever remain a fund for the use of the Tuskegee Normal and Industrial Institute.

PD Con. 965 BTW Papers DLC.

From Mary Elizabeth Preston Stearns

College Hill P.O. Masstts Jan'y 24th 1896

My Dear Friend— Your letter of the 17th *inst.* was most welcome.

It was a cross to have missed sight of you, when last in Boston. Day after day I watched for your coming — eagerly. There was so much of profound interest to talk over — and you always renew my hope, and faith as Gen'l Armstrong did as all such souls do. Even in touch with the unseen mighty Power — working "both to will, and to do."

The night you addressed the crowd of eager listeners in Boston, my people went in to hear also. It is my penalty to years, and shattered health, that such satisfactions are no longer mine; but the enthusiastic report stirred my heart like a trumpet.

Martha (the cook, col'd) said she would have *walked* ten miles, rather than have missed it. "Such eloquence, they never heard."

It seems to have stirred the hearts and pocket to a remarkable degree.

Just in the moment of triumph your Barn was in flames, and those precious cows, (I love cows) going down in an awful baptism of fire! I felt this loss for you all most keenly. Am glad there was "*some* insurance." But the cows! the cows!

I have been thinking of a Permanent Scholarship in memory of Olivia as a tribute from me. What do you say to it?

I want to see the dear children very much. Some little Christmas gifts were waiting your coming; as also for Portia. Had I known her address I would have sent hers. Now that you have given it, I shall send for her, when the weather is suitable for the trip.

My love to Mrs. W. I will try to get the pictures she desires; if she will wait a bit. Christmas was too much for me. I broke down from over-work, and *that* is the reason you did not hear from me. Writing was too much for me. Last Tuesday, I was 75. Love to the dear Boys. Ever faithfully yours,

Mary E. Stearns

ALS Con. 112 BTW Papers DLC.

From James Nathan Calloway

Washington, D.C., Jan 25, 1896

Dear Mr Washington— Inclosed find a copy of letters from Gov & Supt of Education of Ala. Also a copy of the House bill. I have not succeeded in getting to see Senator Morgan[1] but I have an appointment with him for 8 this evening. Mr Morse[2] has promised his support and says if we get the democrats to champion the cause it will go through like a flash. I am having several copies of the Gov. letter made and putting them into the hands of members both from south and north.

T. T. Allain promises to get the Ill. members to vote for our measure.

As far as possible keep me informed of your address that I may reach you by telegram. Also of your important meetings that I may not call you at a time when due somewhere else. I shall try to raise our bill on calender. Yours truly

J. N. Calloway

ALS   Con. 112   BTW Papers   DLC.

[1] John Tyler Morgan.
[2] Elijah Adams Morse (1841-98) was a Massachusetts Republican congressman from 1889 to 1897. A stove-polish manufacturer, Morse had run for lieutenant governor on the Prohibition party ticket in 1877, and also served in the state senate from 1886 to 1887.

From Amanda Ferguson Johnston

Malden W Va   Jan 25th, –96

Father is still alive send twelve dollars.

Mrs. Amanda Johnson

TWSr   Con. 539   BTW Papers   DLC.

From Amanda Ferguson Johnston

Malden W Va   Jan 29 1896

Father is Dead.

Mrs Amanda Johnson

HWSr   Con. 539   BTW Papers   DLC.

From Atwell Theodore Braxton[1]

Meharry Med. College, [Nashville, Tenn.] Jan. 31, '96

Dear Mr. Washington: I am quite sure you will be, perhaps, the least bit surprised when you read this letter I have hastily prepared to send by Mr. T. N. Harris.[2] I hope to graduate within a few days and it is my intention to take the state board examination as I intend practicing at Birmingham, Ala. I have an impediment and it is that a young physician cannot pass without an influential friend to help him. Here are the words of one of the oldest white physicians in Nashville

"You cannot hope to practice medicine in Ala., as it is rumored that the physicians have decided that they have about enough Drs. & I have a set of the last questions of the examination given in Bhm, and there is not a prof. of any of the med. col. & Drs. of Nashville that could pass it and in order to pass you must be strongly recomended by a leading physician who has a friend on the board."

I have asked Mr. Harris to look after this matter for me & he will explain matters in full.

I am confident that I could pass without a recomendation on fair questions, but it seems that North Carolina, Virginia & Alabama has adopted this unfair plan after they have found out that a colored man could climb the other bars they put up to keep him out. Respt.

A. T. Braxton

ALS   Con. 114   BTW Papers   DLC.

[1] Atwell Theodore Braxton graduated from Tuskegee in 1892 and then went to Shaw University, Raleigh, N.C., where he was a student and instructor of printing from 1892 to 1894. He graduated from Meharry Medical College in 1896 and established a practice as physician in Columbia, Tenn.

[2] Thomas Nathaniel Harris graduated from Tuskegee in 1889 and went to Montgomery, Ala., where he taught printing at the Alabama State Normal School and ran a printing business from 1890 to 1894. He then went to Meharry Medical College to study medicine and dentistry, graduating in 1897. He was a dentist in Henderson, Ky., and later a physician in Montgomery before moving to Mobile in 1899.

From Elliston Perot Morris[1]

Philad[elphia]   2 mo 6. 1896

Dear Friend   I am very glad to know of thy proposed visit to Philada, and shall hope that we may meet at that time. My immediate object in writing this is to speak relative to Friends Freedmens Assn work at Christiansburg Va. I hope this may reach thee in time to allow thy route north, being so arranged, that thee may stop *there,* on the way, and be able to give our Board some late information of the work being done, and to consult with us at a meeting of the Board to be called whilst thee is in the City, so that we can more intelligently decide on our future efforts. As I doubt not this may entail some *additional* outlay, I will add that our association will wish to return it.

The School is not as large as formerly, and we do not understand its great falling off since 1st of the year as shown by our last report — nor does the attendance, & averages seem as good as we would like. A suggestion has been made by Thweatt[2] that we close school a week earlier than usual, so that the Teachers might all go to Tuskagee Exercises — as they went to Atlanta & had the week before & after Christmas we hardly think it would be best to again shorten the time & expect to so write.

We sincerely wish we could see a Hampton, or a Tuskagee school at Christiansburg, with all the interest & enthusiasm of either. Are we wrong in thinking it is a neighborhood where such a school would flourish. I do sincerely hope thee will be able to stop over there, & believe a good deal of our future may depend on thy so doing. Please write me on receipt of this & say what day it would suit thee to meet with Friends Freedmens Board — we generally meet at 12.15 but wd try to have another hour if it suited thee better. Any day, but Thursday. Truly thy friend

Elliston P. Morris

ALS   Con. 119   BTW Papers   DLC.

[1] Elliston Perot Morris (1830-1914) was a Philadelphia Quaker philanthropist who contributed regularly to Tuskegee and was active in peace movements. He was president of the Friends' Freedmen's Association, and it was this office that brought him into frequent contact and correspondence with BTW. Founded in 1862 to aid black schools in the South, the Friends' Freedmen's Association eventually abandoned all of its educational work except that at Christiansburg Academy.

Becoming upset with the academy's decline, Morris asked BTW to suggest ways of improving the school. BTW recommended appointment of Charles Lives Marshall, an 1895 Tuskegee graduate, to take charge of the school in 1896. Marshall modeled it after Tuskegee, and BTW and Robert C. Bedford made frequent visits of inspection. The school took the name Christiansburg Normal and Industrial Institute.

2 Hiram H. Thweatt.

From James Sullivan Clarkson[1]

New York, N.Y., February 7, 1896

Personal and Private

My dear Friend: I address you in confidence to talk a little further on the Presidential situation. Our conversation at Atlanta left a deep impression upon me, and it has been much in my thoughts since. As I said to you then, the responsibility of men like yourself and Professor Wright[2] and all your strong men, especially those who have been developed in the last ten years under the evolution of the great problem of human rights, is the most serious resting upon any people at this time. Others may choose lightly as to the next candidate for President. To you and your people, face to face with the fact that the new President in the next four years will largely determine in fact the solution of this problem for this generation, it is the gravest of questions and the most serious of decisions. No Federal law is now left in protection of your rights. On the temperament of the next President, on his fidelity to the doctrine of human rights, on his courage, his readiness and willingness to see every opportunity and to utilize every circumstance, depends very largely the fate of your people for this generation. An indifferent man in the White House would be even worse to you than an open foe. A man of inertia would not be a friend. You must have a man of conviction, alert, watchful, always guarding the interests of Southern Republicans and the negro race, and surrounding himself with men of similar conviction and backbone, and appointing to the Federal offices in the South men of like courage and ability and fidelity. I know the timidity of many Northern leaders on this question. When I was in the Post Office Department I found the President a courageous man, and yet, tainted with something of prejudice from his Virginia ancestry, unwilling when it came to the test to put colored men in any high or responsible office. Under my own limitations in the Post Office Department I was able to appoint over eleven hundred of your race as postmasters, route agents, letter carriers, etc., and I was also able to influence the appointment of many of them in the revenue service. The only office of high class that I was able to induce President Harrison to give to your people was that of Collector of the Port of Galveston, Texas, and it took four months of effort to induce him to appoint Mr. Cuney,[3] whose record there, fine and faithful in every respect, approved my judgment fully.

I had two motives in standing for this sort of fidelity to your people. First, our party is pledged to it in fellowship and brotherhood and conviction; second, it was due to your people to be given the chance to demonstrate their capacity for citizenship and sharing equally in the honors and burdens of the Republic. I feel it the highest duty of the Republican party toward your struggling race, which has made such remarkable advancement in the last thirty years — the most rapid of any race in history — both to encourage it as it is moving forward into higher civilization, and still more to demonstrate to the whole Republic and to the world the competency of your people for intelligent citizenship and capacity for office holding. In your address at Atlanta, which analyzed this problem with as much of philosophy as power, you made clear to your people that the negro problem is a different one since the close of the war and that it is constantly changing and must be met constantly from different standpoints of view. To a President the problem is to be dealt with as one of circumstance and opportunity. More, for instance, can be done for your race in one State than in another, or in one community in a certain State than another. More can be done for certain men in your membership than for others — which is a truism for your race as well as my own. You were the first of the leaders among your people to emphasize these changing phases of this great problem, and the truths must have sunk deep in the hearts of all who follow you.

As I said to you at Atlanta, as this problem is now largely a new one, and as such very strong men have been developed under its new conditions, it seems to me an absolute necessity that the strongest men you have developed under these new features ought to be in the convention at St. Louis — men like yourself and Professor Wright, and others I could mention. A Republican National Convention is an arena in which the progress of your race can be demonstrated more effectively than in any other — demonstrated, I mean, as to its growth and ability in conviction, in higher character, and in all the nobler things of life. For your people are a very different people to-day from those of 1860 and 1870. No duty could be higher upon you than to improve the quality of the men you send into this national arena. Your best men coming there to operate with the men in the North whom you know to be sincere, who you have reason to believe will stand steadfastly by your interests after the election as well as in the convention, can serve your people more than is possible to them in any other way in this campaign, for it is doubtful if the South can give many electoral votes to the party next November. In this connection, without detracting in the least from any of the other candidates, and frankly saying that I consider all of them worthy of the great office, I wish to impress upon you the superiority, in my judgment, of Mr. Allison[4] on this great question. You know fully as well as I the influence of environment upon anyone. Allison was born on the Western Reserve, and gained his first notions on that high ground of human freedom. His parents before him were abolitionists. He went to Iowa in the early fifties, and ever since he has been always a part and for thirty years the leader of that State in political sentiment and political action. Iowa is holy ground on the question of human rights. The first decision of its Supreme Court when it became a State set up the immortal doctrine afterwards adopted by the Republican party in the nation that no slave should be allowed to come into free territory without himself becoming free. Ever since the State has been faithful to this great doctrine. It never cast a vote in Congress during the days leading up to the war and to emancipation that was not on the side of human rights. Allison entered Congress in 1862, and was the friend and counsellor of Lincoln, and has been in Congress during all the legislation following emancipation. The State of Iowa a year before any other State or the nation enfranchised the negro. As a State it was settled largely by Quakers and New England abolitionists. John Brown went there frequently to renew his faith in the days he was beginning his struggles in Kansas. He recruited in Cedar County, Iowa, the Coppick boys[5] and others for his fight at Harper's Ferry; and afterwards when the Governor of Virginia made a requisition on the Governor of Iowa the requisition was refused. I mention these things

to you, and many others which might be quoted, to show that Senator
Allison not only by his environment but by his own demonstrated
leadership for thirty years, is a faithful, courageous, and wise friend
of your race. Iowa was made sacred ground in all the years before
the war by the underground railroads across its surface, on which
fleeing slaves from Texas, Arkansas, and Missouri found their way
to freedom in Canada. My father's house was one of the stations,
and I as a boy played a part in helping hundreds of these poor people
on their way to liberty. It is this sort of a State and this sort of a
people that says to you and all of your race that in Allison you would
find a friend in the highest place, as you have always found him a
friend and defender in every place he has held. I think you know,
aside from this record avouching his superiority on this question, that
I could not recommend to you or to any of your people a man who
would not be true to your interests. I am entitled to no credit for any
views that I hold upon this subject, for it comes down to me in the
blood of all my ancestors and has been my training in the thirty years
I have been in politics in Iowa. I had the fortune to be a member of
the committee on resolutions that drafted the plank declaring for
negro suffrage in Iowa, and for twenty-five years I edited a paper in
that State never wavering from this line. I can see no course in conscience, humanity, or civilization, saying nothing of the pledges of the
Republican party, other than to stand faithful and courageous on
every phase of this question. I am anxious to see the next President
redeem, and if possible sanctify, the pledges of the Republican party
to the negro race. This can be done in many ways, and I hope to see
some of the representative men of your people given high position, both
because the Republic can receive the best sort of service from them,
because it is due to your race to have this opportunity to show its
progress in civilization, and because it is necessary in the demands of
civilization itself. I would like to see a President who had the courage
to select from your people a member of his Cabinet — and you have
several men perfectly able to fill up faithfully the great duties of such
a high place.[6] In any event, I want to see a man who will, as I said
at the outset of this letter, utilize every opportunity and circumstance
to help your people forward in the noble struggle they are making to
develop their ability and secure their proper place in the Republic.
This letter I address to you in the frankness and confidence of friend-

ship, but I am ready to stand to its sentiments in public or private. I shall be glad to hear from you at any time, and to have any suggestions you may desire to make. I hope to see you at the St. Louis convention, if not as a delegate as a visitor, and I shall be glad to make you acquainted with many of the prominent men in our party.

I have dictated this letter just as I am leaving for the train, and it will be signed for me by Mr. Barnes, my secretary. Sincerely yours,

James S. Clarkson

TLSr Con. 1 BTW Papers DLC.

[1] James Sullivan Clarkson (1842-1918) grew up in Brookfield, Ind., learning the printer's trade from his father. Moving to Iowa, Clarkson became a compositor and eventually editor and owner of the Des Moines *Register*. An active Republican, he was postmaster of Des Moines from 1871 to 1877 and was a member of the Republican national committee from 1880 to 1896. A champion of the spoils system and opponent of the Civil Service Commission, Clarkson had his opportunity for important national office after 1888, when he backed the successful presidential candidate Benjamin Harrison. In 1889-90 Clarkson was first assistant postmaster general, and he used the title of "General" for the rest of his life. He acquired the nickname of "The Headsman" because he replaced Democrats with Republicans in fourth-class post offices at the rate of 30,000 a year. It was in this period that he first sought BTW's advice on southern black appointments.

Moving to New York in 1891, he was president of a bridge construction company. In 1902 Theodore Roosevelt, who had once fought Clarkson as a civil service commissioner, brought the old spoilsman out of political retirement, appointed him surveyor of customs of the port of New York, a position he held until 1910, and put him in charge of important political matters. Among other duties, Clarkson had principal charge of black federal appointments and black political strategy, with the advice of Roosevelt and BTW. Long an advocate of black civil rights, Clarkson claimed that in his youth in Indiana he had been a conductor of the Underground Railroad. He and BTW worked together effectively in opposing the "lily-white" movement in state Republican conventions in the South. BTW became suspicious, however, when Charles W. Anderson reported that Clarkson also conferred with "the enemy," the followers of William Monroe Trotter. After the 1904 campaign Clarkson played a less prominent part in black Republican affairs, and he retired from political life in 1910.

[2] Richard Robert Wright, Sr. (1855-1947), of Mandingo and Cherokee ancestry, was born a slave on a Georgia plantation. He became in the course of his life a teacher, author, newspaper owner and editor, college president, organizer of educational institutions and associations, political activist and appointee, and, in his sixty-sixth year, organizer and president of a bank in Philadelphia. In 1868, when General O. O. Howard asked students of an Atlanta freedmen's school what message he could bring to the school children of the North, Wright cried out: "Tell 'em we're rising!" His enthusiasm won Wright instant fame, and Howard and others frequently told the story of "the black boy of Atlanta." John Greenleaf Whittier wrote a poem eulogizing the youngster's spirited reply:

O black boy of Atlanta!
But half was spoken:
The slave's chain and the master's
Alike are broken.
The one curse of the races
Held both in tether:
They are rising, — all are rising,
The black and white together!

("Howard at Atlanta," in Whittier, *Complete Poetical Works*, 348-49.) After he graduated from Atlanta University, Wright frequently accompanied Edmund Asa Ware, the university president, on his fund-raising trips north, billed as "the black boy of Atlanta," a characterization he continued to exploit for the rest of his life.

Graduating in the first class of Atlanta University in 1876, Wright became the principal of a school in his boyhood home of Cuthbert, Ga. After receiving his A.M. from Atlanta University in 1879, he became the first principal of Ware High School in Augusta. Ten years later he was appointed the first president of the Georgia State Industrial College in Savannah, where he served until his retirement in 1921. Though Wright followed in general the Tuskegee educational policy, his inclusion of the classics in the curriculum ultimately caused conflict with the trustees, who unsuccessfully tried to oust him. Wright and BTW had a mutual high regard for each other; in 1907, BTW wrote William Jennings Bryan at Wright's request, praising his colleague as "a conservative and sensible man." (BTW to Bryan, July 12, 1907, quoted in Haynes, *Black Boy of Atlanta*, 85-86.)

Wright was a delegate to the Republican national conventions from 1876 through 1900 and again in 1908. In 1879 he bought a weekly newspaper in Cuthbert and moved it to Augusta. Wright built the *Sentinel*, also called the *States Rights Sentinel*, into a significant state political organ for black rights, and through it and the influence gained by his many other activities he won political preferment. He served as a special agent in the Interior Department, and as a U.S. deputy marshal for the southern district of Georgia. After declining McKinley's offer of the post of minister to Liberia in 1898, Wright was during the Spanish-American War a paymaster of the Georgia State Volunteers, with the rank of major. During World War I, the governor of Georgia appointed Wright chairman of the Colored Association Council of Food Production and Conservation.

Acting on the suggestion of his eldest son, Richard Robert Wright, Jr., Wright moved to Philadelphia after retiring from his college presidency in 1921. There, with the aid of his children, he founded the Citizens and Southern Bank, naming it after a white bank in Savannah where his daughter had been insulted. In a few years Wright merged the bank with a trust company to form the Citizens and Southern Bank and Trust Company, the only wholly black-owned bank in the North at the time. Among the many projects Wright sponsored for the recognition of blacks was the issuance of a postage stamp honoring BTW in 1940.

[3] Norris Wright Cuney (1846-98) was the leader of black Republicans in Texas for the two decades prior to his death. He was born near Hempstead, Tex., one of eight children of Colonel Philip Cuney, a white planter, and his slave Adeline Stuart. At thirteen, Norris and two of his brothers were sent to Pittsburgh to school. The boys were to have attended Oberlin, but the Civil War cut off their funds. Soon after the war Cuney settled in Galveston, where he was active in Reconstruction politics and held minor political posts. He was a school official

in Galveston County, sergeant-at-arms of the Texas legislature, and from 1872 to 1882 inspector of customs at Galveston. In 1882 he was elected a Galveston alderman. He was a delegate to every Republican convention from 1872 to 1896 and national committeeman from 1885 to 1896. In the Benjamin Harrison administration he was collector of customs at Galveston from 1889 to 1893. An energetic organizer and congenial companion, almost singlehandedly he held the line against exclusionist efforts by the "lily-white" Republican faction in his state.

4 William Boyd Allison (1829-1908) was a Republican from Iowa and a member of the U.S. House of Representatives from 1863 to 1871. He served in the U.S. Senate from 1873 until his death. Though some blacks believed that Allison's old-fashioned Republicanism would make him a protector of their civil rights, black delegates to the Republican convention in 1896 generally cast their votes for William McKinley, Allison receiving only 35½ votes.

5 Edwin Coppoc (1835-59) and Barclay Coppoc (1839-61), born in Ohio, moved to Kansas in 1858, where they became acquainted with John Brown. Both took part in the raid on Harpers Ferry, and Edwin was captured, convicted, and hung. Barclay escaped to Kansas, continued his antislavery activism, joined the Third Kansas Infantry, and was killed in the Civil War.

6 Shortly after McKinley's election in 1896, Clarkson wrote to John E. Bruce, the black journalist: "I have noticed the talk about putting one of your people in the Cabinet. I agree with you that it is probably not done sincerely; yet I do think it is something that might be done wisely. If I were President I would select someone like Booker Washington at this special juncture in human affairs, for the reason that he or some man like him has as much ability as the average member of the Cabinet, and for the further and greater reason that it is time for the Republican party to make some such assertion as this by way of emphasizing and re-declaring its apparently waning faith in the equality of men. . . . But if I were in McKinley's place I would appoint a colored man in the Cabinet from the South, and also a Democrat of the best class." (Clarkson to Bruce, Nov. 25, 1896, John Edward Bruce Papers, NN-Sc.)

To Butler H. Peterson

[Tuskegee, Ala.] Feb. 8th, 1896

Mr. Peterson: The Council has considered with care and deliberation your connection with the outbreak that occurred in the teachers meeting called and presided over by Mrs. Kaine a few afternoons ago. We have considered your statements with those of three other teachers who were present at the meeting, and from the evidence we gather the Council comes to this conclusion: first, that you showed disrespect to the institution by your words and general attitude in that meeting. The school cannot permit any teacher to decide when he or she should be called into a meeting and when not, nor can the school permit the teachers to be the judge of what matters should be discussed in these meetings. In this respect we consider that your words and actions on this occasion were in direct opposition to the best interests of the school. Secondly: we find that you are in error about any suggestion being made first by Mrs. Kaine that those who were not in harmony with the policy of the school should go away. From the evidence it is clear that Mrs. Kaine simply coincided with this suggestion made first by some one of the teachers. Your action in this matter is so serious in its relations to the welfare of the school that we are of the unanimous opinion that it is the proper thing for you to make a written apology that the Principal can read before the body of teachers before whom the offence was committed. This apology can be read in your presence or absence as you choose. In addition to this decision we have taken into consideration your previous conduct in relation to the school and feel that your action was largely a result of a loss of temper, nevertheless we cannot permit such an offense which strikes so directly at the foundation of our school to go by unnoticed. We should like the matter settled before the end of the day.

Booker T. Washington

TLpS Con. 135 BTW Papers DLC.

From Thomas Jefferson Morgan[1]

New York, Feb. 14th, 1896

Dear Brother: I am in receipt of your favor of Feb. 10th, inviting me to attend the Annual Negro Conference at Tuskegee, Ala., March 5th, 1896. I thank you heartily for the courtesy of the invitation and should be very glad to be present, but my official engagements render it impossible.

I have watched the work of these Conferences, from year to year, with great interest, and I am inclined to think that in the main they are doing good. I have, however, feared that possibly you are unconsciously lending your influence, and the influence of your school, and the influence of these Conferences, toward encouraging the pernicious idea that Industrial education of a low grade and the improvement

of the economic conditions of the Negroes, is the chief end to be aimed
at, and that the higher education of the Negroes, College training that
gives breadth and culture is not to be expected nor desired. I do not
mean to say that you teach this deliberately, but you encourage this
thought, as it seems to me, by the undue emphasis which you lay
upon Industrial Education and the improvement of economic conditions. These are desirable but I think they will come as the result of
higher training and that they do not of themselves necessarily constitute the basis of growth and prosperity for the Negro race. If I read
aright the history of education in this country it teaches one very important lesson, that the masses of the people, white or black, have been
and are to be reached from above, and that the great institutions like
Harvard, Yale and Brown, Princeton and others, have wrought for
the elevation of all of our people and secured an advancement which
would have been impossible without their aid. If I am wrong please
set me right. Fraternally yours,

T. J. Morgan

TLS Con. 119 BTW Papers DLC.

1 Thomas Jefferson Morgan (1839-1902) commanded black troops during the
Civil War and championed the cause of the black soldier. An ordained Baptist
minister and educator, he became corresponding secretary of the American Baptist
Home Mission Society in 1893, and edited that organization's monthly magazine.
In 1898 he wrote *The Negro in America and the Ideal American Republic*. In
this work, an enlightened defense of black rights, he called for racial and sexual
equality and for the same schooling for blacks as for whites, including higher
education of both sexes.

From James Nathan Calloway

Washington, D.C., Feb 19, 1896

Dear Mr Washington Your letter has just reached me. I have just
seen Chairman of Land Com. of House, Mr Lacey,[1] and he thinks
there is no chance to get our bill before the House before 1st of
March. I shall push forward, however, and see if we cant get it in
next week.

If Council and Patterson come they will do us great damage and
themselves no good. The bill for the whites is going to pull heavily
upon ours when in the House.

The land Com. is really oppose[d] to it. Ours is carrying it. I will wire you Friday if we can get a hearing Monday. Yours

J. N. Calloway

ALS Con. 115 BTW Papers DLC.

[1] John Fletcher Lacey (1841-1913) served in the Union Army during the Civil War and later was a Republican member of the U.S. House of Representatives from Iowa from 1889 to 1891 and 1893 to 1897.

From Henry William Blair

Washington, D.C. February 21st 1896

My Dear Sir: I take the liberty to enclose a copy of speech in which is incorporated an article by Dr Mayo,[1] which states with substantial truth the effect of the agitation for the enactment of the Blair Education Bill into law. If ~~in addition~~ to the effect of this general awakening to the importance of common school education could have been added the influence of the money proposed to be distributed we should have seen a complete revolution in the general condition of the South within ten years — as great as under the operation of existing causes can result in the next fifty.

The movements to curtail suffrage while denying the means to acquire the higher qualifications for its exercise, are merely efforts to disfranchise those who have only the suffrage such as it now is between them and practical slavery. Disguise it as we may, the man who living in a Republic is not a voter is not a freeman, and no improvement in his material condition ever will be permanent unless he votes.

There is everywhere a feeling that now is the time to revive the agitation for the Blair Education Bill. Everybody knows what the measure is and that is a great deal. It is as important to the white race as to the colored people. It will be easy if you endorse this measure with vigor and enthusiasm at your Conference at Tuskegee, to combine the political sentiment of the South of all parties in favor of this bill and to carry it into the political conventions now being held everywhere for the selection of Delegates to the Presidential Conventions. The bill could be endorsed in the platforms of the parties as the one united purpose and desire of the South and I feel sure that during the next administration this measure could be carried and the future be made forever secure.

Your wonderful address at the Atlanta Exposition together with the embodiment of your great life-work in the Industrial Institute point you out as the one man whose endorsement of this movement will make it successful, and the opportunity for its conspicuous inauguration at the Conference seems to be Providential. I feel sure that you will gladly assume this responsibility which can not be evaded any more than your special qualification for its discharge can be denied. I am not now in political life and have no purpose of a personal nature, nor have I ever entertained one in my public life. But I know that in this idea of national aid to common school and Industrial Education is the only hope of the poorer classes, that is of the masses of the people of the South and in many other parts of the country the common school is not properly supported by the state. The notion must eventually fall unless it has the power & exercises it temporarily to educate or to assist to educate while the state & the parent fail in the discharge of this first duty of one generation to another. Will you not my Dear Sir, *do this thing?* I enclose a substantial copy of a resolution which has been adopted in some of the Republican Conventions in North Carolina & I am told that the movement is on foot in several of the states & rapidly increasing. If you should voice and endorse it in such way as may seem best to you in your Conference I feel sure that it would at once become general and that within five years the Blair Education Bill would become the law of the land. By the provisions of the Bill itself the money to each state is to be "applied to the use of the *common* and *industrial* schools therein, under the direction of the Legislature thereof, & so as to equalize the privileges of all without regard to race or condition in life.["]

Unless this is done I can see nothing in sight which is likely to arrest the increasing movement for the disfranchisement of the colored race. The opportunity is evident as the sun in heaven.

The old leadership of the colored race is passing away. The new generation is here and it is charged with a tremendous duty, not inferior to that discharged so well & nobly by those now passed and passing away. Ere long it will be too late — and at best the work of ten years will be extended over a dreary century to come if we are now unfaithful. I know that you will pardon me for thus addressing you, but I have given of my life and fortune and of my blood in this cause beyond most other men and I would gladly die to see this work done, without which the sacrifices of the past may ultimately be lost. Sincerely & Respectfully   Your Obt Ser't

Henry W. Blair

ALS   Con. 114   BTW Papers   DLC.

¹ Amory Dwight Mayo.

From James Sullivan Clarkson

New York, N.Y., February 25, 1896

Confidential

Dear Friend: I cannot tell you the pleasure, personal as well as political, that your letter of the 18th gives to me. I am sorry not to have been in New York during your presence there so that I could have had a personal conference with you. I also desired very much to attend the exhibit that I understand your Institute made in that city. Your letter simply confirms the impression that your conversation at Atlanta gave me, that you are alive to the responsibility of your leadership of your people, and that they may safely trust in your wisdom and fidelity alike. I hope to see you before long, meantime I want to say to you in the confidence of the friendship that exists between us, that the strongest leaders of the party are of the opinion now that Allison stands in the situation to win. He has enough first choice and he has the second choice of a strong majority of the Convention. I will say to you again and leave it to time to vindicate the sincerity of my judgment, that in him as President your people would find shelter and defense. He stands for the great doctrine of human rights and liberty. I have just discovered lately that the Supreme Court of the State of Iowa, way back in the year 1839, when this Nation was so cowardly before the slave power that few people and no states dared to proclaim the doctrine of human liberty, made a decision in the case of Ralph, a slave who had been brought from Missouri to work in the lead mines of Iowa, to the effect that when a slave set his foot on free soil he became free himself. I will have made a copy of this and send to you and such other cherished friends of mine among your people, as Prof. Wright, Col. Pledger,¹ Prof. Dent² and others. I am inclined to think that it was the first decision that set up this immortal doctrine, afterwards adopted by the Republican party, and under the blessing of God and the wisdom of Abraham Lincoln, finding its fruition in the Emancipation Proclamation. I cherish the thought that Iowa, my home where my children were born, made as its first decision of its supreme court this noble and courageous opinion in the face of what was then an almost universal subservience to slavery with all its cruelties and enormities. For this was the first decision of the first supreme court of the Territory, and stands on the records of our jurisprudence as the first formal utterance of Iowa as a Territory. Ever since our state has followed this doctrine. Allison has been potential in our politics for thirty-five years, and every step we have made in this direction has been with his counsel, and nearly all of it under his leadership. What he advised in Iowa he has supported in Washington. I shall send you also with this first decision, a copy of a speech that he made in behalf of the negro sufferage in Iowa, on the stump in 1864. Again renewing my thanks, and frankly confessing the pleasure and encouragement your letter gives me, a letter which I shall preserve together with the letters that I have from Frederick Douglas as something to be transferred to my children, I am, Sincerely yours,

James S. Clarkson

TLS Con. 116 BTW Papers DLC.

¹ William A. Pledger, the son of a slaveowner, was one of the most influential Republicans in Georgia, serving as chairman of the state executive committee. He graduated from Atlanta University, and later practiced law and edited newspapers in Athens and Atlanta. Pledger was president of the Afro-American Press Association, vice-president of the Afro-American Council, and he attended every Republican national convention from 1876 to 1900. He alternated between conciliation and militancy in his pursuit of black civil rights, calling "only for justice" and then advocating black economic self-sufficiency. Pledger found the doors closed when he tried to gain political preferment from President Roosevelt in 1902, though his good friend, T. Thomas Fortune, interceded for him with BTW. The Tuskegean dispelled Pledger's suspicions, however, and within months the errant Georgian was back in the fold to stay until his death in 1904.

² T. M. Dent, a black educator, was active in Republican politics in Georgia. A delegate to the Republican national convention in 1896, he served on the credentials committee. In 1897 he sought BTW's endorsement of his candidacy for minister to Haiti. Dent had first met BTW at a teachers' convention in Columbus, Ga., and later saw him at the Atlanta Exposition, where he was an acting commissioner.

To Charles Gordon Ames[1]

[Tuskegee, Ala.] Feb. 29, 1896

My Dear Mr. Ames: I learn that applications have been made to the American Unitarian Association board of directors by several schools for the Frothingham Fund, which as you perhaps know has been coming to the Tuskegee Institute ever since the Fund was established. The last time I saw Mr. Reynolds[2] he told me that it was his hope that this Fund would continue to come to Tuskegee as long as the school merited it by its work. I find very much to our disadvantage at this time, that there is a prevailing opinion that Tuskegee gets all the money that it needs and that our treasury is overflowing. You cannot realize how exasperating it is to have such an impression abroad when we practically live from hand to mouth each day. During the last fourteen years I have not been able to take a single week of vacation on account of the pressing needs of the institution. We are being hurt in this way, one person feels that everybody else is giving to Tuskegee consequently it is not necessary for him to give; then we are failing to receive a good deal of money from orthodox individuals and churches that we might receive but for our liberal position and help that we receive from Unitarian institutions. To fail to receive help we ought to receive from orthodox bodies and then failing to receive help from Unitarian sources will prove pretty disastrous to us. I do not think it helps the cause in the South to take money from one Institution to give to another, especially when it simply means that so much additional time has to be spent by the principal away from the school to get money to replace that which has been taken away. In the end the cause is not benefited. If one or two institutions can be gotten on their feet with somewhat of an assured income then the cause will be greatly helped. The trouble at Tuskegee now is, that we do not know where we are to get two-thirds of our support at the beginning of the year.

I hope you and the members of the board will consider this matter carefully in making your decision.[3] Yours truly,

Booker T. Washington

TLpS   Con. 135   BTW Papers   DLC.

[1] Charles Gordon Ames (1828-1912) was a prominent Unitarian minister. He

served during the 1870s as editor of the *Christian Register*. In 1888 he became pastor of the Church of Disciples in Boston and served there until his death.

2 Grindall Reynolds.

3 The directors of the American Unitarian Association met on Apr. 14, 1896, and divided the Frothingham Fund between Tuskegee Institute and the Calhoun school. Tuskegee received $800 and Calhoun $216. (George Batchelor to BTW, Apr. 17, 1896, Con. 114, BTW Papers, DLC.)

An Article in *Our Day*

[Tuskegee, Ala., February 1896]

A NEW EMANCIPATION

When a black man hates a white man he narrows and degrades himself. When a white man hates a black man he narrows and degrades himself. If for no higher reason each should love the other in self-protection. Does one of my readers wish to experiment with himself? I want the experiment not so much for the benefit of the negro as for himself. Suppose, by reason of environment and early teachings, one has been disliking the negro, has been refraining from helpful contact with him, has always treated him as a degraded and unworthy creature. Let one who has thus felt and acted resolve to make a change. Experiment on himself. It will require a hard effort, much struggle and much prayer, but the result is worth the effort.

Mind you, my plea is not for the sake of the negro, but for the white man.

*   *   *   *

A man is not free when he is compelled for any reason to hate this man and love that one simply because of some difference in the tincture of the skin, or peculiar shape of the nose, or curl of the hair. There are thousands of white men, and black men, too, in America whom I want to help set free — I want to help make them free to love the world. Show me a man that dislikes another human being on account of his race or color and I will show you a man who is weak, who is holding back his own growth, his own development, who is repressing and cramping the best that is in him. Let the soul loose! Do not make it a slave. Let it grow. No one can realize the happiness that comes from such growth out of race narrowness into a love of humanity till he has tried the experiment on himself.

*   *   *   *

It is only as the soul has opportunity unbounded and unfettered to do its best work that we have great and lasting deeds performed. Take Whittier, Longfellow, Lincoln — and the name above all, Christ; would their names live in all history had their sympathies been narrowed and confined to this or that race? I would permit no man to drag down my soul by making me hate him.

*   *   *   *

This growth, I repeat, can only come as a result of daily effort, daily struggle by rising daily on "stepping stones of our dead selves," but the happiness, the sense of freedom is worth the price paid. No one who has thus made the struggle and has thus freed himself would go back for any consideration into the old slavery. Let us try at once the experiment.

Booker T. Washington

PDSr *Our Day,* 16 (Feb. 1896), 69-70. The same issue (pp. 79-84) also contained another article by BTW, "Out of Bondage," a typical account of BTW's rise from slavery to become head of an educational institution.

From John W. Browning[1]

Baltimore, March. 2nd 1896

My Dear Mr. Washington: I have your letter of Feb. 28th, and reply to it without delay. I am highly pleased to have you come at the appointed time and have secured Mr. Robinson's church for that evening.[2] If you are to leave here the same evening or early next morning for Tuskegee, can't you come here early in the day of the 18th? I know you are pressed for time, but it is greatly desired.

No, in my judgment, it would not be wise for you to stop at the Mayor's[3] house, as these colored people (and some of the whites, too, for that matter) are so queer, I fear it might operate against you and prejudice them to you and your noble work. It is true, my home is an humble one, but to it no man is more welcome than yourself — not even a brother. I feel free to speak to you on this point, and do not believe it would be discreet, although it would be perfectly appropriate that you pay your respects to the Mayor, and possibly, take tea at his home if he suggests it, but to stop there while here would not meet the approval of our people.

Whatever expense you will be put to please let me know and I will arrange for its immediate forwarding to you if you request it. I have just seen Mr. Robinson and he is as delighted as myself to know you are coming and will speak at his church as you proposed some time ago.

Drop me a postal when you are to pass through this city again and I will come to the station to see you and have a word with you. I shall see the Mayor in due time and convey your message to him. Very likely I shall see him tomorrow or Wednesday.

I hope the Presbyterian meeting, at which I see by the papers you are programmed to speak Tuesday night, will be of much profit to you. Hoping to hear from you soon, and wishing you continued success, I am, Yours truly,

J. W. Browning

ALS Con. 114 BTW Papers DLC.

[1] John W. Browning was a Baltimore druggist and president of the Booker T. Washington Business Association.

[2] BTW spoke on Mar. 18 at St. John's A.M.E. Church. The pastor was probably David Robinson, a member of the board of directors of the Booker T. Washington Business Association.

[3] Alcaeus Hooper, mayor of Baltimore from 1895 to 1897.

From William Miller Beardshear[1]

Ames, Iowa   March 5, 1896

Dear Sir: Your letter in regard to a colored graduate is duly received. We graduated a colored man a couple of years ago, Mr. G. W. Carver.[2] He made such standings in Horticulture, that he has been retained as an assistant in the horticultural department of the experiment station work. He is a thorough christian gentleman and scholar. We can give him iron-clad recommendations. Any school would be fortunate in securing his services. Sincerely,

W. M. Beardshear

TLS Con. 114 BTW Papers DLC.

¹ William Miller Beardshear (1850-1902), minister and educator, was president of Iowa State College of Agriculture and Mechanic Arts from 1891 until his death.

² George Washington Carver (1861-1943) became Tuskegee's most famous faculty member and a partly mythical symbol of black achievement in science. Born a slave in Diamond Grove, Mo., he was kidnapped as an infant along with his mother and sister. Their owner, Moses Carver, sent a man to track the abductors. The other slaves were not found, but when the tracker returned with the sickly George, the owner paid for him and reared him with kindness. George Carver left home at fourteen to attend school in Neosho, Mo., and later worked and studied in wanderings through Kansas, Minnesota, Colorado, and Iowa. After attending Simpson College, Indianola, Iowa, he studied at Iowa State College in Ames, graduating in 1894. Ames was an important center of agricultural education, and Carver knew there three future U.S. secretaries of agriculture, James Wilson, Henry C. Wallace, and Henry Agard Wallace. He spent two more years studying for a master's degree, meanwhile working in the botany department at the greenhouse. While at Ames, Carver also was co-author of two articles describing experiments with rust inoculation and parasitic fungi, with one exception the only technical publications of his career.

When BTW wrote Carver in the spring of 1896 seeking to secure him for Tuskegee, he anticipated by almost a year the establishment at the institute of a federal/state agricultural experiment station. Carver began at Tuskegee also as a teacher and head of the agriculture department. He quickly proved his ineptitude as an administrator, however, and later indicated little interest in teaching classes, so gradually BTW delegated these responsibilities to others and allowed Carver free rein to experiment, to publish bulletins on applied agriculture as related to conditions in rural Alabama, and to teach some students informally as they worked under his direction. Carver was also considered an eccentric local character, and he played the part, knitting his own socks, living on the second floor of a girls' dormitory which he entered by the fire escape, singing in a high voice at Sunday school, and wearing various flowers and weeds in his buttonhole to advertise their properties. He had in his career acquired skill as a painter and pianist, and at Tuskegee he painted many watercolors and oil paintings, most of them still lifes. He donated several pianos to the school out of his salary, which as a reclusive bachelor he did not spend, and he fiercely defended BTW and the school whenever it was attacked.

Carver had what he once called "a passion for flowers," but it was his association with the peanut that made him famous. In 1916, the year following BTW's death, he published a Tuskegee experiment station bulletin, *How to Grow the Peanut and 105 Ways of Preparing It for Human Consumption.* Little in it was new; the Department of Agriculture had issued two more comprehensive bulletins on peanut cultivation and consumption, and Carver freely acknowledged his debt to numerous cookbooks. He continued his interest in the peanut. In 1920 he appeared before the convention of the United Peanut Association of America to talk about "The Possibilities of the Peanut," exhibiting substitute milk, coffee, stains, and others of the more than 145 applications he claimed for the peanut. In 1921 he testified before the House Ways and Means Committee for the United Peanut Association's effort to include peanuts in the Fordney-McCumber tariff bill. Over the years he developed other peanut products, including a vanishing cream that he used to massage victims of infantile paralysis. His fame as a masseur spread, and on a usual day he gave four or five massages to afflicted persons, though he himself did not claim that peanut oil had any restorative powers. Carver was unable, despite many efforts, to add to the commercially successful peanut products. The Carver Products Company in 1923, the Carver Penol Company in 1926, and the Carvoline Company in the 1940s all were unsuccessful.

Carver was not outstanding as a scientist or as a promoter of new commodities, but he did contribute to the education of the community served by Tuskegee Institute. Both on the campus and off, he taught such needed lessons as diversification of crops, soil-building crops, and the avoidance of erosion by proper cultivation. Through the Tuskegee Negro Conferences, exhibits, demonstrations, and clearly and simply written publications Carver communicated the importance of improved agricultural methods.

One factor in Carver's wide acceptance among white Americans as "the Negro scientist" was his accommodation to white stereotypes about black behavior. His extreme humility, his slight, stooped frame, and his attribution of his discoveries to divine guidance presented the picture of the kind of black scientist whites could accept without any feeling of being threatened. The hailing of George Washington Carver not only obscured the more solid scientific accomplishments of such men as Charles Drew and Daniel Hale Williams, but also obscured Carver's real and important work in agricultural education. (Mackintosh, "The Carver Myth.")

From William J. Bailor[1]

Harrisburg, Pa., Mar. 6, 1896

Dear Sir. I had hoped to have heard from you, before this, as I did not know where you were.

The reason is that I wanted to hear your opinion on the Quay[2] matter.

Deputy Sec. of State, Mr. Barnett,[3] wrote to you some time ago, but did not receive any reply. I hope you will answer his letter. All Quay's friends here want you to use your influence for the Senator at the Convention.

Hoping to hear from you at an early date. I remain   Sincerely

W. J. Bailor

ALS Con. 114 BTW Papers DLC.

[1] William J. Bailor published the Harrisburg *Sentinel Gazette* from 1894 to 1896.

[2] Matthew Stanley Quay (1833-1904), an editor and longtime politician, was a Republican senator from Pennsylvania from 1887 until his death. He managed Harrison's presidential campaign in 1888 and was a member of the executive committee of the Republican national committee in 1896.

[3] James Elder Barnett (b. 1856) was deputy secretary of state of Pennsylvania from 1895 to 1897 and state treasurer from 1899 to 1902, when he returned to private law practice.

From James Nathan Calloway

Washington, D.C. March 6 96

Dear Mr Washington   I saw Mr. Goodwyn[1] yesterday and had a talk about our matter in Congress. He is very kindly disposed toward it but does not want it to pass until he is seated. I will see Aldrich[2] tomorrow and see what he is doing. In the mean time I am pushing our bill in the Senate. I find that it is to be discussed before Senate Com. again today. That is the report is to be made up there today.

Wheeler[3] is trying every body to get in his bills. Patterson is still here. I hope to do something one way or other early in next week.

If this thing is to wait until Aldrich is seated I had better come home. I will write you as soon as I find out. Yours

J N Calloway

ALS   Con. 115   BTW Papers   DLC.

[1] Albert Taylor Goodwyn (1842-1931) was in Congress from 1896 to 1897 after he successfully contested the election of James E. Cobb. Later he was elected chief of the United Confederate Veterans.

[2] William Farrington Aldrich (1853-1925), who was seated on Mar. 13, 1896, rather than his brother Truman Heminway Aldrich (1848-1932), who was seated on June 9, 1896. William served in Congress from 1896 to 1897, 1898 to 1899, and 1900 to 1901, gaining his seat each time after contesting the election of others. He was owner and publisher of the Birmingham *Times* and served as a delegate to the Republican national convention in 1904.

His brother Truman served in Congress from June 9, 1896, to Mar. 3, 1897, having successfully contested the election of Oscar W. Underwood, and later served as postmaster of Birmingham from 1911 to 1915. Truman was also a delegate to the 1904 Republican convention. Both men had successful careers in mining and manufacturing, and Truman was vice-president and general manager of the Tennessee Coal, Iron and Railroad Company after 1892.

[3] Joseph Wheeler (1836-1906) was a West Point graduate who served in the Confederate Army. In 1880 he served one year in Congress, but his election was successfully contested. Later he was elected to the House from Alabama and served from 1885 to 1900. His service as a major general of volunteers in Cuba during the Spanish-American War was symbolic of the reunion of the sections.

To Adella Hunt Logan

[Tuskegee, Ala.] Mar. 7, 1896

Mrs. Logan: For some time I have had in mind having some one come to Tuskegee with a view of looking thoroughly through our class room work and reporting on its condition. I have not however, up to the present, arranged with any outside person to do this. It occurs to me that perhaps you might be able to take a week or ten days in making this investigation. At the outset I am trying to say that it is very difficult to find persons to do such work for the reason that there are such few persons who can entirely separate themselves from the individual whose work she is looking into, such an examination means nothing unless the examiner is strong enough, I might add has a heart hard enough to shut her eyes against everything except facts. Taking this view of the case I should like to have you go into each class, look into each class room teacher's work on the place long enough to give a report as to the fitness of each teacher. Such an investigation will prove of the greatest service to the school and might just as well be done by you as any outside person. Of course if you can undertake it I should like such report to mention the weak points as well as strong points and make suggestions for remedying present evils. I want to know just whether or not we are doing the best work, and the only way to know is to have it thoroughly looked into by an outside person once in a while. Of course the school will be willing to pay you whatever is reasonable for this service. I should like an early answer to this communication.

Booker T. Washington

TLpS Con. 135 BTW Papers DLC.

From Timothy Thomas Fortune

Jacksonville, Fla., March 7, 1896

Dear Mr Washington: I have just finished reading your splendid address (in the Mail and Express) at the Home Mission Rally in New York.[1] It is worthy of you and of the great occasion.

Mrs. Matthews,[2] in a recent note to me, spoke of "the publication of *The Black Belt Magazine,* published at Tuskegee, as the outgrowth of a suggestion of Mrs Washington about a woman's magazine, and she asked me how I would like to edit such a magazine. That reminds me of a long talk I had with Dr Frissell last Summer, in which I suggested that I could take the *Workman* and make it *the* authority on Afro-American education in the South and Hampton the literary center. He thought mighty well of the idea, but the old barnacles who control affairs were averse to the change, and so we dropped the matter.

Now why can't we do it with Tuskegee? *The Black Belt Magazine* I could make indispensable to all the friends and patrons of Southern education in the South. With Mrs Matthews, Mrs Josie Washington[3] and myself on the spot, I could command the cream of the literary talent of the race. And you would be a great power in it. We could easily make Tuskegee the center of the literary thought of the Southern educational work.

There are a few other routine things I could do at Tuskegee, in the way of lectures once a week on fiscal, economic and social subjects, in line with the literary studies necessary to a proper editing of the magazine.

If you want to talk it over I will stop by Tuskegee within the next ten days and do so. I shall be leaving here soon perhaps to Texas by way of Atlanta, so I will thank you to wire me here on receipt of this as to whether you think it worth while to talk the matter over. Perhaps Mrs Washington and Mrs Matthews have already said something to you about it. I think it a very important matter, one which would be of great service to you and Tuskegee and the race at large.

With kind regards for you and all the house, Your Friend

T Thomas Fortune

ALS Con. 116 BTW Papers DLC.

[1] The address at Carnegie Hall on Mar. 3. (See above.)
[2] Victoria Earle Matthews (1861-1907), born a slave in Georgia, was left behind by her runaway mother during the Civil War, but after the war her mother returned to her nine children. In 1872 they moved to New York, where Victoria received four years of schooling. In 1879 she married William Matthews. After some years of intense reading in the library at her place of employment, Mrs. Matthews began writing for T. Thomas Fortune's New York *Globe* and New York *Age.* She also did free-lance writing for the New York *Times,* New York *Herald,* and other white newspapers.

An active feminist, she founded the Women's Loyal Union of New York and Brooklyn, concerned with black women's rights, particularly fair employment. In 1897 she founded the White Rose Mission, a social center for black migrants patterned after the white settlement houses for immigrants. The mission taught sewing and cooking and black history. BTW helped Mrs. Matthews to raise funds and visited the mission. In 1895 Mrs. Matthews was, with Josephine St. Pierre Ruffin and Margaret Murray Washington, a founder of the National Federation of Afro-American Women, which combined the following year with another body to form the National Association of Colored Women. She selected and edited *Black Belt Diamonds: Gems from the Speeches . . . of Booker T. Washington* (1898).

3 Josephine Turpin Washington.

A Bill before the United States Senate

[Washington, D.C.] March 10, 1896

To grant lands to the State of Alabama for the use of the Industrial School for Girls of Alabama and of the Tuskegee Normal and Industrial Institute.

Be it enacted by the Senate and House of Representatives of the United States of America in Congress assembled, That the governor of the State of Alabama be, and he is hereby authorized to select, out of the unoccupied and uninhabited lands of the United States within the said State, twenty-five thousand acres of land, and shall certify the same to the Secretary of the Interior, who shall forthwith, upon receipt of said certificate, issue to the State of Alabama patents for said lands: *Provided,* That the proceeds of said lands when sold or leased shall forever remain a fund for the use of the Industrial School for Girls of Alabama, located at Montevallo, Alabama.

SEC. 2. That the governor of the State of Alabama be, and he is hereby, authorized to select, out of the unoccupied and uninhabited lands of the United States within the said State, twenty-five thousand acres of land, and shall certify the same to the Secretary of the Interior, who shall forthwith, upon receipt of said certificate, issue to the State of Alabama patents for said lands: *Provided,* That the proceeds of said lands when sold or leased shall forever remain a fund for the use of the Tuskegee Normal and Industrial Institute.

PD Con. 10 BTW Papers ATT. Original destroyed. The bill was S. 2461, 54th Cong., 1st Sess. It was reported from the Committee on Public Lands by Senator Samuel Pasco (1834-1917) of Florida.

To Nathan B. Young

[Tuskegee, Ala.] Mar. 11, 1896

Mr. Young: You must have noticed in the meetings this week that one teacher said that he did not know it was the custom of the school to take into account the matter of correcting spelling and grammar in connection with the ordinary class room work, and another teacher said that he did not know the matter of spelling, grammar, etc., entered into the matter of marking the students. You can see that such expressions from teachers give me the impression that there is need of great improvement in the matter of looking into the class room work *closely.* You see six months have passed away and at the end of six months to have teachers report that they are not acquainted with a rule of such vital interest to the class room work is rather surprising. Such defects can only be remedied by you looking in detail into the work of each teacher, going into *their classes, often looking* into their papers, etc. I do not mean to say that this is not done to some extent now, but I am sure that this needs to be emphasized more in the future than it has been in the past. I depend on you to keep close contact with the work of each individual teacher and the proper results can only be obtained by a close individual inspection of each teacher's work from week to week. It might be well for you to remain with one teacher several days or a week in order to get that teacher in the right track and correct defects.

Booker T. Washington

TLpS   Con. 135   BTW Papers   DLC.

From Nathan B. Young

Tuskegee, Ala. Mch 11, 1896

Mr. Washington, I was as surprised as you that any teacher did not understand that all written work is to be graded with a view to *spelling* — not to grammar, however, for no such regulation regarding grammar exists. I have made it plain to the teachers the policy of the school in this matter; and therefore feel no responsibility for any one's not understanding it.

The question of supervision, raised in your note, is yet an open question. How far shall a supervisor direct the work of the teacher. Shall he go into the minutiae of showing a teacher how to grade examination papers, how to conduct this or that recitation and such questions of detail, which doubtless if entered, will destroy all freedom, all personality on part of the teacher.

I much prefer the method which I pursue here, and pursued before coming here, of holding the teacher responsible for results, going on the presumption that the teacher has sufficient teaching ability to direct the details of her work, and to take and apply the suggestions offered in private conversations and in teacher's meetings, or institutes, in my mind, the only successful way of procedure on part of the supervisor.

If, among the corp[s] of teachers, there is one who is so obtuse, or so *conceited* as not to take suggestions, the duty of the supervisor is to recommend (only after fair consideration in view of *results*) the removal of said teacher.

I try to supervise the work of my associates in such a way as to leave them the largest possible freedom in selecting their *methods,* in offering suggestions as well as in receiving them. I want them to feel free to *come* to me for suggestions, as freely as I go to them with suggestions. In a word, I strive for the co-operation of the teachers, to impress upon them that I am their *co-worker,* not their *director,* or their brains.

I go to their class-room sufficiently often to know what they are doing, and *how* they are doing — to gather general information as to the progress of the work, and of the difficulties in the way. Finding difficulties, we set about to devise a remedy.

If I *go* into further details, I cross or check the teacher's individuality. Class-room supervision is a delicate piece of work, and needed to be done with the greatest precaution, else the work will be marred by useless personalities &c.

I have made this lengthy statement, not because I take any exception to your note, but to give you my notion of the functions of my office, regarding the class-room work of the teachers especially, and thus to explain my policy in dealing with them. Experience has taught me that this is the best policy for me, and I can not adopt any other.

Hoping that I have made my position plain, and pledging to continue doing what I can toward perfecting the work of this department, I am   Respectfully,

Nathan B. Young

ALS   Con. 123   BTW Papers   DLC.

From Henry Clay Reynolds[1]

Washington, D.C. Mch 11th 1896

Dr Sir   I think the sooner you come up, the better. I found on my return efforts were being made to have our bills "laid on the shelf" and it was only by defying Patterson & Eldridge[2] that we could prevent something of the kind being done, and Judge Cobb[3] acted very manly about it, told Patterson if that was his object had as well go home &c. I feel sure bill will go thro Senate & be ready to come to house in a few days. So now is in my opinion the time to do our work and try to pull it thro'. Respt &c,

H. C. Reynolds

ALS   Con. 112   BTW Papers   DLC.

[1] Henry Clay Reynolds (1838-1903) was the president of the Girls' Industrial School for whites at Montevallo, Ala. He worked with BTW to secure a grant of Alabama coal lands to aid state schools. A Democrat, Reynolds did most of the lobbying in Washington, D.C., and in Alabama, but relied on BTW's political contacts especially with Republican congressmen. Tuskegee and Montevallo eventually excluded other schools from the bill and gained the land for themselves. In 1899 Reynolds's quick sale of the land at a low price and various conflict-of-interest charges brought his downfall as head of Montevallo.

[2] Edwin R. Eldridge was president of the white state normal school in Troy, Ala. The school opened in 1896 and Eldridge was in the competition with BTW, Reynolds, and others for the federal land grant.

[3] James Edward Cobb (1835-1903) was a lawyer from Georgia who settled in Tuskegee after the Civil War. In 1874 he was elected judge of the ninth judicial district. He served five terms in Congress beginning in 1886, but his seat in the Fifty-fourth Congress was contested on grounds of fraud and ballot-box stuffing. In 1901 Cobb was a member of the Alabama constitutional convention, and voted for restrictive suffrage measures.

From Henry Clay Reynolds

Washington, D.C. Mch 12 1896

Bill passed senate today come at once need you now.

H. C. Reynolds

HWSr   Con. 539   BTW Papers   DLC.

From Timothy Thomas Fortune

Jacksonville, Fla., March 13, 1896

Dear Prof Washington: I have your favor of the 11th instant and am glad, as I am always, to have a line from you.

As to the magazine project I acquiesce in your determination of the matter without argument. You have plenty of burden to stagger under in these times of money stringency, and if you donot see how the magazine could be made self-sustaining under the circumstances the wise course is not to undertake the venture. I understand fully what the cost of such a venture would be and I know how tight the money market it is. Some other time we shall talk it over.

I am thankful for the reassurance that I am always welcome at Tuskegee. I always find it pleasant to be there. As I am to be in Georgia soon I may look in on you for a few days.

I am glad that Mrs. Matthews is still with you and active along literary lines and apparently happy and busy. She is a estimable woman.

I am satisfied with my work in the South, which is drawing to a close, from the point of results. I have not been wise in money matters, but I have made friends who will stand by me in the future. Matters are going my way and am gratified to know that you are still pushing matters in the direction indicated by me. I shall not hesitate to call on you when I need help. My ticket to Washington expires March 31, and I don't think I am going to be able to use it before May 15, as Pledger wants me in Georgia until April 30. I enclose it; if you can get it extended to May 31 all right; if not return it, and if I don't use it within the limit I will return it to the main office with my thanks.

Have it returned to my box here and if I shall have gone away it will be promptly forwarded. I may attend the Alabama State convention. With kind regards for you all, Yours truly

T. Thomas Fortune

ALS   Con. 119   BTW Papers   DLC.

Two Extracted Versions of an Address before the Bethel Literary and Historical Association[1]

[Washington, D.C., Mar. 17, 1896]

The saddest thing in the condition of the colored man to-day is that he takes no part in the industrial life of this country. I was in a Northern city the other day, and I saw a church being erected by the hard-earned pennies of our race, but the contractor would not let a colored man drive a single nail. The white men had made all the building material, and the colored people were paying them to build the church, because they had no contractors in their own race competent to do the work.

It also seems that we are losing our hold on the industries we used to control. Some years ago, in the North, the colored barber had a monopoly on his trade. He did not put his brains into the business, as he should have done, and the white man is gradually taking the business away from him. If you go to New York to-day you can hardly find a colored barber.

If you go to Atlanta, where a few years ago there was nothing but colored horse-shoers, you will see signs of "Veterinary Horse Shoeing." And you will not find two black horse-shoers there. The white man knows more about the anatomy of the horse's hoof and he shoes the animal in a scientific manner. There is no room for the old negro horse-shoer. Only a few years ago in Atlanta you could see the old colored uncles going around the streets with a long pole and a white-wash brush and bucket. If you had them come in and white-wash your house they would wash the ceilings and the walls and the carpets, and the furniture. They gave no thought to their work. But if you

137

look for those old colored men now you will find instead the white "house decorator," who understands something about the blending of colors, and who never drops a spot on the carpet or the furniture. The old man with his bucket and his long pole is not wanted.

Our mothers and sisters, who once were the recognized laundresses of the country, are losing their business. I was in Chicago recently and sent my laundry away in the morning and in the evening it was returned. Down South I used to send it away Monday morning, to my old colored washwoman, and I was lucky to get it back Saturday night. How long can our people hold the laundry business if the young men who are graduating from these industrial schools do not come South and build electric laundries to compete with the white man, who has a machine now in which he washes 100 shirts an hour.

To-day 85 per cent. of our people live from agricultural pursuits, and we have but two scientific farmers in the whole race. But you may ask what is being done for this race at Tuskegee. The race is being educated to realize that the relations between the races will only improve so far as the negro improves his education. He must produce something which the white man wants before he will be recognized.

Washington *Post,* Mar. 18, 1896, 3.

[Washington, D.C., Mar. 17, 1896]

If our education means anything, if our young men and women have any object in life, this object should be to lift up the masses who dwell in so large measure on the plantations of the south. If tonight you will place yourselves in the place of the colored men and women of the south you can better appreciate what I shall say.

We have got to make an effort to better our condition. We must remember that our position is a peculiar one. The relations that should exist between the two races are still unsettled.

It has taken the white race one thousand years to reach its present high plane, and if we are wise we will take advantage of some of the advances made by them.

LOT OF THE NEGRO

Our people in the south are finding out that the world is getting very practical, and they care very little about what a man knows, but they do care what he does with his knowledge.

The negro produces almost every bale of cotton that is raised in the south, but let him go to a factory where cotton goods are manufactured, whether it be in Massachusetts, Rhode Island, North Carolina or Mississippi, and ask for work, and the door will be shut in his face. There are but two or three states in the south where the negro can ride in a first-class railroad coach, but let that negro go into the shop in Massachusetts where that coach is made and he will be turned out of the place.

I have often wondered why it was that fully one-half of the money earned by the Georgia negro farmer had to be spent in the north for corn and pork and other necessaries of life, which the farmer must have to support himself and his family during the year, but I never could understand the matter until I went into Indiana a few months ago. There I saw a white farmer in a field riding on some kind of a machine, of the use of which I then knew nothing. The man was riding on the machine, to which were attached two spirited horses, and the man's principal occupation seemed to be to keep the horses from going too fast. Not only was the man in the comfortable position to which I have referred, but he had an umbrella to cover his head, to protect him from the rays of the sun. I analyzed that machine, and I found that it ploughed the ground, laid out the rows, and planted two rows of corn at a time.

ONE-GALLUS MAN

A short time afterward I was down in Georgia, and I saw a negro farmer planting corn. He had an old mule attached to an antiquated plough, and dragging behind was a pole about five feet long. Every little while the mule would stop, and then the farmer would reach behind, take up the pole and beat the mule. This would cause the animal to move on again, but before going far it would be necessary for the man to stop the mule and repair the harness, which was made partly of leather and partly of rags. This he would fix up, but in a little while it would become necessary to make some repairs to the plough. And it would not be much longer before the farmer would have to stop to fix his pants, for our negro farmers are all one-gallus fellows, who are used to making repairs while at work to their trousers.

Thirty years ago there was scarcely a white barber to be found in the city of Baltimore, Philadelphia, New York or Boston. Today there is not a first-class barber shop in one of them that is owned by a colored man. The latter failed to realize that he must progress with the times. He was satisfied to have a dingy shop on a side street. The white man came along, saw an opportunity for making money, rented a nice, bright room on a front street, fixed it up with improved chairs, hung pictures on the walls, and took all the colored man's trade. The name of the craft was changed; the colored man was a barber, the white man styled himself a tonsorial artist, but he took the colored man's trade all the same.

EVEN THE WASHERWOMAN

Our mothers and sisters in the south who now make their living at washing and ironing will lose even that occupation unless they will develop progress with the times. I was in Chicago a short time ago, and one Monday morning at 6 o'clock I sent my laundry from my room to be washed and ironed. At 5 p.m. of the same day it was returned to me in perfect condition. How does this compare with the course pursued in the south, where you send your laundry to the washwoman at 6 a.m. Monday and get it back possibly by 6 p.m. Saturday? Some of these days an enterprising northern white man will go into Atlanta or Montgomery or some other city and start a steam, or electric laundry and the occupation of the washerwoman will be gone.

Washington *Evening Star*, Mar. 18, 1896, 12.

1 BTW spoke before an audience of blacks and whites at the Metropolitan A.M.E. Church on M Street in Washington, D.C.

From Jabez Lamar Monroe Curry

Washington, D.C. 20 March/96

Personal

My dear Sir— Pres. Gilman was much pleased with his interview with you, and he wishes you to *put in writing* your strong views as to the unadvisability, or as you say, "the evil," of this "new departure." I hope you will do so. It will be for his eye alone, and you will lose nothing by this *confidential* utterance. It is important that you write at once, so that he will have it before our Board meets.

I am glad you have such clear & pronounced views as to the folly and wrong of making spasmodic, local, emotional efforts for meeting a great problem. We are moving forward hopefully, systematically, on broad and sure lines, not as fast as we could wish, but safely, surely, *permanently,* and we have the *proofs of progress.*

Such *men* as you & I know what ten years have done. Why cast contempt on our work and spend valuable money for the relief of individual cases or neighborhood suffering? I hope you will *see* Gov Northen[1] and communicate with Bishop Galloway,[2] Jackson, Miss.

Remember me kindly to teachers and pupils. I remember pleasantly & gratefully my last visit. The only drawbacks were your absence and the time wasted in speaking. Yours very truly

J. L. M. Curry

ALS Con. 187 BTW Papers DLC.

[1] William Jonathan Northen (1835-1913) was governor of Georgia from 1890 to 1894. A paternalist in racial matters, he worked after the Atlanta Riot in 1906 to improve race relations in the South.

[2] Charles Betts Galloway (1849-1909) was a Southern Methodist Episcopal bishop. At one time editor of the New Orleans *Christian Advocate* (1882-86), he was a prolific writer on religious and social topics. He was a founder and president of the board of trustees of Millsaps College, Jackson, Miss. He was also a trustee of Vanderbilt University, Tougaloo College, and the John F. Slater Fund.

At the Conference for Education in the South in Birmingham in 1904, Galloway defended the blacks' right to education and legal protection, saying: "We cannot have a democracy for one class of our population, and a despotism for the other." The carpetbaggers, he said, poisoned "the spirit of one race and aroused the fierce antagonism of the other." At the same time, he specified the conditions that whites would insist upon: no social mingling of the races, separate churches and schools, the whites to retain political control, and the blacks to remain in the South as "natives not intruders." (Conference for Education in the South, *Proceedings of the Seventh Session,* 30-32.)

To Hollis Burke Frissell

Tuskegee, Ala. Mar. 24, 1896

Personal and Private

My Dear Dr. Frissell: I deem it fitting to let you know my views regarding the work that the Washington ladies[1] are planning to [do] in connection with the Slater Fund. I had a long talk with both Dr. Curry and Dr. Gilman last week. Dr. Curry feels it considerably that so much stress has been laid upon the work of these ladies in the last number of the Southern Workman. He feels that perhaps the matter has been overstated and unduly emphasised, but this is not the main object of my letter. Until very recently I have not understood fully the plan and scope of these ladies' work, and I am free to say that if I understand it now I do not agree with what they propose to do. When they first suggested the matter of helping I supposed that they were going to help Dr. Curry strengthen the domestic work already being done in the institutions aided by the Slater Fund, but I find their plan to be something different. It seems that if anything has been made clear during the last 25 or 30 years in connection with the missionary work in the South, it is that we must depend for reaching the masses upon the education of strong leaders in central institutions, these leaders of course to go out and reach directly the masses. All of the large religious bodies have more and more dropped off their local work and have concentrated more and more their efforts in larger institutions. You and I both know that when Dr. Haygood had charge of the Slater Fund it was not nearly so effective as it is now for the reason that Dr. Haygood scattered it among too many small institutions whose influence was not felt three miles from the center. At the price of a great deal of hard work, at the risk of incurring much personal dislike, Dr. Curry has moved steadily on the plan of concentrating the fund in a few institutions with the view of turning out stronger men and women. If we are to reach the masses of our people they are to be reached with the young men and women who go out from these larger institutions. I cannot see how the greatest amount of good can be accomplished for the race by spending money in three or four cities in a manner that will reach at most only 50 or 100 individuals when at the same time there will be hundreds of other places entirely untouched. I fear that the plan that the ladies propose working upon is beginning at the wrong end. Dr. Curry I am quite sure has the feeling that in view of the fact that he has stood loyally by Hampton and Tuskegee, that now we ought to stand by him in his plan and not suffer so far as our influence can prevent it, this fund to be scattered and its influence ultimately curtailed. He feels that if these ladies begin scattering money in one or two states very soon it will spread to other states and very soon the money will be scattered and no tangible results come from it. I say, of course confidentially, to you that Dr. Gilman is opposed as strongly as Dr. Curry to this new movement. The matter is to come up at the meeting of the Slater Fund board April 7th and whatever is done must be accomplished before that date.

Mr. George E. Wood[2] is now here helping us in regard to our trade school buildings, etc. Yours truly,

Booker T. Washington

TLS BTW Folder ViHaI. A press copy is in Con. 135, BTW Papers, DLC.

[1] Mrs. Elizabeth C. Hobson and Mrs. Charlotte Everett Hopkins. BTW opposed their suggestion that every southern state should receive money from the Slater Fund to establish several centers for the teaching of domestic science, as already planned for Virginia and Alabama. In the early 1890s, after the passage of the second land-grant college act, Dr. Curry sharply reduced the number of Slater Fund recipients from about forty schools to a dozen. The result was considerably enlarged donations to Tuskegee, one of the favored, and the demise or severe curtailment of the industrial departments in a number of previously supported institutions. BTW always opposed any expansion of Slater Fund activities that might threaten the substantial Tuskegee appropriation. (See Alice J. Kaine to BTW, Nov. 30, 1895, above; *Southern Workman,* 25 [Mar. 1896], 43-44; Meier, *Negro Thought,* 95-96.)

[2] George E. Woods, a New York architect, had drawn up the plans and specifications for Hampton's Armstrong-Slater Memorial Trade School building.

To Daniel Coit Gilman

[Tuskegee, Ala.] Mar. 25, 1896

Personal

Dear Sir: Since my conversation with you a few evenings ago on what I suppose may be termed the "new movement" of the Slater Fund Board, I have decided to put into writing for your eye, the objections to or evils of the new departure.

If the history of the work among our people in the South during the last thirty years has made any one thing clear to all the religious and other organizations having work in the South, it is that the masses of the people are to be reached and helped through the sending out of strong well trained leaders from central well equipped institutions who will show the masses how to lift *themselves up.* All of the religious denominations immediately after the war, began by spending a few hundred dollars in two or three dozen local communities, but they soon learned that such work was not the most effective and soon began the policy of concentration.

This lesson has been learned at great cost. It does not seem wise at the end of thirty years that the Slater Fund Board should repeat the same mistake.

2nd. In this Southern work, nothing is so much to be guarded against as the unwise expenditure of money because conditions in a local community happen to awaken one's sympathy. One on visiting the South for the first time and finding a community where there are fifty families who mortgage their crops and are in debt, and at the same time finds that these families do not know how to sew or cook, is tempted to spend money in helping to pay the debts and in teaching these families how to cook and sew. In this case some temporary good is done, but it is a mere "drop in the bucket." There are half a million families in the same condition. The influence of money thus spent does not radiate three miles from that special community. The same amount of money spent in relieving the local needs of this community, if spent in some central well equipped institutions would educate ten or a dozen selected men and women who would go out and reach a dozen communities and show the people how to raise themselves up.

3rd. The matter of training leaders in the larger institutions is not an experiment. The evidences of the wisdom and value of such concentration are apparent on every hand in the South.

4th. Dr. Curry has given long, careful and patient study to this whole problem in the South and I feel that there is no man in the North or South who understands it in all its ramifications as he does, and I do think that his word and wish in all such matters should have the greatest weight.

As you know when Dr. Curry took hold of the Slater Fund he found the income scattered here and there among dozens of institutions many of which were merely local and inefficient. By a wise and careful policy of selection and concentration he has brought the Slater Fund to the point where its value is being felt in every part of the South. In dropping off a good many small and other inefficient institutions Dr. Curry incurred the personal dislike of individuals in many cases, but notwithstanding this Dr. Curry has bravely carried out his policy and we are now seeing the good results. It would be little short of folly to go over this same road again it seems to me. Not only has Dr. Curry pursued the policy of concentration, but all who have studied and watched the effect of the Peabody and Slater Fund, realize the value of Dr. Curry's policy of using these two funds in a way to *stimulate* institutions to do the best work, letting them understand that they will be helped in proportion as they help themselves. In this way we are fast reaching the point where a few schools will be on their feet to the extent that they can serve as models for others.

5th. The fact that Dr. Curry is a Southern man of broad and liberal views gives him an advantage in dealing with this problem that few realize. The colored people have the greatest faith in him. The Southern whites have the highest regard for him. He speaks to Southern people individually and through the Southern State legislatures and other influential bodies concerning their duty to the Negro in a manner that no other man could do, and his influence and help in this direction is very noticeable and salutary. Thus he is placed in a position to understand the problem in all of its relations, and is of the greatest help to both races. Any change that may result in setting aside or interfering with Dr. Curry's policy I feel would be a *set back* to the whole work in the South. Yours sincerely,

Booker T. Washington

TLpS   Con. 135   BTW Papers   DLC.

To Nathan B. Young

[Tuskegee, Ala.] Mar. 26, 1896

Mr. Young: I am now engaged in reorganizing the various departments of the school for next year. There are some vital matters in connection with your work and attitude towards the school that must be changed otherwise I decide that it is best that your connection with the school cease at the end of the present year. My position in respect to the students and the public is peculiar, and I must see that every one does the highest service in benefitting the students, and must get rid of any obstacle that prevents this result.

In the first place you do not respect authority and this defect is fatal in an institution where the will and policy of the Principal are expected to be carried out even in the remotest corner of the school in the actions of teachers and students through the head of a depart-

145

ment. In the first place, you seem to lack that delicacy of mind that should enable one to detect even without formal order, the policy and wish of the one in charge of the school, and seek without pressure to carry out the policy. This is at the foundation of all successful organized effort. There is no escaping or disregarding it; when we do, chaos is the result. Teachers under you see you disregard or disrespect the requests or wishes of the Principal and they in turn end in treating you the same way, and thus a sure start is made on the road to ruin. To be more clear I give a few examples: Some months ago I asked that special attention be given all through the school to the matter of cleanliness. You did not co-operate in this in a hearty and effective manner. Not only this, but those directly in charge of some part of the cleaning reported to me more than once that you were opposing my policy, and would not co-operate. Almost no attention was given to my request as to the cleanliness, order and attractiveness of the class rooms, etc., until I went into several rooms myself and had the janitor put my policy into effect. Your lack of willingness and co-operation in this matter were apparent all through the school, even now the class rooms, as to cleanliness, care of lamps, etc., are in but moderate condition. During the last two years it has been the policy of the school to give special attention to the examination, grading and classifying of the students in order that our class work may become more *simple and thorough* — so that our students will know what they know. This policy you have not co-operated in carrying into effect until very recently. Last year I took great pains to explain to you and all the teachers my wish in regard to the teaching of mathematics, especially in the teaching of denominate numbers, to have the teachers have the students measure an actual acre, or furlong, or pile one cord of wood, and weigh an ounce, and keep on hand the vessels for measuring a gill, etc. With perhaps one or two exceptions I find that no respect has been paid to this request, and teachers go on about as usual.

Some months ago I announced to the teachers that you and Mr. J. H. Washington would be asked to put into operation the correlating of the literary and industrial work to a larger extent; almost no progress has been made in this as you saw by a letter I sent you a few days ago from the Superintendent of Industries that he expressed himself as feeling that you would not co-operate. Besides this, as many as four different teachers told me in person that you went so far in an academic meeting as to ridicule the use of the term "dove tail" which

I had used. Of course this gave these teachers to understand that your heart was not in the matter. For the first and only time in the history of this institution, I have recently had the experience of having a teacher openly refuse in a public meeting of teachers, to carry out a simple request. This refers to your actions in refusing to make an announcement to the academic teachers in regard to uniformity in marking. So to-day you stand before the body of teachers in open defiance of my wish. Had nothing else ever occured that alone would be sufficient reason for this communication. No institution that tolerates such actions on the part of teachers, and especially a member of the Executive Council where there should be none but the most trusted and loyal, is fit to live.

Another thing that needs close attention, is more systematic oversight of the work of teachers with a view of bringing about uniformity to a larger extent in aims and methods. To bring about a change in this matter, one will have to speak frankly, directly and plainly to teachers regardless of whether he secures their good-will or ill-will. The time to correct such evils is *at the time*. There is some good teaching now being done and some very poor teaching; much of the poor teaching you should have corrected before now or reported the individuals to me. I depend upon you for this, and if you do not correct evils or report them promptly to me the teaching will mean little. To illustrate I give below an extract from Mrs. Logan's report to me of Mr. Hoffman's[1] class work:

"Mr. Hoffman, Botany. Subject, Roots. 'What are roots?' Answer. 'Mistletoe!' Not systematic, not full, evident lack of plan. Class kept only about 12 or 20 minutes. Another class. Botany. This class seemed uncertain about the work assigned; roots finally agreed upon as the subject, but the lesson began with a lichen. Then the invisible flower was discussed upon a little. Roots were taken up after all. Language of teacher and class inaccurate and often incorrect. Lack of system in recitation. Few of the class called upon for any part of the lesson. No board work at all, very little accomplished. This is about what was observed each time the classes in botany were visited."

You should have had this poor teaching stopped or reported Mr. Hoffman to me. Neither has been done, and the poor teaching continues. To stop at once such poor teaching is one of the main duties of the head teacher.

No teacher does himself justice to remain connected with an institution with whose methods and policy he cannot give the hearty, earnest and conscientious co-operation. What is in a man's heart is not long in showing itself in an unmistakeable manner to the outer world.

To be still more plain, the impression prevails to a large extent that you are not loyal to the work of the school.

When one is not happy and hearty on his work, his spirit of fault finding, sourness, complaints, insinuations, soon spread among other teachers and they as a result of the contagion form themselves into groups and with this spirit in them can not render the best service. In such a case there is but one thing to do, for it costs no more to pay teachers who have the right spirit than those who have the wrong attitude.

Thus I think I have put matters clearly before you. In justice to you as well as to the school I have thought it best to be very frank for in no other way can one person understand another.

One trouble with you is that you worry and chafe unnecessarily especially over the matter of criticisms and suggestions. If one has the feeling that it is degrading to receive suggestions, orders, or criticisms, he will always be unhappy and lose a large percent of his usefulness.

I do not send this communication expecting argument or refutations, for I am convinced of the justice of my position and have made up my mind [what] to do.

If after patient consideration you can see your way clear to make a complete change in all the matters to which I have referred, I shall be glad to have you retain your present position — otherwise it is best it be vacated at the close of the present school year, June, 1st, 1896.

I would not be doing my duty to the school did I permit the present state of things to exist, especially in view of the fact that I am compelled to be away from the school a large part of the year and I am compelled to perform my work almost wholly through the members of the Executive Council and there must be only such persons as I have my complete confidence in and share my desires as to the policy and work of the institution.

In making the foregoing statements I do not overlook for a moment the many points in which you do your work well — especially in regard to promptness, business-like methods, and several other matters that I might mention in which you give satisfaction. With the defects to which I have referred out of the way, there is no reason why you should not prove of the highest service to the institution, but I repeat that it is best in the long run to be very frank as it saves trouble and misunderstanding. Yours truly,

Booker T. Washington

TLpS   Con. 135   BTW Papers   DLC.

¹ John Wesslay Hoffman.

From Andrew F. Hilyer[1]

Washington D.C., Mch 28/96

My Dear Mr. Washington— Yours of the 26th acknowledging receipt of Nash. Times and referring to letter in Wash. Post criticising your Bethel Literary Speech[2] just received. I did not send you the paper containing the article in question because I feared that you, not knowing its inconsequential source, might be unduly annoyed by it. I hoped that it would escape your notice. I do not know the author. But have seen the name signed, several times before, to discordant screeds pertaining to the Race question. I can imagine circumstances similar to this under which your annoyance would be justifiable. But I do not think the present case is one. It is always annoying to be misunderstood when there is no excuse for it, and exasperating to be wilfully misrepresented; but they are incidental to a career like yours. In the present instance the writer was so hard up for something to criticise that he drives his peg and then hangs his argument upon it. He states in his letter that he was not present and did not hear your speech but read it as reported in the papers. This discounts his statements. I did not think it worth a reply nor did any of your friends here, as no one has noticed it and it has fallen flat.

I can assure you, on the other hand, that your speech made a profound impression in Washington. You amply justified the best expectations and you and Tuskegee have made a host of friends here. The article in question will do you no harm whatever. All such opposition will tend to unite and awaken your friends. I have the photos, magazines &c you so kindly loaned me for my Star article and was about to return them to you as requested. But I determined to keep them a while longer and in a little while, perhaps after Congress adjourns I can get them used in an article in some other paper. My kindest regards to Mrs. Washington, tell her I asked for some more of her Leaflets, but have not received them. Fraternally yours.

Andrew F. Hilyer

ALS   Con. 119   BTW Papers   DLC.

¹ Andrew F. Hilyer was born in slavery in Monroe, Ga., and educated in Omaha and Minneapolis. He received his A.B. from the University of Minnesota and his Bachelor and Master of Laws degrees from Howard University in the early 1880s. At that time he began his long career as an accountant in the U.S. Treasury Department. An active participant in the Bethel Literary and Historical Association, Hilyer in 1892 founded the Union League to promote the "moral, material and financial interests of the colored people . . . by encouraging a spirit of practical cooperation." (Meier, *Negro Thought,* 45.) Until 1900 he published a directory of black workers in Washington, hoping it would facilitate their employment in black businesses. In addition, Hilyer was a trustee of Howard University, a member of the National Negro Business League and the NAACP, and was secretary to the executive committee for the Negro exhibit at the Jamestown Exposition in 1907.

² As Hilyer observed, Thomas A. Sembly, a waiter, misconstrued BTW's remarks, charging him with saying that "the colored man's lack of inventive genius accounts for his non-recognition by the whites" and "that the negro is incapable of utilizing his brain to pecuniary advantage." (Washington *Post,* Mar. 21, 1896, 11.)

To Elliston Perot Morris

[Tuskegee, Ala.] Mar. 30, 1896

My Dear Sir: I visited Christiansburg Mar. 21st as suggested by you.

In one respect I found an improvement as compared with my last visit. This improvement was noticed in a slight advance in the scope and amount of industrial work, especially was this true of sewing and cooking. The attendance was not quite up to the previous years for the reason as the teachers told me, that the people for local reasons had been poorer during the last two years.

The thing that I would criticise most adversely is the want of cleanliness, thrift, order. There were almost no signs of thorough sweeping, dusting, scrubbing, keeping up repairs, etc. These are the lessons that our people need.

There is still too much tendency toward the superficial or top heavy work. The industrial is not given an equal chance with the literary work.

Now as to the question as to whether the school can be broadened and made more effective as you desire at Christiansburg. There are some obstacles but I believe that a much more effective work could be done at Christiansburg than is now being done. If I could choose a place to start a new school I should not choose Christiansburg, but should put it in the heart of Georgia or Alabama or Louisiana, or where there were more colored people and where they are more needy. But the main reason I should select a new field is the fact of Capt. Shaffer's[1] stand. He does not oppose the school actively but he is not actively in favor of it. I cannot but feel that his neutral position in view of his past interest in the school and in view of his large influence all through that region, is hurtful. Still if the present property cannot be disposed of, the next best thing is to make the best of things as they are at Christiansburg. While I hardly think it possible for the work to be developed to the point that your board has in mind, I do think it possible with the right man at the head for the work to be put on a much more effective footing, especially along industrial lines. The industrial work made strong and effective would go a long way toward counteracting Capt. Shaffer's indifference.

If you still favor the plan, I see no reason why the Tuskegee school could not take hold of the school at Christiansburg in the way you suggested when I was there, but to bring the school up to the point of efficiency that you outlined to me would require an expenditure of $1,800 or $2,000 a year. At first a large proportion of the additional amount would have to go into repairs, outfit, etc. I have a first rate man in view for the position of Principal in case you decide to make the change. The man that I refer to, would I think soon bring about a new state of things. The teachers now there, except the principal, seem to be persons that could be moulded into new channels. One or two more additional teachers would be needed. I should like to hear the decision of your board as early as possible as it will not be easy to secure good teachers after April.

If I can be of further service please use me.

Unless necessary I prefer that my name not be used in connection with this report. Yours truly,

Booker T. Washington

TLpS   Con. 135   BTW Papers   DLC.

[1] Charles S. Schaeffer (1830-99) of Germantown, Pa., became an administrator of the Freedmen's Bureau after the Civil War. Stationed in Christiansburg, Va.,

he took an active part in aiding blacks by establishing a school and also by preaching at black Baptist churches. Schaeffer supported the school out of his own pocket after the Freedmen's Bureau was dissolved. Gradually the administration of the school came under the control of the Friends' Freedmen's Association of Philadelphia, and Schaeffer withdrew from active participation in its affairs in order to concentrate on his role as minister.

From Timothy Thomas Fortune

Atlanta, Ga., March 31, 1896

Dear Mr. Washington: *Our friends in the north* want me to establish a newspaper here which shall cover the whole South and which they will back until I can get it on a paying basis.

You know my opinion of longer residing in the north. I write now because you are my good friend and I want your candid opinion of the undertaking. We shall not abandon *The Age*. It will do in the north what we do in the South with the *Southern Age*. If I go into the undertaking I shall want your active support in all directions, and if you approve of it I wish you to dictate *at once* a letter to the paper expressing your approval of the movement and stating in your way the work it can do for the good of the race.

I wired Mrs. Matthews yesterday to come here because I need her help in the project. With kind regards for you and Mrs. Washington, Your friend

T. Thomas Fortune

ALS   Con. 119   BTW Papers   DLC.

From William Edward Burghardt Du Bois

Wilberforce, O. Wednesday, 1 April 96

Dear Mr Washington: I have been for some time seeking a leisure hour in which to answer you[r] kind letter of the 17th January — but leisure hours are scarce here. I feel that I should like the work at Tuskeegee if I could be of service to you. My idea has been that there might gradually be developed there a school of Negro History and social investigation which might serve to help place, more and more, the Negro problem on a basis of sober fact. I think that in time various northern colleges like Harvard, Chicago, Johns Hopkins, and the U. of Penn. would join in supporting such a movement. What do you think of it?

At present I do not know just how I could be of service. I can teach most primary and secondary branches — preferring of course, History, Economics, Social Problems, &c. It seems to me that some elementary courses in these lines would be needed at Tuskeegee. I have had an indication that I may possibly expect an offer from the Univ. of Pennsylvania to conduct an investigation as to the condition of the Colored people of Philadelphia, for a year. This, it might be, would [be] a good introductory year's work after which if needed I could come to Tuskeegee and perhaps have the active aid of a great college like the Univ. of Penn. In any case I am willing and eager to entertain any proposition for giving my services to your school. As to salary I know the embarrassment of all southern schools: at the same time I shall, in the future, have to care for two i.e. I expect to marry this spring.

Hoping to hear from you at your convenience, I remain   Sincerely Yours,

W. E. B. Du Bois

ALS   Con. 116   BTW Papers   DLC.

From Charles William Anderson[1]

Albany, New York   April 1st 1896

Dear Sir: Let me inform you that your bill went to the Governor on yesterday, and was signed this A.M.[2] I assume from your letter and the Governor's conversation, that you have a perfect understanding with the commission — therefore I have thus far exercised my offices in pushing the bill through, and have said not a word to the members of said commission. As the bill is now a law, you can proceed. Yours Truly,

Charles W. Anderson

ALS   Con. 116   BTW Papers   DLC.

¹ Charles William Anderson (1866-1938) was probably born in Oxford, Ohio, though the 1870 census indicates Tennessee. He attended public schools in Oxford and Middleton, Ohio, the Spencerian Business College in Cleveland, and the Berlitz School of Languages in Worcester, Mass. Anderson moved to New York City in the late 1880s and in 1890 was a gauger in the customs house. From 1893 to 1895 he was private secretary to the state treasurer, and from 1895 to 1898 chief clerk in the state treasury. He was supervisor of accounts for the state racing commission from 1898 to 1905. At BTW's suggestion, President Theodore Roosevelt appointed Anderson collector of internal revenue in 1905 for the district that included Wall Street. In this responsible post Anderson performed so well that he remained in office for ten years, being among the last of the black Republican officeholders removed by President Wilson. Anderson again served the state of New York as supervising agent of the agriculture department from 1915 until 1922. In that year President Harding appointed him collector of internal revenue in the third district of New York City, and he served in the post until retirement in 1934.

An important element in Anderson's political preferment was his party activities. From the time of his arrival in New York in the 1880s until his retirement, he was the principal organizer among black Republicans. He was a founder and longtime president of the Colored Republican Club of New York City, for which he established a clubhouse and affiliation with other black Republican clubs that he organized in the rest of the state. He was for ten terms a member of the New York state Republican committee, and a delegate-at-large to three Republican national conventions. In the 1904 convention, Anderson was the floor manager of the pro-Roosevelt black delegates under BTW's leadership.

Anderson's friendship with BTW, which began about 1895, continued and deepened until BTW's death in 1915. Anderson and BTW were not only political allies but close personal friends, Anderson's humor and wit helping to relax the stiffer BTW. Washington promoted Anderson's political career, and Anderson reciprocated with many favors. Anderson shared BTW's conservative outlook, or at least his political orientation, and he aided the Tuskegean in New York by keeping a close watch not only on anti-Washington groups but on those who were favorable to Washington but who acted in ways that would embarrass the chief. Anderson was a self-made man with a limited education, but his hard work and sharp intelligence made him one of the most successful black politicians of his day, a leader of the New York black community.

² By an act of the New York legislature, the state gave to Tuskegee Institute the property of the New York exhibit at the Atlanta Exposition. Anderson's good offices in arranging for this began a lifelong close friendship with BTW.

To the Faculty Committee on the Course of Study

[Tuskegee, Ala.] Apr. 3, 1896

To the Committee on Course of Study: I have examined with some care the course of study as outlined by you for the coming year. The changes already made by you are in the direction that I have indicated as being desirable on several occasions in the various teachers meetings, but I am convinced that still more decided changes need to be made in the direction of giving the students fewer studies so that they can concentrate more of their time and strength upon the studies that are more fundamental, especially do I wish this to apply to the students in the lower classes. With this in view I wish the committee just as soon as possible to go over the entire course of study again, and just as soon as this has been done please submit it to me. I make the following suggestions: Writing wants to be given a prominent place, also spelling with a regular text book. Geography and language lessons I think should be taken out of the C Preparatory classes. I do not think anything will be gained by dividing the Preparatory classes into grades and shortening their periods of recitations. I am convinced that more good can be accomplished by giving them as much time as they are now having upon a few studies and that the work should be so planned that one teacher can have charge of one study running through all of the classes just as far as possible. The B Middle class it seems to me at present still has too many studies. I also wish you to arrange for the Seniors to elect certain studies by the advice and consent of the Council in the Senior year. Nature study as it is now taught I do not think should be given a place. I also wish the committee to consider whether or not it would not be well to arrange in some way for the teaching of mental arithmetic. It is my request that the committee concentrate as much of their time on this work early next week as possible. Most of these suggestions are based upon fourteen years of experience. Some things these years have settled and we are now to the point where I do not think we should waste time in making mistakes that we have previously corrected at great loss to the school. The committee should consider seriously whether or not we could afford to give vocal music to the students in the preparatory classes, if it is going to deprive them, as now seems the case, of time that should be spent in getting hold of the more fundamental studies. I wish the committee would be a little more definite in mapping out the course of study not leaving so much in foot notes.

Booker T. Washington

I wish the committee to consider whether it is wise to give the Bible and rhetoricals to the very low [classes?].

TLpS Con. 135 BTW Papers DLC.

From Elliston Perot Morris

Philad[elphia] 4 mo 3.1896

Esteemed Friend   I telegraphed Wednesday night — *my* belief that the plan named in your Report could be carried out, and also wrote by that nights mail. The Friends Freedmens Assn Board were notified to meet today, and your report was then read to them; they continue to wish to place Christiansburg under your Tuskagee care & oversight, & feel sanguine of success, and that they can agree to furnish Two Thousand Dolls p[er] Ann[um] besides the free use of the School Building there. We all feel that when we had the subject under consideration at the Providence Building a month or two ago, that the 20th of this month was named as the date of our Annual Meeting, & we feel a *promise* was kindly *given,* that you would arrange to be there. The Phila Yearly Meeting of Friends is a large body whose sessions commence on April 20th and many are in the city, especially from the states of Pennsylvania, New Jersey & Delaware. Monday Evening is always the day for holding the Freedmens Annual Meeting, and all other evenings of the week are occupied by other organizations. We all feel that much depends upon your presence *that night,* whether we can put new life into the cause, or only partially revive the work of this once large & effective organization. Do not let me urge too strongly, but *I* & *we all* feel it *most important* for the cause, that *you* shd be with us. I telegraphed again today after the Board meeting. Your telegraph did not reach here till *after* the Board had adjourned. Please *think it well over again* & *wire reply,* for we want timely notice to be given to secure a *full* house, I am very truly

Elliston P. Morris

I would add that we shall expect to bear your expenses.

ALS Con. 119 BTW Papers DLC.

From George Washington Carver

Iowa Agr. College   Ames Ia   4-3-96

Dear Sir: I have just returned from a lecture tour and found your letter awaiting me.

I will finish my masters degree in scientific agr. this fall, and until then I hardly think I desire to make a change, although I expect to take up work amongst my people and have known of and appreciated the great work you are doing. Mississippi has been negotiating with me for some time (Alcorn A. &. M.). I was ready to go this spring, but a long line of exp. work has been planned of which I will have charge and from the educational point of view, I desire to remain here until fall. Very respectfully

Geo. W. Carver

P.S. Should you think further upon this matter I can furnish you with all the recomendations you will care to look over.

ALS   Con. 115   BTW Papers   DLC.

From Oscar Wilder Underwood[1]

Washington, D.C. April 4, 1896

Dear Sir: Your letter of the 1st inst. received this morning. Mr. Aldrich[2] stated to me two or three days ago that he was willing to ask the Speaker[3] that the bill in favor of the Tuskegee and Montevallo schools might be called up by unanimous consent for passage. If he can do this I have no doubt that I can get the bill through on the floor.[4] I am satisfied that although Gen. Wheeler is anxious to get some relief for his school at Florence, he will do nothing to prejudice the passage of our bill. Yours truly,

O W Underwood

TLS   Con. 112   BTW Papers   DLC.

[1] Oscar Wilder Underwood (1862-1929), a Democrat from Birmingham, Ala., served in the U.S. House of Representatives from 1895 to 1915 except for a brief

time in 1896 when his seat was contested by Truman H. Aldrich. He was senator from Alabama from 1915 to 1927.

2 William Farrington Aldrich.

3 Thomas Brackett Reed (1839-1902).

4 As a member of the Committee on Public Lands, Underwood recommended passage of the Tuskegee Institute land bill (H.R. 4706) on Feb. 15, 1896, stating that "Similar bills have passed Congress in aid of schools in other states." (*House Report,* vol. 2, 54th Cong., 1st Sess., 1895-96, RG233, DNA.)

From William Edward Burghardt Du Bois

Wilberforce, 6 April, '96

Dear Mr. Washington: I have been wanting to have you as my guest when you visit the University in June but living in the building as I do I had no place. My friend however, Lieutenant Young[1] of the US. Army, and mother, cordially unite in inviting you thro' me to be their and my guest at their residence. Answer at your convenience and let us know when you arrive that we may meet you. Sincerely,

W. E. B. Du Bois

ALS   Con. 116   BTW Papers   DLC.

1 Charles Young (1864-1922) was the most successful of the early black graduates of West Point in forcing reluctant whites in the Army to grant him the rank his services warranted. Born in Mayslick, Ky., he moved with his family nine years later to Ripley, Ohio. He studied in the public schools, Wilberforce University, and at the U.S. Military Academy from 1884 until graduation in 1889, when he was assigned to the black Nineteenth Cavalry on frontier duty in Nebraska and Utah. From 1894 to 1898 he taught military science, French, and mathematics at Wilberforce. Young returned to the Tenth Cavalry during the Spanish-American War and participated in its rescue of the Rough Riders at San Juan Hill; he also served in the Philippines. From 1912 to 1915 he was military attaché in Liberia, where he reorganized the Liberian Frontier Force into an effective military unit. He also commanded a squadron in Pershing's punitive expedition against Pancho Villa in Mexico. When the United States entered World War I, confronted with the problem of what to do with a full colonel who was black, the Army solved its dilemma by relieving Young of duty on account of ill health, June 22, 1917. The Army claimed that Young's case of Bright's disease would incapacitate him, but Young rode on horseback from Wilberforce, Ohio, to Washington, D.C., to protest and to prove he was healthy. Black public opinion was so stirred by the episode that Young was recalled to duty on Nov. 6, 1918. In 1919 he returned as military attaché to Liberia, where he died of "blackwater fever."

To William Boyd Allison

Tuskegee, Ala. Apr. 10, 1896

Personal and private

Dear Sir: I am not active in politics and do not expect to be, and have no claim upon your time or attention. I simply write to assure you that I am doing in a rather quiet way whatever I can in connection with our mutual friend, Mr. Clarkson, to bring about your nomination for the presidency at the St. Louis Convention. I am basing my action on the ground that I consider you a wise, conservative and sincere leader, & one who can be depended upon to do the right thing in connection with the interests of the race to which I belong. Yours truly,

Booker T. Washington

TLS   William B. Allison Papers   Ia-HA.

From George Washington Carver

Ames, Iowa, 4-12 1896

My dear Mr Washington: Yours of 4-1 just received, and after a careful consideration of its contents, I now venture a reply. It is certainly very kind of you to take the interest you have in me.

Of course it has always been the one great ideal of my life to be of the greatest good to the greatest number of "my people" possible and to this end I have been prepareing my self for these many years; feeling as I do that this line of education is the key to unlock the golden door of freedom to our people.

Please send me catalogues and any other data you may have with refrence to your institution, so I may get some idea of the present scope of your work, and its possible and probbable extension.

I should consider it a very great privilege to have an interview with you, but cannot say if I will be in the west or no. As among the prospective locations I accepted a position within the shadow almost of your own institution, and nothing more remained to be done but the election to the chair, but said election was defferd until spring, and will take place very soon now. So if you are prepared to make me an offer now it shall receive my first consideration.

I am so glad you met our dear Bro. Marshall. I dearly love him.

Should I not accept the position above mentioned I will be here at the college all summer except when my occupation calls me away.

At the next writing I hope to give you a more deffinite answer.

May the Lord bless you and prosper your work.

Geo. W. Carver

ALS Con. 116 BTW Papers DLC.

To John Gale[1]

[Tuskegee, Ala.] Apr. 14, 1896

My Dear Sir: As you know your daughter[2] has been a teacher in this institution since last September. I have just been forced to ask for her immediate resignation, and I deem it fitting to acquaint you with the facts in connection with this matter. First, it is but right to say that in her class work we have found her efficient and very promising. Almost from the first we found her inclined to associate on terms of too much freedom with the young men who are here as students. You can easily realize that in an institution like this a line must be drawn between teachers and students in many respects, otherwise teachers have no influence over the students. Owing to her youthfulness and want of experience on more than one occasion I talked to her personally about this mistake, and she has been talked to from time to time by our lady principal, my wife and others concerning this same matter, and each time she has promised that she would not be guilty of the same mistake again. In all I am sure she has been spoken to five times by various officers concerning this offense. Last Saturday night she remained off the school grounds clandestinely in company with a young man student at least two hours in direct violation of the policy of the school. When spoken to about her action in this respect she was guilty of outright deception and falsehood. There is not the slightest doubt about the truth of this statement and I think she will be frank enough to tell you herself she was guilty of not only making the mistake of persistently associating improperly with students but of deception in connection with her action last Saturday night. I think it will do her good for you to insist upon her telling you the whole truth concerning this matter. You cannot realize how deeply it pains me to be compelled to take this action. Only a few days ago I had told her that we should be glad to give her employment during the coming school year. This I should not have done had I not felt that she could be of great use to us next year. It is due your daughter to say that in connection with this matter there is not the slightest suspicion of any immorality in this matter, no one feels that there is the least ground for any such thought. I hope you will excuse the liberty I have taken in speaking so plainly to you in this matter, but I have done as I should like one to do me if I were placed in the same circumstances. Yours truly,

Booker T. Washington

TLpS   Con. 135   BTW Papers   DLC.

¹ John Gale was a florist in Tewksbury, Mass.
² Annie F. Gale taught freehand drawing and physical culture at Tuskegee during the 1895-96 school year.

To Charles Lives Marshall

[Tuskegee, Ala.] Apr. 16, 1896

Dear Mr. Marshall: You perhaps know something about the Christiansburg Institute at Christiansburg, Va., of which Mr. H. H. Thweat has been principal for some years. That school hereafter is to be under the direct control of this institution, and the teaching force which now numbers four or five is to be enlarged to six or seven persons. Mr. Thweat is not to be principal after this year, and we have decided to ask you to become principal of this school. The salary we will offer you will not be a very large or tempting one, but this new field will be a very good one for excellent work. If you are at all inclined to accept this work let me know and I shall give you the facts concerning the salary, work, etc. Yours truly,

Booker T. Washington

TLpS   Con. 135   BTW Papers   DLC.

To George Washington Carver

[Tuskegee, Ala.] Apr. 17, 1896

My Dear Sir; Yours of April 12th is received and I hasten to reply.

First, I would say that, the John F. Slater Fund Board trustees have decided to establish an Agricultural School in connection with this institution and the plan for the building is now being gotten out by an architect who was sent here for that purpose a few days ago. It will certainly be the best equipped and only distinct agricultural school in the South for the benefit of the colored people. In a conversation with one of the members of the Board a few days ago when in New York, it was his idea that we should be compelled to get a white man to take charge of this department as he thought there was no colored man in the country fitted for such work. You perhaps know that at present all of our teachers are of the colored race. Now we very much prefer to have a colored man in charge of this new department and feel that you are the man for the work. If we cannot secure you we shall be forced perhaps to put in a white man. We have already in connection with our faculty a gentleman who is well fitted to take charge of the dairying, in fact we have a dairy department now that is in reasonably good condition.

If you are willing to come here we can pay you one thousand dollars ($1000.00) a year and board, board to include all expenses except traveling. This perhaps to you may not seem a large salary, but from the first we have made a policy of trying to get teachers who come not only for the money but also for their deep interest in the race.

I repeat, I do not think you will find a field in the South that offers such effective work as Tuskegee. We have between 700 and 800 students who come to us from 19 states. So far as material is concerned we have the pick of the South. So great is the desire to come here that we refuse admission to about as many students now as we admit.

If the terms I have named are not satisfactory we shall be willing to do anything in reason that will enable you to decide in favor of coming to Tuskegee. We have secured over half of the money for the Agricultural Building and will doubtless get the other within a few months. Your decision to come to us would push the matter much faster. Yours truly,

Booker T. Washington

TLpS   Con. 135   BTW Papers   DLC.

A Memorandum

Tuskegee, Ala. April 18, 1896

Hereafter families having girls living with them whose names are on the school roll, will be expected to have head of family accompany the girl to and from chapel at night whenever the boys and girls are permitted to go together. In cases where families find it more convenient, they can send the girls to Alabama Hall to fall in line under the same regulations as the girls now living in Alabama Hall.

Families whose girls attend night school are cautioned to use every precaution possible to see that the girls get safely to and from night school. Where this matter is not given strict attention, families cannot expect to retain girls who come to the Normal School.

Booker T. Washington

TLS Con. 116 BTW Papers DLC.

From John Gale

Tewksbury, Mass., Apr. 18, 1896

Dear Sir, Yours of the 14th inst. was received today, but it pained me to learn that my daughter's leaving the institution was under such undesirable circumstances. I was sorry to hear that she had so often violated the rules of the institution, but more than all was I grieved to know that she had been found guilty of deception. Ever since she has been old enough to know the right from the wrong, I have *never* in any instance found her guilty of the sin of falsehood, and this is the first instance in which she has ever been complained of for such an offense.

I heard from her last week and she spoke of getting on nicely and spoke of her re-appointment if she so desired, so it seems as if these five misdemeanors which you spoke of, must have come quite close to-gether.

My daughter, not-with-standing having been entirely educated in the north, always was very enthusiastic in the work of enlightening our race. On the street, by pleasant, descriptive talks of the different agencies of nature; at home, by reading pleasing books at gathering[s], and no matter where she was she always seemed to want to impart some of her knowledge to some one less talented than herself.

She is young, and having been raised in the north, naturally her habits and ways are northern; and you, who have visited the north so frequently, undoubtedly know that the *social* habits are far different here than they are in the south. I have lived in the south, myself and know to a certain extent the difference existing between these two section[s] of the country in regard to the *social* standpoint.

I have done all I could for my daughter in the way of giving her a normal education, and I feel satisfied that she has done her best in the way of instructing, as long as she was in your employment as a teacher.

I know it was hard for her to give up her easy, social manner and take up the cold, formal manners of the south.

My daughter is past twenty-one and is old enoug[h] to know right from wrong, and I do not beleive she would wilfully do what she knew was wrong.

If she has erred I thank you for notifying me.

Will you please answer immediately and state full particulars. Yours very respectfully

John Gale

ALS Con. 117 BTW Papers DLC. Docketed: "Mrs. W. ansd this fully."

From Robert Curtis Ogden

Philadelphia   April 28, 1896

My dear Mr. Washington, The Hon. John S. Durham[1] has for some time pursued a course of historical study with Prof. John Bach Mc-Master, of the University of Pennsylvania, and has recently prepared a course of lectures having to do with the Negro and American history, certain questions concerning Cuba, and other valuable historical sub-jects. I was so much impressed with the importance of Mr. Durham's work that I made an arrangement through Dr. Frissell for the delivery of the lectures at Hampton. They were not treated merely as lectures but a portion was adapted to class-room work, as will partially appear by a scrap from one of Mr. Durham's letters that I enclose herewith.

The opportunities that I have had for understanding the nature and results of Mr. Durham's work indicate it to be very valuable and it has been deeply appreciated at Hampton.

These experiences raise the inquiry in my mind whether the same course could not be very advantageously pursued at Tuskegee and, should you approve, I desire to offer a contribution of $100. that you can apply to securing Mr. Durham's services. The request for his assistance will have to come from yourself and my suggested contribution must be confidential. If the arrangement is made it is likely that you will have to introduce the lectures and studies within a period of about one week. Upon receipt of information that this suggestion meets your approval and is being put into practical operation, I will remit the proposed amount.

I imagine that Mr. Durham would come to Tuskegee for the sum named, $100.00, paying his railroad fares each way, but his entertainment at the School to be without expense. The amount left for him after travelling expenses are paid would of course be very moderate.

On the evening of Friday next, our exhibition here will close. You will have to do your best towards securing influence from your end of the line for free transportation of the merchandise on return. Possibly this may have been already arranged for; if so, it would be well to place the evidence of it in my hands, or Mr. Taylor's, so that we can secure the shipment by the Pennsylvania R.R. Co. from this place. I have an impression that the exhibition here has planted seeds of influence that will bring forth fruit in the future. Yours very truly,

Robert C Ogden

The latter subject confirms my telegram of this date.

TLS   Con. 116   BTW Papers   DLC.

[1] John Stephens Durham (1861-1919) was a black lawyer from Philadelphia and a close friend of BTW. After taking degrees in science and civil engineering at the Towne Scientific School (University of Pennsylvania), Durham was a teacher and then a journalist, becoming assistant editor of the white Philadelphia *Evening Bulletin*. In 1890 he became U.S. consul at Santo Domingo and from 1891 to 1893 served as U.S. ambassador to Haiti and chargé d'affaires in Santo Domingo. Returning to Philadelphia, he gained admission to the bar in 1895. While maintaining a private practice in Philadelphia he studied history under John Bach Mc-Master at the University of Pennsylvania. About 1900 he took a position with the Department of Justice as assistant attorney and represented the United States

before the Spanish Treaty Claims Commission in Cuba. In 1905 he left government service to supervise a Cuban sugar plantation, a position he held until 1910. He tried repeatedly to gain a judgeship in a Spanish-speaking U.S. territory, but was thwarted, perhaps because of his marriage to a white woman. From 1910 to 1913 Durham lived in Munich, Germany, practicing international law and advising American and European interests on investment in the Caribbean. He moved to London in 1913 and practiced law there until his death.

Durham occasionally lectured and wrote on racial themes, urging that blacks receive training in skilled occupations which offered the best chance for independent development. He cooperated with BTW and Emmett Jay Scott in their attempts to introduce sugar cultivation to Liberia in order to give that country a commercial and industrial base.

To Oliver Otis Howard

Tuskegee, Ala. [April 1896]

My Dear Sir: By this mail I send you a marked copy of the New York Age which may interest you.

I am glad to say that our friend in Congress, Mr. Aldrich, with whom I had rather a stormy interview, has changed completely around and has been made to see some of his errors. He is now heartily in favor of our bill and is doing all he can to pass it. I have no doubt but that the bill will pass in a few days. Both Mr. and Mrs. Aldrich are deeply interested in our school work.

I thank you very much for your interest and help in our work. Yours truly,

Booker T. Washington

TLS   Oliver Otis Howard Papers   MeB.

An Article in *Our Day*

[Tuskegee, Ala., April 1896]

OUR NEXT DOOR NEIGHBOR

It is too much the tendency to curse the heathen of another race that is our next door neighbor, and pray and work for the heathen of the same race who are thousands of miles away. Not long ago I heard a Southern clergyman praying in a most earnest manner that the gospel might be sent to the millions in Africa, and just right across the street there were negro families just as much in need of Christ's life as any in Africa, and they had never been touched by the minister.

* * * *

There are numbers of white men in the North and West who pray earnestly that the race problems in the South may soon be solved, who never think of solving the race problem in their own offices, stores or factories. Let the colored boy who sweeps the office or runs errands in a bank or factory feel that one day he may become a clerk or a cashier in the bank or a partner in the factory, and you make a new boy of him. The ambition and the talents of thousands of colored boys and girls are being smothered and cramped, simply because they feel that there is a limit to their aspirations.

* * * *

Said a colored porter to me on a Pullman car a few days ago, when I refused his invitation to take a drink of whisky: "all a colored man can do is to drink whisky and play cards." If that porter could have felt that one day he could become the conductor or a superintendent of a division, how different would have been his ambitions.

* * * *

There are thousands of white men North and South, who pray earnestly for the salvation and comfort of the negro's soul in the future world, who never think of turning over their hand to give the negro a chance to make his body comfortable in matters of public travel and accommodation in this world.

* * * *

Not long ago I heard a white man protesting that he did not want to ride in the same railroad coach with a dirty negro, yet this same white man seemed to forget that between Washington City and New Orleans there is no public place outside a Pullman car, where a colored man is allowed to wash and become clean while traveling.

Let us apply more and more the Golden Rule, "as ye would have men do unto you do ye even so unto them." I fear the negro is ahead of the white man in this.

Booker T. Washington

Our Day, 16 (Apr. 1896), 190-91.

From Timothy Thomas Fortune

New York, May 6, 1896

Dear Friend: I got home yesterday, pretty well used up after the long campaign, and was surprised to find that our people are all broken up over the apparent sweep of the McKinley[1] boom. However, I am in good humor with myself and the rest of mankind. I am still wrestling with that southern newspaper question and shall not decide it until I see my way out. I notice that many of our papers are going to your support against crazy attacks of crazy men controlling unwie[l]dy pens in patent back newspapers.

Unless something drops we shall have McKinley for our candidate. Of course I regret this, as most of our friends are in the other camp. However, it is the fortunes of war.

With kindest regards for you and Mrs. Washington and the youngsters of the dear home. Your friend,

T. Thomas Fortune

ALS   Con. 119   BTW Papers   DLC.

[1] William McKinley (1843-1901), twenty-fifth President of the United States, was the first of several presidents on whom BTW had some influence. Though BTW had worked for McKinley's rival, William B. Allison, for the Republican nomination in 1896, he publicly endorsed McKinley against the Democrat William Jennings Bryan. BTW was mentioned as a possible cabinet member, though there is no evidence that either he or McKinley took it seriously. BTW recommended a number of black politicians for presidential appointments. At the Chicago Peace Jubilee in 1898 he was the President's guest at a luncheon, and later that year he entertained McKinley and a large party of dignitaries at Tuskegee.

From George Washington Carver

Ames, Iowa, 5 8 1896

My dear Sir, Yours of Apr. 27th received and contents duely noted.

It affords me great pleasure to be identified as one of the faculty of Tuskegee.

Now as to the time of my coming my *post graduate* work has been arranged to run through[ou]t the college year which closes in Nov. And I would nescessarily have to readjust my work in some way, if needs be.

As I stated in a former letter I will have some pretty extensive collections along various economic lines to bring down and it requires some little time to get them ready and cary my course of study too; however if vitaly important I can arrange to come at your opening or shortly after.

Please send me your little publication *The Southern Letter,* and charge the same to me and I will settle for it when I come down. Or any other paper that notes the progress of the proposed building and the news in general concerning the school.

May the Lord pour out His choicest blessings upon you, and your work. Yours for Christ

Geo. W. Carver

ALS   Con. 116   BTW Papers   DLC.

To John Henry Washington

[Tuskegee, Ala.] May, 11, 1896

Mr. J. H. Washington: I wish to call your attention to several important matters in connection with our farming. These matters I wish you not only to consider yourself but to lay them before Mr. C. W. Greene.

First, I call your attention to the increased expense in connection with our farming. Formerly the farm manager had the management of the brick yard, stable, fruit growing, etc. Within the last few years we have taken from the farm manager the brick yard, the stable and the fruit growing. All this has greatly added to the school's expense. These changes have been made with a view of giving the farm manager more time to devote more directly to farming, especially to the growing of vegetables. While there has been an improvement in the number of vegetables grown, still we are far from the point of satisfaction. One weakness is, that there is not enough of forcing vegetables, I mean we go too much on the principle of the common farmers all through the South rather than on the principle of wide awake truck gardeners. Hereafter I wish it to be thoroughly understood that we are to plant seeds for vegetables earlier and if the seeds are lost on account of the cold weather the school will bear the expense. It is a great deal cheaper to lose a few seeds now and then than to receive practically no vegetables or very few vegetables during the time that the school is in session.

I also call your attention to the poor plowing that is now being done on many parts of the farm. One has but to examine much of this plowing to see that instead of being deep first class plowing it is merely in many cases just scratching of the ground. This comes about in many cases I think because the plowing is not followed closely and inspected hour by hour by the farm manager. If you will also go into the large field of vegetables near the barn and examine the snap beans you will find that they are suffering for want of work, that the ground is hard about them and it is impossible for vegetables to grow while in that condition. You will also see that the students have pretended to work many of these vegetables and it has not been faithfully and carefully done. This is owing to the fact that they are not closely superintended by the farm manager. The school pays these students just as much for poor work as for good work and it is very hard on our school treasury if we have to pay these students and get very little return for vegetables. No one can examine the vegetables in the field that I have mentioned without getting the idea that I have, that there is a want of forcing our vegetables to the front in the way that first class wide awake truck gardeners do. We still hold on too much to the old worn out methods of farming. I also call your attention to the number of bushes or undergrowth that are springing up on various parts of the farm that detract greatly from the looks of the farm.

You will note that I have called attention before to several of these matters. I hope it will not be necessary to do so again.

Booker T. Washington

TLpS Con. 135 BTW Papers DLC.

From Emmett Jay Scott[1]

Houston, Texas   May 22d 1896

My Dear Sir: I enclose to you under separate cover copies of The Daily Post and Texas Freeman of this city containing references to the Afro American State Fair to be given in this city August 25 to 29. I am vice

president of this association and am commissioned to invite you to
deliver the opening address at the Fair grounds, August 25. Your
reputation is [in] Texas is the very best and I am glad to say that I
am one who has given you the fullest meed of praise for the good work
you are doing for the race. This fair contemplates a representation of
what the race is accomplishing in Texas along industrial and agricultural, as well as along educational lines; and I am sure your sympathies
are in accord with the objects of this project. I shall be very glad to
have a reply at as early a date as possible and almost feel that I'd like
to heartily urge you to accept this invitation. The whites as well as the
blacks of this section are very desirous of having you come to Texas,
and I beg to suggest that it would be a trip that will prove mutually
beneficial. Yours very truly —

Emmett J. Scott

P.S. I shall be glad to have you indicate what your terms and conditions are to come this way.

ALS   Con. 113   BTW Papers   DLC.

¹ Emmett Jay Scott (1873-1957) was BTW's private secretary from 1897 until
BTW's death in 1915. Born in Houston, he attended Wiley College in Marshall,
Tex., from 1887 to 1890, when he left to become a journalist. Scott was a reporter for the white Houston *Post* for three years. In 1894 he founded his own black
weekly, the Houston *Freeman*. Scott managed so well the publicity for BTW's
visit to Houston in June 1897 that a few days later BTW offered him a position
as private secretary. After some indecision, Scott accepted, arriving at Tuskegee
on Sept. 10, 1897. When he reported for work, BTW assigned him two stenog-
raphers and a large stack of correspondence to answer. He had never dictated
before, but by late afternoon Scott presented BTW with the sheaf of letters for
his signature. The chief signed all but two, which he sent back for redrafting, and
commended Scott on his ability to express BTW's thought and style.

Soon Scott became BTW's close friend, confidant, and agent. He scanned the
white and black press for information important to BTW, served as his emissary
on confidential missions, stood as watchdog at Tuskegee during BTW's absences,
and subordinated his own ideas and interests to those of his superior. In 1909 he
was sent as one of three U.S. commissioners to Liberia during that country's diplomatic and economic difficulties. In 1912 the Tuskegee trustees elected Scott the
secretary of the institution.

Scott increasingly carried the load of BTW's heavy correspondence, and many
blacks believed that he went beyond BTW in attacking the Tuskegean's enemies
and interfering unduly in the affairs of black newspapers. Scott's submerged ambition also came to surface in a number of business investments, including the Afro-
American Realty Company of Harlem, the *Voice of the Negro* magazine, the
African Union Company, and the Standard Life Insurance Company.

After BTW's death, the Tuskegee trustees bypassed Scott to make Robert R.
Moton BTW's successor. When the United States entered World War I, Scott

became special assistant to the Secretary of War in charge of black affairs. Scott was an effective go-between but not a leader in this turbulent period of race relations. In 1919 he became secretary-treasurer of Howard University, a position he held for many years.

Scott's dream of personifying the goals of BTW, however, rested on his business activities. He knew the black business community well, for throughout its first fifteen years he was secretary of the National Negro Business League. His chief personal business ventures continued to be in real estate, insurance, and banking, all under black auspices.

Throughout his life Scott was also an active Republican, beginning in Texas in the 1890s, when he was for a time the secretary of Norris Wright Cuney. In the Tuskegee years this political involvement was subordinated to BTW's role as a party leader during his lifetime, but Scott organized his own black faction of Republicans from the 1916 election to the 1950s. In the wake of Woodrow Wilson's segregation policies, Scott worked to organize the black vote for Charles Evans Hughes. Throughout the 1920s and 1930s he served on the Colored Advisory Committee and other committees of the party. In 1941 the Republican party "loaned" Scott to one of its largest financial backers, John G. Pew, president of the Sun Shipbuilding Company at Chester, Pa. This non-union company established an all-black shipyard with Scott in charge. As he directed this work, Scott also organized blacks for the Republican party. When the yard was closed in 1945, Scott retired to Washington, D.C. (Waller, "Emmett Jay Scott.")

From Robert Curtis Ogden

Philadelphia   May 23, 1896

My dear Mr. Washington, I can hardly express my regret that we did not meet yesterday after you left the conference.[1] I was detained from the earlier part of the afternoon session and got in to the meeting just after you had left. I had not the slightest suspicion that you would leave before evening or I should have taken pains to have seen you. Can you not write about the subject upon which you desired to speak to me?

I was interested very much in yesterday's proceedings and in my remarks at the time of presenting the diplomas I gave expression to the thought that is now uppermost in my mind, viz: that there is not now a sufficient comprehension in the minds of the negro population as to the risk of losing the industrial position now held by the race. Of course they need not fear competition in the low grade of agricultural labor, but the higher positions of skilled labor and industrial leadership it seems to me must be grasped within a decade and tenaciously held, or they will be lost forever. Possibly my anxiety upon this point intensifies my feeling concerning it.

I am today in receipt of some very excellent recommendations from Mrs. Washington regarding Mr. Durham's lectures and I hope to make some use of them for his advantage. Yours very truly,

Robert C Ogden

TLS Con. 120 BTW Papers DLC.

[1] The fourth annual conference of Hampton graduates on May 22, 1896, the day after commencement. BTW attended the conference, described the Alabama crop-mortgage system, urged the cultivation of business habits, and at the end of the meeting made a plea for educated young people to devote themselves to the cause of the masses. He said: "Don't let the subject be befogged by the question what kind of an institution a man has been through. Whatever kind it may be, a larger proportion of its graduates should give the force of their educated powers to industrial advancement. When we enter the field of industry, there is where competition with the white race is. And who are standing the brunt of that competition? Our ignorant masses; and it is time for our educated young people to realize that more and more they must bring the force of their education to bear in this direction, or we shall lose our hold on the industries of the country." (*Southern Workman*, 25 [July 1896], 132-37.)

To Jabez Lamar Monroe Curry

Tuskegee, Ala. May 26, 1896

My Dear Sir: In reply to your letter of May 20th asking my opinion regarding the advisability of closing the Peabody Trust, I would say that in a word it is my belief that the Fund will accomplish more good for the South in its present form than in any other. The policy of stimulation — "you do so much for yourself and I will do so much for you" — heretofore pursued by the Trustees of this Fund, has helped the South more than any other one agency. Through the various agencies put in motion by the Agent of the Peabody Fund the South has continually held up before it the highest and best things in education. Yours truly,

Booker T. Washington

TLS   J. L. M. Curry Papers   A-Ar.

From Charles William Eliot[1]

Harvard University, Cambridge, May 28th, 1896

Private

My dear Sir, Harvard University desires to confer on you at the approaching Commencement an honorary degree; but it is our custom to confer degrees only on gentlemen who are present. Our Commencement occurs this year on June 24th, and your presence would be desirable from about noon till about five o'clock in the afternoon. Would it be possible for you to be in Cambridge on that day?

Believe me, with great regard, Very truly yours,

Charles W. Eliot

TLS Con. 116 BTW Papers DLC.

[1] Charles William Eliot (1834-1926) was president of Harvard from 1869 to 1909. He was an important reformer of the American college curriculum. Eliot's racial attitudes were characteristic of many American intellectuals who made a distinction between political equality and social equality. While some black students did attend Harvard during Eliot's tenure, there was no attempt to integrate blacks into Harvard society. Eliot supported BTW's political accommodation as well as industrial education for blacks. Eliot had the ability to rise above his own racism, however, and when BTW received hostile criticism for dining with Theodore Roosevelt at the White House in 1901, Eliot remarked: "I select my companions and guests, not by the color of skins, but by their social and personal quality." (Hawkins, *Between Harvard and America,* 182.) In 1906 Eliot visited Tuskegee Institute on its twenty-fifth anniversary.

To Robert Curtis Ogden

Tuskegee, Ala. May 30, 1896

My Dear Mr. Ogden: I too was very sorry that I missed seeing you at Hampton. I made quite a hunt for you but missed seeing you.

There were two points that I wanted to emphasize concerning Mr. Durham's lectures.[1] In the first place, he has made a very thorough study of the subject of American history in its relation to the progress of the Negro, or turning it around, the Negro's relation to American history. He treated it in a way to prove the value of Hampton and Tuskegee's work showing that we are proceeding along the line of nature. His lectures are also the strongest kind of pleas for what we contend for in our people taking hold of the positions in skilled labor and industrial leadership. I think if at an opportune time, you and Mr. Frissell lay the importance of these lectures before the Slater Fund Board Trustees that they would be inclined to employ Mr. Durham to give these lectures at all of the schools, some 12 in number I think, aided by this Board. I also think it will be well if you could bring such influence to bear on Dr. Gilman that would cause him to issue one of these lectures in pamphlet for[m] under the head of the "Occasional Papers" of the Slater Fund Board, I think you have seen some of these papers. Mr. Durham is a valuable and strong man in all these race matters and we should use him in a larger measure than we have in the past. He seemed happy while here and more than anxious to be placed in a position where he could be of more service to the race than he has in the past. I confess I fell quite in love with him. Yours truly,

Booker T. Washington

TLS Con. 1 Educ. Ser. R. C. Ogden Papers DLC.

¹ The six lectures given at Hampton Institute and Tuskegee Institute were published in 1897 as *To Teach the Negro History: A Suggestion.* Durham stressed the growth of job opportunities for blacks, tracing their development from the jobs available to slaves in the field, in the mansion house, and as skilled labor. Scorning those who still practiced the decadent morality of their slave masters, he praised the mechanics and small businessmen of the black community, contending that they were generally the descendants of skilled laborers. Durham reminded the students that it was the American tradition to start at the bottom, and he urged them to regard their struggle for greater job opportunities as the emancipation movement of their day.

To Charles William Eliot

Tuskegee, Ala. June 1, 96

Dear Sir: Your favor of May 28 informing me of the desire of Harvard University to confer an honorary degree upon me at the next Commencement — June 24, is received. In reply I would say that the information is a great surprise to me. I shall be present at the time you name. Yours Sincerely

Booker T. Washington

ALdS Con. 123 BTW Papers DLC.

From Fannie Merritt Farmer[1]

Boston, Mass. June second 1896

My dear Mr Washington, Miss Lillian Heywood[2] will graduate in our Normal Class of '96. Having had years of practical experience in cookery, and having done excellent theoretical work at our institution I feel [able] to conscientiously recommend her to fill the position of which you write. Very truly

Fannie Merritt Farmer

ALS Con. 116 BTW Papers DLC.

[1] Fannie Merritt Farmer (1857-1915) was director of the Boston Cooking School from 1891 to 1902, when she opened her own school, Miss Farmer's School of Cookery. Her recipes and cookbooks are still widely used in America.

[2] Lillian Heywood was in charge of the teachers' home at Tuskegee during part of the 1896-97 school term.

From Isabel Eaton[1]

Fisher's Island, N.Y. June 10, 1896

Dear Sir, I have just been appointed to a fellowship given under direction of the Univ'y of Penna, by the terms of which I am to reside next year at the Philadelphia College Settlement and from that as a point of appliance am to investigate the "industrial opportunities of the colored population of Philadelphia."

I suppose that you can tell me better than any other man in the country just what are the best things written on the "Negro Problem" in America, and as I hope to make the work count in a practical direction & *hope to* accomplish something for the men in Phila. who are working under all sorts of disadvantages, I have ventured to write and ask you to send me a list of, say, the best half dozen things — (either books or short articles) — to give a good all round idea of the chief aspects of the problem.

With sincere thanks in advance, for the references, I am Very truly yours,

Isabel Eaton

ALS Con. 116 BTW Papers DLC.

[1] Isabel Eaton (d. 1938?) wrote the "Special Report on Negro Domestic Service in the Seventh Ward, Philadelphia," which appeared as a supplement to Du Bois, *The Philadelphia Negro*. A graduate of Smith College in 1888, Miss Eaton received an M.A. from Columbia University in 1898. She worked for many years with the College Settlement Association in New York, Philadelphia, and Chicago.

From Warren C. Coleman

Concord, N.C., June 18 1896

Dear sir: This will inform you that we have decided to erect a Cotton Mill at Concord, N.C. to be operated by colored laborers. The books have been open for subscriptions only a very short time and shows upwards of the amount of $10,000, already subscribed, with a steady increase and a bright future. One southern white man subscribed 21 shares of $100. each and the citizens generally are manifesting great interest and subscribing liberally. We have bargained for a site of 100 acres of very desirable land. We now propose to introduce the subject to the friends abroad for their consideration and support. Knowing you as we do to be a man of worth, talent and influence and one who is interested in the industrial development of the race, we hope that you will help by influencing those around you and by sending us your subscription, not as a donation but as stockholder. Investments in the enterprise would within a short time pay 15 to 20 per cent dividend. We are operating a colored Building & Loan Association in connection. One hundred Dollars is a share. Subscriptions to this may be paid in monthly instalments of $1.00 per share in advance, or 25/100 weekly per share in advance. This is also in a progressive state.

For further information and circulars address

W. C. Coleman

ALS Con. 115 BTW Papers DLC.

From Isabel Eaton

Fisher's Island, N.Y. June 19, 1896

My dear Sir. Please accept my most hearty thanks for your kind and very helpful letter.

I shall certainly write to President Gilman and to Gunton's Magazine as you suggest and I shall consider myself very fortunate indeed if I may have the personal advice of Mr. Durham when I go to Philadelphia. Thank you very much for naming him to me and for suggesting conferring with him. I am sure such a conference will prove fruitful, for I know enough to feel certain that the best friends of the colored race are themselves colored men, just as I have already found the best friends of the working men are themselves working men. It's a matter of understanding and sympathy, and I am sure Mr. Durham will help me to help his own people, as you have so kindly done.

Since you are so kind as to suggest it I will write to you again in the early fall, if I find myself at a loss for the next pointer in the way. I trust that my work may be fruitful of something practical. To study this, or any serious question, for any reason except that something may be *done* to help, seems to me inhuman. With sincerest thanks again. Very truly yours,

Isabel Eaton

ALS   Con. 116   BTW Papers   DLC.

An Interview in the Washington *Post*[1]

[Washington, D.C.] June 21, 1896

I find that a colored man who possessed education and property and character is treated with about as much respect by the Southern white people as a white man under similar circumstances. A good and forceful illustration of this occurred a few days ago in the city of Montgomery, Ala., where the butchers of the city organized themselves into a club for the furthering of their interests. While a majority of the butchers are white Southern men, still two of the members are colored men, both former slaves. In the organization it is interesting to note that one of these colored men was made chairman of the committee on rules and another on an important committee. This recognition of these colored men came about from the fact that by their energy and industry, coupled with common sense, they had secured such a large proportion of the trade of the city of Montgomery that it was not possible for them to be left out of this organization and its purpose carried out; so colored people all through the South will receive such recognition in proportion as they make themselves felt in the business world.

SOCIAL MATTERS CARE FOR THEMSELVES

A man is not going to be invited to join a business organization unless he has business that makes him of value in the commercial world. Of course a colored man is not taken into the families in a strictly social way in the same way that a white man is, but such social intercourse is a matter that will take care of itself, and no sensible man worries about that. There are many things in connection with public travel and other public conveniences that are very annoying at present to the colored people, but I believe all of these will pass away in proportion as the colored people become educated and refined. I believe that the forcing of the colored people to ride in a "Jim Crow" car that is far inferior to that used by the white people is a matter that cannot stand much longer against the increasing intelligence and prosperity of the colored people.

You ask me for some of my personal experiences in connection with my travels. My main work, of course, is on the grounds at Tuskegee. While this is true, especially within the last twelve months, I have been kept away from the school work a good deal by invitations to speak in various parts of the country. While speaking of these invitations, I might add that invitations to speak literally pour in upon me from all parts of the country. Were I to accept one-half of the invitations I receive I would not remain on the school grounds a single day, but I tell all that Tuskegee and its work must be first with me, and I only speak at places where I can have an opportunity of serving the cause of the colored people in some way. I have received recently very tempting offers from the various lecture bureaus to put myself at their disposition for public lectures, but these I have refused.

POLITELY TREATED IN PULLMAN CARS

Speaking of traveling in the South, while in most of the Southern States there is a separation made in the cars so far as white and colored people are concerned, I have found no trouble in securing accommodations in the Pullman palace cars, and what is a curious and interesting fact in connection with this is that, while for the ten years that I have ridden in the Pullman palace cars with Southern white people, I have not in the slightest manner been insulted or been treated in an ungentlemanly way by them. This, I think, grows out of the fact that only the most refined Southern men and women patronize the Pullman palace cars.

A great deal of stress is often laid upon the importance of educating the masses of the colored people in order to solve the problem in the South. Equally as much stress should be laid upon educating the masses of the poor white people because until the masses of the poor whites are educated there cannot be the greatest peace and harmony between the two races. In all my contact and experience with various classes of white people in all parts of this country I have invariably found that it is the ignorant and poorly educated white people who are inclined to turn up their noses at the negro; there is no difference in this respect between the Northern and Southern white people — I mean that the ignorant and poor white man, whether North or South, seems to have a certain amount of contempt for the negro, while the prosperous and intelligent white man is much more inclined to treat the negro in the way that one man treats another.

DINED WITH CHAUNCEY DEPEW

My experience is that the greater a man is the more easy he is to approach. I have had the privilege of meeting President Cleveland, Vice President Stevenson, and all the members of the Cabinet. Only a few days ago while riding on the train in the South, one of the members of President Cleveland's Cabinet heard that I was on the train and he voluntarily sought me out and introduced himself and made himself most agreeable during the entire journey. A few days ago while in New York City I was invited to dine with Mr. Chauncey M. Depew, and I saw nothing about him to indicate that my color was in any degree offensive to him. A few days ago when in the city of Baltimore I was invited by the Mayor of that city to be his guest while in that city. I mention all of these matters not out of an egotistic spirit, but simply to show that the time is fast coming when colored people will be appreciated and respected in all parts of this country just in proportion as they make themselves of value — commercially and educationally, or by reason of their culture and refinement. I emphasize industrial education because I think history teaches that, after all commerce is the great forerunner of peace and civilization.

Washington *Post*, June 21, 1896, 25.

[1] John Gilmer Speed, who conducted the interview, praised BTW for his "abundant common sense rather than any flashing brilliancy." BTW had not become vain following his 1895 Atlanta address, the interviewer noted, though not since Frederick Douglass had a black man "made so deep an impression in the country." (Washington *Post*, June 21, 1896, 25.)

From Martha H. Willis[1]

Tuskegee, Ala., June 21 1896

Dear Mr Washington: I have just left Maggie. She is feeling particularly blue this morning. She is still very weak aside from this I think she is very much better. The thing that will make her well soonest will be to be with you. She worries over your absence a great part of the time.

She wishes me to ask you to send money so that she may come and be with you as soon as she is able to travel. I think she will be very much happier if she is where she can see you. Her honeymoon is not over yet.

She is down stairs now and is looking very well indeed to have been so ill as she was.

She has generally a very good appetite; but to day something seems to have upset her stomach and she does not seem to want to eat, in consequence of it.

Davidson went to Opelika with Mr & Mrs Penney today. Baker is over to the Penney's and I occasionally hear him giving commands. Both of the children are quite well.

I expected my children this morning; but I was disappointed.

I hope you keep well. Do not feel anxious about Maggie now; for she is getting along extremely well. Very Sincerely

M. H. Willis

ALS   Con. 123   BTW Papers   DLC.

¹ Martha H. Willis, a close friend of Margaret Murray Washington, was reported in the 1900 census as a thirty-five-year-old black schoolteacher, widowed, with three children.

From John Stephens Durham

Philadelphia, June 23, 1896

My dear Mr. Washington: I am ashamed that a letter from you should reach me before any acknowledgment from me of my many obligations to you for your many kindnesses to me while your guest in the South and since. I have not been well and I have been seriously disturbed in mind in trying to decide as to my future. Of this, however, I shall speak later in my letter.

I am very glad indeed to have your concurrence with my reply to Bishop Tanner. The great wonder is he should have gone out of his way to endorse any inferior negro standard in scholarship. I think you do yourself a great injustice when you include your case in the same class with that which the Bishop attempts to defend. There can be no doubt that the high mark of recognition which you receive at Harvard University will have the approval of all men familiar with your work. I for one do most heartily congratulate you. Do send me a copy of the newspaper containing the report of the exercises.

I shall be very glad to meet the young woman¹ who comes to do special work among our people here in Philadelphia. I have no doubt the work is in capable hands as I regard Smith² to be thoroughly up to standard. Of course I regret that both Dr. DuBois and Mr. Tucker³ should have been set aside. I know Tucker to be an unusual man. Dr. DuBois has a good record, I believe.

I must shortly decide whether or not I shall make a contract to go to the West Indies to live. On the one hand it means the giving up of much that is dear to me and the abandoning of a career which I have been ambitious enough to hope would some day develop into one of usefulness. On the other hand, it means the opportunity to make some money, where in this country I cannot make my living expenses. You can appreciate my perplexity. I shall let you know my decision as soon as I shall have reached it.

Can you not stop in Philadelphia on your way South? I should be greatly helped by a talk with you, apart from the pleasure which I always have in seeing you. I am, Very truly yours,

John S. Durham

TLS Con. 116 BTW Papers DLC.

[1] Isabel Eaton.
[2] Smith College.
[3] Possibly Miles Tucker, a Philadelphia teacher.

An Address at the Harvard University Alumni Dinner[1]

Cambridge, Mass. June 24, 1896

Mr. President and Gentlemen: It would in some measure relieve my embarrassment if I could, even in a slight degree, feel myself worthy of the great honor which you do me to-day. Why you have called me from the Black Belt of the South, from among my humble people, to share in the honors of this occasion, is not for me to explain; and yet it may not be inappropriate for me to suggest that it seems to me that one of the most vital questions that touch our American life, is how to bring the strong, wealthy and learned into helpful touch with the poorest, most ignorant, and humble and at the same time, make the one appreciate the vitalizing, strengthening influence of the other. How shall we make the mansions on yon Beacon street feel and see the need of the spirits in the lowliest cabin in Alabama cotton fields or Louisiana sugar bottoms? This problem Harvard University is solving, not by bringing itself down, but by bringing the masses up.

If through me, an humble representative, seven millions of my people in the South might be permitted to send a message to Harvard — Harvard that offered up on death's altar, young Shaw, and Russell, and Lowell and scores of others, that we might have a free and united country, that message would be, "Tell them that the sacrifice was not in vain. Tell them that by the way of the shop, the field, the skilled

183

hand, habits of thrift and economy, by way of industrial school and college, we are coming. We are crawling up, working up, yea, bursting up. Often through oppression, unjust discrimination and prejudice, but through them all we are coming up, and with proper habits, intelligence and property, there is no power on earth that can permanently stay our progress."

If my life in the past has meant anything in the lifting up of my people and the bringing about of better relations between your race and mine, I assure you from this day it will mean doubly more. In the economy of God there is but one standard by which an individual can succeed — there is but one for a race. This country demands that every race measure itself by the American standard. By it a race must rise or fall, succeed or fail, and in the last analysis mere sentiment counts for little. During the next half century and more, my race must continue passing through the severe American crucible. We are to be tested in our patience, our forbearance, our perseverance, our power to endure wrong, to withstand temptations, to economize, to acquire and use skill; our ability to compete, to succeed in commerce, to disregard the superficial for the real, the appearance for the substance, to be great and yet small, learned and yet simple, high and yet the servant of all. This, this is the passport to all that is best in the life of our republic, and the Negro must possess it, or be debarred.

While we are thus being tested, I beg of you to remember that wherever our life touches yours, we help or hinder. Wherever your life touches ours, you make us stronger or weaker. No member of your race in any part of our country can harm the meanest member of mine, without the proudest and bluest blood in Massachusetts being degraded. When Mississippi commits crime, New England commits crime, and in so much, lowers the standard of your civilization. There is no escape — man drags man down, or man lifts man up.

In working out our destiny, while the main burden and center of activity must be with us, we shall need, in a large measure in the years that are to come, as we have in the past, the help, the encouragement, the guidance that the strong can give the weak. Thus helped, we of both races in the South, soon shall throw off the shackles of racial and sectional prejudice and rise, as Harvard University has risen and as we all should rise, above the clouds of ignorance, narrowness and selfishness, into that atmosphere, that pure sunshine, where it will be our highest ambition to serve MAN, our brother, regardless of race or previous condition.

PD   Con. 955   BTW Papers   DLC.

[1] BTW was one of thirteen persons receiving honorary degrees at Harvard that day. By custom, the names of recipients were kept confidential until the moment of their announcement, and the students' applause was a measure of their popularity. Washington received applause equaled only by that for General Nelson A. Miles. It was at the alumni dinner that evening, when each recipient made a short speech, however, that Washington shone. According to the later recollection of Roger Baldwin, BTW won his audience by his first sentence: "I feel like a huckleberry in a bowl of milk." (Reminiscences of Roger Nash Baldwin, Oral History Research Office, Columbia University, 1954.)

From Margaret James Murray Washington

Tuskegee Ala   June 24–96

Accept heartiest congratulations from.

Maggie

TWSr   Con. 539   BTW Papers   DLC.

From Mary Elizabeth Preston Stearns

Medford near Boston, June 25th 1896

Dear & Honored Friend. Glory! Hallelujah!

I salute your Race, through the devotion and inspiration of your character wh' has secured this recognition, this triumph of your deservings.

The wise angels of Anne Radcliffe and John Harvard rejoice today, in the crowning achievement of their work for civillization, and humanity. A nearer one; a dearer one holds this crown over your head. My first thought, after you was the Sainted *Olivia. Would* that she might have rejoiced with us for the meaning of that event wh' marks an epoch in History, and adds a new, and needed dignity to our oldest University of learning.

Verily — the "stone that President —— *rejected,* has become the head of the corner" for a true Republic!

My soul is filled with thanksgiving for the new morning dawning for all the children of men; for all the sons and daughters of God.

Present my congratulations to Mrs Washington, and believe me, proudly, with "High Humility" — always your friend

Mary E. Stearns

ALS   Con. 122   BTW Papers   DLC.

An Article in *Our Day*

[Tuskegee, Ala., June 1896]

WHO IS PERMANENTLY HURT

The United States Supreme Court has recently handed down a decision[1] declaring the separate coach law, or "Jim Crow" car law constitutional. What does this mean? Simply that the separation of colored and white passengers as now practiced in certain Southern States, is lawful and constitutional.

This separation may be good law, but it is not good common sense. The difference in the color of the skin is a matter for which nature is responsible. If the Supreme Court can say that it is lawful to compel all persons with black skins to ride in one car, and all with white skins to ride in another, why may it not say that it is lawful to put all yellow people in one car and all white people, whose skin is sun burnt, in another car. Nature has given both their color; or why cannot the courts go further and decide that all men with bald heads must ride in one car and all with red hair still in another. Nature is responsible for all these conditions.

But the colored people do not complain so much of the separation, as of the fact that the accommodations, with almost no exceptions, are not equal, still the same price is charged the colored passengers as is charged the white people.

Now the point of all this article is not to make a complaint against the white man or the "Jim Crow Car" law, but it is simply to say that such an unjust law injures the white man, and inconveniences the

186

negro. No race can wrong another race simply because it has the power to do so, without being permanently injured in morals, and its ideas of justice. The negro can endure the temporary inconvenience, but the injury to the white man is permanent. It is the one who inflicts the wrong that is hurt, rather than the one on whom the wrong is inflicted. It is for the white man to save himself from this degradation that I plead.

If a white man steals a negro's ballot, it is the white man who is permanently injured. Physical death comes to the negro lynched — death of the morals — death of the soul — comes to the white man who perpetrates the lynching.

Booker T. Washington

Our Day, 16 (June 1896), 311.

¹ Plessy *v.* Ferguson, 163 U.S. 537 (1896), established the "separate but equal" doctrine not only in transportation but in public accommodations and education until its overthrow in Brown *v.* Board of Education, 347 U.S. 483 (1954).

From Francis William Fox¹

Westminster England   6 July 1896

Dear Sir   Mr George Dixon² of Great Ayton has kindly favored me with your name & address, thinking you may know of some suitable American who could undertake the superintendence & management of our agricultural Industrial Mission which it is proposed to establish in one of the Islands of Zanzibar or Pemba to employ & train the liberated slaves when we have obtained the abolition of the legal status of slavery in those Islands.

The superintendent would have under him native overseers but he will have to learn Swahili & the Languages.

The climate is much the same as that of the Bermudas in the West Indies.

I should be glad to hear from you by an early post if you know of any individual who would be suitable & who would be disposed to take the management of such an Agricultural enterprise?

He should be a decided Christian man. Yours faithfully

Francis Wm Fox

Since writing the foregoing I have recd your letter of the 26 June to Mr Dixon in which I see you have written about our friend Mr H S Newman.³ Mr Newman is absent on the Continent for two weeks or so. In his absence I may say the salary offered would be about £*150* per annum to commence with some 150 native Africans would be employed on Farm which would be a coconut & cloves plantation.

ALS Con. 116 BTW Papers DLC. Docketed: "Mr. Logan thinks you had better have this letter. Nothing has been done about it. E[stelle] M. J[ackson]."

¹ Francis William Fox (1841-1918) was the son of a banker of Kingsbridge, Devonshire. An active Quaker throughout his life, Fox became an engineer with an international clientele, and this led him into peace activities. A visit to Egypt in 1884 to discuss construction of irrigation works, for example, led to efforts to bring peace in the Sudan and Abyssinia. Fox sought to abolish the slave trade in Africa, and this led to an interest in the agricultural-industrial mission in Zanzibar and Pemba. Fox later turned his interest to Quaker missions in China and to the cause of European disarmament. (De Montmorency, *Francis William Fox.*)

² See above, 2:45.

³ Henry Stanley Newman (1818-1908) was a prominent Quaker of Leominster, England, and justice of the peace in Hereford County. He was editor of *The Friend,* a Quaker newspaper, from 1892 until his death. Newman traveled widely in Europe, America, and Africa. He took special interest in freeing the slaves on the islands of Zanzibar and Pemba.

An Address before the National Educational Association¹

[Buffalo, N.Y., July 10, 1896]

THE INFLUENCE OF THE NEGROES' CITIZENSHIP

Mr. President, Ladies and Gentlemen: The discussion of the educational needs of the South would not be complete without a consideration of the condition and the needs of the seven millions of the race which I have the honor to represent. It is interesting to know the number of suggestions that have been made within the last thirty years looking towards improving the condition, or getting rid of the negro in this country. I remember about a year ago when a ship set sail from the port of Savannah, Georgia, bound for Liberia, Africa, that the news was flashed from one end of this country to the other, "Now the negro problem will very soon be solved in this country as the negroes have decided to return to Africa, the land of their fathers." But those persons who reasoned thus forgot that that same morning down south, before breakfast, at least six hundred more negro children were born. And so the problem will not be disposed of in that way.

I was on a train in the west a few days ago and sat by the side of a gentleman who was very earnest in his endeavor to convince me that the negro after all was fast disappearing in this country; that he was fast being swallowed up by the white man; that he was fast becoming bleached out, as it were, and that after a while there would be no such thing as a negro in America. Now, I do not know as you have noticed it, but the moment it is proven that a man has even 1 per cent. of African blood in his veins, he becomes a negro; he falls to our pile; in the count we claim him every time. The 99 per cent. of Anglo-Saxon blood is not strong enough to overcome the 1 per cent. of African blood; the 99 per cent. counts for nothing and we claim the man. So you see we are a stronger race than you are; we have a greater power of attraction and absorption, and at that rate we will ultimately absorb you. I have a good friend down in Georgia who argues very strongly from the platform, and in the press, that the way to solve the negro problem is to set aside a territory in the West, and put him into it, and let him grow up a race unto himself. Now, there are two slight difficulties about that suggestion. In the first place you would have to build a wall about that territory to keep the black men in; in the second place you would have to build a much higher wall to keep the white man out. In fact, if you were to build ten walls about South Africa, you could not keep the white man out of there if he heard there was any gold in it. No, my friends, none of these suggestions will do. There is but one way to solve the negro problem, as there is but one way to solve all problems. Treat the negro as a Christian gentleman, no more, no less. If you educate his head and hand and heart, he will take care of himself.

But there are reasons why we have some rights here. We are the only people, when you come to think of it, we are the only citizens of this country who ever came here by a special invitation and by a special provision. Your race came to this country against the protests of the leading citizens at that time. Having been so important to the prosperity of this country that we had to be sent for at great inconvenience and expense on the part of yourselves, do you think we are so foolish as to leave now? No, we have a mission here and part of that mission

is to help lift you up; to help make you better; to help you live Christian lives, and wherever you lack civilization to help give it to you.
I suspect you think we have a pretty hard job on our hands. But we
are not discouraged by any means.

But seriously, at Tuskegee, in connection with the work to which I
have given my life, we have from the first tried to make a thorough,
systematic study of the actual condition and needs of the people by
whom we are surrounded, and shape our educational work in a way
to improve and bring up the condition of the people about us. Now,
the temptation is, I think, with educational work, as in all work, to do
that for the people which has been done for people for thousands of
years, very often forgetting the actual need and conditions of the people
by whom we are surrounded. I remember that I was in Boston some
time ago and there talked to a young colored man who was studying
medicine in one of the New England medical colleges. I asked this
young man what branch of medicine he was giving special attention
to and I remember his reply that he was "making a specialty of the
study of nervous diseases." I asked him where he expected to practice
medicine after he finished, and he said he was "preparing to practice
medicine among the colored people down in the Mississippi bottoms."
I said to him, "My friend, did it ever occur to you that not one black
man in a hundred thousand ever has any trouble with his nerves?
Did it ever occur to you that the race in the Mississippi bottoms has
not yet advanced to that delightful stage of civilization where he is
troubled very much with nervous prostration?" Now, do not understand me to say that in the future we are not going to be just like you,
afflicted with nervous prostration and everything else. We may have
it, just as you do now, fifty or a hundred years to come; but fortunately
or unfortunately we haven't gotten there yet.

But what are the actual needs of the people in the black belt of
the South? I refer to those who are on these large cotton, rice, and
sugar plantations, rather than those in the cities and larger towns. A
large majority of the people on these plantations are ignorant, without
habits of thrift. They are industrious but they are in debt; they have
mortgaged their crops to keep them alive and they are attempting to
pay a rate of interest that often ranges from 15 to 40 per cent., and,
of course, they come out at the end of the year in debt. The schools
in the plantation districts are rarely in session more than three months.
The scholars are often taught in places which bear little resemblance

to anything like a school building. Each colored child in this cotton district receives this year from the public fund for his education about ninety cents. I do not know how it is in this state, but I think you will find in the state of Massachusetts that each child has spent on him for his education each year between $18 and $20. Ninety cents for the black boy of Alabama, and $18 for the white boy of Massachusetts.

Now, as to morals and religion. During slavery the people reasoned something like this, "My body belongs to my master, and taking master's chickens to feed master's body is not stealing." One old colored man whom his master caught stealing his chickens said to the master, "Well, now, massa, you's got a few less chickens, but you's got a good deal more nigger."

Now our people are attempting to apply something of that same kind of logic to this mortgage system that obtains in the South, and it is not hard for you to realize some of the results of that kind of reasoning. It is not hard for you to understand something of the moral and the religious condition of the people where so large a proportion of them are forced to be born, to eat, sleep, drink, cook, to get sick and die in one room from year to year. But what is the remedy for that condition of things. If in the providence of God the negro got any good out of slavery, he got the habit of work. In that respect he is different from most of the races among whom missionary effort is made. I know we have a class of people around the railroad stations and the corners of the streets and in the bar-rooms just as you will find among any people. We have some black sheep in our flock as there are in all flocks. I mean to say that the rank and file of our people on these plantations of the South are working along from year to year, but without advancement by reason of their ignorance and want of skill. Their labor is confined to the lower forms. At Tuskegee we are trying to develop the head, and hand, and heart of 800 young men and women in such a way that they will also be able to do what is called higher forms of work. I know in this country it is everywhere regarded as all right for the negro to work at the lower forms of work. There is no trouble about his raising cotton in the Mississippi bottoms; but the trouble comes when the negro attempts to work that cotton — to follow it from the field through the gin up into the factory, and from there up into Massachusetts where it is woven into the higher fabrics. Whenever the negro attempts to enter the shop or factory in the state of Massachusetts where the cotton is manufactured into the form of fabrics, the door of that factory is likely to be slammed in his face. The same thing is true in Georgia and Alabama, so far as these higher forms of the manufacture of cotton is concerned. There is a law or custom, in some parts of the South, that prevents the black man from riding in a first-class car, even when he has a first-class ticket. Let that same black man apply in a shop of the North, where that same first-class car is manufactured, and they will put the black man out of that shop if he attempts to take a part in the manufacture of that first-class car. There is no trouble about the negro working in the pig iron or getting it out of the mine in its raw form, but the trouble comes when he attempts to follow that pig iron until it gets into the form of watch springs. Then the door is shut in his face. We want to bring about such skill, such intelligence all over this country among the black people, that their labor will not be confined as it is at present, to the lower forms only.

Another trouble is that after the negro works he does not know how to utilize the results of his labor. What he earns gets away from him, on these plantations, for whiskey, snuff, cheap jewelry, and in a hundred other ways which I haven't time to mention. I have often gone into these one-room cabins where I have found clocks for which these people have paid, on the installment plan, as high as twelve or fourteen dollars, while everything in that cabin aside from that clock would not be worth that much money. In nine cases out of ten there would not be a single member of that family who could tell nine o'clock from twelve o'clock by that timepiece.

I repeat, what is the remedy for that condition of things? Ten years ago in Alabama I could have shown you a community just such as I have attempted to describe, where the people were in debt, mortgaging their crops, living from hand to mouth, with school three months in the year, taught in a rough-looking cabin. But ten years ago there went out from our institutions men trained in head, and heart, and hand, and they went there at their work in a plain, simple way. These graduates taught these unfortunate people to come to their weekly meetings, and in these meetings taught them how to economize and save money instead of paying it out for whiskey and snuff. Every one of them began, and soon they were building better houses; then they built a school house and had school more than three months in the year. And so that work has gone on during these ten years. I wish I could take you into that community and show you these people almost out of debt, owning their own homes to a large extent; living in houses of three or four rooms with well-cultivated farms and the advantages of church and Sunday school.

I could there show you a community that has been revolutionized in its educational, moral, and religious life. No one gave these people a single dollar from the outside with which to bring about this improved condition. Every improvement took place by reason of the fact that these people had these leaders, these guides, who induced them to make a change in their methods; showed them how to take their money which had hitherto been scattered to the winds for mortgages and whiskey and snuff, and use it in the direction of their own civilization. My friends, if I know anything about this problem in the South, it is that this kind of work is what we have to look to for our salvation. I was in one of these communities six months ago and I saw not only a change like that, but in addition to that I saw one white man in that community, a southern white man who forty years ago owned at least 100 slaves. That white man had been so won over to believe in education that he had taken $400 that year out of his pocket and contributed it towards building an excellent school-house for the colored people in the community. I was on one of these cotton plantations some time ago and I saw an old man, at least seventy years of age, living in misery, filth, and poverty. As I glanced about that old man's surroundings and saw how he was living in a crude log cabin, I said, "My friend, it seems to me that if you were worth your freedom you would have improved during the thirty years that you have been free." And the old colored man looked up into my face and said, "Mr. Washington, I want to improve, I want a change, I want to have something for my wife and children before I die, but, Mr. Washington, I do not know how; I do not know what to do first." That old man looked up into my face and said that, and as I looked into his lean and haggard countenance I realized as I had never realized before, the terrible curse of slavery upon my people. The greatest injury slavery did us, as a race, was to deprive us of the opportunity to exercise the little executive power that we might have had; a slavery, which, had it continued, would have been the destruction of the Anglo-Saxon race. For 250 years we have been taught to depend on somebody else, for food and clothing, for shelter, and for every move we made in life. You cannot expect habits with a growth of 250 years to be gotten out of a race in twenty-five or thirty years. Unless we can educate the children and give the older ones the benefit of good example and wise counsel, you will find little change in the future. However, you will find a great improvement has taken place within the last few years in these communities in the south.

Now, some people have had the idea that all that was needed in the South was some one to organize a Christian church on one of these plantations, and another on another plantation, and they felt that the problem would thus be settled on those plantations. But it was not; no substantial improvements can be accomplished in that way. I will tell you, my friends, that in Alabama — I do not know how you find it here — but in Alabama it is a mighty hard thing to make a good Christian of a hungry man.

You know as a race, we are rather emotional; we have a good deal of feeling about us, and we feel our religion in a way that you do not. I believe the average black man can feel more religion in ten minutes than the average white man can in a day. You beat us in some things, but I believe when it comes to feeling we can beat you. Down south when a person gets converted, we look for him to exhibit a great change in his conduct and make some manifestations of it in a visible form. If he does not do that we become skeptical about his religion and we say, "He has got the white man's religion." Now, this emotional side of our nature rather tempts us to spend a good deal of our time preparing in a certain way to live in the next world, which is all right. But I notice you not only prepare for the next world, but you take good pains to prepare for this world also. That is one of the differences between us. The average sermon you hear preached to the people on the cotton plantations is made up of an imaginary and vivid description of heaven. Our preachers like to preach and sing about living in a great, big, white mansion — that is, these people who live in little log cabins down in this world. They like to think and sing about wearing golden slippers in the next world while they trudge along barefooted in this. On the sugar plantation down in Louisiana they have a song they like to sing which says:

"O, give me Jesus and take all this world —"

and the white man in Louisiana generally takes the black man at his word.

The white man down there gets about all the negro has except his hope and his religion. I do not speak with irreverence; yet, after eating and sleeping with my people and coming into contact with them under all conditions and circumstances night and day for fourteen years on these plantations of the South, I think I have learned this, that the way to teach them to have the most of Jesus in a permanent form is to teach them to mix in with their religion some practical ideas which will bring about an improved material condition. Give them the benefit of well-directed industry, a house with two or three little rooms and a little bank account. The negro can appreciate that as well as a white man does, and in proportion as they mix these things with their religion you will find they have a practical Christianity that is worthy of the name. These are some of the lessons which we are trying to push forward at every opportunity, although we meet with some prejudice. At one time the late Hon. Frederick Douglass was making a great speech in the South and he began to warm up to his subject as only Frederick Douglass could do. There happened to be in an out-of-the-way corner two persons who seemed unusually interested in what Douglass was saying. One was an American, and the other an Irishman. The Irishman said, "Be jabers, who is that making such an eloquent speech?"

The American said, "That is Frederick Douglass, the great negro orator."

"You do not mean to say a negro can speak like that, do you?"

"Oh well, he is not a negro, he is a mulatto, a kind of half negro."

"Be jabers, if a half negro can speak like that what in the world can a whole negro do?"

Now, my friends, I claim that during the last thirty years in which we have been in partial possession of our freedom we have not had an opportunity to become even half men and women. But if we meet with the same help, the same encouragement in the future that we have in the past, we are not only going to become whole negroes, but, what is better, we are going to become whole, helpful American citizens.

But what of your white brethren in the South, those who are still suffering the consequences of American slavery for which you and they are responsible? What was the task you asked them to perform — to return to their desolate homes after years of a relentless war, to face blasted hopes, a shattered industrial system and devastation everywhere. You asked them to add to their burdens that of preparing, in education, politics, and economics, for citizenship, four millions of their former slaves. That the South staggered under the burden, made mistakes; that disappointment in a measure has been the result need surprise no one. This country has never yet realized, has never yet comprehended, its duties to the millions of people in the South known as the poor white people. It needs no prophet to tell the condition of the future when the poor white boy in the country districts of the South is in school but three months a year, and your boy is in school nine or ten months; when the poor white boy in these country districts often has but one dollar's worth of education and your boy $20 worth; when in the south he enters a reading room or library perhaps two or three times a year, while your boy finds a reading room or library in every hamlet, almost every house. The poor white boy of the south hears a lecture not more than once in two or three months, while your boy can hear a lecture or sermon every day of the year. My friends, there is no escape from it, you must help us raise the character of our civilization or else you will be lowered with it. No member of your race, in any part of this country, can harm the weakest or meanest member of my race without the proudest and best blood in the Anglo-Saxon race being degraded. When the South is poor you are poor. When the South is ignorant, you are ignorant. When the South commits crime, you commit crime. Mere abuse will not bring a remedy. It seems to me the time has come when we should arise in this matter above party or race or section into the atmosphere of the duty of man to man, Christian to Christian, citizen to citizen; and if the negro who has been oppressed and denied rights in a Christian land can help you, North or South, to rise into this better atmosphere of unselfishness and Christian brotherhood, he will have indeed a sufficient recompense for all that he has suffered at your hands. So long as there is ignorance among the poor white people of the South, so long there will be crime against the negro and crime against our boasted civilization.

In considering this matter I thank God that I have grown to the point through the opportunity which your generosity has given me and those like me; I have grown to the point where I can sympathize with the white man as much as I can sympathize with the black man. I always tell our students when they go out into the world to work, never to feel themselves above the white man. I thank God that I have grown to the point where I can sympathize with the southern white man as much as I can sympathize with the northern white man. To me

"A man's a man for a' that."

I believe, as a race, we strengthen ourselves at every point in extending this symmetry, for no race can go on cherishing hatred and ill-will toward another race without being lowered and degraded in all of those elements that go to perpetuate a strong, growing, and generous manhood and womanhood. I propose, in other words, that no race or individual shall drag me down by making me hate him.

This problem will work itself out in the South in proportion as the negro's skill and intelligence and character can produce something the white man wants or that the white man respects; hence the value of industrial education. One race respects another in proportion as it contributes to the markets of the world. When you consider that question closely, one white man don't care a great deal about another white man unless he has got something that he wants in the way of culture, or influence, or property, or sometimes a daughter. The black man who has a mortgage on a dozen white men's houses will have no trouble in his intercourse with the white men. The black man who spends $10,000 a year in freight charges with one of the southern railroads can select his own seat in the railroad coach, or else a Pullman palace car will be put on for his special accommodation. When the black man develops to the point where by reason of his knowledge and improved skill in agriculture he can produce forty bushels of corn alongside of the white man producing but twenty in the same kind of soil, then the white man will come to the black man to learn. They will sit down and talk about it, and I believe the black man will be a good friend to the white man. When the black man has $50,000 to loan, he will never want for friends and borrowers among his white neighbors. It is meet, it is right that all the privileges guaranteed to us by the constitution be sacredly guarded; but it is vastly more important that we be prepared as a race for the exercise of these privileges. Those who suffered and fell on the field of battle performed their duty faithfully and well. But a duty remains for you and me. The mere fiat of law could not make a dependent man an independent man; could not make an ignorant father an intelligent father; could not make one race respect another. These results will come to the negro as to all races, by beginning at the bottom and gradually working up towards the highest civilization. My friends, by reason of ignorance, by reason of our freedom beginning at the top instead of at the bottom, the burden has been too heavy for many to carry; the opportunities have been too great. We have spent time and money in political conventions, making idle political speeches, that could have been better spent in becoming leading real estate dealers and leading carpenters and truck gardeners, and thus have laid an imperial foundation on which we could have stood and demanded our rights.

In conclusion, my friends, I make no selfish appeal; it is a plea to save yourselves. The negro can better afford to be wronged in this country than the white man can afford to wrong him. We are a patient, humble people; we can afford to work and wait. There is plenty for us to do away up in the atmosphere of patience, forbearance, forgiveness, and goodness. There the workers are not many and the field is not overcrowded. If others will be little, we can be great. If others would be mean, we can be good. If others can push us down, we can help push them up. If ever there has been a people in this world who have observed the Bible injunction, "If thy brother smite thee on one cheek, turn to him the other also," that people has been the American negro.

To right his wrong the Russian hurls his dynamite, the Frenchman applies the torch as in the French Revolution, the Indian flies to his tomahawk; but the negro must lie by, must be patient, must forgive his enemies, and depend for the righting of his wrong upon his midnight moans, upon his songs, upon his four-day prayers, and upon an inherent faith in the justice of his cause. If we may judge the future by the past, who will dare say that the negro's course is not the better one. Think of it, my friends; we went into slavery a piece of property and we came out American citizens; we went into slavery pagans, we came out Christians; we went into slavery without a language, we came out speaking the proud Anglo-Saxon tongue; we went into slavery with the slave-chains clanging about our wrists, we came out with the American ballot in our hands. Progress is a law of God and progress is going to be the negro's eternal guiding star in this fair land.

National Educational Association, *Journal of the Proceedings and Addresses of the Thirty-fifth Annual Meeting Held at Buffalo, N.Y., July 3-10, 1896* (Chicago: University of Chicago Press, 1896), 208-17.

[1] BTW's address was billed as the highlight of the last day of the convention, and one newspaper said his session was the "most crowded" of all. (Unidentified clipping, [July 11, 1896], Con. 1029, BTW Papers, DLC.) The Buffalo *Courier* reported that BTW spoke twice on the evening of July 10, to more than 5,000 people. (Buffalo *Courier*, July 12, 1896, 11.)

An Interview in the Buffalo *Courier*

[Buffalo, N.Y., July 10, 1896]

"I was born in bondage in Virginia before the War had fairly got underway. When a child, I removed to West Virginia, and was educated in the Hampton Institute, in that State. Fourteen years ago I went to Tuskegee, Ala., to become principal of the Normal Institute (then in its infancy), in that place. We have built the institute up by hard work and contributions from well inclined people, until this year we have 800 students, learning how to take care of themselves and becoming men, under our guidance. Most of our buildings were of brick, made by our students, and all of the labor was performed by them. So far, we have sent 300 graduates into the world, equipped to battle with life's tribulations and uphold and lead their race on to better and nobler things.

"This is my second visit to Buffalo. I was here some four years ago, and I am strongly impressed with the evidence of growth, push, and prosperity that I see about me. I believe there is a strong sentiment in Buffalo, in fact, in Western New York, for the colored man, and it gratifies me to be thus impressed. I am only sorry that I was unable to reach here early in the week so as to be present at all of the deliberations of the N.E.A. I consider these annual conventions an educator for the educator, and I am pleased to learn that as many as 40 colored teachers from all parts of the country have been present at the convention here in Buffalo. These meetings between the colored and white teachers do much to help both races. A great many white people know only the colored man of the bar-room, of the street corner, or the servant behind some hotel counter, but these conventions serve to bring together the better and more intelligent white and black people, and the white teachers go away with new impressions and thoughts about the black man and black woman. They have seen and talked with cul-

tured and college-bred black people, and the effect on the future relationship between the two races cannot help but benefit both, and particularly the former."

"What do you think of the nomination of Mr. Bryan[1] on a silver
platform by the Democratic party?" [he] was asked.

"Bad, very bad," was the reply. "I cannot see how any merchant
or citizen, who has the interests of his country at stake, can vote for
Bryan and a silver platform. It may catch a few Irishmen, who might
confound Bryan with O'Brian, but it is a losing ticket up to date, and
a demoralizing platform. The Democrats should have nominated a
well known Eastern statesman upon a gold basis, and then there might
have been a chance for success."

Buffalo *Courier,* July 12, 1896, 11.

[1] William Jennings Bryan (1860-1925) was the Democratic candidate for president in 1896, 1900, and 1908. He was U.S. Secretary of State from 1913 to 1915.

From Walter Hines Page[1]

[Boston] July 15, 1896

Dear Mr. Washington: Here is your manuscript.[2] It came while I
was away in Buffalo, and one member of our staff took the little
liberties with it that you will discover, all of course subject to your
approval. These are mere matters, as I take it, of verbal change, on
which I myself lay exceedingly little stress. My notion is that if you
will strike out from the shoulder, broadening the application of the
principle that you have worked out so as to show in the next part of
your article that this principle which has made a success of Tuskegee
is really the proper principle for education in the whole south without
reference to race — this I am sure will meet a very hearty response,
and will throw your work where it properly belongs, among the great
forces of our time and not simply the force of the work done at a
single institution.

Of course I make this simply as a suggestion; but the ATLANTIC is,
if you will permit me to say so, as important a platform as a man can
stand on, and I wish it to serve you to the very best advantage. Please
let me have your completed manuscript at the earliest hour you can,

because we have little time now to get it to press properly. I wish to give it a place of distinction in the number we are making up.

Come in to see me at any time, and believe me, Very heartily yours,

Walter H. Page

TLSr Copy   W. H. Page Papers   MH.

¹ Walter Hines Page (1855-1918) was a distinguished editor, publisher, and diplomat. Though a northern resident during most of his career, he maintained a lively involvement in southern affairs. Born in Cary, N.C., he was the son of a farmer who owned a few slaves but was a Unionist and thus gave his son a maverick heritage.

Page studied at Bingham Academy, Trinity College, Randolph-Macon College, and Johns Hopkins, where he was a graduate student in Greek for two years. After experience as a reporter for several years, Page returned to his home state, acquired control of the Raleigh *State Chronicle,* and launched an iconoclastic campaign against the shibboleths of the Old South and in favor of racial justice, business hustle, and the New South. After two years of trouble he gave up his paper and moved to New York.

After considerable success as editor of *Forum* and the *Atlantic Monthly,* in 1899 Page became a partner in the newly formed Doubleday, Page and Company. The following year he founded *The World's Work,* a news monthly, of which he was editor until 1913.

An early supporter of Hampton Institute, Page was one of the founders of the Conference for Education in the South and was an active member of the Southern Education Board, using these agencies for a renewal of his effort to reform the recalcitrant South. Page believed that the northern millionaire philanthropists and their allies among southern educators and progressives might reconstruct the South where armies and politicians had failed. Page was one of the organizers of the Rockefeller Sanitary Commission, founded in 1909 to eradicate hookworm, the "germ of laziness," in the South. His publication of *Up from Slavery* and several other of BTW's books reflected a commitment to BTW's methods of dealing with race problems.

A longtime friend and ardent supporter of Woodrow Wilson, Page became in 1913 the ambassador to Great Britain. An intense Anglophile, Page worked after the outbreak of World War I to eliminate causes of Anglo-American friction. His advice to the President was uniformly pro-British, and he was frequently exasperated during the neutrality period at what he viewed as vacillation on Wilson's part. After the United States entered the war, Page undermined his health through overwork and died.

² BTW's article, "The Awakening of the Negro," appeared in *Atlantic Monthly,* 78 (Sept. 1896), 322-28. Much of the article was included in chap. 6 of BTW, *The Future of the American Negro* (Boston, 1899). See below, vol. 5.

To Emily Howland

Crawford House   Boston, July 19 1896

Dear Miss Howland: After your very generous help of a year ago I hoped not to call Tuskegee's needs to your attention for a long time, but the agitation of free silver &c. makes it very hard for me to get money this summer, notwithstanding I am working harder than I ever did in my life. For want of a comparatively small amount the work at Tuskegee is really suffering. Whether you can help or not I knew you would not mind my saying this to you.

This will be my address for some days. Yours Sincerely

Booker T. Washington

I speak at Chautauqua Aug 1.

ALS   Emily Howland Papers   NIC.

From Portia Marshall Washington

[Washington, D.C.] July 22, 1896

My dear Papa: I am here in Washington at last. I did not get car sick until after I came and then I came down. To day is my first day up. I am still weak but I am getting along pretty well.

Mamma has been pretty well and she says look for her Saturday or Monday. I think she is pretty nervous yet.

Please excuse bad writing my hand trembles so. Dont be worried. Everything is all right.

Much love to you, Your loving daughter,

Portia

ALS   Con. 17   BTW Papers   DLC.

From Portia Marshall Washington

[Washington, D.C.] July 24, 1896

My dear papa; Mamma has been feeling so badly that she asked me to write to you. She has gone out riding with Dr. Tancil[1] to see a little of Washington. She woke up feeling very badly this morning so Dr. Tancil took her for a drive. She said it was all she could do to go to those meetings and every time [at] night when she came home she was sick.

Yesterday we went to a charming little place on the Cheasapeake bay. I went in bathing nearly all morning, and would have gone in the after noon also if mamma had been willing. I enjoyed myself very much. Mamma had a very restful time.

I am simply in love with Washington & wish I could see more of it. I hope some day when you come here to stay any lenght of time you will bring me with you.

You may expect us Monday.

With much love, I am, Your loving daughter

Portia

P.S. I met a Miss Plumer[2] who used to go to school at Wayland with you. Also several of my mothers and your school mates.

P. M. W.

ALS Con. 17 BTW Papers DLC.

[1] Arthur W. Tancil, a graduate of the Howard University Medical School in 1886, was attending physician at the dispensary clinic of Freedman's Hospital in 1899.

[2] Nellie A. Plummer.

From Paul Laurence Dunbar[1]

Dayton Ohio, July 31st. 1896

Dear Sir: Yours of late date received with great pleasure. I thank you for your words of encouragement and congratulation. I think that you for one can thoroughly understand what all this means to me after a long and hard fight. I have gotten nothing without working for it and have contested every bit of the ground over which I have passed. With Best wishes, I am   Sincerely Yours,

Paul Laurence Dunbar

TLS   Con. 116   BTW Papers   DLC.

¹ Paul Laurence Dunbar (1872-1906), born in Dayton, Ohio, became the foremost black poet of his era. He attended Steele High School in Dayton, where he was president of the literary society and editor of the *High School Times*. Unable to pursue his ambition of becoming a lawyer, he began working as an elevator operator. Meanwhile his poems appeared in the Dayton *Herald,* and in 1892 he published at his own expense a collection entitled *Oak and Ivy,* selling the booklets to the people who rode the elevator. In 1895, with the help of two sponsors from Toledo, he published *Majors and Minors,* which was favorably reviewed by William Dean Howells in *Harper's Weekly* in 1896. The book then began to sell very well, and in 1896 he published *Lyrics of Lowly Life,* considered his best collection. His success then assured, he began to lecture and write full time, and he traveled in 1897 to England. From 1897 to 1898 he served as an assistant in the Library of Congress. In 1902 Dunbar was separated from his wife, Alice Ruth Moore, better known as Alice Dunbar Nelson, after five years of marriage. At this time Dunbar's health declined, partly because of alcoholism, and he returned to Dayton, where he died in 1906. His other works include *The Sport of the Gods* (1898), *The Uncalled (*1899), *The Love of Landry* (1899), and *The Fanatics* (1901). Dunbar had a rather close if sometimes strained relationship with BTW. Dunbar recognized that industrial education was no panacea, but he saw in BTW a great leader and in Tuskegee a great endeavor worthy of several laudatory poems. (Brawley, *Paul Laurence Dunbar.*)

From Henry Stanley Newman

Leominster, [England] 3 Augt 1896

Dear Brother— I have received your letter & have thought it over. You are doing a grand work in the South, for which I praise God. I have been to Hampton when dear Genl Armstrong was there. I have been to Captain Pratt's.¹ I have stayed at Southland College, Ark. You ask what Salary we can offer for a Missionary for Pemba. We do not want a man who comes for salary & we cannot make an offer. Such men had better stay in the States, but on *Pemba* are *87,000* slaves, snatched from their village homes in the heart of Africa, & transported by the wretched Arabs to the Clove Plantations on the fertile island of Pemba. Our Government has promised that they shall be freed. Our Government has last week been holding a Council in London to make arrangements to carry out its promise. The next few months will probably see the emancipation accomplished. But there is not one single missionary in the whole island to stand by the coloured people in the crisis of emancipation. It is a habitation of cruelty & of darkness. We want forthwith to establish a *Christian Industrial Mission,* in the name of Jesus who died for them, among these people. We want to purchase a plantation, pay the people wages, establish schools, erect a church, & let the light of the gospel of Jesus Christ shine upon them. Give them a new hope, offer them a new life, create within them new aspirations for a higher & better estate than they have ever yet known. Give them a chance. Providence has given you a chance in the South. We want a smart business man who can run a plantation intelligently, economically. Let him [be] imbued with the Spirit of Christ, & we will undertake his support. Have you the man? Yours on behalf of the oppressed in the Crisis of emancipation.

H. S. Newman

ALS   Con. 120   BTW Papers   DLC.

¹ Richard Henry Pratt.

From William Jenkins

Tuskegee   Aug 7/96

Dear Mr Washington: I am afraid that you misunderstood the import of my letter. I did not ask for an increase of salary; at least I did not intend to do so. I realize what a struggle you are having in trying to make both ends meet.

No one is less willing than I am to embarass you at this time by clamoring for an increase of salary. My object in alluding to the matter at all was simply to call your attention to the fact that I am unable after two years trial to support my family on the $433.00 which I receive as salary even with house rent thrown in; and that I hoped for better things for the future. I prefer to wait until your return to lay our grievances before you concerning our Commissary charges and the embarrassments caused by unfulfilled promises. Not wishing to monopolize any part of your time by complaints I shall await your return. Your friend

Jenkins

P.S.

Politics are warm here. Lives have been threatened.

To see men going by here heavily armed has been a rather common sight of late.

It seems as if some one is bound to be hurt before the excitement fully dies out.

Old man Baxley formerly of Tuskegee but now of Tallapoosa County stole the ballot box from a precinct near Franklin. The Populites threatened to kill him. Last night about fifteen Tuskegeeans heavily armed went out to guard the offenders house.

They returned this morning; no harm having been done.

I shall speak at Sweet Gum to-morrow on invitation.

I should have said that Ben Walker with about 250 populites came to town August 1st, and after Walker had made one of the most abusive speeches that I have ever heard, repaired to the Court House and signed a paper declaring to have a fair election or lose their lives in the attempt. Result: fairest election ever had. Walker seized one of the boxes because the manager refused to come to town same night of election. Result: box thrown out. Marx[1] was probably elected by Negro votes. Your friend

Jenkins

ALS Con. 118 BTW Papers DLC.

[1] Simon Marx, a Tuskegee merchant, was elected sheriff of Macon County.

From George Washington Albert Johnston

Tuskegee, Ala., Aug. 10. 1896

My Dear Uncle, Your letter received O.K. I am very glad to know that Aunt Jacobum[1] is getting on very well. I hope she will be able to stand the operation. The children are doing very well indeed. We are having some hot weather here now. I received the 10.00 to go on Marx's note. As soon as Mr. Logan can pay me any of the first installment on his house I will get somewhat straight. I have the first floor of Mr. Logans house framed and 3/4ths of the second floor. I have also begun on the chimneys. I shall do all in my power to make both ends meet though perhaps I may be a little behind. My report will reach you at Boston by Friday. I have a fine Chester White Yorkshire pig by our white one. Uncle John is ill at present but I guess he'll be out soon. Mr. Marx is sheriff. A White man was lynched near Tallessee[2] last night for stuffing ballot boxes. The populites have threatened to kill several others, among the number are two prominent whites in town. The pigs are looking alright. Tell Aunt Jacobum that Baker and Davidson both send love. The[y] are wild over their belts and caps she sent.

I hope you are getting on well. Your Nephew

Geo. W. A. Johnson

ALS   Con. 118   BTW Papers   DLC.

[1] Johnston's nickname for Margaret James Murray Washington.
[2] Tallassee, Ala.

To Emily Howland

Crawford House   Boston, Aug 27 1896

Dear Miss Howland: Your very kind letter is received and it gives me a very pleasant surprise. You are very kind and generous to think and act in this way toward Mrs. Washington and myself. We should not accept this gift in the way you suggest except that anything that help[s] restore Mrs. Washington to health helps the cause in the South.

Please do not think that I was disappointed in the least in not receiving a collection. The privilege of being in your house and of speaking to those people was compensation.

In spite of the hard times I think I shall get through the summer very well. So far I have gotten more money than I did last summer. I believe that no cause that is worthy to live dies.

Mrs. Washington stood the severe operation very well and she is now in a *very* encouraging condition.

I think I know the physician who wrote you and I shall explain the matter to him.

I go South next week, but Mrs. Washington will have to remain here till Oct. She asks to be remembered to you. Yours Sincerely

Booker T. Washington

ALS   Emily Howland Papers   NIC.

A Statement to the Christian Endeavor Society

[Tuskegee, Ala., Sept. 3, 1896]

I hope every member of the Christian Endeavor Society will be brave this year — be full of Christian courage. In many parts of our country it requires much courage for a Christian to take a poor black boy by the hand and lead him to the Sunday school or Christian Endeavor society. Often the one who does this will be laughed at or scorned by others. But no person was too black or forsaken to make Christ ashamed to take him by the hand. All over this country there are promising boys and girls with black skins who sink into the mire simply because no one has the Christian courage to take them by the hand and lift them up. Let us all this year throughout the world show that we are one in Christ by heroic deeds as well as by words.

How often as a poor black boy have I passed the doors of churches and Sunday schools and heard the grand old song, "Come to Jesus," welling up from hundreds of throats, and at the same time if I, a poor black boy, had obeyed the command, and entered that church or Sunday school, I should have been put out by force, if necessary.

If is often easier to send a few pennies to help the poor black boy in Africa than it is to show the Christlike spirit to the little black boy just around the corner of the street.

Golden Rule, Sept. 3, 1896, 3.

From Albert G. Davis

Montgomery Ala. Sept 10th '96

Dear Prof: I am an applicant for Swayne School[1] in this city, and have received the endorsement of many leading citizens. It matters not how much I am endorsed, if my Alma Mater withholds her endorsement, I will be seriously handicapped in the race when all the other applicants are receiving the generous and unqualified endorsement from the various institutions from whence they graduated.

Please send at once as nice a letter as possible endorsing my candidacy to Hon. A. D. Sayre[2] Sec'y Board of School Examiners. The election of Principal of Swayne School is soon to be held, and it is absolutely essential that all my papers be submitted as early as possible. Do not send the letter to me but to Mr. Sayre. I leave for Birmingham Ala tonight. *Please write me there* what you have done. My wife is sick so that I cannot remain here any longer. Yours gratefully

Albert G. Davis

ALS   Con. 116   BTW Papers   DLC.

[1] Swayne School in Montgomery was founded by the American Missionary Association during Reconstruction. It was named for General Wager Swayne, then in military command of Alabama and in charge of black education. One of the largest schools of its kind, it was subsequently absorbed by the State Normal School for Colored Students in Montgomery.

[2] Anthony Dickinson Sayre, born in Tuskegee in 1858, was admitted to the Montgomery bar in 1880, thus beginning a political career that included service in the state legislature and as an associate justice of the Alabama Supreme Court. He was a member of the Montgomery Board of Education from 1891 to 1911. The youngest of his six children, Zelda, married F. Scott Fitzgerald.

To Nathan B. Young

Tuskegee, Ala., 9, 16, 1896

Mr. Young: I did not understand and do not now understand, that it is the wish of the committee on the course of study to have the phsycology dropped out of the course of study. The matter was discussed last year but it was not determined that this change be made. I desire that the phsycology remain in the course much in the same

way that it has been heretofore. The arrangements heretofore existing
between myself and Mr. Peterson have been satisfactory. I like to
come into contact with the Seniors in this study when I have an opportunity. I like to know the Seniors and like to have them know me.
I find that most of them have already purchased their books and do
not understand that the study is to be dropped. I wish you would
notify me when you have decided on the hour for the recitation.

B. T. W.

TLI Con. 116 BTW Papers DLC. Young replied on the bottom of the
letter: "You may meet them the third hour in the morning — 10:40 to 11:20 in
Room 4 Porter Hall. Unless you desire to have the committee to *reconsider* their
action in the matter of pedagogy, you need not call them. I have followed *im-
plicitly* their decision regarding the course in every particular; and am sorry if
you think otherwise. Resp'y, Nathan B. Young."

From Shepherd Lincoln Harris[1]

Tuskegee Ala. Sept. 21/96

Mr. Washington: I went to town this A.M. and saw Mr. Simon Marks[2]
and told him of the affair and he told me that I was not charged for
shooting at all, only for the concealed weapon.

He also told me he would make the fine just as low as it could be
made just on the account of the School.

He told me to come back on to morrow and he would have the matter settled before Judge Hurt.[3]

Mr Washing if you think you can have the matter settled for less
than I can I wish you would take the matter in hand and settle it.
I am sure you can do more with it than I can.

Now Mr Washington I have not the money right now, but I waunt
you to settle the affair. And I am sure I will have it in short. I sent
for it this morning rather a part of it, even if it does not get here time
enough I will stop out of school and make it; but I am satisfied of
geting it.

Please let me know what you will do about the matter. Obblige

S. L. Harris

ALS Con. 117 BTW Papers DLC.

[1] Shepherd Lincoln Harris, a member of the A middle class in 1896, graduated from Tuskegee in 1899 and went to work as a carpenter in Maysville, S.C. He was among the first group from Tuskegee that sailed for Africa in November 1900 to introduce cotton raising under the direction of the German government in Togo. Harris died of fever there in August 1902.

[2] Simon Marx.

[3] William H. Hurt, a Civil War veteran and former tax collector in Macon County, was a probate judge of the county. In 1899 he was a member of the state legislature.

From Matthew T. Driver

Tuskegee, Ala., Sept. 22 1896

My Dear Sir, I enjoyed the talk that you gave the students in the Chapel yesterday very much, but for one thing. I think you do the industrial teachers an injustice when you say to the students that when they shall have mastered their trades by putting brains etc. into it, that they can demand high salaries, when they are being taught by those who receive no more and in many cases less than ordinary mechanics. As I look at it, you are saying to the students that the teachers you have are not masters of their situations. I have heard this criticism made by students, and outsiders, both, white and colored. Respectfully yours

M. T. Driver

ALS   Con. 116   BTW Papers   DLC.

A Speech at the Institute of Arts and Sciences[1]

[Brooklyn, N.Y., Sept. 30, 1896]

DEMOCRACY AND EDUCATION

Mr. Chairman, Ladies and Gentlemen:

It is said that the strongest chain is no stronger than its weakest link. In the Southern part of our country there are twenty-two millions of your brethren who are bound to you by ties which you cannot tear asunder if you would. The most intelligent man in your community has his intelligence darkened by the ignorance of a fellow citizen in the Mississippi bottoms. The most wealthy in your city would be more wealthy but for the poverty of a fellow being in the Carolina rice swamps. The most moral and religious among you has his religion and morality modified by the degradation of the man in the South whose religion is a mere matter of form or emotionalism.

The vote in your state that is cast for the highest and purest form of government is largely neutralized by the vote of the man in Louisiana whose ballot is stolen or cast in ignorance. When the South is poor, you are poor; when the South commits crime, you commit crime. My friends, there is no mistake; you must help us to raise the character of our civilization or yours will be lowered. No member of your race in any part of our country can harm the weakest and meanest member of mine without the proudest and bluest blood in the city of Brooklyn being degraded. The central ideal which I wish you to help me consider is the reaching and lifting up of the lowest, most unfortunate, negative element that occupies so large a proportion of our territory and composes so large a percentage of our population. It seems to me that there never was a time in the history of our country when those interested in education should more earnestly consider to what extent the mere acquiring of a knowledge of literature and science makes producers, lovers of labor, independent, honest, unselfish, and, above all, supremely good. Call education by what name you please, and if it fails to bring about these results among the masses it falls short of its highest end. The science, the art, the literature that fails to reach down and bring the humblest up to the fullest enjoyment of the blessings of our government is weak, no matter how costly the buildings or apparatus used, or how modern the methods in instruction employed. The study of arithmetic that does not result in making someone more honest and self-reliant is defective. The study of history that does not result in making men conscientious in receiving and counting the ballots of their fellow men is most faulty. The study of art that does not result in making the strong less willing to oppress the weak means little. How I wish that from the most humble log cabin schoolhouse in Alabama we could burn it, as it were, into the hearts and heads of all, that usefulness, service to our brother, is the supreme end of education. Putting the thought more directly as it applies to conditions in the South: Can you make your intelligence affect us in the same ratio that our ignorance affects you? Let us put a not improbable case. A great national question is to be decided, one that involves peace or war, the honor or dishonor of our nation — yea, the every existence of the government. The North and West are divided. There are five million votes to be cast in the South, and of this number one half are ignorant. Not only are one half the voters ignorant, but, because of this ignorant vote, corruption, dishonesty in a dozen forms have crept into the exercise of the political franchise, to the extent that the conscience of the intelligent class is soured in its attempts to defeat the will of the ignorant voters. Here, then, on the one hand you have an ignorant vote, and on the other hand an intelligent vote minus a conscience. The time may not be far off when to this kind of jury we shall have to look for the verdict that is to decide the course of our democratic institutions.

When a great national calamity stares us in the face, we are, I fear, too much given to depending on a short campaign of education to do on the hustings what should have been accomplished in the schoolroom. With this preliminary survey, let us examine with more care the work to be done in the South before all classes will be fit for the highest duties of citizenship. In reference to my own race I am confronted with some embarrassment at the outset because of the various and conflicting opinions as to what is to be its final place in our economic and political life. Within the last thirty years — and, I might add, within the last three months — it has been proven by eminent authority that the Negro is increasing in numbers so fast that it is only a question of a few years before he will far outnumber the white race in the South, and it has also been proven that the Negro is fast dying out and it is only a question of a few years before he will have completely disappeared. It has also been proven that crime among us is on the increase and that crime is on the decrease; that education helps the Negro, that education also hurts him; that he is fast leaving the South and taking up his residence in the North and West, and that the tendency of the Negro is to drift to the lowlands of the Mississippi bottoms. It has been proven that as a slave laborer he produced less cotton than a free man. It has been proven that education unfits the Negro for work, and that education also makes him more valuable as a laborer; that he is our greatest criminal and that he is our most law-abiding citizen. In the midst of these opinions, in the words of a modern statesman, "I hardly know where I am at." I hardly know whether I am myself or the other fellow. But in the midst of this confusion there are a few things of which I feel certain that furnish a basis for thought and action. I know that, whether we are increasing or decreasing, whether we are growing better or worse, whether we are valuable or valueless, a few years ago fourteen of us were brought into this country and now there are eight million of us. I know that, whether in slavery or freedom, we have always been loyal to the Stars and Stripes, that no schoolhouse has been opened for us that has not been filled; that 1,500,000 ballots that we have the right to cast are as potent for weal and woe as the ballot cast by the whitest and most influential man in your commonwealth. I know that wherever our life touches yours we help or hinder; that wherever your life touches ours you make us stronger or weaker. Further I know that almost every other race that tried to look the white man in the face has disappeared. With all the conflicting opinions, and with the full knowledge of all our weaknesses, I know that only a few centuries ago in this country we went into slavery pagans: we came out Christians; we went into slavery pieces of property: we came out American citizens; we went into slavery without a language: we came out speaking the proud Anglo-Saxon tongue; we went into slavery with the slave chains clanking about our wrists: we came out with the American ballot in our hands. My friends, I submit it to your sober and candid judgment, if a race that is capable of such a test, such a transformation, is not worth saving and making a part, in reality as well as in name, of our democratic government. It is with an ignorant race as it is with a child: it craves at first the superficial, the ornamental, the signs of progress rather than the reality. The ignorant race is tempted to jump, at one bound, to the position that it has required years of hard struggle for others to reach. It seems to me that the temptation in education and missionary work is to do for a people a thousand miles away without always making a careful study of the needs and conditions of the people whom we are trying to help. The temptation is to run all people through a certain educational mold regardless of the condition of the subject or the end to be accomplished. Unfortunately for us as a race, our education was begun, just after the war, too nearly where New England education ended. We seemed to overlook the fact that we were dealing with a race that has little love for labor in their native land and consequently brought little love for labor with them to America. Added to this was the fact that they had been forced for two hundred and fifty years to labor without compensation under circumstances that were calculated to do anything but teach them the dignity, beauty, and civilizing power of intelligent labor. We forgot the industrial education that was given the Pilgrim Fathers of New England in clearing and planting its cold, bleak, and snowy hills and valleys, in providing shelter, founding the small mills and factories, in supplying themselves with home-made products, thus laying the foundation of an industrial life that now keeps going a large part of the colleges and missionary effort of the world. May I be tempted one step further in showing how prone we are to make our education formal, technical, instead of making it meet the needs of conditions regardless of formality and technicality? At least eighty per cent of my pupils in the South are found in the rural districts, and they are dependent on agriculture in some form for their support. Notwithstanding in this instance we have a whole race depending upon agriculture, and notwithstanding thirty years have passed since our freedom, aside from what we have done at Hampton and Tuskegee and one or two other institutions, not a thing has been attempted by state or philanthropy in the way of educating the race in this industry on which their very existence depends. Boys have been taken from the farms and educated in law, theology, Hebrew, and Greek — educated in everything else but the very subject they should know the most about. I question whether or not among all the educated colored people in the United States you can find six, if we except the institutions named, that have received anything like a thorough training in agriculture. It would have seemed, since self-support and industrial independence are the first conditions for lifting up any race, that education in theoretical and practical agriculture, horticulture, dairying, and stock-raising should have occupied the first place in our system. Some time ago when we decided to make tailoring a part of our training at the Tuskegee Institute, I was amazed to find that it was almost impossible to find in the whole country an educated colored man who could teach the making of clothing. I could find them by the score who could teach astronomy, theology, Greek, or Latin, but almost none who could instruct in the making of clothing, something that has to be used by every one of us every day in the year. How often has my heart been made to sink as I have gone through the South and into the homes of the people and found women who could converse intelligently on Grecian history, who had studied geometry, could analyze the most complex sentences, and yet could not analyze the poorly cooked and still more poorly served bread and fat meat that they and their families were eating three times

215

a day. It is little trouble to find girls who can locate Pekin and the Desert of Sahara on an artificial globe; but seldom can you find one who can locate on an actual dinner table the proper place for the carving knife and fork or the meat and vegetables. A short time ago, in one of our Southern cities, a colored man died who had received training as a skilled mechanic during the days of slavery. By his skill and industry he had built up a great business as a house contractor and builder. In this same city there are thirty-five thousand colored people, among them young men who have been well educated in languages and literature, but not a single one could be found who had been trained in architectural and mechanical drawing that could carry on the business which this ex-slave had built up, and so it was soon scattered to the wind. Aside from the work done in the institutions that I have mentioned, you will find no colored men who have been trained in the principles of architecture, notwithstanding the vast majority of the race is without homes. Here, then, are the three prime conditions for growth, for civilization — food, clothing, shelter — yet we have been the slaves of form and custom to such an extent that we have failed in a large measure to look matters squarely in the face and meet actual needs. You cannot graft a fifteenth-century civilization onto a twentieth-century civilization by the mere performance of mental gymnastics. Understand, I speak in no fault-finding spirit, but with a feeling of deep regret for what has been done; but the future must be an improvement on the past.

I have endeavored to speak plainly in regard to the past, because I fear that the wisest and most interested have not fully comprehended the task which American slavery has laid at the doors of the Republic. Few, I fear, realize what is to be done before the seven million of my people in the South can be made a safe, helpful, progressive part of our institutions. The South, in proportion to its ability, has done well, but this does not change facts. Let me illustrate what I mean by a single example. In spite of all that has been done, I was in a county in Alabama a few days ago where there are some thirty thousand colored people and about seven thousand whites; in this county not a single public school for Negroes has been open this year longer than three months, not a single colored teacher has been paid more than fifteen dollars a month for his teaching. Not one of these schools was taught in a building worthy of the name of schoolhouse. In this county the state or public authorities do not own a dollar's worth of school property — not a schoolhouse, a blackboard, or a piece of crayon. Each colored child had spent on him this year for his education about fifty cents, while one of your children had spent on him this year for education not far from twenty dollars. And yet each citizen of this county is expected to share the burdens and privileges of our democratic form of government just as intelligently and conscientiously as the citizens of your beloved Kings County. A vote in this county means as much to the nation as a vote in the city of Boston. Crime in this county is as truly an arrow aimed at the heart of the government as crime committed in your own streets. Do you know that a single schoolhouse built this year in a town near Boston to shelter about three hundred students has cost more for building alone than will be spent for the education, including buildings, apparatus, teachers, of the whole colored school population of Alabama? The commissioner of education for the state of Georgia recently reported to the state legislature that in the state there were two hundred thousand children that had entered no school the past year, and one hundred thousand more who were in school but a few days, making practically three hundred thousand children between six and sixteen years of age that are growing up in ignorance in one Southern state. The same report states that outside of the cities and towns, while the average number of schoolhouses in a county is sixty, all of these sixty schoolhouses are worth in a lump sum less than $2,000, and the report further adds that many of the schoolhouses in Georgia are not fit for horse stables. These illustrations, my friends, as far as concerns the Gulf states, are not exceptional cases or overdrawn.

I have referred to industrial education as a means of fitting the millions of my people in the South for the duties of citizenship. Until there is industrial independence it is hardly possible to have a pure ballot. In the country districts of the Gulf states it is safe to say that not more than one black man in twenty owns the land he cultivates. Where so large a proportion of the people are dependent, live in other people's houses, eat other people's food, and wear clothes they have not paid for, it is a pretty hard thing to tell how they are going to vote. My remarks thus far have referred mainly to my own race. But there is another side. The longer I live and the more I study the question, the more I am convinced that it is not so much a problem as to what you will do with the Negro as what the Negro will do with you and your civilization. In considering this side of the subject, I thank God that I have grown to the point where I can sympathize with a white man as much as I can sympathize with a black man. I have grown to the point where I can sympathize with a Southern white man as much as I can sympathize with a Northern white man. To me "a man's a man for a' that and a' that." As bearing upon democracy and education, what of your white brethren in the South, those who suffered and are still suffering the consequences of American slavery for which both you and they are responsible? You of the great and prosperous North still owe to your unfortunate brethren of the Caucasian race in the South, not less than to yourselves, a serious and uncompleted duty. What was the task you asked them to perform? Returning to their destitute homes after years of war to face blasted hopes, devastation, a shattered industrial system, you asked them to add to their own burdens that of preparing in education, politics, and economics in a few short years, for citizenship, four millions of former slaves. That the South, staggering under the burden, made blunders, and that in a measure there has been disappointment, no one need be surprised.

The educators, the statesmen, the philanthropists have never comprehended their duty toward the millions of poor whites in the South who were buffeted for two hundred years between slavery and freedom, between civilization and degradation, who were disregarded by both master and slave. It needs no prophet to tell the character of our future civilization when the poor white boy in the country districts of the South receives one dollar's worth of education and your boy twenty dollars' worth, when one never enters a library or reading room and the other has libraries and reading rooms in every ward and town. When one hears lectures and sermons once in two months and the other can hear a lecture or sermon every day in the year. When you help the South you help yourselves. Mere abuse will not bring the remedy. The time has come, it seems to me, when in this matter we should rise above party or race or sectionalism into the region of duty of man to man, citizen to citizen, Christian to Christian, and if the Negro who has been oppressed and denied rights in a Christian land can help you North and South to rise, can be the medium of your rising into this atmosphere of generous Christian brotherhood and self-forgetfulness, he will see in it a recompense for all that he has suffered in the past. Not very long ago a white citizen of the South boastingly expressed himself in public to this effect: "I am now forty-six years of age, but have never polished my own boots, have never saddled my own horse,

have never built a fire in my own room, have never hitched a horse."
He was asked a short time since by a lame man to hitch his horse, but
refused and told him to get a Negro to do it. Our state law requires
that a voter be required to read the constitution before voting, but
the last clause of the constitution is in Latin and the Negroes cannot
read Latin, and so they are asked to read the Latin clause and are
thus disfranchised, while the whites are permitted to read the English
portion of the constitution. I do not quote these statements for the purpose of condemning the individual or the South, for though myself a
member of a despised and unfortunate race, I pity from the bottom of
my heart any of God's creatures whence such a statement can emanate.
Evidently here is a man who, as far as mere book training is concerned,
is educated, for he boasts of his knowledge of Latin, but, so far as the
real purpose of education is concerned — the making of men useful,
honest, and liberal — this man has never been touched. Here is a citizen in the midst of our republic, clothed in a white skin, with all the
technical signs of education, but who is as little fitted for the highest
purpose of life as any creature found in Central Africa. My friends,
can we make our education reach down far enough to touch and help
this man? Can we so control science, art, and literature as to make
them to such an extent a means rather than an end; that the lowest
and most unfortunate of God's creatures shall be lifted up, ennobled
and glorified; shall be a freeman instead of a slave of narrow sympathies and wrong customs? Some years ago a bright young man of
my race succeeded in passing a competitive examination for a cadet-
ship at the United States naval academy at Annapolis. Says the young
man, Mr. Henry Baker, in describing his stay at this institution: "I
was several times attacked with stones and was forced finally to appeal
to the officers, when a marine was detailed to accompany me across
the campus and from the mess hall at meal times. My books were
mutilated, my clothes were cut and in some instances destroyed, and
all the petty annoyances which ingenuity could devise were inflicted
upon me daily, and during seamanship practice aboard the *Dale* attempts were often made to do me personal injury while I would be
aloft in the rigging. No one ever addressed me by name. I was called
the Moke usually, the Nigger for variety. I was shunned as if I were a
veritable leper and received curses and blows as the only method my
persecutors had of relieving the monotony." Not once during the two
years, with one exception, did any one of the more than four hundred

cadets enrolled ever come to him with a word of advice, counsel, sympathy, or information, and he never held conversation with any one of them for as much as five minutes during the whole course of his experience at the academy, except on occasions when he was defending himself against their assaults. The one exception where the departure from the rule was made was in the case of a Pennsylvania boy, who stealthily brought him a piece of his birthday cake at twelve o'clock one night. The act so surprised Baker that his suspicions were aroused, but these were dispelled by the donor, who read to him a letter which he had received from his mother, from whom the cake came, in which she requested that a slice be given to the colored cadet who was without friends. I recite this incident not for the purpose merely of condemning the wrong done a member of my race; no, no, not that. I mention the case, not for the one cadet, but for the sake of the four hundred cadets, for the sake of the four hundred American families, the four hundred American communities whose civilization and Christianity these cadets represented. Here were four hundred and more picked young men representing the flower of our country, who had passed through our common schools and were preparing themselves at public expense to defend the honor of our country. And yet, with grammar, reading, and arithmetic in the public schools, and with lessons in the arts of war, the principles of physical courage at Annapolis, both systems seemed to have utterly failed to prepare a single one of these young men for real life, that he could be brave enough, Christian enough, American enough, to take this poor defenseless black boy by the hand in open daylight and let the world know that he was his friend. Education, whether of black man or white man, that gives one physical courage to stand in front of the cannon and fails to give him moral courage to stand up in defense of right and justice is a failure. With all that the Brooklyn Institute of Arts and Sciences stands for in its equipment, its endowment, its wealth and culture, its instructors, can it produce a mother that will produce a boy that will not be ashamed to have the world know that he is a friend to the most unfortunate of God's creatures? Not long ago a mother, a black mother, who lived in one of your Northern states, had heard it whispered around in her community for years that the Negro was lazy, shiftless, and would not work. So when her boy grew to sufficient size, at considerable expense and great self-sacrifice, she had her boy thoroughly taught the machinist's trade. A job was secured in a neighboring shop. With dinner bucket in hand and spurred on by the prayers of the now happy mother, the boy entered the shop to begin his first day's work. What happened? Had any one of the twenty white Americans been so educated that he gave this stranger a welcome into their midst? No, not this. Every one of the twenty white men threw down his tools and deliberately walked out, swearing that he would not give a black man an opportunity to earn an honest living. Another shop was tried, with the same result, and still another and the same. Today this promising and ambitious black man is a wreck — a confirmed drunkard, with no hope, no ambition. My friends, who blasted the life of this young man? On whose hands does his blood rest? Our system of education, or want of education, is responsible. Can our public schools and colleges turn out a set of men that will throw open the doors of industry to all men everywhere, regardless of color, so all shall have the same opportunity to earn a dollar that they now have to spend a dollar? I know a good many species of cowardice and prejudice, but I know none equal to this. I know not who is the worst, the ex-slaveholder who perforce compelled his slave to work without compensation, or the man who perforce compels the Negro to refrain from working for compensation. My friends, we are one in this country. The question of the highest citizenship and the complete education of all concerns nearly ten million of my own people and over sixty million of yours. We rise as you rise; when we fall you fall. When you are strong we are strong; when we are weak you are weak. There is no power that can separate our destiny. The Negro can afford to be wronged; the white man cannot afford to wrong him. Unjust laws or customs that exist in many places regarding the races injure the white man and inconvenience the Negro. No race can wrong another race simply because it has the power to do so without being permanently injured in morals. The Negro can endure the temporary inconvenience, but the injury to the white man is permanent. It is for the white man to save himself from his degradation that I plead. If a white man steals a Negro's ballot it is the white man who is permanently injured. Physical death comes to the one Negro lynched in a county, but death of the morals — death of the soul — comes to the thousands responsible for the lynching. We are a patient, humble people. We can afford to work and wait. There is plenty in this country for us to do. Away up in the atmosphere of goodness, forbearance, patience, long-suffering, and forgiveness the workers are not many or overcrowded. If others would be little we can be great.

If others would be mean we can be good. If others would push us down we can help push them up. Character, not circumstances, makes the man. It is more important that we be prepared for voting than that we vote, more important that we be prepared to hold office than that we hold office, more important that we be prepared for the highest recognition than that we be recognized. Those who fought and died on the battlefield performed their duty heroically and well, but a duty remains for you and me. The mere fiat of law could not make an ignorant voter an intelligent voter; could not make one citizen respect another; these results come to the Negro, as to all races, by beginning at the bottom and working up to the highest civilization and accomplishment. In the economy of God, there can be but one standard by which an individual can succeed — there is but one for a race. This country demands that every race measure itself by the American standard. By it a race must rise or fall, succeed or fail, and in the last analysis mere sentiment counts but little. During the next half-century and more my race must continue passing through the severe American crucible.

We are to be tested in our patience, in our forbearance, our power to endure wrong, to withstand temptation, to succeed, to acquire and use skill, our ability to compete, to succeed in commerce; to disregard the superficial for the real, the appearance for the substance; to be great and yet the servant of all. This, this is the passport to all that is best in the life of our republic, and the Negro must possess it or be debarred. In working out our destiny, while the main burden and center of activity must be with us, we shall need in a large measure the help, the encouragement, the guidance that the strong can give the weak. Thus helped, we of both races in the South shall soon throw off the shackles of racial and sectional prejudice and rise above the clouds of ignorance, narrowness, and selfishness into that atmosphere, that pure sunshine, where it will be our highest ambition to serve man, our brother, regardless of race or past conditions.

Ernest Davidson Washington, ed., *Selected Speeches of Booker T. Washington* (New York, 1932), 60-77. A newspaper version with a few variations appeared in the Brooklyn *Eagle*, Oct. 1, 1896, 4. In revised form it appeared in *The Future of the American Negro*. See below, vol. 5.

[1] Washington's address was the opening one of the Brooklyn Institute's series at Association Hall. The hall was crowded and enthusiastic. "Mr. Washington is an erect and sinewy young man of about medium height, with closely cropped hair and a manly face that impresses one particularly by its frankness and modesty," said a

reporter. "He has fire, humor, pathos and, what is more rare among colored speakers, logic. He spoke from manuscript, mainly; when he left it it was to tell one of his humorous stories or to point an argument by illustration." (Brooklyn *Eagle*, Oct. 1, 1896, 4.) About two months later BTW may well have read from the same manuscript when he gave a talk on "Education and Democracy" at the Twentieth Century Club in Boston. (Boston *Herald*, Nov. 25, 1896, 6.)

From Heli Chatelain[1]

Newark, N.J., Oct. 5/96

My dear Mr. Washington, Please accept my thanks for agreeing to represent the colored people of this country on the Board of the Philafrican Liberators' League. At the last meeting of the Directors, on June 8, many names were proposed and approved for the few vacancies left on the Board, yours in the number. At the next meeting, the names previously approved will be sifted and those who are known to be willing to accept, will be elected. I think you will pass without the least difficulty. I shall notify you, as soon the election is over.

You ask what the League expects of you. *Your name,* which you have given, is the only positive requisite. A Director who is not a resident of New York and can therefore not be expected to attend the meetings, is not expected to do any more than his interest in the work prompts him to do. But, if there is nothing more than his occasional vote on important matters, which the League has a right to *expect* from a Director, there is much, that I, as planner of the League, see that you *may* do, and which I earnestly hope you *will* do. And first, I hope you will *realise* that all you do to advance the solution of the problems concerning the American negro, is a direct or indirect contribution to the solution of parallel problems in Africa; that, as Dr. Frissell puts it, "Your cause is ours, and ours is yours" that what helps one helps the other; that great as your Mission already is in these United States, it is to affect a far wider circle than you perhaps have thought of, that your real "sphere of influence" embraces the whole continent of Africa, and even the millions of negroes in Brazil and other South-American States, who have not yet come in touch with our Evangelical civilization. Wherever white and negro come in contact, there is a racial problem. Even where there is next to no color line, as among the Portuguese, some friction and antagonism is inevitable, and the negro naturally is the greatest sufferer.

While I sat listening to the debate at the last Hampton Conference of graduates, I was continually struck with the fact that the condition of things in our South is in many respects the same as that of large sections of the African continent; that what I had realized to be needed in Africa is also needed here, and that Hampton and Tuskegee are, to say the least, on the right track. The mistakes made here are also made, with very good intentions, in Africa. It was really the discovery of the good that I might do in the South that revealed to me the good that institutions like Hampton & Tuskegee may do for Africa.

Practical as you are, you probably wish some hints concerning the *concrete* things you *may* do, at no distant date for the cause represented by the League.

(1) Snatch now and then a moment, to *read* the literature which we will supply on African slavery. The mere fact that there are at least 50,000,000 slaves in Africa, and that the slave-trade claims, according to the computation of the British & Foreign Anti-Slavery Society, an annual tribute of 500,000 lives, should interest one like you in a responsible effort to organize American (and Negro) participation in a movement for the removal of that colossal evil. Evidently, the emancipation of the 5,000,000 of American negro slaves is but a stepping stone to the liberation of the 50,000,000 of African slaves.

(2) In private conversation and in public addresses impress when it fits in, the fact that "slavery is not yet dead."

(3) Interest your students in this cause. Solid facts about Africa, and about the great events that are taking place there, will do them more good than all the rubbish that is talked and written about Liberia.

(4) I hope that, when the time comes, you will help us to get, perhaps from among your graduates, well-trained and hard working colored mechanics and farmers able to teach their hand craft to their African brethren. Is it too much to hope that as you, branching off from Hampton created Tuskegee, so one branching off from Tuskegee may become the founder of a similar institution in some part of Africa?

If you have not yet got "Africa and the American Negro" (Gammon Theol. Seminary) I advise you to get it. In my paper on African slavery, therein published, you will find a general view of the principal aspects of the world's open sore.

It is probably not necessary for me to develop the main points of my plan of work as stated in the pamphlet "The Open Sore of the World." Your experience enables you to add, in a moment, flesh, skin and life to that skeleton.

With believing prayers for God's blessing on your grand work, I remain   Fraternally yours

Heli Chatelain

P.S. I send you a few copies of our pamphlets for distribution. If you can use more, let me know how many.

ALS   Con. 115   BTW Papers   DLC.

¹ Heli Chatelain was born in Morat, Switzerland, in 1859. Crippled for about twenty years, he spent his time learning European languages. In 1883 he moved to the United States, regained his health, and took part in a missionary journey to West Africa. Chatelain expanded his interest in linguistics and folklore to include Africa, and was the author of *Folk-Tales of Angola* (1894). In 1896 he founded the Philafrican Liberators' League for the purposes of ending the slave trade and founding colonies of freedmen in Africa. On July 23, 1897, a group including Chatelain sailed for Angola, where they established a settlement. Among BTW's acquaintainces who supported the League were H. B. Frissell, Lyman Abbott, Josiah Strong, and William E. Dodge.

From Ernest Howard Ruffner¹

Baltimore, Md. Oct. 9th. 1896

Dear Sir: Under our agreement for the rent of the Malden field² the final payment of $25. is now due. As it is my intention to hold the rent at its present figures no reduction will be made.

But, if you will send me a receipt from Mr. W. J. Edwards³ of Snow Hill Ala, for $15., which I contribute for the help of his very praiseworthy efforts there, I will send you a receipt for the $25. yet due me. The unpaid $10. you may consider my contribution to you, personally, for your services at Tuskegee. We all feel an interest in your enterprise. Very truly,

E. H. Ruffner

TLS   Con. 701   BTW Papers   DLC.

¹ Ernest Howard Ruffner (1845-1937) was the son of BTW's benefactors in Malden, W.Va., General Lewis Ruffner and his wife Viola Knapp Ruffner. A graduate of Kenyon College and West Point, Ernest Ruffner spent his entire

career in the Army Corps of Engineers at Charleston, W.Va., Baltimore, Charleston, S.C., New Orleans, Cincinnati, and elsewhere, in charge of river and harbor improvements. After his retirement in 1909, Ruffner resided in Cincinnati.

2 For many years BTW rented a plot for the use of his sister Amanda Ferguson Johnston, who raised chickens there.

3 William Junior Edwards graduated from Tuskegee in 1893 and became principal of Snow Hill Industrial Institute.

From Walter Hines Page

Boston, 14 Octr 1896

Dear Mr. Washington: A letter was sent to you by Messrs H. M. & Co.[1] yesterday, very regretfully declining to publish the book of addresses. This house is not the natural or the best channel for a book so made up, which would not find its sale through the regular channels of the book-trade.

I know that you will be here before a great while, & I have held your ms. till you come or till you send word where it may be sent.

I have a notion — yet somewhat vague — of a possible book in a different form — not speeches, but a history or narrative, with some peculiar features — about Tuskegee — which I should like to talk over with you. Let me know when you will be here. Very Sincerely Yours,

Walter H. Page

ALS   Con. 116   BTW Papers   DLC.

1 Houghton, Mifflin and Company.

To Hollis Burke Frissell

Tuskegee, Ala., Oct. 23, 1896

Dear Dr. Frissell: During the present week we are having a visit from Mrs. B. K. Bruce,[1] of Washington, wife of ex-Senator Bruce. We are finding her visit very helpful in every way. She is a woman of fine sense and refinement, there is no nonsense about her. I thought perhaps you might like to have her visit Hampton and speak to the students as a whole or to the girls alone. She has spoken to our students very acceptably, and this afternoon speaks to the teachers alone. To-morrow she speaks to the girls alone, besides speaking to several classes. Her Washington address is, 2010 R St., N.W. Yours truly,

Booker T. Washington

TLS BTW Folder ViHaI.

[1] Josephine Beall Wilson Bruce, the daughter of a Cleveland dentist, taught school in Cleveland before marrying Blanche Kelso Bruce in 1878. After her husband's death in 1898, Josephine Bruce became Lady Principal at Tuskegee Institute, serving from 1899 to 1902.

From John Quincy Johnson

Princeton N.J. Oct 23. '96

Dear Mr Washington: During the sesquicentennial exercises here, I called to see Dr Gilman. He said it was the idea of the Board that the pamphlet should deal principally with the Mortgage system, showing how Jews loan money to the colored people at great rates of interest & thus keep them hard pressed. In Bullock Co the Jew is not operating to any considerable extent. He did not read my pamphlet, but sent it to Dr. Curry, whose letter concerning the work I received. Dr Gilman would like me to rewrite it according to the line suggested by Dr Curry. I have been looking for the MSS. since I received your letter but it has not yet reached Princeton.

Best wishes for your health   I am   Yours Truly

Jno Q. Johnson

ALS Con. 130 BTW Papers DLC.

A News Item in the *Outlook*

[New York City, Oct. 24, 1896]

By invitation of the President and students, Booker T. Washington, the colored Principal of the Tuskegee Institute in Alabama, delivered an address recently before the Faculty and students of Trinity College in North Carolina. Although Trinity College is an old Southern white college, and this is the first time he was ever invited to address a Southern white college, Mr. Washington says that he and the half-dozen colored citizens who accompanied him were treated with the greatest courtesy, and his address was received with marked enthusiasm. As he left the college grounds the students assembled on the campus and gave him their college yell in a most hearty manner.

Outlook, 54 (Oct. 24, 1896), 745.

From Thomas Junius Calloway

Boston, Mass. October 29th, 1896

Dear Mr. Washington: I have just called upon Gov. Wolcott[1] and he declines to speak at the Trinity meeting for the reason that he has a uniform rule not to accept any appointments to speak on Sunday, because if he did not, as a public man, he would never have any Sundays to himself. That he has only broken this rule one time, and that was at a meeting in the interest of Hampton and Tuskegee. He expressed anxiety as to the condition of Mrs. Washington's health, and asked, as well, concerning yourself.

I have now arranged one hundred and twenty dates for meetings, or at least I have one hundred and twenty dates from which to choose. Of course it will not be possible to hold a hundred and twenty meetings in six weeks, unless we should hold three a day. However, the prospects are that we shall have a very full campaign, but as to its financial results, I cannot prophesy. The Atlanta Quartette and Fiske Quartettes are already in the field, and an agent for Hampton is making dates, so that the prospects are that the field will be very warm. I am inclined to believe that the larger places are going to be so over-run that the better chances will be in the smaller communities, and hence I have not to any great extent, made special efforts to confine the appointments to the cities.

I have just had a conversation with Dr. Courtney,[2] relative to the banquet which the Progressive Club have proposed to tender you. He has consulted with Mr. Lewis[3] and others, and the feeling is that it would be unwise for you to have anything to do with the parties represented by this club. Mr. W. H. Scott,[4] the president of the Racial Protective Association has pronounced himself so frequently and so pointedly as opposed to the Tuskegee method and your speeches in general, that it is not believed that he has anything good in view. Dr. Courtney thinks that you would be in danger of being denounced right in the meeting in case you made your usual line of speech. The writer of the letter has called upon me, and I have deferred him until I hear from you.

I enclose you a letter from Asheville, No. Carolina. I think it would be better if you would write to him something definite in the matter.

I thought I had written you that I had arranged with Dr. Gordon[5] to have a meeting of the Trustees at his house on December the 15th, the morning after the public meeting.

I am finding it necessary to make several definite engagements for you during each week, but am trying to make them so that you will be within an hour or two's ride of Boston. Very truly yours,

Thos. J. Calloway

TLS   Con. 116   BTW Papers   DLC.

[1] Roger Wolcott (1847-1900) was governor of Massachusetts from 1896 to 1900. The son of a leading Boston merchant, he graduated from Harvard College in 1870 and Harvard Law School in 1874. After serving in the Boston Common Council and the state legislature, he became lieutenant governor in 1893 and governor in 1896.

[2] Samuel E. Courtney.

[3] William Henry Lewis (1869-1949) was one of the "Talented Tenth" of blacks who by education and ideology were unlike BTW but who found it mutually rewarding to work with him. Born in Berkeley, Va., the son of former slaves, Lewis attended Virginia Normal and Industrial Institute in Petersburg. With money earned as an errand boy in Congress and by work in hotels and restaurants, Lewis entered Amherst College in 1888. He became class orator and captain of the football team. In 1892 and 1893 he played football for Harvard while attending law school there, and was named All-American. For some time after receiving his law degree, Lewis coached the Harvard team. Lewis's athletic prowess as well as his intellectual ability naturally made him a hero to the Harvard alumnus Theodore Roosevelt. When Roosevelt became governor of New York, he invited Lewis to stay overnight at the governor's mansion. BTW was placed in something of a dilemma when, in their early conversations after Roosevelt became President in 1901, Roosevelt urged BTW to work closely with Lewis, who was the type of black leader he sought to appoint to federal office. Lewis had been one of a group of Boston critics of BTW, but he quickly made his peace with the Tuskegean and worked with him not only in politics but in other racial matters. Roosevelt in 1903 appointed Lewis assistant district attorney in Boston, and in 1911 Taft ap-

pointed him assistant attorney general, the highest appointive post held by an American black man up to that time. He became one of the few black members of the American Bar Association, through the intervention of the Attorney General. Returning to private practice, he did some legal work for the NAACP.

⁴ William H. Scott (d. 1910), a black minister of Woburn, Mass., was a close associate of William Monroe Trotter, the militant editor of the Boston *Guardian*. Scott helped to found the *Guardian,* was president of the Boston Suffrage League, and led the Massachusetts Racial Protective Association. (Fox, *Guardian of Boston,* 29, 110.)

⁵ George Angier Gordon (1853-1929) was pastor of Old South Church, Boston, from 1884 to 1927, and was the author of many religious tracts. From 1892 to 1909 he was a trustee of Tuskegee Institute.

From Blanche Kelso Bruce

Washington, D.C., Nov 12 1896

My dear Mr Washington: Your valued favor of Nov. 3 was recd due course of mail. McKinley is elected and we are all happy, and hopeful of the future.

I mailed you a copy of the Post the other day in which the editor speaks of you and me.¹ Whatever may have been the purpose of the writer, one thing is certain — that the mention of colored men in connection with such positions does the race no harm, but may be productive of much good.

The office to which I shall aspire is the one indicated by you, but for reasons which you fully appreciate I do not deem it wise at this time to give publicity to my intentions in this direction. We shall discuss this matter fully when I see you. Present our warmest regards to Mrs Washington. Sincerely Yours

B. K. Bruce

ALS Con. 116 BTW Papers DLC.

¹ The Washington *Post* claimed that William McKinley owed a debt to black Americans for his election and that he should consider appointing a black to a cabinet position. The *Post* named Blanche K. Bruce and BTW as the two most logical black candidates for Secretary of Agriculture. (Washington *Post,* Nov. 7, 1896, 6.)

From Joseph Oswalt Thompson[1]

Tuskegee, Ala., November 14 1896

My dear Sir, I received a copy of the Washington Post, of the 7th inst, this morning, which makes a suggestion that I fully endorse.

It is, that a colored man be given a cabinet Portifolio in the incoming administration, and gives sound reasons to sustain its position. The Post rightly maintains that the colored man has ever remained true to the Republican Party no matter in what part of the United States he may reside and that without his support the Republicans could not have won this last great victory, inasmuch as the Negro holds the balance of power in seven of the middle and western states.

Therefore in acknowledgement of the support of these eight millions of People, the Republican Party should tender them some material recognition. Your name, together with Senator Bruce's, was suggested and I hasten to offer whatever assistance I can render and to devote what influence I may have with Alabama Republicans to have that honor bestowed on *you*. You are, according to my opinion, most fitted of all your Race to occupy that high position of honor, in as much as you have been placed as the foremost man of your people wherever your utterances have been heard or read.

Not only would it prove a blessing to your race, that (though still in the full vigor of young manhood) you have already done so much for but also would it prove that a Negro can hold one of the highest political positions in our Nation and at the same time retain his love and respect for the southern People among whom he was born and has always lived. Such sentiments expressed in public speeches would forever do away with the race problem. If you decide to offer for this political honor, which I hope you will do, advise me and I believe Alabama Republicans to a man will give you their support and endorsement.

Wishing you success in all of your undertakings   I am, Your friend,

J. O. Thompson

ALS Con. 122 BTW Papers DLC. On stationery of the Thompson Hardware and Grocery Co., J. O. Thompson, manager.

[1] Joseph Oswalt Thompson (b. 1869), member of a prominent merchant and cotton-growing family of Tuskegee and brother of the Democratic congressman

Charles Winston Thompson, was the family's only Republican. He was chairman of the Macon County Republican organization and for eight years of the Alabama Republican committee, as well as postmaster of Tuskegee. In 1902 President Roosevelt, at BTW's suggestion, appointed him collector of internal revenue for Alabama and made him one of two referees on presidential appointments and other party matters in Alabama. A strong partisan of Theodore Roosevelt, Thompson was removed from office in 1912 by President Taft.

From Emmett Jay Scott

Houston Texas, Nov. 15/1896

My Dear Sir: I am pleased that you have accepted an invitation to speak in Texas, but am very sorry that only at two places can you speak. You must pass through Houston going to Prairie View and so I shall arrange to have you speak as suits your conv[en]ience here either going to, or returning from that place. The two points are only 46 miles apart, and transportation is easily had every five, or six, hours. Of course, we shall correspond again before that time and I shall be delighted to be advised that you can make at least a week's tour of Texas. These people are anxious to meet you — whites and blacks alike. Very sincerely yours.

Emmett J. Scott

ALS Con. 113 BTW Papers DLC.

An Address at the Opening of the Armstrong-Slater Memorial Trade School

[Hampton, Va., Nov. 18, 1896]

A while ago I spoke at the dedication of a colored orphan asylum in the city of Cincinnati. After I had spoken, one of its donors sitting near me whispered to me: "It was the ambition of my life that this building should be in all its parts the product of colored artisans. But after the foundation was laid I couldn't find enough Negro brick masons, Negro carpenters, plasterers or tinsmiths to complete the building, so I had to turn it over to mechanics of another race — some of them from another country."

My friends, it is just so all over this country. These industries that have been our very life blood are slipping away from our hands. And here it seems to me we have a new opportunity to recover our hold on them.

One value of industrial education is in the fact that without it we are likely to get hold of a superficial culture. In proportion to our means we have more culture than any other people. But culture out of all proportion to our means, culture without a decent home and a bank account means very little.

I will illustrate to you my meaning. I was invited the other day to attend a wedding among our people. I sat in the church, and as the bride came walking up the aisle, I saw something coming creeping and trailing five yards along the floor after her. That had to be turned around into place before she could be married, of course, and then, after the ceremony was over it went creeping and trailing after her out of church. We were invited to the wedding supper provided at the house of [a] friend. There I saw a row of carriages filling the street from one corner to the next — one would have thought the President of the United States was getting married. The wedding supper cost $75 or $100. Then we were invited to get into the carriage and accompany the couple to the door of their new abode. What kind of a house do you suppose that bride and her five yards of trail went home to? I followed that whole thing to a little one roomed log cabin which the bridegroom rented for $2 a month. That [is] the sort of thing I mean by too much culture in proportion to our means. For months that bride and groom must have been dreaming about grocers' bills, and dress makers' bills and tailors' bills and all sorts of bills.

How did people marry in New England two hundred years ago? The young man bought his license for 75 cents and they went to the minister's house and were married quietly, and then went home to the groom's farm and went to work: and their fortunes grew and grew, and they saved their money, and by and by they built a better house and they sent their children to college and today their descendants are counted among the most highly cultured in the world.

Let us begin as they began — get down to hard pan, and rise from a solid foundation, get some property, get good homes, so we can enjoy our religion. Religion tastes mighty good when you have a decent home and decent clothes and proper food. And all this means religion to us, for it means industry and morality and right living.

I wish all the young men and young women here tonight, and all the fathers and mothers, would realize the fact that there is actual need among us of men and women who can support themselves. There are two kinds of sight you know: hindsight and foresight. A great many more people have hindsight than foresight. We want to have foresight, to support ourselves. The colored people are in need of food and clothes. I don't mean they are starving, you can't starve a colored man. But sometimes we — don't starve, but we feel terribly uncomfortable!

Do you know that from eighty to eighty-five per cent of the colored people in the Gulf States depend entirely on agriculture for a living? Yet how many have we educated in agriculture since emancipation? We have educated many in theology and law and medicine — and that is all right — but we have educated hardly any in agriculture, in the line eighty per cent of them must follow in life.

A young colored man who lately graduated at an Agricultural College in Iowa had three positions offered him before he got his diploma. When a college graduate finishes his classical course, he may look for a position — diploma in hand, and look and look — till whiskers grow on the bottoms of his pantaloons. I know of six positions now waiting for young colored men who can give instruction in scientific agriculture; as many for instructors in mechanics; as many more for instructors in cooking.

I was in a Western college a while ago and among its twelve hundred students, I saw many who were taking courses in agriculture and mechanics. There were two colored young men among the students. I thought of course they were taking either an agricultural or mechanical course. How I rejoiced that they had such an opportunity. I asked the President of the college, "What course are those young colored men taking?" "Oh" he replied, "they are studying — oratory!" Understand me. I don't mean that a colored man hasn't the same right to study oratory that a white man has. I claim the best chances for my people, equal to those of any race. But when you take your oratory down South where our people are in need of food and clothes and decent homes, your oratory won't live down there. But if you can teach men and women how to live and how to make a living, then, in ten or twenty years, they can go to an evening entertainment and pay for it and enjoy it. That is the foundation we've got to lay for our culture. An old-time preacher was once teaching a Sunday-school class. A young fellow sat there fresh from college. The old preacher was explaining to the class how Pharoah got drowned in the Red Sea and the children of Israel were saved.

"You see, brudderin, dose chillen of Israel, dey crossed dat sea soon in de mo'nin', while de ice was hard, but ole Pharaoh he came too late, de ice all melted." The young collegian said, "Mr. Pastor, I've been to college and I've studied geography, and geography teaches us that water can't freeze in a country like Egypt, near the equator."

"Oh, you knows a lot," said the preacher — "I've just been spectin we'd hear from you. Dis time I've been speakin' of, brudderns, was fore dere was any jogafry, or any quators either."

Now here at Hampton we have all the time been removing artificial layers, getting down to bed rock, if we go on as we have begun there is a bright future before us.

I fear nothing of trouble between the races. We can go on without fear of that. And there is nothing to prevent us from being better than any who would do us harm. Let us be great whoever else is small. If the white man hates us, let us give him love in return for hate. If others are mean, let us be good. I have grown to the point where no man shall drag me down to hate him. No man can hate another without degrading himself. If others would push us down, let us help them up. And then, more and more shall we see repeated what we have seen and heard on these grounds today.

Southern Workman, 25 (Dec. 1896), 241-42.

From Daniel Augustus Straker[1]

Detroit, November 19th 1896

My dear friend: The mail brings me to day your published report of "Tuskegee Normal and Industrial Institute." It is a grand showing and reflects much credit on you for the noble work you have done.

You have done more than raise money for the work the past year. You have uplifted the Negro race in America, aye, the World over.

Your plan of Negro advancement has met with general approval. There is but one thing more in my humble opinion to make the trestle board complete, and let the laborers go to work, and that is — Like opportunity for the Negro to work with his fellow white citizen; but I recognize that the work you are doing is necessarily preparatory. Go on, and God will bless you, and protect you in all your doings. It seems that God's protection is especially needed, when I tell you that Rev. J. J. Smallwood,[2] President of Claremont, Va., Temperance Institute has been publicly denounced as a fraud and a cheat in the Detroit Journal. I hope he can make a complete defense. If not, what a mill stone will be around your neck.

I am glad to see you spoken of for a Cabinet place in President Elect McKinley's Cabinet.

I am sorry to inform you that I retire from public Office, January 1st 1897, owing to factional strife among the colored citizens of this City. They were two other colored Candidates. They were warned that if they continued, the opposition to me, the race would lose the place entirely; yet they continued, and the place has gone — perhaps forever — a white man was chosen. I sought a Third Term upon the ground that two white officials were seeking the same. My colored opponents denied me the right to claim equal rights with the white men, claiming Third Terms also. How strange and inconsistent. The white men got each a third term; but with the assistance given by my colored opponents, I was defeated in the Convention.

Let me hear from you. Madam joins me in best regards for you and family. Very truly yours.

D Augustus Straker

TLS Con. 112 BTW Papers DLC.

[1] Daniel Augustus Straker (1842-1908) was born in Bridgetown, Barbados, and received an excellent education there. He moved to the United States in 1867 or 1868 and taught in a freedmen's school in Louisville, Ky., for two years before entering Howard University Law School. Graduating from Howard in 1871, Straker served briefly as stenographer to General O. O. Howard before becoming a clerk in the U.S. Treasury Department for several years. In 1875 he was appointed inspector of customs at Charleston, S.C., but resigned to open a law practice in Orangeburg, S.C., the following year. He was elected to three successive terms in the South Carolina legislature beginning in 1876 but was denied his seat because it was claimed he was not an American citizen, though he was naturalized. Straker was dean of the law school of Allen University in Columbia, S.C., from 1882 to 1887. His aspiration for public office and his effort to maintain his civil rights were thwarted in a period of disfranchisement and proscription in the South.

Straker moved to Detroit in 1887 and began a law practice there, and he quickly rose to become Detroit's leading black attorney and politician, twice being elected to serve as Wayne County circuit court commissioner.

A well-known essayist, Straker contributed to many black journals during his day and counted among his six books a biography of Toussaint L'Ouverture. As one historian has commented: "In both prose and politics, Straker trod a path that wandered between the activism of W. E. B. Du Bois and the accommodation of Booker T. Washington." He often urged blacks to agitate for their civil rights but also cautioned that blacks in the South should not engage in politics as long as they were disfranchised. (Katzman, *Before the Ghetto,* 189-94.)

[2] BTW's friend Emily Howland pursued an energetic campaign for several years to have Smallwood denounced in every northern city where she could learn that he was soliciting funds for his school, which she claimed was entirely or nearly nonexistent.

Margaret James Murray Washington to Ednah Dow Littlehale Cheney

Tuskegee, Ala., Nov. 23–'96

My Dear Mrs. Cheney: I have meant to write you more than once since I came home but I find that I am obliged to consult my strength every little while.

I am writing you now of a matter which concerns me and the rest of women of my race. I want your advice.

You know as much about this separate car business in the South as I can tell you. The southern people, of course, make these laws — The Rail Road Officials have little or nothing to do with them. I think the change will come only as the sentiment of the Southern white man is changed. Another thing, the southern women keep up this thing. They are behind the men because their education is more limited — they have little to do except to nurse their predjuices. They do not object to the colored woman who is their servant but they especially object to colored people who are not thus located.

I have wanted to get a petition but we have no money to pay for its presentation and thus we are hedged in here. We have no colored legislators in the states where the law exists except one in Tennessee. I want to petition for first and second class fare.

I hear that the Executive Board of the National Council of Women

meet in Boston this winter to prepare for their meeting next year. I
have thought our cause in this matter might be helped, by having a
Colored woman to appear in this Council, to present, not only this
question but she might represent us in a general way. I understand
that organizations of southern white women will not enter the Federation nor the Council of white women, because there they are opposed
to colored organizations entering these clubs. Even if this is true, there
would be southern women in the audiences. I have no cencure for the
northern white woman, if we have any friends at all, they are but
the great organizations such as the W.C.T.U the national Council,
the Federation &c managed by northern white women if they were
inclined, could do more in the direction of correcting evils or indig-
nities against the colored women than they. I do not belong to the
agressive class but I believe if such women, as Miss Willard,[1] Mrs.
Henrotin[2] Mrs. Dickinson[3] and others were to show a little less fear
of their southern sisters, these conditions of which I speak would be
altered. They are anxious to make their organizations succeed as to
numbers money &c and I think this is correct but the sacrifice of free
speech ought not to be given up. I can not tell you how I have felt
since Miss Willard has taken up the Armenian question, not that she
should not do this but it is so strange that these people who have no
special claim upon this country should so take possession of the hearts
of northern women, that the woman of color is entirely over looked.
These great religious papers are painfully silent upon this indignity and
yet they preach to us to be Christians — I must confess I can not
understand it. Thousands of young Colored live a living death under
these things, they can not be otherwise. The colored women have organized themselves into an association in order to correct certain evils
among women and girls and to bring about needed reforms. The first
year we met in your city, in July, we met in Washington. The women
who live north object to coming south to hold a meeting because of the
travel. This is where work must be done for this is where the great
mass of the colored women are. When I think of this state of affairs
I feel as if I must do something if it is only to open my heart to someone as I am doing tonight. I can not rest.

I hope you will think of us Mrs. Cheney and if you can see any
way to help if only by telling me what you think of an attempt to
create a sentiment against.

You know I promised last spring to send you those exhibits. I do not know that I can do so for I have been from home so long and now I do not move around very much.

I hope that you are well and that this winter is to be to you, a good one. Yours very respectfully,

Mrs. Booker T. Washington

ALS   Ednah Dow Cheney Papers   MB.

[1] Frances Elizabeth Caroline Willard (1839-98), temperance leader and feminist, was a co-founder of the National and International Councils of Women in 1888, and of the General Federation of Women's Clubs in 1889. She was president of the Women's Christian Temperance Union from 1879 until her death. Under her leadership, the WCTU was involved in a wide range of liberal causes, including the social deprivations of southern blacks.

[2] Ellen Martin Henrotin (1847-1922), wife of a bank president, was active in labor and social reform movements and was a prominent club woman in Chicago. She was president of the General Federation of Women's Clubs from 1894 to 1898. Later she sought to unionize women workers and to investigate and eliminate prostitution. She also served on the executive committee of the Amanda Smith School for Negro Girls in Harvey, Ill.

[3] Mary Lowe Dickinson (1839-1914), poet and novelist, was president of the National Council of Women from 1895 to 1897.

George Washington Carver to the Tuskegee Financial Committee

Tuskegee Ala. 11-27-96

Messrs of the finance Com.: Some of you saw the other day something of the valuable nature of one of my collections. I have others of equal value, and along Agr. lines.

You doubtless know that I came here soley for the benefit of my people, no other motive in view.

Moreover I do not expect to teach many years, but will quit as soon as I can trust my work to others, and engage in my brush work, which will be of great honor to our people showing to what we may attain along science, History literature and art.

At present I have no rooms even to unpack my goods. I beg of you to give me these, and suitable ones also, not for my sake alone but for the sake of education. At present the room is full of mice and they are into my boxes doing me much damage I fear.

While I am with you please fix me so I may be of as much service to you as possible.

Also I am handicaped in my work. I wanted a medical journal the other day in order that I might prescribe for a sick animal. It was of course boxed up, couldn't get it. Trusting you see clearly my situation and will act as soon as possible I remain most Resp. yours

Geo. W. Carver

ALS Con. 115 BTW Papers DLC.

From Samuel McCune Lindsay[1]

Philadelphia, Nov. 28th 1896

Dear Sir: Enclosed please find the proof-sheets of the schedules which have been adopted for the Investigation into the Condition of the Negroes in Ward Seven of the City of Philadelphia. We desire to make this investigation as thorough as possible and to have the results in such shape as to be comparable with similar work undertaken in other cities. The work is being done by Mr. W. E. B. Du Bois, Ph.D. (Harvard) and Miss Isabel Eaton, B.L. (Smith), under the direction of this department of the University which will print all results worthy of publication.

Will you kindly examine the enclosed proofs and return them at once with any corrections or suggestions which in your judgment will add to the value of the investigation?

The proofs will be held until December 2nd, and corrections arriving later than that date, will be unavailable. A complete set of the final schedules will be sent to you. Yours very truly,

Samuel McCune Lindsay

TLS Con. 129 BTW Papers DLC.

[1] Samuel McCune Lindsay (1869-1959) was a pioneer American sociologist with a Ph.D. from the University of Halle (1892). An expert on housing and labor economics, he was appointed instructor in sociology at the University of Pennsylvania in 1894. He was responsible for the appointment of W. E. B. Du Bois

to study blacks living in Philadelphia's seventh ward, a study which resulted in Du Bois's pioneering book, *The Philadelphia Negro*. From 1902 to 1904 Lindsay was commissioner of education of Puerto Rico, while retaining his chair in sociology at the University of Pennsylvania. He moved to Columbia University in 1907, remaining there until his retirement in 1939.

From Timothy Thomas Fortune

Jacksonville, Fla., Dec 1, 1896[1]

Dear Friend: I don't think you want to go into the Cabinet or think that a man of ours can get there. I would be glad if you would drop a line to Major McKinley at once endorsing Col. A. E. Buck[2] of Georgia as the Southern member. If he gets there *we* shall have a friend at court. As things now stand Henry Clay Evans[3] of Tennessee, a rank cuss, has the inside track.

Why haven't I had a line from you. Peterson[4] sent me the Boston Herald Editorial. I sent it back marked "go."

My father is a shade better. How is Mrs Washington? Yours truly

T. Thomas Fortune

ALS   Con. 116   BTW Papers   DLC.

[1] Fortune wrote a similar letter to BTW on Dec. 2 which he addressed to BTW in Boston rather than Tuskegee.

[2] Alfred Eliab Buck (1832-1902), a Union veteran who had served with black troops, held a number of Republican appointive posts in Alabama during Reconstruction and was a congressman from 1869 to 1871. Moving to Atlanta in 1874, he remained an active Republican officeholder. He was U.S. minister to Japan from 1897 to 1902. Washington may have recommended him for this appointment. (See BTW to Fortune, Dec. 6, 1896, below.)

[3] Henry Clay Evans (1843-1921), a Union veteran, settled in Chattanooga after the war and quickly prospered as a railroad car manufacturer. He was twice elected mayor of Chattanooga and served in Congress in 1889-91 as a Republican. In 1897 he became U.S. commissioner of pensions, and in 1902 consul general in London.

[4] Jerome Bowers Peterson (1860-1943) was Fortune's partner in the New York *Freeman* and New York *Age* from 1887 until 1904, when he secured a federal appointment, first as consul at Puerto Cabello in 1904-5 and then in the New York office of the Internal Revenue Service. Later he was employed on the *Age* by Fred R. Moore, until his retirement in 1933.

From Warren Logan

Tuskegee 12/4/1896

Dear Mr. Washington: A committee from the legislature was here yesterday — not quite as many were in the party as we were expecting, yet there were thirty in the party including the speaker of the house, Col. Clements[1] and Major Culver,[2] Commissioner of Agriculture.

The party reached Tuskegee at one thirty and after dinner at the hotel came out to the school and went through all of the industrial departments. After completing the round of the departments they assembled in the pavilion and a few of them spoke to the school. Those who spoke publicly and privately expressed themselves as very much surprised and gratified at what they had seen at the school and said that they would do all in their power to help the school in its effort to have an Experiment Station established here. Mr. Campbell, Judge Hurt and Milo Abercrombie[3] came out from the town and went around with the committee. Mr. Campbell made a speech to the committee telling something of the early history of the school.

I believe that the visit of the committee will help us very greatly in every way.

I think Mr. Hare[4] cannot be commended too highly for the part which he took in the affair. He will follow up our bill in the legislature and I have no doubt but that it will go through but as the legislature adjourns for recess next week it is not likely that the bill can be pushed through until the legislature re-assembles in Jan. Very truly yours,

Warren Logan

TLS Con. 118 BTW Papers DLC.

[1] Newton Nash Clements (1837-1900) was born in Tuscaloosa and graduated from the University of Alabama in 1858. He studied law at Harvard University but never practiced that profession, pursuing instead his interest in cotton planting and manufacture. From 1870 Clements served almost continuously in the state legislature for twenty-five years. He was elected speaker of the house four times and was instrumental in developing the bill establishing the state school system. In 1880 Clements was appointed to fill a vacancy in the U.S. Congress, but lost the bid for renomination in 1881.

[2] Isaac Franklin Culver, born in Sparta, Ga., in 1830, moved to Alabama with his family as a young man and became a cotton planter in Bullock County. After serving in the state legislature from 1878 to 1882, Culver spent the next six years as Bullock County superintendent of education and president of the state agricultural society. From 1896 until 1900 he was state commissioner of agriculture.

³ Milo Bolling Abercrombie, Jr., of Tuskegee, was for many years probate judge in Macon County.

⁴ Charles Woodroph Hare (b. 1857) was a Baptist minister and lawyer who was active in local affairs in Tuskegee after settling there in the early 1890s. He was a member of the city council and editor of the Tuskegee *News*. He also served on the board of trustees at Tuskegee Institute from 1896 until after BTW's death. Hare accompanied BTW to the White House in 1898 to invite President McKinley to visit Tuskegee.

To Timothy Thomas Fortune

Crawford House, Boston, Mass. Dec. 6, 1896

My Dear Mr. Fortune: I have yours of December 2nd. In regard to Col. Buck, I am going to see Major McKinley in person in January; would it not be better to speak to him at that time about Col. Buck? I will do whatever you think is best. I am glad to know you think so highly of him. I am not acquainted with either him or Mr. Evans. You ought to get a good position out of this administration, you deserve it, you are too honest, however, to succeed in politics as politics are going these days. I am getting a lot of fun out of the cabinet matter.

Matters look brighter here financially.

You speak of being in Jacksonville until February. Our Negro Conference occurs Feb. 24th. Will it be possible for you to come by and drop in upon us? I will look out for expenses in that case. Shall be here for ten days. I am glad to hear that your father is better. Yours truly,

Booker T. Washington

TLS   Con. 116   BTW Papers   DLC.

From William E. Benson[1]

Kowaliga, Ala., Dec/6/96

My Dear Mr. Washington: Yours of a recent date to hand. You will, perhaps, be surprised to learn that some one set my store on fire about 2 o'clock Tuesday morning while I was at home preparing to leave

243

for Montgomery, and burned up every thing I had save what was on my back and in my Iron Safe. My stock of goods over $2300.00, my photo stock, & negatives — all belonging to myself and your school — three cameras included worth over $200.00 — my bed-room contents, clothes, a fine machine which had just been put in for Matilda who had opened up a sewing room and all my private trinkets, gifts books &c. Loss over $3000 — not a cent insurance. I had tried to get insurance but couldn't as you know what a time papa had trying to insure his milling establishment. They have been afraid of our property ever since. It was all result of envy and jealousy between *mean* negroes and poor white *trash.* You know how much help we are to this community and how hard we have labored to help our people here but it seems that there is an element here that is determined to keep us from succeeding. We have lost on that spot over $6000 within last 5 years. We look for the mill and school building to go next.

You can imagine my state of mind after laboring and sacrificing for a year and paying of all my debts — to have my goods, which was all that was left as a result of my labor, swept away by the fire.

I had thought of applying to you for work at Tuskegee. Then it occurred to me that I might do some good for our school here in the north. I had intended sending you a set of pictures (13 in all) showing every step of our work here by the patrons from cutting stock in woods to the building as it stands but only made one set for Mrs Kaine and had just carried them home to send her before the burning occurred.

I am pretty well discouraged and would be glad of any word of encouragement from you. Yours truly,

Wm E. Benson

ALS Con. 114 BTW Papers DLC.

1 William E. Benson, born in Kowaliga, Ala., graduated from Howard University in 1895 and founded the Kowaliga Academic and Industrial Institute the following year. Five years later he organized the Dixie Industrial Company, which owned 10,000 acres, several mills and stores, and 1,300 acres in farms, property which Benson hoped would develop into a self-sufficient black community. The possibility of black-owned businesses and black-owned land, he expected, would halt migration to the cities and end the deprivations of seasonal employment. While urging blacks to economic self-sufficiency, Benson demanded of whites the equal protection of property and equal justice before the law as "the least" they should grant the blacks. For a few years BTW was one of Benson's trustees, but in November 1898 he suddenly resigned, despite efforts of Emily Howland, Hollis Burke Frissell, and Francis J. Garrison to persuade him that Benson was an example of the Tuskegee philosophy of self-help. Benson was a good friend of Du Bois, who

nonetheless criticized the Kowaliga school in *The Crisis,* particularly for maintaining a white board of trustees. Shortly before he died, in 1915, Benson was involved in a fight with the trustees over financial matters.

From Charles Barzillai Spahr[1]

New York, Dec. 10th, 1896

Dear Sir: Dr. Abbott desires me to thank you very heartily for your letter concerning Governor Johnston.[2] The message which you inclose is of great interest to us and throws just the light on the situation which we desire. Your own view also is one to which Dr. Abbott attaches great weight and though you express it very briefly he thanks you most cordially for the expression. Yours very truly,

Charles B Spahr

An associate hands me another letter received during my absence from the city. It will be brought before Dr Abbott. We thank you for all the trouble you have taken.

CBS

TLS   Con. 122   BTW Papers   DLC.

[1] Charles B. Spahr (1860-1904) studied economics at Leipzig and took a Ph.D. at Columbia University. He was on the editorial staff of the *Outlook* from 1886 to 1904.

[2] Joseph Forney Johnston (1843-1913), governor of Alabama and U.S. senator, was born in Lincoln County, N.C., and moved with his family to Talladega, Ala., before the outbreak of the Civil War. Enlisting in the Confederate Army when he was seventeen, Johnston was wounded four times before he was mustered out as a captain. After admission to the bar in 1866, Johnston practiced law in Selma until 1884, when he moved to Birmingham to assume the presidency of the Alabama National Bank and there began his profitable political and business careers. Birmingham, which had been little more than a railroad crossing thirteen years before, was then in the midst of a business boom resulting from the exploitation of its iron and coal resources. Johnston quickly expanded his financial and managerial interests, becoming the first president of the Sloss Iron and Steel Company, one of the principal pioneer manufacturing firms.

An active Democrat, Johnston was chairman of the party's state executive committee and was elected governor for two consecutive terms, serving from 1896 to 1900. Johnston was proud of his administration's efficient tax policies, increased public school expenditures, and successful program for out-of-state capital investment in Alabama businesses. But a major controversy over the need for a new state constitution marred the personal success of Johnston's tenure. The movement for revision, initially based on tax reform to facilitate industrial development, soon focused on using the constitutional convention to disfranchise blacks. Though in favor of the convention at first, Johnston led the opposition when he feared that rigid voting requirements would also disfranchise the poor whites, his principal constituents. His position brought party censure and probably lost him the senate nomination in 1900. In 1907, however, he was appointed to fill a senatorial vacancy, and he was elected to a full term two years later.

BTW apparently wrote to Lyman Abbott about Johnston's message to the state legislature which advocated ending the convict-lease system, paroling convicts for good behavior, and speedy trials for severe crimes. The last proposal was designed partly to reduce the number of lynchings by keeping mobs from taking the law in their own hands, for a frequent argument of lynch mobs was that the law was too slow and uncertain a remedy. Johnston also urged an upgrading of the Alabama educational system. The *Outlook* used BTW's observations in an editorial. (*Outlook,* 54 [Dec. 19, 1896], 1131.)

To the Editor of the Boston *Transcript*[1]

Tuskegee, Ala. [ca. Dec. 15, 1896]

To the Editor of the Transcript: If there are those who would like to help brighten the Christmas days of the children connected with the plantation schools in the Black Belt of the South and will send to me Christmas cards, etc., new or old, I will see that they are sent to our graduates who are teaching on these plantations among a class of people who will have little to remind them of Christmas.

Booker T. Washington

Boston *Transcript,* Dec. 19, 1896, 17.

[1] BTW customarily sent a similar letter to various northern papers every Christmas season.

From Timothy Thomas Fortune

Jacksonville, Fla., Dec 18, 1896

My Dear Friend: I have your favor of the 15th instant and appreciate very highly the sentiments you express concerning myself and the incoming administration. I shall be reluctant to seek any preferment, because of the grand scramble our *common* men make, for place and the opposition I always encounter from the Bruce-Lynch crowd all along the line. I certainly should not ask for any position ever held by an Afro-American, and no outsiders should know I was in the hunt. I should like to be the American representative of the International Board of Arbitration in Egypt or Consul to Jamaica, W.I. when we meet we can talk it over.

If we dont get Buck in the cabinet we may get Hanson, and we shall be on the inside in the either case.

I am real glad to learn that Mrs. Washington improves daily and I hope she may soon be entirely well. My father's condition remains unchanged. I have sent an editorial to The Age give Chase[1] of the Washington *Bee* a ripping up the back for his foolish and ungenerous attacks on you. With kind regards, Yours truly

T. Thomas Fortune

I have done no special work for 8 weeks and am broke, but hopeful. Could not lecture for Prof Wright[2] today on account of unfavorable change in father's condition on Thursday.

F.

ALS Con. 116 BTW Papers DLC.

[1] William Calvin Chase (1854-1921) was born in Washington, D.C., and was mostly self-educated. Ten years old when his father died, Chase moved to Massachusetts but later returned to Washington to work in the Government Printing Office and begin a career as an editor. Chase edited the Washington *Argus* and *Free Lance* before taking over the Washington *Bee*. Lacking a consistent ideology, he lashed out in all directions. The *Bee*'s motto was "Honey for friends and stings for enemies," and the editorial policy reflected Chase's personal journalism and frequent changes of direction. Chase was among BTW's earliest critics after the Atlanta Exposition address in 1895. In 1900 Chase reversed himself and began to publish Washington's speeches and give him other favorable notice. Then, in late 1901, Chase discovered BTW was supporting Robert H. Terrell rather than himself for appointment to a District of Columbia judgeship. He turned against Washington for five years, going so far as to support William Monroe Trotter against BTW after the Boston Riot. In 1906, by an elaborate strategy that involved installing a spy/provocateur in Chase's office, BTW inveigled Chase into accepting BTW's subsidies and publishing matter favorable to the Tuskegean. From that time until BTW's death Chase was loyal to Washington editorially, though he often grumbled at the crumbs that fell from the master's table. Chase was encouraged in this direction, undoubtedly, by the financial aid from Tuskegee and the fact that his militant former friends regarded him as a traitor, but a recent detailed study of Chase's accommodation to BTW suggests that a part of this ambivalent man's nature and thought always responded favorably to BTW's racial program. (Harlan, "Secret Life of BTW," 410-11; Chase, " 'Honey for Friends, Stings for Enemies.' ")

[2] Richard Robert Wright, Sr.

To Timothy Thomas Fortune

Tuskegee, Ala., Dec. 26, 1896

My dear Mr. Fortune: Enclosed I send you an editorial taken from this week's Independent.[1] I must confess that I am greatly disappointed and rather startled by the tone and spirit of this editorial. It seems wholly unlike the Independent. I cannot think that Dr. Ward[2] wrote this editorial. I very much hope that you will see your way clear to give it some attention in the editorial columns of your paper. I do not know whether the writer means to intimate that I am seeking a cabinet position or not, but this is a matter of small consequence, but it is the spirit of the editorial to which I refer. I might say to you in this connection that I have never turned my hand over in connection with this matter of the cabinet agitation. I have said to several of my friends that I felt that no harm could come to the race by reason of the agitation, on the other hand I think good will be accomplished, but I am willing that you should know privately that Mr. McKinley has no position within his gift that I would think of accepting were it offered. Yours truly,

Booker T. Washington

TLS Con. 116 BTW Papers DLC.

[1] The editorial in *The Independent*, "The Negroes' Fool Friends," first attacked "misguided" efforts to pension former slaves. Then it advised blacks: "It is not to their honor to be soliciting appointive offices on the ground of color, when they can do better work for their race as teachers, etc. Some of their fool friends are suggesting that Booker T. Washington be put into the Cabinet. Why so? He has found his niche, is doing splendidly where he is; but he has no experience that would fit him to be Secretary of State, or of the Interior, or Attorney-General, or Postmaster-General.... The time will come when Negroes will have their share of competent men. But let them first give themselves to the most honorable labor of elevating their people; and, if they want office, let them seek elective rather than appointive offices. The fact is, that we do not like office seekers, white or black, very much. It is better when the office seeks the man." (*The Independent*, 48 [Dec. 24, 1896], 10-11.)

[2] William Hayes Ward (1835-1916), editor of *The Independent*, was a graduate of Andover Theological Seminary, a former church missionary and college teacher, and a distinguished Orientalist. He was an abolitionist in his youth, and after the Civil War he continued his fight against racial intolerance and encouraged blacks to publish in his magazine. Ward gave the keynote address at the National Negro Conference in 1909 at which the NAACP was formed. When Ward died, William S. Scarborough, president of Wilberforce University, wrote: "He has virtually devoted his life to the interests of the race, to its emancipation, to its education,

to its struggle, to its ambitions, to its possible future, without a particle of prejudice." (*The Independent,* 87 [Sept. 11, 1916], 386.)

To Timothy Thomas Fortune

Tuskegee, Ala., Dec. 26, 1896

My dear Mr. Fortune: Yours of December 18th has been forwarded to me from Boston. I reached home day before yesterday after an absence of about six weeks.

I think after things get settled in Washington after the 4th of March we can put on foot a plan to carry out your wishes in regard to going abroad. To me it seems pretty evident now that either Allison or Mr. Andrew D. White[1] will be appointed Secretary of State, in that case we shall be all right. I am personally acquainted with Mr. White and I feel that what I say would go a long ways in your favor, and Mr. Allison knows the stand that both you and I took in regard to his nomination so in either case I do not see how things would miscarry if we keep our eyes open and our hands at work.

I thank you very much for what you have done in regard to Chase. I never read his paper and hence am not conversant of the nature of his attacks, but I thank you sincerely for taking the matter up. Of course you can easily understand that I am misquoted in all kinds of ways, for instance I saw an article a few days ago in a San Francisco paper which purported to be a quotation from my Richmond speech in which I advised colored men and women not to take up the professions, I have never done anything of the kind.

If I can be of any service to you in a financial way during the sickness of your father I shall be glad to do so. I realize what it means for you to be tied up in this way. I trust however that by this time your father is on the road to recovery. Yours truly,

Booker T. Washington

TLS Con. 116 BTW Papers DLC.

[1] Andrew Dickson White (1832-1918), historian, was the first president of Cornell University, serving from 1865 to 1885. During that period and later, he held several high-level diplomatic posts. In 1896 White published his two-volume work, *A History of the Warfare of Science with Theology in Christendom.*

From Timothy Thomas Fortune

Jacksonville, Fla., Dec 31, 1896

My Dear Prof Washington: Your favor of the 26th came this morning and I thank you for the Independent clipping. I will go after it in the Age. I think Dr Ward wrote the article. He certainly wrote the last two sentences of it. He gets very cranky sometimes, but his heart is in the right place. The discussion of your name in connection with the Cabinet will do you good. *You did not start it and you can't stop it.* And you are in a position where you cannot decline a[n] honor which has not been offered you. You can afford to stand still and let the whole business proceed. Yours truly

T. Thomas Fortune

ALS Con. 116 BTW Papers DLC.

From George Washington Lovejoy

Mobile, Ala. Dec. 31st 1896

My Dear Mr. Washington: I received your letter asking me to see the Senitor and Representatives of my county, now members of the Legislature, and use what infuence I have to get them to vote favorable to the bill, that is now before the Alabama legislature, for the purpose of establishing an Agricultural Experiment Station, in connection with the Tuskegee Normal School.

I assure you that I will call upon these gentlemen at once, and do what I can to have them see, that this is the proper thing to do for us.[1]

I am personally acquainted with all the members of the legislature from my county, and on the best friendly terms with them.

Three of them are brother lawyers, and treat me with that curticy belonging to fraturnal brother.

I will report to you how they talk after I have seen them all.

Hoping that the vote may go as we wish.

Best reguards for you, your work and all. I am respectfully Yours,

Geo W. Lovejoy

ALS Con. 118 BTW Papers DLC.

An Article in *Our Day*

[Tuskegee, Ala., December 1896]

CHRISTIANIZING AFRICA

"Cape Town, Aug. 7. — Details have just been received here of the decisive victory won on Wednesday by the seven hundred British troops composing Colonel Plumer's column, over a native force estimated to have numbered from 5,000 to 7,000 men. The latter fought most desperately and bravely, charging up within a few yards of the British rapid fire guns.

"About 500 of the Matabele warriors were slain during the engagement.

"At 6 o'clock on Wednesday morning, a force of about 700 men, whites and natives, cavalry, infantry and artillery, all under British officers, marched to the Umlugu valley.

"But when the screw guns began crashing case-shot into the enemy, tearing wide, bloody gaps in the ranks, and the deadly Maxim rattled its hail of lead into the heaving, serried masses of the rapidly moving impis, the natives wavered in their charge, and a moment later the rush was stopped and they began to give way, leaving heaps of dead and wounded."

The brief extracts quoted above from the press dispatches tell their own story. Such dispatches are nothing unusual. They can be seen almost weekly.

With such an object lesson before us, why need Christians wonder that Africa is not Christianized faster. What is the crime of these heathen? Why are they thus shot down — mowed down by the acre. Simply because God has given them land that some one else wants to possess — simply because they are ignorant and weak.

On the very day, perhaps at the very hour that the British troops were mowing down those Africans simply because they tried to defend their homes, their wives and their children, hundreds of prayers were being offered up in as many English churches that God might convert the heathen in Africa and bring them to our way of thinking and acting. What mockery!

Have not these Matabele warriors as much right to lay claim to the streets of London, as the English have to claim the native land of these Africans? What England has done every Christian (?) nation in Europe has done.

On one ship a half dozen missionaries go to use the Bible and prayer book — in the next ship go a thousand soldiers to use the rifle.

Can we wonder that the Africans hesitate about exchanging their religion for that of the Anglo-Saxon race?

Booker T. Washington

Our Day, 16 (Dec. 1896), 674-75.

From Stephen E. Moses[1]

Anniston, Ala., Jan. 4–'97

Dear Sir Your letter recd. In reply to same I saw Senator Abercrombie.[2] We discussed the appropriation feature of Tuskegee bill. His honor, he assured me would publicly support the bill as a whole, that his Committee would both endorse and support the same, that he thought it would undoubtedly pass both houses. The only point "pro or con" whether some of Senators thought appropriation too large. Say if you think considerately have your representative to add "a reductory appropriation provis[i]on" then there will be no *doubt* of its passage. Truly Yours

Stephen E. Moses
Prin. High School

P.S. Anniston celebrated Jan 1st here right. You as it were, were honored as riding a cream colored horse, the leader of the race, and the procession. Made the walk in ring. It was my pleasure to be in Atlanta the same day. R. R. Wright, the orator, made an antagonistic speech — of a prejudicial nature. He attempted to arouse public sentiment against "some one" as if "he" was against higher education. In his effort he made you more prominent. He caused people to know you who did not. The while speaking some one cried out Hurra for Booker T. Washington. The house yelled out. The Georgia Negro is jealous of Our Washington but they will have to get in the procession for he is their leader, and a safe one. Yrs

S. E. M.

P.S. Dont give up Tuskegee to go in McKinley cabinet. Stay with Tuskegee, & in Ala.

S. E. M

ALS   Con. 131   BTW Papers   DLC.

¹ Stephen E. Moses, according to city directories, was principal of the Seventeenth Street School in Anniston, Ala., one of three black public schools in the city in 1898. His wife Della also taught in the school. Sometime after 1914 Moses relinquished the principalship to be a teacher, and in 1924, perhaps in partial retirement, he held a position as cashier of the school.

² John William Abercrombie (1866-1940) was a leading Alabama politician and educator for three decades. A graduate of Oxford College and a law graduate of the University of Alabama, Abercrombie was an Alabama state senator from 1896 to 1898. From 1898 to 1902 he was state superintendent of education, and had many contacts with BTW. He was president of the University of Alabama (1902-11), a U.S. congressman (1913-17), and an official of the Department of Labor in the Wilson administration. He was again state superintendent of education from 1920 to 1926. Though often conservative in political matters, Abercrombie was a consistent champion of educational progress.

To Timothy Thomas Fortune

Tuskegee, Ala., Jan. 16, 1897

My dear Mr. Fortune: A few days ago I sent you from some point in the West a letter containing the check to which your previous letter referred. I did not remember your post office address and so sent it to the general delivery; I hope you received it all right.

I have just gotten home and shall be here for some months.

It seems now a certain thing that Sherman¹ will be in charge of the State Department. He is as cold as an oyster and I do not think we can expect anything from him. I learned however that there is a chance of my friend, Mr. Henry White,² being connected with the State Department, perhaps as first assistant, if this is true we shall be all right as he is an excellent friend of mine. Yours truly,

Booker T. Washington

TLS   Con. 129   BTW Papers   DLC.

¹ John Sherman (1823-1900), after a long and distinguished career in the U.S. Senate, was Secretary of State briefly in 1897-98.

² Henry White (1850-1927) was a career diplomat from the 1880s through World War I, holding a number of positions in European countries and advising President Woodrow Wilson during the Versailles Peace Conference in 1919. Mc-Kinley appointed him first secretary in the London embassy.

From Timothy Thomas Fortune

Jacksonville, Fla., Jan 18, 1897

Dear Friend: Your favor of the 16th instant was received this morning. I wrote you on Wednesday last acknowledgment of check from Milwaukee and last night I wrote you concerning Chase and the Bee and my father.

I am glad you are home for a while. My father is still between life and death.

We are likely to go to smash on the Cabinet make up. Sherman, John D. Long,¹ Nathan Goff,² Henry C. Payne,³ R. A. Alger,⁴ C. N. Bliss.⁵ It is a regular mugwump affair as far as we are concerned. I shall wait and see what the Cabinet is before opening my mouth one way or the other. But it is simply outrageous to put old John Sherman in the State department. With kind regards, Yours truly

T. Thomas Fortune

ALS   Con. 116   BTW Papers   DLC.

¹ John Davis Long (1838-1915) was Secretary of the Navy (1897-1902). He had previously been governor of Massachusetts (1880-82) and congressman (1883-89).

² Nathan Goff (1843-1920) of West Virginia was Secretary of the Navy briefly in 1881, a congressman (1883-89), a circuit judge (1892-1913), and a U.S. senator (1913-19).

³ Henry Clay Payne (1843-1904), a railroad entrepreneur and Wisconsin politician, was postmaster of Milwaukee from 1876 to 1886. From 1902 to 1904 he was Postmaster General and one of Theodore Roosevelt's chief advisers on patronage matters. In this role he worked closely with BTW and James S. Clarkson against the southern "lily-white" Republicans.

⁴ Russell Alexander Alger (1836-1907), a former governor of Michigan, was McKinley's Secretary of War from 1897 to 1899. From 1902 until his death he was a U.S. senator.

⁵ Cornelius Newton Bliss (1833-1911), a successful textile manufacturer in New York, was Secretary of the Interior (1897-99) and treasurer of the Republican national committee (1892-1908).

From John Wesley Cromwell[1]

Washington, D.C., Jan. 19, 1896[7]

Confidential

Dear Sir: The inclosed circular and card are sent you at the suggestion of Rev. F. J. Grimke with the request that you give us your cordial coöperation.

Several gentlemen, among them, Dr. Alex. Crummell, Rev. F. J. Grimke, Rev. A. P. Miller, Rev. J. [H.] A. Johnson, Paul L. Dunbar, Kelley Miller,[2] J. L. Love, W. B. Hayson and your humble servant, organized provisionally and temporarily, "The American Negro Academy"[3] and decided to hold a meeting sometime in the early part of March for the perfection of the organization.

Of this meeting you will receive due notice. Trusting to hear from you at an early date, I am   Yours Respectfully,

J. W. Cromwell

ALS   Con. 116   BTW Papers   DLC.

[1] John Wesley Cromwell was born in Portsmouth, Va., in 1845 and moved with his family to Philadelphia in 1851, after his father obtained their freedom. In 1864 he graduated from the preparatory department of the Institute for Colored Youth and taught at various times in Pennsylvania, Virginia, and the District of Columbia. In the late 1860s, while in the grocery business in Portsmouth, Va., he became active in Reconstruction state politics. In 1871 he moved to Washington, D.C., where he entered Howard University Law School, graduating in 1874. From 1872 until 1885 Cromwell was a clerk in the Treasury Department. When the Democrats assumed control under President Cleveland, Cromwell was charged with "offensive partisanship," for publishing the Republican *People's Advocate*, and was dismissed from government service. Within a few months after its first issue, in 1876, Cromwell became the proprietor of the *People's Advocate*, later moving its place of publication from Alexandria, Va., to Washington, D.C. Later he was editor of the Washington *Record*.

Cromwell supported black economic progress and industrial education, self-help and racial solidarity in the 1880s and 1890s, and defended BTW in 1895 before the Bethel Literary and Historical Association, of which he was a founder. By 1903, however, he was an anti-Washingtonian and a believer in political means of racial advancement. Cromwell was the author of *The Negro in American History*, a biographical study published in 1914.

[2] Kelly Miller (1863-1939), a professor at Howard University, sought to maintain a compromise position in the polarized ideological debate between BTW and his militant black critics. Born in Winnsboro, S.C., the son of a black tenant farmer and his slave wife, Miller secured some education at Fairfield Institute, entered Howard on a scholarship, and graduated in 1886. He studied mathematics at Johns Hopkins for two years and served on the Howard faculty from 1890 to 1934, first

as a mathematics professor, then as dean of the college of arts and sciences, and finally as professor of sociology from 1918 until he retired.

Miller occupied middle ground in the debate between advocates of higher education and industrial education. He thought both were necessary and useful, and he had nothing but praise for Tuskegee Institute. On the issue between BTW's accommodationism and the more outspoken advocacy of black rights, Miller criticized BTW's policies as too pacific to protest fundamental rights, while he called the militants quixotic. He believed race progress would come through an alternation of the two approaches. Miller's moderation reflected his academic detachment but also stemmed from his feeling that blacks were losing half their strength in internal strife. Symbolic of Miller's middle way was his membership on the boards of both the NAACP and the National Urban League. (Kelly Miller, "Washington's Policy," in Hawkins, ed., *BTW and His Critics,* 49-54; Meier, "Racial and Educational Philosophy of Kelly Miller," 121-27.)

³ The American Negro Academy, consisting of forty members, was founded at Washington in 1897 by a gathering of black scholars and writers at the invitation of Alexander Crummell. When Crummell died in 1898, W. E. B. Du Bois succeeded him as president. The broad aim of the academy was to foster black literature, scholarship, and the arts, not only to counter the materialistic trend symbolized by BTW's industrial education, but to develop a coherent black civilization. It published a series of papers on racial themes.

To Hollis Burke Frissell

Tuskegee, Ala., Jan. 23, 1897

Dear Dr. Frissell: We are very glad to hear that you are to be with us at the Conference. Let me hear from you as soon as practical who will come instead of Miss Ludlow. I am very sorry to hear about the trouble with her eyes. Notwithstanding the condition of her eyes we shall be glad to [agree to] her coming and feel that she can be of great service to us even if she has to use the typewriter.

The War Department has granted Captain Romeyne¹ permission to visit us once a month for the purpose of helping in our military instruction. He has been here for a week and has just left this morning and is very glad to hear of your coming. Yours truly,

Booker T. Washington

TLS BTW Folder ViHaI.

¹ Henry Romeyn (1833-1913). (See above, 2:100.) BTW bent his rule of not having white instructors on campus to gain the part-time services of Romeyn during the 1897 school year. In his letter to Nelson A. Miles, commander-in-chief of the Army, BTW said: "Capt. Romeyn is a very good friend of ours and has consented

to come to us and give our young men this instruction without compensation."
(BTW to Miles, Dec. 26, 1896, Item 74 4636, Box 270, RG94, DNA.)

From Timothy Thomas Fortune

Jacksonville, Fla. Jan. 23, 1897

My Dear Friend: Your letter of the 20th instant was received this morning and I am glad to have it. I appreciate the sympathy which you and Mrs. Washington extend to me under the trying circumstances I find myself. My father's condition grows more hopeless every day and the doctors say the end may come any moment. He has aneurism of the main aorta, and of course there is no remedy for it. He has a very unusual constitution and will force, or he would have been dead months ago.

As soon as I can collect my thoughts I will think out the article of the Sun, in a general as well as specific statement of the case. I swipe Chase right and left in the leading editorial in the current issue of The Age. He is a slippery article in debate but we hope to keep pace with him.

Mr. Hanna's[1] desire to go into the Senate has complicated the whole Cabinet situation. But for that John Sherman never would have been thought, because he is too old and has too many political obligations of his own. Either Tracy[2] or Woodford[3] of New York would be useless to the race. Payne of Wisconsin, Alger of Michigan, Goff [and] Sherman of Ohio would constitute a cabinet from which we should have nothing to expect. I hope your friend Mr White may come in somewhere. But we cannot reach an idea of where we stand until the whole slate is made up and announced.

You were very right in not seeing Major McKinley under the circumstances. The visit would have been promptly and widely misconstrued.

I notice what you say of the date of the conference and shall want to be with you, but cannot say now. I shall have to pin down to hard grinding as soon as I have relief from the situation here.

With kind regards for you and Mrs. Washington, Yours truly

T. Thomas Fortune

ALS   Con. 128   BTW Papers   DLC.

¹ Marcus Alonzo Hanna (1837-1904), the Ohio iron manufacturer who managed McKinley's campaign for the presidency in 1896, was appointed senator from Ohio when John Sherman vacated the seat to become Secretary of State.

² Benjamin Franklin Tracy (1830-1915), Secretary of the Navy under President Benjamin Harrison. In 1897 he was badly defeated for mayor of New York.

³ Stewart Lyndon Woodford (1835-1913) of New York was minister to Spain in 1897 during the delicate period of negotiations preceding the Spanish-American War. In 1898 he returned to private law practice and a directorship of the Metropolitan Life Insurance Company.

From Blanche Kelso Bruce

Washington, D.C., Jan 25 1897

My dear Mr Washington, Many thanks for your letter of the 22 inst. enclosing your reply to Mr Manning.¹

I understand that there are several white and two Colored men candidates for Reg. of the Treasy. Having once held that office and given entire satisfaction to all concerned, and supported as I shall be by some of the best men in the land, I feel that my chances are good. But I shall rely very much upon the impression made by your proposed visit to Canton,² and the conclusion to which you shall then arrive. I have unlimited confidence in your judgment, and your ability to personally present the case to Maj McKinley.

I may add that friends in several of the states have written letters asking my appointment to some important official position, but they have not, as far as I know, designated a particular position. Sincerely Yours

B. K. Bruce

ALS   Con. 124   BTW Papers   DLC.

¹ Joseph Columbus Manning, a white radical, helped organize the Alabama Populist party in 1892 and was a leading party spokesman. In 1894 he was a leader of the Kolb faction of agrarians. Faced with lack of political support for a third party and frustrated with fraudulent elections, Manning vacillated between the Republicans and the Democrats. He urged fusion with the Republicans and fought against disfranchisement by organizing in 1895 the Southern Ballot Rights League. Early in the twentieth century he supported the Constitutional League's efforts for universal suffrage and equal rights. Spurred by the Springfield Riot in 1908, a group of whites and blacks issued a call for a conference the following year to discuss methods of protecting blacks' civil and political rights. At the National Negro Conference, which was in fact the organizational meeting of the NAACP, Manning spoke on the "Effect on Poor Whites of Discrimination against

Negroes" and of the control of the ballot by the white oligarchy: "It is to-day as impossible for the opposition majority of whites, without including the blacks, to overthrow this political despotism of the minority in the state of Alabama as was it impossible for the Negro in that state to free himself from the manacles and chains of chattel slavery." (National Negro Conference, *Proceedings, 1909,* 209.) In 1919, obviously swept up in the Red Scare, Manning charged the NAACP with Bolshevism and expressed fear that socialism would attract blacks.

Manning's relationship with BTW was stormy. On Jan. 16, 1897, he wrote BTW indicating his desire to be register of the Treasury and urged him to enlist the support of blacks on account of Manning's work for equal suffrage rights. (Con. 131, BTW Papers, DLC.) Thinking that because he supported equal rights BTW would support him, Manning was disappointed when the only federal job he could secure was the postmastership at Alexander City, his home town. Manning often attacked BTW's accommodationism, and it was obvious that ideologically the two men had little in common.

[2] Canton, Ohio, home of President-elect William McKinley.

From Blanche Kelso Bruce

Washington, D.C., Feby 1 1897

My dear Mr Washington, I highly appreciate your thoughtfulness and kindness in sending me the enclosed letter. It puts me on my guard and indicates the character of contest we must make. Bishop Arnetts[1] son is, as far as I know, the only colored candidate for the place, but he can hardly be considered in my way. Of the white candidates, a dozen in number, Col Buck is the most formidable. He is a strong friend of McKinly, having given him loyal support at St Louis. I believe, nevertheless, with a little judicious management on our side, we shall succeed. I am not idle. I shall have strong support from the Senate. I look forward with interest to your visit to Canton. You are, for the best reasons, the only colored man that I desire to speak to the Maj in my interest in person, before his inauguration. You will tell him what we want, and why we want it. Sincerely Yours

B. K. Bruce

ALS Con. 272 BTW Papers DLC.

[1] Benjamin William Arnett, an A.M.E. bishop, was a staunch Republican and adviser to President William McKinley on black political appointments. Born in Brownsville, Pa., in 1838, Arnett taught school there before becoming active in politics and religion. In 1879 he was appointed chaplain of the Ohio House of Representatives, and he served as a member of that body from 1885 to 1887. He fought to repeal discriminatory laws, and sponsored the Civil Rights Act of 1886,

which repealed the notorious "Black Laws" in the state. Arnett also backed the educational bill advocated by the WCTU. He served pastorates in Toledo, Cincinnati, and Columbus, becoming a bishop of the A.M.E. church in 1888.

From John Henry Washington

Tuskegee, Ala., Feb. 1, 1897

Mr. B. T. Washington, Principal: In connection with the change about to be made in my work I submit the following:

Since my connection with this Institution in 1885 I have been moved around from one place to another, and have never been told that these changes have been made because I did not give satisfaction in the work taken from me. I have been moved from seven different places, and the change that is now to take place will be eight. It is not to my credit, but greatly against me, to have so many changes made. Some people like to move around from one place to another to keep people from seeing their failures, but I do not. In whatever place you have thought best to put me I have always tried to do my best. It seems that nearly in all of the eight changes made, that they had been made after I had gone through the roughest of the work and about gotten to the place to reap the results of my effort. During the last three months I have looked forward with great hopes to what we might get from the farm within the next two years with Mr. Carver's help.

I do not think it fair to have me go on with the work these several years with such poor opportunities, and just at the time we have built up the soil, fenced the land, and secured a capable helper and adviser, to take the work from me. I had much rather leave, so that the matter will get off of my mind.

If Mr. J. N. Calloway had shown, since he was appointed Business Agent, great tack and ability in business; or since he took the Marshall Farm from me, great fitness for farming or any promise of securing more from the Home Farm in the next two or more years than will be done with my recommendations under similar circumstances, I could then see reasons for such steps. I do not object in the least to giving up the farm work to any one, but I must protect myself. You have acknowledged Mr. Calloway's unfitness to run the Boarding Department, or to make a good Business Agent. The Institution pays him, at the lowest calculation, nin[e]ty dollars per month to run the Boarding Department, Marshall Farm, and to serve as Business Agent, and pays me sixty-six dollars per month to superintend 25 departments with a house.

I submit two propositions to you, though I prefer the first:

Give me a good live assistant who understands farming or mechanical work and seventy-five dollars per month for the next two years, and I will give you as large an increase from the farm as any one.

2nd If you still think it unwise for me to superintend it, I will take the shops, sewing departments, brickyard and construction, and do Mr. Palmer's[1] work with the boys for eighty dollars per month. In either case the school is to furnish me a house etc. as it now does. Very truly,

J. H. Washington

TLS Con. 129 BTW Papers DLC.

[1] John H. Palmer joined the Tuskegee faculty in 1894 as assistant superintendent of industries. He was business agent for the school during the 1898-99 school year and then served for many years as registrar.

From Blanche Kelso Bruce

Washington, D.C., Feby 4 1897

My dear Mr Washington: I desire to keep you informed as to every move that may be made in regard to the matter in hand. Friends, some real and some pretended are now suggesting my name for Asst Secretary of one of the departments. The arguments used by them are neither weighty nor satisfactory. Both my inclination and judgment move me to adhere to our original program, while I am as well qualified for the discharge of the duties of Asst. Secy. as most of those who are seeking these positions — their equals, no more nor less, I am specially fitted to discharge the duties of Register of the Treasury. I gave entire satisfaction when I held that office, and there would be no criticism of my reappointment to it, in fact, it seems to be what the country expects. Aside from these considerations, the office is as dignified as the majority of the Asst secretaryships, and in the minds of our people it is a larger office, and actually carries with it more political influence than any subordinate position in the government. These are the grounds of my preference for the office. If we insist, as we shall, we shall succeed. Yours truly

B. K. Bruce

ALS Con. 272 BTW Papers DLC.

To Thomas Brackett Reed

[Tuskegee, Ala.] Feb. 5, 1897

My dear sir: Both of us are engaged in the industrial education of the youths of the South. Both the white race and the Negro race was the sufferer by reason of slavery, both are now trying to regain what was lost by putting our respective races upon a permanent industrial footing. This can only be done through industrial education such as both of us are seeking to give in our institutions. The State of Alabama is too poor to do all that it wants to do for the education of the white and colored people. What we ask of the Government in the way of land would largely put both of our institutions on their feet and at the same time the Government would not feel the loss. In the end speculators and others will secure these valuable lands and the children of the state will perhaps reap very little if anything by reason of their sale. There is an exceptional chance to put every dollar resulting from the sale of the 25,000 acres of land each which we ask, into the education of the head, hand and heart of the white and colored youths of the South. Will you help us by letting our joint bill pass? We make this last joint appeal to you. Yours truly,

Booker T. Washington

TLpS Con. 135 BTW Papers DLC.

From John Langalibalele Dubé[1]

Brooklyn N.Y. Mch 7th 1897

Dear Sir/ You will perhaps be surprized to hear from a stranger, but I have heard of your good work in the South at Tuskegee Alabama.

My friend Mrs. Mitchell told me of you & your work. I am very much interested in just the same work that you are for my people the Zulus of So. Africa. I am here preparing to return & start a school of an industrial character among them. I desire to have an interview with you for I wish to visit both Hampton and Tuskegee before my return to my native land. I heard through my friends that you are to speak at Dr. Gregg's ch. tonight but I am engaged for the evening and cannot possibly see you. Are you to be any where in Greater N.Y. tomorrow Monday & at what time can I call upon you? Please drop me a card early to-morrow morning so that I may have the pleasure of seeing you. If you will read this note before the bearer has left you can tell him the time you will be at leasure to see me. Trusting for a favorable response tomorrow I am Sir   Yours truly

John L. Dubé

ALS Con. 127 BTW Papers DLC.

[1] John Langalibalele Dubé (1871-1946), educator, journalist, and politician, was often called the "Booker T. Washington of South Africa." His grandmother Dalida Dubé was one of the first black converts to Christianity in South Africa. Dubé's father was a Congregational minister of Inanda Church in the 1870s and an influential Zulu spokesman. Educated at Natal and then at Oberlin College from 1887 to 1892, John Dubé returned to Africa and established several native schools at Incwadi, Natal. He returned to the United States in 1897 and visited Hampton and Tuskegee during the summer. He was ordained a Congregationalist minister in New York City in 1899. Returning to Natal, in 1901 Dubé established at Ohlange the Zulu Christian Industrial School, modeled after Tuskegee, with financial assistance from white philanthropists in America.

In 1903 Dubé founded and edited *Ilanga lase Natal* (*Sun of Natal*), one of the first black-oriented newspapers in his country. Through his paper Dubé often criticized the government for unjust policies regarding the Zulus. Dubé founded the Natal Native Congress, the central political organization of the Zulus, and after the Bambata Rebellion in 1906, was a founder of the South African Native Congress, later called the African National Congress. For several years Dubé was a leader in protests against the increasing racism in South Africa.

In many ways Dubé's career paralleled that of BTW, and he often appeared in contradictory roles. An advocate of industrial education and political accommodation, Dubé nevertheless was an important force in shaping the lives of more militant and independent Africans such as James Gumede, president of the African National Congress in the 1920s and a leading South African Communist. In 1932 Dubé founded the Bantu Business League, whose aims closely followed those of BTW's National Negro Business League.

From William James[1]

Cambridge [Mass.] March 8. 1897

Dear Sir, You are probably aware that we are to be associated together in bearing the oratorical brunt of the day at the unveiling of the Shaw[2] monument on decoration day in Boston.

My own invitation came to me as a great surprise for neither my ambition nor my avocations had lain in the direction of public oratory. But I had to pick up the challenge thrown down, and shall do the best I can. With your proved powers on hand the day can't be a failure anyhow.

It has seemed to me that, since on all such occasions much depends on there being a good *ensemble,* with all its parts in keeping with each other, it might be well, if your own oration is not already written, to see a copy of mine so far as I have it composed. I don't know whether in the moralizing remarks at the end, placing civic virtue above military courage, I am at all touching on your province. I hope not. Possibly you may rather not read it, for fear of interfering with your own spontaneity — I can imagine that feeling. Possibly you may be glad to have it. Possibly you may have critical suggestions to make. If so pray make them frankly — they will be of great help to me. The task is a hard one. I mean to keep the MS. unlooked at till May, and then revise and finish it by adding one page of final peroration.

I trust that the Lord and the good cause will see us both happily through the scrape! Don't send back my MS. if you have any use for it, as I have another copy. Respectfully and sincerely Yours,

Wm James

ALS Con. 272 BTW Papers DLC.

[1] William James (1842-1910), the Harvard psychologist and philosopher, was one of the leading academic intellectuals of his time.
[2] Robert Gould Shaw. (See above, 1:347.)

From Alonzo Homer Kenniebrew[1]

Tuskegee, Ala., Mch. 25 1897

Dear Prof: I have been waiting to hear the results of the medical examination before writing you and this A.M. my hopes were realized. The report came to me and I passed the board representing the State of Ala. with a very good average. The dif. averages ran as fol. Surgery 75.5 Obstetrics 87, Physiology 83, Chemistry both org. & Inorg. 98.% Anatomy 85.5% &c.

You are aware of the difficulty of passing an Ala. examination, but I think it quite practicle and only requires one to be well prepared.

I heard from Dr. Courtny a few days ago concerning the Hospital and he was waiting an ans. from Supt. of the City Hospital about me getting the position there & said that he would let me know as soon as possible about it.

Of course Mr Washington I will be compelled to look to you for financial aid as I am now about out, but my expenses are all paid. That necessary for me to get through the Hospital would have to come out first years sal'y at The T.N.I.I. It takes six weeks to complete the Post graduate course but I would be glad to spend two months if possible in the service. Let me hear from you, I am   Your obt. servant,

A H Kenniebrew

ALS   Con. 272   BTW Papers   DLC.

[1] Alonzo Homer Kenniebrew, an 1891 graduate of Tuskegee, graduated from Meharry Medical College in 1897. He returned to Tuskegee as resident physician and teacher of physiology and nurse training until 1901. In 1899 he married Leonora Love Chapman, the Lady Principal at Tuskegee. He established himself as a physician in Jacksonville, Ill., and he and his wife continued their strong interest in Tuskegee.

From Richard Theodore Greener

Washington, D.C., Mch. 26th 1897

My dear Mr. Washington, I have been on the point of writing to you several times, regarding an endorsement of me for a political position but had some natural doubt, if you cared to endorse anybody having been so prominently and properly mentioned for recognition yourself.

But yesterday I was shown a letter of yours endorsing Mr. Allain[1] of La. and I concluded it would not be unreasonable for me to make my first draft on our friendship since 1884.

I shall be a candidate for an advanced position, one never held by a colored man, an "Envoy Extraordinary and Minister Plenipotentiary," and I shall go to the President with the backing of the Nat'l. Repub. Com. May I ask a letter addressed to the President, stating how long you have known me, and what your opinion is of my character, fitness and training for the position I seek. You may recall that, in spite of active work in each National Campaign from 1872 until and including 1896, with the exception only of 1888, I have been an active worker, and never have held an office of high political trust. This, too, in spite of the fact that in 1876, I lost both position, and money and political prospects, by my advocacy on the stump in S.C. of Hayes and Wheeler. In the last campaign as in 1892, I went in and earned my spurs anew, as if I had never had any claim before. I have the medal awarded by Mr. Hanna for my work in the Western Colored Bureau, and such letters regarding the quality and number of my speeches, as would be considered flattering. I am not anxious to get a long list of endorsements and not alarmed at the lateness of this request. I feel there will be no great hurry in filling the colored appointments: but on the contrary, great precaution will be taken to secure good men. This is proper and natural.

If you shall find yourself at liberty to write me such a letter as I have indicated I shall be deeply indebted, and take it as an evidence of that friendship, which has, so far as I know, always subsisted between us. Please address me, at no. 27 Chambers St., New York City. Very truly Yours,

Richard T. Greener

ALS   Con. 128   BTW Papers   DLC.

1 Theophile Tarence Allain.

To Isabel Howland

Grand Union Hotel, New York, Mar. 28, 1897

Dear Miss Howland: I want to thank you for your excellent article concerning the "Jim Crow" cars which was published in the New York Tribune a few days ago.[1] I think it will help. Yours truly,

Booker T. Washington

TLS   Isabel Howland Papers   Sophia Smith Collection   MNS.

[1] Isabel Howland's letter to the editor, in the New York *Tribune,* Mar. 21, 1897, 7, described segregated railroad cars as "one of the most galling [institutions] to which the negroes are subjected." She emphasized the filth and the degrading conditions in Jim Crow cars, which, because they were also the only coaches where smoking was permitted, contained white men who drank and swore as well as smoked, and behaved in ways not permitted in the white cars. She said that when BTW rode trains out of northern states into the South, he rode in the regular coaches, but when he boarded the train in the South he was forced to enter the Jim Crow car. She ended her letter with the quotation from Justice John M. Harlan's dissent in the *Plessy* case in 1896.

To Warren Logan

Grand Union Hotel, New York, March 30, 1897

Dear Mr. Logan: I telegraphed you today that I thought it would be all right to give Mr. Loeb[1] the notes to which you refer in your letter. I very much hope that every effort possible is being put forth to stop the enormous expenditure of money for outside food both for the people and animals. I hope that something is being [done] from the farm in both of these directions. This matter should be constantly kept before all parties concerned.

I regret very much that Mr. Grimmett[2] has found out that I am to be in Washington on the 5th. I have tried to keep my being there quiet as I cannot undertake to see the President in behalf of all who want me to do so, to attempt this would simply be to make myself a nuisance to the President. I shall be willing to help Mr. Grimmett all I can in any reasonable way. I have already given him strong letters of endorsement. I think it best for you to give him no direct answer concerning my position in this matter. If he sees me in Washington I shall be glad to do what I can for him but I cannot undertake to make any promise as to what I can do as I am to be there for a few hours only. Yours truly,

Booker T. Washington

TLS Con. 12 BTW Papers ATT. Original destroyed.

[1] J. Loeb and Bro., wholesale grocers in Montgomery, Ala.

[2] James A. Grimmett, a Republican, sought BTW's help in securing an appointment as federal marshal under McKinley. He served three terms as postmaster of Tuskegee, 1881 to 1885, 1898 to 1902, and 1912 to 1913.

From Caroline H. Pemberton[1]

[Philadelphia] 3-30-97

My Dear Mr Washington   What I wanted to get from you was some information on the mortgage system among the colored people, how & why it became so prevalent, if an excessive rate of interest is charged, & if it amounts practically to your people paying an exorbitant rent for everything they occupy.

I have in my mind also two things to say to you, & being of Quaker descent, when the spirit moves, I must speak.

One is to remember that your race needs you & cannot afford just now to have you kill yourself off by over work. Public speaking in our climate is destructive to throat & lungs, & you need to be careful.

The other point is, don't despise the sentiment which many of us entertain towards your race. It is all very well to appeal to the head when you want to convince, but to draw money out of pockets, like Mr Fitzsimmons you must aim at the heart. It seems to me that an appeal to help the negro rise into successful competition with the white man is a kind of pill that needs a *little* coating of sentiment, and if you leave out all the sentiment, what have you left but the antagonism of races, each jealous of the other?

I say this at the risk of being called a sentimentalist, which I am not. There is a difference between sentiment & sentimentality. I do not know that I could successfully distinguish between the two, but I am sure that you could, & you are in no danger of becoming a sentimentalist. Patriotism is a sentiment which we place above commercial interests, and beside it, many of us place our interest, sympathy & reponsibility for the negro, there seems a connection between the two, which we cannot afford to lose sight of if we hope to do our duty.

But I assure you my sentiments do not prevent my appreciating the manliness, common sense & clear logic of your arguments & your attitude, only I do not think it would be wise for you to cast out sentiment altogether from your speeches. Very Truly Yours

Caroline H. Pemberton

ALS   Con. 132   BTW Papers   DLC.

¹ Caroline H. Pemberton was a Philadelphia writer and social worker. In 1896 she wrote *Your Little Brother James,* which explored the social influence theory of delinquency, and in 1899 *Stephen the Black,* a story of race relations sympathetic to blacks. From 1897 to 1899 she was a member of the eighth section board of directors of the Philadelphia public schools and was secretary of the Negro Educational League. She frequently corresponded with BTW, and visited Tuskegee.

From Richard Theodore Greener

Phila., Penna., April 5, 1897

My dear Washington, I found your kind note awaiting me here, on my arrival yesterday. I had hoped to see you in W. but have been away so long, my presence is now demanded at home.

I have such a natural diffidence about asking influence, I really would not have applied to you, had I not found your letter as I told you. As you know me so much better than many others, mere lip service is not necessary between us. And yet I should take it as a favor, should you see the President, to say a good word for me. I have done all the work necessary to success; but I have found several times in my life, that was not all that was needed.

Thanking you for your promptness and generous words, I am, as ever, Sincerely Yours,

Richard T. Greener

ALS   Con. 128   BTW Papers   DLC.

To Warren Logan

Grand Union Hotel, New York, April 9th, 1897

Dear Mr. Logan: I have received your letter regarding Dr. Mayo, and I hope you will give him every chance possible to see the class work.

In a letter to me Miss Jackson[1] mentions the fact that Dr. Mayo had not been properly taken care of while there.[2] Perhaps you might see Miss Jackson and find out in what particular he has not been properly looked after.

Sometime next week Miss Caroline H. Pemberton, of Philadelphia, will reach Tuskegee. She is a writer of a good deal of ability and note. I wish you to give her every opportunity to see the school also see that she has an opportunity to go to Mt. Meigs, and also see the work Mrs. Washington is doing on Russell plantation and anything else that you think it well that she might see. I have asked Mrs. Washington to let her stop at my house. Please see that some one meets her at Chehaw or at Tuskegee. Yours truly,

Booker T. Washington

TLS   Con. 12   BTW Papers   ATT.   Original destroyed.

[1] Estelle M. Jackson.
[2] Apparently Mayo visited Tuskegee twice during his stay in Alabama of a month or more.

To William James

Grand Union Hotel, New York, April 14th, 1897

My dear sir: It was very kind and thoughtful in you to send me a copy of your oration. It will be of great service to me in preparing my own. Only a few days ago I decided to write you on one point and that is, I feared perhaps since several poems have been written on Mr. Shaw's life and death, that both of us might be tempted to use the same line of poetry. I shall not read your oration until I have finished my own and then I shall go through yours carefully with a view of seeing if in any way mine is too much like yours in any respect. I think you understand that my address is to be a short one and it will be general in its nature. Such occasions are a great trial to me and the nervous strain is very hard to bear, and I shall be glad when it is all over, and I shall have to depend upon you very largely for the success of the occasion.

This will be my address during the next two weeks. Yours truly,

Booker T. Washington

TLS   William James Collection   MH.

From Blanche Kelso Bruce

Washington, D.C., 4/15 1897

My dear Mr Washington. Many thanks for your letter[1] to the President. It comes at the right time — just when the Senate is making strong efforts for me.

Information just recd is to the effect that my appt has been determined upon, but when it will be made, I cannot say, but believe it will occur in a few days. My wife is up again, and sends her best wishes. Sincerely yours

Bruce

ALS   Con. 124   BTW Papers   DLC.

[1] This letter was not preserved in either the McKinley Papers, DLC, nor the BTW Papers, DLC.

From William James

Cambridge [Mass.] April 16th [1897]

Dear Mr. Washington   Your letter is at hand and I can well understand why you should wish to write your oration freely before comparing it with mine. I may tell you in advance that I have quoted no poetry in it, and that speaking for the donors of the monument, as I suppose myself to be, I have given nearly half my time to a recital of Shaw's and the regiment's history. You need therefore not be explicit at all concerning these facts. My words are as "abolitionist" in tone as anyone can desire. I feel also as if it were no longer necessary to keep flourishing the old conventional sentimentalisms about the war, and I have tried to shape the thing towards a sort of mugwump conclusion — mugwump in the sense that the daily civic virtues which save countries from getting into civil war are more precious to the world than the martial ones that save them after they get in.

My idea has been that your discourse would be larg[e]ly one on political morality and possibly on the future relations of the two races in our midst.

One has got to keep in touch with the instinctive reactions of the audience so that immid[i]ate oratorical effect may not be damped. But with tact many a bitter pill may be sugar coated. And it seems to me that between us we have a good opportunity of raising the occasion to something a little higher than the usual flourishing of proper names and the flag, which are sure to bring down conventional applause. But the problem is a delicate one; and I hope you will take these words of mine, not as suggestions to yourself but only as expressions of my own state of mind. Believe me   faithfully yours

Wm James

ALS   Con. 272   BTW Papers   DLC.

To Warren Logan

Grand Union Hotel, New York, April 19th, 1897

Dear Mr. Logan: Hereafter I wish you would see that all donations sent by Mr. Henry Villard,[1] of New York, are put in the general fund rather than the scholarship fund. In this connection I will say that Mr. Villard criticised us rather severely for giving our students studies which they cannot or have not mastered. He says he received sometime ago a scholarship letter from one of the students mentioned in which this student mentions the high studies she was pursuing and others higher that she meant to pursue the coming year, and at the same time this letter showing evidence of the most glaring errors by reason of misspelled words and other inaccuracies. All this goes to show the importance of our making our course of study just as simple as possible and have everything done thoroughly.

If the finance committee has not already done so, I wish very much that you would have it make an estimate of the monthly expenses of the school during the summer on the basis to which you have now reduced expenses. As I have said in my former letter, these expenses must be reduced to the lowest point possible. I do not think it necessary to pay any teachers except Mr. Gregory[2] at the brickyard, those who have charge of the farms and those connected with the building of the chapel, and what office force is absolutely necessary. I do not think we can be too radical in this matter. Yours truly,

Booker T. Washington

Enclosed find check for $25.

TLS Con. 12 BTW Papers ATT. Original destroyed.

[1] Henry Villard (1835-1900) was a prominent journalist, railroad promoter, and financier. He married Helen Frances Garrison, daughter of the abolitionist William Lloyd Garrison. Their home at Dobbs Ferry, N.Y., was a center for various humanitarian and reform activities. Villard's son Oswald later was a close adviser to BTW and one of his closest contacts with abolitionist-oriented donors to black education.

[2] William Gregory of Dick's Creek, Macon County, Ala., graduated from Tuskegee in 1887 and joined the faculty in 1888. He taught brickmaking from 1893 to 1906 and for many years thereafter was a custodian at the school.

From Daniel Hale Williams[1]

Washington, April 21 1897

My Dear Mr Washington— Your very kind letter of 19th received and I want to thank you for your interest in the matter under consideration. I want to especially thank you for letter to Mr Bliss.[2] It is humiliating to be put in these positions, but I feel that it is only for a short time. In case my arrangements come out all right can your man come May 1st. Is he a level headed fellow, and what particular lines do you want him directed in. How long do you wish him to be here? Tell me plainly your wishes in regard to him so that we can have a mutual understanding about him. I have thought that it might do some good to give to the country your impression of Freedmens Hospital as spoken of in your letter. I would only do so with your kind permission. I have a scheme for your hospital and training school. You can build a monument there and care for thousands of those poor people who would die for the want of surgical attention. My plan would make the enterprise almost self supporting. You could draw work from all over the South. I would stand for the success or failure of the work. Keep me posted as to your movements. I want to talk this over before you go South. I may be in N York next week. With regards   Sincerely Yours

D H Williams

ALS   Con. 272   BTW Papers   DLC.

¹ Daniel Hale Williams (1856-1931) was the leading black physician of his time. Born in Pennsylvania, after his father's death he made his way to Janesville, Wis., where he was taken in by the family of Harry Anderson. Williams received an M.D. degree from Chicago Medical College in 1883 and began his practice in Chicago. In 1889 a Republican governor appointed Williams to the Illinois State Board of Health, and during these years he was also a member of the powerful Hamilton Club of Chicago, a Republican organization with a few black members. Seeing the need for a Negro-controlled hospital both for treating blacks who could not be admitted to any existing hospital and for training black nurses and doctors, Williams founded Provident Hospital in Chicago in 1891. It was there that Williams made medical history in 1893 by performing the first successful open-heart surgery in the United States.

In the 1890s Williams became associated with Freedmen's Hospital in Washington, D.C. Founded during the Civil War to serve freed slaves moving into the nation's capital, Freedmen's remained under federal direction at the end of Reconstruction when many similar hospitals reverted to local control. Under divided authority and a prey to politics, the hospital was a shambles. The position of chief surgeon was a political appointment, and although the incumbent, Dr. Charles B. Purvis (a man trained in the pre-bacteriological era of medicine), fought to maintain himself in power, Williams secured the job. Despite Purvis's continued opposition, Williams reformed the hospital, instituting modern nurse-training and internship programs, both of which he had pioneered at Provident. Finding white professional medical organizations closed to him, he founded in Jan. 1895 the Medico-Chirurgical Society of Washington, and in December of that year assisted in the formation of the National Medical Association. With McKinley's election in 1896, Williams had to fight to retain his position at Freedmen's.

Williams met BTW in 1895 at Atlanta during the organization of the National Medical Association, and after touring Freedmen's Hospital in 1897, BTW asked Williams to help organize medical care at Tuskegee. Williams, who saw the need for medical training institutions for southern blacks, jumped at the opportunity to turn the Tuskegee infirmary into a real hospital. Such enthusiasm was more than

BTW desired, and he responded very coolly to the proposal. Williams continued to prod BTW, but finally he turned his attention to Meharry Medical College in Nashville, Tenn., where he established surgical clinics and the basis for a modern medical school before returning to Chicago and Provident Hospital. The relationship between Williams and BTW remained strained, though the two men did cooperate from time to time.

Williams was increasingly cut off from his black constituency by his success in white medical circles. Aided perhaps by his lightness of color, in 1912 he was appointed associate attending surgeon at the prestigious St. Luke's Hospital in Chicago. After bitter political wrangles within the black community, Williams was forced to resign his position at Provident Hospital in 1912. He continued his brilliant surgical and medical career, but increasingly he became a social recluse. He was at odds with the philosophy of BTW, for he felt that the most talented of the race should be educated as professionals who would then be accepted by whites as equals. Though he had originally spurned the Niagara Movement, Williams left the largest portion of his estate to the NAACP when he died in 1931. (See Buckler, *Doctor Dan.*)

2 Cornelius Newton Bliss.

From Daniel Hale Williams

Washington, April 28th, 1897

My Dear Mr Washington: Your kind letter of 26th inst has just been received and I want to thank you for your kind interest in the affairs of Freedmen's Hospital. We are also in receipt of a letter from your Dr B,[1] at Tuskegee, he wrote me that he would start for here the 28th. I wrote him that he had better wait until I had some official matter settled, I thought it better to wait until I had something more definite from Secretary Bliss, I do not like the tone of his note to you, "No prospect of an immediate change" dont mean much in politics it might mean tomorrow or next day, if you wish to have your man come on such an assurance it would be agreeable to me, but it dont satisfy me, I am about disgusted with the whole thing, it is not worth the annoyance that one is subjected to. I want you to always to feel assured that anything you write to me is sacred, and that it would never be exposed to public gaze or published without your permission. I am sorry that I could not go to New York this week, I went to Pittsburgh Sunday to do some surgical work and just returned yesterday. Whenever I find a young colored man trying to advance himself in Surgery I take great pleasure in assisting him. The doors of Pittsburgh's largest hospital swung easily to colored men Sunday, and I feel safe in saying that prejudice will not soon cut a figure in hospital work in Pittsburgh. I send you the letter that I have just [received] from the young Doctor in Pittsburgh in reference to the trip, he was one of my Internes last year. I hope that this will find you well, Very Sincerely Yours,

D. H. Williams

TLS Con. 135 BTW Papers DLC.

¹ Should be K. for Alonzo Homer Kenniebrew.

From Edward Thomas Devine[1]

New York May 1st, 1897

My dear Sir: You are no doubt aware that there are several fraudulent collectors who regularly visit Northern cities in the interest of schools and colleges for colored persons. In some instances there is a small school to support the claim, and in other instances the institution seems to exist only in the person of the canvasser. We have been compelled to report unfavorably to our members about several of these institutions, but we do not wish to appear antagonistic to negro education or to prevent charitable contributions for its support.

It has occurred to me that it would be of advantage for us to have a list of perhaps eight or ten good schools, in different states and affiliated with different religious denominations, that can be vouched for by those who are familiar with the actual work done by the schools. I do not mean necessarily to exclude small enterprises, provided they are honestly and efficiently conducted, and it would be of great service to us if you could send us the names of a few such schools known by yourself to be worthy of commendation, and if you could put me in the way of securing similar information from any Southern state with which you do not happen to be acquainted. Possibly you could have the entire list prepared for us by some one upon whom you could rely.[2] If so this would be very greatly appreciated and would enable us to serve the cause of progressive and intelligent negro education in a more positive manner. At present we have only the satisfaction of knowing that we have prevented to some extent the success of some fraudulent schemes. Very sincerely yours,

Edward T. Devine

TLS   Con. 127   BTW Papers   DLC.

¹ Edward Thomas Devine (1867-1948) was born in Union, Iowa. He received a Ph.D. degree from the University of Pennsylvania in 1893 and became active as a teacher, author, and civic leader. At the time of this letter Devine was general secretary of the Charity Organization Society of the City of New York, and later he headed many kinds of disaster relief work, edited *Survey* (1897-1912), and wrote several books.

² Attached to the letter is a list, not in BTW's hand, of schools in Alabama (Mt. Meigs Institute, People's Village School in Mt. Meigs, Snow Hill Institute, and Talladega College) and Georgia (Atlanta University, Spelman Seminary, Clark College, Morris Brown College, and Clay Street Normal and Industrial School in Thomasville). The list may have been part of a larger one.

From Cornelius Nathaniel Dorsette

Montgomery, Ala., 5/2nd 1897

Dear Prof Washington   I have just learned of a remark from "Old" Dr Mayo. Viz. That the State normal school here, was 25 yrs ahead of your school in its Academic Dept! — he is completely under Pats.¹ controlle & I thought might interfere in some way with your Peabody & Slater fund should he continue such a lie, when he goes North. So if you see the old cuss have him "put on brakes." Hastily yours

Dorsette

ALS   Con. 272   BTW Papers   DLC.

¹ William Burns Paterson.

From Daniel Hale Williams

Washington, May 2nd, 1897

My Dear Mr Washington: Your letter of 27th, was received and I was as usual pleased to hear from you. I can hardly share with you the feeling you express of the Interior Department, as we are having such newspaper clippings as you will find enclosed.[1] There is no doubt that a hard fight is being made for the place by the spoil hunters. The fight is much harder than it was when you were here. Dr Kenibrew came a few days ago, I was not quite ready for him but I think it will be all right in a few days. We made application to the Civil service Commission for permission to appoint him for three months. We were informed yesterday that we would have the authority in a few days, in the meantime he has been put to work learning the routine hospital duties. I see plainly that he needs everything in a practical way, I shall have a plain practical talk with him in a few days, after he wears a little. I would suggest that you write him a plain practical letter in regard to him spending every moment in hard work, insist on his taking notes on all of the detail work, in the hospital and training school. His teaching has all been theoretical, he now needs hard drill on working lines. I hope this will find you well. Very truly yours,

D H Williams

TLS Con. 135 BTW Papers DLC.

[1] The enclosure was an unidentified clipping which read: "Washington, April 28. It is reported on good authority that Dr. D. H. Williams is to be succeeded as surgeon-in-chief of the Freedman's hospital in this city by Dr. Curtis, a well-known colored surgeon of Chicago.

"If the nomination is made it will be due to Senators Mason and Cullom, who have been working for Dr. Curtis. Dr. Williams is a Chicago man and secured his appointment through the late Secretary Gresham.

"It is ascertained that two Chicago men made an effort for the recordership of deeds for the District of Columbia, an office which is also held to be a special plum for colored men. Seward French was the candidate of Senator Mason and Senator Cullom presented Major Buckner, the understanding being that if an Illinois man could get the place the two senators would come to an understanding. The President, however, gave both senators to understand that the place was provided for from another direction."

To the Editor of the New York *Evening Post*

Tuskegee, Ala. [May 3, 1897]

Sir: The President of the Alabama State Convict Board, the Hon. S. B. Trapp,[1] is making an earnest effort to put good reading matter

into the hands of the hundreds of convicts now in the Alabama penitentiary, coal mines, chain gangs, etc. To this end Mr. Trapp has asked
me to aid in the establishment of permanent libraries in the various
places where the convicts are kept.

If persons who wish to help establish these libraries will send books
(new or old) to me I will see that they are put into the hands of Mr.
Trapp for the purpose named. When the books are sent it should be
stated that they are for the penitentiary library. Books containing easy
reading matter would be most useful.

Booker T. Washington

New York *Evening Post,* May 6, 1897, 5. The letter also appeared in the Washington *Post,* May 7, 1897, 9.

¹ Sydenham B. Trapp, a Georgia-born Confederate veteran, after many years
in Louisville moved to Montgomery, Ala., in 1882 as manager of the Montgomery
and Eufaula Railroad. In 1885 he went to Anniston, where he was a partner of
Braxton Bragg Comer in a wholesale grain and commission business. While
Comer became so discouraged by the high freight rates that he sold out to Trapp,
the latter apparently made his peace with the railroads, for he became director
of the Louisville and Nashville Railroad.

From Blanche Kelso Bruce

Washington, D.C., May 5 1897

My dear Mr Washington, I told you when you were here the last time
that should any change occur in the situation that I would write you.
Well, the change seems to have occurred. From information received
from a friend yesterday, it seems that the office will likely go [to] another, but to whom we do not know.

Well, we have made a good fight, contested every inch of the ground,
and if the battle is lost, it is only because victory was not in the situation. I thank you most sincerely for the zeal with which you worked
for me. You could not have done more.

We trust you and Mrs Washington are enjoying good health.

Present the madame our regards. Very truly yours

B. K. Bruce

ALS Con. 124 BTW Papers DLC.

From Victoria Earle Matthews

New York   May Tenth, 1897

Dear Sir: I have just received three large Scrap-Books, by express from Tuskegee (at no cost to my self). These with the addresses and clippings already in my possession will enable me to compile the volume,[1] discussed by us, I trust to your satisfaction and *approval.* I regret exceedingly my continued feebleness, but, I am assured, that e'er long I will be my self and doubtless will find my self, fundamentally stronger by the enforced rest of during the past three weeks. I will set to work at once, and if all goes well will try to have volume in hand by September. I am indebted to you for suggestion concerning Nashinville, also your generous encouragement in the matter of handling them.

I appreciate more than I can tell you the confidence reposed in me evidenced by intrusting to my care your valuable collection of clippings. I will be careful of them, trusting you are well and hoping to see you soon again I am   Sincerely Yours,

Victoria Earle Matthews

ALS   Con. 131   BTW Papers   DLC.

[1] This volume was *Black-Belt Diamonds: Gems from the Speeches, Addresses, and Talks to Students of Booker T. Washington,* selected and arranged by Victoria Earle Matthews (New York: Fortune and Scott, 1898), reprinted in 1969 by Negro Universities Press. The excerpts, usually of one or two sentences, were intended to illustrate such principles or sentiments as "Spread Sunshine," "Patience," or "The Little Green Ballot" at the teller's window. One excerpt, for example, stated: "There are a million and a half black men in the South who have never worn a necktie, but send them to school and educate them and they will want neckties, cuffs, and, instead of the bare floors in their little log-cabins, they will want carpet in neat frame houses" (p. 33). Some gems shone more brightly than others, as in an excerpt on lynching: "Physical death comes to the one Negro lynched in a county, but death of the morals, death of the soul, comes to the thousands responsible for the lynching" (p. 98).

From Elijah Winchester Donald[1]

Boston   May 14, 1897

My dear Mr. Washington, It must be nearly time for the Trinity Church Prize to be awarded; and in order that you may do it with satisfaction to the recipient, I enclose you my cheque for twenty-five dollars, to assist you in the pleasing proceeding.

I hope to see you on the occasion of your visit to Boston to make the address on the unveiling of Shaw's monument. I told St. Gaudens[2] the other day that he would better understand his long delay in finishing the Shaw statue when he should have heard you speak; and that he will then understand that Divine Providence stayed his hand in the execution of his task until you should be full grown and come to your prime as an orator. After your oration, I shall ask St. Gaudens whether he does not think I told him the truth.

With love to Mrs. Washington and the children, I am, Ever sincerely yours,

E. Winchester Donald

TLS   Con. 127   BTW Papers   DLC.

[1] Elijah Winchester Donald (1848-1904) was an Episcopal clergyman. A graduate of Amherst, Donald was rector of the Church of the Ascension in New York City from 1882 to 1893, when he became rector of Trinity Church, Boston, until his death. He was a warm supporter of BTW, who often spoke at his church.

[2] Augustus Saint-Gaudens (1848-1907) was a highly acclaimed sculptor, excelling in statuary and reliefs, who was honored in Europe and in the United States with many commissions and awards. Among his most famous works are statues of Lincoln in Chicago, of General Sherman in New York City, and the Henry and Marian Adams monument in a Washington, D.C., cemetery.

To Charles G. Harris

[Tuskegee, Ala.] May 22, 1897

Mr. Harris: You will recall that when I was consulting you in Washington regarding taking the position here that I told you very plainly that it was my wish to have the plantation singing emphasized, and you will also recall once, and I think twice, that I have spoken to you since being here that I wished one third of all the public singing, both the choir and the school, to be plantation singing. This request, which is the policy of the school, I do not think you are carrying out. It is a plain business matter. I have been perfectly frank with you in stating my request and I do not think it necessary to repeat them or to take my time to make further requests in the same direction. The plain fact is that the plantation singing is not being practiced and used in the way that the policy of the school requires. When I have spoken to you about it you have always spoken very pleasantly and expressed an intention to carry out my wishes but in actual practice my wishes are not being carried out. There is almost no plantation singing in the chapel except when I make a personal request for it. Besides the singing of many new and original songs on the part of the school there are many old and beautiful songs that the choir might sing pretty often. I hope you understand that a person with so many duties as I have cannot be expected to repeat a request of this kind very often. Yours

Booker T. Washington

In this connection I desire to say that, your services both in the class room and in the general musical work are satisfactory to the school. The singing of the choir especially is good. The weak point is in the direction that I have mentioned. It would also be a great help if you could give more attention to the bringing up the general singing of the school, I mean the congregational singing, but in the main I repeat that your work is satisfactory.

TLpS Con. 282A BTW Papers DLC.

To Blanche Florence Saffold[1]

[Tuskegee, Ala.] May 27, 1897

Miss Saffold: I cannot be consistent in performing my duty as principal of the institution and let you remain in its employment since you violated in the way that you did the trust imposed in you in communicating official business to a student. All during this past year the tone and dignity of the institution have been lowered by reason of the fact that the office business and the work of the teachers in their meetings has been in some way communicated to the students. In view of all the institution has suffered in this regard I cannot feel that it is right to re-employ a teacher who has in such a manner violated its confidence. I trust however that you will not let your action discourage you and in the future you will let it prove a valuable, tho it may seem a severe, lesson. Those persons entrusted with the communications that come into the office have the reputation of the school largely in their keeping and the violation of this trust means more than you can realize. I hope that another year you may find employment and be successful in making a position for yourself that will be creditable to the institution as well as profitable to you.

Booker T. Washington

TLpS Con. 282A BTW Papers DLC.

[1] Blanche Florence Saffold graduated from Tuskegee in 1896 and worked one year as a clerk in the principal's office.

To Lettie Louise Nolen Calloway

[Tuskegee, Ala.] May 27, 1897

Mrs. Thos. J. Calloway: I am informed that Miss Jackson in your presence, and in the presence or hearing of a student or students, made the statement or statements to the effect that the Principal or Council, or both, were forced by threats on the part of the Senior Class to give Albert Shoots[1] his diploma, and that Miss Jackson further stated that the action of the Senior Class in this matter was the right thing. Will you be kind enough to state in writing on this same sheet of paper, whether or not my information regarding Miss Jackson is correct. I hardly need add in this connection that if such statements were made that there is absolutely no truth in them so far as my knowledge is concerned, but whether Miss Jackson made true statements or not has little to do with the object I am seeking. An early answer will greatly oblige. Yours truly,

Booker T. Washington

TLpS Con. 282A BTW Papers DLC.

[1] Albert Jasper Shootes of College, Ga., attended Georgia State College after graduation from Tuskegee in 1897. In 1901 he was in charge of the tailor shop at the State Normal School, Tallahassee, Fla.

To Estelle M. Jackson

[Tuskegee, Ala.] May 27, 1897

Miss Jackson: You are well aware of the fact that your conduct up to the close of the year has been the subject of criticism to the extent that it was a question whether or not you ought to be retained in the employment of the school. Remembering however, your valuable office work and other good qualities, I advised you to take a vacation and return at the beginning of the next school year with the hope that the vacation would prove of such benefit to you as to enable you to be a different woman in the future. For some months I have been in possession of the fact that the office business, as well as the business of the council and faculty meetings, have been made common property among teachers and students but have not been able to locate the person who was guilty of this indiscretion. The fact that you were guilty of talking of the office business in the presence of teachers and students in itself was a grave offense, and when we add to that the one of misrepresentation it is still more great. All such actions on the part of one connected with an office or a teacher tend to degrade the tone of the institution and to make its official work common property and for these reasons I am forced to say to you that your services will not be required from this date. I regret to make this known to you all the more because of the fact that in your office work in many respects you have proven yourself a very valuable and faithful person. You possess a strong and quick mind and if you had controlled yourself, especially your *talk,* you could have made yourself a very valuable woman in connection with the work of the institution. I hope however that this action will not tend in any way to discourage you. You are still young and have an opportunity to profit by the mistakes that you have made during this year and I trust that wherever you may go in the future that you will bear in mind that I shall be interested in your progress and success. Yours truly,

Booker T. Washington

TLpS   Con. 282A   BTW Papers   DLC.

From William James

Cambridge [Mass.] May 30. 1897

Dear Mr. Washington, My wife and I have wished to invite you to stay with us during part at least of your sojourn, but having invited some relatives from a distance we had no spare room. The relatives at last send word they can't come, and it would therefore give us great pleasure, unless you are otherwise pledged, to have you come to us tomorrow evening, and stay as many days as you can. Possibly you might thus see a little more of Harvard University than your commencement day experiences showed you.

I wish I had your speech — you have suggested no modifications in mine — so I have just forged ahead, improving considerably, I think, the draft I sent you.*

Hoping you may come, I am very sincerely yours

Wm James

* But it is *you* whom we all count on to save the country!

ALS   Con. 272   BTW Papers   DLC.

A Speech at the Unveiling of the Robert Gould Shaw Monument[1]

Boston, Massachusetts, May 31, 1897

Mr. Chairman and Fellow-Citizens: In this presence, and on this sacred and memorable day, in the deeds and death of our hero, we recall the old, old story, ever old, yet ever new, that when it was the will of the Father to lift humanity out of wretchedness and bondage, the precious task was delegated to Him who, among ten thousand, was altogether lovely, and was willing to make himself of no reputation that he might save and lift up others.

If that heart could throb and if those lips could speak, what would be the sentiment and words that Robert Gould Shaw would have us feel and speak at this hour? He would not have us dwell long on the mistakes, the injustice, the criticisms of the days

> "Of storm and cloud, of doubt and fears,
> Across the eternal sky must lower;
> Before the glorious noon appears."

He would have us bind up with his own undying fame and memory and retain by the side of his monument, the name of John A. Andrew,[2] who, with prophetic vision and strong arm, helped to make the existence of the 54th regiment possible; and that of George L. Stearns, who, with hidden generosity and a great sweet heart, helped to turn the darkest hour into day, and in doing so, freely gave service, fortune and life itself to the cause which this day commemorates. Nor would he have us forget those brother officers, living and dead, who by their baptism in blood and fire, in defence of union and freedom, gave us an example of the highest and purest patriotism.

To you who fought so valiantly in the ranks, the scarred and scattered remnant of the 54th regiment, who with empty sleeve and wanting leg, have honored this occasion with your presence, to you, your commander is not dead. Though Boston erected no monument and history recorded no story, in you and the loyal race which you represent, Robert Gould Shaw would have a monument which time could not wear away.

But an occasion like this is too great, too sacred for mere individual eulogy. The individual is the instrument, national virtue the end. That which was 300 years being woven into the warp and woof of our democratic institutions, could not be effaced by a single battle, as magnificent as was that battle; that which for three centuries had bound master and slave, yea, North and South, to a body of death, could not be blotted out by four years of war, could not be atoned for by shot and sword, nor by blood and tears.

Not many days ago in the heart of the South, in a large gathering of the people of my race, there were heard from many lips praises and thanksgiving to God for His goodness in setting them free from physical slavery. In the midst of that assembly, a Southern white man arose, with gray hair and trembling hands, the former owner of many slaves, and from his quivering lips, there came the words: "My friends, you forget in your rejoicing that in setting you free, God was also good to me and my race in setting us free." But there is a higher and deeper sense in which both races must be free than that represented by the bill of sale. The black man, who cannot let love and sympathy go out to the white man, is but half free. The white man, who would close the shop or factory against a black man seeking an opportunity to earn an honest living, is but half free. The white man, who retards his own development by opposing a black man, is but half free. The full measure of the fruit of Fort Wagner and all that this monument stands for will not be realized until every man covered with a black skin, shall, by patience and natural effort, grow to that height in industry, property, intelligence and moral responsibility, where no man in all our land will be tempted to degrade himself by withholding from his black brother any opportunity which he himself would possess.

Until that time comes this monument will stand for effort, not victory complete. What these heroic souls of the 54th regiment began, we must complete. It must be completed not in malice, not in narrowness; nor artificial progress, nor in efforts at mere temporary political gain, nor in abuse of another section or race. Standing as I do today in the home of Garrison and Phillips and Sumner, my heart goes out to those who wore gray as well as to those clothed in blue; to those who returned defeated, to destitute homes, to face blasted hopes and shattered political and industrial system. To them there can be no prouder reward for defeat than by a supreme effort to place the Negro on that footing where he will add material, intellectual and civil strength to every department of State.

This work must be completed in public school, industrial school and college. The most of it must be completed in the effort of the Negro himself, in his effort to withstand temptation, to economize, to exercise thrift, to disregard the superficial for the real — the shadow for the substance, to be great and yet small, in his effort to be patient in the laying of a firm foundation, to so grow in skill and knowledge that he shall place his services in demand by reason of his intrinsic and superior worth. This, is the key that unlocks every door of opportunity, and all others fail. In this battle of peace the rich and poor, the black and white may have a part.

What lesson has this occasion for the future? What of hope, what of encouragement, what of caution? "Watchman tell us of the night; what the signs of promise are." If through me, an humble representative, nearly ten millions of my people might be permitted to send a message to Massachusetts, to the survivors of the 54th regiment, to the committee whose untiring energy has made this memorial possible, to the family who gave their only boy that we might have life more abundantly, that message would be, "Tell them that the sacrifice was not in vain, that up from the depth of ignorance and poverty, we are coming, and if we come through oppression out of the struggle, we are gaining strength. By the way of the school, the well cultivated field, the skilled hand, the Christian home, we are coming up; that we propose to invite all who will to step up and occupy this position with us. Tell them that we are learning that standing ground for the race, as for the individual, must be laid in intelligence, industry, thrift and property, not as an end, but as a means to the highest privileges; that we are learning that neither the conqueror's bullet nor that of law, could make an ignorant voter an intelligent voter, could make a dependent man an independent man, could give one citizen respect for another, a bank account, nor a foot of land, nor an enlightened fireside. Tell them that, as grateful as we are to artist and patriotism for placing the figures of Shaw and his comrades in physical form of beauty and magnificence, that after all, the real monument, the greater monument, is being slowly but safely builded among the lowly in the South, in the struggles and sacrifices of a race to justify all that has been done and suffered for it."

One of the wishes that lay nearest Col. Shaw's heart was, that his black troops might be permitted to fight by the side of white soldiers. Have we not lived to see that wish realized, and will it not be more so in the future? Not at Wagner, not with rifle and bayonet, but on the field of peace, in the battle of industry, in the struggle for good government, in the lifting up of the lowest to the fullest opportunities. In this we shall fight by the side of white men, North and South. And if this be true, as under God's guidance it will, that old flag, that emblem of progress and security, which brave Sergeant Carney never permitted to fall on the ground, will still be borne aloft by Southern soldier and Northern soldier, and in a more potent and higher sense, we shall all realize that

> "The slave's chain and the master's alike are broken;
> The one curse of the race held both in tether;
> They are rising, all are rising —
> The black and the white together."

PD Con. 955 BTW Papers DLC. The speech also appeared in the *Tuskegee Student,* 11 (July 1897), 1, 4.

¹ For BTW's account of the ceremonies, see above, 1:106-12, 347-49.
² John Albion Andrew (1818-67), Civil War governor of Massachusetts.

From Albert Bushnell Hart

Cambridge, Mass. May 31 1897

Dear Mr Washington: Can you join a small company of gentlemen to meet Professor Woodrow Wilson at dinner at the Colonial Club, Cambridge, at half past six on Wednesday, June second? Sincerely yours,

Albert Bushnell Hart

ALS Con. 129 BTW Papers DLC.

A Message to the People of the North¹

Tuskegee, Alabama [May 1897]

I wish to ask each person in the North who reads these lines to put himself in the place if he can of the Negro and the Southern white man as often as possible. After he has done this let him ask God to help him do the thing that will result in [re]moving all bitterness of heart and that will help lift the load of ignorance that now weighs down most parts of the South. Yours Sincerely

Booker T. Washington

ALS Con. 977 BTW Papers DLC. At the top of the sheet in BTW's hand were the words "Our day   May, 1897."

¹ The message appeared as a facsimile of BTW's autograph in *Our Day,* 17 (May 1897), 214. It preceded an 11-page biographical sketch of BTW by George T. B. Davis and a 5-page account of the Tuskegee Negro Conferences by R. C. Bedford.

From Alonzo Homer Kenniebrew

Washington, 6–1 1897

My dear Prof. I have spent one very profitable month in Freedman's Hospital and beginning a new one. I have had under my care one hundred and twenty six patients of different diseases; and all of my time in the day & part of the night is spent in my ward studying the effects of drugs & courses of diseases and with such an able guide as Dr D H Williams, the greatest Negro Sergeon living, I have been successful in acquiring a reasonable degree of practicle skill in managing ailments of the most dangerous nature. And I have given two hrs. a day to examination of urine, milk & foodstuffs. I get to witness & assist in all operations performed, which are many. Please suffer me to say for the first time in medical history was an abdominal section performed on a colored woman for Ovarian Cystoma, last Sabbath morn. Dr. D. H. Williams was the operater & I was allow to assist. Many distinguished Operators were present to witness this so called phenomena as it will go down in history. I hope to be able to perform the same operation alone when I leave here.

I was pleased to read an account of the T.N.I.I. commencement in the "Washington Post" a few da[y]s, since. The "Post" is the leading daily in the District.

I will write again next month. Yours for success,

A. H. Kenniebrew

ALS   Con. 130   BTW Papers   DLC.

From Emmett Jay Scott

Houston. June 3, 1897

My Dear Mr. Washington: For fear of not being able to converse with you for any length of time I desire to hand you this note.

I have worked our lecture up so that all our citizens are expectant and waiting for you; and I hope that you will find yourself in good form. I hope that the long trip from Tuskegee and the work at Prairie View will not have you feeling worn and tired. I also hope that you will not give up the manuscript of your speech at P.V. — if you are to deliver the same speech here, as I can use it in the *"Post"* — our daily city newspaper. I also desire to request rather *firmly* that you accept no proffers of hospitality from anyone representing the Afro-American Fair Association of this city. These people are chagrined because they were not able to secure you to speak under their management. They have thrown every concievable barrier in my way to defeat the plan to make your lecture the huge success I have every reason to think it will be. I understand they're expect[ing] to meet you at P.V. and prevail upon you to put yourself in their hands when you arrive yon. Prof Blackshear[1] & all others can tell you of my hard work to make your appearance here a success. Our leading educators — state & city — have been invited & will be with us. I am also very anxious to have you stay with Mrs. Scott and myself over Saturday. Our people are very anxious to honor you — & I hope you can afford to accept it. I shall be glad to welcome you at the depot when you come down from P.V.

Well — this is all. I hope to have your absolute acquiescence in the matters herein mentioned. Yours very truly —

Emmett J Scott

ALS Con. 272 BTW Papers DLC.

[1] Edward Lavoisier Blackshear was born in Montgomery, Ala., in 1863 and graduated from Tabor College in Iowa in 1881. Moving to Texas, he was principal of a black high school in Austin from 1883 to 1896. Governor James S. Hogg appointed him president of Prairie View Agricultural and Mechanical College. An admirer and supporter of BTW, he sought to model his school after Tuskegee. Blackshear lacked BTW's gift for diplomacy, however, and he was forced by Governor James E. Ferguson to resign after he campaigned for Ferguson's opponent. (Woolfolk, *Prairie View*, 122-59.)

Margaret James Murray Washington
to Warren Logan

Crawford House, Boston   June 4 [1897]

Dear Mr Logan. I send this letter & order. I have written & thanked them. You may simply send receipt.

I wish you would send $5.00 for me to Mrs. Lucy Brown Macon

Miss. It is my mother, and I meant to have asked you to do this before I left but I forgot it. Please do not delay it longer than absolutely necessary. I shall not write her for she is very aged and ne[r]vous and if the money did not reach her the day after the letter she would be upset. Send it by Post Office Order.

The audience was wild over Mr. Washingtons speech. The Governor[1] rose to his feet & cried Three Cheers for Booker T Washington. You would have been pleased at the sight.

I hope that both you and Mrs Logan will get a little rest this summer. I was never so tired in my life. I do not think I can ever call myself rested again.

Please attend to this matter as soon as possible. Yours truly

Mrs W.

ALI   Con. 12   BTW Papers   ATT.   Original destroyed.

[1] Governor Roger Wolcott at the unveiling of the Shaw monument, May 31, 1897.

From William James

Cambridge, Mass., June 5, 1897

Dear Mr. Washington: I hope you got back safely, none the worse for wear and tear. Your speech has left the most enthusiastic expressions of delight behind it. I hear nothing on all sides but praise of it and of you, and I only hope that such things will not turn your head. What *I* particularly admired it for, apart from the nobility and elevation of its sentiments, is its simplicity and brevity. To say *one* thing, strongly, is after all the rule for the orator; every digression and excursion simply weaken the effect. The sentiment of the whole day here was very extraordinary. I think it took everyone by surprise that it should have been so intense and pathetic. After all, it was the last wave of the war breaking over Boston — "the tender grace of a day that is dead" etc. The subject was so humane and ideal and symbollical that the whole celebration seemed to float off into the realms of poetry. What struck me most in the whole thing was the faces of the survivors of the 54th and 55th, such excellent, patient, furrowed old citizens as they were. I enclose the note which, by mistake, was not mailed on Sunday night, and I hope that this week's meeting will not be our last. With regards to Mrs. Washington, believe me, Very truly yours,

Wm. James

TLS Con. 129 BTW Papers DLC.

From J. Francis Robinson[1]

Cambridge, Mass. June 6th 1897

My dear Mr Washington: We thought you would call, upon the occasion of your recent visit to Boston and spend at least ½ hour with us But alas! however we will not be angry with you this time providing you don't neglect us when you are here again. We are still calling public attention to your sentiments and the nature of your work as we are a thorough convert to your views upon the race question. But I give you no new information when I tell you that the New England Negroe does not share that opinion with us and whenever he is given opportunity whereby he might show how widely different his views are from ours he embraces it with alacrity as was the instance of my address before the League and later since the "Shaw Monument unveiling" when I took occasion to once again advise the Negroes to conservatism and imitation of B. T. W. as the one way of conquering race prejudices and antagonism. I had two lawyers to conquer the other night namely lawyers Edwin G. Walker[2] and Clement G. Morgan[3] and I floored them. I told them that you did not style yourself as the leader of the race But by merit, industry, and strict integrity had won your way to the front ranks Just as any of us will have to do before we will be given the place in the public confidence that you enjoy &c, &c, &c. I was overwhelmed with joy at your Music hall speech, surpassing as you did our most sanguine expectation not a few of the so called smart Negroes, who had declared that you would'nt be equal to the situation went home with drooping heads being compelled to admit that yours was an able, eloquent, and manly speech. It did my very heart good. It is not strange that the address has attracted wide attention and has called forth the praise of the press and pulpit all over the country. You have the faculty of saying the right word at the right time, which is like "apples of Gold and pictures of Silver." I hope you had a good

11

time in Texas. Please accept my earnest congratulations and very best wishes for your continued success. Please ask Mrs Washington if she recd. the book sent some time since and oblige. Faithfully and Admiringly Your Friend

J. Francis Robinson

ALS Con. 133 BTW Papers DLC.

¹ J. Francis Robinson resided in Fort Worth, Tex., 1892-96, where he edited *The Organizer.* He briefly held a pastorate in Halifax, Nova Scotia, lectured for a while, and then became pastor of the Mount Calvary Baptist Church in Norwich, Conn., from 1900 to 1907. Robinson often corresponded with BTW, praising the work of Tuskegee and asking to become BTW's lieutenant. He was miffed that BTW did not seem to appreciate his true worth.

² Edwin Garrison Walker, son of the famous black abolitionist David Walker, was a Boston lawyer. He served one year in the state legislature. He was a Democrat, and when Governor Benjamin F. Butler sought to appoint him a judge he was blocked by the Republicans. (Daniels, *In Freedom's Birthplace,* 100, 120, 451.)

³ Clement Garnett Morgan, born in Georgia, attended Atlanta University and Harvard, graduating from the college in 1890 and from the law school in 1893. He was a member of the Cambridge common council in 1895-96 from a predominantly white ward and alderman for two years. Twice nominated for the legislature, he failed to win election. Aligned with the "Boston radicals" against BTW, Morgan was W. M. Trotter's counsel in the Boston Riot trial. At the secret Carnegie Hall Conference in Jan. 1904, Morgan represented the Boston radicals. He was the leader of the Massachusetts wing of the Niagara Movement, but about 1906 he quarreled with the other fiery spirit of Boston militancy, Trotter, and thus weakened the effectiveness of the movement. (Daniels, *In Freedom's Birthplace;* Fox, *Guardian of Boston;* Rudwick, *W. E. B. Du Bois.*)

From Sophia Burroughs Agee

Handley W.Va. June 7, 1897

dear Booker   It has been a long time since I heard from any one at Tuskegee. I have been very sick and allso Sallie but we are geting a bout now. Sallie is well but I am not very well. Booker will you please send me a paire of shoes, I am in need of them very bad. a few more little thing that I need some plane dresses and some under ware. give my love to all the familey and John. times has been very hard hear and geting a little better. write me soon from your dear Aunt

Sophie Agee

ALS Con. 124 BTW Papers DLC.

To William James

Tuskegee, Ala. June 9, '97

Dear Prof. James: Your very kind favor of June 5, has reached me and you do not know how very much I appreciate your generous words. It was a privilege for me to come into contact with you in the way that I did. It gives me an acquaintance which I shall try to not let slip from me.

I enjoyed very much your strong address. You had by far the most difficult task, but I think that both of us may congratulate ourselves that the task was performed so well as it was. After all it is a privilege to have a part in the closing scenes of our great war.

Mrs. Washington and I both are very grateful to you and Mrs. James for the invitation to be your guests while in Boston. Both of us hope at some time to see you at your home. Yours truly

Booker T. Washington

ALS   William James Collection   MH.

From Robert Lloyd Smith[1]

Austin, Texas. June 9 1897

Prof Booker T Washington, The effect of your speech at Prairie View and Houston is far reaching. A good many who had an idea that industrial education was designed to continue the Negro as a hewer of wood and drawer of water have had their eyes opened and now know that it is the profoundest statesmanship and the soundest philosophy.

As for myself — I have already expressed to you the great effect your wonderful plea had on me. It did something that never was done before in my history — I allowed my ears to influence my will more than my eyes.

My trip to Tuskegee was a wonderful revelation but your speech was even more so.

I am going to work along certain lines that I'm sure will meet your hearty approval.

I want to start this coming fall a poor boys school. I want to fix it so that every poor boy or girl can go to this school and that every one of them shall have to work.

Since I left you, I have gone home and called a council and we have decided that we should make a start.

As soon as this session closes (about June 16) I want to see if I can not arrange to purchase a tract of land convenient to our village and prepare to open a school for poor boys in the fall. I think we could at once give instruction in three trades and in improved agricultural methods. We want to make the terms within the reach of all who really want to secure an education.

I think if we could get $1200 we could push the Improvement Society work and also run the school. I have had the offer of several of our best teachers to work for very small wages. For instance Prof Holmes of P.V. and his dear wife has offered more than once to come over and work for very little more than board. I couldnt have him make such a sacrifice however.

We can secure instruction in carpentry and blacksmithing from two splendid mechanics at a cost not to exceed $25 each per month. All these are men of means and are in love with the work. We could get a lady assistant who would give instruction in sewing for about $25 per mo or less. All these people want to see the Negro of this state trained in hand head and heart.

If we could get the $1200 to run the school and prosecute our other work, I am sure it will be the best investment in education anybody can make in this state.

The sum is not a large one. I simply want to employ a few teachers. Our own people would erect necessary buildings for a small work. A part of this money would be used by me in traveling over the state, organizing the people and a great work in Christian Civilization can be done.

I am of the opinion that with the reputation as a teacher I have gained in this state, if I succeed in *doing* anything and you would act as a member of the Board of Trustees, I myself could raise a good deal of money right in the state.

I have a constitutional objection to asking help unless there is something done. Its easier to ask and obtain help of friends but its very hard for me to even ask a stranger to help to put on foot an enterprise that is yet to demonstrate its usefulness. I speak now of the school.

As soon as this legislature adjourns (about June 16) I will be ready to set out on a lecturing and organizing tour on Improvement Society work.

I want a complete outfit about a dozen more pictures which I will have well mounted thus affording a practical illustration of what can be done under efficient organization & direction. I want to meet our Summer Normal Schools (they last about 6 wks), educational meetings and religious gatherings. As you are no doubt aware I am gladly welcomed and could get an hour at any gathering of colored people in the state.

I think that I should spend the summer at this work lecturing, distributing literature, and organizing and in the fall I should throw myself with all the energy of my being into the work of founding a Little Tuskegee at Oakland.

This is a long letter but I'm through now. If you write *at once* direct to Austin; if you wait until next wk. send answer to Oakland Texas. With much love   I am   Your friend

R. L. Smith

P.S. Keep all the material of your life together. Somehow I feel that if I outlive you I must be your Boswell.

R. L.

ALS   Con. 134   BTW Papers   DLC.

[1] Robert Lloyd Smith (1861-1942), a Texas educator, agrarian leader, and politician, was a model of self-reliance to whom BTW often referred as the right type of black leader. Born in Charleston, S.C., the son of a black teacher in the local public schools, he attended Avery Institute (1871-75), the University of South Carolina (1875-77), and Atlanta University, where he graduated in 1880. After teaching for five years in the Georgia public schools, Smith moved to Oakland, Colorado County, Tex., as principal of the Oakland Normal School. He was also a member of the county board of school examiners. To promote self-help and mutual help, he founded the Oakland Village Improvement Society. Since the community was engaged largely in farming, Smith organized the Farmers' Improvement Society in 1891 to help farmers improve their agricultural and business methods and strengthen their political voice. Its official organ was the magazine *Helping Hand*. The Woman's Barnyard Auxiliary worked to improve poultry and swine raising, gardening, and dairying. In 1906 Smith founded the Farmers' Improvement Agricultural College at Wolfe City on land owned by the society. Since his attitude and methods were similar to those of BTW, Smith became active in the Tuskegee Negro Conferences soon after their founding in 1892, and he was later an active participant in the National Negro Business League.

Smith was active in politics, serving in the state legislature from 1895 to 1899 as the last black legislator in Texas until 1966. His first speech was against a separate-waiting-room bill. As soon as Theodore Roosevelt became President, BTW began to urge a federal appointment for Smith. Roosevelt temporized because of opposition to Smith among the "lily-white" Republicans who dominated the party in Texas, but from 1902 to 1909 Smith was deputy U.S. marshal for the eastern district of Texas. He was a trustee of the Anna T. Jeanes Foundation. In 1914 he started an overall factory. In 1916 he was put in charge of black agricultural extension work in Texas. In the 1920s he was a member of the Southern Interracial Commission, which campaigned against lynching. He spent his last years in Waco, Tex. (Carter, "Robert Lloyd Smith and the Farmers' Improvement Society," 175-76, 190-91; Brewer, *Negro Legislators of Texas,* 101-4, 120-21.)

To Joseph Forney Johnston

Tuskegee, Ala., June 13, 1897

My dear sir: I write to express my gratitude and to thank you for your noble and courageous efforts in preventing the three colored persons charged with crime in Decatur from being lynched. I feel that this move on your part will go a long ways towards blotting out mob law in Alabama. Yours truly,

Booker T. Washington

TLS Governor Letter File G38 A-Ar.

From Emmett Jay Scott

Houston, Texas June 14, 1897

My Dear Mr. Washington: I read with pleasure the letters addressed to "The Post" and to myself. I thank you much for your generous references to our state. We all love it — in spite of the numberless acts which conform neither to logic, nor to justice. I have ordered copies of newspapers sent you containing references to the speech and yourself. My wife joins me in kindest regards. We hope to entertain you again if ever you are fortunate enough to come this way. I have many letters from over Texas, asking for engagements for you. I hope you can come again this fall.

May I prefer a request for a photograph of yourself to go in our house? Mrs. Scott has requested me to ask you. Very Sincerely Yours,

Emmett J. Scott

ALS   Con. 133   BTW Papers   DLC.

From Albert Bushnell Hart

Cambridge, Mass. June 14, 1897

Dear Sir: I was very sorry not to have seen you when you were in Boston. I hope you will give me quite an early notice of any contemplated visit — for I am quite anxious to see you, with especial reference to Professor DuBois, who it seems to me ought naturally to find his field of labor associated with you. Sincerely yours,

Albert Bushnell Hart

ALS   Con. 129   BTW Papers   DLC.

From Jabez Lamar Monroe Curry

Washington, D.C., 15 June 1897

My dear Sir— I am at home after an absence of two weeks and find your two letters.

1st. I shall leave on 17th for Bar Harbor, where we expect to remain two or more months. Should you visit that place this summer, I shall be more than pleased to see and confer with you. I am glad to hear of your work at reorganization. Some changes are desirable & you know best how to make them.

2d. I have heard of the effort to remove Prof. Paterson[1] and Prof Young[2] has been associated with the movement in all the letters which have reached me prior to yours. If he be not the right man, he ought to be removed, but not on the ground of his color.

Gov. J.[3] has written me several letters lately and he is greatly stirred up on the School question. To him I have written plainly and frankly in reference to the rascalities practiced on the Negroes in some of the Counties of the Black Belt. He will always listen to you. Kindly & with appreciation. Yours sincerely

J. L. M. Curry

ALS   Con. 272   BTW Papers   DLC.

1 William Burns Paterson.
2 Nathan B. Young.
3 Joseph Forney Johnston.

An Article in *Leslie's Weekly Illustrated*

[New York City, June 17, 1897]

THE SHAW MONUMENT

A few days ago I received a letter from an ex-Confederate soldier, now residing in Charleston, South Carolina, who was in the battle at Fort Wagner. In this letter this white gentleman told me that soon after Colonel Shaw was shot he cut a button from his uniform, before his body was thrown in the trench with those of his dead black soldiers. He further added, now that all was over, he would like the privilege of presenting this button to the family of Colonel Shaw.

Within the last month I saw in New York an ex-Confederate soldier from South Carolina, with an empty sleeve, pleading before a committee for money to be used in educating the black people of South Carolina.

Not long ago I saw in Boston a black officer who lost a leg at Fort Wagner, walking the streets arm in arm with an ex-Confederate white soldier with an empty sleeve, from Kentucky, who had come to Boston to secure money with which to maintain an orphan asylum, in which this white man was a teacher, under the control of a black superintendent.

When I was asked, a few weeks ago, by a Boston committee to deliver an address on the 31st of May at the unveiling of the statue on Boston Common in memory of Colonel Robert Gould Shaw, I was impressed with the change that had taken place in the sentiment of the people of Massachusetts since Colonel Shaw was asked, more than thirty years ago, by Governor John A. Andrew, to form a negro regiment. But a change has come not only in Massachusetts, but throughout the country, since that time, as the incidents with which I began this article indicate more clearly than anything I can say.

It would be hard for any white man to appreciate to what an extent the negro race reveres and idolizes the name of Colonel Shaw. Not so much for what he did as for the principle for which he stood. Recently, I have had the privilege of reading a private letter written by Colonel Shaw's mother[1] to Major George L. Stearns, who was largely instrumental in recruiting and forming the Fifty-fourth (Massachusetts) Regiment of colored troops. In this letter Mrs. Shaw says: "It will be the proudest day of my life when I can see my only boy at the head of a negro regiment." At this distance few can realize what such an expression meant at that time. Here we have the only son of one of the most cultivated and distinguished families in the North willing to resign a position in a successful white regiment to cast his fortune with a negro regiment. There were but few in the North who favored the experiment of making the negro a soldier, and still fewer who favored putting the negro soldier on absolute equality with the white soldier. There were few who thought the negro would be a success as a soldier. His courage and ability were doubted. Beyond all this, he belonged to a servile race. It was the open boast of the Southern soldiers that negro soldiers would be given no quarter — that if captured, both they and their officers would not be dealt with in accordance with the rules of civilized war. In making his decision all this Colonel Shaw had to face. When Governor Andrew and his father once made him see that it was his duty to head the negro regiment he did not hesitate for a moment. Neither the danger on the battle-field nor the threatened loss of social position had weight with him. He counted his own life as nothing if it might be used in saving the country and freeing the black man. Soon there came to his aid as officers dozens of men who represented the bluest and best blood in the North. From the time that Colonel Shaw organized this black regiment until the present, the negro has been a success as a soldier, as is proved by the fact that there are now several fine colored regiments enlisted in the regular service. Besides, every Southern State now has several companies of colored militia. In Alabama there is a colored regiment that is on the same footing as the white regiments of that State.

Colonel Shaw succeeded in making the negro a soldier because he had faith in him as a man. Any one will succeed in dealing with the negro who has faith in him in any capacity.

As all truly brave men are, Colonel Shaw was generous to the enemy. Nothing in his army career seems to have given him so much pain as the fact that by the orders of a superior officer he was compelled to burn the town of Darien, Georgia. In his letters he repeatedly referred to this as being an act against which his whole nature rebelled. If he lived to-day none would be more anxious and active to blot out all cause for difference between North and South.

Few, if any, monuments erected in this country — now that the full meaning of Colonel Shaw's deeds and death are understood — will possess a wider and more genuine interest for all classes than that which has just been dedicated in Boston. In every act the black regiment justified Colonel Shaw's faith in it. In the war there were no braver deeds than those performed by the negro soldiers at Fort Wagner. Soon after the battle one of the wounded soldiers wrote that if the giving of his life would have saved that of Colonel Shaw he would have gladly given it.

With all his faults the negro has never proved himself ungrateful, nor has he ever betrayed a friend. During the war he betrayed neither the Yankee nor the Confederate when his honor as a friend was at stake. The negroes are most grateful to the committee in Boston who have secured this magnificent monument, and by their efforts to secure property, education, and character, they are trying to prove to the world that the precious sacrifices that have been made in their behalf were not in vain.

Booker T. Washington

Leslie's Weekly Illustrated, 84 (June 17, 1897), 397.

[1] Helen B. Shaw.

From Edward T. Devine

[New York City] June 23rd–1897

My dear Sir: Within a few days the Evening Post of this city expects to publish an article upon the subject about which we have exchanged one or two letters, the special point being to emphasize the necessity of discriminating in the charitable support of schools for negroes. The special cause is the arrest of two men, Fremont & Chesire, who have been for three or four years collecting money apparently in considerable amount for the so-called Fremont Polytechnic School in Alexandria Va. There is no such school in existence and the representations that have been made are absolutely fraudulent. I believe the men have been living in New York City most of the time. They were discharged yesterday by the Magistrate as the evidence in regard to the non-existence of the school was not quite sufficient technically to hold them; but the Principal of another school in Alexandria which really does exist is here to-day and I am expecting to place his testimony, together with the other evidence before the District Attorney in the hope that the Grand Jury will indict them. There seems to be no other way to force the matter on public attention.

I spoke to the representative of the Evening Post who called to see me yesterday about the list which you had been kind enough to prepare for us and was asked whether they could not publish it in the article which they are preparing. I suppose that you will probably have no objection to this but preferred to ask you before giving it to them. If you will be kind enough to reply immediately I will regard it as a special favor.

In the same connection the Post would be very glad to have from you any remarks on the general subject that you might wish to publish. It is rather a good opportunity to make an appeal to the New York public for support of legitimate and sensibly conducted institutions.

Congratulating you upon the work of your own Institute, I am, Very sincerely yours,

Edward T. Devine

TLS Con. 127 BTW Papers DLC. Written on stationery of the Charity Organization Society of the City of New York.

From Henry Villard

New York, June 28, 1897

Dear Sir: In accordance with your request, I enclose my check for $100., but I feel obliged to attach a condition to this contribution.

You will remember that in a conversation with you when you were our guest, I expressed a strong deprecation of the attempts made at the Atlanta University to give young men and women of your race a regular university education such as is obtained at the highest institutions of learning in the North, when they were not by previous training prepared to receive it. I also then expressed to you my gratification that you, as I then supposed, confined yourself at Tuskegee to giving the pupils an elementary education coupled with a training in domestic arts, agriculture and mechanical trades so as to qualify them to support themselves and open their way to material independence and set a good example of self-reliance and success in life to their race. In other words, I was under the impression that no studies beyond the common school range were followed at your institution, and you said nothing to correct it.

It was a most disagreeable surprise therefore to receive last December the letter of which I enclose a copy and which contained the positive proof that the very practice I criticized is being also followed at Tuskegee. The letter also affords a striking illustration of the very hurtful results which must inevitably come from such a false method of education. For, here is a young woman, who evidently not only has an insufficient knowledge of English grammar and is even unable to spell correctly, and yet writes me that her last studies have been in: "Natural Philosophy, Ancient History, Algebra and Grammar," and that in the next quarter there will be added to them "Civil Government and Rhetoric."

To make sure that my conclusions from this evidence before me were justified, I discussed the subject with President Gilman of John[s] Hopkins University a short time since. He not only confirmed my inferences, but himself expressed the strongest disapproval of the travesty of higher education, which is being enacted at Tuskegee, and gave me some ludicrous instances of the mental confusion produced there by the pursuit of classical studies on immature minds, which he had drawn out by personal examination of pupils.

The letter from Mrs. Booker, accompanying the enclosure, gave me the first intimation that my contribution was used for the education of a particular pupil. As this is contrary to my conviction of what is best for the institution, I make it a condition of the present and future ones that they shall be devoted to the general purpose of your school.

Requesting a confirmation of this, I remain, Yours truly,

H. Villard

HLS   Con. 31   BTW Papers   ATT.

From Samuel Thomas Mitchell[1]

Wilberforce, Ohio, June 28, 97

My Dear Bro: In recognition of your high personal merit and splendid achievements by which you have obligated a whole race to yourself, Wilberforce University joins Harvard & confers the degree of Master of Arts.

We all wish you every prosperity & exaltation. Fraternally,

S. T. Mitchell

ALS   Con. 272   BTW Papers   DLC.

[1] Samuel Thomas Mitchell (1851-1901) was president of Wilberforce University from 1884 to 1901. Born in Toledo, Ohio, he attended public schools in Cincinnati and graduated from Wilberforce in 1873. From 1875 to 1884 he was principal of Lincoln Institute (now Lincoln University) in Jefferson City, Mo. He helped to organize the black state teacher's association. Then he worked successfully for a bill to allow black teachers in the major cities of Missouri. As president of Wilberforce he was a successful money-raiser, securing from the state funds for a normal and industrial department at Wilberforce. This allowed the state, at the risk of joining church and state, to pretend that it was providing equal college opportunities for black citizens at Wilberforce.

From Robert Lloyd Smith

Austin, Texas. [ca. June] 1897

Dear Friend   I know that it was asking a good deal to have you add another to your family but if you can see your way to do it I can promise you some startling *results*. For instance, take the town of Oakland. The Negro has nothing like it in Texas. I dont mean to say that there are not better homes more intellectual and wealthier Negroes in other places. I think there are, but there is not another place anywhere that I have heard of, where the blacks and whites are segregated in which the *blacks* are so *nearly raised* to *the standard* of *the whites* and that standard a high one. Now when I began work a few years ago I had no such influence as I have today. I can go to a town to day and get a big meeting and organize on a permanent footing in 36 hours. Why? My work as a teacher — Two hundred and fifty trained teachers sent out at a cost of nothing to the state — This work done with one assistant a part of each year. The character of my students was so high and their work so satisfactory that many county judges in South Texas recommended me for principal of Prairie View last year without ever having seen me. Why cant you do it now? Physically unable to do what I have done again — and to teach and travel too.

I honestly think that if I can do something in the line I have indicated the state itself will grant aid possibly in two years. I dont want to weary you but you know what it is to begin an undertaking and you know also that is it the friendly hand at the outset that *counts*.

Now if you will take hold of us even in a small way I promise you *results* that will absolutely surprise you if God spares my life. I will change your next conference into a picture gallery that will give a great impetus to the work that you are doing. I'll give you *results*. I hate like the mischief to beg — I think if you take hold of this — You will have no difficulty whatever in procuring the means to prosecute it especially after the next conference. I guess you see how I stand in Texas. I have worked very hard for my people and have been at *no expense* whatever to them. I have organized now about 30 societies two less than double what we had in Feb. when I was at Tuskegee. I can do a great work here and will do it under your patronage if you say so and *will not worry you* continually. I want a good poor mans school in Texas. I can do it more easily more cheaply and more quickly than anybody else in this state that I can think of and I am now pleading for a *start* along industrial lines in Texas independent of state *exclusive* control.

Now then, suppose you try what I can do in one year with about $600 for school and $600 for ~~industrial~~ Village Improvement Work. I could easily spend $1200 in Improvement Society work but I would rather divide it into two equal parts. I will make this proposition to you. If I dont *satisfy you* as to results, Ill pay you the money back.

Thats the best I can do. Ill go to work the 15th of July and spend my time on the road. Texas is a big state and until the annual convocation which takes place in Oct (2nd Wednesday) I will keep on moving. With the means to do this at my command I think I ought to have 5000 persons, some improved homes, some purchase of land &c and at least 100 societies by that time. If we succeed and get a great gathering you might come over and give us a good talk. A talk with my crowd means *results*. You'll *see* it after a few months.

Now Ive written a long letter and I do hope you will see this as I see it and will take hold of it. I have worked hard in this state without ever having recd any aid and now that I see a ray of light for God sake dont close it. You can succeed in doing untold Good here at small cost with the assurance that if things dont pan out I'll take the responsibility of returning the money to you or whoever it comes from. Of course you will not understand this as a begging letter or me as a begger or anything like that. It is a plain business proposition to encourage the planting & growth of those ideas for which Booker T Washington stands as their greatest living champion and exponent.

Thanks for book I read it with great interest. Our society was organized in 1891. I must have made a mistake at Conference.

Now lets have a big thing at Conference of 98 — Respectfully & Cordially and I may add Hopefully Yours

R. L. Smith

ALS Con. 134 BTW Papers DLC.

From Joseph Oswalt Thompson

Tuskegee, Ala., July 2, 1897

Dear Sir, Yours dated Chicago, 26th ult. just to hand. I appreciate very much the interest you are manifesting in my behalf.

While in Washington I met Ex. Congressman Murray of South Carolina. You will remember him as the successful contestant for Col. Elliot's[1] seat and the man for whom our Representative, at that time, Capt. Goodwyn, voted to seat.

I made myself known to him as your friend and the choice of Capt. Goodwyn and it was he who introduced me to P.M. Gen'l.

307

Mr. Walker² at Montgomery and Mr. Russell³ here have had a good deal to say about me allowing myself introduced to the P.M. Gen'l by a colored man. Their idea was to predudice my white friends against me but they have not accomplished anything further than to weaken themselves with the colored Republicans who see the contemptable attitude they have placed themselves in.

While in Washington I circulated a petition among the Ala. Republicans there and nearly every one signed it. Such men as Dr. Moseley,⁴ Dr. Pettiford,⁵ Wm. Stevens, Judge Horn and Col. Reese⁶ and many others who happened to be there.

The P.M. Gen'l told me after listening to my statement about the trade made by the present encumbent with Judge Cobb, the Congressman then, to pay to Mrs. J. J. Mosley the sum of $25.00 per month out of her Office, that he would remove them when I established that fact. I then saw Col. Youngblood⁷ and he asked me not to push the case until after Congress adjourned and he would have me put in. I have furnished him with the proof of the statement made [by] the P.M. Gen'l.

If it would be possible for you to do so I am sure it would hasten my appointment if when Congress adjourns you will run down to Washington — see Col. Youngblood & P.M. Gen'l and have case called up.

Out of the past 12½ years you will remember the Republicans have only had 2 yrs. 10 months administration of this Office. S. Q. Hale (Dem) was P.M. 6 years then M. S. Russell (Rep) was P.M. 2 years 10 mos. and the Howards⁸ have been in nearly 4 years.

This is one place when the Dems have always put Reps. out before their time expired, while on the other hand the Republicans have allowed the Dem's. to serve out time. We think turn about fair play. I hope you will state this fact to the P.M. Gen'l when you see him.

What ever extra expense you may incur in making the trip to Washington, keep a memorandum of it and I will re-emburse you when you return home as I of course do not expect you [to] go there in my behalf without defraying expense.

I feel that you will do me more good at this time than anyone. I remain   Your friend

J. O. Thompson

ALS   Con. 135   BTW Papers   DLC.

¹ Robert Brown Elliott (1842-84) was born in Boston of West Indian parents. After elementary education in Jamaica he attended a London academy and Eton and studied law in London. Returning to the United States during Reconstruction, he became a newspaper editor in Charleston, S.C., and served in the constitutional convention of 1867, the legislature, and Congress (1869-71, 1873-74). He was noted for his eloquence in defense of black civil rights and against the Ku Klux Klan. He later was a U.S. Treasury agent in Charleston and New Orleans. In 1898 he asked BTW's help in founding at Beaufort, S.C., the Sea Island Agricultural and Industrial School. (Elliott to BTW, Apr. 25, 1898, Con. 139, BTW Papers, DLC.)

² Benjamin Winston Walker.

³ Morgan S. Russell was postmaster of Tuskegee from 1891 to 1893.

⁴ Robert Alexander Moseley, Jr. (1841-1900), born in Montevallo, Ala., served in the Confederate Army until he suffered a severe head wound at the battle of Murfreesboro. He returned home, studied medicine, and became a physician and druggist. The founder of five Alabama newspapers, he switched his allegiance from the Democratic to the Republican party in 1872. A delegate to the Republican national conventions in 1876, 1880, and 1884, he was chairman of the Alabama Republican state committee from 1888 to 1896. His support of fusion with the white Populists in 1892 led to a rival faction of black regular Republicans headed by William J. Stevens. Moseley held several appointive federal offices in Alabama and died of illness contracted while U.S. consul general at Singapore, 1899-1900. He worked jointly for BTW and Henry Clay Reynolds as a lobbyist and helped gain passage of the bill granting Tuskegee Institute and the Montevallo school federal land in 1899.

⁵ William Reuben Pettiford. (See above, 2:360.)

⁶ Warren Stone Reese was born in Sycalauga, Ala., and joined the Confederate Army at a young age. He was promoted to colonel at the age of nineteen by General Joseph Wheeler for gallantry at the battle of Chickamauga. He lived in Montgomery after the Civil War as a planter and cotton commission merchant. He was mayor in 1888-89, and the unsuccessful fusion candidate for the U.S. Senate in 1896.

⁷ William Youngblood (b. 1844) was an auditor in the Treasury Department in Washington from 1897 to 1899. He and former governor Lewis E. Parsons were leaders of the "lily-white" faction of Alabama Republicans. In 1901-2, when BTW had gained the ear of President Roosevelt, he worked to remove Youngblood and other lily whites from control of the party in Alabama.

⁸ Benjamin F. Howard was postmaster of Tuskegee from 1893 to 1895, and Sally Howard was postmistress from 1895 to 1898.

From Emmett Jay Scott

Houston, Texas. July 2, 1897

My Dear Mr. Washington — I have your favor of June 29th and note contents. Replying to same beg to say that I am so situated that I can

favorably consider a proposition from you looking forward to my association with you in the capacity of Private Secretary. I shall be glad
to have a line from you advising me when I shall be expected to begin
service; also whether provision will be made for wife and self at Tuskegee; and such other matters as you may think I deserve to know.
An early reply will be appreciated by me. Mrs. Scott joins me in good
wishes for your continued health and prosperity. Very sincerely yours,

Emmett J. Scott

ALS   Con. 272   BTW Papers   DLC.

From John Stephens Durham

Parker House, Boston, July 3, 1897

My dear Dr. Washington: I regret very much that I missed you when
I called at your hotel this morning. I shall remain in this evening and
I trust that you may find it convenient to drop in after seven or half
past to meet my wife.

I enclose a very bad proof of an article which will appear in the July
issue of the A.M.E. Church Review.[1] It is an abstract of a fragment of
my talks to the Hampton and Tuskegee students a year ago. My recollection is that you thought well of this part of my studies. If my plan
be approved, I trust to put those talks in the form of a pamphlet:
"To Teach the Negro History" and to distribute the screed privately
among the graduates of both institutions. I am deeply interested, therefore, in having your frank judgment and I have brought on the proof
for that purpose. Trusting to see you, I am   Very Sincerely Yours,

John S. Durham

ALS   Con. 127   BTW Papers   DLC.

[1] Durham's article, "Three Growths," *A.M.E. Church Review,* 14 (July 1897),
121-30, concluded that the establishment of trade schools and the movement to
open factories, workshops, and businesses were in harmony with natural economic
development. Durham discussed the different economic roles of slaves and how
they evolved after the Civil War. He had high praise for the ex-slave craftsmen
and suggested that schools such as Tuskegee continued that tradition.

To Henry Villard

Crawford House, Boston, Mass. July 5th, 1897

Dear sir: I should have sent an earlier reply to your kind favor of June 28th, but have been forced to be away from my mail for more than a week. I wish to thank you for your donation and shall see that it is used as you request.

I very much hope that you will take the time to look further into the work being done at Tuskegee. With me it has been a life work and I have tried to do things that I thought was helping my people.

I have seldom had occasion to discuss with any one the details of our course of study. I have always said that our course of study was similar to that of the Hampton Institute and as so many of our friends have been to Hampton and seen the work there, I have as a rule thought that this was the best way of explaining our course of study. If you will compare the course of study at Hampton with our own I think you will find little difference. So far from encouraging what are usually termed classical studies at Tuskegee I have always opposed the introduction of such studies there, and in doing so have for a number of years received the adverse criticism of numbers of my own race. Still I have never given way to this and expect to give my time and strength to the keeping of the work at Tuskegee in a simple form and trying to do well what we attempt.

You will find at Tuskegee as [at] most schools I think, those who have imperfectly mastered what they have gone over, especially will you find those who are weak in spelling and the use of the English language, and it is for this reason that I have never permitted any language to be taught at Tuskegee except English. You will find those at Tuskegee as in the case of the girl who wrote you, whose youthful ambition tempt[s] them to overestimate their own work and intentions. For example, she spoke of taking up "Rhetoric" soon. The fact is there is no rhetoric as a text book taught at Tuskegee. It was in the course a number of years ago, but I found that the students needed the time in the study of simple English grammar and so took rhetoric out of the course. This girl speaks of intending to study Civil Government. The term as it stands seems ambitious. To appreciate what it means at Tuskegee one would have to see the work done. There it means little more than the giving of the student an idea of the divisions

311

of federal and state government — something that is done in all our first class public schools. The girl in question speaks of singing classical music from Handel, Mozart, etc.; this simply means that she is in our school choir and sometimes I presume the selections are from these authors.

In our course of study there now are several changes that I would like to make in the direction of simplicity and perfection, but I cannot make them for the reason that we receive an appropriation from the State and those who finish our course at Tuskegee are expected to have studied the things required for a first grade state teacher's certificate. But were this restriction removed I do not mean to say that I would make any great change — were I permitted I should attempt less in mathematics.

Your letter calls my attention to the fact that the names used in our catalogue are misleading in several cases and give an exaggerated idea of what is attempted in the actual instruction. For example, under the chemistry our students are taught the most simple elements mainly with a view of using it in agriculture. From first to last the industrial work is the thing most emphasized at Tuskegee and the class room seems in a large measure to help the industrial work. Since my conversation with you last spring I have taken out the subject embraced under the head of "Economics" in the enclosed course of study though the work was given in a simple way.

In conclusion I would say that your criticism has done us good and I thank you for it. I think in a large measure you would get a different idea of our work if you could spend some time on the grounds and see the earnest way which our students take hold of their work. This I hope you will sometime be able to do.

I shall be glad to have at any time further suggestions from you. Yours truly,

Booker T. Washington

TLS   Henry Villard Papers   MH.

JULY · 1897

From Seth Low[1]

New York   July 8th, 1897

My dear Mr. Washington: I am glad to learn that you have secured the $30,000 necessary for your Trades School Building. I enclose my cheque for $1,500, in accordance with my pledge, with pleasure. Yours sincerely,

Seth Low

I shall be glad to know who have joined me in this enterprise.

TLS   Con. 130   BTW Papers   DLC.

[1] Seth Low (1850-1916) was a trustee of Tuskegee Institute from 1905 until his death, and after 1907 was president of the board of trustees. After graduation from Columbia University at the head of his class in 1870, he entered his father's shipping firm and become a senior member of it by the time of its dissolution in 1887. Thereafter he devoted his time to public service and politics. An active Republican, he was elected mayor of Brooklyn in 1881 and 1883. He reformed the city's civil service, school system, and finances. In 1884 he was a Mugwump supporter of Grover Cleveland, a defection that denied him the further support of many Republicans. From 1890 to 1901 he was president of Columbia University, where he centralized graduate training and arranged for the affiliation of Barnard College and Teachers' College with the university. In 1901, in a reaction against Tammany corruption, Low was elected mayor of New York. He sought to reduce patronage corruption by civil service reform, and sought to make more efficient the transportation and electrical services of the city. Low served only one term as mayor, but he remained a leading figure in Progressive politics in the state.
As a trustee of Tuskegee, Low was obsessed with a mission to bring greater efficiency into the operation of the school and particularly its agricultural operations. As a gentleman farmer in upstate New York in his spare time, Low claimed some expertise in operating a farm. Believing that blacks were disdainful of work because of their reaction against the labors of slavery, Low sought through Tuskegee and Tuskegee methods to bring blacks into the American mainstream by teaching them how to work hard and effectively. Low's energy and devotion as a trustee were equaled within BTW's lifetime only by William H. Baldwin, Jr. Low's behavior, however, was sometimes overbearing toward BTW and members of the Tuskegee staff. In his obsession with efficiency and detail, he failed to lead and encourage, and his concern with training for agricultural pursuits left little room for the higher aspirations of blacks or for technological changes of the future. (Kurland, *Seth Low*, 323-27.)

From J. H. Coleman

St. Louis Mo   July 12 1897

Mr Washington Sir   It affored me great Pleagure in riteing to you this after noon to ask of you your opinion on the subject of so many of our People being lynch. Mr. Washington it a shame an Disgrace on the Negro race in Many Respects tha ar lynch for crymes that Wood not Send them to the Penn tha Have gone so far as to Take our Wemoms out an lynch them. Must we as men stand that. Who Have our females got to Depend on for Protection if we don't study some Plan to stop this linching. We Have ben taught to live Peaceful an on the other hand the White People ar Uniting to Gether against us. Hear in this city the Whites meets evry Week to formulate Some Plan against the Negro.

On one of there Meeting a White Gentleman got the floor an spok in the favor of the Negro an he was ousted out of the Meeting at once. Dear sir I think it Wood be a good idear for our Peple now to be taugh How to unite an Protect life an Propety an Protect our femeals if some of us have to looze our life. Mr. Washington if we do not Protest against this Why after While tha Will come to our Schools an take our Teachers out an mob Them an also come to our Homes an take our Wives an Daughters out an male treat them. Great meny of our People ar being lynch on faulst Repots Mr. Washington. Please send me some of your Books showing the Diffrence Persitions that the Graduates of Tuskegee Hold an if it cost eny thing i Will send you the Price at once soon as i get them. Hope to hear from you at once because I am verry much Disturbe the Way our People ar being treated.

J. H. Coleman

ALS   Con. 126   BTW Papers   DLC.

From Samuel May

Leicester, Mass. July 22/97

Dear Mr. Washington, Yesterday two papers came to me from Illinois. One was the Chicago "Daily Inter Ocean" of July 17th, the very first article in which was a two-column communication to the editor signed by "Ida B. Wells-Barnett."[1] She had been to Urbana, Ohio, to inquire into the case of the colored young man, Mitchell, lately put to death there by a mob which broke into the jail, and this was her statement concerning it.

The other paper was from Shelbyville, Ill., in which was mentioned the fact that you are to attend a meeting, early in August, in the neighborhood of that town, at a place called Lithia Springs.

It comes to me as a duty from which I cannot escape, and to which I seem to be compelled by the power above me — "which makes for righteousness" — that I should see to it that you are informed of this state of things; that you may not go into that neighborhood without being made fully aware of the facts thus far ascertained; and that you may have time to consider them carefully, before being called to speak of them at Lithia Springs, as you will probably be.

The difficulties of the case are obvious; but the word of God, and our Christian duty to our brother man, spoken as you are wont to speak them, and which grace will still be given you to speak them, are sufficient for all difficulties.

I enclose Mrs. Wells-Barnett's communication.

I find no editorial comment in the Chicago paper upon *this* case; but there is one upon a late Southern lynching, which I cut out & enclose.

Much to sadden us, dear Mr. Washington, but we *must keep* our *faith,* our *hope,* our *patience, and our courage,* "speaking the truth in love." Always yours,

Samuel May

ALS   Con. 131   BTW Papers   DLC.

[1] Ida B. Wells-Barnett wrote a vivid account of the lynching in Urbana, Ohio, of Charles Mitchell for allegedly raping a white woman. Mitchell had turned himself in when informed that he was a suspect. A mob of 5,000 persons took Mitchell from the jail and hanged him. Attempts by the militia to save Mitchell resulted in the deaths of three of the mob. (Chicago *Inter Ocean,* July 17, 1897, 9.)

To Warren Logan

Crawford House, Boston, Mass. July 27th, 1897

Dear Mr. Logan: I notice that arrangements are being made by the city council of Tuskegee to support a public school for the white people. I wish you would go at once before the council or see the members individually, and arrange for the colored schools to receive support from the city fund. I wish you would press this matter or use Mr. Hare[1] or any one else that you think proper to help. Mr. Adams[2] also might help you. Now is the time to push this matter otherwise we will lose. Keep me informed of your progress. Yours truly,

Booker T. Washington

TLS   Con. 12   BTW Papers   ATT.   Original destroyed.

[1] Charles Woodroph Hare.
[2] Lewis Adams.

From Samuel Somerville Hawkins Washington

Tuskegee, Ala., Aug 3d 1897

Dear Sir: Though no responsibility for the care of the sick rests with me for next year I should regret to see any epidemic at Tuskegee that may with proper precautions be avoided or at least made comparatively light.

You are no doubt aware of the large number of small pox cases in B'ham and that there are now in Montgomery over 30 cases not confined to any one section of the town but springing up every where. The disease has been in the state for more than six months and has been going from community to community — the very mild type in which it has manifested itself having made the authorities somewhat lax in dealing with it. The disease manifests itself in four distinct types — the mildest of which is called discrete — this is the type that has been in the State and there has not been a single death from it. Should it get into the school here at Tuskegee the confluent type is almost bound to show itself and you would expect a large death rate.

You can hardly keep it out of Tuskegee as it has been so general in the State. The worst season for it is the winter. The best thing to do is to prepare to meet it. You ought to have a *number* of people *now* engaged in removing trash & weeds from, and throwing lime around your buildings in considerable quantity. You ought to commence vaccinating at the rate of 20 a day at once. I would not recommend any greater number as there is always more or less sickness attending vaccination. Many of the towns in the State have waked up to the urgency of the situation & are taking just such steps as I have outlined to you. If you are prompt in giving instructions in this matter I can at least give you one week's service. I could have written you two days earlier but Jewett has been down with *typhoid* fever and has demanded very much of my time.

I have talked the matter over with Mr. Logan. Hoping you will understand that I have no interested motives other than for the general good of the public and the school   I am very truly yours

S. S. H. Washington

ALS   Con. 135   BTW Papers   DLC.

From Emmett Jay Scott

Houston, Texas, Aug. 6/1897

Dear Mr. Washington: I have your favor dated July 26 and mailed August 1st. Replying thereto, I beg to say that I cannot accept the terms of your offer. The amount of salary offered is too small for serious consideration, especially now since I find that Mrs. Scott cannot be with me there next year; and must be provided for here at Houston, while I am at Tuskegee.

I am not unmindful of the great opportunities offered me by being associated with you, but I should try to be so valuable as to merit a sum, for salary, greatly in excess of what you offer. Thanking you most cordially for your much appreciated offer and regretting the necessity which precludes acceptance of it, I am, Yours very sincerely —

Emmett J. Scott

P.S. If you decide to come to Texas again soon I shall be glad to hear from you. Mrs. Scott sends regards.

EJS

ALS   Con. 272   BTW Papers   DLC.

The Introduction to *Progress of a Race*

Tuskegee, Ala. August 8, 1897

The Progress of a Generation in the history of the Negro is the most fascinating study modern times possesses. Springing from the darkest depths of slavery and sorrowful ignorance to the heights of manhood and power almost at one bound, the Negro furnishes an unparalleled example of possibility. In the pages following, the authors have performed a duty at once difficult and needful — that of following the rise of the Negro through the different stages of his career. It is a task that merits respect, commands attention, and is, unhappily, too seldom attempted.

The task of a biographer of a people is too frequently a thankless one. In sifting out the conflicting elements which present themselves for his consideration he is apt to injure tradition. In using material which he thinks best he is likely to upset preconceived ideas of theorists. His work must be the result of careful thinking and an astonishing amount of *finesse* and diplomacy.

The historian of the Negro race has all this and more too. He must, in addition to the other duties which devolve upon him in his work, be able to prophesy and foresee the days to come. For the progress of the Negro is far from completed — it is yet in its incipient stage — and the eyes of the prophet must discern whither the road leads, upward or downward.

The unprecedented leap the Negro made when freed from the oppressing withes of bondage is more than deserving of a high place in history. It can never be chronicled. The world needs to know of what mettle these people are built. It needs to understand the vast possibility of a race, so much despised and so thoroughly able to prove without blare and flourish of trumpet its ability to hold its own and compete, after only thirty years of life, with those of centuries of lineage.

The dawn of new life is again gleaming behind the horizon. After the words were spoken which pronounced the Negro free, he hesitated a minute, then sprang towards the highest place at once. It was not many days before he was heard from in all positions, in all walks of life; he was in high government positions, his name was on the most exclusive professional roles, yet the common horde lingered in surprised helplessness, wondering what next. Such a state of affairs, though brilliant, was without foundation and could not last. In building the structure of his race-life the Negro had begun at the top. The cupola could not last without a foundation; the work was shaking without a firm support. Of late years this is being realized, and we are turning our attention to the foundation work. It may be that some are blind to the crying needs of an absolute and unwrenchable foundation in the soil of the state, but those whose eyes are opened must realize that we can advance no further, or do no better work, until we have paused and implanted ourselves firmly. The progress made thus far has been magnificent, but like the house built upon sands. Ere we add another gable or tower to its structure we must insure it against the lash of the storm's fury by placing a solid rock beneath its surface.

This is where the progress of the Negro leads us today — to pause in the brilliant meteoric advance and stride forward henceforth as a solid phalanx of earnest, industrious toilers, for a merited place in the world's array of nations. By the work-shop, the well-tilled farm, the scientifically conducted dairy, the mechanic's well-done work, our advance is now being noted. From gaining the wondering curiosity of the world for a chosen, brilliant few, we are compelling its respect and admiration for ourselves as a whole, as a people upon whom the stigma of idle dreaming can no longer be laid.

Thus, while the authors record in these pages the progress of the Negro within the past generation, let us hope that when another quarter century has passed away the race's biographer may have a still more promising story to tell. Let us hope that it will be a story of a people taking part in the affairs of a nation — not in isolated cases, but as an integral part of a magnificent whole. Let us hope that there will be manufacturers, as well as senators; good and successful business men, as well as politicians; reputable artisans, as well as literateurs; millionaires, as well as laborers. Let us hope that the wave of industrial feeling now extending over the country may find its culmination in the unmistakable and solid foundation of a magnificent people, and crystallize a race into conformation with the highest standard reached by man in the present age.

Booker T. Washington

H. F. Kletzing and W. H. Crogman, *Progress of a Race* (Atlanta, Ga., Naperville, Ill., and Toronto, Ont.: J. L. Nichols and Company, 1897), v-vii.

From Albert Bushnell Hart

Boston, Aug. 10, 1897

Dear President Washington: Owing to absence from the city today is the first time that I have been able to call at the Crawford House: and I find that you have left. I will with pleasure send you a contribution in a few days.

Have you no place for the best educated colored man available for college work? Prof Du Bois is a man in whom I have much confidence, based on long acqua[i]ntance. His book on the slave trade is very scholarly and able. He is a man of character. One reason why I have for years been interested in him is that I expect him to be a force in the uplifting of his race.

He has had an appointment from the University of Pennsylvania, fellowship from Harvard, and study abroad from the Slater Fund. It seems as though the time has come for his own race to give him an opportunity. I feel sure that you yourself will find in him a competent aid in your great work.

Will you not let me know as soon as you come to Boston next time? I want to know you, and to have you acquainted with some of my friends. Sincerely yours,

Albert Bushnell Hart

ALS   Con. 272   BTW Papers   DLC.

From Emmett Jay Scott

Houston Texas   August 23/1897

My Dear Sir: In confirmation of my message by wire to you today I desire to reiterate that it will be impossible for me to come to Tuskegee for less than eighty ($80) dollars per month. I would not expect board, room, etc. free in addition to this amount. I find myself very anxious to accept an offer that will allow the close association with you that your offer implies, but I cannot be wholly unmindful of my own best interests. I have a good place offered me which will pay me the amount mentioned above, but I have not accepted — pending the settlement of this matter. Let me hear from you and be assured of my entire appreciation of your interest in me. Regards for personal success and prosperity. Yours truly and faithfully,

Emmett J. Scott

ALS   Con. 272   BTW Papers   DLC.

From Robert Charles Bedford

Beloit, Wis   Aug 26 1897

Dear Prof Of course you will read Dr Crummell's article in the Independent of Aug 19 "The Prime need of the Negro Race" and the Independent's hearty endorsement of the same in an editorial note.[1] It is alright except for the covered inference that Tuskegee does not believe in the "Higher Culture." A glance among our graduates revealing such characters as Miss Bowen Harvey Wood Lovejoy Wilborn Harris Canty Stewart, Kitty Baskin, Kinniebrew Robt Taylor Long Marshall and many others show that the genius of the Tuskegee method is not to ignore the advanced education but wherever it is in a man to inspire him to it. I hope nothing will swerve you from your course. You are right and the best people are with you. Only those who cannot or will not for some selfish reason understand your position are even secretly against you. No one dare openly oppose you. How much I think of the school now in this opening of a new year. I do pray that it may be a year marked with great wisdom and freedom from mistakes of every kind. You are very much in the thoughts of the masses of the people. I am pleased with your article in Golden Rule Aug 26. Shall send my article tomorrow. Yours

R. C. Bedford

ALS   Con. 124   BTW Papers   DLC.

[1] Alexander Crummell's article stressed the attainment of "civilization" through "Higher Culture." Crummell defined civilization as "indicative of letters, literature, science and philosophy." He explained: "In other words, that this Negro race is to be lifted up to the acquisition of the higher culture of the age. This culture is to be made a part of its heritage; not at some distant day, but now and all along the development of the race. And no temporary fad of doubting or purblind philanthropy is to be allowed to make 'Industrial Training' a substitute for it."

The editors of *The Independent* endorsed Crummell for showing that the "prime need of the Negro race is not industrialism but civilization." They added: "It is the influence of a thoroughly educated small minority of their people which they need; such an education as a college would give as distinct from an industrial school — an education which will give the best brains the power to lead intelligently. We must not forget that for the Negro the choicest work is that of the college and professional school, which make ministers, doctors, lawyers and teachers. Then add all the industrial education of the mass that you can." (*The Independent,* 49 [Aug. 19, 1897], 1-2, 14.)

Extracts from an Address in Indianapolis[1]

[Indianapolis, Ind., ca. Aug. 28, 1897]

The whole South recognizes the value and far-reaching [effect] of the educational and religious work being done by the church which you represent, and my race is especially grateful to you for your efforts in lifting it up. Of all the agencies in the South for the elevating and strengthening of my race, we count Knoxville College, your work in Wilcox county, Alabama, at Norfolk, Va., and elsewhere among the most important.

In a large measure the Negro race in this country is in the position of a sick man. This being true, it does but little good to bemoan the cause of his sickness and why he remains so; but the sensible thing to do is to find out the actual condition of the patient and apply the remedy; and in doing this it must be borne in mind that it is with an ignorant race much as with a child. It craves at first the superficial, the gewgaws of life, the shadow, rather than the substance. In this you must be patient with my race.

It must be borne in mind that in the gulf states, where the bulk of our people live, 85 per cent of them are in the rural districts, where they are difficult to reach except by special effort. In these plantation districts three-fourths of them live on rented land, mortgage their crops and dwell in small one-room cabins, at the same time trying to pay an interest on their indebtedness that ranges between 15 and 40 per cent.

I was in a county in Alabama not long ago where no public school for black children had been in session longer than three months; the state did not own a single schoolhouse, a blackboard nor a piece of crayon. No colored teacher in this county had been paid more than $16 a month for his work. In this county each colored child had received only 31 cents for his education for one year. Think of it, 31 cents in that county for the education for one year of a black child, and compare it with the $20 a year which each child receives for his education in this part of the North. And yet, my friends, crime in that county in Alabama is just as truly an arrow aimed at the heart of the republic as crime committed in your own streets; a vote in that county is as potent for weal or woe as one cast for the governor of your state.

On many of these plantations as many as six, eight and even ten persons, of all ages, sexes and conditions are often found living in one room. The effect of all this cannot produce a very high state of morality or christianity. Out of this industrial, educational and moral condition grow crimes committed by black men and white men, in other words, the degradation of both races.

Indianapolis *Freeman,* Aug. 28, 1897, 4.

[1] BTW spoke before a meeting of the Young People's Christian Union and, according to the Indianapolis *Freeman,* he was received "with indescribable enthusiasm."

An Interview on Lynching in the Indianapolis *Freeman*

[Indianapolis, Ind., Aug. 28, 1897]

I think that with the advancement of the race the question will settle itself. The men that are lynched are invariably vagrants, men without property or standing.[1] Lynchings seem to come in waves and it is hard to say whether they are on the increase. If the record of the last six months is to be taken as a criterion, I should say that they were increasing. There are undoubtedly some lynchings that are never reported by the Associated Press. The disregard for the life of a Negro in the South is only manifested by the lower class of the whites, the intelligent whites showing no difference of sentiment on this point than those of the North.

There is in my opinion no chance for a race war in the future. The indications are favorable for an early breaking up on political lines. I do not believe that politics in the South will be divided on race lines much longer. Economic issues must eventually divide them as the intelligent people of the white race are divided. The colored race predominates in South Carolina, Mississippi and Louisiana, but as to the race controlling governmental affairs in those states, I think the man who has the property, the intelligence and the character, is the one who is going to have the largest share in government, whether he be white or black or whether he lives in the North or South. What I favor is the industrial development of the colored race, and that in order to achieve this development the colored man must learn to work his own salvation.

Indianapolis *Freeman,* Aug. 28, 1897, 4.

¹ The *Freeman* commented that BTW was wrong to assume that only vagrants were lynched, but agreed that in general most criminals were "of the lower order of mankind."

From William R. Morris and Jasper Gibbs

Minneapolis, Minn., Aug. 31st 1897

Our Dear Mr. Washington, The enclosed clipping was cut from the Minneapolis Tribune of this morning.¹ Thinking that this is erroneous and not a correct quotation of what you said or intended to say, we therefore send it to you that you may read it, and if you care to make any explanation whatever we will take great pleasure in having the same published in the columns of the paper in which this clipping appeared. Having, as you know, the highest regard for you and the cause you represent, we are entirely unprepared to admit the veracity of what seems to be at least a partial justification of the wholesale lynching of the Negroes in the South. We are satisfied that the effects of such a statement, which purports to be from you, will not only act as an incentive for greater and more horrible outrages in the future, but will also have a tendency to lessen the sympathy and influence of Northern sentiment which is decidedly — as you are aware — against all such outrages, whether they be black or white vagrant victims, and favors the enforcement of law and order. Please let us hear from you at your earliest convenience, as we do not wish you to appear in a false position in this community. Sincerely yours,

Wm R Morris and Jasper Gibbs

ALS   Con. 131   BTW Papers   DLC.

¹ The Minneapolis *Tribune,* Aug. 31, 1897, 4, ran the same interview that had appeared in the Indianapolis *Freeman,* Aug. 28, 1897, above.

From William Burns Paterson

Montgomery, Ala. Sept 3, 1897

My dear Friend: I believe the desire to have peace and good-will between our Schools is mutual. We have mutual friends. I therefore deem
it my duty to inform you that if a discussion of the work or management
of the two schools comes up before my Board it is not of my doing,
nor with my consent.

In a letter written this week to the Chairman of my Board, Mr.
Young says "The contrast between the two schools is painfully sharp."
Also that my retention in the school is a violation of well established
"Southern policy." Of course you are not responsible for what he says.

Mr. Hare also, in a letter written in behalf of clients, brings up the
question of "social equality" the one thread running through all the
fabrications presented by Mr. Young's friends. Now you are not responsible for Mr. Hare either, but he is a Trustee of your school, and
I think it poor policy for him to charge our Board with encouraging
this so called "social equality" by retaining white teachers.

I confess to you that I was pleased with what you did in regard to
this matter some weeks ago, and it was and is my intention to forgive
and forget the offence given to me at B'gham four years ago.

I propose to bear this in mind in whatever takes place now.

I am getting old enough to love peace, but if these gentlemen want
some amusement, they can have it. I am here on the ground, and know
the situation.

In the meantime, I want your friendship and good-will. I want to
see you prosper and am with you in every effort to make better citizens
out of your people. Very truly

W. B. Paterson

ALS   Con. 272   BTW Papers   DLC.

From Emmett Jay Scott

Houston Texas, Sept. 4th 1897

My Dear Mr. Washington: As soon as I received your telegram from
Boston, advising me that I should hear definitely from you on the

Fourth or Fifth — I took the train at once and went to Galveston to confer with Congressman Hawley and to San Antonio, to see Mr. Cuney. These gentlemen are *political* friends of mine. I only arrived this evening at 5 o'clock and was handed a copy of each of your telegrams. Mrs. Scott tells me that she sent you a telegram last night telling you of my absence from the city. I hasten to reply to both of them. As I wrote to you before I am not only anxious, but more than willing to come to Tuskegee, but I find just *at this time* that I am handicapped by conditions. I have sought to control the post-mastership at this place and am assured positively that it will turn out alright. Mr. Hawley who is the only republican congressman from Texas is with me and is the McKinley manager in Texas. They insist that my going just at this time will be to sacrifice those friends — both white & black, who have sustained me at all times, and under all circumstances. The appointment is to be made for Houston about the 21st of September. If I go at this time I shall vacate the chairmanship of the county executive committee and sacrifice their candidate just about the time that his appointment is assured.

I hope you see just what my position at this time is. But in spite of this I will come *at once* if you cannot, or rather are not disposed to allow me until the 21st, to come there. Is it not possible to supply my place until that time? I am not unconscious of the fact that I am asking almost too much of you since you have acceded to my every request. Then I know too that my place can be easily supplied if you are not willing to forbear longer. I shall be glad to have a wire from you upon receipt of this, either asking my immediate presence, or granting this request for a little longer stay here. I beg to assure you that I am not insensible to the consideration shown me by you and I shall more than deserve it by hard work and assiduous devotion to you and your interests. Very Faithfully Yours,

Emmett J. Scott

P.S. If you can make no arrangement for less than a month, I shall be satisfied & will come thirty days from this time.

ALS   Con. 272   BTW Papers   DLC.

From Blanche Kelso Bruce

Washington D C   Sept 8/97

My dear Friend Washington, A thousand thanks for your telegram. It shall be acted upon as soon as the President arrives. I had a pleasant talk with the Secretary of the Treasury[1] today, and feel that he is my friend. I shall push things with vigor now.

Mrs B. starts to Nashvill[e] Saturday, 12th inst. where she will meet Mrs Washington. I trust our ladies may accomplish more in their conventions[2] than we men have thus far done in ours. Sincerely yr frd

B. K. Bruce

ALS   Con. 124   BTW Papers   DLC.

[1] Lyman Judson Gage (1836-1927).

[2] The third annual meeting of the National Association of Colored Women met Sept. 15-17, 1897, at the Howard Congregational Church in Nashville. Mrs. BTW was chairman of the executive committee, and Mrs. Bruce was on the resolutions committee. The sixty-three delegates represented twenty-six clubs. BTW made a short speech on the second day. Among the resolutions adopted were condemnations of both rapists and lynchers, a call for humanization of the convict-lease system, commendation of the WCTU, and a petition to state legislatures to repeal the Jim Crow car laws. (Nashville *American,* Sept. 16, 1897, 8; Sept. 17, 1897, 5; Sept. 18, 1897, 5.)

From John Langalibalele Dubé

Brooklyn N.Y. Sept. 10th '97

My dear Sir: Can I use your name as indorsing my work. I have recently visited your establishment. I shall be pleased to hear favorably. Yours very truly

John L. Dube

ALS   Con. 127   BTW Papers   DLC.

From William Hannibal Thomas[1]

Everett Mass. Sept. 13th, 1897

Dear Mr. Washington: It is my judgement that a department of Domestic Industry would prove a valuable addition to Tuskegee Institute. My notion is this; if Tuskegee would train a class say of 100 colored girls, for capable and efficient household service, you could easily place them in leading white families in the North, and where each girl through faithful and loyal service, would prove a valuable ally of Tuskegee; in fact, I can see with hundreds of girls scattered over the North in the employ of white people, that your labors would be lessened and the income of the school vastly increased. The servant girl question, is the problem of the North; at present, our families depend on foreign help, which is more or less incompetent and unreliable; now if a movement could be started, whereby trained and honest colored girls could take the place of this class of help, the benefit would be incalculable both to themselves and to the colored race, and from my knowledge of Northern people, I am satisfied that a greater interest would be shown in a movement of this sort, than in any other. I trust you will see your way clear to do something in this direction, and if you like, we will confer more fully in regard to it the next time you come to Boston.

I published an article on the characteristics of Negro christianity in the July number of the "United Brethren Review," if you would like to see it, write to Rev. W. J. Shuey, Dayton, Ohio, and ask him to send you a copy, I know you will enjoy it. Trusting you are in good health, I am   Very truly yours,

Wm. Hannibal Thomas

TLS   Con. 135   BTW Papers   DLC.

[1] William Hannibal Thomas (b. 1843) was of mixed ancestry that included several blacks, although Thomas usually passed as a white man. His parents' home was a station on the Underground Railroad in Ohio. He enlisted in the Ohio infantry during the Civil War and later joined a black regiment, losing his arm as a result of a battle injury. From 1865 to 1868 he studied theology and worked on religious newspapers. Several years later he was practicing law in South Carolina. In 1876 he was elected to the South Carolina legislature and later became a colonel in the National Guard. Thomas moved north in the 1880s, living near Boston. In 1901 he wrote a scurrilous anti-Negro book, *The American Negro*.

To William R. Morris and Jasper Gibbs

[Tuskegee, Ala., ca. Sept. 14, 1897]

My Dear Friends: Replying to your favor of Aug. 31 I would say that I should have answered more promptly, but have been sick for several days to the extent that my physician forbade my doing any work.

I thank you very much for giving me an opportunity to set matters right in regard to the press dispatch which has been very widely disseminated purporting to give my views regarding the matter of lynching. I would say that this dispatch is an example of many others which have misrepresented me. When once such matters get into the newspapers through the press bureaus it is almost impossible to do anything that will modify their influence. I might on some occasion have said that most of the people lynched in the South were of the worthless or vagrant class, but if any one understood by this expression that I meant to justify lynching or lawlessness he was certainly far from understanding my views or position. I condemn in the strongest terms lynching for any cause. I believe that the most miserable and most unfortunate being, whether black or white, should have the fullest protection of the law, and that lynching under any circumstances is to be condemned. Nothing is hurting our country so much today as the reign of lawlessness, which shows itself through the medium of lynching. While I condemn in the severest terms those who are guilty of committing outrages upon women, I claim that they should have a fair trial, which is the only protection to our civilization. Yours truly,

Booker T. Washington[1]

Minneapolis *Tribune,* Sept. 18, 1897, 5. The newspaper ran BTW's letter under the headline "Sets Himself Right."

[1] Morris and Gibbs replied, saying that they had arranged for the newspaper to display BTW's statement over his signature. They wrote: "We do not propose to suffer anything to go unanswered that comes to our notice that in any way reflects upon your fidelity, integrity and sound judgment." (Morris and Gibbs to BTW, Sept. 18, 1897, Con. 131, BTW Papers, DLC.)

A Petition from Tuskegee Students

[Tuskegee, Ala.] October 7, 1897

Sirs: We believe heartily in the spirit of work which characterizes the Tuskegee Normal & Industrial Institute. This condition we would not change if we could. We would have no less work; but we feel sure that if you will give the matter a few seconds consideration, you will agree with us that we ought to be given more time for recreation. We feel that Tuskegee ought to hold her own, even in the field of athletics, which is not true now, because of the fact that our teams do not have time for proper practice.

We cannot finish a game of ball between the hours of three and four. We therefore petition that we be given Saturday afternoons, say from three o'clock till tea for base ball and other games.

Hoping for a favorable reply, we remain, Yours truly,

TLS Con. 864 BTW Papers DLC. The petition was signed by 259 Tuskegee students, and addressed to BTW and members of the Executive Council.

An Excerpt from the Diary of Claude Gernade Bowers[1]

Indianapolis, Oct. 20 [1897]

Oct 20 This afternoon as I was walking down Penn. St, I met Brooker T. Washington, reading a newspaper in front of The Denison. I talked with him for awhile concerning his magazine article and found that he had sent it last Saturday. Its delay is probably due to the prevalence of yellow fever in the south.

Tonight I heard him address a monster convention of the Christian church people.[2] He is a magnificent orator — one of the Phillips type. His style is mostly conversational. Now and then as he becomes especially eloquent his voice rises and his form expands. His voice is rough in the higher scale but that is lost sight of in what he says. He has a limitless store of original antedote gleaned from personal expierence with which he keeps his audience in a constant roar. I noticed one man on the platform — an old grey haired man — who went into fits over the stories. He would press his sides, stamp his feet, and scream with laughter. I took down a few of his stories which I here record

"Its a mighty hard thing to make a good christian out of a hungry man."

"The colored men down south are very fond of an old song entitled 'Give me Jesus and you take all the rest.' The white man has taken him at his word."

"A white man once asked a negro to loan him 3 cents to get across the river. The colored man replied 'Boss, I knows yous a white man, and Boss I knows yous got moah sense dan dis yeah niggah. But Boss I aint goin to lend you no three cents. Boss you say you haint got no money. Well Boss a man whats got no money is as well off on one side of the river as on de other . . .' "

"Weve got a few black sheep in our flock."

"A negro was once heard to say, 'Oh Lod, de sun am so hot, and de ground am so hard, and de sun am *so* hot, I beleive dis heah darky am called to preach.' "

"A friend of mine who went to Liberia to study conditions once came upon a negro shut up with-in a hovel reading Cicero's orations. That was all right. The negro has as much right to read Cicero's orations in Africa as a white man does in America. But the trouble with the colored man was that he had on no pants. I want a tailor shop first so that the negro can sit down and read Cicero's orations like a gentleman with his pants on."

"I can't tell the exact day or place of my birth. But I have fairly conclusive evidence that I was born, some-time and some-where."

"There seems to be a sort of sympathy between the negro and a mule. Wherever you find a negro you are very apt to find a mule some-where about. I feel somewhat lonesome tonight. A colored man was once asked how many there were in the family. He replied, 'Five of us. My-self, my brother and three mules.' "

"We were the only race that came here by special invitation. Your race came over here against the protest of the leading citizens. We were so important to your interest that you had to send for us at a great cost and inconvenience. Now that we have been brought here at so much cost, it would be very ungrateful for us not to oblige you by staying here."

"A slave was once called up before his master who thus addressed him — 'Bill your soul belongs to God and your body belongs to me.'

331

'Yess — Hows dat mas'er?' 'Your soul belongs to God, and your body belongs to me.' 'Wars I come in mas'er?'

"One Sunday afterwards during a violent rain, Bill was seen running bare-headed through the rain — his hat tucked under his coat. His owner called him up and asked him why he did not put on his hat. 'Oh, mas'er, dis yeah niggahs soul belongs to God, my body belongs to mas'er, but de hat belongs to dis heah niggah.' "

He spoke for 1 hour and ½, and left at 2 A.M. for his Alabama home for fear that the yellow fever might shut him out.

Holman Hamilton and Gayle Thornbrough, eds., *Indianapolis in the "Gay Nineties": High School Diaries of Claude G. Bowers* (Indianapolis: Indiana Historical Society, 1964), 98-100.

[1] Claude Gernade Bowers (1878-1958), journalist, historian, and diplomat.

[2] BTW spoke before a convention of the Christian Church to a packed audience of 3,000 at City Hall. The Indianapolis *Freeman* reported that "When Mr. Washington was introduced the audience gave him a rousing reception, waving their handkerchiefs and otherwise manifesting their pleasure." (Indianapolis *Freeman*, Oct. 30, 1897, 1.)

From Arthur L. Macbeth[1]

Charleston, S.C., October 21 1897

Dear Sir: I send you on this mail seven different views of Charleston Cotton Mills and operatives (colored) the white ones were not in the picture. I had lots of red tape to unwind before I could get the interior views. I trust they will prove satisfactory to you. Having the negatives now, I can make you additional prints at half price hereafter; there are two other Factories in this City (the Cradle of Cecession) that are operated by negro help — the Charleston Knitting Mills, and the Charleston Shoe Factory. Very respectfully,

Arthur L. Macbeth

ALS   Con. 131   BTW Papers   DLC.

[1] Arthur L. Macbeth was a black photographer in Charleston, S.C.

From Viola Knapp Ruffner

Charleston S.C. Oct 30/97

Dear Booker   Yours in time. Promptness is a virtue I do this from necessity. You know people have dropped dead without warning. Such was my case, only in falling, I struck my head on the bed post, which brought back life, & then for 5 months did not leave the bed, then up a little, then in bed for 7 mo[n]ths, suffering as no one knows. The worst is, eye sight gone almost entirely. I can see this only because it is black upon white. I think it will soon end. Life cannot endure much more. When, & how old were you when you came to my house? Did you teach in M.?[1] The young seem to have no ambition there every thing seems without life. I hope you will continue to prosper & that your children will rise up & call you blessed. They will be educated there I suppose, & help to do what you are doing. You must excuse blank paper, as sight will not hold out. Respects to your wife & self from your old friend

V. Ruffner

ALS   Con. 272   BTW Papers   DLC.

[1] Malden, W.Va.

George Washington Carver to Mrs. W. A. Liston[1]

[Tuskegee, Ala., ca. October 1897][2]

As nearly as I can trace my history I was about 2 weeks old when the war closed. My parents were both slaves, Father was killed shortly after my birth while hauling wood to town on an ox wagon.

I had 3 sisters and one brother. Two sisters and my brother I know to be dead only as history tells me, yet I do not doubt it as they are buried in the family burying ground.

My sister mother and myself were kucluckled, and sold in Arkansaw and there are now so many conflicting reports concerning them I dare not say if they are dead or alive. Mr. Carver[3] the Jentleman who owned my mother sent a man for us, but only I was brought back, nearly dead with whooping cough with the report that mother & sister was dead, although some sauy they saw them afterwards going north with the soldiers.

My home was near Neosho Newton Co Missouri where I remained until I was about 9 years old. My body was very feble and it was a constant warfare between life and death to see who would gain the mastery.

From a child I had an inordinate desire for knowledge, and especially music, painting, flowers, and the sciences Algebra being one of my favorite studies.

Day after day I spent in the woods alone in order to collect my floral beautis and put them in my little garden I had hidden in brush not far from the house, as it was considered foolishness in that neighborhood to waste time on flowers.

And many are the tears I have shed because I would break the roots or flower of off some of my pets while removing them from the ground, and strange to say all sorts of vegetation seemed to thrive under my touch until I was styled the plant doctor, and plants from all over the country would be brought to me for treatment. At this time I had never heard of botany and could scerly read.

Rocks had an equal facination for me and many are the basketsful that I have been compelled to remove from the outside chimney corner of that old log house, with the injunction to throw them down hill. I obeyed but picked up the choicest ones and hid them in another place, and some how that same chimney corner would, in a few days, or weeks be running over again to suffer the same fate. I have some of the specimens in my collection now and consider them the choicest of the lot. Mr. & Mrs. Carver were very kind to me and I thank them so much for my home training. They encouraged me to secure knowledge helping me all they could, but this was quite limited. As we lived in the country no colored schools were available so I was permitted to go 8 miles to a school at town (Neosho). This simply sharpened my apetite for more knowledge. I managed to secure all of my meager wardrobe from home, and when they heard from me I was cooking for a wealthy family in Ft. Scott Kans. for my board, clothes and school privileges.

Of course they were indignant and sent for me to come home at once, to die as the family doctor had told them I would never live to see 21 years of age. I trusted to God and pressed on (I had been a Christian since about 8 years old). Sunshine and shadow were profusely intermingled such as naturaly befall a defenceless orphan by those who wish to prey upon them.

My health began improving and I remained here for two or 3 years, from here to Olatha Kans. to school, from there to Paola Normal School, from there to Minneapolis Kans. where I remained in school about 7 years finishing the high school, and in addition some Latin & Greek. From here to Kans. City entered a business college of short hand and typewriting. I was here to have a position in the union telegraph office as stenographer & typewriter, but the thirst for knowledge gained the mastery and I sought to enter Highland College at Highland Kans. was refused on account of my color.

I went from here to the Western part of Kans. where I saw the subject of my famous yucca & cactus painting that went to the Worlds Fair. I drifted from here to Winterset Iowa, began as head cook in a large hotel. Many thanks here for the acquaintance of Mr. & Mrs. Dr Milholland,[4] who insisted upon me going to an art school, and choose Simpson College for me.

The opening of school found me at Simpson attempting to run a laundry for my support and butchering to economize. For quite one month I lived on prayer beef suet and corn meal, and quite often being without the suet and meal. Modesty prevented me telling my condition to strangers.

The news soon spread that I did laundry work and realy needed it, so from that time on favors not only rained but poured upon me. I cannot speak too highly of the faculty, students and in fact the town jeneraly, they all seemed to take pride in seeing if he or she might not do more for me than someone else.

But I wish to especially mention the names of Miss Etta M. Budd[5] my art teacher Mrs. W. A. Liston & family, and Rev. H. D. Field & family. Aside from their substantial help at Simpson, were the means of my attendance at Ames.

(Please fix this to suit)

I think you know my career at Ames and will fix it better than I. I will simply mention a few things.

I received the prize offered for the best herbarium in cryptogamy. I would like to have said more about you Mrs. Liston & Miss Budd but I feared you would not put it in about yourself and I did not want one without all.

I received a letter from Mrs. Liston and she gave me an idea that it was not to be a book or anything of the kind this is only a fragmentary list.

I knit chrochet, and made all my hose mittens ect. while I was in school.

If this is not sufficient please let me know, and if it ever comes out in print I would like to see it.

God bless you all,

Geo. W. Carver

AMS Con. 138 BTW Papers DLC.

¹ Mrs. W. A. Liston, a former student at Simpson College, became a friend and benefactor of Carver when she learned from Etta M. Budd that he needed help to stay in school. She provided him with lodging and some household items and encouraged others to support Carver's laundry business. She continued her interest in Carver when he transferred to Iowa A & M in 1891, visiting him there. Mrs. Liston persuaded school officials to allow Carver to eat with the other students rather than in the basement with the hired help.

Mrs. Liston, at BTW's request, asked Carver for a sketch of his life. Carver wrote this account for her unaware that it was to be sent to BTW. Mrs. Liston wrote to BTW: "You can use any thing in it that is of int[e]rest to you, but I must add that incidents of most int[e]rest to me are left out by him." She thought that Carver might have been saving some episodes for a book. "The sever[e] trials misstreatment and hardships I know about are omit[t]ed," she wrote. "If I could see you," she continued, "I could relate many strange incidents and special interventions of Divine providence." (Liston to BTW, Nov. 1, 1897, Con. 130, BTW Papers, DLC.)

² The original was dated "1897 or thereabouts" in another hand, perhaps at a later time.

³ Moses Carver, who had owned George's mother, and his wife Susan had no children of their own and raised George and his brother Jim. The Carvers made it clear to the youths that they were not slaves and were free to leave at any time.

⁴ John Milholland was a medical doctor in Winterset, Iowa, and his wife was director of the church choir there. Carver took singing lessons from Mrs. Milholland, and he taught her painting. The Milhollands became Carver's closest friends and encouraged him to enter Simpson College.

⁵ Etta M. Budd befriended Carver and was instrumental in getting him to study at Iowa A & M, where her father, J. L. Budd, was head of the horticulture department.

To Herbert Wrightington Carr[1]

Tuskegee, Ala., Nov. 6th 1897

Dear Sir: Few persons who have not been engaged in educational work among my race in the South can appreciate just how far clothing of any kind can be made to go in helping students to secure an education and at the same time not cultivate a dependent spirit in the students.

Shoes, even if very much worn are very helpful as they can be repaired in our shoe shop.

If your church Sunday school any society or individual can help us along this line we shall be most grateful.

Of course our greatest need is the $50 with which to pay the tuition of each student, but clothing will greatly help. Yours very truly,

Booker T. Washington

TLS   Courtesy of Helen Carr, Annisquam, Mass.

[1] Herbert Wrightington Carr (1867-1915) was a Universalist minister who served parishes at Fort Plain, N.Y., Stamford, Conn., Framingham, Mass., and Manchester, N.H. He had a lifelong interest in the cause of black advancement in America.

To Edward Atkinson[1]

Tuskegee, Ala. Nov. 7th, 1897

My dear sir: I hope you will pardon the delay in answering your letter of recent date. I could not put my hands on the information for which you wrote before today.

By this mail I send you a book called "School History of the Negro Race"[2] which contains some facts bearing upon the Negro's progress. I have turned down the pages where this information can be found. I do not know how accurate these figures or statements are. In some cases I feel that they are exaggerated; for example, I know we often see in print figures purporting to represent the Negro's wealth, but I cannot understand how these figures can be accurate. There are only two states so far as I know that keep the Negro's and white people's property separate on the tax books, these states are Georgia and Virginia and Virginia I think only recently begun to do this, hence I do not see how except in these two states we can judge accurately as to the Negro's taxable property.

In some inexplainable way, before I got through reading it, the clipping which you sent me containing the Mississippi gentleman's statement was mislaid, and I should be very grateful if you will send

me another one as I am intensely interested in it and want to read it
for future use.

The book which I send you belongs to the public library in Tuskegee which has just been opened in town. It is, so far as I know, the
only public library free to all races in Alabama. You will therefore
please return the book when you are through with it.

If I can serve you further please be kind enough to command me.
Yours truly,

Booker T. Washington

TLS   T. E. Atkinson Collection   MHi.

¹ Edward Atkinson (1827-1905), a Boston industrialist and economist, was a
founder of the Boston Manufacturers' Mutual Life Insurance Company. A sound-
money advocate, in 1887 he served on a presidential commission under Cleveland
to study the problems of bimetallism.
² Written by Edward Augustus Johnson.

To Gilchrist Stewart

[Tuskegee, Ala.] Nov. 9th, 1897

Mr. Stewart: I am glad to note that in some respects you are giving
more attention to the details of your work, and I hope the improvement
will continue. There are some things that I wanted to say to you regarding your work sometime ago but refrained for the reason that I
did not want to seem to discourage you by mentioning too many things
at the beginning when everything was new. But I do not think it fair
to you or the school to defer longer.

For some reason you do not seem to comprehend the nature and
scope of your work, whether this is because you have not the proper
interest in your work or for lack of ability I do not know, at any rate
the result is the same to the school. To give you an idea of how far
you are at present from answering the purpose that I had in view when
you came, I would say that your work has required as much of my
personal attention and caused me as much anxiety as that of all the
other teachers on the place combined during the same length of time.

To speak frankly, to me and to the members of the Executive Council, you seem either ashamed or afraid of your work. I shall not at-

338

tempt in this note to go into details concerning all the matters in which you do not give satisfaction; I shall mention one or two matters which will illustrate many others. At the bottom of everything is the fact that *you do not respect authority.* For example, I have said to you on several occasions, and Mr. Carver has done the same thing, that it was important for you to *remain with your students when at work,* that is what we had you come here for. Notwithstanding this request, you do not go to the barn in the morning and remain there while the cows are being milked. *You do not go to the dairy room in the morning and remain there while the milk is being separated and the butter churned. You are not at the dairy to receive the milk bought from outside persons.* The whole matter of separating, churning and buying milk is left completely in the hands of students except when you step in for a few minutes much as a visitor would do.

I will tell you in a word what we want in the position that you are now attempting to fill. We want a man who puts his whole soul into the work — who gives it his thought night and day — who can teach the theory of dairying in the class room, and who is not afraid after his teaching to put on his dairy suit and go into the stable and *remain with* the students while they are milking, and then go into the creamery and take hold in a whole souled way and show the students how to do their work. We want a man who is so much in love with the work that he thinks it just as important for him to *remain with students* while they are milking and separating the milk as it is for the academic teacher to remain with his class while they are reciting arithmetic. We want a person whose soul is so deeply in love with his work that it is a pleasure for him to co-operate and obey orders, who looks so closely after every detail of his work that matters will not [get] so out of order that others will have to be constantly calling his attention to defects, and to whom orders will not have to be continually repeated by the farm director or myself. We want one who is continually planning for the improvement and perfection of his work. This is what we want in this position and we can accept nothing else.

After taking time to carefully consider the matter, if you think you can meet these requirements we shall be glad to have you remain, otherwise it is best that your business connection cease at the end of fifteen days.

I do not want you to think that I am unreasonable with you. I realize that the hours for the dairy work are out of the ordinary hours of work and for that reason I shall expect you to have reasonable time to yourself during the day.

Personally I am interested in you and it pains me deeply to be forced to speak to you in the way that I do, but I can not refrain from it and do my duty to this institution. I have taken the deepest personal pride in your coming here, and had hoped that you would build up a department here that would be an honor to the school and yourself and [it] has given me the deepest pain personally to note how matters have gone. You are a young man and still have a chance to redeem yourself here, but you cannot do it by living on the edges of your work, but your whole mind and activity will have to be put into it. We can be satisfied with nothing short of the highest and most conscientious service.

Booker T. Washington

TLpS Con. 282A BTW Papers DLC.

From Henry Clay Reynolds

Montevallo, Ala. Nov-14-97

Dear Sir: Yours of the 11th received and contents noted. I think you are correct in regard to Secretary Wilson's[1] presence in our State being of service to us. I will endeavor to be at your place on the date mentioned and it will afford me great pleasure as I have been so busy that heretofore I have not been able to pay my respects to your institution. I will go to work at once as you suggest on the bill and I am pretty sure that it will be best to double it and unless I hear from you to the contrary I shall proceed on that line. I am determined never to give this up and I have the utmost faith in its ultimate success.

Wishing you all the good fortune that you deserve in your noble efforts, I am, Sincerely   Your friend,

H. C. Reynolds

TLS Con. 133 BTW Papers DLC.

[1] James Wilson (1836-1920), Iowa politician and U.S. Secretary of Agriculture (1897-1913). Wilson promoted agricultural experiment stations, farm demonstrations in the South, and cooperative extension work in agriculture and home economics. He also expanded the department's scientific research and services to both producer and consumer.

From John A. Hertel

Naperville, Ill., Nov. 15, '97

Dear Sir: Replying to yours of the 5th inst. We wrote you some time ago that your letter was forwarded to our office at Atlanta, and we have heard from our manager and hence wish to write you more particularly regarding your prospective book entitled "Story of your life."

You understand that we are at present pushing our new book "Progress of a Race" extensively, it has been our method of handling a few articles at a time and then put on more energy and hence we do not think it would be advisable to put on another book short of one year. Kindly write us by return mail and state how soon you will have manuscript of your book ready. If you would be willing to postpone the publication of this book until about next year by this time, we should be glad to take hold of it provided we could agree on terms. We should also like to know about how large the book will be. If you would allow us to make a suggestion we would say a book that would sell at $1.00 would perhaps command the largest sale. A book of the nature you speak, would if properly gotten up, fairly well illustrated, and vigorously pushed, command a pretty good sale.

Shall be pleased to hear from you again.

J. A. Hertel

TLS Con. 131 BTW Papers DLC.

To John Henry Washington

[Tuskegee, Ala.] 11, 17, 1897

Mr. J. H. Washington: I hope you will use a great deal of time in approving or disapproving the rate of wages paid the students. I am sure that we are now paying too much, and you have the liberty to make such changes as you think best. The amount paid the night students is quite an item and I want it reduced considerably.

B. T. W.

TLpI Con. 282A BTW Papers DLC.

From Robert Curtis Ogden

New York, November 17, 1897

Dear Mr. Washington: I do not know when circumstances will make it possible for me to realize my long cherished desire to visit the Tuskegee School; that privilege is at present denied me and I therefore regret that I cannot accept your attractive invitation to attend the opening of the Ste[a]rn's Agricultural Hall at Tuskegee.

It is borne in upon my mind with increasing intensity that the colored people of this country have not only their destiny in their own hand but that they are rapidly approaching a crisis which is to largely determine their future happiness and influence.

The issue is moral and industrial. Unless the industrial position is held the moral position will be greatly weakened. The Afro-American must rise to the point where he will not only secure all the labor that is at present in his hands but will also make such an advance as to rapidly develop scientific and mechanical experience. He must mix his brawn with brain. He must not only be able to toil but to design: He must not only serve but he must be served; he must be the employer of the members of his own race, and maintain his work and theirs up to the level of the competition of the age; otherwise he will be a declining factor.

Scientific agriculture and technical knowledge of trades are the prime factors in the solution of the industrial problem; but these factors need to be developed with tremendous intensity throughout the land, and especially the South, that the chance may not slip away from the race before the emergency is realized.

Congratulating you upon the progress of Tuskegee, I am, Very truly yours,

Robert C Ogden

TLS   Con. 129   BTW Papers   DLC.

From Jabez Lamar Monroe Curry

Washington, D.C., 24 Nov. 97

Dear Mr Washington— I saw Sec. Wilson today and he is quite much interested in our proposed visit. A Mr Curtis, newspaper correspondent, will accompany us. We propose to reach Atlanta on Monday morning — address the Legislature at 11 — and in the afternoon go on to Tuskegee, according to your suggestion. The Southern Railway promised us this morning to send a trip pass to Mr Wilson. I do not know how to reach the Pullman "close corporation."

Allow a suggestion. You will have present Sec Wilson, Govs Johnston & Northen, Superintendents Glenn & Turner, and perhaps others. Do not speak your meeting into a failure. Mr Wilson is the central figure. Give him the best time and as much as he wants. Gov. Johnston cannot be ignored. Gov. Northen is a Slater Trustee and one of the most practical farmers in Georgia. As for myself, I can say a few words after Mr Wilson closes, or all of us can be silenced. I shall be satisfied with 10 or 15 minutes, towards the close.

Do not magnify the Tuskegee meeting at night to the prejudice of your occasion. *The two must not conflict.* We go South for your benefit & the night meeting for Tuskegee people can be shoved aside without detriment. Yours very truly

J. L. M. Curry

ALS Con. 272 BTW Papers DLC.

To Elizabeth E. Lane

[Tuskegee, Ala.] Nov. 27, 1897

Miss Lane: It comes to me on good authority, that you have been recently talking about Dr. Kenniebrew both in the presence of teachers and students, in a tone and manner that is calculated to do Dr. Kenniebrew harm as the school physician.

If at any time you or any one else connected with the school know anything concerning the actions and character of any student or officer of the school that is hurtful if you would report it to the office I should

343

be very grateful. In doing this you would really be accomplishing some good for the school. If you know anything against the character of Dr. Kenniebrew that unfits him for the position he now holds, it is your duty to speak to the proper authorities, otherwise to say nothing. Dr. Kenniebrew is a young man and one of our own graduates, and it should be a pleasure to each teacher to do all in his or her power to build him up rather than to tear him down.

While speaking to you on the subject of gossip, I might as well be plain with you. It is the general impression of teachers on the place, and I share the same opinion, that you are too much given to hurtful gossip. I have recently expelled a girl from the school for starting gossip concerning a teacher, and I am determined to be no less severe with teachers than with students in this respect.

There is no reason why the excellent opportunities that all of us have here for doing good should be largely neutralized by the uncalled for gossip of a few individuals, and I am determined to stop it at any cost.

You are a useful and able woman. Few persons here are capable of so much helpful unselfish work as yourself and few persons do so much to help others as yourself. Your work is in every way satisfactory, only you seem to have let this unfortunate habit of gossip fasten itself upon you to the extent that it nullifies much of the good that you do.

If you will just turn yourself and make an effort to find good things to say of people when you have no real facts to report to the office, you will make yourself of the greatest value to the school.

I speak to you frankly because I feel it to be my duty both as principal of the school and as your friend.

Booker T. Washington

TLpS   Con. 282A   BTW Papers   DLC.

From William R. Hammond[1]

Atlanta, Ga. Nov. 30. 1897

Personal

Dear Sir— I am in receipt, through my friend Dr. Boggs,[2] of your letter indorsing me for judicial appointment by the president,[3] and beg to thank you for the same. I will ask you, if you please, to keep the matter quiet, as it may transpire that I will not be a formal applicant for the office.

It has been my desire and effort, all my life, to be a fair and just man, and I have tried to give expression, with fearlessness, to my convictions even when my friends thought it imprudent to do so. I will send you a re-print of some letters published by me in 1894 and 1896, and if you feel inclined to do so, I would appreciate it if you will send a copy to the president and ask his personal attention to them. I have been told by friends that the publication of these letters kept me from going on the Supreme Bench of my own State.

My special efforts, in behalf of the colored people, as shown by my connection with their college at Savannah, on which I have served for many years, without compensation, and to which I have given much of my time, I think would entitle me probably to special consideration from the leaders among them, who are in position to appreciate such things. If in view of these considerations, you would write a personal letter to the president, Stating that you thought my appointment would be appreciated by the colored people, I would be glad.

I remember your speech at the opening of the Exposition here, which was eminently sensible, and have frequently spoken of it as the best delivered on that occasion, though my friend and college class-mate, Judge Emory Speer, also spoke.

With sentiments of esteem, I am, Yours truly —

W. R. Hammond

ALS   Con. 272   BTW Papers   DLC.

¹ William R. Hammond (b. 1848) of Georgia was a lawyer and judge of the superior court in Atlanta (1882-85). In 1888 he made an unsuccessful bid for the state senate on the anti-saloon platform, then returned to private law practice.

² William E. Boggs was chancellor of the University of Georgia from 1888 to 1899. Born in India in 1838, the son of a Presbyterian missionary, he returned to South Carolina with his family and graduated from South Carolina College in 1859. He graduated from Columbia Theological Seminary in 1862, became a Presbyterian minister, and was a chaplain in the Confederate Army. He served as a Presbyterian minister from the end of the war to 1888, and again after his resignation as chancellor.

³ BTW wrote to McKinley on behalf of Hammond's appointment as a U.S. circuit judge. (John Addison Porter to BTW, Dec. 15, 1897, Con. 132, BTW Papers, DLC.)

From Emmett Jay Scott

Tuskegee, Ala., Dec. 4/1897

My Dear Mr. Washington: The enclosed matters are handed you for your attention. I send under separate cover matters sent by Judge Hammond and Edward Atki[n]son.

Atlanta Journal — Dec. 3 — has a squib — with flashing headline — "He differs with Booker Washington. Colored Professor of Latin and Greek Believes in Higher Education for the Negro."

Some fellow named J W Gilbert, Payne's Institute, Augusta spoke of you as "preaching narrow and erroneous ideas.["]¹ About ten lines. Springfield Republican has nice sketch & Asso. Press report & cut of bldg. Everything goes well. Hope you'll take good care of your health. Yours Respectfully —

Emmett J. Scott

ALS   Con. 133   BTW Papers   DLC.

¹ John Wesley Gilbert of Paine Institute, Augusta, was reported in the Atlanta *Constitution,* Dec. 3, 1897, as a speaker at a church meeting in Atlanta. He criticized BTW as advocating that "the negro only needs an industrial education and that he should consume his life in drawing water and hewing wood."

From John Addison Porter

[Washington, D.C.] December 6, 1897

My dear Sir: The President has noted with pleasure the contents of your favor of the 4th instant¹ and wished me to thank you sincerely for your cordial reference to the appointment of Hon. B. K. Bruce. Very truly yours,

John Addison Porter
Secretary to the President

TLSr   McKinley Papers   DLC.

¹ BTW's letter was not preserved in either the McKinley Papers, DLC, or the BTW Papers, DLC.

The Introduction to *Magnolia Leaves*[1]

Tuskegee, Ala., December 6th, 1897

I give my cordial endorsement to this little "Book of Poems," because I believe it will do its part to awaken the Muse of Poetry which I am sure slumbers in very many of the Sons and Daughters of the Race of which the Author of this work is a representative.

The Negro's right to be considered worthy of recognition in the field of poetic effort is not now gainsaid as formerly, and each succeeding effort but emphasizes his right to just consideration.

The hope, I have, is, that this Volume of "Poems" may fall among the critical and intelligent, who will accord the just meed of praise or of censure, to the end that further effort may be stimulated, no matter what the verdict.

The readers I trust will find as much to praise and admire as have I done.

Booker T. Washington

PDSr   NN-Sc.

[1] Mary Weston Fordham, *Magnolia Leaves: Poems* (Charleston, S.C., 1897).

From Blanche Kelso Bruce

Washington, D.C., Dec 7 1897

My dear Friend Washington. Accept my most sincere thanks for your letter to the President. It is exactly what is needed to bring about the result desired.

Have a number of our friends do the same thing.

I am working in the same line. Sincerely yours

B. K. Bruce

ALS   Con. 124   BTW Papers   DLC.

From Adella Hunt Logan

Tuskegee   Dec. 8–'97

Dear Mr. Washington: I wish to express to you my sincere thanks for your anxious thoughtfulness and kindness during my recent severe illness.

I am able to be up now but am too weak to leave my room.

Our dear friend Dr. Dorsette actually died.[1] It does seem too bad that such skill and usefulness should come to such an untimely end. How we shall miss him, all of us but especially those of us who have always seen good in him despite his numerous faults and weaknesses.

Of course we regret that none of us could be with him during his last hours.

I do not mean to make it necessary for you to take any of your valuable time to answer this letter but I must call your attention to a book the reading of which I am just completing in connection with my C.L.S.C.

Have you read the Social Spirit In America by Prof. Henderson of the University of Chicago? If you have not done so I am quite certain you would like to read it in part at least. No doubt you know that in it he mentions you and Tuskegee. The book is published by Flood and Vincent, Meadville Pa. If you care to read these striking sections I should be glad to mark my copy — to save your time and strength — for your consideration.

Mr. Logan and Mrs. Washington are still in Montgomery.

So far as I can know in my shut in condition every thing is going well here. Very sincerely yours,

Adella H. Logan

ALS   Con. 272   BTW Papers   DLC.

[1] Cornelius Nathaniel Dorsette died unexpectedly on Dec. 7, 1897. His funeral was a grand affair, with the Capital City Guards and the Order of the Knights of Pythias marching in the ceremony ahead of more than sixty vehicles. Margaret Murray Washington, Warren Logan, and Robert C. Bedford represented Tuskegee Institute at the services. ("Death of Dr. C. N. Dorsette," PD, Con. 170, BTW Papers, DLC.) Bedford wrote to BTW that "I never in my life saw so large a number of people at a funeral as at Dr. Dorsette's. It was a most charming day and both sides of the street from the ch[urch] to the cemetery were lined while many windows were open and full of gazing people. Whites were nearly as prominent as the colored." (Bedford to BTW, Dec. 14, 1897, Con. 124, BTW Papers, DLC.)

A News Item in the Atlanta *Journal*

[Washington, D.C., Dec. 11, 1897]

SOME GOOD ADVICE FOR MCKINLEY
FROM A VERY SMART NEGRO

Booker T. Washington, the founder and head of the Industrial School for Colored People at Tuskegee, Ala., advises the men of his race to keep out of politics and not to seek for office. "Don't try to govern the country," he says to them, "until you know how. Educate yourself and take care of your own interests and promote your own fortunes and leave the interests of other people to be cared for by men of education and experience."

Mr. Washington came to this city the other day to have an interview with the president, but was not able to do so, owing to the latter's absence in Canton. He would have advised the president, says the Washington correspondent of the Chicago Record, against the appointment of colored men to office in the south. He says that it stimulates an ambition among their friends and the members of their race generally to seek a living by politics instead of by the trades and other industries, and has a demoralizing influence. At the same time it provokes hostilities among the whites and keeps alive race prejudices. The only career Mr. Washington sees for his race is in industrial and agricultural education.

Atlanta *Journal,* Dec. 11, 1897, 4.

From Emmett Jay Scott

[Tuskegee, Ala.] Dec 13 [1897]

The article from the Atlanta Journal — published Saturday which I send you is a plain misrepresentation and seems to me to call for some denial from you. It's outrageous in its evident purpose to put you in false light.

EJS

ALI   Con. 133   BTW Papers   DLC.

From Jabez Lamar Monroe Curry

Washington D.C. 14 Dec. 97

My dear Sir— This letter raises a question which I purposed to ask an answer to, when with you at your great meeting, but I had not the opportunity. Who is Stearns, and what has he done to deserve this great honor? The Institution should be named Washington-Jesup, or Washington-Slater, or something memorial of Founder and chief Benefactor.

I do not see any special appropriateness in attaching the honored name of Armstrong to the Institute. He was a great & good man and made his impress indelibly on you, but should not have all the honors. No one more than himself would have shoved aside, refused, such monopoly of honor.

Your meeting was a grand success. The conjunction of Federal & State officers was unique and suggestive & valuable.

A greater future is before you. Keep three things always in view.
1. Improve every year the teaching. It is the teacher, the teacher, who makes the man or the woman.
2. Five hundred worthy representatives will be more honorable for yourself and Institution and more useful to the race and the country than 1,000 superficially educated & little or no capacity for leadership.
3. Let all your financial operations — buying, borrowing, consuming, &c. be on strictest business principles. Do not go in debt. Do not borrow at usurious interest. Do not put yourself in power of bank, or merchant, Jew or Gentile.

With best wishes & regards   Yours sincerely,

J. L. M. Curry

ALS   Con. 272   BTW Papers   DLC.

From Edgar Webber[1]

Nashville, Tenn., Dec. 17 1897

Dear Sir: I have this morning mailed you a copy of the Nashville *American* of today containing an account of the proceedings of the

National Federation of Labor now meeting in our city, in which a statement alleged to have been made by you was challenged and created considerable discussion.[2] Thinking that the matter might be of some interest or perhaps importance to you, I thought I would forward you the paper containing the account.

You will remember me as the young man who as President of the Students Lecture Bureau of Fisk invited you to make an address here which you did over two years ago. Yours very truly,

Edgar Webber

ALS   Con. 135   BTW Papers   DLC.

[1] See above, 1:xvii-xix.

[2] During the national convention of the American Federation of Labor at Nashville in 1897, northern and southern delegates discussed the relationship of blacks to the labor movement. Delegate Henry Demarest Lloyd reported that BTW had stated that "trade unions were placing obstacles in the way of the material advancement of the negro," and proposed in answer a resolution that the A. F. of L. welcome all laboring men regardless of "creed, color, sex, race or nationality." Such a resolution, he said, would be "the complete answer to any and all such false assertions." Lloyd added that "he . . . did not ask our Southern friends to take the negro to their breast, but he did ask them to give to the negro the same bargaining power with capital that we accord to the white workers." Samuel Gompers, Peter J. McGuire, and others defended the unions against charges of exclusion. McGuire suggested, according to a newspaper report, that BTW was trying to "put the negro before the public as the victims of gross injustice and himself as the Moses of the race." Lloyd's resolution, however, was adopted by a ruling of President Gompers that no vote was necessary. Southerners appealed the ruling, but a vote sustained the chair. (Nashville *American,* Dec. 17, 1897, 2; American Federation of Labor, *Proceedings of the Seventeenth Annual Convention, 1897,* 82-83.)

From Henry Clay Reynolds

Washington, D.C. 12/17 1897

Dr Sir   I have your letter. Sorry I missed you, but all OK at last I believe. I was told by Plowman[1] at 1 PM you had gone back to Boston. He was mistaken. When you came to 201 E Cap'l I was upstairs. I did go out, they supposed I was already gone. I tried to find Cecil Browne[2] but failing had an appt with Bob Mosely, so kept that. Well its now 10 PM, just got back from a visit to Speaker Reed. Had a long talk ¾ of an hour discussed all round. Said He was pleased with all I said, told me all his views & objections. I told Him He was mistaken in some things. Finally said "well I wont promise you but I will say I think far better of it all than I have," we parted good friends. I like him very much. He s a *grand man,* and if He ever gets nom' for Pres' Ill vote his ticket any how, land or no land. He told Mosely "He liked me" and Mosely beleives He'll do us right. I then went to see your friend Walker of Tuskeege at National Hotel. I will try to come back in Jan'y and somehow I am of opinion we'll get it thro'. I went to see Sen Morgan, but gone to bed, I dont know how He's getting on, but I think He'll pull bill thro' all O.K. I go home tomorrow, Will stop over Monday in Milledgeville Ga to see the school there. I hope you are getting on as well as usual. with best wishes   Your friend

H. C. Reynolds

ALS   Con. 133   BTW Papers   DLC.

¹ Thomas Scales Plowman (1843-1919) was a member of the U.S. House of Representatives from Alabama from Mar. 4, 1897, to Feb. 9, 1898, when William F. Aldrich successfully contested his seat.

² Cecil Browne, born in 1855 in Montevallo, Ala., was a member of the Alabama House of Representatives (1882-83, 1896-97), the Alabama Senate (1884-86), and the constitutional convention of 1901. In 1910 he became a city judge in Talladega. His wife was the daughter of Robert A. Moseley.

To Hollis Burke Frissell

Crawford House, Boston, Mass. Dec. 18, 1897

My dear Dr. Frissell: I have your letter of December 15th and in reply would say that, I shall be glad to speak at the meeting in New York on February 18th and shall reserve that date.

I am very glad that Dr. Curry was so pleased with what he saw at Tuskegee in connection with the opening of our agricultural building. I think by far it was the most interesting and encouraging occasion we have ever had. We got hold of not only the leading white people but the masses of the common white farmers in a way that we have never done before; there were four or five hundred of these common white people present and they seemed deeply interested. The speeches made by Secry. Wilson, Dr. Curry, Gov. Johnston, Gov. Northen and Commissioner Glenn were all good.

Two articles of mine, or rather one article which Dr. Ward writes me he is going to divide into two parts, will appear soon in the New York Independent.[1] I have taken up the whole subject of industrial education without referring to either Hampton or Tuskegee so far as I now remember the article, and I hope you will have time to glance over what I said. I sent this article to the Independent because I fear the Independent has never fully appreciated what we are trying to do through industrial education. I had a very pleasant note from Dr. Ward saying that he would publish the article. Yours truly,

Booker T. Washington

TLS   BTW Folder   ViHaI.

[1] These appeared on Jan. 27 and Feb. 3, 1898. (See below.)

An Interview in the Chicago *Inter Ocean*

Washington, D.C., Dec. 20 1897

Booker T. Washington, the negro who has won a place as a leader of his race by his work at Tuskegee, Ala., in teaching the colored people that it is better to learn trades than to seek political and professional careers, was at the capital today looking after a bill to grant 25,000 acres of government land in Alabama to the Tuskegee Agricultural and Industrial Institute.

Mr. Washington believes that if some of the unoccupied land of the South could be given to such schools it would be a double benefit to that section. It would convert land which has remained unoccupied for many years into prosperous farms, and it would enable him to carry out his plan of encouraging negroes to take small farms and become independent and free from the bondage of the lease system which keeps them in practical slavery.

Mr. Washington has for several years been carrying out a plan of helping negro families to buy farms of a few acres. He bought a large tract of wild land, divided it up into ten acre tracts, and sold these to men who had graduated from his agricultural school, on terms that enabled them to pay for the land and make improvements. In this way he established a model farm community where the negro farmers were independent landholders. It was an object lesson to the poor negroes of the Black Belt and all through that section the negro farmers became ambitious to become landholders. Such white men as Senator Morgan, Governor Johnston of Alabama, and ex-Governor Northen of Georgia look upon Booker T. Washington as a man who is doing more than any other individual to settle the race question by making the negroes enterprising and progressive farmers. Mr. Washington could get his bill passed but for the fact that some of the Southern Senators want to tack on a rider giving an equal amount of land to several white schools. The same argument does not apply to these and the House will not accept the rider.

*   *   *   *

Mr. Washington was surprised to learn from a Chicago paper that he was in Washington two weeks ago, and urged President McKinley not to give offices to the negroes because they must be kept on the farms and in the trades, and discouraged from political ambition. Mr. Washington smiled as he read this announcement in the Chicago Record, and then said it must be a part of the scheme of those opposed to negro suffrage to prejudice the President against recognizing the negroes of the South. "I have not been in Washington before for several months," said Mr. Washington, "and when I was here and saw the President I put in my best effort to have him recognize the colored man and appoint a negro to the position of register of the treasury. I am glad to note that President McKinley has appointed a negro to this office, and one who stands on his own merits as a man and a Republican. No one can say that ex-Senator Bruce was given an office simply because he is a negro, and one can point to it as an evidence that the negro is recognized in national affairs just the same as the white man. It will have a great educational effect in the South for the poor negroes to be able to see the name of a negro on every treasury note and silver certificate that comes into their hands. Our money goes everywhere, and the negro who earns a dollar by hard work in the field or factory can read the name of B. K. Bruce, a negro, on the dollar bill he receives in wages. It shows that negro that he has an interest in the government; that this is not a white man's government, as demagogues tell him, but is a people's government. It also teaches him that the negro can rise here just as well as the white man if he has the energy and ambition to do it. It gives him confidence in the government, makes him a better and better satisfied citizen, and gives him an ambition.

*　　*　　*　　*

"It has been the custom of white teachers to hold up to their pupils the possibility of every one of them reaching the exalted position of President. That incentive to study and work and right living has been offered to the white youth ever since the government began, and preachers and political orators today point to the career of Lincoln and Garfield and McKinley as illustrating the possibilities of American manhood. But they have not held up such inducements to the colored youth. We have not had the opportunity to tell our negro boys that if they grow up to be good men and able men they may be President or Senator or Governor. No such incentive is held out to the negro youth. It will be a rift in the cloud that hangs over the negro politically, to see the name of a negro on every treasury note which he earns. It will show him that there is a chance for him, and that all the honors of public life are not denied to his race. I used just this argument to President McKinley in urging him to appoint a negro like ex-Senator Bruce as Registrar of the Treasury. I pointed out the educational effect it would have with the poor negroes in the South who are sometimes discouraged with the outlook. I am glad to have this opportunity to go home and hold up a silver certificate or treasury note and point to the name of a negro on it, and tell my 600 negro boys that a negro has his name on every dollar bill and every hundred dollar bill issued by the government as money. It may give them more confidence to know that these promises to pay by Uncle Sam are indorsed by a negro. But seriously, I think it will have an educational value among our people in the South which the people of the North can hardly understand or appreciate.

*　　*　　*　　*

"I have never been opposed to the negro's holding office or positions of trust anywhere. I hope to see the day when men will be appointed or elected to office without regard to race or color, but on their merit as men. I hope that some day the test will be manhood, and I want the negroes to be ready to share in the contest of manhood. I have discouraged young men without education or business training from seeking political places as janitors simply to be on the salary list. I have tried to show them that their first ambition should be to take care of themselves by having a trade or business career. I have urged young negroes in my school to become scientific farmers or skilled mechanics, that they might be certain of an earning capacity greater than they would have without this knowledge. I have tried to show them that this is the first step toward independence. I want them to go out from school independent men, fully competent to compete with any other men they meet. The professions are crowded, and I encourage them to seek the trades and the farm first. When they are independent on the farm or in a trade, they can seek any other advancement for which they have an ambition.

*　　*　　*　　*

"But I am not opposed to the negro's holding office. If he is qualified I believe he ought to have the same chance as the white man. I don't want him to ask office because he is a negro, nor do I want him denied office because he is a negro. Let the test be ability, and citizenship, and manhood. If there is a community where the majority of the patrons want a negro postmaster and the negro candidate has their confidence, I think he ought to be appointed. You can't have the American principle of rule by majorities carried out in any other way. You can't take a community where there are 1,000 negroes and 100 white men and allow the white men to say that a negro shall not be postmaster without changing the rule of American government that the majorities shall rule. I prefer, however, to see the negro stand on his own footing, and work out his own salvation. He can do that best by beginning at the bottom and making himself the equal of every other man in his community. If he is the best and most successful farmer in his township, or the most skilled mechanic in his town, he will be in a position to stand on his rights. The man who has what another man wants is always more independent than that other man. I want the negro to get what the white man wants, then he will have no trouble. I never saw a negro molested by a white man if the negro held a mortgage on the white man's house.

*　　*　　*　　*

"The negroes of the South are gradually learning this. They no longer fear an educational test of citizenship. They have been ambitious to learn, and in Alabama and Georgia they have no fear of a fair educational test. They have no fear of a fair test in Mississippi, but unfortunately the Mississippi law does not provide a fair test. It provides that a man shall either be able to read a section of the constitution or be able to understand it when read to him. This leaves the whole question in the hands of the judges of election. The negro is compelled to read and explain. The white man is said to understand anything if the judges want him to vote.

"But I wish you would say that I am not here to ask President McKinley not to appoint negroes to office, nor am I here to urge him to appoint them. I am not a politician, but I would like to see the same political rights accorded to all citizens in holding office as well as at the polls."

Chicago *Inter Ocean*, Dec. 21, 1897, 7.

From Ollie Meadows

Farm, W.Va. Dec 22, 1897

Dear Sir   I thought I would write to you, but I dont expect you no me but know mamma   She was a Fergeson befoure she was married, and I always hear her talk abought you and I often hear Prof Prillman[1] speak of you. mamma is always talk abought how she useter play with you when she was little, I guess you will be suprised to hear from me but I saw you when you was hear abought four years ago. mamma would like to see you very much   I go to the West Virginia Instute Prof Prillman is my teacher   mamma wants me to come there to go to school. I am 14 years old my other sister is in Prairre Ala going to school with my Aunt Alice   Answer soon   I will close   your loving Cousin Ollie Meadows.

ALS   Con. 131   BTW Papers   DLC.

[1] Byrd Prillerman, born a slave in 1859 in Franklin County, Va., traveled in 1868 to West Virginia on foot and settled near Sissonville. He was twelve years old before he began school. He studied under a Hampton graduate and in 1879 began teaching at Sissonville. After attending Knoxville College, he taught in the Charleston, W.Va., schools until 1892, when he and Christopher H. Payne opened the West Virginia Colored Institute. He taught English there until 1909, when he became president. He was active in civic work and in educational associations, once serving as president of the West Virginia Teachers' Association. In 1912 BTW, whose career paralleled Prillerman's in many ways, spoke at the institute and said of Prillerman: "I have known your Principal for a number of years. I have always

admired and loved him. I admire and love him first, because of his modest bearing. He is one of the few men who have learned that the sign of true worth, the sign of true greatness, is in modesty and simplicity, and I want to congratulate you that you have such a principal for this institution." Prillerman helped to care for BTW's sister Amanda in her last days and spoke at her funeral.

To Edward Ware Barrett[1]

Tuskegee, Ala. [December 1897]

Personal

Dear sir: I thank you for your letter of recent date regarding my Chicago address. I had seen editorials bearing upon it in two or three Southern daily papers until your very kind letter came I had not decided to say anything for publication. Especially in view of the fact that such papers as the Age-Herald, the Advertiser, and the Mobile Register, had said nothing of an adverse nature thus seeming to indicate by their silence that they still had faith in me. I appreciate fully the harm that could result from any mistake on my part, and also the false position that any hypocritical utterances or actions on my part would place you and others in, who have so generously stood by me. It is this latter consideration mainly that has made me decide to send you the enclosed short article for publication.

I want to thank you personally for calling the matter to my attention. When I am in Birmingham I shall see you and talk the whole matter over in a more satisfactory manner than I can now write. Yours very truly,

[Booker T. Washington]

ALd Con. 272 BTW Papers DLC.

[1] Edward Ware Barrett was born in Athens, Ga., in 1866. Though he studied civil engineering at Washington and Lee, Barrett early began the newspaper career he pursued all his life. He rose from typesetter to city editor at the Augusta *Chronicle* before going to Washington in 1888 as correspondent for Henry Grady's Atlanta *Constitution.* After covering China and Japan for the *Constitution* and the New York *World,* Barrett bought control of the Birmingham *Age-Herald* in 1897 and was its editor until his death in 1922. During his Washington days, Barrett was political secretary to Speaker of the House Charles F. Crisp, and was thereafter involved in Democratic party affairs, serving as delegate to all but one national convention from 1892 through 1916, and as a member of the executive committee of the Democratic national committee in 1921.

From William A. Pledger

Atlanta, Ga., Jan. 6th 1898

My Dear Mr. Washington, I have your letter or rather telegram of this date and shall try to be in your town on Saturday morning. If I should have to go on to Washington without seeing you you must bear in mind that I will be at your command when there as same as if I had seen you before going. You must in the future feel that I can be commanded by you without being seen by you. I told Fortune that I was satisfied that his theory of you was the correct one. I am your friend and when you need me call me. I shall stand by you in the future and you shall see it. I think that I shall get over on the Saturday morning train, but if I should not — talk to me freely by letter. Fortune will tell you that I am no hypocrit. What I am I am. You take care of the youth at your school and I will take care of the wise-acres. You see me work and when you are pleased remind me that you are a prop. Yours Sincerely,

W. A. Pledger

TLS   Con. 144   BTW Papers   DLC.

From William E. Benson

[Kowaliga, Ala.] Jan 7th 1898

Dear Mr. Washington: I herewith enclose the endorsement which you gave me some time ago. I endeavored to have you feel my exact position this afternoon, with regard to your withdrawing the endorsement which I have so extensively advertised and honorably sustained, and which now, because of these facts, to withdraw at so critical a time would be unpleasant for both of us, because I cannot have your letter to back up the footing that I have even *already* made. In this case it were better that you had not given me a letter at all; and even though I had not made so great headway as I have with your endorsement as a basis to work on, however poorly I might have succeeded it would have been *genuine,* and I should not now find myself standing in space with no conceivable support, nor evidence of any by which I could have reached such a position. However, I do not contend for the letter, still I cannot see how you could give anybody *my* endorsement, which is as I consider purely individual and not general. I fully appreciate your point in not having out too many letters &c, but if you notice you do not make an appeal for me at all but simply by testifying as to my individuality gives *me* an opportunity to make an appeal. It was from this view that I asked your consideration this after-noon, and as you did not give me any definite understanding, I return the letter with the request that it be forwarded me to the address given, if you should decide to let me keep it. Yours very sincerely

Wm. E. Benson

ALS Con. 136 BTW Papers DLC.

To Mary Elizabeth Preston Stearns

[Tuskegee, Ala., ca. Jan. 8, 1898]

My dear Mrs. Stearns: I put this letter in type so that you will have no trouble to read it.

After you have read it I fear you will become very much disgusted, and disappointed in me.

But I think you have faith enough in me to know that I am trying to do that which is for the best interest of the school, and were it not for the fact that I know your deep interest in our work will cause you to be willing to make any reasonable personal sacrifice, I should hesitate to write you. What I refer to is regarding the name of the new agricultural building.

When you and I discussed the naming of the new agricultural building I was not aware that the Slater Fund trustees had any special plan or desire regarding the name of the building. It now turns out that from the first it has been the wish and plan of the Slater trustees to have all the buildings erected at their suggestion at Hampton and Tuskegee bear the name: "Armstrong and Slater Memorial" (Agricultural Building) &c. You will, I think, remember that I told you that the Slater Fund trustees are to give us $3000 annually for the support of the Agricultural building and when we get the Trades

Building erected they are to give us an additional amount for that. For this reason you can see that it is important that their wishes be regarded otherwise we may find ourselves without support for these new departments.

These trustees want these buildings to bear the names "Armstrong" and "Slater" for the reason that it was Gen. Armstrong who first started the idea of industrial education and Mr. Slater gave the money from which these new departments are to be permanently supported.

Our executive committee in connection with myself feel that your deep interest in the school will make you willing to agree to any change that will best serve the school, although in this case it must cause you a great deal of annoyance.

For the reasons mentioned we want your permission to transfer the name of "George and Mary Stearns Hall" to a brick building now called Armstrong Hall[1] and let Gen. Armstrong's name go to this new building according to the wishes of the Slater Fund trustees.

We want very much to have one of our large and important buildings commemorate for all time your generous help and deep interest in Tuskegee as well as the unselfish and patriotic services rendered to our whole country by your husband. This is just and fitting. I hope to hear from you soon.

Mrs. Washington and the children are well. Yours Sincerely

Booker T. Washington

ALdSr   Con. 147   BTW Papers   DLC.

[1] Mary Stearns urged BTW to leave the name as it was. She believed Armstrong's name was one "that cannot be spoken too often; too reverently; or too long." (Stearns to BTW, Jan. 14, 1898, Con. 701, BTW Papers, DLC.)

From Victoria Earle Matthews

Borough of Brooklyn   Jan 8th 1898

Dear Mr Washington   I thank you most sincerely for your gracious favor, brought me by this morning's mail. That such endorsement from you will serve me in the matter of developing and advanceing an Industrial institution here. I need not tell you my plan is to be enabled to secure a good sized house. The upper part of which to be used as a temporary lodging house for women and girls coming from the South or other parts to New York in search of work. These persons to be prepared for work in families to be located in churches of their choice and in general be looked after by respectable women until they make association of a proper and wholesome nature. The lower part of the house to furnish place for classes in domestic sewing dressmaking, milenery, cooking, marketing — in other words, common sense housekeeping a daily kindergarten and manual training for boys — also lectures in regard to domestic service for young men and boys — in time other departments — trades and professional branches — (typewriting Stenography, book keeping ect). The building to have a reading room, Library and Gymnasium.

Long before I made a public move this was my idea. I realized when in Tuskegee as never before the need for such work in New York City but my faculties were so torn and disordered by my son's departure that I not only did not know how to start but had not the tact to seek advice from authorities when chance and fortune offered. I felt to turn to you, something ever restrained me, for I felt it were imposition and would look as though I were trading upon friendship and the fact that I had been a guest in your house. Then I did not feel to calculate too much upon my influence here to make the idea arouse commendation and co-opperation. This point I think has been clearly demonstrated. The idea will take the sustained interest of the past 9 months [to] settle that. My great anxiety now is to work on a plan, calculated to stand the wear and tear. I feel that the success or failure of this work now depends upon the method I proceed by. Any plain talk you may feel to give me I will be under lasting obligation to you. In no wise am I sensitive. I am anxious not to fail in the end. My unspoken or unwritten — heretofore, hope is, to see the Tuskegee System as far as one not reared in Tuskegee can bring about with needed local additions in New York City.

Thank you again most heartily and wishing you every success and happiness I am sincerely yours

Victoria Earle Matthews

ALS   Con. 143   BTW Papers   DLC.

From Mary Elizabeth Preston Stearns

Tufts College, near Boston   Jan'y 10th 1898

My Dear Friend, Your letter is at hand announcing the conditions requiring the withdrawel of the names of "George and Mary Stearns" from the "Agricultural Building."

I hasten to assure you, that the prosperity of "Tuskegee" outranks any personal, or private interest I might have in the matter.

You are quite right in yielding to the superior claims of the "Slater Trustees."

It goes without saying — that my noble Husband, who gave his life, and fortune for the overthrow of Slavery; and the elevation of the Colored Race, would not wish his name to shadow even the financial prosperity of the humblest effort in behalf of the supreme aim which enlisted his devotion.

I cannot help regretting the publicity attending the announcement of our names at the "Dedication ceremonies," and I trust you will put us right before the world — for, I must confess to not a little embarrassment in the matter.

With kind regards to Mrs Washington, whose letter shall receive acknowledgement, when I am able to hold my pen — as is evident by this writing, I am *not*. Ever Cordially Yours.

Mary E. Stearns

ALS   Con. 701   BTW Papers   DLC.

From Warren Logan

[Tuskegee, Ala.] Jan 11 '98

Mr Washington, I find that the estimated monthly expense of the institute is $12,500.00. This estimate is based on the operations for Oct. and Nov. and includes purchases of every kind, salaries, labor etc.

For the summer months, I think ⅖ of this amount per mo. will perhaps cover the cost of running the school.

Warren Logan

ALS   Con. 142   BTW Papers   DLC.

From Victoria Earle Matthews

New York. Jan. 12–1898

My Dear Mr Washington. Please accept my sincere thanks for your kindness in putting my work before Mr Ogden with such splendid results. I hardly knew what to say when Miss Moore[1] handed me the check for $50.00. Yesterday we went and thanked Mr Ogden he was very gracious assured us that he was deeply interested in such work and "my friend Mr Washington" he said something about having confidence in his judgement ect ect. We both felt very important at that moment for having been brought to his notice by you. Again I thank you. Oh yes — your name gave us quite an opening at the headquarters for Kindergarten Supplies whither we went, after talking awhile I asked for reduced rates for missions & — telling him of the work — I said I want to plant a "minature Tuskegee" in 97th st. immediately he wished to know if I knew of your work — knew you — had ever been South, and a multitude of questions. You can imagine my answers — he has very great respect for your name. When we asked the price of what we had selected — to our great delight he made us a nice contribution and said he intended doing more for us in the future.[2] It may not be right to send you so long a letter, but I am so encouraged — and I thought you'd be pleased to hear about our good fortune. When you come up on the 12 Feb. kindly plan to give me 30 minutes. Sincerely yours

Victoria Earle Matthews

ALS   Con. 143   BTW Papers   DLC.

[1] Alice Ruth Moore Dunbar Nelson (1875-1935), social worker, educator, and poet, was born in New Orleans and graduated from Straight University in 1892. While teaching school in Brooklyn, N.Y., she was active in the work of Victoria Earle Matthews's White Rose Mission. In 1898 she married Paul Laurence Dunbar but the marriage lasted only until 1902. From 1902 to 1920 she was head of the Howard High School English department in Wilmington, Del. In 1916 she married Robert John Nelson, a newspaper editor. She founded the Delaware Industrial School for Colored Girls in 1924, and in 1928 she became executive secretary of the American Interracial Peace Committee and associate editor of the *A.M.E. Church Review*. Among her published works were *Violets and Other Tales* (1895) and *The Goodness of St. Rocque* (1899). Despite their brief and stormy marriage, Alice Dunbar Nelson helped to keep Paul Laurence Dunbar's work alive by giving readings of his poetry.

From William Henry Baldwin, Jr.

New York, Jan. 21st., 1898

Dear Mr. Washington: I will take pleasure in talking fully with Mr. Daniel C. Smith when he calls.

I had a half hour's talk with Mr. Jessup, and I think the interview was helpful all 'round. It is important to name that new agricultural building after Mr. Armstrong or Slater or both. Have you written to the people in Boston to ask for the privilege of changing the name? It would be necessary to make a clean breast of the whole matter, even if you have to offer to return to them their subscriptions; but a letter well worded, or, better, an interview, should produce satisfactory results.

I have had some correspondence with Mr. Reynolds, of Montevallo School, and have also had satisfactory correspondence with Speaker Reed; and I am satisfied the Speaker will not oppose or take any action to influence an adverse report, provided the Committee make a report. It will have the fullest and fairest consideration. Please let me know at once the final date for the conference. Yours very truly,

W H Baldwin Jr

TLS   Con. 792   BTW Papers   DLC.

From Oscar Wilder Underwood

Washington, D.C., Jan. 24th, 1898

Dear Sir: Your favor of the 21st. inst. received. I have made an appointment to take the matter of the grant of twenty-five acres[1] to your school and the school at Montevallo up before the Public Lands Committee next Friday. I will read your letter to them and I believe confidently that we can get a favorable report. I think the bill will pass if we can get Mr. Reed's recognition. Yours truly,

O W Underwood

TLS   Con. 147   BTW Papers   DLC.

[1] Actually 25,000 acres.

An Article in *The Independent*

[New York City, Jan. 27, Feb. 3, 1898]

INDUSTRIAL TRAINING FOR THE NEGRO

PART I

Since the War no one object has been more misunderstood than that of the object and value of industrial education for the Negro. To begin with, it must be borne in mind that the condition that existed in the South immediately after the War and that now exists is a peculiar one, without a parallel in history. This being true, it seems to me that the wise and honest thing is to make a study of the actual condition and environment of the Negro and do that which is best for him regardless of whether the same thing has been done for another race in exactly the same way. There are those among our friends of the white race, and those among my own race, who assert with a good deal of earnestness that there is no difference between the white man and black man in this country. This sounds very pleasant and tickles the fancy; but when we apply the test of hard, cold logic to it, we must acknowledge that there is a difference, not an inherent one, not a racial one, but a difference growing out of unequal opportunities in the past.

If I might be permitted to seem, even, to criticise some of the educational work that has been done in the South, I would say that the weak point has been in a failure to recognize this difference.

Negro education immediately after the War in most cases was begun too nearly at the point where New England education had ended. Let me illustrate. One of the saddest sights I ever saw was the placing of a three hundred dollar rosewood piano in a country school in the South that was located in the midst of the "Black Belt." Am I arguing against the teaching of instrumental music to the Negroes in that community? Not at all; only I should have deferred those music lessons about twenty-five years. There are numbers of such pianos in thousands of New England homes; but behind the piano in the New England home, there were one hundred years of toil, sacrifice and economy; there was the small manufacturing industry started several years ago by handpower, now grown into a great business; there was ownership in land, a comfortable home, free from debt, a bank account. In this

"Black Belt" community where this piano went, four-fifths of the people owned no land, many lived in rented one-room cabins, many were in debt for food supplies, many mortgaged their crops for the food on which to live, and not one had a bank account. In this case how much wiser it would have been to have taught the girls in this community how to do their own sewing, how to cook intelligently and economically, housekeeping, something of dairying and horticulture; the boys something of farming in connection with their common school education, instead of awakening in these people a desire for a musical instrument which resulted in their parents going into debt for a third-rate piano or organ before a home was purchased. These industrial lessons should have awakened in this community a desire for homes and would have given the people the ability to free themselves from industrial slavery to the extent that most of them would have soon purchased homes. After the home and the necessaries of life were supplied could come the piano; one piano lesson in a home is worth twenty in a rented log cabin.

Only a few days ago I saw a colored minister preparing his Sunday sermon just as the New England minister prepares his sermon. But this colored minister was in a broken-down, leaky, rented log cabin, with weeds in the yard, surrounded by evidences of poverty, filth and want of thrift. This minister had spent some time in school studying theology. How much better would it have been to have had this minister taught the dignity of labor, theoretical and practical farming in connection with his theology, so that he could have added to his meager salary, and set an example to his people in the matter of living in a decent house, and correct farming — in a word, this minister should have been taught that his condition, and that of his people, was not that of a New England community, and he should have been so trained as to meet the actual needs and condition of the colored people in this community.

God for two hundred and fifty years was preparing the way for the redemption of the Negro through industrial development. First, he made the Southern white man do business with the Negro for two hundred and fifty years in a way that no one else has done business with him. If a Southern white man wanted a house, or a bridge built, he consulted a Negro mechanic about the plan, about the building of the house, or the bridge. If he wanted a suit of clothes, or a pair of shoes made, it was to the Negro tailor or shoemaker that he talked.

Secondly, every large slave plantation in the South was, in a limited sense, an industrial school. On these plantations there were scores of young colored men and women who were constantly being trained not alone as common farmers, but as carpenters, blacksmiths, wheelwrights, plasterers, brick masons, engineers, bridge builders, cooks, dressmakers, housekeepers, etc., more in one county than now in the whole city of Atlanta. I would be the last to apologize for the curse of slavery; but I am simply stating facts. This training was crude and was given for selfish purposes and did not answer the highest purpose because there was the absence of literary training in connection with that of the hand. Nevertheless, this business contact with the Southern white man, and the industrial training received on these plantations, put us at the close of the War into possession of all the common and skilled labor in the South. For nearly twenty years after the War, except in one or two cases, the value of the industrial training given by the Negroes' former masters on the plantations and elsewhere was overlooked. Negro men and women were educated in literature, mathematics and the sciences, with no thought of what had been taking place on these plantations for two and a half centuries. After twenty years, those who were trained as mechanics, etc., during slavery began to disappear by death, and gradually we awoke to the fact that we had no one to take their places. We had trained scores of young men in Greek, but few in carpentry or mechanical or architectural drawing; we had trained many in Latin but almost none as engineers, bridge builders and machinists. Numbers were taken from the farm and educated, but were educated in everything except agriculture; hence they had no sympathy with farm life and did not return to it.

The place made vacant by old Uncle Jim, who was trained as a carpenter during slavery, and who, since the War, had been the leading contractor and builder in the Southern town, had to be filled. No young colored carpenter capable of filling Uncle Jim's place could be found. The result was that his place was filled by a white mechanic from the North, or from Europe, or from elsewhere. What is true of carpentry and house building in this case, is true, in a degree, of every line of skilled labor, and is becoming true of common labor. I do not mean to say that all of the skilled labor has been taken out of the Negro's hands; but I do mean to say that in no part of the South is he so strong in the matter of skilled labor as he was twenty years ago, except, possibly, in the country districts and the smaller towns. In the more northern of the Southern cities, such as Richmond and Baltimore, the change is most apparent; and it is being felt in every Southern city. Wherever the Negro has lost ground industrially in the South, it is not because there is prejudice against him as a skilled laborer on the part of the native Southern white man, for the Southern white man generally prefers to do business with the Negro as a mechanic rather than with a white one; for he is accustomed to do business with the Negro in this respect. There is almost no prejudice against the Negro in the South in matters of business, so far as the native whites are concerned, and here is the entering wedge for the solution of the race problem. Where the white mechanic or factory operative gets a hold, the trades-union soon follows, and the Negro is crowded to the wall.

But what is the remedy for this condition? First, it is most important that the Negro and our white friends honestly face the facts as they are, otherwise the time will not be far distant when the Negro in the South will be crowded to the ragged edge of industrial life as he is in the North. There is still time to repair the damage and to reclaim what we have lost.

I stated in the beginning that the industrial education for the Negro has been misunderstood. This has been chiefly because some have gotten the idea that industrial development was opposed to the Negro's higher mental development. This has little or nothing to do with the subject under discussion; and we should no longer permit such an idea to aid in depriving the Negro of the legacy in the form of skilled labor that was purchased by his forefathers at the price of two hundred and fifty years in slavery. I would say to the black boy what I would say to the white boy, get all the mental development that your time and pocketbook will afford — the more the better; but the time has come when a larger proportion — not all, for we need professional men and women — of the educated colored men and women should give themselves to industrial or business life. The professional class will be helped in proportion as the rank and file have an industrial foundation so that they can pay for professional service. Whether they receive the training of the hand while pursuing their academic training or after their academic training is finished, or whether they will get their literary training in an industrial school or college, is a question which each individual must decide for himself; but no matter how or where educated, the educated men and women must come to the rescue of the race in the effort to get and hold its industrial footing. I would not have the standard of mental development lowered one whit, for with the Negro, as with all races, mental strength is the basis of all progress; but I would have a larger proportion of this mental strength reach the Negroes' actual needs through the medium of the hand. Just now the need is not so much for common carpenters, brick-masons, farmers and laundry-women as for industrial leaders, men who, in addition to their practical knowledge, can draw plans, make estimates, take contracts; those who understand the latest methods of truck gardening and the science underlying practical agriculture; those who understand machinery to the extent that they can operate steam and electric laundries, so that our women can hold on to the laundry work in the South that is so fast drifting into the hands of others in the large cities and towns.

PART II

It is possible for a race or an individual to have mental development and yet be so handicapped by custom, prejudice and lack of employment as to dwarf and discourage the whole life, and this is the condition that prevails among my race in most of the large cities of the North; and it is to prevent this same condition in the South that I plead with all the earnestness of my heart. Mental development alone will not give us what we want; but mental development tied to hand and heart training will be the salvation of the Negro.

In many respects, the next twenty years are going to be the most serious in the history of the race. Within this period it will be largely decided whether the Negro is going to be able to retain the hold which he now has upon the industries of the South, or whether his place will be filled by white people from a distance. The only way that we can prevent the industries slipping from the Negro in all parts of the South, as they have already in certain parts of the South, is for all the educators, ministers and friends of the Negro to unite to push forward, in a whole-souled manner, the industrial or business development of the Negro either in school, or out of school, or both. Four times as many young men and women of my race should be receiving industrial training. Just now the Negro is in a position to feel and appreciate the need of this in a way that no one else can. No one can fully appreciate what I am saying who has not walked the streets of a Northern city day after day seeking employment, only to find every door closed against him on account of his color, except along certain lines of menial service. It is to prevent the same thing taking place in the South that I plead. We may argue that mental development will take care of all this. Mental development is a good thing. Gold is also a good thing, but gold is worthless without opportunity to make it touch the world of trade. Education increases an individual's wants many fold. It is cruel in many cases to increase the wants of the black youth by mental development alone, without at the same time increasing his ability to supply these increased wants along lines at which he can find employment.

I repeat that the value and object of industrial education has been misunderstood by many. Many have had the thought that industrial training was meant to make the Negro work, much as he worked during the days of slavery. This is far from my idea of it. If this training has any value for the Negro, as it has for the white man, it consists in teaching the Negro how rather not to work, but how to make the forces of nature — air, water, horse-power, steam and electric power, work for him, how to lift labor up out of toil and drudgery into that which is dignified and beautiful. The Negro in the South works, and he works hard; but his lack of skill, coupled with ignorance, causes him to do his work in the most costly and shiftless manner; and this keeps him near the bottom of the ladder in the business world. I repeat that industrial education teaches the Negro how not to work. Let him who doubts this contrast the Negro in the South toiling through a field of oats with an old-fashioned reaper, with the white man on a modern farm in the West, sitting upon a modern "harvester" behind two spirited horses, with an umbrella over him, using a machine that cuts and binds the oats at the same time — doing four times as much work as the black man with one-half the labor. Let us give the black man so much skill and brains that he can cut oats like the white man, then he can compete with him. The Negro works in cotton and has no trouble so long as his labor is confined to the lower forms of work — the planting, the picking and the ginning; but when the Negro attempts to follow the bale of cotton up through the higher stages, through the mill where it is made into the finer fabrics — where the larger profit appears, he is told that he is not wanted. The Negro can work in wood and iron and no one objects so long as he confines his work to the felling of trees and the sawing of boards, to the digging of iron ore and making of pig iron; but when the Negro attempts to follow his tree into the factory where it is made into chairs and desks and railway coaches; or when he attempts to follow the pig iron into the factory where it is made into knife blades and watch-springs, the Negro's trouble begins. And what is the objection? Simply that the Negro lacks skill coupled with brains to the extent that he can compete with the white man, or that when white men refuse to work with colored men, enough skilled and educated colored men cannot be found able to superintend and man every part of any one large industry, and hence for these reasons we are constantly being barred out. The Negro must become in a larger measure an intelligent producer as well as a consumer. There should be a more vital and practical connection between the Negro's educated brain and his opportunity of earning his daily living. Without more attention being given to industrial development we are likely to have an overproduction of educated politicians — men who are bent on living by their wits. As we get further away from the War period the Negro will not find himself held to the Republican Party by feelings of gratitude. He will feel himself free to vote for any party; and we are in danger of having the vote or "influence" of a large proportion of the educated black men in the market for the highest bidder unless attention is given to the education of the hand, or to industrial development.

A very weak argument often used against pushing industrial training for the Negro is that the Southern white man favors it, and, therefore, it is not best for the Negro. Altho I was born a slave, I am thankful that I am able so far to rid myself of prejudice as to be able to accept a good thing whether it comes from a black man or from a white man, a Southern man or a Northern man. Industrial education will not only help the Negro directly in the matter of industrial development, but it will help in bringing about more satisfactory relations between him and the Southern white man. For the sake of the Negro and the Southern white man there are many things in the relation of the two races that must soon be changed. We cannot depend wholly upon abuse or condemnation of the Southern white man to bring about these changes. Each race must be educated to see matters in a broad, high, generous Christian spirit; we must bring the two races together, not estrange them. The Negro must live for all time by the side of the Southern white man. The man is unwise who does not cultivate in every manly way the friendship and good-will of his next-door neighbor, whether he is black or white. I repeat that industrial training will help cement the friendship of the two races. The history of the world proves that trade, commerce, is the forerunner of peace and civilization as between races and nations. We are interested in the political warfare of Cuba and the Sandwich Islands because we have business interests with these islands. The Jew that was once in about the same position that the Negro is to-day has now complete recognition, because he has entwined himself about America in a business or industrial sense. Say or think what we will, it is the tangible or visible element that is going to tell largely during the next twenty years in the solution of the race problem. Every white man will respect the Negro who owns a two-story brick business block in the center of town and has five thousand dollars in the bank. When a black man is the largest taxpayer and owns and cultivates the most successful farm in his county, his white neighbors will not object very long to his voting and to having his vote honestly counted. The black man who is the largest contractor in his town and lives in a two-story brick house is not very likely to be lynched. The black man that holds a mortgage on a white man's house which he can foreclose at will is not very likely to be driven away from the ballot-box by the white man.

I know that what I have said will likely suggest the idea that I have put stress upon the lower things of life — the material; that I have overlooked the higher side, the ethical and religious. I do not over-look or undervalue the higher. All that I advocate in this article is not as an end, but as a means. I know as a race we have got to be patient in the laying of a firm foundation, that our tendency is too often to get the shadow instead of the substance, the appearance rather than the reality. I believe, further, that in a large measure, he who would make the statesmen, the men of letters, the men for the professions for the Negro race of the future, must, to-day, in a large measure, make the intelligent artisans, the manufacturers, the contractors, the real-estate dealers, the landowners, the successful farmers, the merchants, those skilled in domestic economy. Further, I know that it is not an easy thing to make a good Christian of a hungry man. I mean that just in proportion as the race gets a proper industrial foundation — gets habits of industry, thrift, economy, land, homes, profitable work, in the same proportion will its moral and religious life be improved.

I have written with a heart full of gratitude to all religious organizations and individuals for what they have done for us as a race, and I speak as plainly as I do because I feel that I have had opportunity in a measure to come face to face with the enormous amount of work that must still be done by the generous men and women of this country before there will be in reality, as well as in name, high Christian civilization among both races in the South.

To accomplish this, every agency now at work in the South needs re-enforcement.

The Independent, 50 (Jan. 27, 1898), 105-6; (Feb. 3, 1898), 145-46. This article was revised for inclusion in *The Future of the American Negro.* See below, vol. 5.

An Article in the *Southern States Farm Magazine*

[Baltimore, Md., January 1898]

THE BEST LABOR IN THE WORLD

Many persons who have never lived in the South and want to move to the South, get the idea that the presence of the negro in the South in large numbers is a disadvantage.

I have just returned from a visit to the State of Vermont. While there I attended a convention in which the subject of domestic help was discussed. Several persons in the meeting stated that they had tried to get satisfactory help among all the representatives of foreign countries who flock to America; in despair they sent South for negro help, and in every instance they stated that the result had been satisfactory.

It may be that I, a member of the negro race, cannot speak without bias on this subject, but I believe I can do so. I believe I have grown to the point where I can love a white man as much as I can love a black man. I believe that I can sympathize with a Southern white man as much as I can sympathize with a Northern white man. To me "a man is but a man for a' that and a' that."

The negro race has several characteristics which the average Northern or Western man does not appreciate or know. In the first place, with few exceptions, the Northern people see the worst side of negro life in the colored people who are in the Northern cities and towns. The negro race should not be judged by these.

The negro race has a genuine interest in this country — in the South. It is his home, and he is going to remain in the South. He is not here to grab a few dollars and then return to some foreign country. Then the negro, when treated right, can be trusted when made to feel that confidence is put in him. During our late war no Southern or Northern soldier who confided in the negro was betrayed. Even where an individual negro is inclined to be dishonest on general principles, when valuables are entrusted to him he will not betray the trust except in rare instances. The negro is used to the climate and the soil of the South, and he is at his best when cultivating this soil. If he is treated fairly, paid good wages and is paid promptly, there is no farm laborer in this country that will excel him.

The negro is not given to strikes and lock-outs. He believes in letting each individual be free to work where and for whom he pleases. He has the physical strength to endure hard labor, and he is not ashamed or afraid to work.

The negro, like the white man, has his faults, but he can be educated out of them. He is too quick to spend his money for gew-gaws. He likes to go on excursions, he likes to go to town on Saturday, but these faults, if dealt with in the right way, can soon be cured.

It is very seldom that the black man on the farm becomes a drunkard. He likes his whiskey on Saturday and Sunday, perhaps, but he seldom becomes a drunkard. On this, as on all subjects, the negro is willing to take the advice of anyone who gets and deserves his confidence.

The charge is often made that the educated negro will not work. Some years ago there seemed to be some foundation for this charge. Soon after his freedom, when the negro was intoxicated with his new ideas of liberty, not knowing what it meant, and when he did not feel the responsibilities of freedom, many negroes had the idea that to get education was to be put into a condition where labor would not be necessary. But all this is changing. In 1881, when I started the Tuskegee Normal and Industrial Institute at Tuskegee, Ala., parents would not send their children because they said they did not want their children taught to work. Now a revolution has been wrought in this matter. Here at Tuskegee we have about 1000 students, and every one of them is learning some trade or industry. Every parent who sends his son or daughter requests that they be taught some industry in connection with their academic training. So great is the demand from all parts of the South for this that we are compelled to refuse admission to hundreds each year. For example, our students cultivate 700 acres of land each year. Not only this, but they are being taught farming, dairying, horticulture, truck gardening, etc., and there is a positive enthusiasm about it. Of the forty-two buildings on our grounds, all except four have been erected by the labor of the students. While erecting a building some are taught brick masonry, others brickmaking, plastering, carpentry, tinsmithing, etc. In all we have twenty-six different industries in constant operation. I ask any white school in the country to show a better record in regard to labor. When the negro is properly taught he learns to love labor instead of despising it. The negro throughout the South is beginning to see the dignity and beauty in labor.

He who would succeed with negro labor must let the negro see that he is treated as a man, not as a brute. If he is given a decent house for himself and family, and not made to work an unreasonable number of hours during the day, he will repay anyone in high profits who thus treats him and at nearly one-half the cost paid to Northern white farm help.

Sooner or later this country is going to realize that it has at its very doors the best labor that the world has seen.

The vast unoccupied lands in the South, with its mellow climate and the strong and willing arm of the negro, are simply waiting for those with capital, foresight and faith to step in and occupy.

Conditions at the South are too often misunderstood by Northern and Western people in another direction. Those who get their information from newspaper dispatches alone are likely to get the impression that there is continual friction between the white and colored people in the South. The fact is that the newspaper reports, as a rule, give the worst side. Outbreaks of lawlessness are widely reported, while the evidences of friendly relations now to be found in every part of the South are seldom referred to. In most sections of the South there is little, if any, trouble between the two races. As the colored people continue to grow in intelligence, property, thrift and character there will be less trouble. And still more will friction disappear as the white people grow in the same direction. Within the last few months I have attended several county fairs. In each case I found both the white and colored people making exhibits together, and there was the most friendly rivalry. In one case the fair was in charge of the colored people, but the white people made exhibits and some of them acted as judges. In another case colored people were awarded first prizes over their white competitors; one colored man won the prize for the best bushel of corn and another for the best cow.

At the Tuskegee Normal and Industrial Institute a few days ago we had the annual opening of our new agricultural hall. The secretary of agriculture, a republican, was present and spoke; the governor of Alabama, a democrat and ex-Confederate soldier, was present and spoke; also the State commissioner of agriculture. Besides, there were hundreds of the best white farmers, together with hundreds of colored people. There was the most friendly feeling shown throughout the day. These are only a few of the many evidences of the growing friendship of the two races.[1]

Southern States Farm Magazine, 5 (Jan. 1898), 496-98. An AMf of this article is in Con. 864, BTW Papers, DLC. BTW capitalized "Negro" throughout; the magazine editors printed the word in lower case.

[1] Charles William Dabney, president of the University of Tennessee and an editorial contributor to the *Southern States Farm Magazine,* wrote to BTW praising this article. "I am glad that you have spoken out so plainly and strongly," he wrote. "What a pity," Dabney lamented, "that all of our institutions for the 'brother in black' are not upon the same basis as yours." He told BTW that "I am convinced that your policy is the only true one, and that they must all come to it." He believed that "a vast deal of money and honest work has been wasted in trying to make literary men, or teachers, or preachers out of colored boys which should have been expended in teaching them how to be independent." (Dabney to BTW, Dec. 30, 1897, Con. 127, BTW Papers, DLC.)

From George Washington Henderson

New Orleans, La., Feb. 2 1898

Dear Mr. Washington: Last Spring when I started a series of meetings in the interest of the common people you were kind enough to say in response to an invitation, that though prevented by prior engagements from accepting, you would come another year, should the invitation be re-extended.

I write you now to claim the fulfilment of this promise.

Our movement has now assumed an organized shape under the name of the Society to promote the public health, the public morals and popular education and general progress. Our central idea, however, is education in its various forms, and in line therewith our first task is to secure from the state the establishment of a normal and industrial school. Not much can be done for our public schools till we have more and better qualified teachers.

A Constitutional Convention to place the suffrage upon an educational basis meets in this city Feb. 8. We intend to ask that Convention to provide for a normal school.

We have taken our stand on this subject of education to fight the battle for the rights of our citizenship. A Memorial a copy of which is enclosed will be presented.

Our plan is to have a popular meeting at the time the subject of education is taken up by the Convention, to endorse this Memorial, and we wish you to address this meeting, and, if possible, we will get you a chance to address the Convention. In this we have the co-operation of influential white gentlemen — among them Senator D. M. Sholars[1] whom you may remember.

Our Memorial has already been endorsed in strong editorials by every influential paper in this city.

The time cannot now be definitely stated, but we think the last part of Feb. or the first of March.

A formal communication from our Secretary will be sent you.

We assume your expenses, and you will be cordially entertained at Straight University.

May I hope for an early and favorable reply? We shall need you whether we get a hearing before the convention or not. Our object is to create a strong public sentiment in the hope that if we fail before the Convention, we may succeed before the legislature later on.

Trusting that you will have a successful Conference this year as usual, and assuring you of my presence in spirit if not in body I remain, Very Cordially Yours–

Geo. W. Henderson

ALS   Con. 140   BTW Papers   DLC.

[1] Dennis M. Sholars (b. 1854) was a white attorney in New Orleans, in partnership with Charles A. Schreiber.

To Edward H. Weston[1]

[Tuskegee, Ala.] Feb. 3, 1898

Mr. Weston: Considering the fact that you have been spoken to several times in regard to your relations with the girl students and the further fact that you have not ceased communicating with the girls as shown by a recent letter, I deem it best that the school have your resignation take effect from this date. The dignity of the whole corps of teachers is lowered by the action of one that is classed as an officer of the institution. I am very sorry personally to be forced to take this action but I am sure that you have had plenty of warning as to what the policy and wish of the institution is in such matters and I cannot suffer the institution to be injured by the action of a single individual. I hope that you will not let this discourage or dishearten you and that you will learn a lesson from this that will be valuable to you in the future. If I can be of service to you at any time please let me know.

Booker T. Washington

TLpS Con. 282A BTW Papers DLC.

¹ Edward H. Weston was a stenographer in the business agent's office at Tuskegee Institute from 1897 to 1900. Despite BTW's letter he remained on the staff until 1900, when he suddenly resigned and married a pregnant employee of the Tuskegee sales room. (See Warren Logan to BTW, June 19, 1900, and Logan to BTW, June 20, 1900, below.) In July 1900 Weston was in Richmond, Va., seeking employment from BTW's friend Giles B. Jackson. (Jackson to BTW, July 27, 1900, Con. 176, BTW Papers, DLC.)

From George Washington Henderson

New Orleans, La., Feb. 10 1898

Dear Mr. Washington: Your kind letter is at hand. I thank you very much for it, and for the efforts you are making to help us. We are at a critical juncture in our history; much with reference to the future depends upon our success or failure.

You anticipated our wishes in urging Dr. Curry to come to our aid. I have written him a letter, but possibly it will not reach him before his arrival.

Our aim is to have you address both our people and the Convention, but we are unable at this moment to assure you of a hearing before the Convention. Senator Sholars is working with us to this end, and when Dr. Curry comes, we will invoke his help. We feel quite confident of success, and will let you know at the earliest moment. Should we fail to get you before the Convention, we will get the Convention

379

before you — that is, we will see that many of the delegates shall have a chance to hear you. There will be no difficulty in bringing this to pass. Consequently in any event, you will need to have both barrels of your gun loaded.

I will write you again as soon as I can get matters in a more definite shape. Very Truly Yours–

Geo. W. Henderson

ALS   Con. 140   BTW Papers   DLC.

A Grocery Receipt

New York, Feb 14 1898

Sold to Mr. Booker T. Washington, TUSKEGEE, ALA.

3	jar Quinces	.85
3	" Peaches	.85
1	20 oz Pineapple	.45
1	bot Bartlett Pears	.55
9	lb. can Petit Beurre	2.02
1	can Lobster	.32
1	" Turkey	.42
1	" Tongue	.35
2	lb. tin Corn Beef	.25
2	" " Roast "	.25
1	can Shrimp	.25
1	" Sardines	.30
1	doz Anheuser Busch	1.25
1	" Bass	2.00
1	bot Glenlivet	1.50
1	" Wise's Irish	1.50
1	bot. One Star Hennesy	1.45
1	" Rock & Rye	1.00
1	bot. Waldorf Oroloso	.90
1	" Jockey Club	1.00
		17.46

HD   Con. 126   BTW Papers   DLC.   On stationery of F. A. Cauchois & Company, 40 East 42nd Street.

An Open Letter to the Louisiana Constitutional Convention[1]

Tuskegee, Alabama, Feb. 19, 1898

TO THE LOUISIANA STATE CONSTITUTIONAL CONVENTION: In addressing you this letter, I know that I am running the risk of appearing to meddle with something that does not concern me. But since I know that nothing but sincere love for our beautiful Southland, which I hold as near to my heart as any of you can, and a sincerer love for every black and white man within her borders, is the only thing actuating me to write, I am willing to be misjudged, if need be, if I can accomplish a little good.

But I do not believe that you, gentlemen of the Convention, will misinterpret my motives. What I say will, I believe, be considered in the same earnest spirit in which I write.

I am no politician; on the other hand, I have always advised my race to give attention to acquiring property, intelligence and character, as the necessary bases of good citizenship, rather than to mere political agitation. But the question upon which I write is out of the region of ordinary politics; it affects the civilization of two races, not for a day alone, but for a very long time to come; it is up in the region of duty of man to man, of Christian to Christian.

Since the war, no State has had such an opportunity to settle for all time the race question, so far as it concerns politics, as is now given in Louisiana. Will your Convention set an example to the world in this respect? Will Louisiana take such high and just grounds in respect to the Negro that no one can doubt that the South is as good a friend to the Negro as he possesses elsewhere? In all this, gentlemen of the Convention, I am not pleading for the Negro alone, but for the morals, the higher life of the white man, as well. For the more I study this question, the more I am convinced that it is not so much a question as to what the white man will do with the Negro, as to what the Negro will do with the white man's civilization.

The Negro agrees with you that it is necessary to the salvation of the South that restriction be put upon the ballot. I know that you have two serious problems before you; ignorant and corrupt government on the one hand, and on the other, a way to restrict the ballot so that control will be in the hands of the intelligent, without regard to race.

With the sincerest sympathy with you in your efforts to find a way out of the difficulty, I want to suggest that no State in the South can make a law that will provide an opportunity or temptation for an ignorant white man to vote and withhold the same opportunity from an ignorant colored man, without injuring both men. No State can make a law that can thus be executed, without dwarfing for all time the morals of the white man in the South. Any law controlling the ballot, that is not absolutely just and fair to both races, will work more permanent injury to the whites than to the blacks.

The Negro does not object to an educational or property test, but let the law be so clear that no one clothed with State authority will be tempted to perjure and degrade himself, by putting one interpretation upon it for the white man and another for the black man. Study the history of the South, and you will find that where there has been the most dishonesty in the matter of voting, there you will find to-day the lowest moral condition of both races. First, there was the temptation to act wrongly with the Negro's ballot. From this it was an easy step to dishonesty with the white man's ballot, to the carrying of concealed weapons, to the murder of a Negro, and then to the murder of a white man, and then to lynching. I entreat you not to pass such a law as will prove an eternal millstone about the neck of your children.

No man can have respect for government and officers of the law, when he knows, deep down in his heart, that the exercise of the franchise is tainted with fraud.

The road that the South has been compelled to travel during the last thirty years has been strewn with thorns and thistles. It has been as one groping through the long darkness into the light. The time is not distant when the world will begin to appreciate the real character of the burden that was imposed upon the South when 4,500,000 ex-slaves, ignorant and impoverished, were given the franchise. No people had ever been given such a problem to solve. History had blazed no path through the wilderness that could be followed. For thirty years, we wandered in the wilderness. We are beginning to get out. But there is but one road out, and all makeshifts, expedients, "profit and loss calculations," but lead into the swamps, quicksands, quagmires and jungles. There is a highway that will lead both races out into the pure, beautiful sunshine, where there will be nothing to hide and nothing to explain, where both races can grow strong and true and useful in every fibre of their being. I believe that your Convention will find this

382

highway; that it will enact a fundamental law which will be absolutely just and fair to white and black alike.

I beg of you, further, that in the degree that you close the ballot-box against the ignorant, that you open the school house. More than one half of the people of your State are Negroes. No State can long prosper when a large percentage of its citizenship is in ignorance and poverty, and has no interest in government. I beg of you that you do not treat us as alien people. We are not aliens. You know us; you know that we have cleared your forests, tilled your fields, nursed your children and protected your families. There is an attachment between us that few understand. While I do not presume to be able to advise you, yet it is in my heart to say that if your Convention would do something that would prevent, for all time, strained relations between the two races, and would permanently settle the matter of political relations in our Southern States, at least, let the very best educational opportunities be provided for both races; and add to this the enact-ment of an election law that shall be incapable of unjust discrimination, at the same time providing that in proportion as the ignorant secure education, property and character, they will be given the right of citi-zenship. Any other course will take from one-half your citizens interest in the State, and hope and ambition to become intelligent producers and taxpayers — to become useful and virtuous citizens. Any other course will tie the white citizens of Louisiana to a body of death.

The Negroes are not unmindful of the fact that the white people of your State pay the greater proportion of the school taxes, and that the poverty of the State prevents it from doing all that it desires for public education; yet I believe you will agree with me, that ignorance is more costly to the State than education; that it will cost Louisiana more not to educate her Negroes than it will cost to educate them. In connection with a generous provision for public schools, I believe that nothing will so help my own people in your State as provision at some institution for the highest academic and normal training, in connection with thorough training in agriculture, mechanics and domestic econ-omy. The fact is that 90 per cent. of our people depend upon the common occupations for their living, and outside of the cities 85 per cent. depend upon agriculture for support. Notwithstanding this, our people have been educated since the war in everything else but the very thing that most of them live by. First-class training in agriculture, horticulture, dairying, stock-raising, the mechanical arts and domestic economy, will make us intelligent producers, and not only help us to contribute our proportion as taxpayers, but will result in retaining much money in the State that now goes outside for that which can be produced in the State. An institution that will give this training of the hand, along with the highest mental culture, will soon convince our people that their salvation is in the ownership of property, industrial and business development, rather than in mere political agitation.

The highest test of the civilization of any race is in its willingness to extend a helping hand to the less fortunate. A race, like an individual, lifts itself up by lifting others up. Surely no people ever had a greater chance to exhibit the highest Christian fortitude and magnanimity than is now presented to the people of Louisiana. It requires little wisdom or statesmanship to repress, to crush out, to retard the hopes and aspirations of a people, but the highest and most profound statesmanship is shown in guiding and stimulating a people so that every fibre in the body, mind and soul shall be made to contribute in the highest degree to the usefulness and nobility of the State. It is along this line that I pray God the thoughts and activities of your Convention be guided. Respectfully submitted,

Booker T. Washington

PDSr Con. 955 BTW Papers DLC.

1 Both the New Orleans *Picayune*, Feb. 21, 1898, 4, and the New Orleans *Times-Democrat*, Feb. 21, 1898, 4, published BTW's letter. In a brief editorial, the *Picayune* said: "Its doctrines are sound, its conclusions are just and temperate, and the *Picayune* fully indorses them." The *Times-Democrat* acknowledged the extreme antipathy of some members of the convention toward permitting blacks to vote at all and had little hope for BTW's plan that suffrage be based on property or education, not on race. Agreeing with BTW, the paper said that the suffrage clauses "should be straightforward and free from all fraud or trickery."

From Daniel Webster Bythewood[1]

Beaufort S.C. Feb 26th 1898

Dear Sir: I have read with intense interest your Article on Industrial Training for the Negro. We endorse your doctrine and feel that we cannot well get along without such training in our section of the country.

We are living in a rich country so far as the soil is concerned, with little or no skill among the working classes to command it. Our streets are sometimes thronged with a beggarly element, possessing acres of land not having sufficient skill to eke out an honest, respectable living.

The great problem with us, in this section, is what shall we do with this beggarly element that feed themselves a few months in the year and beg the balance.

Were it not for fish and oysters, things that really grow without cultivation, the situation would be most apalling sometimes. Agriculture is fast becoming a lost art among our people. Our older mechanics that have mastered the situation and bore the burden in the heat of the day for thirty years are passing out and we find none or at least few that are prepared to take their places.

We doubt not that during thirty years of freedom the Negro is fast losing one of his strongest lines of salvation — viz. the Industrial Art. I asked one of my members a few months ago, who plants about five acres of land in cotten, how much cotten he expects to get or does he get from so many acres and his reply was "about one bale and a half of lint cotten."

Think of a rich plain country bringing only one bale and a half to five acres of land. Land that ought to bring easily one bale to an acre. What we want to do is to teach this man's son to command better results from the soil than his father.

This is not an abnormal circumstance. Now to the point. Mrs A. H. Christensen[2] a resident of Beaufort and who also has a home in Brookline Mass. is agitating the matter of an Industrial school here for the Negro and we are all anxious for it but we want you to suggest some plans for organization and operation. If you will do this you will confer a great favor on us and a blessing upon our people. Mrs A. H. Christensen met your wife during last summer. You do not know me and as near as I can tell you who I am is to wit, I am a graduate of Lincoln University. I was there some years ago when you delivered the annual address for the Philosophian Literary Society. Mr. Alton Bythewood who attended your School last year is a first cousin of mine.

Kindly let me hear from you at once. Yours for the best things for the race,

D. W. Bythewood

ALS Con. 137 BTW Papers DLC.

¹ Daniel Webster Bythewood was born in Madison, Fla., in 1865 and moved with his family to Beaufort, S.C. He graduated from Lincoln University in 1889 and received an S.T.B. degree there in 1892. For the next two years Bythewood taught at Beaufort High School and then became superintendent. For many years, beginning in 1897, he was pastor of the Tabernacle Baptist Church of Beaufort, preaching that blacks would only progress when accorded full civil rights.

² Abbie H. Christensen probably moved to Beaufort, S.C., from Brookline, Mass., in 1896.

To Margaret James Murray Washington

[Tuskegee, Ala.] March 5, 1898

Mrs. B. T. Washington: In my efforts to get funds for the support of the school this year, it occurs to me that perhaps some of the teachers might count it a privilege to make a contribution towards the support of the school. If you can see your way clear to help in this way, I shall be glad of anything that you can contribute. Yours truly,

Booker T. Washington

TLS Con. 15 BTW Papers ATT. Original destroyed. Margaret Washington wrote on the letter: "Mr. Logan, Will you please take $5.00 five dollars from my acc. for this. Mrs. W. Mch. 10–98."

To William Jenkins

[Tuskegee, Ala.] Mar. 6, 1898

Mr. Jenkins: After giving the matter the most thorough consideration, the six teachers who have had the matter in charge — all of whom are your personal and official friends — are unanimous in the decision that owing to the charges brought against you by two girl students and the evidence found to sustain these charges, that it would not be best for you nor for the school for you to longer remain connected with it.¹

In informing you of this decision I think I am safe in saying that it is the most painful duty that I have been called upon to perform during my connection with the institution.

I have never had one whom I considered a more reliable and close personal friend nor do I believe that this institution has ever had one connected with it, who at all times under all circumstances has watched and sustained its interests and whose heart was so deeply in the work. All these facts add to the pain of the decision on the part of those who have so long and pleasantly associated with you and your family. I hope that you will not let this unfortunate affair discourage and dishearten you. You are a young man and can still find a way to accomplish good in the world. If I can consistently serve you in any capacity at any time I shall be very glad to do so. I shall always feel under personal obligation to you for many kindnesses. Yours truly,

[Booker T. Washington]

Please turn your department over to. . . .

TLp   Con. 282A   BTW Papers   DLC.

[1] In the spring of 1898, thirty-eight-year-old William Jenkins, head teacher of the academic department at Tuskegee, was charged by two girl students with making sexual advances. Jenkins's longtime friendship with BTW and his wife and his outstanding service to the school for many years made it particularly hard for BTW to dismiss him. After his dismissal, Jenkins tried to organize a faculty and student protest. Twenty-six faculty members notified BTW that they believed Jenkins was innocent, and a number of students demanded his reinstatement. BTW wrote Warren Logan that he would ignore the faculty protest, and he thought it unwise "to have students meddling with such affairs." (BTW to Logan, Mar. 9, 1898, Con. 15, BTW Papers, DLC.)

From Henry D. Davidson[1]

Centreville. Ala. March 7th 1898

My dear Sir: There is an organization at Springfield Ohio, known as the Anti-Mob & Lynch Law Association, with Messrs W. H. Dickson[2] E. T. Butler[3] & S. E. Huffman[4] as President, organizer & Sect. respectively. It has for its object the suppression of the mobbing and Lynching of colored men in the U.S. This to be done by *petitioning the various Legislatures* of the several states and the *National Congress* at Washington to so *enact* or *amend* the Laws to bring about a halt of these audacious atrocities. I write to ask — as I consider you one of the leading thinkers of our Race — if you think that such is a wise proceedure to accomplish any good, and to assertain as to whether you have any acquaintance with the above organization. What do you think of it? An early reply will greatly oblige me. Yours very truly.

H. D. Davidson

ALS   Con. 127   BTW Papers   DLC.

¹ Henry D. Davidson, a schoolteacher, born in Alabama in 1869.
² William H. Dickson, a blacksmith, born in Tennessee in 1840.
³ President of the National Agitator Printing and Publishing Company, publisher of the Springfield *National Agitator,* a black weekly newspaper.
⁴ Samuel E. Huffman, a porter, born in Kentucky in 1858.

From George Washington Henderson

New Orleans, La., Mar. 9 1898

Dear Mr. Washington: The Convention has been so absorbed in considering the Suffrage that we have been unable to get a hearing yet.

The Committee on Education will probable give us a hearing soon now, as the Suffrage question will probably be out of the way in about a week.

Would it be possible for you to come here about 15th? Or how soon could you come?

It has been impossible for us to fix a date till now, and even now we are unable to be specific.

I think, however, that it will be all right if you can come in about a week or ten days.

We hope to get you a chance to speak before the Convention, and influential white gentlemen think the best way is to have you here on the ground before we make formal application.

I thank you for your wise and able letter. It was very well received by the press here, and I am sure will do us good.

Dr. Curry gave an address of remarkable power and courage. No one could have spoken more plainly, and his address was well received by the Convention.

Please let me hear soon. I note with great satisfaction the splendid success of your last Conference. It was not possible for me to attend. Cordially Yours–

Geo. W. Henderson

ALS   Con. 140   BTW Papers   DLC.

To John Davis Long

Tuskegee, Alabama. March 15, 1898

My dear sir: In times like these it is easy to grow excited. I do not write in a spirit of excitement, but from a genuine wish to be of service to our country, should events so shape themse[l]ves as to make this service needed. In common with all good citizens the Negro race abhors war, but should war be forced upon us I belie[v]e that the Negro race is in a position to render a service to our country that no other race can.

The climate of Cuba is peculiar and danger[o]us to the unaclimated white man. The Negro race in the South is accustomed to this climate. In the event of war I would be responsible for placing at the service of the government at least ten thousand loyal, brave, strong black men in the South who crave an opportunity to show their loyalty to our land and wo[u]ld gladly take this method of showing their gratitude for the lives laid down and the sacrifices made that the Negro might have his freedom and rights. Yours obediently,

[Booker T. Washington]

~~In saying this I am not unmindful of the fact that my race has suffered and still suffers wrongs, but when the welfare and honor of country~~

ALd   Con. 161   BTW Papers   DLC.

From John Stephens Durham

San Pedro De Macoris, Republica Dominicana, March 15, 1898

My dear Mr. Washington: It is too rich to keep, that story about the return of the Montgomery tin smiths to work with the students. That is the stuff and it is the biggest lesson which Tuskegee has ever taught to my knowledge. I have read with the deepest interest the clipping which you send me in your welcome letter of the tenth ult referring to the discussion at Federation Congress. Gompers[1] is at bottom all right. His management of the Cigar makers Union was as fair as possible. When he plunged into general leadership, however he began to trim. McGuire[2] is a low demagogue at heart and he shows it in the small personality which he injected into the discussion. I have been hammering at those same fellows for the past fifteen years. General Armstrong thought my editorials inexpedient; but, in our warm discussions of his ideas of race differences — and they were always of the most friendly nature — we invariably ended with my remark that the best authority as to where the shoe pinches is the man wearing the shoe. I have been through it all — from my place behind the white man's chair to square competition with him in professional and business life. My experience tells me that the labor unions — fighting as they are for equality of opportunity for their own people and denying it to us — offer the most vulnerable point of attack for us. I may be wrong; but I think the general tone of newspaper comment among the white editors will support my unhesitating belief in the American spirit of fair play. When a large firm in Philadelphia declined to consider my application to put a colored girl behind one of its counters, our little society went directly to the organization to which the greater number of the girls employed belonged. Minton, Mrs. Coppin and I told them that the application had been denied on the ground that the white employees would object. We stated our case and asked them to consider the matter and take a vote at the next monthly meeting in our absence. The girls voted all right and we went back to the firm with the report of the vote. The colored girl secured the place.

I am glad to know all you say about Fortune. I am writing him by this steamer and so will send no message.

Mrs. Durham is pleased to hear from you and joins me in sending greetings to Mrs. Washington and you. She will go north as soon as the fever season threatens and will doubtless be ahead of me. She will be at 4816 Florence Avenue, West Philadelphia, after the middle of May and will be pleased to see you should you be in Philadelphia.

I am working like a fiend. Our cane is poorer this year than last and the price is lower. We are trying to make up the difference by better work than I was able to do as a green hand a year ago. As I have ten cents in every dollar of profit, you can imagine how absorbed I am in this year's work. I have been quite ill too and that fact makes the work seem draggy when really we are doing very well.

Do let me hear from you when your many occupations will give the time. Truly yours,

John S. Durham

TLS Con. 146 BTW Papers DLC.

[1] Samuel Gompers (1850-1924), an English-born cigar maker, was a founder and first president (1886-94, 1895-1924) of the American Federation of Labor. Despite his belief in the class solidarity of labor, Gompers shared in the racial bias of his society, and the A.F. of L. unions generally excluded blacks.

[2] Peter J. McGuire, another A.F. of L. leader.

From Josephine Beall Wilson Bruce

Washin[gton] D.C. Mch 15 1898

Mr Bruce is very sick indeed have telegraphed for Roscoe.[1]

Mrs. B K Bruce

HWSr   Con. 539   BTW Papers   DLC.

[1] Roscoe Conkling Bruce (1879-1952), the son of Blanche Kelso Bruce and Josephine B. Wilson Bruce, was named for the U.S. senator from New York who led the fight for seating B. K. Bruce as senator from Mississippi. From 1896 to 1898 R. C. Bruce attended Phillips Exeter Academy, and from 1898 to 1902 he attended Harvard, where he studied the humanities and was elected to Phi Beta Kappa. In his third year, however, on BTW's advice, he began the study of education. He graduated magna cum laude and delivered the 1902 class oration. In the fall of 1902, at the age of twenty-three, Bruce became the head of the academic department at Tuskegee.

In 1906 he moved to Washington, D.C., as a supervising principal of the black public schools, and the next year became assistant superintendent in charge of black schools. Following the Tuskegee philosophy, Bruce established trade schools for boys and girls and recommended the founding of an agricultural school. His successful efforts to establish the first black junior high school and to develop a black teachers' college reflected the influence on him of Charles W. Eliot. In addition, Bruce fought to establish his autonomy as the head of the black schools. Bruce was able to keep the support of the white superintendent and school board, but he was never popular with the black professional class of the city. His emphasis on vocational and industrial education and his frequently dogmatic personnel policies aroused these black citizens to organize the Parents' League and seek Bruce's removal from office. A board of education investigation of Bruce's administrative capacity in 1921, after a sex scandal in the black schools, cleared Bruce of all charges. Bruce resigned soon afterward and became principal and teacher of the Brown Creek District High School in Kimball, W.Va. In 1923 he returned to Washington, D.C., to manage his farm. During the Depression Bruce managed the Paul Laurence Dunbar Apartments, an unsuccessful Rockefeller-financed middle-class cooperative in Harlem. He was later involved in several real-estate ventures.

To Josephine Beall Wilson Bruce

[Tuskegee, Ala.] Mar 18 1898

You have our deepest sympathy in your great bereavement. Your husband was great, good and true. May God give you strength to bear your sorrow.

Booker T. Washington

AWS   Con. 539   BTW Papers   DLC.

From John Davis Long

Washington, March 18, 1898

My dear Mr. Washington: I write to acknowledge the receipt of your letter, tendering your services, in case of an emergency, and your readiness to enlist ten thousand men in the cause of the national defense.

Permit me to express my very great appreciation of the patriotic spirit you have manifested and the admirable manner in which you have written. Very truly yours,

John D. Long

TLS   Con. 142   BTW Papers   DLC.

To Hollis Burke Frissell

Tuskegee, Ala., 3, 19, 1898

Dear Dr. Frissell: When in New York a few days ago Mr. W. Bayard Cutting[1] spoke to me rather strongly about the importance of something being done to stop the very large number of persons who are going North to represent small schools in the South; he says that the matter is fast becoming disgusting to many generous people and that if it is not stopped it will hurt the whole cause permanently. Is it not practical for the Hampton board of trustees to put on foot some plan that will help in this matter?

I hope you have invited Mr. Cutting to attend the Hampton Commencement, he wants to do so and I am sure will go if you urge him. Yours truly,

Booker T. Washington

TLS   BTW Folder   ViHaI.

[1] William Bayard Cutting (1850-1912) was a New York financier. He served on the U.S. Civil Service Commission in 1896-97 and was a trustee of Columbia University from 1880 until his death.

From Benjamin J. Bridgers[1]

Macon Ga. March 19th 1898

my dear sir   It was with much regret that I read your letter of the 15 inst stating you could not be with us on the 15 of nex month as your present in this city would meet with the warm welcome of both white and colord. now as there will be a District meeting of the Anti Mob & Lynch Law Association held in this city on th 27 day of may I beg to no if you can manage to be with us on that night to Address the people on mobbing & Lynching and the General condition of the Country. we would be glad to have you with us that day. however as I fine that most all of the big men that speaks in Macon makes it night so that the working class of men can have a chance to heare them night would be best. let me no by early mail if you will come and speak for us at night. If so I shall try to secure the opera house for you to speak in, or some other place that will hold the multitude that will turn out. I am yours awaiting further favors

B. J. Bridgers
Grand Deputy Anti Mob
and Lynch Law Association

ALS   Con. 137   BTW Papers   DLC.

[1] Benjamin J. Bridgers was reported in Macon city directories as a black preacher, and in the 1900 census as president of a black orphanage.

393

From Timothy Thomas Fortune

Winston N.C., March 24, 1898

Dear Friend: I got here in good shape at 1:30 today, but has been raining ever since I got here.

I see that the President has appointed Lyons[1] to succeed Bruce, and it seems to me that he was *indecently hasty* in filling the vacancy, as Bruce was only buried the day before. But perhaps you and I are too sensitive on these high matters of *political morality,* or immorality as the case may be. I am sure there is nothing of that sort of politics in me nor in you. I hope before you leave for the North you will see to it that Mr. Saffold has those other "Talks" made up, so that I can have them when I am in New York April 2.

Dr. Rainsford[2] was a very pleasant companion up.

With kind regards for you and the family, Yours truly

T. Thomas Fortune

I have just finished dictating a column article on the dedication for The Sun,[3] but can't tell what manner of thing it is until the stenographer fetches it in, which he promises to do by 6 oclock. I am afraid that it will be too late for the Sunday edition.

F

ALS   Con. 139   BTW Papers   DLC.

[1] Judson Whitlocke Lyons, a leading black lawyer and politician, was born in Burke County, Ga., in 1860. He received a law degree from Howard University in 1884, was admitted to the Georgia bar the same year, and practiced in Augusta. A member of the professional-class, light-skinned black elite, Lyons was one of the few black politicians who opposed BTW's philosophy and influence. He received appointment as register of the Treasury in 1898 because he and other black delegates in the 1896 convention cast their votes for McKinley. Lyons managed to secure BTW's support for his reappointment in 1901 after Roosevelt became President. BTW discovered, however, that Lyons had expressed sympathy for W. Monroe Trotter after the Boston Riot in 1903, and he turned his considerable influence against Lyons. Lyons retained his seat on the Republican national committee until 1908, but he lost his position as register in 1905.

[2] William Stephen Rainsford, who delivered the principal address at the dedication of the Tuskegee chapel, was rector of St. George's Episcopal Church in New York City, the church of J. P. Morgan.

[3] Entitled "A Cathedral in the Black Belt," Fortune's article appeared in the New York *Sun,* Apr. 3, 1898, 6. He declared the chapel one of the finest church edifices in the South. He characterized Rainsford's address as endorsing the Tus-

kegee philosophy of educating the head, hand, and heart, and urging blacks to cultivate good relations with their white neighbors. A highlight of the ceremony was the singing of plantation songs by the Tuskegee Institute choir in the excellent acoustics of the new chapel.

From William Jenkins

Tuskegee Ala. Mar. 24/98

Dear Sir: Now that everything pertaining to my trial has quieted down, and second sober thought has had an opportunity to assert itself; I appeal to you, in justice to all parties concerned, for a re-hearing of my case. The ruin of my reputation may be of small moment to you; but it is a matter of life & death to me & mine.

I present the following reasons for my request:

1. The result of the Ethel DuVall charge should have been determined by facts rather than by belief — knowing that the presumption is usually with the woman.
2. The charge in Ethel's case was *not sustained*.
3. The combining of two cases so very unlike in every aspect was unjust, to say the least.
4. In the latter case I pleaded guilty, in part to indiscretion. No immorality was intended or shown.
5. I must have been convicted upon the first or second charge, not both. If upon the second, then I cannot but feel that the punishment was excessive.
6. As matters now stand the impression has gone forth that I attempted to commit rape. It is in your power to right this great wrong that has been done me and my family.

Mr. Washington you cannot afford to allow this great wrong to go unrighted. Respt.

Wm. Jenkins

ALS   Con. 141   BTW Papers   DLC.

To William Jenkins

[Tuskegee, Ala.] 3, 26, 1898

Mr. Jenkins: I have received your note of March 24th, and have considered it with care. There is nothing in reason that I would not give or do in order to change the present status of your case. It can not give you much more pain than it does me.[1]

You must bear in mind that we have not declared you guilty of the charge or charges, but we find that your name and the reputation of the school were so connected with the charges that to keep you here simply meant the ruin of all that we are trying to do.

Unless some new facts can be brought to light, to re-connect you with the school will simply mean the downfall of the school.

You will remember that on more than one occasion you have reminded me of the harm that has been done the school by the retaining of Mr. Penney. Now to add another case to this when in the minds of the committee the facts are more hurtful would simply be to ruin us all.

I feel just as tenderly and sorely for you as one individual can feel for another, but I cannot go beyond what I know to be right. If I can serve you further in the way of getting a position I shall be glad to do so.

You cannot class this case as a court case. In court it is true a charge must be proven, in a school when conditions are such that a teacher loses his usefulness there is nothing left but to act as we have. Yours sincerely,

Booker T. Washington

TLpS   Con. 282A   BTW Papers   DLC.

[1] BTW seems to have been sincerely compassionate. In November 1898, Jenkins was secretary of the Citizens' Commercial Union in Montgomery, which was run by BTW's friends including J. W. Adams, a Tuskegee trustee.

From William Jenkins

Tuskegee   Mar. 26 '98

Dear Sir: I still maintain that whenever a teacher or preacher becomes involved in a scandal his or her usefulness is impaired and for the good of the cause he or she should seek new fields of labor, whether guilty or innocent.

It is the manner of my taking off of which I complain. You will hardly find a disinterested person but who will say that I should have been given an opportunity to resign after the conflict was fairly settled; so that I could have found employment in the South along the line of my chosen profession.

I do not belong to that class of despoilers of homes that prey upon the virtue of our young girls. But the action of your committee has placed me thus.

I am willing to leave the matter with you & your God.

I have only one final request to make and that is that you will assist me in procuring work.

I ask this in behalf of my dear wife who is surely sinking under this great strain. Respectfully

Wm Jenkins

ALS   Con. 141   BTW Papers   DLC.

From William Watson Thompson[1]

Tuskegee, Ala., Mch 27 1898

Dear Sir: How many volenteers do you think your school could and would furnish in case of necesity to protect Mobile. My reason for making this request is that I want to communicate with Gov Joseph Johnston on tomorrow, and want to know about how many men Tuskegee can furnish on short notice. yours at command

Wm W Thompson
Mayor

ALS   Con. 147   BTW Papers   DLC.   Written on stationery of the Thompson Livery Co., W. W. Thompson, proprietor.

397

1 See above, 3:306. Thompson was sheriff of Macon County from 1892 to 1896 and from 1902 to 1906. He was mayor of Tuskegee from 1897 to 1899.

From Carleton Bartlett Gibson[1]

Columbus, Georgia   March 30, 1898

Dear Sir: Your work in the education of the young people of your race has been, you will permit me to say, so magnificent, and the results of your work so far in advance of anything that has been accomplished by any other institution in the South, that progressive educators do well to look to your excellent institution for advanced *practical* methods of teaching along the line of industrial training. I have given much study to the question of the education of the colored people of our city, and while I believe in a liberal policy in their education, I believe that we are not accomplishing the best results for them by confining them to the identical line of work undertaken in the white schools. We ought to work in some industrial and manual training even in our public school course.

As this matter will be brought before our Board on April 14 will you be kind enough to give me some helpful information.

First. What two lines of training do you consider most helpful to our colored youth, and at the same time most practical in a public school course, in point of cost and equipment?

Second. What is the cost of equipping such a school in teaching force and appliances for about forty pupils?

If this matter can be made of sufficient interest to our Board it is probable that a committee from the Board may wish to visit your institution. Yours very truly,

C. B. Gibson

TLS   Con. 183   BTW Papers   DLC.

1 Carleton Bartlett Gibson (1863-1927), as superintendent of the public schools of Columbus, Ga., from 1896 to 1909, was in many respects a white counterpart of BTW, seeking to train white cotton-mill children for the work they were to do. Born in Mobile, he was a graduate of the University of Alabama. After several educational administrative posts in Alabama, he moved to Columbus, where he became principal of the high school in 1894 and superintendent in 1896.

Gibson's inquiry of BTW and later visit to Tuskegee were part of his preparation for reorganizing the Columbus schools. In 1900, with financial aid from George

Foster Peabody, Gibson established the Primary Industrial School, which used few textbooks, had no grades or fixed course of studies, and had a term of twelve months. The school substituted tools and benches for textbooks, and some twenty lines of handicraft were taught. Other factory towns followed Gibson's example, notably Augusta under the leadership of Lawton B. Evans.

In 1909 George Eastman called Gibson to the presidency of the Mechanics Institute at Rochester, N.Y. His services as a Red Cross worker in Germany and Poland early in World War I undermined his health. Returning to the South after the war, he became principal of the Savannah public schools.

From William Watson Thompson

Tuskegee, Ala, Mch 31 1898

My Dear Sir: The Gov requests me to express to you his thanks for your offer of cooperation in case of necesity. Respect Yours

Wm W Thompson
Mayor

ALS   Con. 147   BTW Papers   DLC.

To Warren Logan

[Aboard Congressional Limited, Pennsylvania Railroad] April 1 1898

Dear Mr. Logan: I have it direct from a Cabinet officer that war is sure.

Reduce every expense to *lowest point*.

B. T. W.

ALI   Con. 15   BTW Papers   ATT.   Original destroyed.

From Mary Elizabeth Preston Stearns

Tufts College P.O. Masstts   April 2d 1898

Dear Friend, Ever since yours of the 28. ult. came to hand I have wanted to thank you for the "Open Letter," as well as your kind one

399

to me. Would to Heaven, that the former could have found the welcome that the latter received in all true sincerity and regard! Nothing could be more convincing than your wise, and kindly words.

The madness which refused such an appeal is a fearful condition that can only result in disaster, terrible to contemplate.

The Newspapers had given only a brief report of your Letter, or I had failed to see any other — and I am most glad to own it in permanent form.

Yes, as you suppose, the exciting events of the last weeks have overwhelmed me with dread and anxiety. War, is such a calamity — so unworthy of our better civillisation that it never occurred to me that I should live to see my country engaged in another, so crushing to all *my* joy in life. Tho' followed by sublime results for the oppressed; for which we sacrificed all private affections and interests.

I agree with you, had President McKinley been allowed to carry out his beneficent ideas, war might *possibly* have been averted. Can we be sufficiently grateful to the Ruler of the Universe, for that glorious *Man* and model President? Imagine Bryan! Horrors! All, that kindly; patient; judicious; magnanimous offers to Spain that could be made, that faithful Guardian of the People's welfare extended in the noblest spirit. But Spain, blind with *pride:* and deaf with *hate:* brutalised by centuries of crime: treachery; and cruelest oppression, could not understand this lofty and straightforward dealing. The frightful tragedy of the "Maine," stung the people to white heat; while the "Nemesis of Fate," was luring its besotted victim to destruction.

There is a retribution for crime that is sure as gravitation, and we may be the avenging angel as Senator Hoar said "St Michael and the Dragon." Four Hundred years, Spain has tortured *humanity*. She has supped full of horrors and signed her own Death warrent. Alas! how much innocent blood must be shed: how many hearts and homes wrecked forever! The old, old expiatory sacrifice.

The Naval battle yesterday would seem to point a speedy termination of hostilities. Heaven grant it!

This injustice of the Louisiana business, is full of peril; and I am worried about the terrible result. Think of the millions upon millions, spent in this War, and Tuskegee and Hampton without an endowment!

Well, we cannot help it. Let us pray that we may live long enough, to say as my hero Husband did, after the War for "Emancipation." "It was worth all it *cost*."

Give my love to the dear Boys, and Mrs Washington, and believe me faithfully Yours,

Mary E. Stearns

ALS   Con. 146   BTW Papers   DLC.

From Samuel S. Gilson[1]

Pittsburgh, Pa., April 2nd 98

Dear Sir   Will you please tell me to what denomination you belong? It was stated here recently in a public meeting that you were a Unitarian. I do not believe it, and I wish to correct the statement.

Let me know something as to your faith, and church connection, that I may use it to our interest. Expecting an early reply, I am, Yours Respectfully

(Rev) S. S. Gilson (DD)

ALS   Con. 140   BTW Papers   DLC.   Written on stationery of the *Presbyterian Banner.*

[1] Samuel S. Gilson (b. 1842) was a Presbyterian minister and principal of East Liberty Academy.

To Warren Logan

Grand Union Hotel   New York, April 5 1898

Dear Mr. Logan: War now seems sure. Buy nothing except *absolute necessities*. Live on the farms in every way as far as you can. Yours Sincerely

Booker T. Washington

ALS   Con. 15   BTW Papers   ATT.   Original destroyed.

From Edward Elder Cooper

Washington, D.C., April 5 1898

Friend Washington   I have just read in the Appeal an article under the caption "Blowing Hot and Cold" in which editor Taylor[1] makes the remarkable statement that I show him a letter from you in which you asked me to boom you for a place in the McKinley cabinet. This is an infamous lie and I shall so state it in this weeks Colored American.

You never wrote me such a letter and it would be impossible for me to show anyone a letter which I never received. I did boom you and the late B K Bruce as cabinet size race timber but it was not from any suggestion from you.

I write this letter for your own as well as my protection. Very Sincerely,

E. E. Cooper

ALS   Con. 138   BTW Papers   DLC.

[1] Charles Henry James Taylor (1856-99) was born in Alabama, lived for a time in Savannah, Ga., and attended the University of Michigan. Taylor moved to Kansas City, Kan., where he practiced law and edited the Kansas City *World*. An active Democrat, he was appointed assistant city attorney in 1885 and briefly was minister to Liberia during Cleveland's first administration. With other black Democratic leaders, Taylor thought blacks should vote their interests rather than continue in blind loyalty to the Republican party. In 1889 Taylor called for conciliation with the South: "I have never known a respectable committee of colored men to ask in a respectful manner for a favor from the rulers of the South but what it was instantly granted." Pursuing the economics-before-politics argument, Taylor urged blacks to become self-reliant: "It makes me sick to hear Negroes sending up baby appeals as though they were never to grow to manhood, whereasing and resolving in halls about their wrongs, when they themselves do more to perpetuate these evils than anybody else." (Taylor, *Whites and Blacks,* 28, 51.)

After he returned from Liberia in 1887, Taylor practiced law in Atlanta, where he also edited the *Southern Appeal* and wrote for southern white newspapers. Returning to Kansas City in 1890, Taylor continued his law practice and edited the *American Citizen.* Taylor was recorder of deeds for the District of Columbia from 1894 to 1897 and then returned to Georgia, where he edited the Atlanta *Appeal* until his death. (Meier, *Negro Thought,* 32, 36, 82.)

From Timothy Thomas Fortune

New York, April 6, 1898

Dear Friend: I enclose the Appeal article which I thought I had in the batch yesterday. I also enclose a letter from Cooper bearing on one statement in the article. Thus far I have not deemed it wise and judicious to bother with Taylor, as it is true that we can't play with mud without getting some of it stuck to you. Return the matter, and next week I may decide to use the charge and the refutation. It may be wise and good to get these two fakes and liars pulling each others hair.

I had to stop by Mrs. Matthews on the way over yesterday about a current publication for today and she said she wanted 9,000 words out of your Sunday talks to complete her collection which she says the Putnams are to consider. I have written her word that some of Saffold's notes have just reached me and that she may cull them if she wants to. Is that right? I also wrote her that in view of the fact that we are to publish the addresses we would have been glad to consider the matter of handling her collection. The publication of hers by Putnams will certainly affect the sale of ours.

Please return the Taylor-Cooper and the Louisiana matter as soon as you have finished with them.

I am feeling rather firm in all directions today. Your friend

T. Thomas Fortune

ALS Con. 139 BTW Papers DLC.

From Daniel Webster Bythewood

Beaufort S.C. April 7th 1898

Dear Friend: I herewith enclose you a script containing the plan of our school. We shall be glad if you might make any suggestions that are helpful to us. We shall be glad also with your consent to be considered or designated as a branch of "The Tuskegee Industrial Institute." You will at the proper time be called upon to supply or name the man for the principalship. We shall hope to begin work next Fall D.V.

We were deeply grateful for the contribution sent, but we regret to say that we have mislaid the same or some one has kindly consented to keep it for us. Will you kindly cancel the duplicate or stub and send us the amount? We shall feel greatly favored. Send the Amount direct to Capt N. Christensen,[1] the treasurer of our board of trustees.

Capt N. Christensen of Bft. S.C promises the land to the Amount 125 Acres. He is a strong sympathizer and promises to be a great bene-factor of the school. What we need is money for construction and operation.

Since my communication with you we have organized our board. I have been elected president of the same, Rev. G. M. Elliott[2] Secre-tary, Capt N. Christensen, Treasurer.

We shall be glad to hear from you at your earliest convenience. Yours fraternally,

D. W. Bythewood

Plan of proposed School.

In view of the lamentable condition of ignorance, superstition, pov-erty and vice prevailing among many of the people on our Sea Island plantations it [is] proposed to establish a school on Port Royal Island after the Tuskegee plan.

This school in its beginning shall chiefly aim to instruct the people in better cultivation of land, care of stock and improved manner of living, and as it progresses it will hope to add instruction in carpentry, bricklaying, printing and other trades, besides teaching the women and girls cooking, sewing nursing and home-making.

At least three hours a day shall be devoted to the study of English branches, especially reading, writing and arithmetic.

Above all this school shall endeavor to accomplish the moral eleva-tion of our people of the Sea Islands of South Carolina.

For this undertaking we earnestly solicit the prayers the sympathy and the financial aid of every lover of humanity.

ALS Con. 137 BTW Papers DLC.

[1] Niels Christensen, Jr., son of Abbie H. Christensen. (See Bythewood to BTW, Feb. 26, 1898, above.) He was an active promoter of black schools in the Sea Islands for many years.
[2] George M. Elliott.

From Timothy Thomas Fortune

New York, April 8, 1898

Dear Friend: I have your letters of the 6th and 7th instants, with enclosures, which latter I return herewith. The Times Democrat editorial is very strong, and I am disposed to regard the matter from that standpoint rather than the one you seem to regard it. There is no saving grace in the law as it stands. The vicious thing about it is that it was enacted for *the expressed purpose of disfranchising Afro-Americans* and not to place the suffrage in the keeping of the *intelligence* of the State, a justice for which you made your plea. The enactment as it stands is entirely immoral and vicious. I regret the misplacement of the Picayune, as I wanted to write a special article based upon the text of the law. But never mind about it.

I quite agree with the view you take of the Taylor matter. I shall give him no more publicity than possible.

I have written Mrs Matthews that she can have the use of the talks in my possession. We shall have to talk over the situation in view of her publication.

I have the nervous shakes today and am afraid I shall not be able to get up this afternoon. If not I shall try to do so Sunday afternoon. Yours truly

T Thomas Fortune

ALS   Con. 139   BTW Papers   DLC.

From Max Bennett Thrasher[1]

Boston, Mass. Apr. 20th. 189[8?]

Dear Mr. Washington, Your second letter is at hand. The offer which you make is very attractive. I would dearly like to go, for many reasons. If I was doing newspaper work, now, I could plan to go just as well as not, for one month or six. As I am situated now I don't see very well how I can. If I was to leave here it would have to be permanently. I am not particularly well pleased with the place here, but at the same time I should not feel that I ought to give it up unless I knew that I was pretty sure of a permanent position after I completed that trip with you.

What I would like to do would be to have an office position, sub-editorial or semi-editorial, preferably on some weekly paper, where my work would assure me a moderate salary, and leave me some time for outside literary work, or such work as you propose. If it was not for my father I could take more risk, but as he is dependent upon me for support I feel that I must have some kind of a steady place. Oddly enough I had been thinking, before your first letter came, that I would write and ask you to keep me in mind and see if you did not have a chance to recommend me for some such position. It is possible that some such opportunity may present itself, and that might make it possible for me to go with you. I shall be glad to hear from you again, and if you should happen to come on to Boston please let me know, by wire, if necessary, so that I can see you. If you are to be there until May 10th, I may be able to get on there to see you. I wish it might be arranged in some way, for aside from the pleasure of going with you I know the experience would be very valuable for me. With good wishes, Very truly yours

M. B. Thrasher

TLS Con. 183 BTW Papers DLC.

[1] See above, 1 :xxiv-xxvi.

A Draft of an Address at Hampton Institute[1]

[Hampton, Va., Apr. 21, 1898]

When I came upon these grounds — no, I will not say: when I came upon these grounds — when I came back home this morning, I thought of the changes that had taken place since I came here years ago with 50 cents to begin my education. The advanced steps taken here are indicative of the progress of the Negro race.

Though the line of progress may seem at times to waver now advancing, now retreating, now on the mountain, now in the valley, now in the sunshine, now in the shadow, but the aim has ever been forward, and we have gained more than we have lost. If to-day, we have fewer political conventions we have more economic gatherings, if we have fewer political clubs, we have more building and loan associations, if we cherish fewer air castles, we own more acres of land and more homes than has ever been true in the history of the Negro race, if we have fewer men in Congress, we have more merchants and more leaders in commerce.

The progress along material lines is marked, yet the greatest lesson that we have learned during the last two decades is that the race must begin at the bottom, not at the top, that its foundation must be in truth and not in pretense. We have learned that our salvation does not lay in the direction of more political agitation or in hating the Southern White man, but that we are to find a safe and permanent place in American life by first emphasizing the cardinal virtues of home, industry, education, and peace with our next door neighbor, whether he is White or Black.

But I should be false to my race and myself were I to seem to set meets and bounds upon the ambition and activities of the Negro. No, no, not that. But if I could, I would have my fellow students, and the generous donors of this Hall of Domestic Science, and our brave, good friend, Dr. Curry, the representative of the Slater Fund Board, bear in mind that in helping us along the lines indicated by Hampton, that in sending these men and women out every year into the school room, into the shop, on the farm, into the field of domestic science, Hampton is making men and women who are shaping the laws and customs of our country just as truly as he who sits in congressional halls. In this greater parliament of man, the Negro has his opportunity and through it he will blaze a way to the exercise of every privilege that belongs to him as an American citizen.

In saying what I have, I am not for a minute unmindful of the depths of poverty, ignorance and immorality in the far South, that must be penetrated before the race will be on a safe footing.

The Negro, in common with all good citizens, abhors war, and regrets the present disturbed condition of the country. What need the Nation may have for our service, I know not, but this I know, that whether in slavery or in freedom, the Negro has always been loyal to the Stars and Stripes, and should the clash of arms come, the Negro, with voice and sword, will be found by the side of his late Southern master, willing to lay down his life for his country's cause.

TM Con. 959 BTW Papers DLC.

¹ BTW spoke at Hampton's thirtieth anniversary celebration, and his address appeared in the next issue of the *Southern Workman*. Because this typed draft of his address differs significantly from the printed version, both versions are reproduced. It is not clear if the changes in the printed version resulted from BTW's editing or the editing of the staff of the *Southern Workman*.

The Printed Version of an Address
at Hampton Institute

[Hampton, Va., Apr. 21, 1898]

I am sure my friends will never forgive me if I attempt to detain them any length of time this evening. When I came into this room I found what I wanted to say said so often and so well it seemed an imposition for me to undertake to speak. But I was taught while at Hampton to obey the order given even if you are to be the sufferers.

I wish the remarks of Mr. Starnes¹ might be printed and sent throughout our land, for he has presented most earnestly, most strongly, most logically, most wisely the needs of our race.

When I came on these grounds — no, when I came home, for I never feel so much at home as at Hampton, I could not help but think of the changes that had taken place here since I first came with a capital of fifty cents to begin my education. It makes me think of the census taker who went to see an old colored woman. She said, "Well, what you white people want to know now?" The gentleman said "I want to take your census." "You done got electric lights so the white man can see everything de niggers do, got de telephone so you can hear every ting he say, and now you come here to take the nigger's senses away from him!" Now the changes that have taken place here are in a measure indicative of the forward step taken by the Negro race in this country, though their line may have sometimes advanced and sometimes have retreated, sometimes have wavered, now up in the mountains, now down in the valleys, now in the sunshine, now the shadow, but the aim has ever been forward, and we have gained more in these years than we have lost in the march. We have fewer political conventions, more economical conventions; fewer political clubs, more building and loan associations; fewer classes in Latin and Greek, more in agriculture, and are buying more homes and farms than ever before in the history of our race. We have fewer men in Congress today, but more men as merchants, more men as leaders along material lines. The greatest lesson we have learned is that the race must begin at the bottom and not at the top, that the foundations of our life must be laid in truth and not in pretence, and that we must find our place by emphasizing the cardinal virtues that make the true home life of any people, whether black or white.

I would be false to my race were I to set a limit to the development of the race, but on the other hand I would have the students, trustees, and donors understand that in helping us along the lines indicated by Hampton, and in sending out its students throughout this South to help our people, Hampton in doing this is helping them to make the laws that shape the customs of this country as truly as the men who sit in congressional halls, for in the larger parliament of men they find opportunities for showing their manhood and thus to blaze a way to fuller opportunity as American citizens.

I have always loved Hampton and I love her more and more, because she is not only giving the Negro knowledge, but is seeing and reaching the needs of the race as no other institution is doing.

My friends, don't let us be discouraged. If others be little, we can be great; if others be mean, we can be good; if others push us down, we can push them up; if others excel in hating, let us excel in loving; if others excel in cruelty, let us excel in kindness, for it is along these lines that we can work our way to salvation in this country.

Southern Workman, 27 (May 1898), 106.

[1] A. J. Starnes of New Orleans, a member of the Hampton graduating class, spoke at commencement on "What Education Is Needed for the Negro." (*Southern Workman,* 27 [May 1898], 103-6.)

To Emily Howland

Grand Union Hotel, New York, April 23rd. 1898

Dear Miss Howland: Please excuse my typewritten letter. I have been away from Tuskegee several weeks making my headquarters here, hence your letter of the fourteenth has only reached me.

I wanted very much to attend the Friends Meeting in Philadelphia but was prevented from doing so by the present war excitement, which makes it necessary for me to work very hard in order to get a little money.

I shall let you know when the remaining five hundred dollars for the building is needed. I expect to remain here until the tenth of May.

I prefer to wait until the end of the school year before speaking to you more definitely about Kowaliga. I will then be more sure of my ground. The school at Kowaliga has made good progress, I think, considering everything, but one of the troubles is that these young people don't want to wait for things to grow in a natural way. I have had to speak with Benson rather plainly about several matters lately and I think it will do him good.[1] Mr. Calloway[2] seems to let Benson take charge. He, Mr. Calloway, is more level headed but I try to watch them just as closely as possible, and by the end of the year I will know more about them. I think it very likely that the American Missionary Association will assume the support of two teachers there. This will be a great gain for them and will, in a measure, insure the permanency of the school.

Our last Conference was by far the best that we have held and good results are now showing themselves on every hand.

Were Mrs. Washington here, I know she would like to be remembered to you. She keeps very well this year, notwithstanding her hard and constant work. Both Davidson and Baker are at home. We hope you can visit Tuskegee again before long. Yours truly,

Booker T. Washington

TLS   Emily Howland Papers   NN-Sc.

[1] Howland gave BTW her opinion of Benson earlier when she wrote: "Mr. Benson is young and ardent, his enthusiasm is fine, but he is the child of wealth, for his environment, so we cannot expect practical work-a-day wisdom from him." (Howland to BTW, Apr. 14, 1898, Con. 155, BTW Papers, DLC.) Later she urged BTW to help Benson learn "the secret of leadership, which is self-effacement, as you have done. . . ." (Howland to BTW, May 20, 1898, Con. 701, BTW Papers, DLC.)

[2] Clinton Joseph Calloway (b. 1869) graduated from Fisk University in 1895 and became principal of the Kowaliga Academic and Industrial Institute the same year. In 1901 he joined the faculty of Tuskegee Institute in the agriculture department, where he served in the bureau of nature study and as Negro Conference agent before becoming director of the extension service in 1905, a position he held for more than twenty-five years. Under Calloway's direction the Jesup Wagon, a traveling exhibit of agricultural information, reached many Black Belt farmers.

APRIL · 1898

To the Faculty of Harvard University

Grand Union Hotel, New York, April 23 1898

To the Faculty of Harvard University: It gives me pleasure to recommend to you for admission to the university Roscoe Conkling Bruce, the son of the late Hon B. K. Bruce who was one of the most eminent and useful men that our race has ever produced. Mr. Roscoe Conkling Bruce, is a young man of the highest character and is in every way earnest and worthy. In thoroughness, application and scholarship he stands high as his record at Exeter Academy abundantly proves. Yours Respectfully

[Booker T. Washington]

ALd   Con. 161   BTW Papers   DLC.

From James B. Stone[1]

Worcester, Mass. April 29, 1898

Dear Sir: I write you as the leading representative of your race, some thoughts that have come to me, since the present war became a certainty. You may not agree with me, but it seems to me that the Southern Negro as a race are missing a great opportunity. Let me say here that the writer is the son and grandson of the early friends of your race, whose father's and grandfather's houses were stations on the "Underground Railroad" in the Forties and Fifties, that he himself is a "Grand Army" man and he writes from the natural stand-point of such ancestry and association.

The Army that is to occupy Cuba has no fear of the Spaniard but it does dread the climate of Cuba with its fevers and malaria. The government hesitates to-day as to its policy from the same feeling. Could they to-day land an army of 50,000 men exempt from malarial fever in Cuba, this war with its waste of life and treasure, to all concerned, Spaniard and Cuban, as well as ourselves, not to mention the starving women and children of the reconcentrados; would speedily cease with its purpose accomplished.

Without such an army, all thought of occupation of Cuba must be

411

postponed until the Fall, with the existing condition aggravated by the blockade, to continue during all the intervening months, unless the government decides to occupy now and accept battle with the Cuban climate paying the fearful penalty of thousands of American lives to save other thousands of Cuban lives whose needs are greater than ours.

During the prevalence of an epidemic of Small Pox, the services of a man that has had it and is therefore proof against another attack, are invaluable. From the standpoint of human and military economy to-day, a Southern Negro is worth as much as three Northern White-men.

Herein lies the opportunity of your race to render your country a great service and gain to yourselves a name and fame that seldom occurs. Demand the honor and privilege that an army for the immediate occupation of Cuba shall be recruited from your race and particularly from the Gulf States, and request also that your officers should be taken as far as practical from Confederate Veterans.

Such an event and such a combination would not only be of vast service to the country of which you are a part of and owe much to, but especially would it redound to your honor and benefit as a race. Your race are joint occupants of the soil with the descendants of another race, that but a generation ago, were your masters. An act of war made you free, an act of Congress made you Citizens. The progress of your race in its march toward an independent achievement of higher civilization has been watched with pleasure and surprise.

War makes history fast and you have the opportunity today to acquire at a bound and by a few months' service that which otherwise would require the patient work of years. I want to see you on better terms with your white neighbors, the welfare of both requires it, and there is no surer nor quicker way for two races of men to win mutual respect and esteem than to fight together against a common enemy. This Cuban Campaign is to my mind the golden opportunity for your race. Will you let it pass you by? Yours truly,

James B. Stone

TLS Con. 1 BTW Papers DLC.

¹ James B. Stone (1844-1921) was an engineer and schoolteacher in several states. He resided in Worcester from 1884 until 1905. During the Civil War he was a musician in the Seventh New Jersey Infantry.

Ida Belle Thompson McCall to
Margaret James Murray Washington

Birmingham, Ala, April, 30, '98

Dears Mrs. Washington: You will probably be surprised to get this letter. It is purely business. It is reported here that Mrs. Alice Mason[1] of this place has been employed to teach at Tuskegee. This woman is most certainly not fit to be there. She has a very, very bad reputation here. Has been separated from her husband and during this time it seems that she was talked of as being intimate with Mr. Parker. And too, there has been a scandle about her and another man here. She wears short hair and rides the wheele in short skirts. During Mardi Gras she wore men's clothing in the streets. The woman may go to Tuskegee and do all right but just think of such a woman being a member of the Faculty. I know how you are inclined to look upon things of this sort but I'll tell you Tuskegee cannot afford to employ such characters. I shall write Mr. Washington.

Hope you are quite well these busy days. I meant to see you before you left for Montgomery but failed to do so. Thank you very much for the outing[2] you gave me for Edith, it was not enough to make her a dress but I made her a pretty little sack which she traveled in.

I think I am getting stronger. Yours,

Ida T. McCall

ALS Con. 143 BTW Papers DLC.

[1] Alice Mason was not appointed to the Tuskegee faculty.
[2] Outing flannel.

From Ida Belle Thompson McCall

Birmingham, Ala, April, 30, '98

Dear Mr. Washington: I hear that you are going to, or have already employed Mrs. Alice Mason as one of the teachers at Tuskegee. Dr. Washington[1] told me that you had written him regarding her character but that he should tell you that he knows nothing about her. It is simply because it is not good policy in his case.

The woman has a bad reputation here. She is certainly not the sort of character to come in contact with our girls. She is on the sensational "New Woman" order.

I should certainly be sorry to see Mrs. Mason connected with Tuskegee in any way at all. Respectfully,

Ida T. McCall

ALS   Con. 143   BTW Papers   DLC.

¹ Samuel Somerville Hawkins Washington.

To James B. Stone

[Tuskegee, Ala.] 5, 6, 1898

My dear sir: Replying to your favor of April 29th I beg to say that, I find myself in entire sympathy with the sentiments of your letter. I feel, and have felt, that the present war offers an opportunity for the colored man in the South to give to the government an example of patriotism that would not be lost upon it, but unfortunately the quota apportioned to the several states has been made up entirely of white volunteers, the governors of nearly all the Southern states having declined to accept colored volunteers, the state of Alabama, however, and the one exception if I remember right, has only agreed to accept two companies of 86 men each. As for myself, I offered to raise a regiment among the colored people of the Gulf states, but this matter has been placed entirely in the hands of the governors of the several states as you are well aware. I regret very much that it is not possible for us to co-operate in the grand work of freeing the oppressed of Cuba from the thraldom which has held them, but it is a condition and not a theory which confronts us. Yours truly,

Booker T. Washington

TLSr Copy   Con. 146   BTW Papers   DLC.

From Willis Brewer[1]

Washington, D.C. 9 May 1898

Sir   Yrs of the 8th came today. You tell me I *"don't* know that some time ago a bill was introduced in Congress" to give your school public land, and that "all the Alabama delegation seems to be in favor of it." When you become *impertinent* I prefer you would exercise yr talent on some one who likes it better than I do.[2]

W Brewer

ALS   Con. 138   BTW Papers   DLC.   Written on stationery of the U.S. House of Representatives.

[1] Willis Brewer (1844-1912), a Confederate veteran and Democratic politician of Montgomery, Ala., served in the U.S. House of Representatives from 1897 to 1901, and afterward returned to Montgomery to practice law.

[2] Emmett Jay Scott wrote to Brewer in BTW's absence explaining that Brewer must have misinterpreted BTW's meaning and no impertinence was intended. (Scott to Brewer, May 12, 1898, Con. 145, BTW Papers, DLC.) H. C. Reynolds wrote to BTW that Brewer was opposed to all appropriations and had opposed the Tuskegee bill the year before. Reynolds believed that Brewer's opposition was not a serious matter and that "if we have Messrs. Reed and Lacey on our side the bill will doubtless pass." (Reynolds to BTW, May 24, 1898, Con. 145, BTW Papers, DLC.)

From Frederick Taylor Gates[1]

New York   May 9th., 1898

My dear sir: I duly received your esteemed favor giving synopsis of your address. I now desire to become thoroughly acquainted with your whole financial system. This would involve the annual report of your Treasurer, pretty fully itemized and showing in detail your annual receipts and expenditures. You will remember that in our little conversation at Montclair I specially invited a list of the principal annual donors, with their contributions. This is something that Mr. Rockefeller almost always requires but is held confidential with this office. In many cases these lists are published as a part of the Treasurer's report. Where not published we always make it a matter of special inquiry. I should be glad if you could furnish me such a list. Your financial statement also should include a full statement of your obligations, if any, in the way of debts. Yours very truly,

F. T. Gates

TLS Con. 146 BTW Papers DLC.

¹ Frederick Taylor Gates (1853-1929), a Baptist minister, was John D. Rockefeller's philanthropic agent from 1893 to 1912. He had previously served as corresponding secretary of the American Baptist Education Society (1888-93). He investigated in detail the many appeals for funds, and he showed such acumen that Rockefeller brought him also into his business dealings as an analyst.

An Address before the Union League Club of Brooklyn¹

[New York, May 14, 1898]

I assure you that I did not come here to make a speech, supposing that our policy was to be one of silence. But I am glad to be here and to show my gratitude, and I may say the gratitude of my race to the guest of this evening for the wise, patient, statesmanlike manner in which he has represented our country in a foreign land under very trying and difficult circumstances. [Applause.]

It is a long way, my friends, from a Virginia slave plantation to a Union League Club dinner. [Applause.] It is a long way from the organization of the Fifty-fourth Colored Regiment in Massachusetts some thirty-five years ago, amid the protests and the curses of a great part of the people of this country, to the point where Gen. Fitzhugh Lee said a few days ago that he would like to lead a colored regiment in the present war. [Applause.] In the midst of the present controversy, I do not forget that perhaps my race has one advantage. While we are debating who shall occupy certain portions of this continent, I beg to remind you that the negro is the only race that ever came to this country by reason of special invitation. [Laughter.] Your unfortunate race came here against the protest of the leading citizens of America in 1492, [laughter and applause] while we seem to have been so important to the prosperity of this country that we had to be sent for. [Applause.]

I know not what the country may have for my race to do in this war, but this I do know, that whether as private citizens or as soldiers, whether in slavery or in freedom, we have always been loyal to the Stars and Stripes, [great applause] and you will find the members of my race throughout the South ready to stand by their former masters on the battlefield and fight for the honor and security and freedom of this country. [Applause.]

And I beg of you to remember that while your young men are going to fight a foreign foe, there are hundreds and thousands of young men of my race in lonely log cabins fighting the battles of this country against ignorance and superstition and poverty, just as bravely and just as truly as those who go to fight against Spain. In time of war, in time of peace, whether we are ignorant and poor or not, we are going to be true to the best interests of this country, as a race. [Applause.]

New York *Times*, May 15, 1898, 2.

[1] The New York *Times* reported that BTW spoke before a crowd of more than 4,000 people attending a reception for General Stewart Lyndon Woodford, who had just returned from Spain after a year as American minister. Speechmaking was kept to a minimum, but John S. McKeon, the club president, said the rule against speeches would be broken "in favor of one who had traveled 3,000 miles to be with Gen. Woodford at this gathering." The New York *Times* reported that BTW's speech "evoked volleys of cheers." (New York *Times*, May 15, 1898, 2.)

From Amanda Ferguson Johnston

Malden West Va   May the 16/98

Mr Washington. the Church Aid Sosiety Sends many thanks to you for the Dollar you sent us

Mr Washington we want you to speak for us when you Come Home Let us know at once what Date you Can so we Can get the Hall   we want to Do Something for your School

Pres. Amanda Johnson
Ora Cartney Sectery

Love to all   Kiss Daveson for me   Dont Let Albert go in the ware B. H. send Love to all   Let me Hear from yu at once
it Hailed here to Day.

ALS   Con. 141   BTW Papers   DLC.

From Emmett Jay Scott

Tuskegee, Ala., May 19, 1898

Mr. Washington: I did not every night keep a record of Teachers absent from the Pavilion, but observed closely enough to know that the persons whose names are below were more regularly & persistently absent than others. The abuse, at times, has been flagrant and unpardonable. There were nights when as many as 45 teachers would be absent, and others when it would not exceed 25 absentees, but never less than this number, I think. At the time that it was observed that I was making a list of absentees the attendance improved wonderfully. I regret that I am compelled to make this report:

Mr. Adams	Mr. Claytor	Mr. Craig
Mr. Chambliss	Mr. Cooper	Mr. Conyers
Mr. Driver	Miss Cropper	
Mr. Diggs	Mrs. C W Greene	
Mr. C W Greene	Mrs. J M Greene	
Mr. J M Greene	Mrs. Willis	
Mr. J C Greene	Miss Cooper	
Mr. Gregory	Miss Cropper	
Mr. Gibson	Mrs. Walker	
Dr Kenniebrew	Miss Mabry	
Mr. Jackson	Miss Torbert	
Mr. Lacy	Miss Thomas	
Mr. Menafee	Miss Keith	
Mr. Minter	++	

Mr. Robinson)
Mr. Stevens)   I think I should say in this connection that nearly
Mr. Saffold) all have been absent some. As for myself I have
Jas. E. Scott) been absent about four nights, but each time with
W H Scott) a reasonable excuse. Others are similarly placed, I
Mr. Thomas) apprehend. Yours very truly—
J H Washington)

E J Scott

ALS Con. 145 BTW Papers DLC.

From John Henry Washington

[Tuskegee, Ala.] May 20, 1898

Mr. B. T. Washington: On yesterday I received a note from you to the effect that I had not complied with the policy of the institution, inasmuch as I did not attend the evening prayers. I do not know who is responsible for giving you such information, but I must say with all frankness, that it is false in the highest terms. The person who made the report has either failed to observe my attendance at prayers or has no regard for truth. I feel safe in saying that out of the six evening services held at the school each week, that on an average for the last six weeks I have attended four of the services. I do not mind being reported at any time, or being criticised justly, but I have the highest contempt for false reports. Yours truly,

J. H. Washington

TLS   Con. 146   BTW Papers   DLC.

From Emmett Jay Scott

Tuskegee, Ala., May 20, 1898

Mr. Washington: This note from Mr. JHW forces an issue of veracity that I do not shirk. I regretted very much when I was asked to make you this report, because I knew well the personal feeling that would be engendered, as indeed it has — as I hear echoed from each of the persons to whom you sent your note. I did the duty however conscientiously and had absolutely no regard for persons aside from their absence, or attendance, at the services. I still insist — his strong protests to the contrary — that he has not been present during your absence with the same regularity manifested during your stay here. Yrs truly–

E J Scott

ALS   Con. 161   BTW Papers   DLC.

From Samuel Ebenezer C. Lord[1]

[Tuskegee, Ala.] 21/5/98

Dear Mr. Washington: I believe that I received the *warning* the Faculty gave me for going out of class one evening without permission. It is this sir that I want to tell you concerning my action on that night; I wanted to go to the *closet* and asked my teacher to excuse me, she said she could not. I told her it was impossible for me to stay, endeavoring to impress her with words and the faces I could make as to the importance of the cause, she would not, therefore I told her I had to go and went.

Owing to the predicament which I was in will you be kind enough as to remove the warning before school closes. Respt.,

Samuel E. C. Lord

ALS   Con. 161   BTW Papers   DLC.

[1] Samuel Ebenezer C. Lord from Kingston, Jamaica, was a member of the B middle class in 1897-98. He did not return the following year and did not graduate.

From Samuel Somerville Hawkins Washington

B'ham Ala., May 28th 1898

My dear Mr. Washington: We are anxious that some Colored men from this state should be connected with the Medical Department of the Colored Volunteer forces. We have agreed here on Dr A. M. Brown[1] for surgeon and we have already secured for him the very highest endorsement, both professional and general. We should like to add your endorsement to that of others, and would be glad to have a letter from you to the governer. The appointment is practically certain but in order to strengthen the case we desire to have *yours*.

I had the pleasure last night of blocking a shrewd little game to induce the Colored Company here to elect *white officers*. See Age Herald[2] of this date and note conflicting statements of Sec. Alger with the statement *purporting* to come from Gov. Johnston.

Hoping you are well &c   I am yours very truly

S. S. H. Washington

We do not wish in any way to prejudice any claims that Dr. Dungee[3] may have.

ALS   Con. 147   BTW Papers   DLC.

[1] Arthur McKimmon Brown was born in Raleigh, N.C., in 1867. He received his A.B. from Lincoln University in 1888 and his M.D. from the University of Michigan in 1891. Brown practiced medicine in Bessemer and Birmingham, Ala., Cleveland, and Chicago. During the Spanish-American War he served as assistant surgeon in the Tenth U.S. Cavalry. In addition to his medical work Brown sought improvement of conditions among black convicts, directed a bank, and operated a drugstore. Later he became president of the National Medical Association.

[2] Governor Joseph Forney Johnston undertook in late May 1898 to enlist four companies of black volunteers, one each from the cities of Huntsville, Birmingham, Montgomery, and Troy. The four companies formed a battalion, and the governor was first reported in favor of black officers at the company level, though with white battalion officers, except for the Huntsville company, which was to have all white officers. He reassured white prospective volunteers that they would under no circumstances be required to serve under black officers. Subsequently, however, Johnston announced that he was willing to accept black officers but that the President and the War Department had instructed him to appoint white officers. At meetings in Birmingham and Mobile, black prospective volunteers refused to accept white officers. (Birmingham *Age-Herald*, May 25, 1898, 3; May 27, 1898, 5; May 28, 1898, 5.) Eventually, however, the black volunteers had to accept white officers.

[3] Alfred C. Dungee was born in Virginia in 1862 and later became a physician. While living in Washington, D.C., in 1890 he met BTW, who offered him the job of health department director and teacher at Tuskegee. Though Dungee never took the job, he did move to Alabama and was living in Montgomery at the turn of the century. (BTW to Dungee, Apr. 8, 1890, Con. 106, BTW Papers, DLC.) Like many other physicians of the period, he was also a druggist. He resided in Montgomery until his death about 1919.

From Timothy Thomas Fortune

New York, May 28, 1898

Dear Friend: I asked John Wilson & Son to wire me the probable cost of producing the book, when they should have got the copy. I have there wire today that probable cost would be about $300, half when work begins, balance on delivery. I asked them to rush it for June 15, and we may make it. I have wired you cost and what was needed to start the book in type and hope to hear from you Monday, as I am now anxious to get the book out.

I wired Wilson & Son to forward you my Introduction to the book today. Please read it and make any correction or suggestion [you] may desire. Mrs. Matthews thinks it calculated to provoke antagonism among Southern white men, because of the comparison I draw between you and Grady, but as the comparison is just and truthful to you and Grady I don't see why I should temper my thoughts to the Southern back. But you may take Mrs. Matthews' view. She also objects to "Black Belt Diamonds" as the title. What do you think of it? Let me [know?] about the title and preface at once. My health is fair. Yours truly

Thomas Fortune

I am dropping the first T. in my name.

ALS   Con. 139   BTW Papers   DLC.

From George Washington Carver

[Tuskegee, Ala.] 5-30-98

Dear Sir: In making this report, I think it but fair to you, fair to the school and fair to myself to make this statement of facts.

I assure you that no-one is more deeply intrested in the welfare of the school than myself, and especially my Dept. I have labored early and late and at times beyong my physical strength; have not asked for a private secy. And if you look into my work carefully you will see that I need one quite as much as some who have two.

I had made partial arrangements to enter the Shaw School of Botany, St Louis, from which I hope to take my doctor's degree, a degree that no colored man has ever taken, but your many letters urging the cutting down of expenses, and your desire to have me study the food question, in which I am also deeply intrested, and the very important relationship the farm as a whole stands to the financial side of the school I canceled my engagement with Shaw.

Again — In taking charge of the Agr. Dept. it was my understanding that you wanted it to grow. I have put forth every effort in that direction that time, means and opportunity would permit.

I have been looking forward to a Dept. Second to none in the U.S. in the matters of equipments, methods of teaching and results obtained.

We have great fruit possibillities here, and instead of spending so much money every year in purchaceing trees, vines and shrubery, of various sorts I had planned to do our own budding, layering, grafting and inarching ourselvs, cutting down that expense, and at the same time have fit subjects for the students training and a thing of beauty for visitors both north and south. The landscape feature of our gardens and grounds I expected to have second to none.

Farm

On the farm I expected the same improvements incident to it, Viz. a moddel in every peticular, bending all our energies toward the saving of food on one hand and the production on the other, hoping under favorable conditions of the weather to cut down the hay bill two or three hundred dollars. Mr. Menafee will work in connection with the farm along this line.

Barn

Here we have just decided, and quite wisely, to increase the number of hogs. I am looking forward to the time when we will furnish nearly or quite all of our beef mutton and pork. To do this we must make a steady growth.

To accommodate the number of brood sows we expect to have it will take about 40 new brood pens, which must be built and 3 more open pens, to separate the diffrent hogs, sows, pigs &c. as necessity demands.

In fact I was going to ask you to reccommend to Mr. Chambliss that he must help along that line or be decreased in salary, but not excused altogether, as he is a good man with the cows. If we are going to get the number of hogs we spoke of the above mentioned work must be done, or it will be that much time and expense practically lost.

Besides the dairy herd will always be just as it always has been as long as we bend all of our energies to build it up 9 mo. and demoralize it 3. We have now under Mr. Chambliss nearly 60 cows 30 calvs and the bulls and I had planned to bring all of our dairy stock from Marshall farm as they do so much better here, besides they are not kept track of down at Marshall, and some of them die outright, others are sent up here for beef, and soon we are spending a lot of money for fine cows to repeat the same process, 100 head of stock will if propperly cared for keep any one man busy.

The records for last year are about as follows for the 3 mo vacation, accidents due to irresponsible students. 1 colt value $60   2 cows one worth 75 and the other 30 — $165 saying nothing about the multiplicity of pigs, and a number of calves.

Exp. Station

Here I am working with the smallest and most inexperienced staff of any station in the U.S. having the fourfold object in view that we have. Also with less means to cary on my work. It is impossible for me to do this work without men and means.

Now Mr. Washington, I think it ludicrously unfair to have persons sit in an office and dictate what I have to do and how I can do it. Also to tell me what has been done. If I thought things were to run as they have always run I would not stay here any longer than I could get away. I did not come down here to make experiments to find out what could be done with our Southern Soils. I know what is needed.

You know they said clover would not grow here, scoffed at the sweet potato exp. while they were growing and some even now want to deny the yield because they would not go to see it, (they are among the teachers to). It is the largest yield ever made in the State.

The acorns were bought under rigid protest I was even accused to my face (by a teacher in high authority) as going crazy. Yet Auburn in making up its recent list of valuable hog foods includes the acorn. Miss[.] says "it is one of the most important subjects taken up by any station."

Here are the exact words of my College paper of last mo.

"A short time ago the student gave a biographical sketch of our illustrious alumnus, Mr G. W. Carver '94. A bulletin from the Tuskegee Experiment Station has just reached our desk. This station has but recently been established particularly for the benefit of the colored race of the State and Mr. Carver has been appointed director. His first bulletin treats of the value of the acorn as stock food. He lucidly demonstrates the practical economy of a new interest along this neglected line. Judgeing from the features of this bulletin, Mr. Carver surely is and will be a powerful factor in the development of the 'new South.' "

Mr. Washington I simply want a chance to do what I know can be done, not what I think.

The records from Marshall Farm for the period of 3 years show that

30 heifer calves have been sent to the Farm and only 5 have ever been returned to the dairy.

These were our best calves.

Mr. Holland[1] is given 3 men 4 if needed to tend 10 acres. Mr. Green[2] 10 men to tend 100 acres I have 20 acres in exp. work and not a man given me. I want to conduct some feeding exp. and of course must have responsible men to do them.

I have no further recommendations to make. A number of our finest cows are to drop calvs soon, and during this hot dry weather skill and vigilince must be exercised to save them. I say all this in behalf of my desp.[3] and the best intrests of the school. Respy.

Geo. W. Carver

ALS Con. 138 BTW Papers DLC.

[1] Wiley W. Holland taught in the agricultural department at Tuskegee from 1897 to 1899.
[2] Charles W. Greene.
[3] Carver seems to have intended to write "dept."

To Emily Howland

Tuskegee, Ala., June 1, 1898

My dear Miss Howland: I am sorry that I have been so long in answering your letter. I sent you a note stating that your letter with a draft for $500 had reached us. When your letter came we were in the midst of our Commencement exercises. We are very grateful to you for this gift.

We are planning to have the building ready for use in September. We have felt very severely the war excitement. Our income has been greatly reduced on this account. I do not know where the end will be.

I am unable as yet to give you any definite information regarding Kowaliga. I have asked Mr. Calloway and Mr. Benson for a full statement of last year's income and expenditures together with the vouchers showing how money was spent. This I have not gotten as yet. I think little if any progress has been made towards the completion of the school house since you were at Kowaliga. One thing that makes me a little doubtful about Kowaliga is that Mr. Benson is not inclined to

take advice, and for this reason he does not secure the hearty co-operation of the people in the vicinity of Kowaliga, to say nothing of those
who have had opportunity of a larger experience than he has. I told
Mr. Calloway a few days ago when he was here, that the board of
trustees ought to be called together regularly and a report made, so
that everything would be done in a business and systematic way. As yet
there has been no such meeting. Mr. Benson likes to travel about from
place to place, and I am sure a good portion of what the school receives is spent in this way. I would not for the present wish for you to
speak to him about these weak points. It may be that later on he will
be cured, but as you are one of the trustees I thought it well to let you
know my feelings.

I wish very much you could have been at Hampton at their Commencement. It was in every way an excellent anniversary, and you
would have enjoyed it.

We have just closed our year, and we had a very interesting commencement season.

Under separate cover I send you a marked copy of the Montgomery
Advertiser which contains an account of it.

Mrs. Washington and the children wish to be remembered to you.
I hope it will not be long before we shall see you at Tuskegee again.
Yours very truly,

Booker T. Washington

TLS   Emily Howland Papers   NN-Sc.

From Samuel S. Gilson

Pittsburgh, Pa., June 1st 98

My Dear Bro. Your letter of May 19th is just received. I only returned from the General Assembly last night. I am *sure* you did right
to tell me what you have, and I shall use it to help you in your work.
It was high time to stop the "Unitarian" rumor. When you are in
Pittsburg come and see me. Your friend and brother

S. S. Gilson

ALS   Con. 140   BTW Papers   DLC.

From Jabez Lamar Monroe Curry

Atlantic City, N.J. 3 June/98

Dear Mr Washington— Yours of 29th has been received and I am glad you can do the work the Slater Board requests, without interfering with your paramount duty at Tuskegee and "somewhat as a recreation."[1] It will afford you an opportunity to do good, seldom enjoyed and make the Slater Fund felt as a great educational power. You should publish yourself as representing the Fund and that will, in part, disarm the criticism of rival schools. I have a strong belief that such speeches as you will make will do immense good, if followed, and this you will urge by immediate practical and organized effort. Your addresses will be stimulating & instructive but will be, as most sermons are, like water spilt on dry ground, unless succeeded by organized or associated effort to put in practical execution. Knowing should issue in *doing*. "Right thought, to remain healthy, must ultimately issue in right deed." With your speaking power, knowledge of the negro's wants, excellent good sense, prudence, power of adaptation, I predict most useful results upon both races. Primarily, the Slater Trustees send you on this mission, this crusade, for the uplifting of the Negroes, but the interests of the two races cannot be severed. What uplifts or drags down the one will uplift or drag down the other.

Social, economic, moral and intellectual elevation. What a field for superhuman direction & human effort!

The Negro has false ideas of freedom, of education, of religion, of civil rights, of the true means of progress. He has played long enough upon the time of being led out from Egyptian bondage. The Lord helps those who help themselves. No negro, under forty, was ever practically a slave. Since 1865, African slavery has by law ceased to exist, and yet slavery to habits, to traditions, to ignorance, to superstition, to prejudice, to appetites, may be more tyrannous & degrading than legal slavery, bad & indefensible as that is.

I am glad you will emphasize self-help, self-reliance, self-respect, all along the lines, and that you will encourage the support and improvement of public schools & discourage church schools, and more local, temporary enterprises, and peripatetic mendicants. The State owes education to all her children, and this is the most legitimate tax on property. Provision for free and universal education, the basis of our

427

free institutions, must not be spasmodic, temporary, inadequate, but systematic, stable and adequate. What noble and valuable work Mr Walker[2] has done in Va., in piecing out school terms & closing grog-shops! Longer sessions, better teachers, commodious & clean and beautiful school houses! Some of the costliest are the most untidy. How clean & neat & attractive is the Spelman!

Well, I could write all day on the subject. My heart is in it. God be with you in the work.

Plan your itinerary, in advance. Secure, in advance, cooperation of School Superintendents & teachers and editors and officials and, when possible, of preachers, who are often very ignorant & very narrow & jealous.

I do not see the use of a permanent stenographer — in many places not needed. Newspapers will not publish a full speech, and as you will necessarily make the same speech in different places, you do not care to be confronted with it. In large cities, secure, & pay if necessary a Reporter. I think you should send in advance, a notice of your visit & have the papers generally to speak of your mission. In these war times it will be hard to divert attention to Ed. the chief reformer of nations.

I like the confinement at first to the Southern & So. West. States. Regards to Mrs Washington. Yours sincerely

J. L. M. Curry

ALS   Con. 15   BTW Papers   ATT.   Original destroyed.

[1] The Slater Fund board proposed that BTW and his wife make an extensive speaking tour of the South, covering ten states and about twenty-seven cities over a two-year period, to promote industrial education and spread the work of the Slater Fund. The plan was to have BTW speak to the masses of people in churches and halls, to be followed the next day by Mrs. Washington, who would address an audience of women. (Curry to BTW, n.d., fragment, Con. 142, BTW Papers, DLC; also "Plan of Meetings to be Held in Southern Cities," n.d., Con. 15, BTW Papers, ATT, original destroyed.)

[2] Thomas C. Walker, a Hampton graduate of 1883, had been in the "plucky class" taught by BTW. He taught for six years after graduation and sent twenty-six of his students to Hampton. Studying law under a former Confederate soldier, he passed the bar examination and became a successful lawyer and minor office-holder in Gloucester County, Va. He was a justice of the peace, county commissioner, delegate to the Republican national convention in 1896, and collector of customs for the port of Rappahannock. He led a movement in his county of Negro home-buying, church improvement, and lengthening of the school term. He was also "a strong temperance worker, and through his influence the saloon has been abolished in many counties." ("A Country Lawyer's Work," in Hampton Institute, *What Hampton Graduates Are Doing, 1878-1904,* 98.)

From Chappell Cory

[Montgomery, Ala.] June 3–'98

Dear Sir: By direction of the Governor I have the honor to acknowledge yours of 2nd inst.

The Governor thanks you for your effort to aid him. The enlistment is for two years & he has now probably enough recruits offering to answer the full demand. Very respectfully,

Chappell Cory
Private Sec'y.

ALpS   Governor Letter File G78   A-Ar.

From Timothy Thomas Fortune

Brooklyn, N.Y. June 3, 1898

My Dear Mr. Washington: Your letters of May 31 and June 1 came this morning, but I was so bothered with visitors the whole day that I was unable to answer them at the office, and shall have more opportunity to do so tonight than I shall have tomorrow.

Your letters give me great pleasure. I felt that pressure of work prevented you from answering my letters and was not therefore worried, although I wanted of course to hear from you.

I am glad to say my health continues to improve.

I note what you say about the School Education people. Perhaps our first effort made them tired. All such work should be done with the greatest deliberation.

I am pleased with the collection. I had sample of pages 1, 2 & 3 yesterday in order to decide about style of type and headings, and I was charmed with the beauty of it. So will you be. Of course you must know that I wrote a short appropriate head for each selection. Yes, Mrs. Matthews deserves great praise for her part of the work. But she is dead set against Black Belt Diamonds and wants Gems from Booker T Washington, and I will not have it that way, simply because it does not signify enough and can't be got in one line in the title or at top of the reading page. We have had some stormy times about it. She was at the office when I got there this morning and we spent until 12 30 going over the ground the hundredth time. She finally decided to leave it to me with the hope that I would adopt her view. But I am directing the printers by this mail to go ahead with my view. I think I am right.

Mr Scott sent me $100 on your account and $50 on his. I sent $100 to the printers, who require that as deposit on opening an account. The book will make 150 to 185 pages, and the estimated cost, exclusive of dies for cover and half tone cut and changes in proof, is $250, so I put the whole probable cost at $300. We shall not know the exact cost until the work is finished, which will be about the 15th, as they have promised to rush it. So I hope you will place the balance with me by the 15th and I will render you the account when the printers furnish it.

I am delighted at your estimate of the Introduction. I was conscious that it had plenty of masculinity, and from the business point I thought it would do good in the South by provoking the white papers to take notice of your broad humanity and Americanism as compared with Grady's brutality and narrow Americanism. *It is no concern of mine that he suffers by comparison with you.* It is for us to give our men their proper place *in books*. I am not afraid to do it. Let the struck fellow yell if he wants to. I have ordered, today the printers to go ahead and put the Introduction in type. By the way, you forgot to sign the autograph letter and I shall want you to do so when you are here.

Of course I shall go to Albany with you if I can possibly do so and it will give me the usual pleasure. But with returning health and spirit I am working like a Turk, trying in some sort to make up for lost time.

I don't think Astwood[1] knows his own head from a cabbage all the time.

I shall write to the Southern News company as to your suggestion at once, and I want to see if I can't get Ogden to take an edition.

We are all well at home.

With kind regards for you all   Yours truly

T. Thomas Fortune

See to it that future checks are *certified* as otherwise they are only accepted for collection.

ALS   Con. 272   BTW Papers   DLC.

[1] H. C. C. Astwood, a native of Louisiana, held diplomatic posts as consul at Trinidad and Santo Domingo, before the Senate rejected his appointment as consul

at Calais. He fought against segregation in churches and in schools. He attended the organizational meeting of the Afro-American League in Jan. 1890.

To Frank E. Saffold

[Tuskegee, Ala.] June 4, 1898

Mr. F. E. Saffold: It is important that you keep on foot a regular plan for killing the bed bugs during the summer. Some student should devote his time to this important matter. Yours truly,

B. T. W.

TLI   Con. 13   BTW Papers   ATT.   Original destroyed.

From Willis Brewer

Washington, D.C. 4 June/98

Dear Sir   Yrs of the 7th came yesterday. It is entirely satisfactory. We shall now forget the occurrence, if you please. When you come on here I shall give you points about the bill that will interest you. It won't pass in its present shape I fear.

Write me whenever I can be of use to you. Yrs Truly

W Brewer

ALS   Con. 137   BTW Papers   DLC.

From Elizabeth Evelyn Wright

Denmark, S.C., June 6th 1898

My dear Mr. Washington: I would be very grateful to you if you would advise me concerning this matter; all the steps I take in my work, I usually ask your and Judge Kelley's[1] advice for fear I might make some mistake. I had a letter from Mrs. Steele[2] stateing that Dr. Kellogg[3] would pay the remainder of the sum for the school property

431

if I would agree to deed or put the property under the "American Medical Missionary Association." He wanted also the power of selecting teachers for the work. I must put in writing that I must have the oversight of the work as long as I live or see fit to resign. You can draw some idea of my plans concerning the management of the work when you read the report of the school which I have enclosed in this letter.

I will also say, I do not believe in denominational schools and feel that I can do more for the uplifting of my race by having it strictly independent under a board of trustees.

Please let me hear from you at once as to what you think best for me to do. As "Times" are hard the man from whom I am purchasing has decided to deduct $180.00 from the remainder of the sum which is $1080.00 if I can raise the $900 by July.[4] He also said if I could not raise it by July he would give me more time if I wanted it. Our school was largely attended this term. It ran eight months — the longest a school has ever [been] know[n] to run in these parts. We closed May 26th. The people we[re] highly pleased with the closing — about five hundred persons were present. The people certainly do make me feel very little and ashame[d] when they express themselves as the Denmark School being among the finest schools in S.C. One woman said the closing exercises were the finest she had ever seen and I thought to myself; she has never seen very much. The sermon was preached in the Baptist churchi the pastor wasn't at all willing but the deacons said it must be preached in the church and not in the pavilion which was a rough structure covered with bushes, planned by your humble servant contracted and overseed by Miss Davis. Small boys helped her to do the work and when it was finished the men were surprised to know a woman and children could do so well. I tried to get the men to build it but they were too busy with their farm work.

The school has a beautiful farm and the corn, cotton, potatoes and rice and cane are in a prosperous condition. I hope to realize enough money from the cotton to pay the salary of two teachers for another term and sufficient food to keep five teachers and four students. Miss Dorsey and I are going to remain here all Summer and hope to can many gallons of fruit for the school. We have begun our canning. It is not best for me to remain here I know during the Summer; for last Summer I had the fever and I am told that I will have it each year now unless I leave here, but as I do not get any salary and my means are none, I will have to remain and trust God for what ever may come.

432

My work is hard and some times the way seems dark and I think nothing much will be accomplished, but I am fond of it and have experienced that there is no fun in doing easy things.

I am very anxious to visit Tuskegee and as I have not returned since I left the place which I consider home, I fear you may think I am not interested in what is going on there. I want you to all ways remember I love my Alma Mater and my principal and will ever try to reflect credit upon both. Miss Davis has gone to Birmingham, Ala. for the Summer.

Please remember me to dear Mrs. Washington and the children. Where will Portia spend the Summer? Please send me her address. Also remember me to Mr. J. N. Calloway.

With best wishes for your success & happiness, Sincerely Yours,

Lizzie E. Wright

ALS   Con. 146   BTW Papers   DLC.

¹ Judge George W. Kelley, a black man originally of Rockland, Mass., helped Elizabeth E. Wright in her first effort to establish an industrial school in Hampton County, S.C. He purchased the land and provided bricks and lumber for buildings. Hostile whites burned the lumber, however, and Miss Wright was forced to locate the school elsewhere. She founded Voorhees Normal and Industrial School in Denmark, S.C., in 1902.

² Mrs. Almira S. Steele, a white woman from the North, encouraged Elizabeth E. Wright to teach at her school in Hampton County, S.C., for a year before returning to Tuskegee for her senior year in 1893-94. Mrs. Steele later established a black orphanage in Chattanooga which she conducted for many years.

³ Possibly G. M. Kellogg, a supporter of the American Missionary Association.

⁴ Elizabeth Wright, an 1894 graduate of Tuskegee, personally raised $700 for her school, half of which she solicited from black churches in the area. She purchased land from S. M. Mayfield, a South Carolina lawyer and state senator, and converted an old mansion into a schoolhouse. Also teaching at the school were Lulu Julisees Davis, an 1896 Tuskegee graduate; Miss J. C. Dorsey of Ohio; and J. Merchant of Lexington, Ky. The four teachers had 236 pupils during the 1898 school year. (*Southern Letter*, 15 [June 1898], 4.) By Nov. 1898 Miss Wright was ready to erect a three-story building, and she wrote to BTW asking him to provide plans for the structure. (Wright to BTW, Nov. 18, 1898, Con. 146, BTW Papers, DLC.)

To Frank E. Saffold

[Tuskegee, Ala.] June 7, 1898

Mr. F. E. Saffold: Please arrange for all the boys to bathe at least every other day during the summer. Yours truly,

B. T. W.

TLI   Con. 13   BTW Papers   ATT.   Original destroyed.

From Amory Howe Bradford[1]

Montclair, N.J. June 7, 1898

My dear Mr. Washington: Mr. Gates[2] told me two or three weeks ago of the gift of Mr. Rockefeller[3] to Tuskegee, and he also told me that it was all the result of your address in our church. I am very glad that I have been able to be of a little service to you. Your address was a really noble one, and I am not surprised that it impressed Mr. Gates as it did. You may be sure that you will always have my best wishes. Very sincerely yours,

Amory H Bradford

TLS   Con. 137   BTW Papers   DLC.   Written on stationery of the First Congregational Church.

[1] Amory Howe Bradford (1846-1911), Congregational minister at Montclair, N.J., from 1870 until his death. From 1892 to 1899 he was associate editor of the *Outlook,* and in 1904 became president of the American Missionary Association.

[2] Frederick Taylor Gates.

[3] John Davison Rockefeller (1839-1937) and his descendants were among the principal philanthropic contributors to Tuskegee Institute. In the fall of 1902 he gave the first amount toward the General Education Board, a multimillion-dollar foundation for education. The G.E.B. had an interlocking directorate with the Slater, Peabody, and later the Jeanes and Phelps-Stokes funds, and with the boards of Hampton and Tuskegee. Much of the Rockefeller philanthropy in the South, therefore, reflected the Hampton-Tuskegee philosophy and that of its white supporters.

JUNE · 1898

To George Washington Carver

Tuskegee, Ala., June 22 1898

Mr. Carver: I want the milk report every morning, and on it I want the number of cows milked. I have had no report for this week so far. You and Mr. Chambliss will have to arrange yourselves as to who shall see after this matter but I must insist that it be sent promptly each morning and marked as I have directed.[1] Yours truly,

B. T. W.

TLI Con. 138 BTW Papers DLC.

[1] Carver wrote back on the bottom of BTW's letter that no further trouble with the dairy report would occur, since a new supply of forms had arrived, and that Mr. Chambliss would regularly provide BTW with the information.

Extracts from an Address at Williams College

Williamstown, Mass., June 22, 1898

At Hampton I came into contact with that great soul, Gen. S. C. Armstrong whom Williams College gave to the world. I count it one of the greatest privileges of my life that I am permitted to come here and stand for a few minutes where he stood, to get lessons and inspiration from the college and associations that gave him life and purpose. I honor Gen. Armstrong not only because he was the Savior of my race, but to me he was a dear personal friend and whatever under God I have been permitted to do I owe to his teaching and guidance.

Williams College has done much for the advancement of the world, but I am tempted with no exaggeration when I say, that if Williams had done nothing else than give to the Negro race in this country the man who has lead and pointed the way for its redem[p]tion, this college would have justified all that it has cost in buildings and endowment.

x   x   x   x   x

Amidst the excitement, the glamor, the interest, and deeds of heroism that cluster around our present war, let us not forget that there is a condition in the Southern part of our own country that will demand for years to come our deepest thought and most generous help.

435

Let us bear in mind that Williams and New England will be untrue to the immortal Armstrong, if they permit the work for which he gave his life to remain uncompleted. Let us remember that an edict of war can not blot out ignorance, crime and poverty.

At the present moment there is properly deep interest in the thousands of young men who are going forth from all parts of our country in defense of honor and humanity, but I beg of you to remember that out from Hampton and Tuskegee there are going forth each year hundreds of young men and women into dark and secluded corners, into lonely log school houses, amidst poverty and ignorance, and though when they go forth no drums beat, no banners fly, no friends cheer, they are fighting the battles of our country just as truly, bravely and heroic[al]ly as they who go forth to do battle against a foreign foe.

AM Con. 31 BTW Papers ATT. A typewritten copy of this is in Con. 15, BTW Papers, ATT. Original destroyed.

From J. C. Ladevize

Augusta, Ga., June 1898

Dear friend: From the position which you occupy as a leader among the people we have thought it well to send to you an address, setting forth in plain terms legal battle which we have had in Richmond County relative to our school matter.[1] We have contended that under section 9 and 10 of the law under which our schools are operated, that the Board of Education has no right to establish and run high schools for the whites and deny the same privelege to the colored. We took this case to the Superior courts and you will see that we won. The Board of Education appealed the case to the Supreme Court where we lost. We give the decision in full that you may judge the justice of the methods of reasoning and the conclusions reached. We have decided to appeal the case to the Supreme court of the United States. The decision of the Supreme court of Ga. is clearly in violation of common american law in that it taxes a class of citizens for a certain purpose and then denies them participation in the benefits of the tax money.

We think that a decision from the United States Supreme Court reversing this will greatly benefit us as a race. We have spent about $600.00 in the two cases already heard and feel the need of financial aid to carry the case further. We need about a $1000.00 to take the case up. We appeal to you personally to assist us and also to use your influence with friends to do the same. Does this course of ours meet your approval. If so we would like to have a letter of commendation from you.

Awaiting an early reply we are yours respectfully in this for justice.

J C Ladevize

HLS Con. 142 BTW Papers DLC. Docketed in Scott's hand: "Thoroughly approve of intentions etc. In Fall."

[1] *Cumming* v. *Richmond County Board of Education,* 175 U.S. 528. Three black parents of Augusta, including the sender of this letter, countered the closing of the black high school by seeking an injunction to close the white high school until the black high school was reopened. There had been a black high school until 1897, when the school board closed it, alleging "purely economic reasons." Instead of housing 60 high school students, the building was used for 300 elementary pupils. The lower court granted an injunction forbidding the school board from operating the white high school until there was an equal black facility. The Georgia Supreme Court (103 Ga. 641) reversed the lower court decision.

Associate Justice John Marshall Harlan on Dec. 18, 1899, read the unanimous U.S. Supreme Court decision that the issues in the case showed no abridgment of the equal protection clause of the Fourteenth Amendment. The case as presented did not challenge the doctrine of separate but equal, and Harlan argued that the court was forced to rule on the issue presented. "If, in some appropriate proceeding instituted directly for that purpose," he observed, "the plaintiffs had sought to compel the board of education, out of the funds in its hands or under its control, to establish and maintain a high school for colored children, and if it appeared that the board's refusal to maintain such a school was in fact an abuse of its discretion and in hostility to the colored population because of their race, different questions might have arisen in the state court." The question at issue, the allocation of funds by the school board, was regarded as a state issue, "and any interference on the part of Federal authority with the management of such schools cannot be justified except in the case of a clear and unmistakable disregard of rights secured by the supreme law of the land." Because the decision sanctioned separate and even inferior black schools, it supported the *Plessy* v. *Ferguson* doctrine and extended it to include education.

From John F. Patty[1]

Jesuit Bend, La. July 4th/98

Dear Sir: I am in receipt of your valuable favor dated the 20th of June. The contents of which have been duly considered. In reply, I beg to say, that I will be glad to assist you in having the action of the Constitutional Convention tested by the proper tribunal. I am of the opinion that action will have to be brought by a citizen of this state. Every Negro in the state is interested in this vital issue. The Constitutional Convention didnot reflect the sentiments of the better element of our white people. The letter you sent to the Convention was to the point, and I am glad to say met the approval of a large majority of the people of this state. Please give me an outline of what you think ought to be done. I would advise you to communicate with Rev. A. S. Jackson Pastor of Common st. Baptiste Church Rev. I. B. Scott[2] Editor Christian Advocate and Rev. J. F. Marshall[3] Pastor of Clinton st. M. E. Church. I would ask these men to join you in this good work. Rest assured of my continued interest. I have the honor to remain, Yours truly

J. F. Patty

ALS Con. 144 BTW Papers DLC.

[1] John F. Patty was reported in the 1900 census as a black farmer born in Louisiana in 1854.

[2] Isaiah Benjamin Scott was born a slave in Midway, Ky., in 1854 or 1855. He attended Clark Seminary in 1874-75 and graduated from Central Tennessee College in 1880. Moving to Texas, he held a number of pastorates in the Methodist Episcopal Church. He was a professor at Prairie View State Normal and Industrial College, and in 1893 he became president of Wiley University. From 1896 to 1904 he was editor of the *Southwestern Christian Advocate.* Elected in 1904 a missionary bishop for Africa, he moved to Monrovia, Liberia. Scott was active in Republican politics and was one of BTW's most loyal lieutenants in the Southwest, and later he often sent BTW reports on African affairs.

[3] Julian Franklin Marshall was born near Richmond, Va., in 1847 and studied at Straight University and New Orleans University. He was licensed to preach in 1877, and in 1898 he received a D.D. degree from Wiley University. He later held Methodist pastorates in New Orleans, Shreveport, and Alexandria, La.

An Address before the Christian Endeavor Society[1]

[Nashville, Tenn., July 7, 1898]

THE MUTUAL DEPENDENCE OF THE RACES

At the close of our present war we are likely to find ourselves a very much mixed nation; so much so that I fear it may be a little difficult for the white man to find and identify himself. In fact, I feel rather anxious about the white man in this respect. There is no difficulty with the negro in this regard. He never gets lost in the mixture of colors and races. We have a great advantage over the white man in this respect. You see the instant it is proven that an individual has even 1 per cent. of African blood in his veins he falls to our pile every time in the count of races. The ninety-nine per cent. of negro Anglo-Saxon blood counts for nothing. We claim the man for our race, and we usually get him. It is a great satisfaction to belong to a race just now, when white Americans are likely to find themselves intermingled with the Mongolian and the Malay from the far East and the Latin races from the South — I say that under such circumstances, it is a supreme satisfaction to belong to a race that has such potential drawing power as is true of my race.

At the present moment God is teaching the Spanish nation a terrible lesson. What is that lesson? Simply this: That no nation can disregard the interests of any part of its members without that nation growing weak and corrupt. Though the penalty may have been long delayed, God is teaching Spain that for every one of her subjects that she has left in poverty, ignorance and crime, the price must be paid, if not with the very heart of the nation, it must be paid in the proudest and bluest blood of her sons, and in treasure that is beyond computation. From this spectacle which is now before the world, let America learn a lesson — the most costly product that any State can grow is ignorance, poverty and crime, and I pray God that every city and State in the South may take warning. Every white man in the South is dependent upon every black man in the South, and every black man in the South is dependent upon every white man in the South. There have been placed in the midst of the South eight million negroes, that in most of the elements of civilization are weak. Providence has placed them here not without a purpose. One object, in my opinion, is that the stronger race may imbibe a lesson from the negroes, patience, forbearance, and childlike, yet supreme, trust in the God of the universe. These eight million of my people have been placed here that white man may have a great opportunity to lift himself by lifting up this unfortunate race. The strongest individual is he who is most ready to lift up the weak. The most powerful State is that one which is most ready to make strong the weak. The white South will be intelligent in proportion as the negro is intelligent; it will be in darkness in proportion as the negro is in darkness. Not long ago, on the outer edges of a Southern city, I saw a white child who represented the wealth and culture of a white family surrounded by a group of negro children in the play ground. What these black children are that white child will be in a large measure. If those black children use language which is ungrammatical and impure the white child will do the same. If these black children learn crime the white child will do the same. If disease invades the body of the black child the same disease endangers the life of the white child. My white friends, there is no alternative; we cannot escape the inevitable. Through public schools, through churches and private benevolence, God means that you shall make the highest effort to lift us up, if you would make and keep your civilization pure and permanent. If the negro goes backward in this country he will take you with him.

Amidst the excitement, the glamour, the interests, the deeds of heroism that cluster around our present war, let us not forget there is a condition in this southern part of our country that will demand on the part of every Northern man and every Southern man our deepest thought and most generous help for years to come.

Let us remember that an edict of war cannot blot out ignorance, crime and poverty. At the present moment there is properly deep interest in the thousands of young men who are going forth from all parts of our country, in defense of honor and humanity, but I beg of you to remember that out from our negro colleges, out from Fisk, Hampton and Tuskegee, there are going forth each year thousands of young men and women into dark and secluded corners, into lonely log school houses, amidst poverty and ignorance; and though, when they go forth, no drums beat, no banners fly, no friends cheer, they are fighting the battles of our country just as truly, bravely and heroically as they who go forth to do battle against a foreign foe.

Within the last thirty years — and I might add, within the last three months — it has been proven by eminent authority that the negro is increasing in numbers so fast that it is only a question of a few years before he will far outnumber the white race in the South; and it has already been proven that the negro is fast dying out, and it is only a question of a few years before he will have completely disappeared. It has also been proven that crime among us is on the increase, and that crime is on the decrease; that education helps the negro, that education also hurts him; that he is fast leaving the South and taking up his residence in the North and West; and that the tendency of the negro is to drift toward the lowlands of the Mississippi bottoms. It has been proven that education unfits the negro for work, and that education also makes him more valuable as a laborer; that he is our greatest criminal, and that he is our most law-abiding citizen. In the midst of these opinions I hardly know whether I am myself or the other fellow. But in the midst of this confusion there are a few things of which I feel certain that furnish a basis for thought and action. I know that whether we are increasing or decreasing, whether we are growing better or worse, whether we are valuable or valueless, a few years ago fourteen of us were brought into this country, and now there are ten millions of us. I know that whether in slavery or in freedom, we have always been loyal to the Stars and Stripes; that no school-house has been opened for us which has not been filled; that the two million ballots which we have the right to cast are as potent for weal or woe as the ballots cast by the whitest and most influential man in America. I know that wherever your life touches ours you make us stronger or weaker.

Nashville *American,* July 8, 1898, 7.

¹ BTW spoke before Christian Endeavor delegates representing many states and to an audience of both blacks and whites. The address, according to the Nashville *American,* was well received, with frequent bursts of applause. During the address the electric lights in the building went out momentarily, plunging the audience into darkness. Seizing the moment, BTW remarked: "We are all now of the same color." (Nashville *American,* July 8, 1898, 7.)

John William Dean¹ to the *Tuskegee Student*

Santeago de Cuba   July-7-1898

specil to the Tuskegee Student   while taking a little recreation after a hot battle of the day, I was buisy ingaged in thoughts and while thus being so my mind in that electric speed of its nature gazed most stidfastly upon my kind and most honerable president teachers and school mates at Tuskegee, and while thinking my heart was so filled with that Tuskegee love that I could not avoid writing somthing which I earnesly hope will assist some one in working out their individual honer and a personal credit to every individual who may read it for this brave and most daring patriotic faithful and unsurpassing and

441

graceful Negro race. Which though how long stood with their faces
vailed in a cloud of oppressing misory, who were strangers to fredom,
and by the assistance from both God & man have laid aside those opposing sheckles which thorned their path with woe and all the cursed
things that exist to destroy the happiness of man; and today, I say as
a feuture staff for the race, what Paul said to his apostles let us run with
patients the race that is set before us, think not of the past idle not the
present but ever be ingaged looking to the bright feuture where all of
our hope comfort and prosperity lies, spend not your time away in
idle thinking mischief making nor vain thoughts of pride. I will say to
you my friends ever be mindful of the feuture needs for you, which
you cannot afford to loose, for if you loose now you have lost forever
and your loosing can never be ragained, so wait no longer, the time
for waitting has passed it is no more there was a time when men could
wait their opportunity to improve themselves intelecualy. but the time
for waitting is no more. you must make each day's work fill the space
of that day. I would have you know if you wait now you can never
be exscused from time the world want exscuse you, and therefore you
must be cast aside not only by other nations and races but even by
your own you must be counted a worthless goods.

My loving friends do you know the intire feuture prosperity of the
race depends intirely upon you? you are the pilot you are at the wheel
and if the vessel runs aground the world will charge you with it. therefore I empress it upon you with all of my power to be on the alert,
and guard yourselves against those things that are so destructive to
the progress of our people.

Every other race have give honer and admiration to its own and
today I speake once for my people a word that cant be coverd by
words of no other race on the face of this our vast domane America.
just to stand and think during the battle at Santeago and when the
enemy had the forest morning with the thunder of canons and the hot
bullets of steel and brass around Morrow castle were flying and lighting
like a hail storm, and see how the black troopers of the 9th 10th 24th
and 25th regiments rushed to the front and seeing their comrades
melting like snowdrops in the fire. and then to think how their prosperity is opposed in their homes and a great many other more oppressing things I could not account for their bravery and patriotic love
more than the Negro race must have the freest forgiving and most crist
like heart of any people in time, and could not avoid reflecting back to

the civil war where it was said the love and care of the Negro race could never be canseled and today my friends when I look and study the matter thurily I am compel to say if you my comrads will only stand stu[r]dy press forward aim high the day will soon come when the Negro question will be no more   my heart burns with hope for that hour when my race will be looked down on no more but be on a level playing an active part and honered as one of the topmost rounds of the ladder, and when I look upon such jewels of the race as Miss Josephine Bartlett whose qualities ables her [to] be imployed in one of the largest business houses in chicago, where only the best intelligence in her profession stenografer is tolerated, is interesting chiefly from the fact that it is next to imposible for [a] colored young woman to obtain such impl[o]yment in this free America. I can say the time isnt long, let us say every one to himself that I will do nothing that my race will be ashamed of, or that will impede the progress of a people and the saying of the prophecy that out of the socil disorders of a bondaged race there shall arise a womanhood strong, spirited, and chaste in all the things that make for social uplifting and refinement.

> The shout of we slaved brothers in Cuba.
> Yes rouse Americans and cheer,
> and let your voices be heard,
> Where ever men love liberty
> And prise that sacred word.
> For lo on Santeago's hights,
> Our galant standard waves,
> And fredom dawns on souls of men,
> Who yesterday were slaves.
> Where shafter leads conquering train
> With stern heroic miles,
> Fair Cuba drops her captivi[n]g,
> And lifts her head and smiles
> The proud castilians hirelings bow
> Before rights stern decree
> The pearls of the antilles now
> is fated to be free.

writen by one of your faithful sons in the ninth reg. of cav.

John W. Dean

ALS   Con. 139   BTW Papers   DLC.

¹ John William Dean (1876 [or 1878]-1924) of New Orleans was a junior at Tuskegee in 1897-98. During the Spanish-American War he served in Company M of the all-black Ninth U.S. Cavalry. After his discharge in 1901 he was a laborer and janitor in California.

From W. O. Chase

Chicago, July 9, 1898

Dear Sir: Referring to your telegram of the 28th inst. from Pittsfield, Mass., relative to your being refused a shave by barber on Train No. 15 leaving Boston that date.

I beg to advise you that this matter has been investigated and the barber referred to, dismissed from our service. I regret exceedingly that you had occasion to complain in this respect, and trust that you will not meet with similar experience again. Yours truly,

W. O. Chase
General Supt.

TLS Con. 15 BTW Papers ATT. Original destroyed. Written on stationery of the Wagner Palace Car Company.

To Emmett Jay Scott

Crawford House, Boston, Mass. July 12, 1898

Dear Mr. Scott: The article which you sent, taken from the N.Y. Daily News, is copied indirectly from the Philadelphia Times from an article written by Alexander,¹ who is at Normal. It is so full of misrepresentations and falsehoods that it can have no permanent value. Such exaggerations always, I think, defeat their own purposes. Council is included in the same class of colored people who for ten years fought my idea of industrial education and only came around as he thought it was popular.

For some reason I made the worst speech in Nashville that I ever made before a public audience.² There were a number of contributing causes which were rather accidental. I suppose the colored press in Nashville will go for me.

I wish you to go ahead and get out the Southern Letter as fast as possible. I will send you soon the cut.

In every way possible I wish you to advertise Phelps Hall. I think you can do it through short newspaper paragraphs in the various colored papers. Let me know what the outlook for attendance on Phelps Hall is. Yours truly,

Booker T. Washington

TLS Con. 146 BTW Papers DLC.

[1] Charles Alexander was at that time an instructor of printing and vocal music at Alabama Agricultural and Mechanical College, Normal, Ala., and was also editor of the *Normal Index* and chief of the fire company. He wrote occasional articles for the Philadelphia *Times*, the Washington *Colored American*, the Indianapolis *Freeman*, and other black newspapers. From 1899 to 1901 he was instructor of printing at Tuskegee, and then moved to Wilberforce University as a printer. He went to Boston in 1903 at BTW's request to edit a newspaper BTW had secretly acquired, the Boston *Colored Citizen*, to combat the influence of William Monroe Trotter's Boston *Guardian*. When his newspaper failed, he established *Alexander's Magazine* (1905-9).

[2] The speech before the Christian Endeavor Society on July 7, 1898, above.

From Timothy Thomas Fortune

New York, July 14, 1898

Dear Mr. Washington: I have your favors of the 12th and 16th instants. I would like to see the Albany Argus' publication. I am having printed the slips you suggest to go with the Black Belt Diamonds. They are very necessary and usually go with such publications.

I shall be glad if you can place the article I wrote for the Sun. I placed you on the pedestal where I think you belong.

I hand you Scarborough's letter. He was in and I told him he would go with me. He knows the President personally and with Lyons[1] and Green[2] we should be able to make an impression. I spend my last dollar in taking this step, and if things brighten with you the end of the week I will be glad if you will back me up some. I shall go to Hampton from Washington Sunday night.

The books are moving along all right. My nerves are a hundred percent better today. Yours truly

T Thomas Fortune

ALS   Con. 15   BTW Papers   ATT.   Original destroyed.

¹ Judson Whitlocke Lyons.

² John Paterson Green was born in 1845 of free parents in New Bern, N.C. His father died when he was five years old, and he moved with his mother to Cleveland. In 1870 he graduated from Ohio Union Law School, was admitted to the bar, and began practice in South Carolina. He returned to Cleveland in 1872 and entered Ohio politics, serving in the Ohio House of Representatives for two terms and the Ohio Senate for one term. Green was a delegate to the Republican national conventions in 1872, 1884, and 1896. In 1898 he was appointed agent of postage stamps for the U.S. Post Office Department and remained in that position until 1907, when he resumed his law practice in Cleveland. Though not a racial militant, Green was never an adherent of BTW, and Fortune sometimes referred to him derisively as "Pea Green."

From Robert Alexander Moseley, Jr.

Birmingham, Ala., July 14th 1898

Dear Sir: I expected to have a remittance of $100.00 on account from you this morning — as you promised to send me check from Boston. I told President Reynolds my absolute necessities for this amount *now*. Please hurry it up and oblige. Your friend

R A Moseley Jr

ALS   Con. 14   BTW Papers   ATT.   Original destroyed. Written on stationery of the Birmingham *Times,* R. A. Moseley, Jr., editor and publisher.

From Timothy Thomas Fortune

[Washington, D.C.] New York, July 16, 1898

My dear Friend: Your letter of the 14th was received, and I thank you for it, but I don't think we are going to accomplish anything. Lynch, Lyon and Green were agreed that we should have representation and wanted to make that representation to the President but declined to endorse me or any other candidate, preferring to leave that matter open with the President. I declined to bother with them. Scarborough, Terrell[1] and I went to the White House this morning but we failed as lots of others did to see the President. It is disgusting business all the way through, seeking political favors and I am entirely unsuited to it. White[2] has been in Omaha, but is expected back tomorrow. I shall wait over to see him and go to Hampton Monday night.

I went out to Terrell's yesterday to see Mrs. Washington and of course I was glad to see her. Your friend,

T. Thomas Fortune

ALS   Con. 15   BTW Papers   ATT.   Original destroyed.

[1] Robert Heberton Terrell (1857-1925) was one of BTW's principal lieutenants and advisers in Washington, D.C. Born in Orange County, Va., he moved to Washington in 1865. He graduated cum laude from Harvard College in 1884, and taught for five years at Miner High School while studying law at Howard University. He received his LL.B. degree in 1889, passed the bar examination, and joined the Mississippi Reconstruction leader John Roy Lynch in a law partnership. He married the strong-minded Mary Church, daughter of the wealthy Memphis real-estate owner Robert R. Church, Sr., who spurred her relatively easygoing husband's ambition. Mary Church Terrell, an Oberlin graduate, was more militant than her husband. She fought against racial discrimination at Oberlin and took part in the early meetings of the NAACP. Robert Terrell, after three years as principal of the M Street High School in Washington, became a municipal judge in the District of Columbia in 1902. BTW secured Terrell this position by persuading Theodore Roosevelt that Terrell was a model of the "new Negro" who would replace the old-style black politician. Terrell managed to keep his judgeship until 1925 by appointment of Taft, Wilson, and Harding. The reappointment by Wilson and confirmation by the Democratic Senate was due partly to his circumspect and judicious behavior, which brought him little credit in the black community; but Terrell made his way also through his own ability.

[2] George Henry White (1852-1918), the last of the black congressmen until 1929, was born in Rosindale, N.C. He graduated from Howard University in 1877 and returned to North Carolina, settling in New Bern, where he was principal of the state normal school and studied law for two years before passing the bar examination. In 1880 he was elected to the state house of representatives and in 1884 to the state senate, and from 1886 to 1894 he was solicitor and prosecuting attorney for the second judicial district. In 1896, because of Republican fusion with the Populists, White was elected to Congress, serving there until 1901. White regarded himself as the chief national political spokesman for black Americans; he took offense at his colleagues' racial slurs, and attacked disfranchisement and lynching. He did not stand for election in 1900, but when his term was up in 1901 he vowed that blacks would again return to the national political scene. White unsuccessfully appealed to BTW for sponsorship for a federal job. Settling in Philadelphia, he practiced law, joined the NAACP, and continued to agitate for equal rights. White also founded an all-black town, Whitesboro, N.J., near Cape May.

From Emmett Jay Scott

Tuskegee, Ala. July 16, 1898

Dear Mr. Washington: I note "Bruce Grit's"[1] reference in the Age today to your Albany speech. It's a magnificent tribute. I think he does it extremely well and in every way brought out in thorough style the incidents of importance. I hope you have seen it ere this time.

We have all read it with a great deal of interest. The "Colored American" has not come. I hope it, too, will have a note from Bruce. He is a brainy fellow. I am glad that I know him. We have been very good friends. Yours very sincerely

Emmett J. Scott

ALS   Con. 15   BTW Papers   ATT.   Original destroyed.

[1] John Edward Bruce.

From Rowland Gibson Hazard[1]

Peace Dale, R.I., July 18, 1898

Dear Sir: I last night heard Louis McWilliams[2] speak and sing with the quartet from your school, in our church here, and also heard a graduate of Tuskegee, who said he was now in a school at Cambria, Va., whose name was Long.[3] I thought you would like to hear direct from an auditor as to the impression these young men make.

McWilliams appeared to be in earnest and to be saying something that he had said many times before in very much the same words he had previously used. The impression conveyed was that he had memorized what he had to say, but it was also clear that he had well in mind the impression he wished to convey, and it was decidedly suggestive of hard work and a sincere desire for an education on his part to be applied to the betterment of his race.

Long, I thought, showed considerable ability. He seemed to have done some original thinking, and I recognized, as I supposed, your skillful guidance in some of his courses of thought. He was not too long, and I should say made an excellent impression upon the audience.

The singing was very good, although I confess that the more cultivated the voices of the colored singers become, the less natural sweetness they have. The songs were very well received, and except for a too noticeable monotony in delivery, were very satisfactory. I think, without exception, every song ended by the repetition of the last verse "sotto voce." The people who heard them were much impressed and glad to know so clearly about Tuskegee.

One point, I am sorry they did not bring out, for it is true, I suppose, that there is a semi-military atmosphere about Tuskegee. The singers were a pretty solid looking lot of men, and looked quite military in their simple uniform. If there were enough of these young men to garrison Cuba, it would go a long way towards establishing the place of the Negro in our present political situation. Very truly yours,

R. G. Hazard

TLS   Con. 146   BTW Papers   DLC.

[1] Rowland Gibson Hazard, a member of the prominent Hazard family, wool manufacturers for three generations in Peacedale, R.I.

[2] Sterling Lewis McWilliams, of Allenton, Ala., graduated from Tuskegee in 1900 and became superintendent of industries at East Tennessee Normal and Industrial Institute.

[3] Edgar Allen Long of Cambria, Va., graduated from Tuskegee in 1895 and taught school in Virginia.

From William Henry Baldwin, Jr.

Long Island City, N.Y., July 18th., 1898

Dear Washington: I have your letter of the 15th to-day, and am exceedingly obliged to you for the clipping on the subject of the Negro troops in Cuba.

I am also indebted to you for your book which was received this morning. I shall want to distribute several copies of it, and I have arranged to get them.

I think your idea of getting the papers to take up the Cuban Tuskegee question is a good one. We can get the endorsement from Washington later, just as well as beforehand, and it is important that you should not lose any of the credit. Yours truly,

W H Baldwin Jr

TLS   Con. 792   BTW Papers   DLC.

From Francis Jackson Garrison

Boston, July 18, 1898

Dear Mr. Washington: I have received a letter from my friend Mr. Joseph Sturge,[1] of Birmingham, England, a son of the famous Quaker philanthropist of the same name who was a particular and intimate friend of the poet Whittier, and who was commemmorated by the latter in one of his most beautiful poems. Mr. Sturge has large interests in the island of Montserrat in the West Indies, and supports a school there for the native colored population. He is somewhat exercised in mind because the schooling which has hitherto been given has not seemed productive of the best results, or what seem to him the most desirable results, and he has asked me if I can give him any light on the subject or help him to procure a teacher from this country.[2] I thought I had the letter in my pocket and intended to enclose it with this, but I find that I have left it at home, and will bring it in to-morrow morning. If you can conveniently drop in and see me in the course of to-morrow, or any day that will suit your convenience, I should like very much to talk over this and one or two other matters with you. I am usually here from nine to five, except during my dinner hour between two and three, but on Tuesday mornings I am always occupied between nine and eleven or half past. Yours sincerely,

Francis J. Garrison

TLS Con. 140 BTW Papers DLC.

[1] Joseph Sturge was the son of the famous Joseph Sturge (1793-1859), an English Quaker antislavery crusader whose testimony for seven days on conditions in the West Indies was influential in the passage of the parliamentary act that abolished slavery in the British empire in 1837.

[2] BTW eventually recommended Wesley Warren Jefferson, an 1899 graduate of Tuskegee, who later that year started an industrial school at Montserrat.

From Booker Taliaferro Washington, Jr.

Kowliaga [Kowaliga], Ala July 20, 1898

My Dear Papa; I guess you think that I have forgoten you, but I have not. I received your letter and was very glad to here from you.

450

Ask mamma did she get my letter, I wrote to her last, Papa the two books that you sent me I thank you very much, I read one of them, and I am ready to read the one that is written by you.

Mrs Bond is going Thursday.

We study our lessons every day.

Davidson is going to write soon.

Tell Mamma that I am having a good time.

Miss Hattie and Dave are well, all send love. Your loving Son,

Baker T. Washington

I want you to guess who these two little boys are in the picture.

ALS Con. 146 BTW Papers DLC.

From Thomas A. Harris

Tuskegee, Ala., July 21, 1898

Dear Sir, I desided I would write you the news of Tuskegee. On the night of the 19. Inst. Ransom Powel a young man who use to go to the Tuskegee Normal School, and has been beating about Tuskegee for some four (4) years, Broke into my house and attempted to commit rape on my daughter Leguster, about three (3) O'Clock at night. Great exsitement prevailed at once. He was persued with blood hounds and captured at once after a manful fight with officers and men. They had to shoot him three (3) times. Though the wounds are flesh wounds and not searous, the worst is through the thigh. I think he will live to be convicted. He made a brave fight for liberty. He is now stoping in the Jail of Tuskegee. The white people here wanted the Colored people to mob him. I would not insist on that. I shot at him three (3) time on his leaving my house. I shot the way he went. I could not see him. My shooting caused me to get him. Yesterday was a day of great excitement in Tuskegee. Had not it been for the help of the white people I would not [have] been able to have captured him. Other than what I have said things are quiet here now. My helth is a good eld [deal?] better than it has been. Things are quiet about the School. I hope you are having success in northen work. I hope to hear from you. I am yours Respectfully,

Thos. A. Harris

ALS Con. 140 BTW Papers DLC. Written on Harris's stationery as attorney-at-law.

To the Editor[1] of *Century Magazine*

Crawford House, Boston, Mass. July 27, 1898

Dear sir: If you think it wise I could so rearrange my article now in your hands in a way to make it apply to education for the colored people in Cuba and Porto Rico as well as to their education in our own country. This will be my address for several days. Yours truly,

Booker T. Washington

TLS Century Collection NN.

[1] Richard Watson Gilder (1844-1909) was editor from 1881 to 1909.

From Robert Alexander Moseley, Jr.

Birmingham, Ala., July 27th 1898

Dear Sir: Yours with enclosure rec'd on expense account.

There can be no misunderstanding with us — as Prof Reynolds and I have a complete agreement. I needed $100.00 — and so told him, and he said he would speak to you — and I hoped it would be convenient for you to oblige me by doing so. Again thanking you, and pledging you all I can do, to have the Bill passed next December, I am Your friend

R A Moseley Jr.

ALS Con. 14 BTW Papers ATT. Original destroyed.

From James Carroll Napier[1]

Nashville, Tenn., July-29-98

Dear Sir: Your letter of July 11th was duly received. A little trip in the country and urgent matters of business have caused my delay in making reply. We enjoyed the visit of you and Mrs. Washington to our city and our home, very much indeed. The pleasure which your visit afforded us makes any effort on your part to express thanks unnecessary.

The little matter of the check was promptly attended to the morning after your departure immediately upon my calling upon Mr. Shaw.[2] A day or two thereafter, the enclosed check and receipt were sent me by the young lady in whose hands you had placed it at Fisk University. Mr. Shaw asked me to forward these to him as soon as I received them, but not knowing his address, I failed to do so. I trust that when you forward them to him you will say to him that my failure to do so was due to the fact that I did not have his Boston address.

I think that you have no earthly reason to be dissatisfied with your speech in Nashville. I have heard it spoken of by a number of Nashville people as well as Northern visitors and every one seemed to be highly pleased with the effort.

Your idea of the relations of the races in this country seems to be the popular one and takes well wherever it is expressed whether before a black, white or mixed audience.

My wife and my Mother join me in kindest regards to you and Mrs. Washington and trust that you may again soon, come this way. Yours truly,

J. C. Napier

TLS Con. 144 BTW Papers DLC.

[1] James Carroll Napier, BTW's principal black supporter in Tennessee, was born near Nashville in 1848. He attended local schools until 1859, when he enrolled at Wilberforce and later at Oberlin. After working in the War Department during the Civil War, Napier obtained a clerkship in the Treasury Department and also earned a law degree from Howard University in 1873 and married John Mercer Langston's daughter. In 1870 and from 1878 to 1884 he served on the Nashville City Council. He was on the Republican state executive committee for sixteen years. Napier was a founder in 1903 of the One Cent Savings Bank, where he worked for many years as cashier. While practicing law and engaging in banking,

he was also active in Republican politics, running for Congress in 1898 and leading a fight against the "lily-white" faction of the party in 1900. In 1911 he became register of the Treasury, the highest appointive post in the federal government held by a black man.

Napier was a close friend of BTW and a member of the National Negro Business League, succeeding BTW as its president in 1916. He opposed segregation but accommodated himself to the trends of the day, hoping that hard work and an accumulation of virtues and wealth would someday change the lot of the black man in America.

² Albert Shaw (1857-1947) was editor of the *American Review of Reviews* from 1893 to 1937. A Johns Hopkins Ph.D. in history (1884), he was an enthusiastic advocate of American expansion in the 1890s, an Anglophile, and an active participant in the Southern Education Movement. He joined the Ogden excursions to the annual Conference for Education in the South and was a member of the Southern Education Board and the Slater Fund board. He was an occasional visitor and contributor to Tuskegee.

From William Henry Baldwin, Jr.

Long Island City, N.Y., Aug. 14th, 1898

Dear Mr. Washington: Have just received your communication about Mrs. Spaulding, and will write you in a day or so. I shall be glad to attend a meeting of the Trustees when you get it arranged.

I am right in the midst now of the very thing that I expected to be handling when you called on me in June to go to Tuskegee. The Montauk Camp¹ is being realized and has taken my entire time, day and night, for the last ten days, and will for the next week or so.

I had a talk yesterday with William S. Quigley, of the "Mail and Express." He is going to be sent to Porto Rico and to Havana to take up the industrial side of the natives in Cuba and Porto Rico. I told him all about you and your desire to have some of the Cubans and Porto Ricans sent to Tuskegee to be educated in your industrial methods and have them return to their country and start the same Institutions there. He is a very intelligent man, and was sent to Havana immediately after the blowing up of the Maine, and knows the conditions there quite well. He was very much impressed with what I told him about your work and was anxious to have some of your literature showing what your Institution covers and what you are doing.

I think it would be well for you to send him whatever printed matter you have at once, and write him a letter promptly telling him your desires in that direction. Yours very truly,

W. H. Baldwin Jr

TLS Con. 792 BTW Papers DLC.

[1] Montauk Camp, at the east end of the Long Island Railroad, was an army center of the Spanish-American War. After service in Cuba the Rough Riders and other troops were stationed there.

To the Editor of the *Christian Register*

Tuskegee, Ala. [Aug. 18, 1898]

Industrial Education for Cuban Negroes

To the Editor of the Christian Register: I believe all will agree that it is our duty to follow the work of destruction in Cuba with that of construction. One-half of the population of Cuba is composed of mulattoes or negroes. All who have visited Cuba agree that they need to put them on their feet the strength that they can get by thorough intellectual, religious, and industrial training, such as is given at Hampton and Tuskegee. In the present depleted condition of the island, industrial education for the young men and women is a matter of the first importance. It will do for them what it is doing for our people in the South.

If the funds can be secured, it is the plan of the Tuskegee Normal and Industrial Institute at Tuskegee, Ala., to bring a number of the most promising negro young men and women to this institution to receive training, that they may return to Cuba, and start in the interest of the people industrial training on the island. Tuskegee is so near Cuba that it is conveniently located for this work.

It will cost for the travelling expenses and education of each one of these Cuban students $150 for a year's education.

We are ready to begin the work as soon as funds are secured or guaranteed. In what better or more permanent way can we help Cuba than by educating a number of these people? What I have said of Cuba applies as well to Porto Rico, where over half the population are negroes. Those who would like to pay the whole or a part of the expenses of one of these students can correspond with

Booker T. Washington

Christian Register, 58 (Aug. 18, 1898), 924-25. The letter also appeared in the Boston *Transcript,* Sept. 3, 1898, 15, and other newspapers.

To Emmett Jay Scott

Crawford House, Boston, Mass. Aug. 23, 1898

Dear Mr. Scott: I have received your several communications and I write very hurriedly on the eve of taking the train for Maine.

I note what you say in regard to Dunbar's article.[1] I am very sorry that he has suffered himself to fly off in this way, not because it will do Tuskegee or the cause of industrial education any harm but I regret to see a man discuss something about which he knows nothing. In matters of poetry and fiction Dunbar is a master; in matters of industrial education and the development of the Negro race he is a novice. Mr. Fortune I think is going to answer him in an early issue of the Independent.

I am looking forward with pleasure to my visit in North Carolina and South Carolina. Yours truly,

Booker T. Washington

TLSr Con. 146 BTW Papers DLC.

[1] Paul Laurence Dunbar, "Our New Madness," *Independent,* 50 (Aug. 18, 1898), 469-71, noted: "We are now in the throes of feverish delight over industrial education. It is a good thing, and yet one of which we can easily have too much." The most pointed remark was addressed to Tuskegee. "Any one who has visited the school at Tuskegee, Ala., and seen the efficiency of the work being done there, can have no further doubt of the ability and honesty of purpose of its founder and president. But I do fear that this earnest man is not doing either himself or his race full justice in his public utterances. He says we must have industrial training, and the world quotes him (in detached paragraphs) as saying that we must not have anything else." This was an example of the ambivalence that also manifested itself in Dunbar's poetry. Dunbar later wrote an ode to BTW, the Tuskegee school song, and the ode on the dedication of Dorothy Hall in 1900.

From Warren Logan

Tuskegee, Ala. Aug. 25, '98

Dear Mr. Washington: I have yours in reference to the Dizer Fund. You say this fund now amounts to $8,000.00. Are you not in error in regard to this? Can it be that Mr. Dizer has added $2,000.00 to it during the summer, or that this amount has been added at some former time and not reported by you? The fund according to the books is $6,000.00. I shall make a strong effort to collect the arrearage of interest on outstanding loans by the first of October.

You will remember that we decided to foreclose mortgages of John Ovletrea[1] and L. L. Ivy[2] if not paid by a certain time. Mr. Ivy has been pleading for additional time. He thinks he will be able to get some one to pay the mortgage for him. I have not heard from him for two or three weeks in regard to the matter, and shall take it up again right away. I had the Ovletrea mortgage foreclosed on the first of the month at Abbeville, Henry County. Oveltrea paid absolutely no attention to the letters which I wrote him. I shall endeavor to sell the property at Abbeville, and have asked an attorney there to look after the matter. Yours very truly,

Warren Logan

TLS   Con. 183   BTW Papers   DLC.

[1] John Wesley Ovletrea graduated from Tuskegee in 1893. Originally from Greensboro, Ala., he later taught in Georgia and then became principal of the Harriman Industrial Institute in Harriman, Tenn.

[2] Lewis L. Ivy of Glenville, Russell County, Ala., was a Tuskegee graduate in 1886. He became principal of a public school in Macon, Miss., and also worked as a carpenter.

From George Washington Carver

Tuskegee Ala. 8-27-98

My dear Mr. Washington: I shall do all I can to find some one to help me as I need them badly. I see the necessity more and more clearly, of my being able to go from place to place on both farm & garden to see that as much as possible is produced and then taken care of after *produceing.*

Now I cannot attend to it all.

A man is here from London Eng. to make a specialty of Horticulture and Bible training, he is a good man. I have a number of applications for to learn Horticulture, the young women want to take that & floriculture gardening ect.

I regret we have such a very few tools belonging to the work. I am going to draw some of them and see if the blacksmith cant make them for us.

The Home Farm & Hort. Depts. have put up several tons of dried hay, and we are still cutting and trying to cure although it is very rainy. Marshall F. is sending us all the Teosinte we can use green and putting up nice crab grass hay for winter. The sweet potato crop bids fair to be an enormous yield. Pumpins & squashes did well and we have them now by the many wagon loads, but it rains so and we have no place to store them so they are rotting very fast. I am haveing them culled daily and used as far as I can.

Mr. Washington I hope you will not let any such articles similar to that of Paul L. Dunbar give you a moments uneasiness but simply stimulate you to press on. You have the only true solution to this great race problem. It is only ignorance *mostly* and a bit of prejudice that prompts such articles. Among both white & black, you are living several hundred years ahead of the common herd of both races. Many of our own dear teachers here are just as blind as can be only live in the present 3 or 4 hundred years from now people will know and honor your greatness much more than now because they will have been educated up to it. Pardon me for taking so much of your val. time. May God bless you & Mrs. Wash. Press on. Very Respy.

Geo. W. Carver

ALS   Con. 138   BTW Papers   DLC.

From Frank E. Saffold

Dear Mr. Washington— This is the programme for Wilmington.

You leave Greensboro Monday at 12:15 — reach Wilmington 7:10 that night; drive direct to the home of a Mr Rivera[1] (with whom you and Mrs. W will stop) and step across the street to the St Stephen's A.M.E. Church of which Dr I. S. Lee, an ardent admirer of yours is pastor. You speak at 8:30 — "colored folk's time." Next morning at St Luke's (M. EZ.) 10 a.m. Mrs. Washington to the colored women only, at 11 you speak same place to ministers and teachers. Right here — if your audience be strictly teachers and preachers, I fear you will speak to only a very few, so I have taken the liberty of saying, privately to a number of professional men, Doctors &c. &c. that at this meeting they will be welcomed. Most of the city school teachers are away just now.

St Stephen's where your mass meeting will be is the largest place in town — wont cost you a cent — and I think you will have a good crowd.

Just now Wilmington (that is the colored & white people) is agog and excited because of the statement made by a negro editor here regarding white women[2] — exactly like the Jesse Duke's affair,[3] and how this is going to effect your reception on the parts of the whites I dont know. A lynching, they tell me, is an impossibility at this seaport — the whites therefore are making much political capital out of it and the Wilmington Messenger is exceedingly bitter. Here to my mind is an opportunity for you to — if you care to, bring about a fine feeling between the races. Many have referred to your Atlanta speech as being just the thing to help defeat the force of these Democratic denunciations of the whole race.

I leave tonight for Columbia. More anon.

Saffold

Mr. Taylor will meet you at the depot. My address Charleston is c/o Dr Crum   Columbia c/o J. E. Wallace. I go from here to Charleston that is more direct and I can easily avoid a conflict of dates.

ALS   Con. 146   BTW Papers   DLC.

¹ Thomas Rivera was a black undertaker in Wilmington.

² Saffold did not exaggerate the excitement in Wilmington. Earlier Alex Manly, editor of the Wilmington *Sentinel,* had written an inflammatory editorial about the causes of lynching. He claimed that white women were attracted to black men and that many cases of alleged rape were not rape. Manly suggested that white men keep a closer rein on their women. The Wilmington white newspaper ran an edited version of Manly's editorial every day for a month prior to election day, and it served as an excuse for whites to attack the progressive black community, which by 1898 had gained substantial political and economic power. Following the election, a committee of whites gave Manly an ultimatum to leave town. A black committee responded in moderate terms, but the letter was not received in time to avert violence on Nov. 10. A white mob burned Manly's press and beat and shot blacks throughout the city. More prosperous blacks were given the "opportunity" to sell out and escape the violence. The state militia eventually restored order. No clear estimate emerged of the number of blacks killed, but it was probably between ten and thirty. The next day whites took over the city government, which formerly had included several blacks, and established authoritarian control over the social, political, and economic life of the city for many years.

³ See above, 2:325-26.

From Horace Bumstead

Intervale N.H. Sept. 7, 1898

My dear Mr. Washington: Where can I find a good report of your Ashfield speech? I have read with much satisfaction your brave words about the annexation of Hawaii and one or two other brief extracts, and wish to see the full address if I can. The painful weakness of the reply to your Hawaiian passage which the Congregationalist¹ of last week has made is a testimony to the essential truth of your statement. Yours very sincerely,

Horace Bumstead

ALS Con. 137 BTW Papers DLC.

¹ *The Congregationalist,* 83 (Sept. 1, 1898), 278, commented: "Booker T. Washington, whom the Boston *Transcript* calls the 'Negro Franklin,' made a speech at Ashfield [Mass.] last week which was admirable on the whole, but in which, we regret to say, he said of the United States: 'We went to the Sandwich Islands with the Bible and Prayer-Book in our hands to win the souls of the natives; we ended by taking their country without giving them the privilege of saying yea or nay.' In the first place, the evangelization of Hawaii was a work of individual initiative, not of governmental action. In the second place, the domination of Americans in Hawaiian commercial and social life was the inevitable result of superior physical and mental stamina, not of trickery or brutal disregard of native rights. In the

third place, the overthrow of the monarchy was the just punishment of a ruler who had disregarded her oath of allegiance to a constitution and had deliberately decided to profit by the re-establishment of corrupt practices. Lastly, it is a fact that in 1854 naught but the death of Kamehameha II prevented Hawaiian annexation by the volition of the Hawaiians themselves." (See also the Boston *Transcript*, Aug. 26, 1898, 4.)

About the same time BTW also spoke against the acquisition of the Philippines. He was reported to have said: "My opinion is that the Philippine Islands should be given the opportunity to govern themselves. They will make mistakes, but will learn from these errors. Until our nation has settled the Negro and Indian problems I do not think we have a right to assume more social problems." (Indianapolis *Freeman*, Sept. 24, 1898, 4, quoting from the Springfield *Republican*.)

BTW thought that there were unique difficulties in annexing Cuba. Minimizing the island's race problems in his argument that it should be self-governing, he said: "In bringing Cuba into our American life we must bear in mind that, notwithstanding the fact that the Cubans have certain elements of weakness, they already seem to have surpassed the United States in solving the race problem, in that they seem to have no race problem in Cuba. I wonder if it is quite fair to the white people and the colored people in Cuba to bring them into our American conditions and revive the race antagonism so that they will have to work out anew the race problem that we are now trying to solve in this country." (Indianapolis *News*, Apr. 15, 1899, clipping, quoted in Foner, *Spanish-Cuban-American War*, 2:416-17.)

An Account of Addresses by Washington and Mrs. Washington Delivered at Charleston

[Charleston, S.C., Sept. 12, 1898]

TWO EARNEST ADDRESSES
DELIVERED BY PROF. WASHINGTON AND HIS WIFE
PROF. WASHINGTON SPOKE TO THE PROFESSIONAL AND
BUSINESS MEN OF HIS RACE, HIS WIFE TO THE
COLORED WOMEN OF CHARLESTON

Prof. Booker T. Washington spoke before a very large audience in Zion Presbyterian Church yesterday morning. In the church were nearly all the representative colored ministers and teachers of the city, besides many others. The assemblage paid close attention to the speaker, and seemed to fully appreciate the worth of his advice. He touched strongly upon several points which were not pleasant, but the bad spots in the negro character were brought to light in order that they might be told how to eradicate them.

461

Prof. Washington spoke of the high morality that must prevail amongst ministers and teachers if they hoped to succeed in their work of uplifting the race. He said that it was much better for the colored people to correct and improve their ways within the race than to spend their time abusing another race that is now above it on account of superior education.

The colored boys and girls should be taught useful occupations. The want of employment leads hundreds to immorality and early death. The girls should be taught housework, sewing, cooking and laundry work. The boys should learn to be carpenters, blacksmiths, masons, etc. The young should not regard this instruction as first steps towards "making servants" of them. The wealthiest woman should be able to keep her own house and the colored man with a trade is very much more likely to own his home than one who grew up in idleness.

Speaking of the high death rate of the colored race, as compared with the white in the same cities, Prof. Washington said the chief causes for this difference were bad whiskey, poor food and poor houses. In many of the latter the ventilation was altogether insufficient. He urged the leaders among the colored people to teach and preach cleanliness of body and in the home. He spoke of the alarming mortality of colored infants, less than one year old. The figures showed the ratio to be four to one against the colored race. This certainly must be due to a lack of care and attention, and the employment of unskilled and careless attendants. All these things should be studied by the ministers and teachers, and the colored people should be brought to a realizing sense of their importance.

The speaker was very earnest and his impressive manner and plain statements certainly made his hearers think. After the lecture many of the prominent leaders remained to talk with Prof. Washington and here again they showed their appreciation of his efforts on behalf of the colored people of the South.

AT OLD BETHEL

Mrs. Booker T. Washington spoke to the colored women at Old Bethel M. E. Church yesterday afternoon. Her address was heard by a very large assemblage of women and was a plain, earnest talk upon the condition and prospects of the colored women of the South. In substance Mrs. Washington said:

"I want to say in the beginning that I do not come before you to criticise or find fault especially, but you know that a great deal of harm has been done us as a race by those who have told us of our strong points, of our wonderful advancement, and have neglected to tell us at the same time of our weak points, of our lack of taking hold of the opportunities about us. Praise a child always and he soon gets to the point where he thinks it impossible for him to make mistakes.

"If we wish to help each other let us not only praise ourselves, but also criticise.

"Plain talk will not hurt us. It will lead each woman to study her own condition, that of her own family and so that of her neighbor's family.

"If I can do anything to hasten this study, I shall feel repaid for any effort I may put forth.

"In consenting to come before you women to-day I am influenced by this thought more than anything else: We need, as a race, a good, strong public sentiment in favor of a sounder, healthier body, and a cleaner and higher-toned morality. There is no use arguing; we do not think enough of these two conditions; we are too indifferent; too ready to say: 'O, well, I keep well, my girls and boys behave themselves, and I have nothing to do with the rest of the race!' No nation or race has ever come up by entirely overlooking its members who are less fortunate, less ambitious, less sound in body and hence in soul, and we cannot do it. We must not do it. There are too many of us down. The condition of our race, brought about by slavery, the ignorance, poverty, intemperance, ought to make us women know that in half a century we cannot afford to lose sight of the large majority of the race who have not, as yet, thrown off the badge of the evils which I have just mentioned.

"You are not, I know, surprised to hear me say that the women, young and older, among us, who most need to take caution in the matter of health and character, are the last to take any personal hold. It is no longer a compliment to a girl or woman to be of a frail and delicate mold. It is no longer an indication of refinement in woman to possess a weak and fastidious stomach.

"It was the great French Emperor who declared that the greatest need of France was mothers. And to-day all who are willing to study facts with reference to our growth and strength in this country declare also that the most serious drawback to the race is its lack of a careful, moral and healthy motherhood.

"You have already noticed that I speak of health, then morals; morals, then health; my sisters, these two things go hand in hand, they are interdependent. They must go thus. They must be studied together at this time. They must be corrected at the same time.

"To be a stronger race physically we have got to be a more moral one. We do not want to lose our tempers when we discuss these conditions either. Now that, as women, we may be able to make a move in the direction of improving the race, we have got to take certain facts regarding our health and morals. They are not all from the standpoint of the Southern white man, either, nor are they all from the Northern white man with a Southern soul. You know that we often feel that every white man and woman south of the Mason and Dixon line is a real devil. It is pretty bad down here, I will admit, but there are many very fine and noble Southern white people, women as well as men. It is a Southern man, an Alabama man, at that, who, in part, at least, makes it possible for us to be here together to-day to study our own shortcomings and to try to find a way out of them. I say it is not Southern whites alone who have felt that we should make a move upward, who feel that we are weak in these directions; nor is it the white man alone at all, but our own medical men, our own educators, who also feel and know that there is too great a laxity amongst us. It is not an easy thing to secure accurate data with reference to the race in these particulars, for, in making up the statistics, especially in Southern localities, the health boards have entirely ignored us; of course, many places in the South have had health boards only recently. However, we have evidence sufficient on each of these subjects to condemn us, to make us feel that something must be done; that some step, and that quick, must be made to stay the awful death rate and the alarmingly increasing illegitimate birth rate among our women and girls. This may not apply to a single woman under the sound of my voice, but it does apply to the race, and so far it comes home to you and to me. We cannot separate ourselves from our people, no matter how much we try; for one, I have no desire to do so.

"I do not mean to tell you, or leave the impression, that all of the disease and immorality in the race are confined to what we are pleased to call our poorer classes or second-class folks. There is too much in our higher classes, especially in the case of too many men who are fathers of the girls and boys who, in their turn, will be fathers and mothers of other girls and boys.

"And does hereditary influence count for nothing? Study your own family as far back as your great grandparents and you will agree with me when I say hereditary influence is a mighty power in the formation of character, physical, as well as moral.

"I give you now these facts for five of our large Southern cities: these relate especially to the death rate of colored people in excess of white people: Rate per thousand in city No. 1, colored 36, white 19; city No. 2, colored 36, white 22; city No. 3, colored 37, white 22; city No. 4, colored 32, white 18; city No. 5, colored 35, white 17. This gives us a decrease in race by death rate in these five cities, in excess of the white people, who already so far outnumber us, respectively 100, 63 and a fraction, 68 and over, 77 and over, and 106 per cent. In one of the large Western cities, and this is not Chicago, either, the death rate of colored people is more than twice that of the white people. Pneumonia and consumption are our most deadly foes. They are not standing still, but are on the increase in every city I have mentioned. In one Northern city alone, in one year, out of ten thousand, there was an excess of deaths, caused by pneumonia and consumption, of 135 per cent of colored people over whites; colored dying, 225, and whites, 126.

"The death rate of our children is something to make us tremble. As long as it is so high we cannot hope for much. Numbers count for a great deal in this country. For five years, in one of our largest Southern cities alone, the excess in death rate among colored children under 5 years of age was 163 per cent, while that of the whites was only 32 per cent and a fraction over. In another large Southern city the death rate per cent in excess for colored children over whites is 883.4 per cent. The diseases which are undermining the life of our babies and robbing the race of its future men and women are, cholera infantum, convulsions and still-born. There is an excess in this last disease, still-born, of colored infants over white of 149 per cent per thousand. What a terrible tribute to our womanhood and to our motherhood this is. In another Southern city, not a thousand miles from here, over half the colored children die before they are 12 months old. We are very often inclined to treat this subject lightly by saying that we are a great producing race, but I have no patience with this indifference, for it is simply impossible for any race to balance any such loss as this. And now, more than this, women, we are not so productive as we used to be. I do not know why, I wish I did. I would count no sacrifice too great to bring about a change in this respect. My grandmother had thirteen sons and daughters, every one of whom lived to rear large families. My mother had ten, most of whom have lived long enough, but they have no children. In the whole ten of us, all grown, there are only two children, and they are the children of the youngest girl, who is now 27 years of age, and there has never been more than these, and what is worse, there never will be. Study this race question, this phase of it, and you will find what I say to be true. We have got to change this state of things. Our educated women will not or do not become mothers and our less intelligent mothers let their little ones die, and thus our numbers are each year growing less and less.

"In every city in the country where you observe it you find that we are losing by death more than we are gaining by birth. Immorality, as well as poverty and ignorance, bears its share of the blame for this low state of vitality. It makes us susceptible to all forms of disease and death. We must have a cleaner 'social morality.' A man who has given thought to the moral life of the race claims that over 25 per cent of the colored children born in one city alone are admittedly illegitimate. In a certain locality, in a certain State, another man states that there were during one year 300 marriage licenses taken out by white men. According to the population 1,200 licenses should have been bought by colored men. How many do you suppose were in reality taken out? Twelve hundred should have been secured and only 3 per cent were taken out. Twelve hundred colored men and women, for whom there is no excuse, living immoral lives, handing down to their offspring disease and crime, and only three living in such a way as to advance the race. No spectacle can be more appalling.

"In a certain Northern city only 2 per cent of the people are colored, yet we furnish 16 per cent of male prisoners and 34 per cent [of] female criminals. In another Northern or Northwestern city we make up 1⅓ per cent of the whole city, and yet 10 per cent of the arrests fall on us. Immorality is directly responsible for these crimes, and hence punishment. Immorality is also directly responsible for physical inability to resist crime. Go North or South, East or West, and the numbers of the dens of abandoned women, of profligate men is too large. These are the breeders of disease and the millstone of the race.

"You say there are causes for all these, causes for which we are not responsible. I admit this much, but there are also causes for which we are responsible. And the fact that there are causes ought to make us hopeful, because we have it in our power to remove these causes. It will take time, however, and it will take wise and consecrated women to effect a change along these lines.

"Not only are poverty, ignorance and intemperance the cause of all this misery, but downright negligence, too, plays a large part in these matters. Colored men drive, cut wood, unload ships, etc., all day in the pouring rain, at night they throw themselves onto a bed and sleep without removing their wet clothes. Our women are little or no better. What is a better feeder for pneumonia and all forms of tuberculosis? The men clean streets, sweep and dust great buildings, with no effort to keep the throat clear of dust and dirt. The majority of cases of consumption are not inherent, but are contracted through lack of thought and interest in one's own self.

"How many of our women during their pregnancy make nothing of lifting from one bench to another heavy tubs of clothes, drawing buckets of water, lift great sticks of wood, run up and down stairs, and a dozen other similar things entirely against them. They do not know the laws of health, and they will not learn them. No, I do not say do not work during the months of unborn motherhood; work, even hard work, is good for one, but the manner in which labor is performed is what I criticise.

"As women can we not do something to correct our condition physically and morally? I think we can.

"The average colored person dislikes water, and he won't keep himself clean. He bathes, if at all, once a week — Saturday night — and changes his clothes in the same indifferent way. He seldom uses a tooth brush. He often even neglects to comb his hair, except on Sunday. There is no excuse for this. Bathe at least twice a week, and change the clothes as often, and be sure to clean the teeth at least once a day, and do not forget to comb the hair each day.

"We eat too little or too poor food. We are ready to buy showy clothing, but we stint our stomachs too often. They call us great eaters. Let us eat more and better food. There is very little vitality in grits and gravy. Get fresh fruit, fresh eggs, good meat, etc. These things give strength not only to women, but to their offspring.

"Keep regular hours. Do not stay in church till 12 and 1 o'clock at night. Go to bed at 10, especially if you labor through the day. When you get up in the mornings air the bedding, open up things for

467

a while and let the sunshine in. When the little child comes do not have an ignorant granny, secure a good physician in addition to at least a clean nurse. Apply your lessons of bathing, feeding, sleeping to these little ones, remembering, of course, their age.

"Teach the boys as well as the girls respect for the marriage tie and home. Be companions for your sons and daughters if you would stop the tide of immorality. A young girl has no business out to a party or church or picnic without some older member of her family or woman friend. Teach the boys to come home at night. Teach them the sin of ruining some man's daughter. These lessons can be taught around the fireside at night, from the pulpit, in the school room, in mothers' meetings; and there should be a mothers' meeting in every community. They can be instilled in many ways. Help secure a minister and teacher who will take an interest in the physical and moral improvement of our families, and together with what we women can do and our ministers and teachers, we shall be able to make some progress in the coming ten or fifteen years which will prove to our enemies that our condition physically and morally is nothing inherent or peculiar to race, but rather the outcome of circumstances over which we can and will become masters. In this way and only in this way will [we] satisfy the men and women, both North and South, who still have faith in us. Let us teach our boys and girls some useful occupations, let us insist upon an intelligent and moral ministry, let us employ teachers only who are above reproach, and above all let those of us who have had an opportunity, who have educational advantages, modify our caste lines — stoop down now and then and lift up others."

PROPER APPRECIATION

At the conclusion of the address delivered by Prof. Washington at the Zion Presbyterian Church yesterday morning the following resolutions were presented by the Rev. J. L. Dart[1] and adopted by a rising vote:

"Whereas, the people of Charleston have heard with great delight and benefit the able, instructive and helpful address of Prof. Booker T. Washington, president of the Normal and Industrial Institute of Tuskegee, Alabama.

Resolved, That the people of this city, irrespective of race and color, hail the coming of Mr. Washington among us upon so important a mission as that of the elevation of the negro race as an advanced step in the right direction and as marking the beginning of a new era in the progress of the colored race.

Resolved, That the people of this city return their sincere thanks to Prof. Washington and Mrs. Washington, also to the trustees of the John F. Slater fund, under whose auspices they are commissioned, for the timely advice, helpful suggestions and wise and fraternal sentiments given and expressed by them, and we pledge ourselves to heed the same, act upon them, and thus, with God's help, to endeavor and improve our moral and industrial condition."

After the exercises a reception was given for Mr. and Mrs. Washington in the basement of the church by the Ministerial Union and refreshments were served to all present.

BACK TO TUSKEGEE

Prof. and Mrs. Washington left Charleston yesterday afternoon for Tuskegee. The College opens on Tuesday and the president must be on hand. The visit to Charleston should be long remembered by the colored people of this city and if the plain facts shown forth by this intelligent and earnest couple are taken home by the men and women who heard them, then, indeed, will their mission bear fruit and work not only for the good of the Southern negro, but the entire South.

Charleston *News and Courier,* Sept. 13, 1898, 3.

[1] John L. Dart, born a free black, graduated from Avery Normal Institute in Charleston in 1872. He also attended Atlanta University and Newton Theological Seminary in Newton, Mass. After preaching in the North and in Georgia, he returned to Charleston in 1886 as pastor of the Morris Street Baptist Church. In 1895 he founded the Charleston Industrial Institute. In 1900 he attended the founding meeting of BTW's National Negro Business League in Boston. (Tindall, *South Carolina Negroes,* 205.)

To Jabez Lamar Monroe Curry

Charleston, S.C. Sept 12, 1898

Dear sir: The meetings which we have just finished in this city have been by far the largest and I think the most valuable. There were so many who wanted to attend the meetings in Charleston that I found it necessary to speak three times. Yesterday at three o'clock I spoke to about 1400 people in the Methodist church and several hundred about the windows within hearing distance. At night I spoke to about 1500 in the Baptist church and several hundred on the outside near enough to hear. Monday morning I spoke to about 600 in another church, besides meeting the ministers &c. 800 women attended Mrs. Washington's meeting in the afternoon Monday.

I know that the temptation is to over estimate the permanent value of large meetings, but I find an interest about these meetings that I have not seen before. The people seem to realize that they need help and light in regard to their physical, moral and industrial condition and they almost overwhelm us with their expressions of gratitude. At each place the ministers and teachers have passed a hearty vote thanking you and the Slater Board for these meetings. The ministers and teachers at each place have promised by organized effort to continue what we have begun.

At each place the white people and news papers have taken the deepest interest. You will note that I have placed considerable emphasis upon the industrial side. I have done it for the reason that I find a large idle class in the cities. This idleness leads to immorality and the immorality is largely responsible for a high death rate. In Charleston the death rate is three times as great among our people as among the whites, and among the children between one and six years of age it is almost five times as great.

The number of colored people leaving the country districts and moving to the cities is very large and I fear increasing. Few of these find profitable employment and thus they are lead into crime.

I send you today some more papers bearing upon these meetings. I regret that for the present we shall have to stop this work and return to Tuskegee. We have enjoyed the work so much. Yours Sincerely

Booker T. Washington

ALS   Milton S. Eisenhower Library   MdBJ.

To Emily Howland

Tuskegee, Alabama. Sept. 16, 1898

My dear [Miss] Howland: I have just inspected the addition to the girls' cottage for which you gave us the money. I do not remember that I told you that we concluded that it was best to make a two story cottage of one of our one story cottages. The added story has not improved the looks of the building but has given us nine beautiful large light airy rooms which will add so much to the comfort of the girls. We are so very grateful to you for this help.

I know that you rejoice with us in the close of the war. We found it *very hard* to get money during the war and now shall have to do our best to catch up what we have lost.

Mrs. Washington is quite well and desires to be remembered to you. Yours Sincerely

Booker T. Washington

ALS   Emily Howland Papers   NN-Sc.

To the Editor of the Washington *Colored American*

Tuskegee, Ala., Sept. 20, 1898

I write to correct the impression created by a report sent out of Brunswick, Ga., some days ago in regard to the treatment of Major R. R. Wright[1] by a certain Texas regiment.[2]

The South is responsible for a good many sins, but this special sin charged up against the South, so far as Major Wright is concerned is without foundation. The despatch was evidently manufactured by this Texas regiment for the purpose of home consumption.

It was my pleasure and privilege to be with Major Wright during a portion of his visit through South Carolina and Georgia, and I took especial pains to note the manner in which he was treated by the various southern regiments he was engaged in paying off. I saw Major Wright immediately after he finished paying the troops in Brunswick and he stated to me that he was treated with the utmost courtesy by both officers and men while he was performing his duty as paymaster; that the nearest action bordering upon discourtesy was in the case of one or two officers who came in his presence in the paymaster's tent with their caps on, but when he called attention to this seeming discourtesy the caps were removed at once. In Columbia, S.C., I was with Major Wright on the streets and I took especial pains to see how he would be treated by the South Carolina troops whom he met on the streets in Columbia, and in no instance while I was with Major Wright did any of the privates fail to salute him in the proper manner. As soon as the Colonel of the South Carolina regiment heard that Major Wright had reached Columbia he called at his residence and paid his respects and the next morning came in and drove Major Wright out to the camp where he paid the regiment and was treated with proper courtesy by both officers and men.

Booker T. Washington

Washington *Colored American,* Oct. 1, 1898, 2.

¹ Richard Robert Wright, Sr., was for a brief time in 1898 an army paymaster with the rank of major.

² The *Colored American* had reported that Wright was insulted by soldiers who refused to draw their pay from a Negro. The report stated that southern soldiers objected to the fact that Wright was not in the position of a servant. (Washington *Colored American,* Sept. 17, 1898, 4.)

From William Rainey Harper

Chicago, Sept. 21st, 1898

My dear Sir: The citizens of Chicago have arranged to celebrate the close of the Spanish War and the Peace with which once more our land is blessed. The preparations for the celebration are upon a scale to some extent commensurate with the significance of the event. The President of the United States and the Members of his Cabinet have indicated their interest in the celebration by consenting to be present. The guests of the City on this occasion will include the members of the Diplomatic Corps, many representatives of the United States Senate and Congress and distinguished citizens from all parts of the country. The celebration will include among other features addresses upon appropriate subjects, to be given on Tuesday afternoon, October 18th, at 3:00 o'clock. It is proposed that the larger assembly halls and theatres of the City shall be opened on this occasion and that distinguished gentlemen shall be invited to discuss questions which they themselves may think appropriate for such an occasion. It is still further proposed that these addresses shall be published in permanent form. I write on behalf of the Committee to invite you to make one of the addresses. We desire to give you the largest liberty in the choice of subjects and length of treatment, and shall be pleased to make such arrangements for the delivery of the address as shall be satisfactory to yourself. You may be sure that your audience will number from two to four thousand people.

The celebration will close with a banquet to which there will be invited one thousand guests. This banquet will be arranged upon a larger scale than any that has yet been given in the City of Chicago. In connection with the banquet there will be brief addresses. These addresses also will be published in permanent form.

We sincerely trust that you will co-operate with us in this undertaking. Trusting that I may have the pleasure of hearing from you at once, I remain, Yours very truly,

> William R Harper
> Chairman of Invitation Committee

N.B. It will, of course, give us the greatest pleasure to make all the necessary arrangements for your transportation and entertainment in connection with your visit to Chicago.

TLS Con. 1 BTW Papers DLC. Written on stationery of the National Peace Jubilee. Docketed: "Have promised to speak Sunday night. Could only speak 15 minutes."

To Frank E. Saffold

[Tuskegee, Ala.] 9, 22, 1898

Mr. Saffold: Just as soon as you possibly can I wish you would take measures to see that no brooms in your department are permitted to stand on the floor with the sweeping end downward. See that all brooms are kept in tin pockets on the walls.

> B. T. W.

TLI Con. 13 BTW Papers ATT. Original destroyed.

From William Edward Burghardt Du Bois

Philadelphia   22 Sept 98

My Dear Sir: Your letter of the 18th has just reached me. I think it very probable that I can be in Boston early in December on the occasion you suggest. The final decision must of course come from the authorities at Atlanta but I've little doubt of their willingness to grant me leave of absence for the time. Awaiting further details, I remain Very Sincerely Yours,

W. E. B. Du Bois

ALS   Con. 139   BTW Papers   DLC.

From William J. Barnett[1]

San Luis, De Cuba. Sept. 23rd 1898

Dear sir: Yours of the 26th ult. received, and in reply will say, the newspaper clipping you spoke of in your letter, I did not receive. However, after reading your letter, I came to the conclusion that you wanted me to get 2 men or women (young) that were willing to come to your school, and receive an education, *free,* transportation to be furnished by you.[2] In your reply I would be glad if you would send me the clipping you mentioned in yours of the 26th ult, so I shall be able to give them all information necessary. I await your early reply, I am sir, Yours Resp'tfully

W. J. Barnett
Chief Musician 8th Ill. Inf. Vol.

P.S. Regiment quartered at the above named place condition good, has been quite a large am't of sickness, but glad to say it is on the decrease now.

HLS   Con. 136   BTW Papers   DLC.

[1] William J. Barnett (1869-1906) was a black musician from Jacksonville, Ill. In 1896 he organized the McKinley band to play in the political parades. This band became the Eighth Illinois Infantry Regiment band and went to Cuba with the

regiment. Barnett contracted malaria and was discharged in Apr. 1899. He organized bands in Chicago, St. Louis, and a number of southern Illinois cities. For
years he was leader of the Wallace Brothers circus band, and was secretary-treasurer
for several years of the Chicago Giants, a black baseball team.

[2] Olivia Egleston Phelps Stokes read of BTW's desire to provide an education
for Cuban students and offered to provide tuition and board for two students.
(Stokes to BTW, Sept. 14, 1898, Con. 280, BTW Papers, DLC.)

From Henry Sylvester Williams[1]

London. Eng. 27-9-98

Sir, I am directed by the African Association to call your attention to
this organisation with its Headquarters in London, and to ask your
co-operation & membership.

We are just entering upon our second year of existence & as you
will notice in the Rules which you will find enclosed the object is to
aim at a fuller & perfect sympathy of all our people claiming African
descent.

I take it that you are alive to the necessity of a general union
amongst the children & descendents of Ham, as it would tend to create
a respect for us which today is non est. This the African Assoc. will
endeavor to promote, & to make representations in cases of oppression
effecting our people wherever found.

Hoping to hear from you and from any other who may be interested through you. I remain, Yours truly

H Sylvester Williams
Hon. Sec. Afr. Assoc.

ALS   Con. 148   BTW Papers   DLC.

[1] Henry Sylvester Williams (1869-1911) was the principal organizer of the Pan-
African Conference of 1900. Probably born in Trinidad of black parents from
Barbados, he was educated in Trinidad and was an elementary-school teacher there.
Wishing to study law, he studied in 1893-94 in the law school of Dalhousie Uni-
versity in Nova Scotia. He spent several years in New York City, then migrated to
England and enrolled in Gray's Inn.

It was during Williams's five years as a law student that he and Rev. Joseph
Mason organized the African Association in 1897, which sought to enroll all the
Africans in the British Isles for mutual help. Beginning late in 1898, the association
sponsored a Pan-African Conference to meet in 1900. BTW met with others to

help plan the conference during his visit to London in July 1899, but he found himself unable to attend the conference when it met the following year. Williams did not star as a speaker of the 1900 conference, but his effective administration of it helped to develop Pan-Africanism as a movement. In 1901 on a visit to Kingston, Jamaica, he established a branch of the Pan-African Association.

Williams was admitted to the bar at London in June 1902. Some of his work as a barrister was for West Indian and African clients, but he also had other interests. In 1906 as a member of the Progressive and Labor party, he won a three-year term on the St. Marylebone borough council, where he sought to improve housing conditions of the poor. He returned to Trinidad in 1908, where he practiced law until his sudden death in 1911. (Contee, *Henry Sylvester Williams.*)

To Frank E. Saffold

[Tuskegee, Ala.] 9, 28, 1898

Mr. Saffold: I send you by bearer a sample of the bread which was given the students yesterday for their dinner. You can easily see that such cooking is not only a great waste but is very injurious to the health of the students. I am sure that we are paying enough now for service in connection with the boarding department to have things in first class condition.

I do not think there is any necessity for giving the students so much fat meat as that on this saucer would indicate that they are given.

Booker T. Washington

TLS   Con. 13   BTW Papers   ATT.   Original destroyed.

From John Herbert Phillips[1]

Birmingham, Ala. Sept. 28/98

Dear Sir: We need at once in our schools five teachers. If you can recommend five bright, well educated young women, who have recently completed your course, I will guarantee them places at once. The salary at the start will be small — $25 to $30, per month, but the Board of Education will shortly be in a position to pay better salaries for efficient teachers. Please let me hear from you so that I may report to the Board at its meeting next Monday night. Very Truly

J. H. Phillips

ALS   Con. 144   BTW Papers   DLC.

[1] John Herbert Phillips (1853-1921) was an able superintendent of public schools of Birmingham, Ala., from 1883 to 1921. Born in Covington, Ky., of Welsh parents, Phillips attended schools in Ohio and took an A.M. degree at Marietta College in 1883. Phillips secured favorable legislation and local taxation and attracted able teachers, building an urban school system suited to the rapidly growing coal, iron, and steel center. An industrial high school for blacks was begun in 1899. (Dabney, *Universal Education in the South,* 2:402-7.)

From Isaac Fisher[1]

Aiken, S.C., Sept. 29, 1898

Dear Mr. Washington: You will find enclosed $1.25, money order, which is the balance of my indebtedness to you. As you will doubtless remember, I paid $8.75 of the $10 which I owed you, before I left Tuskegee.

I want to again express my gratitude to you for your personal interest in me while I was at Tuskegee. That interest has even followed me here, for I am certain that the great things which the faculty and students of the Schofield School expect of me, are creations of Miss Schofield's[2] imagination, resulting from your recommendation of me. I pray for strength to come up to the standard which these people have set for me.

On the 15th inst., I closed two months of continuous travelling and negro Conference work in the state. School opens Monday, a week after which, I shall again take the road to be gone about three weeks after which I shall go in the class-room.

I hope to be able, some time, to make a contribution to Tuskegee — I feel that I owe a lasting debt to the school. At present, I am discharging my obligations and getting straight generally and so can't help your work, but I will in some small degree at least, when I am better situated.

When I shall feel that in a measure my work has reflected credit upon Tuskegee, I mean to write you. Until that time, I don't care to have the school hear from me at all. I am going to try to do my best.

Please send me a catalogue, your last financial report and one of those financial statements which I think was prepared when Mr. Smith was at Tuskegee auditing the school's accounts.

Believe me Mr. Washington, I am your sincere admirer and friend,

Isaac Fisher

ALS   Con. 703   BTW Papers   DLC.

¹ Isaac Fisher was born on a cotton farm in Outpost, La., in 1877 and moved to Vicksburg, Miss., in 1886. At Tuskegee he received much personal help from Margaret Murray Washington and graduated at the head of his class in 1898, having won all the school's top honors during his last two years. Because of his outstanding ability, BTW sent him to teach at the Schofield School in Aiken, S.C. There Fisher organized farmers' conferences similar to those held at Tuskegee. In the late 1890s, taking advantage of Fisher's oratorical skill, BTW appointed him Tuskegee's agent for New England. After two successful years, Fisher requested transfer to the South, where he directed the Tuskegee farmers' conferences. He was principal for a short time of the Swayne School in Montgomery before moving to New York City, where he studied the public school system. On BTW's recommendation he then accepted the presidency of the Branch State Normal School in Pine Bluff (Arkansas State Normal School for Negroes), which he held from 1902 to 1911. While there, Fisher won nearly thirty national essay contests. In 1911 he was principal of the East Carroll Baptist Normal and Industrial Institute at Lake Providence, La. In 1914 Fisher became the first editor of the Tuskegee-based journal *The Negro Farmer*. About 1916 he became editor of the *Fisk University News* and taught journalism and debating at Fisk. He was subsequently general secretary of the Hampton Institute YMCA. BTW frequently pointed to Fisher as one of Tuskegee's outstanding graduates.

² Martha Schofield, a Pennsylvania Quaker, founded in 1868 a school at Aiken, S.C., that became the Schofield Normal and Industrial School, under the auspices of the Freedmen's Commission of Germantown, Pa. It used a frame building erected in 1870 by the Freedmen's Bureau until 1882, when a two-story brick building was erected. By the turn of the century the school offered secondary academic training and also courses in carpentry, agriculture, harnessmaking, blacksmithing, wheelwrighting, shoemaking, sewing, cooking, millinery, and laundering. (Tindall, *South Carolina Negroes*, 224.)

From Timothy Thomas Fortune

New York, Oct 1 1898

My dear Friend: I was unable to go to New Haven today as I wished and the doctor advised, because of the mixed political situation here and the fear that I am not just well enough to go away. I am glad to say however that I am feeling in better trim than when I last wrote you and hope to keep on improving.

I had a long chat with Col. Roosevelt[1] this morning on general topics, in the course of which he spoke of you and your work in terms of unstinted admiration. He seems to be a very open and honest man and I rather like him.

Young Benson stopped a moment yesterday with his face turned towards Boston.

With kind regards for you and the family. Yours truly

T. Thomas Fortune

ALS   Con. 139   BTW Papers   DLC.

[1] Theodore Roosevelt (1858-1919), twenty-sixth President of the United States (1901-9), played a significant role in BTW's career. Perhaps the two men had a personal acquaintance earlier than this letter, though there is no evidence of it in the private papers of either. In 1899 BTW and Roosevelt spoke from the same platform at Elmira, N.Y., during the latter's governorship of New York, and BTW sent a congratulatory telegram when Roosevelt was elected Vice-President in 1900. Soon afterward, Roosevelt invited BTW to visit him, confided his desire to be President, and secured BTW's help among black Republicans in return for a promise to help the Negro and the entire South as President.

Roosevelt was planning a visit to Tuskegee with Jacob Riis in 1901 that had to be postponed for five years when he suddenly found himself President on account of the assassination of McKinley. He immediately called in BTW as a consultant on black and southern political matters. During the course of these discussions, on Oct. 16, 1901, Roosevelt invited BTW to dinner with him, his family, and another guest at the White House. This occasioned a storm of editorial attack on Roosevelt, particularly in the southern press. Both men ignored the criticisms, and the excitement soon subsided, to flare up again from time to time. Roosevelt never invited BTW to dinner again, but he consulted him freely on all black appointments and those of many southern whites, and also on his public speeches, messages, and party platform planks on racial and southern matters.

Through his influence on Roosevelt and other highly placed Republicans, BTW was able to place many of his followers in office and thus build a political machine. He used his patronage power in the South to fight the "lily-white" Republican organizations and to replace some old-line politicians with those who shared his business ideals and others who were loyal simply because they were beholden to him. His influence on Roosevelt's utterances and actions in racial matters, however, was negligible, as is shown by the President's order in 1906 dismissing two companies of black soldiers after an alleged riot in Brownsville, Tex. BTW tried to prevent the presidential order, but even though he was unsuccessful he continued to be loyal to Roosevelt.

After his term of office expired, Roosevelt became a trustee of Tuskegee, and, despite the shadow of Brownsville, BTW and Roosevelt remained close friends. In 1912, torn between this friendship and a lifelong Republican loyalty, BTW refused to announce publicly how he intended to vote. After BTW's death, Roosevelt took an active part in the trustees' selection of Robert R. Moton as successor to the principalship. (Harlan, *BTW*, 304-24.)

A Sunday Evening Talk

Tuskegee, Alabama   October 2d, 1898

HOW TO BUILD A RACE

In a great sermon which I once heard Phillips Brooks preach, he used a sentence something like this: "One generation gathers the material and the next generation builds the palaces." He simply meant by that, that one generation laid the foundation for the succeeding generation. The earlier generation is always the one which has to deal very largely with the rougher affairs of life, in order that the next generation might have the privilege of dealing with the higher and finer affairs of life.

I repeat that sentence for the sake of emphasis, for I want you to think about it; "one generation gathers the material and the other builds the palaces." Now this is true of all generations; all people; that one generation has got to lay the foundation for the next generation, and unless the foundation is properly laid — is deeply laid — it is impossible for the succeeding generation to have a very successful career.

I read you a few evenings ago a few extracts from a letter written by our minister to Liberia[1] to a paper published in this country. You remember that among other things, he said that in Liberia uncut ham cost 30 cents, and cut ham 40 cents per pound; lard cost 40 cents; flour was as high as $35.00 a barrel — I fear that if we were in Liberia we would get very little flour bread to eat. Meal costs from $2 to $3 per bushel. They have no wagons built in Liberia; no wheelbarrows, no carts, no bricks, no public roads. What is said of Liberia, is almost true of the Republic of Hayti and of the Republic of Santo Domingo. Both of these countries are in a discouraging condition. Now, what is the trouble, why is there this general want of progress? I simply tell you what you already know, when I say that Liberia, San Domingo and Hayti are among the richest countries in natural resources in the world. Nature has given the inhabitants of these countries immensely rich territories. Then what is the trouble? It is simply this, that these people have not turned their brains to the cultivation of the soil. They have not put their brains into the construction of the agricultural implements and machinery which go toward laying the foundation of a race.

At Tuskegee we emphasize two lines of work; first, normal teaching; second, industrial training, by which we purpose to send out young men and women skilled in all these lines of industrial, agricultural and domestic science and in the fine mechanic arts. We do this not without a purpose, not without thinking; we do it because we have studied the condition of the 8,000,000 of our people in the country, and unless this generation can be wise enough, brave enough, strong enough, to put intelligent brains into these occupations, and thus lay the foundation deeply for the generations that are to come, it is impossible that we shall have a successful race in this country. Without this courage and patience necessary to the laying of this foundation, we shall find ourselves in the same condition as the unfortunate people of Hayti, Liberia and San Domingo.

We cannot say that in these Republics to which I have referred, these people are in this condition for want of education. Of course there is no public school system in either of these places to commend, but from all of them there have gone men to France and England and Germany who are highly educated so far as letters are concerned; especially is this true of Hayti, where the people have been educated in France for a number of generations, and have a high degree of literary education. But practically none have been trained along industrial and scientific lines. Whenever the government of Hayti wants an engineer for her men-of-war, it sends to England or the United States; or for an engineer to build the bridges and other work requiring technical knowledge and skill. Unless you, young men and women, are going to be missionaries along all these lines of development, we cannot hope to have a race that will ever be on its feet. You have got to go out and lay the foundation. We expect you to become leaders in all these important lines. It is not enough that our people get book education, but we must connect with our book learning, industrial development, and no race which fails to do this, will ever get upon its feet.

You are the generation that in a large measure has got to gather the material with which we can lay the foundation for future success along all of these material lines. This we must do, altho in this generation we may not build as many palaces as we might like to build.

I want to be a little more specific in showing you what you have got to do and how you must do it.

One trouble with us is, and the same is true of any young people, no matter what race or condition, one trouble is, we have too many stepping stones. We step all the time, from one thing to another. You find a young man who is learning to make brick, and if you ask him what he intends to do after learning the trade, in nine cases out of ten he will answer, "Oh, I am simply working at this trade as a stepping stone for something higher." You see a young man working at the brickmason's trade and he will be apt to say the same thing. And young women learning to be milliners and dressmakers will tell you the same — all are stepping to something higher. And so, we always go on, stepping somewhere, never getting hold of anything thoroughly. Now we must stop this stepping business, having so many stepping stones. Instead, we have got to take hold of these important industries and stick to them until we master them thoroughly. There is no nation so thorough in their education as the Germans. Why? Simply because the German takes hold of a thing and he sticks to it until he masters it, into it he puts brains and thought from morning till night; he reads all the best books and journals bearing on that particular study, and he feels that nobody else knows so much about it as does the German. Take any of the industries I have mentioned, that of brickmaking. You have the average young man who has been working at this trade at Tuskegee or elsewhere, go into any city in the South and commence working at a brickyard. In nine cases out of ten that young man has no idea of staying on that brickyard.

Now in this and other matters we make a mistake; what we want to do is to learn to make bricks thoroughly. Any of you who are working at that trade should determine to learn all there is to be known about making bricks; read all the papers and journals bearing upon the trade; learn to not only make common handbricks but pressed bricks, fire bricks, in short the finest and best bricks there are to be made. And when you have learned all you can by reading and talking with other people, you travel from one city to another and learn how the best bricks are made. And then when you go into business for yourself, you will make a reputation for yourself for being the best brickmaker in the community, and in this way you will put yourself on your feet and become a helpful and useful citizen. When a young man does this, goes out into one of these Southern cities and makes a reputation for himself, that person wins a reputation that is going to give him a standing position. And when the children of that successful brickmaker come along, they will be able to take a higher position in life; the grand children will be able to take a still higher position. And it all will be traced back to that grandfather who, by his great success as a brickmaker, laid a foundation that was of the right kind.

If you are learning to be a brickmason, make up your minds that you are going to make a success of it. Don't make a "stepping stone" out of the work, saying that next week you are going to take up something better. You make that your profession; succeed in it, learn all there is to be learned about brickmasonry; stick to it until you have learned all there is to be learned about the trade, or as much as anybody can learn about it; and then when you have made a successful mason or contractor of yourself you will be able to build for yourself a fine house and have all the comforts of a refined, cultured home. You can do this by taking this most important industry and making a success of it.

What I have said about these two trades can be applied with equal force to the trades followed by women. Take the matter of millinery; there is no good reason why there should not be in each principal city in the South at least three or four competent colored women in charge of millinery establishments. But what is the trouble? Instead of making the most of our opportunities along these lines the temptation is to be music teachers, teachers of elocution, or something else that nobody has any money to pay for, or have not the opportunity to earn money to pay for simply because there is no foundation. But when the colored people as a mass become successful brickmakers or brickmasons and contractors, they will then be able to put their daughters under the direction of music teachers and elocutionists.

And now, what I have said about these important industries is especially true of the important industry of agriculture. We are living in a country where, if we are going to succeed at all we are going to do so by what we raise out of the soil, and the people in those countries to which I have referred have failed to give attention to the cultivation of the soil, to the invention and use of improved agricultural implements and machinery. Without this no people can succeed. No race which fails to put brains into agriculture can succeed; and if you want to realize the truth of this statement go with me this month into the back districts of Georgia, Mississippi and Alabama and you will find these people almost in a starving condition, slowly starving to death and yet they are surrounded by a rich country.

Are you going to stand still and see these people starve? Are you not willing to make any sacrifice in order to prepare yourself to help these people? I believe you will. Learn all you can about agriculture, about the use of improved machinery, about the science of agriculture. Show them how they can get a living: show them how to so use their land that they will not starve while living on the richest and most productive soil it has been the fortune of any people to live upon.

We must do this. There is no hope for the race unless the young men and women of the race lay hold of these important matters.

I have spoken to you thus plainly because I feel that it is our only salvation as a race, and if any of you can see any other way out I should be very glad to have your advice.

Tuskegee Student, 12 (Oct. 20, 1898), 3-4.

¹ William Henry Heard (1850-1937), schoolteacher, A.M.E. clergyman, and Reconstruction politician in South Carolina, was born in slavery in Elbert County, Ga. Through the lobbying efforts of Bishop Henry M. Turner and others, Grover Cleveland appointed Heard minister resident and consul general to Liberia from 1895 to 1899. While in Liberia he built the first A.M.E. church in Monrovia. In 1908 he became a bishop of West Africa and served there until 1916.

To George William Dixon¹

[Tuskegee, Ala.] October 4, 1898

Dear Sir: I have replied to Hon. John Barton Payne² accepting the invitation of the banquet committee to be present as a guest at the banquet to be tendered to the President of the United States, Wednesday evening, October 19th, and also to Bishop Fallows³ accepting the invitation to deliver an address at the Thanksgiving services, Sunday, October 16th. I am advised that the acceptance of these invitations does not necessitate my sending check for banquet ticket. Yours truly,

Booker T. Washington

TLS Con. 146 BTW Papers DLC. Charles Henrotin, chairman of the

National Peace Jubilee assignments committee, replied on this letter: "You are our guest and will be provided with ticket to banquet on your arrival here."

[1] George William Dixon (1866-1938), a Chicago lawyer, businessman, and banker, and later state senator (1903-7).

[2] John Barton Payne (1855-1935), judge of the superior court of Cook County, Ill., 1893-98. He was Secretary of the Interior in the Wilson administration and chairman of the American Red Cross from 1921 to 1935.

[3] Samuel Fallows.

From Richard Robert Wright, Sr.

College, Ga., Oct. 4th, 1898

My Dear Mr. Washington: I noticed in the New York Age your article with reference to the treatment accorded me by Southern soldiers and I took the liberty to hand it to our morning daily which reproduced it. Your statement is substantially correct and I think will do good. It is not only just but good policy to recognize the endeavors of our white neighbors to treat us courteously, &c. I shudder when I think of the many agencies at work to drive these two people apart and hostile to each other. In mollifying this alleged hostile feeling you are doing philanthropic service as an evangel of peace. If I have had any success in my humble career it has been because of my pronounced effort to see the best side of the Southern white man. In fact I want to see the best side of every man. Our boys and girls must be taught to see something good in the white man south as well as north; in this way we shall teach the white man to see something good in us. For upon peace and good will between the races depends our progress.

I congratulate you not only upon the opportunities which you have, but more upon the splendid use that you are making of these opportunities for the strengthening of the bonds of peace.

My best regards to Mrs. Washington. We are not well. Your friend

R R Wright

TLS Con. 146 BTW Papers DLC.

From Allen Alexander Wesley[1]

San Luis De Cuba   October 5th 1898

Dear Sir— Your letter of the 17th ult just received. In regard to the young persons mentioned I shall take pleasure in trying to find the right kind of persons to come and take up the opportunity presented so generously by you. The poverty of the country is something alarming. The Spanish left the country well nigh starved out.

But these people are heroic and brave some of them loathe the idea of receiving any charity but the majority are forced to take it. There are some of course who like to be fed and clothed by others but this latter class is small indeed. The Government is now issuing out rations to the needy and hundreds of rations are given out daily by our regiment, i.e. some one of our regiment acting as disbursing agent, through our General Ewers.[2]

We are also giving out clothing which has been sent through the Red Cross Society by Cuban sympathizers. We have seen a great change among the people since we have been here. The presence of so many Americans (colored) whom the Cubans i.e. the darker ones, know are their friends seems to have stimulated them to do all they can to improve their appearance. It is a common custom here for the babies to be carried around nude and this does not seem to be confined to the very poor but the others who are not so poor have the same custom and yet since our arrival I think I see an attempt to put some kind of a covering over the children.

The Cubans are a kind and gentle people and the climate of Cuba is indeed the friendship of earth and air, but during the rainy season or when we came here, it rained every day at 2 P.M. The rainy season ends with the 1st day of November and then they say the weather is just lovely. Our regiment has been very fortunate as regards its health. I understand that we are having the lowest sick rate of any regiment on this part of the island. We have about 8% sick. This is with Malarial fever of the intermittent type, and some slight intestinal troubles. We have had our troubles here as in the States, i.e. some persons were envious of our seeming success and endeavored by slander & innuendo to damage our regiment and good name. This caused and examening committee to be appointed by the President and the report of this committee was quite different. This put at rest these carping critics for a little while at least.

The Brigade Surgeon when last investigating the different regiments told me personally as well as others that he had seen but one better hospital on the Island than the one which I had. I have charge of the Medical Department of the 23rd Kansas and the 8th Ill Inf. How long I shall be able to maintain this reputation remains to be seen, because as I understand it just as soon as the yellow fever scare is over there will be a great struggle to get places here and just what man can do and say when he wants a Negro's place has not been written. . . . My hospital is surrounded by *Banana* trees. Palms & Cocoa-nut trees are abundant indeed the Palm is the domestic tree of this part of the island. The tree furnishes the boards for the house i.e. the sides, cocoa nut trees are used for the posts and scantlings and the roof is covered with Palm leaves. I am told that the tree also furnishes salt, i.e. the natives sometimes when short of salt cut the Palm wood into short strips and put them into whatever they wish to season. There are numerous coffee & sugar plantations in this section. The most of the sugar mills here seem to be owned by the French, i.e. Frenchmen came here & got the land in some way and raise sugar in very much the same way it is done in Louisiana.

Excuse this tiresome letter. Remember me kindly to all the Fiskites this of course begins with Mrs. B. T. Washington. Wishing you and your work every success and hoping that I may be able to be of some real service to you   I am   Sincerely yours,

> Major Allen A. Wesley
> Surgeon 8th Ill Inf U.S.V.

ALS   Con. 164   BTW Papers   DLC.   Docketed in BTW's hand: "May get them at Tampa or Key West. Make him no definite promise. Have them ready to send."

[1] Allen Alexander Wesley (1856-1929), born in Dublin, Ind., graduated from Fisk University in 1884 and then attended Chicago Medical College. In 1898 he enlisted as a surgeon in the Eighth Illinois Infantry and was commissioned as a major. While serving in Cuba during the Spanish-American War, he caught malaria and was honorably discharged in 1899. Wesley returned to Chicago, where he practiced medicine until his death.

[2] Ezra Philetus Ewers (1837-1912) was a professional soldier conspicuous for his gallantry in combat. Enlisting as a private in the Civil War, he rose to captain by the end of the war. He was later prominent in the Indian wars, and served in Cuba in 1898.

From Thomas Junius Calloway

Washington, D.C. Oct. 9. 1898

Dear Mr. Washington: I have called on Secretary Long and Secretary War[1] in reference to matter of transportation of persons from Porto Rico & Cuba to this country. I find that if there were any persons now ready to sail an order could with ease be secured for their transportation by first transport, but the plans of the government being entirely unsettled it is not possible to arrange any general plan for future transportation.

However, I was assured by Secretary of War that President McKinley and he had agreed to discuss and agree upon some educational policy for new territory and if Tuskegee has any proposition to offer it will be duly considered. If in the next few months you should wish transportation for a few persons I suggest an application direct to Secty War. In meantime I think any definite plan submitted to President McKinley would meet a warm consideration.

Your telegram directing me to New York City, received. I shall leave just as soon as I can hear from Mr. Logan. I can not now say what my address there will be, but will write you as soon as I arrange same. Very truly,

Thos. J. Calloway

ALS Con. 138 BTW Papers DLC.

[1] Russell A. Alger.

To George Washington Carver

[Tuskegee, Ala.] 10, 11, 1898

Mr. Carver: Hereafter I wish you would have all persons in your division wherever it is necessary insist that students wear overalls, and that the young men be prohibited from working in their undershirts as I find some of them are doing.

Booker T. Washington

TLpS Con. 282A BTW Papers DLC.

From William Henry Baldwin, Jr.

New York, Oct. 11th., 1898

Dear Mr. Washington: Your letter of the 6th to Mr. Smith was referred to me today by Mr. Smith. Of course at first thought it is natural to say that it would be best for Mr. Smith to communicate in all matters pertaining to the auditing department through Mr. Logan; but I think it is a matter worth having a little further consideration. I appreciate fully Mr. Logan's exceptional qualities. From my knowledge of him and through reports of Mr. Smith and others who have been thrown in contact with him, he is a man of rare tact, excellent administrative ability, unquestioned integrity, and, withal, a tower of strength to the work of Tuskegee. But bear in mind that no Treasurer should audit his own accounts! There is no worse combination from a business point of view than to have a cashier or Treasurer his own auditor; and as I feel sure the only reason for your wishing to have Auditor Smith communicate through Mr. Logan is to keep Mr. Logan in touch with the work and also to save Mr. Logan's feelings, I wish to assure you that Mr. Smith would see that the clerks keep Mr. Logan fully advised and will aim to see that they are of more help to him than ever before. I cannot admit that it would be proper for the Treasurer to continue to audit the accounts or to have any direct charge of them; and I hope that you will agree with me and that Mr. Smith may communicate direct with the bookkeepers.

I wonder if you have seen all the good things said about the Tenth Cavalry lately? They came through Long Island City last Friday. I arranged with the Red Cross Society to have sandwiches and hot coffee for them. We fed them in the ferry house. I purchased fourteen hundred cigars for them and altogether we had a very interesting and satisfactory time. I had a nice long talk with their Chaplain, Mr. Anderson,[1] who knows you, and I told many of the men how proud we all are of them. I can say to you positively, without prejudice, they were the finest looking lot of men that have gone through Long Island City, not excepting any troops white or black. There was perfect discipline, and quiet, gentlemanly manners all the time they were at Long Island City.

I am planning to be with you sometime during the first ten days of November, provided the yellow fever does not get to you by that time.

Mrs. Baldwin has promised to go with me. With kind regards, I remain, Yours very truly,

W H Baldwin Jr

TLS Con. 138 BTW Papers DLC.

¹ William Thomas Anderson, born at Seguin, Tex., in 1859, was an A.M.E. minister who served as chaplain of the black Tenth U.S. Cavalry from 1897 to about 1909. He had attended Wilberforce University and graduated from Howard University in 1886. He also graduated from the Homeopathic Hospital College in Cleveland, Ohio, before entering military service. Anderson was a trustee of Wilberforce University.

An Address at the National Peace Jubilee¹

[Chicago, Ill., Oct. 16, 1898]

Mr. Chairman, Ladies and Gentlemen: On an important occasion in the life of the Master, when it fell to Him to pronounce judgment on two courses of action, these memorable words fell from His lips: "And Mary hath chosen the better part." This was the supreme test in the case of an individual. It is the highest test in the case of a race or nation. Let us apply this test to the American Negro.

In the life of our Republic, when he has had the opportunity to choose, has it been the better or worse part? When in the childhood of this nation the Negro was asked to submit to slavery or choose death and extinction, as did the aborigines, he chose the better part, that which perpetuated the race.

When in 1776 the Negro was asked to decide between British oppression and American independence, we find him choosing the better part, and Crispus Attucks, a Negro, was the first to shed his blood on State street, Boston, that the white American might enjoy liberty forever, though his race remained in slavery.

When in 1814 at New Orleans, the test of patriotism came again, we find the Negro choosing the better part; Gen. Andrew Jackson himself testifying that no heart was more loyal and no arm more strong and useful in defense of righteousness.

When the long and memorable struggle came between union and separation, when he knew that victory on the one hand meant freedom, and defeat on the other his continued enslavement, with a full knowledge of the portentous meaning of it all, when the suggestion and the temptation came to burn the home and massacre wife and children during the absence of the master in battle, and thus insure his liberty, we find him choosing the better part, and for four long years protecting and supporting the helpless, defenceless ones entrusted to his care.

When in 1863 the cause of the Union seemed to quiver in the balance, and there was doubt and distrust, the Negro was asked to come to the rescue in arms, and the valor displayed at Fort Wagner and Port Hudson and Fort Pillow, testify most eloquently again that the Negro chose the better part.

When a few months ago, the safety and honor of the Republic were threatened by a foreign foe, when the wail and anguish of the oppressed from a distant isle reached his ears, we find the Negro forgetting his own wrongs, forgetting the laws and customs that discriminate against him in his own country,[2] and again we find our black citizen choosing the better part. And if you would know how he deported himself in the field at Santiago, apply for answer to Shafter and Roosevelt and Wheeler. Let them tell how the Negro faced death and laid down his life in defense of honor and humanity, and when you have gotten the full story of the heroic conduct of the Negro in the Spanish-American war — heard it from the lips of Northern soldiers and Southern soldiers, from ex-abolitionist and ex-master, then decide within yourselves whether a race that is thus willing to die for its country, should not be given the highest opportunity to live for its country.

In the midst of all the complaints of suffering in the camp and field, suffering from fever and hunger, where is the official or citizen that has heard a word of complaint from the lips of a black soldier? The only request that has come from the Negro soldier has been that he might be permitted to replace the white soldier when heat and malaria began to decimate the ranks of the white regiment, and to occupy at the same time the post of greatest danger.

This country has been most fortunate in her victories. She has twice measured arms with England and has won. She has met the spirit of a rebellion within her borders and was victorious. She has met the proud Spaniard and he lays prostrate at her feet. All this is well, it is magnificent. But there remains one other victory for Americans to win

— a victory as far-reaching and important as any that has occupied our army and navy. We have succeeded in every conflict, except the effort to conquer ourselves in the blotting out of racial prejudices. We can celebrate the era of peace in no more effectual way than by a firm resolve on the part of the Northern men and Southern men, black men and white men, that the trench which we together dug around Santiago, shall be the eternal burial place of all that which separates us in our business and civil relations. Let us be as generous in peace as we have been brave in battle. Until we thus conquer ourselves, I make no empty statement when I say that we shall have, especially in the Southern part of our country,[3] a cancer gnawing at the heart of the Republic, that shall one day prove as dangerous as an attack from an army without or within.

In this presence and on this auspicious occasion, I want to present the deep gratitude of nearly ten millions of my people to our wise, patient and brave Chief Executive for the generous manner in which my race has been recognized during the conflict. A recognition that has done more to blot out sectional and racial lines than any event since the dawn of freedom.

I know how vain and impotent is all abstract talk on this subject. In your efforts to "rise on stepping stones of your dead selves," we of the black race shall not leave you unaided. We shall make the task easier for you by acquiring property, habits of thrift, economy, intelligence and character, by each making himself of individual worth in his own community. We shall aid you in this as we did a few days ago at El Caney and Santiago, when we helped you to hasten the peace we here celebrate. You know us; you are not afraid of us. When the crucial test comes, you are not ashamed of us. We have never betrayed or deceived you. You know that as it has been, so it will be. Whether in war or in peace, whether in slavery or in freedom, we have always been loyal to the Stars and Stripes.

PD Con. 955 BTW Papers DLC. This is the version printed at the Tuskegee Institute Steam Press in 1901. A slightly different version also appeared in 1901 in *The Story of My Life and Work.* (See above, 1:119-22.)

1 This speech was one of BTW's most forthright and most successful. The audience of 16,000 was probably the largest of his career. The Chicago *Times-Herald* reported: "At the Auditorium the applause given him made the very columns of the massive building tremble. It sounded more like a roar than cheers and clapping of hands. And it would not cease. Again and again it was repeated." Washington also addressed that same night two overflow crowds in different parts of the city.

His appeal for the conquest of racial prejudice immediately came under attack by the Atlanta *Constitution* and other southern newspapers, which continued until BTW retreated to the Atlanta Compromise formula.

[2] In *The Story of My Life and Work* version the phrase after this point reads: "again choosing the better part — the part of honor and humanity."

[3] The phrase referring to the South did not appear in *The Story of My Life and Work* version. This was probably because of sharp criticism in the southern newspapers.

From William Edward Burghardt Du Bois

Atlanta, Ga., 17 Oct. 1898

My Dear Mr. Washington: I laid your letter before Dr. Bumstead and he returned the enclosed reply. So that I shall be at your service. For the sake of preparing myself I should like to know how many persons & who will take part, & how long I shall be expected to speak — and whether on any particular subject &c &c. Kindly write me at your convenience. Please too return Dr Bumstead's letter. Very sincerely

W. E. B. Du Bois

ALS   Con. 139   BTW Papers   DLC.

From William J. Barnett

San Luis, Cuba. Oct. 18th 1898

Sir: Your letter of recent date received and in reply will say that I have found a young girl and boy, whose parents are willing for them to take the advantage of your liberal offer, to receive an education. Their ages are 14 yrs each. As soon as transportation is furnished they will leave for your school.

Proud to say that I am very well at this writing, have been sick since I wrote you last.

Regiment is in a very good condition, sick rate decreasing. I await your early reply. I am sir   Very Respectfully

W. J. Barnett

ALS   Con. 136   BTW Papers   DLC.

493

From Robert Charles Bedford

Beloit Wis   Oct 20 1898

Dear Mr Washington   I cannot help but congratulate you on your visit to Chicago. It is dangerous to succeed for to avail anything one must always keep on succeeding. I doubt whether any of your public utterances have been more successful than your latest. It is the marvel of all whom I meet that on every occasion you can seem to say just the right word. For all this let us be thankful and praise God. The wisdom of your own course leads me more earnestly than ever to feel the importance of exerting every possible influence on they body of the students and graduates that they may be of like spirit with your self. I may be mistaken but I feel as if I could do the cause for which I have labored so long no greater good than by giving the remainder of my days as far as possible to work among the graduates and former students of Tuskegee and as I am brought in contact with them among all young colored people who are making the future of the race. We must not neglect this work. We must push it, the more vigorously the better. Every day deepens this conviction. I hope you will see Harper's Weekly of Oct 16. It has a double page illustration of the 9th Cavalry charge up San Juan Hill. A painting might well be made from it. The Chronicle today has an excellent editorial on a remark made by you with reference to the Negro as a free laborer. Your addresses are so full of new thought that they will afford endless texts for helpful remarks.

I hope your great success will come forth and rest you and fill your heart with tender gratitude to God and love to all men that you have been so helpfully used in lifting up all men in all lands. Nothing has touched me more deeply than your statement of the gratitude displayed by the Chinese and Corean ministers. Truly when one member suffers all the members suffer with it and when one member is honored all the members rejoice with it. It will be an interesting story there foreign ministers will write home of one born in bondage pleading the cause of their liberty. I hope you will think it best to send the letters to the M & O & Ill Central that I may meet a graduate or student when ever convenient. I will let you know about Prof Grant[1] and other matters as I am able. Your bro

R C Bedford

494

The inclosed came from a little talk in Mr Richardson's[2] office

R C B

ALS   Con. 137   BTW Papers   DLC.

[1] John Cowles Grant.
[2] L. S. Richardson.

A Student's Account of His Summer Vacation

Normal School [Tuskegee, Ala.] Oct. 23–98

Mr. ———: I left Tuskegee, the day after school closed, with the base ball team; for my home (Montgomery Ala). And after playing the two games of base ball that was scheduled with Montgomery; I was to have gone to Hannon. Ala. and work at my trade (Wheel Wrighting) but on account of a bruised finger, I could not go. So on the 15th of June I began work in one of the leading bakery shops of Montgomery. After entering the shop I asked the propriter for a job; the first thing he wanted to know where I was from; and when I told him Tuskegee, he ask me (know) more questions. So I began work at once. There were five of us in the shop; three more colored boys the propriter (German) and my self. The first thing he began to do, was to see if I was honest; by giving me money to buy material, and he would give me more than it would cost always, after testing me a long this line, and my ability to trade and figure, he wanted to know something about Tuskegee, of which I told him in full.

His wife remarked to some white gentlemen in my presence one day, that she never saw a negro so clean about his dress, and polite to every body as I seem to be, in all her life. So time after time they would ask me questions without any sense in them at all; but I would give them a pleasent answer, so they (white men) wanted to know where I had been to school, I told them Tuskegee; and instead of asking me folish questions in the future, they began to ask me certain things about my training here or at Tuskegee, and ask hard questions; and if it had not been for my training in Tuskegee I never would have succeded in answering the questions, controlling my self and keeping my job.

After working there about three weeks the colored boys began to dislike me. First because the white people liked and treated me better than they did them, who had been there for two or three years. In the second place, because I would not act dishonest about a few little things, which would have been for at present for our own personal benifit and from that time I had a hard time in getting along with them during my stay there; but I fix things so they would always treat me wright and pretend that they liked me wether they did or not. He discharged one of them for being empting [impudent?] to me, for I had them in charge though he had been there for some time and could do good work; but his training otherwise was liking. He tried time and again to get me out of my job by offering to work for almost nothing, but he did not succeed. So the propreter told me one day if it was not for the dependence he could put in me; he would be compell to hire some one else, because he could get the same work done cheaper, and there by save money; but he could not depend on them but one day at the time, so he could not full with them.

Then he ask me would I not stay with him all the time, he said he would give me a life time job; but I told him I would not make him any promises; but would stay until I had to leave. And I give Tuskegee the credit for forcing me to work day in and day out regardless to the conditions.

I did not mist work a single day during my three months stay there, but sunday and he wanted me to work then but I would not.

I attended sunday school every sunday except one during the three months I was away from school first as a student, then as a teacher in one of the leading churches of the city.

At the begining of the summer I did not teach any but visited the different churches where I was called on to say something; which I tried to say something that I thought would benifit them. So I began to attend one church, where I was asked to take the first bible class as a teacher, which I did; and they were very sorry for me to leave and come back to school. I found during my vacation, that I needed every particle of the training I had received at Tuskegee to help me hold my own as a man. There was one thing during my vacation I never could under stand, every person that had herd any thing of Tuskegee, after reconizing my features, would ask me want I from Tuskegee, or had I been to school there, they would know me anyhow; but they would never ask any of the other boys whom I was with from other schools, where they were from or whether they had been to school or not. I [How?] they could tell me from the other boys from the different schools I can not tell.

That is a mistery to me yet.

G. W. Henderson[1]

ALS   Con. 864   BTW Papers   DLC.

[1] See above, 2:363.

From Henry Ossian Flipper[1]

Santa Fe, New Mexico, October 23, 1898

Personal, not for publication.

My Dear Professor: I send you, in this mail and under separate cover, a copy of the Brief I have prepared in support of bill, H.R. 9849 (printed on page 1 of Brief) for expunging, from the records of the War Department, the proceedings of my court-martial and for restoring me to the regular Army. I trust you will carefully read the same and learn the truth as to my trial and dismissal from the service.

In sending you this Brief I do so to ask your assistance. It has seemed to me advisable to ask my friends in the different States to write personal letters particularly to Hon. Michael Griffin,[2] author of the bill; Hon. John A. T. Hull,[3] Chairman of the House Committee on Military Affairs, and to Hon. Joseph R. Hawley,[4] Chairman of the Senate Committee on Military Affairs, and such other members of both Houses as may seem advisable, and to urge them to use their best efforts to secure the passage of the bill *as it stands without amendment of any character,* in the interest of the Race, to right the wrong done me and through me every member of the Race. A flood of letters of this character, carefully prepared after reading my Brief, will show more strongly than anything else how our people resent any wrong done to a single one of its individuals and its determination to have that wrong righted.

These letters should be sent so as to reach these gentlemen at Washington about the time Congress convenes in December next.

I do not favor public agitation of the matter in the press or otherwise. Among other strong reasons for this view is the almost certain opposition of the Army itself and of the influential officials of the War Department. The large colony of retired Army officers in Washington, and their families, have an influence I cannot reach or overcome and I do not think there is any need or wisdom in telling these people what I am trying to do.

I wish also to impress upon you the utter futility of writing to or in any other way invoking the aid of the President or of the Secretary of War. The matter is one wholly beyond their jurisdiction, as only an act of Congress can expunge those court-martial proceedings and restore me to the regular Army. I am not seeking appointment of any kind in the volunteer Army. I am seeking vindication and vindication means restoral to my former place in the regular establishment.

Trusting that I shall have your assistance, I am, Very truly yours,

Henry O. Flipper

TLS Con. 146 BTW Papers DLC.

¹ Henry Ossian Flipper (1856-1940) was born a slave in Thomasville, Ga. He attended Atlanta University for a time, and on the recommendation of Congressman J. C. Freeman, a Georgia Republican, he entered the U.S. Military Academy in 1873. Surviving the severe hazing of the white cadets, Flipper graduated in 1877 and was assigned to the Tenth Cavalry, a black regiment. He served at several forts in Indian territory in Texas and was a commissary officer in charge of food, clothing, and supplies. In Aug. 1881 the chief commissary of the Department of Texas informed Col. William R. Shafter that funds Flipper was supposed to have mailed were never received. Though Flipper saw that all the missing money was returned, he was tried in Nov. 1881 for embezzlement. He was not convicted on that charge but was found guilty of conduct unbecoming an officer and was dismissed from the Army in June 1882. Flipper tried on several occasions to have the decision set aside through bills in Congress. In Apr. 1898 H.R. 9849 was introduced by Representative Michael Griffin to annul the court-martial and restore Flipper to his rank. The bill died in the House military affairs committee. The War Department refused to endorse the bill but did not give reasons. Flipper found a new and successful career as a civil engineer and expert in land laws in the Southwest and northern Mexico. Senator Albert Fall of New Mexico called him to Washington as an interpreter and translator for the Senate Foreign Relations Committee, concerning the Mexican Revolution. In 1921 he was employed by the International Alaska Engineering Commission. From 1923 to 1930 he worked for an oil company. He retired to Atlanta in 1930, living with his brother, Bishop Joseph Flipper. (Flipper, *Colored Cadet at West Point,* introduction by Sara D. Jackson.)

² Michael Griffin (1842-99), born in Ireland, served in the Union Army during the Civil War. He was a Republican congressman from Wisconsin (1894-99).

³ John Albert Tiffin Hull (1841-1928) was a Republican congressman from Iowa from 1891 to 1911.

⁴ Joseph Roswell Hawley.

From Collis Potter Huntington

[New York] Oct. 28, 1898

My dear Sir: I have your letter of the 24th and am very much obliged to you for the annual report you enclose, which makes an excellent showing for the School and which I have read with a great deal of interest and satisfaction. I congratulate you on what you have done, what you are doing, and what I am sure you are going to do in the future.

You write about the proposed heating of the building by steam. There is a concern in this city — Baker, Smith & Company — which makes a specialty of this kind of work. They have done a great deal of it for me in the way of heating by steam and by hot water. They could give you some valuable advice about the best way of heating your building, and, as I think I could get passes for them down there and back, it would cost you nothing for the information unless you decided to employ them to do the work. Let me know about this.

The more I hear of the institution at Tuskegee, the more I am pleased with the great good it is accomplishing. It is doing much for the negro race, and the credit for it is due to the practical sense and ability of its guiding spirit — yourself. A few well-organized training-schools modelled — as they well could be — on the one at Tuskegee, would work great benefit to the negro and lift him to a much higher level than he has heretofore occupied. You have studied his disposition and character so thoroughly and you are so accurately acquainted with the direction in which his abilities and tastes run that you ought to be an ideal director of their educational life, and if they follow your advice their rise will be steady and certain. The only question is, Where shall we get another Booker T. Washington for these other schools, or who will take his place when the passing of the years brings him to the end of his useful labors?

I wish you would send me a few of your reports like the one I have, as I think I can distribute them to much advantage. I have heard one party express himself in such a way as to satisfy me that he would be willing to do something towards the construction on the new building for girls you have in contemplation, and I would suggest that you send me a tracing of what you propose to build. It is just possible that I may find somebody who will make the institution a gift of such a structure, and if I can, I shall be only too glad to.

As for myself, I take pleasure in sending you herewith my check for a thousand dollars, which you can use in behalf of the institution in the way that your judgment suggests as being wise and likely to do the most good, and am, with best wishes and kind regards, as always, Sincerely yours,

C. P. Huntington

TLS   Con. 701   BTW Papers   DLC.

From Susan Helen Porter[1]

[Tuskegee, Ala.] Nov. 1, 1898

Dear Sir: I regret to tell you that Pedro Salina[2] was acting dangerously rude in school to-day, notwithstanding the mild and careful treatment which he has received from us.

He is extremely defiant, and does not allow the children to look at him.

He drew a horrid looking knife on two of the little children of his class to-day.

I shall have to ask you to do something concerning this matter as he is exhibiting such a wicked example and disposition.

I was thinking of writing to you earlier, stating that he should have a special teacher as he is unable to keep up with the work of our "First Reader" children. Respectfully,

S. Helen Porter

ALS   Con. 146   BTW Papers   DLC.

[1] Susan Helen Porter was principal of the training school at Tuskegee beginning in 1893. Later she taught history, English, and pedagogy, and was dean of the women's department for many years after 1907.

[2] Pedro Bratu Salina of San Juan, Puerto Rico, was a student in the C preparatory class from 1898 to 1901. He did not graduate.

From Thomas Austin[1]

Tampa Fla., Nov. 1, 1898

Dear Sir: I arrived in Tampa Friday night: Saturday morning I began my commission in Ellinger's, Pino's Ybor's and other Cuban villages. But I am sorry to say that my progress is poor, it is due to the fact that they are more anxious to return to Cuba, than to do anything else. I have explained everything to them and suceeded in getting only one to promise me positively. It seem as though they fail to realize what an opportunity is offered them. Their sentiments are expressed in the words "On to Cuba." I leave to-night for Key West enroute to Havana as I think I can do better there. Please send at once to Key West $25. or $30. so if I find it necessary to go to Havana I may have money enough to pay transportation for a few as far as Key West, then I can waite there for other necessary arrangements. This is to prevent a long stay in Havana.

Hoping an Early reply and success in the future. I am yours

Thomas Austin

ALS   Con. 136   BTW Papers   DLC.

[1] Thomas Austin, of Key West, Fla., was a member of the A middle class in 1898. As he spoke Spanish, BTW commissioned him to recruit Cuban students for Tuskegee. He graduated in 1900 and settled in Key West as a teacher and printer.

From Emmett Jay Scott

Tuskegee, Ala., Nov. 4, 1898

Dear Mr. Washington: I have it in mind to say to you that I think unless the criticism of your speech should become more general than it is that it will not be amiss to give ourselves some time for reckoning just how wide-spread it is. It will be, to my mind, somewhat unseemly to enter into a series of denials etc., as this will be just what some people most desire that you should do, and it will tend to take from your manly plea and stand some of the strength which accentuated and impressed it. I am sure that many are watching with concern and interest to see how *you* will meet this adverse comment. Your speech is made and tells its own story to the intelligent and fair-minded. For the present, it will be well to let it be its own brave defender.

I have thought that Maj. Screws[1] of the "Advertiser" could do us the greatest service by sending Mr. McDavid up here and talking freely with you with reference to the matter. It will be better in every way if the interview is sought instead of being offered. I do not underestimate the mischief that can be done by some of the Southern newspapers, but I fail to note any complete unanimity of criticism. *You* are now a great public character and cannot afford to engage every spiteful sensitive soul that attacks you. But I shall prepare at once the article & have it ready for mailing Saturday evening. Yours sincerely

Emmett J. Scott

ALS Con. 146 BTW Papers DLC.

[1] William Wallace Screws (1839-1913) was an Alabama lawyer and Confederate soldier (the Montgomery True Blues). He became editor of the Montgomery *Advertiser* after the Civil War and transformed it into the most important newspaper in the state.

From Edward Ware Barrett

Birmingham, Ala. November 5, 1898

Dear Sir: You have doubtless seen many comments upon your Chicago speech. It is unnecessary for me to tell you in what newspapers they have appeared. The Age-Herald gladly throws open its columns to you to make a reply to these criticisms upon you and your utterances in Chicago.

As editor of the Age-Herald, I have believed that you have a great work to perform which you can perform better than any living member of your race. I am of the opinion that you owe it to yourself, and to those who have watched your career with so much interest and approval in this and other States, to make a public announcement and explanation at this time of your Chicago speech. I presume the press reports of your speech, which were brief, did not do your sentiments justice. If you see fit to prepare the article I suggest, we will print the same conspicuously in next Sunday's paper.[1] Yours very truly,

E W Barrett

TLS Con. 136 BTW Papers DLC.

[1] See BTW to the Editor of the Birmingham *Age-Herald,* Nov. 10, 1898, below.

From Thomas Austin

Key West Fla   Nov. 5, 1898

Dear Sir: Your telegraph is just received. I arrived in Key West and would of continued on same boat to havana, but after finding out that the city was quarrantined against Key West I would not venture beyond Key West. I found that the pass for the steamboat had to be accompanied with $2.50 each way. I began among the Cubans here but find that they are with the "tide flowing into Cuba." The last boat carried over 300, and the one before that 250.

I had an advertisement published in the Cuban daily paper, you will see the piece mark on the paper sent under another cover. I can get a great many, who are well acquainted with the English language, but I thought probaly you would prefer beginners. I hope by the time general instruction reaches me to be able to start.

I am sure if I went to Havana I could get any number as I am told that there are number of them in Cuba who are yet starving   Yours Respectfully

Thomas Austin

ALS Con. 136 BTW Papers DLC.

To William McKinley

Tuskegee   November 7th, 1898

Dear Sir: According to your suggestion I write to say that the Atlanta people have fixed upon the 14th and 15th of December for their

Peace Jubilee. I shall be in Washington within a few days with some prominent gentlemen from Alabama with a view of trying to perfect definite arrangements for you to visit Tuskegee. I assure you that such a visit will mean more in the bringing together of the two races and the solution of the race problem, which is now the only great question before our country unsolved, than you can realize. Yours truly,

Booker T. Washington

TLS   McKinley Papers   DLC.

From William Henry Baldwin, Jr.

New York, Nov. 7th., 1898

Dear Mr. Washington: The Rev. Mr. Booth[1] handed me this enclosure the other day. I put it in my pocket and neglected to return it. I wish you would do it for me.

I returned this morning and feel much better for my trip. I wish to express to you the feeling of great satisfaction that I have in knowing of the great progress of your work and to feel reassured that you are working absolutely on the right lines. I think of your boys and girls there as being the exponent of the proper solution of your whole race question, and I think of you all as a calm, peaceful, patient, hopeful community. I am sure that every blessing will come to your work, and my constant hope is that you will be spared for many years to teach the world the right ideas about the negro problem.

I returned on the train with Mr. Berry of Atlanta. He is a Charlestonian now living in Atlanta and went to Tuskegee to sell you an ice machine, and, incidentally, to look at the "nigger" school. I found that he was quite as enthusiastic about your work as any human being could be, and he is now determined to raise the necessary funds to get a corliss engine for the shops.

On the train, also, was Mr. George C. Smith,[2] President of the Atlanta & West Point Railroad. I think it would be well to ask him to be a Trustee. He appreciates your modest requests on him for transportation and I do not think that he would feel that you would take any advantage of him if he were to be associated with your school. If you do write him on the subject I would suggest that you invite him, in a simple way, to become one of the trustees for himself, and not because of his position, so that he would not feel that there was any motive except a personal motive.

I send you copy herewith of telegram I have sent to H. M. Atkinson[3] of Atlanta.

"Be sure to invite Washington to address Peace Jubilee. He will say in no uncertain words just what the southern white people want to hear at this critical time. Advise me if you invite him."

I shall look forward to your visit to New York. With kind regards, I am, Yours very truly,

W H Baldwin Jr

Mr. Berry had no faith in your work until he had been there. He thought your school was like Atlanta Schools.

TLS   Con. 1   BTW Papers   DLC.   Postscript in Baldwin's hand.

¹ Probably C. O. Boothe.

² George C. Smith was president and general manager of the Atlanta and West Point Railroad from 1894 to 1900.

³ Henry Morrell Atkinson was born in Brookline, Mass., graduated from Harvard in 1884, and moved in 1886 to Atlanta, where he entered the cotton business. He became a prominent Atlanta businessman and social leader, organizing a power company, railroad, and bank.

From Leonora Love Chapman

[Tuskegee, Ala.] 11-7-98

Mr. Washington: I thank you very much for letting me see these letters. But where will we put them, the girls, I mean.

What on earth, Mr. Washington, will *I* do [with] Cuban girls? Do you suppose I can ever manage them. It has been very easy to stand off and give Major Ramsey sympathy in his management of Pedro, but my heart puts in an extra "beat" at the prospect of having some of the girls to take care of. You know people say, tho I do not agree with them, that girls are harder to manage than boys anyway. However, I will *do my best with them and for them.*

L. L. C.

ALI   Con. 138   BTW Papers   DLC.

To William E. Benson

[Tuskegee, Ala.] Nov. 8, 1898

Dear Mr. Benson: I find myself so much engaged in so many directions that I cannot see my way clear to serve your school as a Trustee any longer. I do not care to serve as a trustee of any institution unless I have time enough to keep up fully with the work being done by that institution in all its details, and for this reason I hope you will consider this as my resignation. Yours truly,

[Booker T. Washington]

TLc   Con. 136   BTW Papers   DLC.

To Allen Alexander Wesley

Tuskegee, Ala., Nov. 8, 1898

My dear Sir: I regret exceedingly the delay in answering the letters from yourself and Mr. Barnett. I hope Mr. Barnett will consider this an answer to his letter as well as to yours. Several matters have taken place recently which have forced me to delay this answer.

In all we wish to get hold of eight students, four boys and four girls if possible. We have already one young man here from Porto Rico which reduces the number that we now want to seven. Sometime ago I heard that desirable students could be gotten at Tampa and Key West, Fla., so we sent a young man to these places to get students, but a letter recently received from him says he is able to get but one desirable student at Tampa and I have not heard from him since he went to Key West. This young man, Thomas Austin, is one of our most reliable students and has had considerable contact with the Cubans and speaks the Spanish language. I have sent him a copy of this letter to you and told him that in case he does not get desirable students at Tampa and Key West to proceed directly to San Luis and place himself under your direction in reference to the matter of students, and that I am sure that you and Mr. Barnett, as well as the other officers of your regiment, will do all you can to assist him in getting hold of whatever number of students is necessary to make up the number to eight.[1] I have also sent Mr. Austin a copy of a letter received from the General Ticket Agent of the Plant System showing the rates at which students can be brought from Cuba here. I also enclose a statement which I thought you might like to use among the parents of these students in reference to our being responsible for their education and careful treatment. Yours truly,

Booker T. Washington

TLS Con. 164 BTW Papers DLC.

[1] BTW wrote to Austin advising him to contact Wesley and Barnett, whom BTW described as "good friends of mine." (BTW to Austin, Nov. 8, 1898, Con. 136, BTW Papers, DLC.)

From Susan Helen Porter

[Tuskegee, Ala.] Nov. 9, 1898

Dear Sir: Miss Cropper[1] and myself are thoroughly convinced that we cannot help Pedro Salina under existing circumstances; as he needs to be helped.

To benefit him means that the other children must be held back and neglected. It requires no greater effort to teach fifty pupils like himself than is required to teach him.

It must be very discouraging to Pedro to be among children whose work he cannot keep up with; nor even understand. I do *not* consider him a hopeless case by any means.

You will please let me know, if you intend to have him remain in the Training School.

Should Austin succeed in securing other Cubans for the school will you have them taught at the Training School also? We had another exhibition of Pedro's temper and cruelty this morning, which excited the entire school.

A few other similar excitements will unfit me for work.

The children of the school are afraid of Pedro after having seen so much of his mischief.

If you desire an explanation of the trouble which occured this

morning the younger Austin[2] and Maj. Ramsey will explain to you.
Respectfully,

S. Helen Porter

ALS Con. 146 BTW Papers DLC.

[1] Lula M. Cropper.
[2] James Stephen Austin of Key West, Fla., in the B preparatory class.

To the Editor of the Birmingham *Age-Herald*[1]

Tuskegee, Ala., November 10, 1898

To the Editor of the Age-Herald: Replying to your communication of recent date regarding my Chicago speech, I would say that I have made no change whatever in my attitude towards the south or in my idea of the elevation of the colored man. I have always made it a rule to say nothing before a northern audience that I would not say before a southern audience. I do not think it necessary to go into any extended explanation of what my position is, for if my seventeen years of work here in the heart of the south is not a sufficient explanation I do not see how mere words can explain. Each year more and more confirms me in the wisdom of what I have advocated and tried to do.

In Chicago at the Peace Jubilee, in discussing the relations of the races, I made practically the same plea that I did in Nashville this summer at the Young People's Society of Christian Endeavor, where I spoke almost wholly to a southern white audience. In Chicago I made the same plea that I did in a portion of my address at the opening of the Atlanta Exposition, for the blotting out of race prejudice in "commercial and civil relations." What is termed social recognition is a question I never discuss. As I said in my Atlanta address, "The wisest among my race understand that the agitation of questions of social equality is the extremest folly, and that progress in the enjoyment of all the privileges that will come to us must be the result of severe and constant struggle rather than of artificial forcing." God knows that both — we, of the black race and the white race — have enough problems pressing upon us for solution without obtruding a social question, out of which nothing but harm would come.

In my addresses I very seldom refer to the question of prejudice because I realize that it is something to be lived down not talked down, but at that great meeting which marked in a large measure the end of all sectional feeling I thought it an opportune time to ask for the blotting out of racial prejudice as far as possible in "business and civil relations."

In a portion of my address which was not sent out by the Associated Press I made the request that the negro be given every opportunity in proportion as he makes himself worthy. At Chicago I did not refer wholly to the south or to the southern white people. All who are acquainted with the subject will agree that prejudice exists in the north as well as in the south. I naturally laid emphasis upon the south because, as we all know, that owing to the large proportion of blacks to whites in the south, it is in the south mainly that the problem is to be worked out. Whenever I discuss the question of race prejudice I never do so solely in the interest of the negro; I always take higher ground. If a black man hates a white man it narrows and degrades his soul. If a white man hates a black man it narrows and degrades his soul.

Both races will grow stronger in morals and prosper in business just in proportion as in every manly way they cultivate the friendship and confidence of each other. Outbreaks of race feelings and strained relations not only injure business, but retard the moral and religious growth of both races and it is the duty of the intelligent among both races to cultivate patience and moderation.

Each day convinces me that the salvation of the negro in this country will be in his cultivation of habits of thrift, economy, honesty, the acquiring of education, Christian character, property and industrial skill.

Booker T. Washington

Birmingham *Age-Herald,* Nov. 13, 1898, 15.

[1] BTW's letter was also reproduced in the Montgomery *Advertiser* on Nov. 15, 1898, and in the Atlanta *Constitution* on Nov. 15, 1898. Robert Charles Bedford wrote BTW from Montgomery that the *Advertiser's* editorial was written by Mr. Glass with Major Screws's approval. Bedford believed that "these men speak from the heart" in their support. (Bedford to BTW, Nov. 15, 1898, Con. 138, BTW Papers, DLC.) The next day Bedford assured BTW that his letter to the Birmingham *Age-Herald* had calmed any criticism in Alabama that might have resulted from accounts of his Chicago Peace Jubilee address. (Bedford to BTW, Nov. 16, 1898, Con. 137, BTW Papers, DLC.)

From J. C. Ladevize and J. S. Harper

Augusta, Ga. Nov. 11–'98

Dear Sir, We wrote you several months ago in regard to taking our High School case[1] to the Supreme Court of the U.S. and asked you to assist us financially in the matter. In reply you stated that you would do so in the Fall of the year. We would be glad to have you make your contribution at the earliest possible date. We are hard at work, trying to do our part of the task.

We have secured the services of the Hon. Geo. F. Edmunds,[2] ex-senator from Vermont, who has kindly consented to argue the case before the Supreme Court without charging us any fee, he simply requires that we pay expenses of court and his actual expenses while in attendance. In addition we have had to employ local counsel. The entire cost will be about $500.00. This we consider very small compared with the good results, which we shall gain by a favorable decision. We have raised already, in Augusta, $200.00 of the required amount.

Mr. Edmunds says in a letter to us I am surprised on general principles that the Supreme Court of Ga. should declare that the colored man can be taxed and denied high school privileges.

Again after reviewing our local attorneys papers, he says I think your case well prepared and that the question is sufficiently well presented to certainly justify you in taking a writ of error and pressing it to a hearing.

These opinions of Mr. Edmunds, coupled with the fact that he charges no fee for services give us great hope that he has everything favorable to our cause. Do what you can for the cause. Respectfully,

J. C. Ladevize
J. S. Harper

ALS   Con. 142   BTW Papers   DLC.

[1] *Cumming* v. *Richmond County Board of Education,* 175 U.S. 528.

[2] George Franklin Edmunds (1828-1919) was a Republican U.S. senator from Vermont from 1866 to 1891. In his first vote in Congress he supplied the one vote needed to override President Johnson's veto of the Civil Rights Act of 1866. He also championed the Ku Klux Klan Act of 1872 and the Civil Rights Act of 1875. Throughout his long tenure, he had an interest in civil rights, railroad and trust regulation, and civil service reform. He resigned in 1891 but continued an interest in public affairs and practiced law in Philadelphia.

From Collis Potter Huntington

New York, Nov. 14/98

Dear Sir: Yours of the 8th, with tracings of the building you propose to put up for your school girls, is received.[1] I wish you would send me a detailed statement of specifications for the building, giving size of the timber etc. and the material of which it is to be built. Mrs. Huntington[2] says she thinks she will erect this building for the girls, so that the cost does not exceed ten thousand dollars. Yours truly,

C. P. Huntington

TLSr Con. 140 BTW Papers DLC.

[1] Huntington Hall, a twenty-three-room brick building of two stories, was officially opened on Nov. 12, 1900.

[2] Arabella Duval Yarrington Worsham Huntington was born in Alabama about 1850. She married Collis Potter Huntington in 1884, when she was about thirty-four and he was sixty-three. When he died in 1900 she inherited $22 million and her husband's interests in philanthropy. In 1913 she married Collis Huntington's nephew Henry, also a railroad millionaire. Mrs. Huntington donated money to Hampton Institute and Tuskegee Institute and also to charities and such causes as the New York women garment workers' strike in 1909. She died in New York in 1924.

From Emily Howland

Gleason Sanitarium, Elmira, N.Y. Nov. 15. 1898

Dear Mr. Washington   Your note of the 9th announcing your resignation from the board of Trustees of Kowaliga School has been forwarded to me here.

I cannot but feel apprehensive, is anything going wrong there? You know that your influence brought it into notice, if you have discovered that it is unworthy we should know it. With kind regards to Mrs. Washington   Cordially

Emily Howland

P.S. You know that I have had one sore trial with an unworthy subject. I do not want any more. O the pity of it.

E. H.

ALS Con. 155 BTW Papers DLC.

From William E. Benson

Kowaliga, Ala., Nov. 18th 1898

Dear Mr. Washington: Your letter of Nov. 8th tendering your resignation as a trustee of our school is just to hand. I shall present it to our Committee and give due consent to the action which we are very sorry to have you take. As you say, I know you are very much engaged in many other directions and I doubt very much — if it were *possible* for you to be less *informed* as to our work at Kowaliga than you are in that of various other enterprises over the country with which you are serving in *some* connection. I am sure we have kept you informed constantly of our work. I wish we could have known of your purpose some months earlier as your name appears on our literature and cannot be changed at a moments notice.

Thanking you for what service you have rendered our community, I am sincerely

Wm. E. Benson

P.S. Of course you will give, to any inquiries, the reason of your action as acknowledged in the letter before me.

W. E. B.

ALS   Con. 146   BTW Papers   DLC.

From Victoria Earle Matthews

New York, Nov. 18 1898

Dear Mr Washington   Thanks for your notice of resignation from Kowaliga Industrial School Trusteeship. I was not aware that my name was still used as I can not never have been able to serve.   I will write Mr Benson to that effect, thanking you again   I am sincerely yours

Victoria Earle Matthews

ALS   Con. 143   BTW Papers   DLC.

A Sunday Evening Talk

Tuskegee, Ala., Nov. 20, 1898

GIVING THE RACE A REPUTATION

I mentioned to you a few evenings ago that many may think the race is now passing through a very trying and discouraging period in its history. A race, like an individual has got to have the right kind of reputation. Such a reputation goes a long way toward helping a race or an individual and when we have succeeded in getting such a reputation, we will find that a great many of the discouraging features of our life will melt away. Now a reputation is what people think we are, and a great deal depends on that. When a race gets a reputation along certain lines a great many things which now seem complex, difficult to attain, and which now seem discouraging, are going to disappear.

I remember in a lecture delivered here some years ago Mr. Chaney[1] spoke of the value of having a reputation in the mechanical world.

The minute you say that an engine is a Corliss engine, people understand that that engine is a perfect piece of mechanical work, perfect as far as human skill and ingenuity can make it perfect. You say a car is a Pullman car. That is all but what does it mean? It means that the builder of that car got a reputation at the outset for thorough, perfect work; for turning out everything in first class shape. And so with a race; you cannot keep back very long a race which has the reputation for doing perfect work in everything that it undertakes.

I spoke to you a few evenings ago about the tendency among many of our people in the Southern States especially to not be willing to stick to anything long. Such a reputation does not help us. And then we have got to get a reputation for economy. Nobody cares to associate with an individual in business or otherwise who has a reputation for being a trifling spendthrift, who spends his money for things that he can very easily get along without; who spends his money for clothing, gew-gaws, superficialities and other things when they have not got the necessities of life. We want to give the race the reputation of being frugal and saving in everything. Then, we want to get the reputation for being industrious. Now remember these three things: Get a reputation for being skillful. It won't do for a few here and there to have it; the race must have the reputation. Get a reputation for being

513

so skillful, so industrious, that you will not leave a job until it is as nearly perfect as any one can make it.

A few days ago I was in the office of Mr. C. P. Huntington, who has the reputation of having fifty millions of dollars. While in his office his private secretary told me that Mr. Huntington very seldom left his office before seven o'clock at night. He was determined to answer every letter that needed an answer. Some of you work until five or six o'clock and think you are having a very hard time of it. You want to get the reputation for that kind of industry, sticking to a job until it is through. If you are performing a task and you see that it should be finished before anything else is done, do not hesitate to prolong your time of work until it is done, even if you are late to your meals to do so, and by this sort of work you will get a reputation for industry that will be of service to you always. And then, you want to make a reputation for the race for being honest — honest at all times and under all circumstances. We have not now got such a reputation. A few individuals here and there have it, a few communities have it; but the race as a mass has not got it. You recall that story of Abraham Lincoln, how when he was postmaster at a small village he had left on his hands $1.50 which the government did not call for. Carefully wrapping up this money in a handkerchief he kept it for ten years. Finally one day the government agent called for this amount and it was promptly handed over to him by Abraham Lincoln who told him that during all those ten years he had never touched a cent of that money. He made it a principle of his life never to use other people's money. That trait of his character helped him along to the presidency. The race wants to get the reputation for being strictly honest in all its dealing and transactions; honest in handling money, honest in all our dealings with our fellowmen.

And then, we want to get the reputation for being thoughtful. This I would emphasize more than anything else. We want to get the reputation for doing things without being told to do so every time. If you have work to do, think about it so constantly, investigate and read about it so thoroughly that you will always be finding ways and means of improving that work. The average person going to work becomes a regular machine, never giving the matter of improving the methods of his work a thought.

He is never at his work before the appointed time and is sure to stop the minute the hour is up. The world is looking for the person who is thoughtful, who will say at the close of work hours, "Is there not something else I can do for you, can I not stay a little later and help you?"

Many of you will go into the various departments to work tomorrow without having given a single thought to the best way of doing your work. This is not the way to get ahead. Go into your work knowing what you want to do, with a well defined idea of your work and day by day you will find yourself not only growing in favor in your instructor's eye, but will be gaining for yourself a reputation for thoughtfulness. Think constantly about the best way of doing your work whether that work be on the farm, in the shop or at the brickyard. The student who does this is the one who is going to get forward very soon.

In speaking of this matter I cannot give you a better example than the career of Mr. Baldwin who was with us a few evenings ago. Twelve years ago Mr. Baldwin was in humble circumstances. Shortly after he began work the person who employed him began to take notice that he was a very thoughtful and suggestive assistant, he came to work a little earlier than the others, and remained a little later than the others. In this way he got a start, made a reputation for thoughtful, conscientious work and before very long he was connected with a railroad in the west. Here he carried his same habits of thrift and industry, and very soon was called to be the vice-president, and general manager of the Southern Railway, one of the largest systems of railway in the country. From this position he was called to the presidency of the Long Island Railroad, perhaps the richest railroad in the country. Now this man who started with practically nothing a little over twelve years ago is receiving a salary of something like $27,000 a year as president of this railroad. Now how did Mr. Baldwin do this? He succeeded because he put his whole heart and soul into everything he undertook. And so as a race we will succeed just in proportion as we make a reputation along all of these lines.

Tuskegee Student, 12 (Nov. 24, 1898), 1, 3.

[1] George Leonard Chaney.

To Emily Howland

Tuskegee, Ala., Nov. 21, 1898

Private.

My dear Miss Howland: I am in receipt of your letter of November 15th regarding my resignation as a trustee of the Kowaliga school. I am very anxious not to get into any controversy with Mr. Benson or with any one else connected with the Kowaliga school and for that reason I wish, unless it becomes absolutely necessary, that you not speak of what I write. When I accepted the trusteeship I did it with the understanding that Mr. Clinton J. Calloway was to be the active and real head of the work there. Mr. Calloway is a man with a good deal of common sense and discretion. Mr. Benson is almost the opposite in character. He is whimsical, spasmodic and rather superficial. I find that Mr. Benson practically runs the school and Mr. Calloway has little or nothing, it seems, to do with it. In order for me to do my duty as a trustee I should have to be persistently looking into affairs and it would require more time than I can at present give. Mr. Benson is not inclined to treat a trustee with that delicate courtesy which is required to keep a trustee interested and I do not feel that I care to run the risk of having my name connected with something that I do not know all about and Mr. Benson is not inclined to keep one informed of the true condition of the school. I have made two or three requests for a financial report but aside from something that Mr. Benson let me use for five or six minutes I have seen no satisfactory report. Of course I presume I could find out the exact condition of the school if I had time to go to Kowaliga and spend one or two days in looking up the true condition of things but this time I have not, and I do not think that a trustee ought to be required to do such a thing. Mr. Benson is not inclined to follow the advice of persons whose experience and years should entitle them to give advice. Mr. Benson is inclined to over-emphasize the work that is being done at Kowaliga through the medium of pictures. He spends the greater part of his time in traveling. I cannot believe that it is right for the North to be called upon to pay the salary and traveling expenses of an individual who is collecting just about enough money to pay his own expenses and that of one other person. In all these matters Mr. Benson is not inclined to take advice. I have told him that if he would content himself by going

516

North once or twice a year and spend a month or so at a time I would gladly give him a letter of endorsement and help him get before the proper kind of people, but he does not do as I suggest and for this and other reasons I wrote him a few days ago that I felt that I could not longer spare the time to act as a trustee. I repeat that I said I could not spare the time for the reason that if I could look into all these matters from day to day I presume that I could keep myself informed of the true condition of affairs to the extent that I could feel safe in acting as a trustee.

Mrs. Washington is quite well and desires to be remembered to you. How much I wish that you could attend our next Conference.

If you are to be in Philadelphia or New York this winter perhaps I can see you as I am to be North for a while after Christmas.

I wrote you to the effect, some weeks ago, that the addition to our girl's building has been completed and the girls are now occupying it. It gives them very much relief. Yours truly,

Booker T. Washington

I have urged Mr. Benson without success to stay at Kowiliga the greater part of the year and put in real work for the school, but instead of real work from day to day he depends largely on some picture of temporary work. His father is a good sensible man but seems to have little control over his son.

B. T. W.

TLS   Emily Howland Papers   NN-Sc.   The postscript is in BTW's hand.

To William McKinley

Tuskegee, Alabama. November 21, 1898

My dear Sir: I note that the Alabama Legislature has just passed a resolution inviting you to visit Montgomery on Saturday, December 17th. I write to say that if for any reason you do not see your way clear to accept the invitation of the Legislature little if anything will be lost in effect by your not accepting as most, if not all, of the members of the Legislature, will be here to meet you. The Governor will also meet you here.

I will send an outline of our program together with some printed matter giving facts about our institution within a few days. Yours truly,

Booker T. Washington

TLS   McKinley Papers   DLC.

From J. W. Adams[1]

Montgomery, Ala, Nov. 22nd, 1898

My Dear Sir: Since talking with you over the phone, I went immediately to see Mr Harris as requested and he heartily agrees to come and assist you with the music; providing you make the necessary arrangements at Washington D.C.

He will gladly come as soon as you notify him to that effect.

I cannot hear any thing, but words of praise from both white and colord for you being so successful in securing the concent of the Pres. to visit your school. You accomplished more than the city of Birmingham with her wealth and influence. I know you remember a few months ago when she attemped to have the Pres. to attend the Jubilee services, but failed in her effort.

Atlanta also had a hard struggle, but succeeded in her effort.

You have accomplished a great deed for the school.

I congratulate you on that masterly explination in the Birmingham Age Hereald of your speech in Chicago. It showed nothing but manhood of the puriest kind: there was no shade of compromise. And I note that it has put a quietness to things.

Please find inclosed check for $3.50 (three dollars and fifty cent) from Mrs H Allen to pay ballance on her son's board (Fredrick Allen).

I wish to state that I have seen the agent of the Western R.R. and he promised to arrange with the authorities in Atlanta for a special train to leave here on the morning of the Pres. arrival in Tuskegee and remain over there until evening and bring us back. I ask that you assist me in making this arrangement, for there are a large number of people from the city who are planing to come up on that day. I am sincerely Yours,

J. W. Adams

ALS   Con. 136   BTW Papers   DLC.

¹ J. W. Adams (b. 1867), a black dry-goods merchant in Montgomery, was an enthusiastic Tuskegee trustee from 1898 to 1905 and one of several aides BTW relied on for information on state and local matters. Adams was also one of the signers of BTW's unsuccessful petition to the Alabama constitutional convention of 1901 in which blacks asked to be given "some humble share in choosing those who shall rule over [them]." Adams sold his business in 1904 and moved to Okmulgee, Indian Territory.

Margaret James Murray Washington
to the Tuskegee Executive Council

[Tuskegee, Ala.] Nov 22 98

To the Executive Council. We have investigated the charge made by Mr. J. B. Washington with reference to the whippings given his sons by Miss Porter. We find that Miss Porter did whip these two boys on the hands with a leather strap. The strap is not a large one and is so made that its effects are distributed and no great injury can be done a child with the strap.

Miss Porter claims that both of these boys refused to allow her to whip them on the hands, stating that their father had said she must not do so. When the boys refused, of course, Miss Porter in order to maintain order in the school was obliged to force the children to obey her.

In questioning Miss Porter we feel safe in saying that she resorts to corporal punishment only, after every other method has been employed.

We go further and say that she is careful not to whip unmercifully. We would advise that Mr. J. B. Washington be reminded that it is not wise to instruct his children to inform Miss Porter how they are to be whipped but that he himself, unknown to the children instruct her with reference to these matters. We further advise that Miss Porter be told that there is complaint against the great amount of whipping and the severity of the same. We also ask that she be cautioned against extremes in both of these — the amt. of whipping and the severity.

Mrs. Booker T. Washington

HLS Con. 161 BTW Papers DLC.

519

From Nathan F. Mossell[1]

Philadelphia, November 23, 1898

My dear Mr. Washington, I have read with regret and chagrin in the public press, statements purported to have come from your lips. I feel sure of your sincere friendship for the race, and I appreciate also that these are trying times and that you occupy a most peculiar position. I do not write this letter with intentions of making an argument against some of the things you are reported to have said. I feel sure that there are many things that you would like to say that it is not prudent for you to say at this time. I have this to suggest, however, that you keep constantly in mind the story that we all have so often heard of the old colored man and the bear, who prayed, "O! Lord, if you can't help me, please don't help the bear; just stand aside;" etc. It seems to me, just at this time, it would be better that you do not say anything, than that you should say some of the things that the newspaper reports you as saying. I hope that you will accept this letter in the spirit in which it is given. We are just now planning in Philadelphia, a large mass meeting to be held in the American Academy of Music, December 1st; speeches will be conservative in character, sectional animosity and prejudices will not be appealed to; the hearts and conscience of the American people will be addressed, in support of good government and in denouncing mob violence without reference to party or section of country. Yours fraternally,

N. F. Mossell

P.S. If you are in sympathy with what we are doing, we would be delighted to have you present at this meeting.

TLS Con. 143 BTW Papers DLC.

[1] Nathan F. Mossell was born in 1856 in Hamilton, Canada, and moved with his family to Lockport, N.Y., in 1865. He received his A.B. from Lincoln University in 1879 and his M.D. from the University of Pennsylvania in 1882. He practiced medicine in Philadelphia and was most noted for the organization in 1895 of the Frederick Douglass Memorial Hospital and Training School.

To William McKinley

Tuskegee, Alabama. November 27th, 1898

Dear Sir: Enclosed I send you an outline of the programme which we have made for your visit here. All classes, black and white, are working together in harmony so as to make your visit do the greatest amount of good possible. I hope this programme will prove in every way satis-factory.

In further answer to the question you asked me as to what points your address here ought to cover, if I might suggest further, I would say that encouraging the colored people to get education, property and character as the basis of their citizenship, suggesting that both races be moderate, reasonable and self-controlled and live on friendly terms are points that I think might be discussed with advantage at this time. I know you will not think that I am presuming in making these sug-gestions and should not do so but for your question. Yours respectfully,

Booker T. Washington

[*Enclosure*]

That the President go to car from banquet in Atlanta and run so as to reach Tuskegee at about 9.30 or 10 A.M.

Will be met at Tuskegee depot by Mayor and town council of Tus-kegee and trustees of the school.

Drive through town of Tuskegee to school.

At school a few minutes will be spent in driving over the grounds getting a general view of them.

Then follows a general exhibition of the school on "floats" or wagons. This to be viewed by the President and visitors from a grand stand.

Speaking in Chapel. President to be welcomed to the State and introduced by Governor Joseph F. Johnston. Singing interspersed be-tween short addresses from members of Cabinet and President of Ala-bama Senate.

Opportunity to shake hands with President.

Light luncheon in town of Tuskegee given by Mayor of Tuskegee at residence of Hon. C. W. Thompson, president of Bank of Tuskegee and member of Alabama Senate.

TLS McKinley Papers DLC.

From William Henry Baldwin, Jr.

Long Island City, N.Y. Nov 27 1898

Dear Washington, Please let me know when you expect to arrive here again.

I am not sure that Calloways[1] method of soliciting will prove to be successful. I want to talk with you about it.

The whole "question" seems to be at a white heat now, and I believe it is a time to strike blows — but not such blows as Fortune would like to strike. I was much disturbed to hear his point of view the other day, in conversation in my office. I don't think you want a Garrison or a Phillips to stir up the question of negro rights. But we want Booker Washington to continue to say what he thinks and does, and check the adverse criticism and the hostility North & South, which comes from lack of knowledge of the ideas you represent.

Give my regards to your household. And believe me, Truly yours

W. H. Baldwin Jr

ALS   Con. 137   BTW Papers   DLC.

1 Thomas Junius Calloway.

To John Addison Porter

Tuskegee, Alabama. November 30, 1898

Dear Sir: I believe you will agree with me that the editor of the Atlanta Constitution has perhaps more to do with making of public sentiment in the South than any one other individual.

I write to ask you to consider, if you think best, with the President the matter of inviting Mr. Clark Howell, editor of the Atlanta Constitution, to accompany the President's party from Atlanta to Tuskegee.[1] I have knowledge of the fact that Mr. Howell will be very glad to accept such an invitation if it is tendered him, and I hope you will not consider my making this suggestion too much out of place. Yours truly,

Booker T. Washington

TLS   McKinley Papers   DLC.

¹ Clark Howell was invited to Tuskegee for the presidential visit, but prior
commitments made it impossible for him to attend. He did, however, send a reporter to cover the event. (Howell to BTW, Dec. 15, 1898, Con. 539, BTW Papers,
DLC.)

From William Jenkins

Montgomery, Ala., Nov 30 1898

Dear Sir: A prominent republican (white) asked me why it was that
all the democratic politicians were being invited to Tuskegee to meet
president McKinley while the republicans have been ignored.

I write to show how every movement at Tuskegee is being watched
here. Sincerely

Wm. Jenkins

ALS   Con. 141   BTW Papers   DLC.

From Timothy Thomas Fortune

New York, Nov 30 1898

Dear Friend: Your letter of the 25th was received and I am glad to
have it. My health is very good but I am very tired and dead broke,
as this race business steals time and cash.

Peaker *is* a good fellow.

No; I am not coming South *just now*. I speak in Philadelphia tomorrow night. I have written it out and it is cork.

I am very sorry about the *Post* interview.¹ The Evening Post is a
sneak and a villian. Mark that.

I understand the Mossell letter. We talked it over when I was in
Philadelphia. *You can afford to say nothing at this time.* Let us talk
up here.

Roosevelt? He is no good, and you will find it out.

We are all well at home.

I want to see you and talk.

Take care of your health. Your friend

T. Thomas Fortune

ALS Con. 139 BTW Papers DLC.

¹ Fortune may have been referring to an item in the New York *Evening Post,* Nov. 16, 1898, 1, announcing a mass meeting organized by Fortune at Cooper Union to protest the race riot in Wilmington, N.C. Fortune was reported to have said that he had invited many other blacks but not BTW: "Mr. Fortune said that the subject was one which was altogether foreign to Prof. Washington's work, and he did not think he would be willing to deliver an address."

He may have referred, however, to the New York *Evening Post,* Nov. 18, 1898, 6, which reported that the mass meeting under Fortune's chairmanship called for a reduction of representation in Congress of southern states denying blacks the right to vote and urged a new amendment to the Constitution strengthening black rights.

The *Post* editorially commented in a way that suggested an interview of BTW: "Infinitely wiser advice to the race is that given by the ablest leader whom it has yet developed. Booker T. Washington not only fails to suggest any effort to secure new laws or constitutional amendments, but he frankly admits that the policy adopted to secure equal rights for the negro in this way thirty years ago has proved a failure. 'It must be apparent at this time,' he says, 'that the effort to put the rank and file of the colored people into a position to exercise the right of franchise has not been a success in those portions of our own country where the negro is found in large numbers.' He sees the reason for this, and thus states it: 'Either the negro was not prepared for any such wholesale exercise of the ballot as our recent amendments to the Constitution contemplated, or the American people were not prepared to assist and encourage him to use the ballot. In either case the result has been the same.'"

Washington's solution to the race problem, the *Post* reported, was "for the negro in every part of America to resolve that his pillar of fire by night and pillar of cloud by day shall be property, skill, economy, education, and Christian character."

To Joseph Forney Johnston

Tuskegee, Alabama [ca. Dec. 1, 1898]

Dear sir: I was very glad to hear through Senator Thompson that you would be here Dec 16, the day that President McKinley visits this institution.

I wish to consult you about the programme before it is finally arranged and will see you regarding the programme some time within the next few days.

I want to thank you most earnestly for the noble words contained in your message regarding education. I do not see how anything could have been stronger or finer and I am sure the whole state feels indebted to you. Yours Respectfully

Booker T. Washington

ALS   Governor Letter File G50   A-Ar.

From William Torrey Harris

Washington, D.C., December 2, 1898

Sir: I write to inform you that at a meeting of a committee of the National Educational Association, held in New York on the 25th instant for the purpose of nominating an Advisory Board to look after the interests of our exhibit of education in the Paris Exposition of 1900 and to advise and assist the United States Commission appointed by the President to take charge of the contribution from this country, you were unanimously chosen by the said committee as a member of that part of the Board to consist of representatives of schools of the fine arts and industrial arts. Will you favor me with an early reply stating whether you accept the appointment?

It is understood that it will not be necessary for the Advisory Board to hold meetings. The secretary of the Commissioner General will consult the several members of the Board by letter and in person from time to time as questions of management arise. Very truly yours,

W. T. Harris

TLS   Con. 146   BTW Papers   DLC.

From William Henry Baldwin, Jr.

Long Island City, N.Y. Dec 4 1898

Dear Washington   I think of you constantly these days. There are so many sore points being rubbed by the public, that I like to think of the healing salve that you manufacture at Tuskegee. Every man or woman who writes or talks on the Negro problem excepts you from their adverse criticisms. Can it be possible that there is any fallacy in your theory, when the Southern white man and woman, and the Northern whites, and the best Southern blacks all agree that it is the only Solution? Fortune and his kind are wrong, I think. No matter what artistic phrases they use, they hide only a bitter resentment against their enemies, and if they are allowed to go on as they have been, will cause a bad setback to their people.

Matters are shaping well for you in this section. Mr Peabody and Mr. Cutting have both said recently that we must do something handsome for Washington, that it is a disgrace to force you to beg for money, etc etc. Col. Dan Lamont[1] is getting much interested. When you come North again I want to prepare a paper that will suit you, and that will stir up the people.

Privately — I think Mr Peabody will give you a dormitory for boys. I have told him the needs. Can't you get up an idea of barracks — it would be a catching idea, and suggest economy. Have a plan ready to take care of 150 or 200 boys, and so planned that it could be extended.

I am afraid I cannot go down to the Jubilee. I am sorry you have not been asked to speak. It means that in the stir up in N.C. & S.C. that the South does not want to recognize the negro at the moment.

Did you see that the Brotherhood of Locomotive Firemen have had a meeting of Firemen at Roanoke and will demand that negroes shall be taken off the engines? It would never have occurred but for the Wilmington troubles.

I tell you again that your course is the only one, and the work must be organized in other states, and you must do it, and *we* must get the money.

I will have a meeting of a few choice spirits at my house when you come up again. Do keep me posted if you see any channel in which I can help you.

Calloway's work is not on the right lines. He *can't* do it, I fear. Give my regards to your good family. Truly yours,

W H Baldwin Jr.

ALS Con. 137 BTW Papers DLC. Docketed: "Took the liberty of showing to Mrs. W. E.J.S."

[1] Daniel Scott Lamont (1851-1905) was private secretary to Grover Cleveland beginning in 1885, and later Secretary of War under Cleveland. He amassed a fortune as a streetcar promoter and investment banker.

December · 1898

From A. B. Barton

Savannah Ga. Dec 4 1898

Dear Sir   you maede a Big mistake. the Negro Have a Rigth to the Ballot Box, are Well the White Peopel do. you must not Say So. I am your Tuly

A B Barton

ACS   Con. 136   BTW Papers   DLC.

From Manuela Gomez

Key West. Dec 6th 1898

Dear Sir: Thanks for your kind letter informing me that my son[1] is enjoying good health and doing well in his studies. I do wish he could continue there, but I am very sorry to inform you that my husband wishes him to be with us in Cuba. I intend to take my family there very soon and beg you to send Juan here where I will remain until he arrives.

It is most kind of you to wish me to send Manuela. I will speak to Mr Gomez about it and if he consents I shall write to you immediately. I assure you, I am Respectfully Yours and most grateful for your kind offer.

Manuella Gomez

HLS   Con. 140   BTW Papers   DLC.

[1] Juan E. Gomez of Havana, Cuba, was a student in the A preparatory class during the 1898-99 school year. In 1907 he was a classmate of BTW Jr. at Dummer Academy, South Byfield, Mass., and then at Phillips Exeter Academy. His first name was often anglicized to John. He died under mysterious circumstances in Liverpool, England, in 1910.

527

From William Henry Baldwin, Jr.

[New York City] Dec 8 98

Dear Washington, I called on Mr. Huntington and had a good talk with him. He is impressed with the fact that you have not lost your head, as so many do in this world, and that you still wear the same sized hat. He spoke of it of his own motion. I believe that if he should see you in a silk hat that he would lose faith.

I passed an evening with Mr. Peabody on your matters. He expects to attend the Conference with Mr. Bayard Cutting! He wants the Hampton & the Tuskegee Trustees to get together soon, and make big strides.

Matters are shaping well.

We both think your circular can be stronger and that a little later will be better than now to send it out. I will give you some suggestions in a day or two.

You must be very busy getting ready for the President. I am to see the Sec'y of War Saturday, and hope to see the Prest. I shall talk to them about Tuskegee.

I passed an hour today with Dr. Albert Shaw of the Review of Reviews. He is always interested in you and your work.

Let me know how you stand for funds as compared with last year.

I will report on the need of restoring funds to endowment in near future.

I believe we may be able to squeeze out of it. I am getting best legal opinions.

With regards to you and all at Tuskegee. Yours ever,

W H Baldwin Jr

ALS Con. 137 BTW Papers DLC.

From Henry Ossian Flipper

Santa Fe, N. Mex., December 12, 1898

My Dear Sir: Your esteemed favor of the 5th inst. enclosing copies of letters from Senator Hawley and Hon. John A. T. Hull, reached me this morning and I hasten to thank you for your efforts in my behalf.

Recent events show, and it has been apparent for some time, that my bill would fail, unless an extraordinary effort were made to have it passed. The disgraceful conduct of the colored volunteers in the south has reduced my chances at least fifty per cent. In Macon, Georgia, a soldier of one of these regiments went into a place of business and asked to be served. He was refused. He went to camp and got about half a hundred of his comrades, came back and undertook to get revenge. Now, in my opinion, this was wholly uncalled for. He was simply inviting trouble instead of trying to avoid it. This statement of the case may not be true, but it is the one published to the country and believed by those to whom we have to look for assistance in such cases as mine. This conduct on the part of the colored volunteers is making the putting of more colored men in the reorganized Army extremely problematical. These soldiers have seemed to think that because they wore the government's uniform they were at liberty to avenge all the wrongs they conceive the white people of the South have ever done to them. The colored officers with them seem to have shared these ideas.

There seems to be no disposition on the part of any one to interest himself in my bill, though they all say I have a strong case and ought to be restored to the service. Mr. Hull, above all others, is the man to push this bill, but he seems to be afraid of it. I have no doubt it would readily be passed, if he would father it. The bill must be passed at this session or not at all. The new Army bill will be passed at this session and before I could get another bill introduced and passed, if at all, by the 56th Congress, the Army will have been reorganized and there would be no place for me. In this view of the case, it seems to me that my only hope is to bring such influence to bear upon Mr. Hull as will induce him to push the bill. This can be done through the President. President McKinley's position is such now that any bill he wants passed will be passed. Can you not see the President, in one of your trips north, lay this matter before him in this light and ask him to endorse the bill and ask Mr. Hull to push it? An intimation of this character from the President will, no doubt, secure the passage of the bill. I am convinced that this is my only chance and hope. I shall ask Hon. Judson W. Lyons, the Register of the Treasury, to do the same thing. You two gentlemen are the only men of our race who can make such a request of the President with any promise of success, and for this reason I appeal to you. Will you do this? I have asked Register Lyons to hand a copy of my brief to the President.

This is the situation as it appears to me and my only hope of success lies along the line I have herein indicated.

With best wishes to yourself and yours, I have the honor to be, Very truly yours,

Henry O. Flipper

TLS   Con. 1   BTW Papers   DLC.

From William A. Pledger

Atlanta Ga   Dec. 14. [1898]

Dear Washington: I will be down either Thursday Evening or Friday morning. Every advantage must be taken to utilize the President at your place. The world is against us. I may come Thursday Evening. No Negro has been permitted to shake his hand here. It would have been a case of "rape."

God bless you & yours. Your friend

Pledger

Tell "Scotty" to look out for me.

ALS   Con. 144   BTW Papers   DLC.

From Timothy Thomas Fortune

Washington D.C., December 14, 1898

My Dear Mr Washington: Your letter of the 10th instant was received and I thank you for writing to Dr Shaw about the article for the January Review. I shall do the work if he gives me the order.

I had a bad attack of grip on Friday last and my doctor advised me to go South. I have got this far on the way to Florida, but I shall not be able to go on before Monday or Tuesday.

Col Pledger writes me that he is to be at Tuskegee tomorrow. The President's visit ought to be worth a great deal to you and your work. I hope much in that regard. The President is a thoroughly despicable

530

character and I despise him, but I am glad that he went to Tuskegee, where he ought to learn something.

The idea of Dr Ward[1] comparing you and your work with that of Crogman, Du Bois and such! It is awful. It is discouraging, coming from that source.

I do not feel very hopeful today; indeed I am blue. Your friend

T. Thomas Fortune

ALS Con. 139 BTW Papers DLC.

[1] William Hayes Ward.

An Address Welcoming President McKinley and Others to Tuskegee Institute[1]

[Tuskegee, Ala., Dec. 16, 1898]

On this occasion I do not trust myself to give expression to the feelings that fill the heart of every white man and [black] man of the south because of the fact that the president of the United States, who has the deepest place in the hearts of every citizen, high and low, the members of his cabinet, the governor of Alabama, the state legislature, together with other distinguished citizens, including our own brave and good-hearted General Joe Wheeler, should lay aside their immediate duties and responsibilities to pay a visit to the town of Tuskegee and to this institution.

We welcome you all to this spot, where without racial bitterness, but with sympathy and friendship, with the aid of the state, with the aid of black men and white men, with southern help and northern help, we are trying to assist the nation in working out one of the greatest problems ever given to men to solve.

In the presence of the chief magistrate of the nation, I am glad to testify that in our efforts to teach our people to put brains and skill and dignity into the common occupations of life, we have not only the active help of all classes of citizens in this little town of Tuskegee, but of the best people of the south. Said our present governor in his recent message to the legislature: "Every dollar given to the cause of

531

education becomes invested capital that cannot be lost or destroyed, but will continue to pay dividends from one generation to another."

These are the words. This is the spirit that governs the action of the present governor of Alabama, and I am sure that no one can more fitly welcome our distinguished guest to the state than Governor Johnston, whom I take great pleasure in introducing.

Atlanta *Constitution,* Dec. 17, 1898, 3.

[1] For BTW's account of McKinley's visit including the speeches of the President, Secretary of the Navy John Davis Long, and Postmaster General Charles Emory Smith, see above, 1:127-34, 378-81; also see Harlan, *BTW,* 286.

From Timothy Thomas Fortune

Washington, D.C., Dec 16 [1898]

Dear Friend: Accept my congratulations upon your splendid address today in welcoming the President to Tuskegee. It was eminently fitting and appropriate, and will enhance your splendid prestige with the people of the Nation. You know how to say the right thing in the right way at the right time.

My health is better. Your friend,

T. Thomas Fortune

ALS Con. 139 BTW Papers DLC.

From Julius Daniel Dreher[1]

Salem, Va. Dec. 16, 1898

Private.

Dear Professor Washington, I was glad that my old friend Mr. Austin[2] remembered Tuskegee in his will. Please let me know whether you have employed counsel to defend the will, which as you doubtless know will be contested. If you have engaged counsel, who is the attorney? We are discussing the question of engaging counsel to represent us.

The recent riots in the Carolinas and the numerous lynchings in recent years weigh on my mind and heart, and I am thinking of preparing "A Plea for Forbearance," which I would offer to *The Century, The North American Review,* or *The Forum.* I would write some pretty plain things and would offend many of my Southern friends; but it does seem to me that this plea for forbearance in dealing with colored people, even in cases *of rape,* ought to be made? Whether I ought to make it, is another question. You know I am a South Carolinian and served in the Confederate army the last year of the war.

Do you know of any riot a shooting affray between whites and blacks where the blacks were the first aggressors?

Can you tell me where I may get reliable statistics of lynchings, with time and cause? I would like also to get the facts about the principal riots in the South for the last two decades. I have no doubt that some one has had clippings of this sort made by a bureau.

Give me your candid opinion of Manly's editorial? If imprudent, was it not still true throughout?

I am glad the President visited Tuskegee. God bless you in your great work!

Please address me at *Selwood, S.C.,* my old home, where I go early next week to take needed rest. With all good wishes   Sincerely yours —

Julius D. Dreher

ALS   Con. 139   BTW Papers   DLC.

¹ Julius Daniel Dreher (1846-1937) was born at Selwood in Lexington County, S.C., and graduated from Roanoke College in Salem, Va. He became professor of English at Roanoke College. During his twenty-five years as president of Roanoke, beginning in 1878, he increased the endowment and improved the school. In the 1890s he gave expression to his racial liberalism in speeches and writings, some of which appeared in national magazines. He served as U.S. consul in Tahiti, Jamaica, Toronto, and Colón, Panama, before retiring in 1924.

² Edward Austin of Boston bequeathed $1,100,000 to charity and education. Harvard received $500,000; Massachusetts Institute of Technology, $100,000; Radcliffe College, $30,000; Roanoke College, $30,000; and Tuskegee, $30,000. Edward P. Clark of the New York *Evening Post* wrote BTW that the bequest should have been reversed, with Tuskegee receiving $500,000 and Harvard $30,000. (Clark to BTW, Nov. 23, 1898, Con. 138, BTW Papers, DLC.) William H. Baldwin, Jr., thought the Austin bequest would encourage others to give money to Tuskegee. (Baldwin to BTW, Nov. 25, 1898, Con. 136, BTW Papers, DLC.)

From William Jenkins

Montgomery, Ala., Dec. 17 1898

Dear Sir: Let me congratulate you upon Friday's *success*. The display gotten up by your institution is the marvel of all who saw it.

Your school was highly spoken of by the president in his speech at Old Ship.

"Pat"[1] was a prime mover in the Old Ship meeting. The motive of the movement was to keep as many people away from Tuskegee as possible. In this the Old Ship meeting was a success, as I verily believe that for this meeting and the president's visit, here, the carrying capacity of the roads would have been sorely taxed. But, after all the meeting helped your work immensely. In addition to what the president said of your work, Mrs. Hereford, Montgomery's sweetest singer, had prepared a patriotic song in which your name, McKinley's and Hobart figured. Its rendition brought tears to the eyes of the president. Nor, was he the only one who was affected.

In the meantime our friend P. fairly wilted. He was the most dejected and disappointed man in the church. I am pleased to know that the members of the union were so royally entertained by you. All returned to the city delighted. Sincerely yours

Wm. Jenkins

ALS   Con. 272   BTW Papers   DLC.

[1] William Burns Paterson.

From John C. Leftwich

Montgomery, Ala., Dec 17th, 1898

My Dear Sir: I regretted very much that I could not come to Tuskegee, up to the very last I tried to go, but could not.

Please allow me to congratulate you on the great demonstration you gave the President and his party in Tuskegee, no doubt you are the wonder of the age.

The colored citizens gave the President a grand reception at the Old ship church, there he was introduced by my self, and I wish to say that I paid you a glowing tribute, which the President bowed to every word I said about you, I am sorry to say that the news-paper left out that part of my speech, the President also spoke in glowing terms of you and your school, which was cheered to the echo, such a demonstration has never been witness in this city before, the people yelled the names of Mckinly and Washington, I am only too sorry that you were not here, we had the church beautifully decorated and under the President picture, hung your picture, which he gazed upon with much interest.

I wish you would send me one of your large lithograph, as I want to place it along with the President in the Government building in this city, great many citizens have requested this to be done.

I hope you have rested and [are] now ready for the battle fray again. I am yours,

John C. Leftwich

TLS Con. 183 BTW Papers DLC.

From Timothy Thomas Fortune

Washington, D.C., Dec 17, 1898

Dear Friend: I have your telegram of even date and I thank you for sending it. I rejoiced that the President's visit was such a pronounced success. You have taught him something he did not know and that is a positive gain to our advantage, for he is no friend to us. His position in his annual message and at Atlanta, in which there is no word of rebuke to deviltry and no note of encouragement for us, is about as cruel and cold blooded as can be imagined. *But we shall out live it and even the possible desertion of the Republican party.* The destiny of a race is not in the keeping of one President or one party or one epoch of history. I have an abiding faith in the future.

I am sorry that I can't come to Tuskegee between now and Jan 1. I am sick with the grip and it would do me good to be at Tuskegee; but I feel that I must be here to the meeting of the Afro-American Council *to do what I can to prevent it from doing something foolish.* And then I am way down in my finances for Jan 1 and Feb 15 account and must pin down here and do a lot of special work and try to pull

535

through. I can't work as well in New York as here because of the superfluous demands upon my time. Here when I am busy I can shut the mob out. After the Council Convention I shall have to go to Jacksonville and get some odds and ends in shape; after that, say in February, I shall go to Tuskegee. Do you still think you will want the lectures on American history for the advanced classes? I am reading along that line and making my notes. Let me know about this point.

I have heard nothing from Dr Shaw.

Mrs. Fortune writes me that she is sick.

With kind regards for you all   Yours truly

T. Thomas Fortune

ALS Con. 139 BTW Papers DLC.

A Sunday Evening Talk

Tuskegee, Ala., Dec. 18, 1898

EDUCATION THAT EDUCATES

Perhaps I am safe in saying that during the last ten days you have not given a great deal of systematic effort in the direction of book study in the usual sense. And when these interruptions come, as they have within the last ten days, taking you away from your regular routine work and study and preparation for routine lessons, the idea that comes to the average person, is that this is time lost so far as it relates to education in the ordinary sense; that it is so much time taken away from that part of one's life that should be devoted to receiving education. And I suppose that during the last few days that question has come to many of you: What are we gaining, what are we getting out of the interruption and irregularity that has taken place on the school grounds within the last week that will compensate in any degree for the amount of book study that we have lost? Now, to my mind, I do not believe that you have lost anything by the interruption; on the other hand, I am convinced that you have gotten the best kind of education. I do not mean to say that we can depend upon it for all time to come for systematic training of the mind, but so far as relates to real education, so far as development of the mind and body and heart are concerned, I do not believe that a single student has lost anything by reason of the irregularity through which you have passed during the last week or more. You have gained in this respect; in making the preparation for the reception and entertainment of the President of the United States and his cabinet, and other distinguished persons, you have had to do an amount of original thinking which you, perhaps, have never had to do before in your lives. You have been compelled to think, you have been compelled to not only put your bodily strength into what you have been doing, and you could not have made the magnificent exhibition of our work unless you had been compelled to do that original thinking and execution. Now the most of you never saw such an exhibition before; I certainly never did. Those of you who had floats that comprehended our agricultural work, our mechanical and academic work, had to put a certain amount of original thought into that planning of those floats in order to make them show up their work to the best advantage; and two-thirds, practically all of you, had never seen such a thing before. And so it was a matter that had to be planned by you, that had to be thought out by you, not only thought out, but put into visible shape.

Now compare that kind of education with the mere committing to memory of certain rules or something else which somebody thought out a thousand years ago, something that somebody originated and thought out and executed a thousand years ago. And that is what a large part of our education really is. As we think of education in the usual sense, it is the mere committing to memory of something which has all along been known before us. Now during the past ten days we have had to solve problems of our own, not problems or puzzles that somebody else has originated for us. I do not believe that there is one connected with this institution that is not stronger in mind, that is not more self-reliant and self-confident, so far as it relates to what he is able to do with his mind or with his hands, than he was ten or twelve days ago. Now there is the benefit that comes to all of us. It puts us to thinking and planning, it brings us into contact with things that are unusual and things which are out of the ordinary, and there is no education that surpasses it. I see more and more that the world will be brought to the study of man, to the study of things, rather than to the study of books; and you will find more and more, as the years go on, that people are going to gradually lay aside books and are going to study the nature of man in a way that they have never done before. I say you have not lost anything. On the other hand, you have gained; you have had your mind awakened, your faculties strengthened, your hand guided.

Now I do not wish to speak of this matter in an egotistical manner, but it is a fact, as I have heard a great many persons from elsewhere mention, their pleasure at meeting Tuskegee students, because they are impressed when they come in contact with a student who has been here, with the fact that he does not seem to be dead or sleepy. They say that when they come in contact with a Tuskegee boy or girl, they come in contact with a person who has had contact with real life. The education that you have been getting within the last few days, you will find, as the years go by, to be a kind that will serve you in good stead all through your life.

Now just in proportion as we learn to execute something, to put our education in some tangible form as we have done during the last few days, just in the same proportion will we find ourselves of value as individuals and as a race. Now those people who came here the other day, the newspaper correspondents, knew perfectly well that we could commit to memory certain lines of poetry, they knew we were able to solve problems in algebra and geometry, they understood perfectly well that we could commit certain rules in chemistry and agriculture; but what interested them most was to see us put into visible form the result of our education. And just in proportion as an individual is able to do that, just in that proportion the individual is valuable to the world. That is the object of the work we are trying to do here. We are trying to turn out men and women who are able to do something that the world wants done, that the world needs to have done, and just in proportion as you can comply with that demand, you will find that there is going to be a place for you — there is going to be standing room. By the training we are trying to give you here, we are preparing you for a place in the world, and when you get to that place, if you do not succeed in it, we are going to so train you that it will not be our fault.

It is a great satisfaction to have connected with a race men and women who are able to do something, not talk about it, not theorize about it, but who are able actually to do something that makes the world better to live in, that enhances the comforts and conveniences of life. I had a good example of this last week. I wanted something done in my office in connection with that work which required a practical knowledge of electricity, and it was a great satisfaction when I called upon one of the teachers to do this, to have him do the work in a careful, praiseworthy manner. It is very well to talk or lecture about electricity, but it is better to be able to do something of value with that knowledge of electricity.

And as we go on increasing our ability to do things of value, you will find that the problem which often now-a-days looks more and more difficult of solution, will gradually become an easier task. Said one of the cabinet members who was here a few days ago, after witnessing this exhibition, that the Islands which this country has taken into its possession during the recent war, are soon going to require the services of every man and woman we can turn out from this institution. And so you will find that, not only in this country, but in other countries, the demand more and more will be for people who can do something. Just in proportion as we can, as a race, get the reputation I spoke to you about a few days ago, you will find that regardless of color or condition, the world is going to give the places of trust and remuneration to the man or woman who can do a certain thing as well or better than any one else. This is the whole problem: Will we prepare ourselves to do something as well or better than any one else? Just in proportion as we can do this, you will find that nothing under the sun will keep us back.

Tuskegee Student, 12 (Dec. 22, 1898), 3-4.

To Hollis Burke Frissell

Tuskegee, Ala., Dec. 19, 1898

Dear Dr. Frissell: Referring further to our conversation in New York I very much hope that you can see your way clear to visit Snow Hill with your stereopticon when you come South in February. I was there about three weeks ago and was deeply impressed with the work that is being done there, especially Mr. Simpson's[1] interest. He has not only brought his whole family around to feel an interest in the colored people as he does, but he is converting the white people in that whole community, and I feel that if you could go there and give an evening to the white people alone it would prove most effective. We must encourage such men as Mr. Simpson wherever we can find them in the South.

539

The President's visit was most successful and effective in every respect. We had the Governor and also the Alabama Legislature present. Yours truly,

Booker T. Washington

TLS   BTW Folder   ViHaI.

[1] Randall O. Simpson.

From Susan Brownell Anthony

Rochester, N.Y., Dec. 19, 1898

My Dear Friends:[1] I am despatching to you a set of my biography, both for yourself and for the library of your splendid school.

I should very much like to have been present when you were escorting the President through the different departments of your institution. It must have made him and the members of his cabinet realize something of the work you are doing for the education and elevation of the colored people of the South.

You have of course noticed the proscription of the Chinese and Japanese from citizenship in the proposed government for the new Territory of Hawaii, and I hope you have also noticed the invidious shutting out of all women from the right to vote or to hold office there. Both propositions, I hope, will be repudiated by Congress, and if not I shall hope that President McKinley will veto the bill on the ground of the preliminary constitution violation of the fundamental principles of our government.

I trust that you are well, and that your family and your school are all prospering. Please accept my kind regards and Christmas greetings for all who abide with you. Very sincerely yours,

Susan B. Anthony

Mr Washington — You will remember of my speaking to you, in Chicago, of the importance of the Colored Women's National League renewing its membership with the National Council of Women of the United States. It holds its next Triennial meeting in Washington in *February or March* — and if the first instalment of their fee is paid — their President & delegate will sit in that meeting — the peers of the officers of the Grand Army Women — & all other societies — then again the Colored Women — would be entitled to a speaker in the *International* Council — of which Countess Aberdeen is President — to be held in London in June 1899.

Indeed there is every reason why that organization shall affilliate itself with the National Council. Mrs Washington — note you must write in if you are not a member already — & oblige —

S. B. A.

TLS   Con. 1   BTW Papers   DLC.   Lengthy autograph postscript.

[1] Addressed to "Mr. and Mrs. Booker T. Washington."

From George Washington Carver

[Tuskegee, Ala.] 12-19-98

Mr. B. T. Washington   I certainly beg your pardon for neglecting or rather forgetting to send you this Cat.

Your talk on last night was a very happy hit indeed, and was just what both teachers and students needed.

This old notion of swallowing down other peoples ideas and problems just as they have worked them out, without putting our brain and origionality into it, and making them applicable to our specific needs must go. And the sooner we let them go, the sooner we will be a free and independent people. Very Respy,

G. W. Carver

ALS   Con. 138   BTW Papers   DLC.

From Leander J. Bryan[1]

Montgomery, Ala., Dec. 19, 1898

Dear Sir: I learn that the President has again sent the name of J. A. Grimmet to the Senate for confirmation as P.M. at Tuskegee Ala.

On account of the long and loyal support given to the Republican party by Capt Grimmet in the days when it tried mens souls to stand up for the cause, in this section of the Country and for the reason that a very unjust and bitter fight has been made on Capt. Grimmet by a certain set of so called Republicans but really by the Democracy I sincerely hope that you will use your influence and best offices to have him confirmed. I am anxious that he be confirmed and I assure that I voice the sentiment of all the old "Guard" who are now left in this Section of the Count[r]y, in the opinion that he ought to be confirmed and also that he is an honest man and merits the place. Thanking you in advance for your best efforts in this matter I am   Truly Yours

L. J. Bryan

ALS   Con. 137   BTW Papers   DLC.

¹ Leander J. Bryan, a white Republican, was federal marshal for the western district of Alabama (1897-1902).

From J. M. Holland¹

Washington, D.C. [Dec.] 20 1898

Dear Mr Washington   I congratulate you on the success of your entertainment of the President and party and trust much good will come of the visit.

I am here to see the President on the solving of the race problem and hoped the good impression made down there would do much toward aiding in the solution. Last night there was a meeting here & our friend Fortune spoke in his usual magnetic manner but I regret to say the advice and language was so foreign to him and what was expected of him that we were sorely disappointed. He has been so dignified so earnest in his plea for law and order in New York while still insisting that these people be given their rights that decided measures be adopted but still on approved lines that the same was hoped for here and I trust the report could be used in a petition both to the President & Congress to show the white man alone was the lawless one but this speech kills it all. It puts it in the power of the opposing party to sustain their declaration. That the larger element of the Race in the South are vicious & must be kept in subjection.

Those who know love & admire him deeply regret it. I feel he has allowed himself to be influenced by the wrong party who have an object other than friendly toward him although he does not see it.

You have great influence over him & I trust you will respect this confidence but use all your power of persuasion to convince him this is wrong. He had won of late and in a short time by keeping on the same line could have led his own race & influenced our people also getting from the Republican party almost what he wanted. It will take a long time to retrieve. I feel this influence over him was exercised to make him kill himself in certain directions because of a desire on their part to lead.

Two men we have in N.Y. whom we admire & are proud of but who are like a pair of Race horses in traces beyond the control of all but their own mood and cannot be led they are Roosevelt and Fortune. We never know what they will do next. I trust Mr Fortunes visit will be one of mutual pleasure and wish you and dear Mrs Washington a Merry Xmas & Glad New Year with many happy returns of the day. Sincerely

J. M. Holland

P.S. Meeting so many you may not instantly recall me but I first met you both at Boston. You later in N.Y. I admired you for your grand work.

ALS Con. 155 BTW Papers DLC.

[1] Mrs. J. M. Holland was a reporter in the woman's department of the New York *Tribune*.

From J. M. Holland

Washington, D.C. [Dec. 21, 1898]

Dear Mr Washington As expected Mr Fortunes speech caused great excitement here. The papers of course gave the worst side of it but he has succeeded in getting a version from himself in "The Star" which will help matters immensely. It has spoilt his prospects politically. Politicians tell me they felt he did so much in his speeches in N Y. etc they were all urging Roosevelt to do something for him in the way of office and from what Roosevelt said to me he expected to do so but now of course it is ended. Too bad just as he was on the verge of success. I understand he mailed you clippings. The truth is C Chase editor of "The Bee" wished to kill him as a leader, got him so drunk and talked this incendiary s[t]uff to him until when he got up to speak he could not separate his own ideas from the others.

Reporters all agree on that. The editor of the Star[1] said when talking to me about it "Fortune was unquestionably drunk Chase has no standing here and our only surprise is he could be influenced by him. It would be better for him to come out like a man & say so many another has been in the same predicament, than blame the poor reporter."

When I went to The White House I did not see the President but I told Sec Porter[2] when he expressed his surprise I told him the truth. He said "I am glad of this explanation & will convey it to the President. Other good men have been in similar condition. It was however unfortunate." So Chase has not done quite all the mischief desired. It however spoilt my work as after the Presidents visit to you I hoped for a very practical interview as to the solving of the problem. As a New Yorker Journalist Republican and one interested in the Race Problem of course I felt it keenly both from its unfortunate effect on my work & from one of my own proffession & city.

Now I think it will be dropped and hope pass over. Theo Roosevelt paid you quite a compliment in speaking of the Mass Meeting to me. He said "I dont believe Washington would approve of them. Fortune may be careful but he needs to be for the Race is doing well now, their friends are doing all they can for them & we can not afford to stir up antagonism just now & I feel Washington will agree with me in this."

Mr Fortune returned to New York.

As the best friend the Race has I tell you this so you will understand the situation & advise our friend Fortune.

This thing aids the Southerners in their effort to disfranchise the Afro-American. Best wishes   Sincerely

J M Holland

Prof John G. Blair is here strongly advocating it.

ALS   Con. 146   BTW Papers   DLC.

[1] Crosby Stuart Noyes, born in 1825, began working on the Washington *Evening Star* in 1855, bought the paper with two partners in 1867, and was its editor and publisher until his death in 1908.

[2] John Addison Porter.

To William McKinley

Tuskegee, Alabama. December 22d, 1898

Dear Sir: Your visit to Tuskegee has resulted in bringing about a sympathy and union between the races of this section that is almost marvelous. We all feel that the impression is permanent. You have helped every black man and white man in the South, and we are deeply grateful to you for your visit and unselfish help, and noble words. Yours truly,

Booker T. Washington

TLS   McKinley Papers   DLC.

From Jabez Lamar Monroe Curry

Naples [Italy] 23 Dec 98

My dear Sir— Distance makes no change in my admiration of, and friendship for, you and, therefore, for personal and official reasons, I like to keep in touch with you. One of my party, a niece, has been seriously ill, on sea and land, for four weeks, and instead of being in Africa, as I had planned, I am here a semi-prisoner in Europe. Tomorrow we hope to sail for Cairo, as the young lady's parents have come over, and her improving health enables us to leave, without any special anxiety.

The few American newspapers which come to us, give me the information of the President's visit to Ga & Ala and I hope he carried out his wishes and saw something of your great work. It will be a life-long regret that I did not have the pleasure of introducing him to an Institution which has so much of my thought and affection.

I hope you have had time to prepare what was requested for one of our "Occasional Papers" series. If not, you must get it ready for our Annual Pamphlet and I will submit it as a part of, or an appendix to, my Report. That may be just as well, for a larger and less individual circulation would be secured.

The troubles in North Carolina and Illinois give increased interest to the "Negro problem," and I am half-inclined in my next Report to discuss the lack of general & educational Statesmanship in connection with Emancipation. The failure of national aid was a great crime and has emphasized the evils connected with ignorant and machine suffrage. I have some very decided opinions on certain phases of the question but in these days of truculent Jingoism and insane lust for territorial aggrandizement and of stupid willingness to incorporate millions of untrained into our citizenship, what the most thoughtful & conscientious may say will fall on deaf ears & prejudiced minds. The paramount question in American civilization, which should take precedence of all others, is how we shall discharge the debt; social, civil, religious, we owe to our Afro-American citizenship.

Best regards to Mrs Washington. Kind remembrance to faculty *and students. Take care of your health*. I shall visit Tuskegee about the first of April. Yours sincerely

J. L. M. Curry

ALS Con. 138 BTW Papers DLC. Docketed: "This is a magnificent letter & I am so glad that Dr. Curry is so cordial & friendly. E J Scott. Jan 9."

To Hollis Burke Frissell

Tuskegee, Ala., Dec. 24, 1898

My dear Dr. Frissell: I have your letter of recent date and thank you for it. It is very generous in you to be willing to give up the Lincoln birthday meeting for Tuskegee. I think too that it will be better to have the two schools represented together on that day and it is very generous in you and the Armstrong people to consent to do that. Please always understand that I am willing to consent to any proposition that you favor that will help either Hampton or Tuskegee, or both. The question as to the soldiers appearing at the meeting was a suggestion which came from Mr. Calloway; I have never favored it very heartily; I think we can get on without the soldier representation.

I certainly hope that your trustees will be able to help us some in the way of endowment fund. I am making especial effort in that way this year and with some prospects of success. Mr. Baldwin has taken hold in a very wholesouled manner and is proving most helpful. I think a joint meeting of the Hampton and Tuskegee board of Trustees in New York would prove most helpful and I shall be willing to co-operate in any way possible. I shall be in New York and Boston from the 1st of January to the 23rd of January and will be at your call at any time if I have several days notice. I think I can easily arrange to meet you in New York on January 6th.

I am very glad to hear that Prof. Brown is pleasing you so much. I have always considered him an exceptionally strong man. We shall be very glad to welcome him to Tuskegee. I have just telegraphed you to the effect that I am to leave here not later than December 30th and wish very much that Prof. Brown can come between now and that date.

The visit of President McKinley has undoubtedly helped this section more than any one event that has occurred lately. It brought the two races together as they have never been together before. Here in Tuskegee every white man and woman in town and vicinity seemed to put themselves at my service and all acted together as one person in making the President's visit a success.

I shall send you within a few days the names of other parties in the Southern cities. I feel that the time is ripe for us to make a campaign in the South, not only with a view of waking up the colored people but the Southern white people as well as to their duty toward the colored people.

By this mail I send you a marked copy of the Birmingham Age-Herald which I thought you might like to see. Yours truly,

Booker T. Washington

TLS   BTW Folder   ViHaI.

Emmett Jay Scott to the Editor of the Boston *Transcript*

Tuskegee, Ala., Dec. 27. [1898]

To the Editor of the Transcript: An editorial[1] that recently appeared in the Transcript with reference to Mr. Booker T. Washington was not intended to do him an injustice, and yet I very much fear that it did. Your editorial implies that the impression has gained currency in some quarters that Mr. Washington has been giving comfort to those who would oppress his race; that to satisfy the enemies of his race he has counselled its political effacement — the surrender of its political rights without resistance or protest.

Those who know Mr. Washington best know that this is not a true statement of his position. His contention is, and has been, that political agitation as a means to an end serves least of all to help the negro. He believes — and many there be who believe with him — that political agitation does his race more harm than the good it is intended to do. He does not believe that the holding of public office [is] itself a need so great for the upbuilding of his race. What he has advised and advocated for his race in the South, however, has been that the negro develop himself in a business way, so that he may make himself felt as a tax-payer and intelligent citizen, to the extent that he will make each Southern white man his friend, to the extent that the Southern white people of his community will encourage and protect him in his voting; in his rights as a tax-payer and citizen.

He has firmly contended that, for his race, it is a matter of more concern to be fully prepared for civic responsibilities than to be forever demanding them. Upon no occasion has he counselled political effacement as has been mistakenly reputed; on the contrary, he does not believe that there should be any surrender in this direction, but to him, and to the more intelligent of his race, the activity is in the direction of more perfect preparation for the duties and responsibilities of today, that the right to those of the morrow may be questioned by none.

Mr. Washington's views and methods have never been so strongly indorsed by all classes and conditions of the colored people, North and South, as they are today; his primacy as a capable, worthy leader, never so fully recognized as now. This is evidenced by the fact that the leading colored newspapers and most representative colored men and women of the country are in hearty, expressed accord with him. Only the present week the three most widely read colored journals contain ringing editorial indorsements of Mr. Washington's position; of his sincere efforts to help his race, and in the way that seems to him best and most easy of accomplishment. As a co-laborer at Tuskegee with Mr. Washington, understanding fully his position with respect to these matters, and with thanks in advance to the Transcript for correction of an impression calculated to do injustice, the foregoing is respectfully submitted.[2]

Emmett J. Scott

Boston *Transcript,* Jan. 3, 1899, 6.

[1] In an editorial, "Our 'Subject Race' at Home," the Boston *Transcript* saw a significance in President McKinley's choice of Tuskegee as a prominent objective of his southern trip, "as Mr. Washington is the colored leader who has counselled submission to the political subjection which has been planned and carried far already in the South, and that able man is incurring much opposition and criticism from the more impetuous of his race for so doing." After praising "the quiet work of Tuskegee" for long-term racial advancement and Washington's "wonderful endowment . . . by nature and the wonderful things he does with it," the editorial contrasted Washington's position with that of Congressman George H. White of North Carolina, who denied that blacks should, "even for policy's sake, put their hands upon their mouths and their mouths in the dust under the political oppressions with which they are visited." (Boston *Transcript*, Dec. 15, 1898, 4.)

[2] Below Scott's letter the Boston *Transcript* responded by reporting that at the Afro-American Council meeting in Washington in Dec. 1898, several speakers, including John P. Green and Ida B. Wells-Barnett, had protested against the non-interference of the federal government under President McKinley in the Wilmington race riot. Green said that "black Judases" whom he could name had advised the President not to interfere, but when T. Thomas Fortune challenged Green to name the Judases he failed to do so.

From Timothy Thomas Fortune

New York, Dec 27, 1898

My Dear Mr. Washington: Your letter of the 23rd instant was received this morning and I am glad to have it. I go to Washington this afternoon and shall remain there at the Southern Hotel (311 Pa. Ave. N.W.) until Jan. 5, unless I change my present plans. If you come on before then let me know there. I am very much pained to have had to bother you about money, because I knew that you had enough bother, but it could not be helped under the circumstances, as I have given more time to other peoples' business since October 1 than to my own — which was contrary to my Winter schedule, but man proposes and God disposes. I shall look for your relief at Washington by the first of January.

I know the woman who wrote the letter you enclosed.[1] She takes more interest in my affairs than she should, and I have already warned her about it three days ago. She is a white journalist stuck on black people. As to the subject she refers to, you have the clippings and my letters bearing on it by this time, and have digested them. The misrepresentation by the newspapers was done by design and preconcert because of my activity in promoting the indignation meetings and to back up the President's Southern position. But the newspaper version served instead to set the people to thinking in the opposite direction and made Congress and the White House squirm.

"The Black Belt Diamonds"? Yes, they have served you well, which was one of my main desires in the publication.

I have been unable to finish up the draft of the Address so that I could send it to you, but I shall weigh well the wise things you suggest in your letter and try to produce a document which will serve our purpose best all along the line.

Mrs. Fortune and Fred are better. Jessie was very much disappointed not to have Portia with her in the holidays. She anticipated the pleasure.

With kind regards for you all, and with the compliments of the season, Yours truly

T Thomas Fortune

ALS   Con. 139   BTW Papers   DLC.

¹ Mrs. J. M. Holland.

From Henry B. Rice

Charleston, West Va., December 28, 1898

My Dear Friend, I have the honor and it gives me supreme pleasure to acknowledge the receipt of a copy of your "Black-Belt Diamonds." I thank you for the book and for your name in it in your own handwriting. God undoubtedly has exalted you to be our Moses. We read about you in the greatest papers and magazines published in our great Country — Washington, Tanner, and Dunbar. We stand before them with uncovered heads. We follow them without questioning their right to lead. Envy and malice may rage and vent their vilest spleen, but the government of our great country takes cognizance of the marvelous progress and work of the leading Negro School in the South located at Tuskegee, Ala., regarding that achievement as the real solution of the most difficult and perplexing social questions that ever engaged the serious attention of the public mind; your calumniators will be among those of us who shall enjoy the blessings and benefits arising from your unswerving devotion to your race in the face of such terrible opposition and obstacles as would have discouraged and hopelessly defeated a less determined and indefatigable spirit long ago.

Our leaders in the political arena are seeking to array us against the whites on account of *their* failure to secure lucrative offices, and when a friend dares to indicate to us the fallacy of their position, they at once seize any death-dealing missile of foul slander and boldly attempt his ruin.

There is no doubt but that "the crisis is upon us"; and we must meet it, led by ambitious, political soreheads, or our own more conservative, disinterested friend — our Moses. God who has raised you up to lead us, will, I trust, enable us to follow you to triumph and success. I highly appreciate your efforts for me as a member of your race. I am Sir   Your old School mate and friend,

Henry Rice

ALS   Con. 145   BTW Papers   DLC.

From Henry Ossian Flipper

Santa Fe, N.Mex., December 28, 1898

My Dear Sir: I am in receipt of your very kind letter of the 21st inst. and thank you for your very kind expressions.

I understand fully how completely your time is filled and did not expect a reply to my letter until your occupations permitted you to write. I have read with great satisfaction the President's address at Tuskegee and the many kind and encouraging things that have been said about yourself and the work you are doing at Tuskegee. You have laid down the lines we must all follow before we, as a race, attain that recognition and place among the American people our political leaders are clamoring for but are doing so little to bring about.

The officer who defended me was at the time Captain Merritt Barber of the 16th U.S. Infantry. We served together at Fort Sill, Indian Territory, and I never saw him again till he came and defended me at Fort Davis, Texas, in 1881. He is now Assistant Adjutant General, Department of the East, Governor's Island, New York, with the rank of Colonel. He was Judge Advocate General under General Benjamin F. Butler, at New Orleans when Butler was in command there. He is a most excellent man, and an able lawyer.

I quite agree with you that letters of themselves do little good. The purpose of the letters I asked you and others to write was this: I received a great many promises from the members of the committee on military affairs last spring when in Washington, and from other members of the House and Senate. The object of the letters was to recall these promises and to show to these gentlemen that my race was interested in having this matter pushed to a successful termination. Politicians often make promises in good faith and then forget them owing to pressure of other business.

General Shafter is the officer who, as Colonel of the 1st U.S. Infantry, preferred the charges against me and prosecuted me. He treated me in the most outrageous manner, confining me in the guard house in violation of express law, violating my personal correspondence, desk, etc. He had many theories for the loss of the money I was charged with embezzling — I had spent it on women, had loaned it to civilian friends about the post, and hundreds of other things that made me appear in the worst possible light as the worst possible felon. All these things Col. Shafter gave to the press etc. When the trial came off he was a different man. His testimony was fair and straightforward and he gave me a most excellent character as an officer. Detailed the various theories he had adopted and followed out and frankly stated that they had all ended in nothing. He is a vain man and can be reached through his vanity. I am almost afraid of him. A word from him in this case would have great weight, a word against me would defeat my bill and a word favorable to me would, I believe, just as certainly secure the passage of that measure. If you are well enough acquainted with General Shafter to do so, you might feel him [out] and if he shows a favorable disposition in the matter, you might ask him to aid us. If you catch him in the right humor, he will consent, I am sure, to aid us. This is a matter, however, which I will leave entirely in your hands.

As to General Miles,[1] I fear his influence might do harm. He is under criticism himself. I do not think he is very favorable to Negro officers.

I appreciate the delicacy of approaching the President in a matter of this character. I believed that such a step would aid me and you and Lyons seemed to me to be the only two men of the race close enough to the President to approach him in this matter. While asking your help, I rely fully on your judgment and what you think best to do will be satisfactory.

As to Mr. Hull, I think it well to leave no stone unturned to bring about our object. Any influence you can bring to bear against him ought, I think, be brought. I expect him to call the bill up in the House and urge its passage. He can do this with more chances of success than any other member, because of his position as Chairman of the Military Committee. Use your influence on him to this end.

This bill must be passed this session. If not, it will be necessary to begin again at the starting point, as the present Congress expires March 4th next. What we do must be done before February 24th next. It will be very difficult to have anything done in the last days of the session. I hope to have the bill passed at the next suspension day in the House, near the end of January. Whatever you can do should be done between now and, say, the middle of January.

Thanking you with all my heart for your interest and help in this matter, and with the best wishes of the season for you and yours, I have the honor to be, Very truly yours,

Henry O. Flipper

TLS   Con. 146   BTW Papers   DLC.

[1] Nelson Appleton Miles (1839-1925) was a well-known Civil War soldier who later conducted various campaigns against the Indians, including the last major confrontation between the U.S. Army and the Sioux at Wounded Knee, S.D. In 1894 he led troops that quelled disorders during the Pullman strike. During the Spanish-American War he directed the occupation of Puerto Rico.

From Collis Potter Huntington

[New York City] December 28, 1898

Dear Sir: Yours of the 24th received and I am very glad all your matters are moving along so pleasantly and that you have begun work on the new building. I will ask Mrs. Huntington to send you a check for five thousand dollars right away, and whenever you need the rest and will let us know, Mrs. Huntington will send you the money.

I note what you say about another engine and boiler needed. I am buying very large amounts of machinery myself and I will make an effort to have some of the manufacturers to send you what you want without charge to you or to me. You are doing a great work, and I think will continue to do good work if you keep on the lines of economy which I believe you have followed all these years. You have a great work to do and it will not be all done when you leave it, and I hope that another Booker Washington will be ready to take your place. A people who have been groping, as you may say, for centuries, can hardly be expected to come upon the highest plane in one generation, and it is with great satisfaction that I look upon the great advance that has been made in the last quarter of a century, and if it will only continue for three-quarters of a century more, I think the whole will be accomplished; and a century is but a short time in the history of a race. Conscientious labor, with the practice of an intelligent economy, always brings good results, but patience and courage are needed with your people — patience to wait until the prejudice against them — and prejudice is a factor to be dealt with, as much as stone walls are, and it can only be removed by time and good conduct — is overcome; and courage to steadfastly continue in the following of those lines and the doing of those things whereby that prejudice is to be removed. Until that time social equality is a delusion and, to say the least, a practical impossibility for your people. I congratulate you on what you have already achieved, and the best wish I can make you, in this Christmas season, is that you may live long to carry on your good work, for I feel certain that your greatest happiness lies in seeing your people advance and prosper. With kindest regards, Yours sincerely,

C. P. Huntington

TLS Con. 146 BTW Papers DLC.

ADDENDUM

To Thomas McCants Stewart

Tuskegee, Ala., February 26th 1892

My dear Sir: I have received your letter and in reply would say that I am sure we do not feel like excusing you on the ground you mention.[1] Of course if your legal business calls you in New York on the week of our Commencement we shall have to submit. You must not let Dr. Derrick scare you out with his stories of Southern railroads. Every wide-awake, intelligent colored man like yourself who comes into the midst of the white people and speaks to them and looks them into the face gives them an object lesson of what the colored people are capable of doing and goes further to break down prejudice than anything else, but I assure you from New York to our place you will not have the slightest trouble on the Pullman Car. I have travelled over that route for 10 years in the Pullman Car and have never had the slightest intimation of any unpleasantness. You can get into a Pullman in New York and come to our place without any change of train, and you can do the same in returning and not a word said. You will be surprised to see how liberal the white people are here owing to the influence of this institution.

I now have the authority to extend the invitation. I certainly hope you will not refuse it. Your speech will be widely reported in Northern and Southern newspapers and you will have an audience of three or four thousand people, including some of the best white and colored people in the State. Enclosed please find stamp for reply. Yours truly,

Booker T. Washington

TLS Scrapbook T. McCants Stewart Papers DHU.

[1] See above, 3:214. Stewart did not speak at the Tuskegee commencement of 1892, but he was the speaker the following year.

BIBLIOGRAPHY

THIS BIBLIOGRAPHY gives fuller information on works cited in the annotations and endnotes. It is not intended to be comprehensive of works on the subjects dealt with in the volume or of works consulted in the process of annotation.

Alabama. *Acts of the General Assembly of Alabama, Passed by the Session of 1892-93.* Montgomery, 1893.

American Federation of Labor. *Proceedings of the Seventeenth Annual Convention, 1897.* New York: American Federation of Labor, 1898.

Bacon, Alice M. *The Negro and the Atlanta Exposition.* John F. Slater Fund, Occasional Paper No. 7. Baltimore: John F. Slater Fund, 1896.

Brawley, Benjamin. *Paul Laurence Dunbar: Poet of His People.* Chapel Hill: University of North Carolina Press, 1936.

Brewer, J. Mason. *Negro Legislators of Texas and Their Descendants.* Austin and New York: Jenkins Publishing Company, 1970.

Buckler, Helen. *Doctor Dan, Pioneer in American Surgery.* Boston: Little, Brown and Company, 1954.

Carter, Purvis M. "R. L. Smith and the Farmers' Improvement Society," *Negro History Bulletin,* 29 (Fall 1966), 175-76, 190-91.

Chase, Hal G. " 'Honey for Friends, Stings for Enemies': William Calvin Chase and the Washington *Bee,* 1882-1921." Philadelphia: Ph.D. dissertation, University of Pennsylvania, 1973.

Conference for Education in the South. *Proceedings of the Seventh Session, Birmingham, 1904.* New York: Wynkoop, Hallenbeck, Crawford Company, 1904.

Contee, Clarence. *Henry Sylvester Williams and the Origins of Pan-Africanism: 1897-1902.* Washington, D.C.: Historical Publications of Howard University, 1973.

Dabney, Charles W. *Universal Education in the South.* 2 vols. Chapel Hill: University of North Carolina Press, 1936.

Daniels, John D. *In Freedom's Birthplace: A Study of the Boston Negroes.* Boston: Houghton Mifflin Company, 1914.

De Montmorency, J. E. G. *Francis William Fox, a Biography.* Oxford: Oxford University Press, 1923.

Du Bois, William Edward Burghardt. *Dusk of Dawn: An Essay toward an Autobiography of a Race Concept.* New York: Harcourt, Brace and Company, 1940; reprint: New York, Schocken Books, 1968.

Dunbar, Paul Laurence. "Our New Madness," *Independent,* 50 (Aug. 18, 1898), 469-71.

Flipper, Henry Ossian. *The Colored Cadet at West Point* (1878). Reprint. New York: Arno Press, 1969.

Foner, Philip S., ed. "Is Booker T. Washington's Idea Correct?" *Journal of Negro History,* 55 (Oct. 1970), 343-47.

———. *The Spanish-Cuban-American War and the Birth of American Imperialism 1895-1902.* Vol. 2. New York and London: Monthly Review Press, 1972.

Fordham, Mary Weston. *Magnolia Leaves: Poems.* Charleston, S.C.: privately published, 1897.

Fox, Stephen R. *Guardian of Boston: William Monroe Trotter.* New York: Atheneum Publishers, 1970.

Gatewood, Willard B. "Booker T. Washington and the Ulrich Affair," *Phylon,* 30 (Fall 1969), 286-302.

Gilbert, Peter, ed. *The Selected Writings of John Edward Bruce, Militant Black Journalist.* Reprint. New York: Arno Press, 1971.

Hackney, Sheldon. *From Populism to Progressivism in Alabama.* Princeton: Princeton University Press, 1969.

Hamilton, Holman, and Gayle Thornbrough, eds. *Indianapolis in the "Gay Nineties": High School Diaries of Claude G. Bowers.* Indianapolis: Indiana Historical Society, 1964.

Hampton Institute. *What Hampton Graduates Are Doing, 1878-1904.* Hampton, Va.: Hampton Institute Press, 1904.

Harlan, Louis R. *Booker T. Washington: The Making of a Black Leader, 1856-1901.* New York: Oxford University Press, 1972.

————. "The Secret Life of Booker T. Washington," *Journal of Southern History,* 37 (Aug. 1971), 393-416.

Hawkins, Hugh. *Between Harvard and America: The Educational Leadership of Charles W. Eliot.* New York: Oxford University Press, 1972.

————, ed. *Booker T. Washington and His Critics.* Lexington, Mass.: D. C. Heath and Company, 1962.

Haynes, Elizabeth Ross. *The Black Boy of Atlanta.* Boston: House of Edinboro, 1952.

Hobson, Elizabeth C., and Charlotte Everett Hopkins. *A Report Concerning the Colored Women of the South.* John F. Slater Fund, Occasional Paper No. 9. Baltimore: John F. Slater Fund, 1895.

Katzman, David M. *Before the Ghetto: Black Detroit in the Nineteenth Century.* Urbana: University of Illinois Press, 1973.

Kletzing, H. F., and W. H. Crogman. *Progress of a Race.* Atlanta, Ga., Naperville, Ill., and Toronto, Ont.: J. L. Nichols and Company, 1897.

Kurland, Gerald. *Seth Low: The Reformer in an Urban and Industrial Age.* New York: Twayne Publishers, 1971.

Locke, Alain Leroy, ed. *The Negro in Art: A Pictorial Record of the Negro Artist and of the Negro Theme in Art.* Washington, D.C.: Associates in Negro Folk Education, 1940.

MacCorkle, William Alexander. *The Recollections of Fifty Years of West Virginia.* New York: G. P. Putnam's Sons, 1928.

Mackintosh, Barry. "The Carver Myth." M.A. thesis, University of Maryland, 1974.

Mathews, Marcia M. *Henry Ossawa Tanner, American Artist.* Chicago and London: University of Chicago Press, 1969.

Meier, August. *Negro Thought in America 1880-1915: Racial Ideol-*

ogies in the Age of Booker T. Washington. Ann Arbor: University of Michigan Press, 1963.

————. "The Racial and Educational Thought of Kelly Miller, 1895-1915," *Journal of Negro Education,* 29 (Spring 1960), 121-27.

National Educational Association. *Journal of the Proceedings and Addresses of the Thirty-fifth Annual Meeting Held at Buffalo, N.Y., July 3-10, 1896.* Chicago: University of Chicago Press, 1896.

National Negro Conference. *Proceedings, 1909.* Reprint. New York: Arno Press, 1969.

Porter, James A. *Ten Afro-American Artists of the Nineteenth Century.* Washington, D.C.: Howard University, 1967.

Rudwick, Elliott M. *W. E. B. Du Bois: Propagandist of the Negro Protest.* Reprint. New York: Atheneum Publishers, 1968.

Starnes, A. J. "What Education Is Needed for the Negro," *Southern Workman,* 27 (May 1898), 103-6.

Taylor, Charles H. J. *Whites and Blacks, or The Question Settled.* Atlanta: James P. Harrison and Co., 1889.

Thompson, Holland. *From the Cotton Field to the Cotton Mill: A Study of the Industrial Transition in North Carolina.* New York: Macmillan Company, 1906.

Tindall, George Brown. *South Carolina Negroes, 1877-1900* (1952). Reprint. Baton Rouge: Louisiana State University Press, 1966.

Waller, James E. "Emmett Jay Scott: The Public Life of a Private Secretary." M.A. thesis, University of Maryland, 1971.

Washington, Booker T. *Black Belt Diamonds: Gems from the Speeches, Addresses, and Talks to Students of Booker T. Washington.* Selected and arranged by Victoria Earle Matthews. New York: Fortune and Scott, 1898.

Washington, Ernest Davidson, ed. *Selected Speeches of Booker T. Washington.* Garden City, N.Y.: Doubleday, Doran and Company, 1932.

Whittier, John Greenleaf. *The Complete Poetical Works.* Boston: Houghton Mifflin Company, 1927.

Woolfolk, George Rublee. *Prairie View: A Study in Public Conscience, 1878-1946.* New York: Pageant Press, 1962.

INDEX

NOTE: The asterisk indicates the location of detailed information. This index, while not cumulative, does include the major identifications of persons annotated in earlier volumes of the series who are mentioned in this volume. References to earlier volumes will appear first and will be preceded by the volume number followed by a colon. Lyman Abbott's annotation, for example, will appear as: *3:43-44. Occasionally a name will have more than one entry with an asterisk when new information or further biographical detail is presented.

Abbott, Lyman, *3:43-44; 225, 245, 246
Abbott, Willis J., 6
Abercrombie, John William, 252, *253
Abercrombie, Milo Bolling, Jr., 242, *243
Aberdeen, Countess, 541
Abolition: in Pemba and Zanzibar, 187-88, 204-5
Abolitionism, 112, 116, 223-25, 411, 450
Abolitionists, 286-87, 294, 363
Abyssinia, 188
Adams, Henry, 281
Adams, J. W., 396, *519; letter from, 518
Adams, Lewis, *2:109; 316, 418
Adams, Marian, 281
Africa, 158; BTW condemns British imperialism in, 251-52; exhibits at Atlanta Exposition, 40; false image at Atlanta Exposition, 41-42; missionaries in, 80-81; slavery in, 223-25; slave trade in, 188
African Methodist Episcopal (A.M.E.) Church, 38, 259-60, 484
A.M.E. Church Review, 310, 364

A.M.E. Zion Church, 21
A.M.E. Zion Quarterly Review, 21
African National Congress, 263
African Union Company, 171
Afro-Alabama Cotton Mill Company, 75, *76
"Afro-American": Edward Wilmot Blyden on use of term, 28; T. Thomas Fortune on use of term, 31
Afro-American Council, 122, 535, 536, 549
Afro-American Fair Association, 291
Afro-American League, *2:357-58; 293, 431
Afro-American Press Association, 122
Afro-American Realty Company, 171
Afro-American State Fair (Tex.), 170-71
Agee, Sophia Burroughs, *2:5; asks BTW for clothing, 294
Agricultural experiment station: at Tuskegee, 250
Alabama Agricultural and Mechanical College (Normal), 39, 445
Alabama constitutional convention, 135
Alabama Hall, 65, 87, 163

Brown, George R., 10

Brown, John, 43, 112, 116

Brown, Joseph Emerson, 15

Brown, W. M., 6

Brown Creek District High School (W.Va.), 391

Brown University (R.I.), 24, 63

Brown *v.* Board of Education, 187

Browne, Cecil, 351-*52

Browne, Hugh Mason, 547

Browning, John W., *2:349; letter from, 125-*26

Brownsville affray (1906), 479

Bruce, Blanche Kelso, *2:411; 36, 38, 227, 246, 346, 394, 402, 411; death of, 392; letter from, 230; name on U.S. dollar, 354-55; seeks BTW's aid in political appointment, 258, 259, 271; seeks political office, 261-62, 327; suggested for McKinley cabinet, 230, 231; thanks BTW for endorsement, 279; thanks BTW for letter of recommendation, 347

Bruce, John Edward, *56, 116, 448; congratulates BTW on Atlanta Exposition address, 55-56; on black advancement, 55-56

Bruce, Josephine Beall Wilson, 226, *227, 271, 327; informs BTW of illness of B. K. Bruce, 391; receives sympathy from BTW on death of B. K. Bruce, 392

Bruce, Roscoe Conkling, *391; recommended by BTW for admission to Harvard, 411

Bruce-Grit. *See* Bruce, John Edward

Bryan, Leander J.: letter from, 541-*42

Bryan, William Jennings, 115, 168, *200, 400; opposed by BTW, 200

Bryce, Lloyd Stephens, *28

Buck, Alfred Eliab, *241, 243, 247, 259

Buckner, John C., 278

Budd, Etta M., 335, *336

Budd, J. L., *336

Buffalo *Courier:* interviews BTW, 199-200

Bullock, Rufus Brown, *3:42-43; 7; congratulates BTW on Atlanta Exposition address, 10, 54-55; message

to Grover Cleveland on opening of Atlanta Exposition, 12

Bumstead, Horace, *3:197-98; 493; praises BTW for stand on Hawaiian annexation, 460

Burr, A. J., 5

Burroughs, James, *2:3; 94

Bush, James E., 76

Butler, Benjamin Franklin, *2:45; 294, 552

Butler, E. T., 387-*88

Bythewood, Alton, 385

Bythewood, Daniel Webster, *386; consults with BTW on black school in Port Royal, S.C., 403-4; letter from, 384-85

Calhoun Colored School (Ala.), 124

Calloway, Clinton Joseph, *410, 425-26, 516

Calloway, James Nathan, *3:105; 88, 433; criticized by John H. Washington, 260; lobbies for Tuskegee land bill, 104-7, 118-19, 129

Calloway, Lettie Louise Nolen (Mrs. Thomas J.), *3:18; letter to, 283

Calloway, Thomas Junius, *3:177; 522, 526, 546; letters from, 228-29, 488

Campbell, George Washington, *2:127-28; 82, 97, 242

Candler, John S., 5

Cansler, Laura Ann, *31

Cansler, William J.: congratulates BTW on Atlanta Exposition address, 30-*31

Canty, James Monroe, *2:372-73; 321

Capital City Guards, 348

Carnegie Hall Conference (1904), 294

Carney, Sergeant, 288

Carr, Herbert Wrightington: BTW solicits clothing from, 336-*37

Carr, William Ramsey, 84, *85

Carter, James Garnette, 48, *49

Carter, Mason, 5

Carter, William Richard, *49; letter from, 48

Cartney, Ora, 417

Carver, George Washington, 126, *127-28, 260, 339; autobiographical sketch of, 333-36; complains of facilities at Tuskegee, 239-40; encourages BTW

Clark College (Ga.), 39, 43, 277
Clarke, Edward Alexander, 66, *67, 96
Clarke Rifles (Ga.), 5
Clarkson, Coker Fifield, 113
Clarkson, James Sullivan, *114, 159,
254; desires black cabinet member,
113, 116; discusses presidential nomi-
nation with BTW, 110-14; urges
support for William B. Allison, 112-
13, 121-22
Clay Street Normal and Industrial
School (Ga.), 277
Claytor, William J., 418
Cleveland, Esther, 11
Cleveland, Grover, 180, 255, 313, 338,
402, 484, 526; congratulates BTW on
Atlanta Exposition address, 50; meets
BTW at Atlanta Exposition, 63; opens
Atlanta Exposition, 3, 11-12
Cleveland, Ruth, 11
Clinton, George Wylie, *21
Clinton Street M.E. Church (La.), 438
Cobb, James Edward, 129, *135, 308
Cochran, John Webster: congratulates
BTW on Atlanta Exposition address,
*20
Coleman, J. H.: writes BTW on lynch-
ing, 314
Coleman, Warren C., 6, *14; urges
BTW to invest in cotton mill, 177
Coleman Manufacturing Company, 14
College Settlement Association, 177
Collier, Charles A., *3:462; speaks at
Atlanta Exposition, 7, 8
Collins, Ellen, *3:110-11; congratulates
BTW on Atlanta Exposition address,
25-26, 33
Collins, Mary, 25
Colonial Club (Cambridge, Mass.), 288
Colored Association Council of Food
Production and Conservation, 115
Colored Methodist Episcopal (C.M.E.)
Church, 24
Colored People's Building and Loan
Association (Hampton, Va.), 59
Colored Republican Club of New York
City, 154
Colored Women's National League, 540-
41

Columbia Theological Seminary (Ga.):
alumni of, 345
Columbia University (N.Y.): alumni of,
177, 245, 313; faculty of, 241;
trustees of, 393
Comer, Braxton Bragg, 100, 279
Common Street Baptist Church (La.),
438
Conference for Education in the South,
14, 141, 201, 454
Congo, 24, 81
Congo Training Institute (Colwyn Bay,
Wales), 81
The Congregationalist: responds to
BTW's position on Hawaiian annexa-
tion, 460-61
Conkling, Roscoe, 391
Constant, Benjamin, 43
Constitutional League, 258
Convict-lease system, 246; condemned
by National Association of Colored
Women, 327
Conyers, Solomon C., 418
Conyers Volunteers (Ga.), 6
Cooper, Edward Elder, *69, 403; on
BTW as possible cabinet appointee,
402; supports BTW, 69
Cooper, Henry E., 418
Cooper, Susan D., 418
Cooper Union, 524
"Coppick boys." *See* Coppoc, Barclay
and Edwin
Coppin, Mrs. Levi Jenkins, 390
Coppoc, Barclay, 112, *116
Coppoc, Edwin, 112, *116
Corliss engine, 513
Cornell University (N.Y.), 249
Cory, Chappell: letter from, 429
Cosmopolitan, 14
Cotteraux, E. P., 6
Cotton mills, 14, 75-76, 99-100, 177,
332
Councill, William Hooper, *2:307-8;
76, 118, 444
Courtney, Samuel E., *2:289; 228, 229,
265
Craig, Arthur Ulysses, 418
Craige, Kerr, 6
Crain, Capt., 5
Creelman, James, *14, 71; reports

Gilmore's Band, 4, 8
Gilson, Samuel S.: asks BTW about religious affiliation, *401; letter from, 426
Girls' Industrial School. *See* Industrial School for Girls of Alabama
Gladstone, William Ewart, 9
Glenn, Gustavus Richard, *3:577; 352; visits Tuskegee, 343
Goff, Nathan, *254, 257
Golden Rule, 321
Gomez, Mr., 527
Gomez, Juan (John) E., *527
Gomez, Manuela: letter from, 527
Gompers, Samuel, 351, 389, *391
Gonzales, Gregorio E., 6
Goode, G. Brown, 6
Goodwyn, Albert Taylor, *129, 307
Gordon, George Angier, 229, *230
Governor's Horse Guards (Ga.), 6
Grady, Henry Woodfin, *2:321; 3, 9, 14, 15, 17, 358; compared with BTW, 422, 430
Grant, John Cowles, *3:506; 494
Grant, Ulysses Simpson, 44
Graybill, James E., 6
Gray's Inn (London), 475
Green, John Paterson, 445, *446, 549
Green, Lydden (or Lytton), 76
Greene, Charles W., *2:54; 169, 418, 425
Greene, James Matthew, *3:246; 418
Greene, John C., 418
Greene, Lottie Virginia Young (Mrs. Charles W.), *3:246; 418
Greene, Sarah F. Peake (Mrs. James Matthew), *3:161; 418
Greener, Richard Theodore, *2:291; seeks BTW's support for political appointment, 265-66, 269
Gregg, Dr., 263
Gregory, William, *273, 418
Gresham, Walter Quintin, 278
Griffin, Michael, 497-*98
Griffin Rifles (Ga.), 5
Grimké, Charlotte L. Forten (Mrs. Francis James), *2:395; 25, 75, 86
Grimké, Francis James, *2:395; 255; BTW reveals role in Thomas A. Harris episode to, 85-86; congratu-

lates BTW on Atlanta Exposition address, 25; letter from, 95-96; letter to, 24-25; questions BTW on role in Thomas A. Harris episode, 74-75
Grimmett, James A., *2:161; 267-*68, 541-42
Gumede, James, 263
Gunton's Magazine, 178

Hagler, Mr., 57
Haiti, 480, 481
Hale, Samuel Q., *3:277; 97, 308
Hamilton, Alexander, 98
Hamilton Club (Brooklyn), 59, 63, 97-*98
Hamilton Club (Chicago), 93, 95, 274; BTW speaks before, 90-95
Hamilton Literary Society, 98
Hammond, William R., 346; seeks BTW's political endorsement, 344-*45
Hampden-Sydney College (Va.), 14
Hampton Normal and Agricultural Institute (Va.), 38, 61, 91, 96, 131, 224, 263, 360, 392, 434, 528, 546; alumni of, 59, 409, 428; Armstrong-Slater Memorial Trade School building, 143; BTW speaks at, 232-35, 406-9; compared with Tuskegee, 311-12; exhibit at Atlanta Exposition, 39, 63; John S. Durham lectures at, 164-65, 174, 175; opening of Armstrong-Slater Memorial Trade School, 232-35
Handel, George Frederick, 312
Hanna, Marcus Alonzo, 257, *258, 266
Hanson, Mr., 247
Hardeman, Eugene, 5
Harding, Warren Gamaliel, 154, 447
Hare, Charles Woodroph, *243, 316, 325; lobbies for Tuskegee land bill, 242
Harlan, John Marshall, 267, 437
Harper, J. S.: letter from, 510
Harper, William Rainey: invites BTW to speak at National Peace Jubilee, 472-73
Harpers Ferry: raid at, 112, 116
Harper's Magazine, 13
Harper's Weekly, 23, 204, 494
Harriman Industrial Institute (Tenn.), 457

lates BTW on Atlanta Exposition
address, 76-*78
McGuire, Peter J., 351, 389
McIntosh, P., 97
McKeon, John S., 417
McKinley, William, 115, 116, *168, 230,
241, 243, 248, 257, 258, 259, 266,
267, 268, 269, 271, 274, 326, 327,
344-45, 346, 347, 349, 354, 355, 357,
400, 402, 421, 445, 446-47, 472, 479,
498, 518, 529, 540, 541; appoints
successor to B. K. Bruce, 394; BTW
mentioned as possibility in cabinet of,
236; informed of T. Thomas Fortune's intoxication in public, 544; invited to Montgomery, Ala., 517-18;
invited to Tuskegee, 503-4; itinerary
of visit to Alabama, 521; praised by
BTW, 492; receives advice from BTW
on speaking in South, 521; receptive
to idea of sending Cuban and Puerto
Rican students to Tuskegee, 488;
T. Thomas Fortune's opinion of, 530-
31; visits Tuskegee, 503-4, 517-18,
521, 522, 523, 524-25, 528, 530, 531-
32, 534-35, 537, 540, 542-43, 544,
545, 547, 549, 551
McKissick, E. P., 6
McMaster, John Bach, 164, 165
Macon, Lucy Brown, 291-92
McWilliams, Sterling Lewis, 448, *449
Magnolia Leaves: BTW's introduction
to, 347
Malaria, 411
Mallory, Hugh Shepard Darby: seeks
BTW's aid in securing black laborers
for southern cotton mills, 99-*100
Mandingo, 114
Mangel, Theodore H., 6
Manly, Alex, 460, 533
Manning, Joseph Columbus, *258-59;
relationship with BTW, 259
Marietta College (Ohio): alumni of,
477
Marietta Rifles (Ga.), 5
Marshall, Charles Lives, *3:455; 110,
151, 160, 321; BTW offers principal-
ship of Christiansburg Normal to, 161
Marshall Farm, 260-61
Martha (a cook), 106

Marx, Simon, *206, 207, 210
Mason, Alice, 413, 414
Mason, Joseph, 475
Mason, William Ernest, 278
Mass, W. C., 5
Massachusetts Bureau of Labor Sta-
tistics, 67
Massachusetts Institute of Technology,
533
Massachusetts Racial Protective Associa-
tion, 229, 230
Matabele warriors, 251, 252
Matthews, Victoria Earle, *131-32, 136,
152, 405, 422; compiles *Black Belt
Diamonds*, 280, 403, 429-30; letter
from, 364; resigns from Kowaliga
board of trustees, 512; thanks BTW
for endorsement, 361-62
Matthews, William, 131
May, Samuel, *2:176; informs BTW of
lynching, 314-15
Mayfield, S. M., 433
Mayo, Amory Dwight, *2:229; 119,
277; visits Tuskegee, 270
Mead, L. P., 6
Meadows, Ollie: letter from, 357
Measles, 84
Mechanics Institute (N.Y.), 399
Medical practice, 290
Medicine: at Tuskegee, 316-17
Medico-Chirurgical Society of Wash-
ington, D.C. (black), 274
Meharry Medical College (Tenn.), 275;
alumni of, 108, 265
Menafee, Crawford Daniel, *3:107; 418,
423
Merchant, J., 433
Methodist Episcopal Church, 438
Metropolitan A.M.E. Church (D.C.),
140
Metropolitan Hotel (St. Paul, Minn.),
101
Metropolitan Life Insurance Company,
258
Migration: of black women from South,
362
Miles, Nelson Appleton, 185, 256, 552,
*553
Milholland, John (Iowa physician), 335,
*336

Old Ship A.M.E. Zion Church (Montgomery, Ala.), *2:459, 534
Old South Church (Boston), 230
Olssen, Jessie Macauley, 43
One Cent Savings Bank (Nashville), 453
The Organizer (Tex.), 294
Our Day: publishes articles by BTW, 124-25, 166-67, 186-87, 251-52, 289
Outlook, 245, 246; reports BTW's reception at white college in South, 227-28
Ovletrea, John Wesley, *457
Oxford College (Ga.; now part of Emory University), 253

Page, Walter Hines, 200-*201; suggests BTW write book, 226
Paine College (Ga.), 24
Paine Institute (Ga.), 346
Palmer, Bertha Honoré (Mrs. Potter), 8
Palmer, John H., *261
Pan-African Association, 475, 476
Pan-African Conference (1900), 475
Pan-Africanism, 56, 475-76
Paola Normal School (Kans.), 335
Parents' League (D.C.), 391
Paris Exposition of 1900, 525
Parker, Mr., 413
Parker, Edward T., 19
Parsons, Lewis E., 309
Pasco, Samuel, 132
Paterson, William Burns, *2:320; *3:77-78; 118, 129, 135, 277, 299, 534; seeks reconciliation with BTW, 325
Patty, John F.: seeks BTW's advice on Louisiana suffrage issue, 437-*38
Paul Laurence Dunbar Apartments (N.Y.), 391
Payne, Christopher H., *2:402; 357
Payne, Henry Clay, *254, 257
Payne, John Barton, 484, *485
Peabody, George Foster, *3:86; 398-99, 526, 528
Peabody Education Fund, *2:153; 145, 277, 434
Peaker, Mr., 523
Pearson's Magazine, 14
Pemba: slavery in, 187-88, 204-5
Pemberton, Caroline H., 268-*69, 270

Penn, Irvine Garland, *3:517; 6, 36, 63, *70
Penney, Edgar James, *3:53; 29, 181, 396
Penney, Estelle C. (Mrs. Edgar J.), 181
Pennsylvania Academy of Fine Arts, 42, 58
Pennsylvania Anti-Slavery Society, 19
Pennsylvania Railroad, 165
People's Advocate (Alexandria, Va., and Washington, D.C.), 255
People's Church (St. Paul, Minn.), 102
People's Village School (Ala.), 277
Perkins Institute for the Blind (Mass.), 51
Pershing, John Joseph, 158
Peterson, Butler H., *3:458; 210; reprimanded by BTW, 116-17
Peterson, Jerome Bowers, *241
Pettiford, William Reuben, *2:360; 308
Pew, John G., 172
Phelps-Stokes family. *See* Stokes
Phelps-Stokes Fund, 434
Philadelphia *Bulletin,* 165
Philadelphia College Settlement, 176
Philadelphia Negro, 177, 241
Philadelphia *Times,* 444, 445
Philafrican Liberators' League, 223-*25
Philippine Islands: BTW on U.S. imperialism in, 461
Phillips, John Herbert: seeks Tuskegee graduates for Birmingham school system, 476-*77
Phillips, Wendell, 287, 330, 522
Phillips Exeter Academy (N.H.), 391, 411, 527
Philosophian Literary Society, 385
Phoenix wheel, 7
Pittman, Portia Marshall Washington, *2:235-37; 106, 433, 550; letters from, 52-53, 202, 203; student at Framingham, 50-51; studies piano, 50; witness to beating, 22
Plant Railway System, 13, 507
Pledger, William A., 121, *122, 136, 530; pledges support of BTW, 359; reports on William McKinley's visit to Atlanta, 530
Plessy *v.* Ferguson (1896), *187, 267, 437; BTW's reaction to, 186-87

annexation of Cuba, 461; on black emigration to Africa, 188-89; on black migration to cities, 470; on black military contribution, 490-92; on black participation at Atlanta Exposition, 60; on black patriotism, 407, 416-17, 441, 490-92; on black poets, 347; on black political appointments, 354-57; on black soldiers, 389, 414; on black-white relations, 372-73, 376; on Christian living, 208; on Christianizing Africans, 251-52; on conflicting race theories, 213-14; on economic and social equality, 179-81; on effects of race violence, 212; on effects of slavery, 193; on emotions of blacks, 194; on evils of race hatred, 92-93; on evils of slavery, 92; on fair treatment of blacks, 376; on growth of Tuskegee, 375-76; on high death rate in cities, 462; on higher education for blacks, 369-70; on his authority as principal, 146-47; on industrial education, 16, 74, 215, 232-35, 366-74; on Jim Crow cars, 179-80, 555; on job discrimination, 139, 167; on loyalty of slaves, 375; on lynching, 187, 221, 298, 323, 329; on manual labor, 10; on mechanized farming, 139; on mechanized laundering, 140; on moral standards at Tuskegee, 378-79; on need for educating white masses, 180; on Plessy *v.* Ferguson decision, 186-87; on poor whites, 196, 218; on public accommodations, 167; on race hatred, 124-25, 196-97, 235; on race progress, 318-19, 406-7, 408-9; on racial advancement, 60-62, 93, 183-85, 287-88; on racial and sectional prejudice, 184; on racial discrimination, 219-20, 287, 370-71; on racial equality, 61-62; on racial prejudice, 508-9; on racial segregation, 192; on racial violence, 382; on religion, 234; on reputation of race, 513-15; on restrictive suffrage, 381; on role at Atlanta Exposition, 46; on role of education, 212; on S. C. Armstrong, 435; on social equality, 16, 56-57, 508; on solution

to race problem, 167, 189; on Spanish corruption, 439; on success of Tuskegee graduates, 92; on trades of women, 483; on U.S. imperialism in Hawaii, 460; on U.S. imperialism in Philippines, 461; on white South, 61-62; optimistic over success of Atlanta Exposition, 15-17, 93-94; plays down sectionalism, 102; race war unlikely, 323; races to be measured by American standard, 184; reaction to reception of Atlanta Exposition address, 24-25; regrets decline of black skilled workers, 137-40; war should not detract from fight against poverty in America, 435-36, 440
—Opponents and critics, 149, 150, 247, 527; criticized for position on industrial education, 117-18, 346, 456; criticized for position on lynching, 74-75, 324; criticized for public utterances, 520; opposed by Clement G. Morgan, 294; opposed by Judson Lyons, 394
—Other black schools, 383-84; as trustee of Kowaliga, 244, 506, 511, 512; criticizes William E. Benson, 425-26, 516-17; E. E. Wright seeks aid of, 431-33; inspects Christiansburg Normal, 150-51, 156; on Kowaliga, 410; opposes distribution of Slater funds to smaller schools, 141-45; rivalry with William B. Paterson, 277; seeks joint meeting of Hampton and Tuskegee trustees, 546-47; selects principal of Christiansburg Normal, 161; William B. Paterson seeks reconciliation with, 325; William E. Benson seeks endorsement of, 359-60
—Personal: anecdotes of, 331-32, 408, 416, 439; compared with Frederick Douglass, 70, 181; compared with Henry M. Turner, 42; compared with Henry W. Grady, 422, 430; concern for campus details, 163, 401, 431, 434, 435, 473, 476, 488; described as Negro Moses, 3, 8, 30, 34, 55, 73, 351, 550-51; described as "New Negro," 36; described as successor to Frederick Douglass, 30, 31; diet, 380;

enjoys notoriety from talk of cabinet position, 243; friendship with Charles W. Anderson, 154; illness, 329; offers financial aid to T. Thomas Fortune, 249; physical appearance, 8-9, 90-91, 93, 101, 222; speaking style, 31, 223, 330-32; thought to be Unitarian, 426
—Politics, 95; advises Theodore Roosevelt, 479-80; advises William McKinley, 349, 521; appeals to Benjamin R. Tillman to support black education, 71-73; considered for McKinley cabinet, 116, 168, 230-31, 236, 248, 250, 402; disclaims interest in political appointment, 248; discusses appointees to State Department, 249, 253; eschews politics, 349; invites William McKinley to Alabama, 517-18; lobbies for Tuskegee land bill, 166, 262; meets William McKinley, 354-55; on McKinley cabinet, 243; on nomination of William Jennings Bryan, 200; on political appointments, 258, 259, 261, 267, 344-45; receives advice from James S. Clarkson, 110-14; receives Adlai E. Stevenson at Atlanta Exposition, 63; receives Grover Cleveland at Atlanta Exposition, 63; secretly endorses William B. Allison for president, 159; welcomes William McKinley to Tuskegee, 531-32
—Public recognition: accepts invitation to speak at National Peace Jubilee, 484; demand for as public speaker, 179; hailed as race leader in Emancipation Day parade, 252-53; invited to address Hamilton Club, 59; invited to be judge at Atlanta Exposition, 45; invited to meet Woodrow Wilson, 289; invited to speak at National Peace Jubilee, 472-73; receives honorary degree from Harvard, 174, 175; receives honorary degree from Wilberforce, 305; receives thanks from city of Charleston, S.C., 468-69; reception at Hamilton Club, 98; reception at Harvard University, 185; reception in Indianapolis, 332; reception in Nashville, 441; suggested as

possible cabinet appointee, 116, 168, 230-31, 236, 248, 250, 402; well received at white college in South, 227-28
—Relationship with faculty, 133; asks head of academic department to resign, 386-87; asks stenographer to resign, 378-79; criticized by Matthew T. Driver, 211; criticizes teacher, 338-40, 343-44; fires clerks, 282-83, 284; forces resignation of teacher, 160-61; makes decision in sexual misconduct case, 396; offers position to George W. Carver, 162; on departmental reorganization, 145-49; receives appeal in sexual misconduct case, 395; receives complaint about handling of sexual misconduct case, 397; receives report on morals of prospective teacher, 413-14; reprimands teacher, 116-17, 145-49
—Speeches: at Charleston, S.C. (1898), 461-62; at dedication of Armstrong-Slater Memorial Trade School (1896), 232-35; at Hampton Institute (1898), 406-7, 408-9; at Robert Gould Shaw memorial, Boston (1897), 285-88; at Williams College (1898), 435-36; before Bethel Literary and Historical Association (1896), 137-40; before Brooklyn Institute of Arts and Sciences (1896), 211-22; before Christian Endeavor Society (1898), 438-41; before Hamilton Club in Chicago (1895), 90-95; before Harvard alumni (1896), 183-85; before National Educational Association (1896), 188-98; before National Peace Jubilee in Chicago (1898), 490-92; before Union League Club of Brooklyn (1898), 416-17; in Indianapolis (1897), 322-23; welcomes William McKinley to Tuskegee (1898), 531-32. *See also* Sunday Evening Talks
Washington, Booker T., Business Association, 126
Washington, Booker Taliaferro, Jr. (Baker), *2:361-62; 53, 106, 181, 207, 410; letter from, 450-51